W9-BKE-925

PLAZAS

LUGAR DE ENCUENTROS

Second Edition

Robert Hershberger
DePauw University

Susan Navey-Davis
North Carolina State University

Guiomar Borrás A.
Thunderbird, The American School
of International Management

With contributions from
Stacey Powell
Auburn University

THOMSON
™
HEINLE

Australia Canada Mexico Singapore Spain United Kingdom United States

THOMSON
✳
HEINLE

PLAZAS
Second Edition
Hershberger / Navey-Davis / Borrás A.

Editor-in-Chief: *PJ Boardman*
Publisher: *Janet Dracksdorf*
Acquisitions Editor: *Helen Alejandra Richardson*
Development Editor: *Viki Kellar*
Senior Production Project Manager: *Esther Marshall*
Assistant Editor: *Heather Bradley*
Editorial Assistant: *Ignacio Ortiz-Monasterio*
VP, Director of Marketing: *Elana Dolberg*
Manufacturing Manager: *Marcia Locke*

Compositor/Project Manager: *Pre-Press Company, Inc.*
Photo Manager: *Sheri Blaney*
Photo Researcher: *Billie L. Porter*
Interior Designer: *John Walker & Linda Beaupré*
Cover Designer: *Diane Levy*
Cover Illustration: *© 2004, Simon Shaw/*
IllustrationOnLine.com
Printer: *Transcontinental/Interglobe Printing*

Copyright © 2005 Heinle, a part of the Thomson Corporation. Heinle, Thomson, and the Thomson logo are a trademark used herein under license.

Printed in Canada.
1 2 3 4 5 6 7 8 9 10   09 08 07 06 05 04

For more information contact Heinle, 25 Thomson Place, Boston, Massachusetts 02210 USA, or you can visit our Internet site at http://www.heinle.com

All rights reserved. No part of this work covered by the copyright hereon may be reproduced or used in any form or by any means—graphic, electronic, or mechanical, including photocopying, recording, taping, Web distribution or information storage and retrieval systems—without the written permission of the publisher.

For permission to use material from this text or product, submit a request online at http://www.thomsonrights.com. Any additional questions about permissions can be submitted by email to thomsonrights@thomson

Library of Congress Cataloging-in-Publication Data

Hershberger, Robert
    Plazas: lugar de encuentros / Robert Hershberger, Susan Navey-Davis, Guiomar Borrás A. with contributions from Stacey Powell. -- 2nd. ed., [student's ed.]
        p. cm.
    English and Spanish.
    Rev. ed of: Plazas / Robert Hershberger ... [et al.]. 2001.
    Includes index.
    ISBN 0-8384-0852-4 (student's ed.) --ISBN 0-8384-0890-7 (instructor's annotated ed.)
    1. Spanish language—Textbooks for foreign speakers—English.
    I. Navey-Davis, Susan.
    II. Borrás Alvarez, Guiomar. III. Title: Plazas. IV. Title.

PC4129.E5P63 2004
468.2'421--dc22   2003071188

	CAPÍTULO preliminar ¡Mucho gusto! 2	CAPÍTULO 1 En una clase de español: Los Estados Unidos 22	CAPÍTULO 2 En una reunión familiar: México 48	CAPÍTULO 3 El tiempo libre: Colombia 76	REVISTA 1 102
CHAPTER					Celebraciones hispanas en los Estados Unidos
COMMUNICATIVE GOALS	• Greet others, introduce yourself, and say good-bye • Exchange personal information (origin, age, address, etc.) • Identify quantities of objects • Ask and answer questions	• Identify people and things in the classroom • Indicate relationships and specify colors • Describe everyday activities • Talk about academic courses and university buildings • Say what you like and don't like doing • Tell time	• Define and ask about family relationships • Indicate ownership and possession • Describe people and things • Indicate nationality • Express physical status • Count from 30 to 100 • Describe daily activities at home or at school	• Describe leisure-time activities • Express likes and dislikes • Express plans and intentions • Describe basic actions, places, and activities in town • Talking about the months, seasons, and the weather	◆◆◆ ¿Necesitas 100.000 pesos? Tenemos un trabajo para ti ◆◆◆ ¿Sociable o tímido? Dos características de la nacionalidad mexicana ◆◆◆ Una nueva visión artística del pintor colombiano Fernando Botero
VOCABULARY	• Greetings and good-byes 4 • Numbers 0 to 30 12 • Interrogative words 14 • The Spanish alphabet 20	• In the classroom 24 • The colors 24 • Foreign languages and other academic courses and majors 31 • University places and buildings 31 • The time and the days of the week 39	• The family 50 • Physical features and personality 59 • Nationalities 63 • Numbers 30 to 100 69	• Sports and leisure-time activities 78 • Places 84 • The months, the seasons, and weather expressions 94	
STRUCTURES	• Subject pronouns and the present tense of the verbs **ser** and **tener** 10, 16 • The verb form **hay** and numbers 1–30 12 • Question words and inflection 14 • The Spanish alphabet 20	• Definite and indefinite articles and how to make nouns plural (Gender of nouns) 29 • Present tense of regular **-ar** verbs 35 • **Me gusta +** infinitive 38	• Possessive adjectives 53 • Possession with **de(l)** 53 • Common uses of the verb **ser** 57 • Agreement with descriptive adjectives 59 • Present tense of **-er** and **-ir** verbs 65 • Common uses of the verb **tener** 67	• **Gustar** + infinitive and **gustar +** nouns 82 • **Ir a** + destination or infinitive 86 • Irregular **yo** verbs 90 • **Saber, conocer,** and the personal **a** 92	
CULTURAL INFORMATION	• El lugar de encuentro: Las plazas 7 • ¿Ser informal o formal? **¿Tú** o **usted?** 9 • El mundo hispano-americano 17	• El español en los Estados Unidos 28 • La educación en Latinoamérica y España 34 • El sistema de 24 horas 41	• Los nombres y apellidos en español 56 • La familia hispana 62	• Los deportes en el mundo hispano 81 • El café en Colombia y en el mundo 89	

	CAPÍTULO 4	CAPÍTULO 5	CAPÍTULO 6	REVISTA 2 192

CHAPTER

CAPÍTULO 4
En la casa:
España   106

CAPÍTULO 5
La salud: Bolivia
y Paraguay   138

CAPÍTULO 6
¿Quieres comer
conmigo esta noche?:
Venezuela   166

REVISTA 2   192

¡Mi casa es su casa!

◆◆◆

Franquicias
latinoamericanas en los Estados
Unidos y en el mundo: Churro
manía

◆◆◆

Curaméricas

◆◆◆

«La casa de Bernarda Alba»,
Federico García Lorca

COMMUNICATIVE GOALS

- Describe the features of your home or personal residence
- Talk about furniture and appliances
- Describe household chores
- Make commands
- State locations and describe feelings
- Describe actions in progress
- Count from 100 and higher

- Identify parts of the body
- Describe daily routines and hygienic practices
- Talk about what you have just finished doing
- Talk about illnesses and health conditions
- Describing people, things, and conditions
- Point out people and things

- Talk about foods and beverages for breakfast, lunch, and dinner
- Make comparisons
- Order food in a restaurant
- Describe past events in detail

VOCABULARY

- Home and furniture 108
- Appliances and household chores   118
- Numbers 100 and above   127

- The human body   140
- Health care (illnesses, symptoms, and medical treatments)   149

- Food and beverages   168
- Dining out   177

STRUCTURES

- Present tense of stem-changing verbs (e> ie, o> ue, e> i)   113
- More idioms with **tener**   116
- Affirmative **tú** commands   121
- **Estar** and the present progressive   123

- Reflexive pronouns and present tense of reflexive verbs   144
- **Acabar de** + infinitive   148
- **Ser** vs. **estar**   152
- Demonstrative adjectives and pronouns   156

- Comparatives and superlatives   172
- Verbs regular in the preterite   180
- Verbs with stem and spelling changes in the preterite   180

CULTURAL INFORMATION

- Gaudí y su obra   112
- Viviendas en Lationamérica y España   120

- Bolivia y la salud   143
- Tradición de hierbas: yerba mate en Paraguay y las hojas de coca en los Andes   155

- La comida típica venezolana   171
- Los postres venezolanos   179

CHAPTER	CAPÍTULO 7 De compras: Argentina 196	CAPÍTULO 8 Fiestas y vacaciones: Guatemala y El Salvador 224	CAPÍTULO 9 De viaje por el Caribe: La República Dominicana, Cuba y Puerto Rico 254	REVISTA 3 284 La magia de los magos ◆◆◆ Experiencias en Santo Domingo, República Dominicana y La Habana, Cuba ◆◆◆ Gigante salvadoreño durmiente ◆◆◆ Mar del Plata, Argentina
COMMUNICATIVE GOALS	• Talk about shopping for clothing • Make emphatic statements about possession • Talk about singular and/or completed events in the past • Make selections and talk about sizes and other shopping preferences • Describe ongoing and habitual actions in the past	• Talk about holidays, events, and activities in the beach and in the countryside • Describe changes in emotion • Inquire and provide information about people and events • Narrate in the past • State indefinite ideas and quantities • Talk about periods of time since an event took place	• Talk about air travel, other types of transportation, and lodging • Simplify expressions with indirect and double object pronouns • Talk about getting around in the city • Give directions and express desires • Make informal requests	
VOCABULARY	• Clothing and fashion 198 • Shopping 207	• Parties and celebrations 226 • The beach and the country 237	• Airline travel 256 • Hotels 268 • Directions 271	
STRUCTURES	• Stressed possessives 202 • Verbs irregular in the preterite 204 • Direct object pronouns 211 • Imperfect tense 214	• Interrogative words 231 • Preterite vs. imperfect 233 • Affirmative and negative expressions 240 • **Hace** and **hace que** 244	• Indirect object pronouns 261 • Double object pronouns 266 • Prepositions and adverbs of location 270 • Formal and negative **tú** commands 274	
CULTURAL INFORMATION	• De compras en Buenos Aires 201 • El tango argentino 210	• Chichicastenango 230 • Arzobispo Óscar Arnulfo Romero 239	• La República Dominicana: Santo Domingo, la primera ciudad de las Américas 260 • Cuba: Escuela Latinoamericana de Ciencias Médicas 265 • Puerto Rico: Estado Libre Asociado 273	

CHAPTER	CAPÍTULO 10 Las relaciones sentimentales: Honduras y Nicaragua 288	CAPÍTULO 11 El mundo del trabajo: Panamá 314	CAPÍTULO 12 El medio ambiente: Costa Rica 346	REVISTA 4 374 Fundación Violeta Barrios de Chamorro ◆◆◆ En Honduras hay trabajo para el verano ◆◆◆ Costa Rica: Recursos naturales para pagar la deuda externa ◆◆◆ Rubén Blades: Cuando una carrera no es suficiente…
COMMUNICATIVE GOALS	• Talk about relationships and courtship • Describe recent actions, events, and conditions • Describe reciprocal actions • Talk about receptions and banquets • Qualify actions	• Talk about professions, the office, and work-related activities • Make statements about motives, intentions, and periods of time • Describe the job hunt, benefits, and personal finances • Express subjectivity and uncertainty • Express desires and intentions	• Talk about rural and urban locales and associated activities and problems • Express emotion and opinions • Talk about the conservation and exploitation of natural resources • Hypothesize and express doubts and uncertainty • Talk about a nature preserve, animals, and endangered species	
VOCABULARY	• Personal relationships 290 • Receptions and banquets 299	• Professions and offices 316 • The office, work, and the job hunt 325 • Personal finances 331	• Rural and urban geography 348 • The environment 356 • Animals and the wildlife preserve 364	
STRUCTURES	• Present perfect 295 • Reciprocal constructions with **se, nos** and **os** 298 • Adverbs and adverbial expressions of time and sequencing of events 302 • Relative pronouns 305	• **Por** and **para** 321 • Subjunctive mood and impersonal expressions with the subjunctive 330 • Formation of the present subjunctive and statements of volition 334	• Subjunctive following verbs of emotion, impersonal expressions, and **ojalá** 353 • Subjunctive to state uncertain, doubtful, or hypothetical situations 360	
CULTURAL INFORMATION	• Los novios en los países hispano-americanos 294 • Las bodas en el mundo hispano 301	• El Canal de Panamá 320 • Protocolo en los negocios en el mundo hispanohablante 329	• Costa Rica: puros igredientes naturales 352 • Costa Rica: Estación biológica La Selva 359	

	CAPÍTULO 13	CAPÍTULO 14	CAPÍTULO 15	REVISTA 5 452
CHAPTER	**CAPÍTULO 13** **El mundo del espectáculo:** **Perú y Ecuador** 378	**CAPÍTULO 14** **La vida pública:** **Chile** 402	**CAPÍTULO 15** **Los avances tecnológicos:** **Uruguay** 430	El Faro del Sur: Luces, cámara, acción ◆◆◆ «Tosca» por Isabel Allende ◆◆◆ La fantasía artística en Perú, Chile y Uruguay ◆◆◆ Mujeres, en cifras (Estadísticas de la Organización de las Naciones Unidas (ONU) sobre las mujeres en América Latina y el Caribe)
COMMUNICATIVE GOALS	• Talk about television and other forms of popular culture • Talk about anticipated actions • Talk about the arts and the vocations of artists • Talk about unplanned or accidental occurrences • Describe completed actions and resulting conditions	• Talk about politics and elections • Talk about future events • Talk about political issues and the media • Express conjecture or probability	• Talk about home electronics and computers • Make statements in the past with the subjunctive mood • Talk about hypothetical situations	
VOCABULARY	• Television programs and movies 380 • The arts and artists 388	• Politics and voting 404 • Political issues and the media 413	• High-tech appliances 432 • The computer 440	
STRUCTURES	• Subjunctive with purpose and time clauses 385 • **Se** for unplanned occurrences (No-fault **se**) 392 • Past participle (as adjective) 394	• The future tense 408 • The conditional 417 • Present perfect subjunctive 421	• Past (imperfect) subjunctive 436 • *If* clauses 444	
CULTURAL INFORMATION	• La cinematografía en Latinoamérica 384 • Oswaldo Guayasamín 391	• El gobierno de Chile 408 • La libertad de prensa 416	• Las telecomunicaciones en Uruguay 435 • Equipos: en la palma de la mano 443	

Apéndices   457

Glosarios   473

Índice   492

Credits   497

ACKNOWLEDGMENTS

We would like to thank Wendy Nelson, former Publisher at Heinle, for her inspiration and confidence in us which were instrumental in both the inception and completion of this project, and to Helen Richardson, Acquisitions Editor, for her hard work, motivation and dedication to the success of this project. A very special thanks to Viki Kellar, whose words of encouragement and help were always present, and to Glenn Wilson for his support. Our gratitude and very special thanks for her hard and meticulous work reflected throughout the book go to Esther Marshall.

Many thanks also go to our native reader, Luz Galante; copyeditor, Susan Lake; copyeditor and proofreader, Margaret Hines; interior designers: John Walker for the design of the chapters and Linda Beaupré for the design of the *Revistas*; cover designer, Diane Levy; illustrator, Dave Sullivan; proofreaders, Patrice Titterington and Soledad Phelan; and to the great team at Pre-Press Co. for the composition and project management.

Reviewers

We are grateful for the comments and suggestions made by our colleagues who reviewed this work during all stages of development. Your contribution to this project makes it truly a community effort and your expertise and experience are reflected on every page.

Plazas First Edition

Ellen Abrams, *Northern Essex Community College*
María Álvarez, *Stetson University*
Diana Álvarez-Amell, *Seton Hall University*
Eileen Angelini, *Philadelphia University*
Marta Antón, *Indiana University-Purdue University at Indianapolis*
Frank Attoun, *College of the Desert*
Miriam Ayres, *New York University*
Helga Barkemeyer, *Montclair State University*
Keith Brower, *Salisbury State University*
Suzanne M. Buck, *Duke University*
Karina Collentine, *Yavapai College*
Richard K. Curry, *Texas A&M University*

John Deveny, *Oklahoma State University*
Doug Duno, *Chaffey College*
Ray Elliott, *University of Texas at Arlington*
José Antonio Fabres, *Saint John's University*
Anna Gemrich, *University of Wisconsin-Madison*
Ana Hnat, *Houston Community College*
Lina Lee, *University of New Hampshire*
Roxana Levin, *St. Petersburg Junior College*
Hilda López Laval, *Chadron State College*
Ernest Norden, *Baylor University*
Gabriela Pozzi, *Grand Valley State University*
Jim Rambo, *DePauw University*

Kay Raymond, *Sam Houston State University*
Steve Richman, *Mercer County College*
Joel Rini, *University of Virginia*
Mirna Rosende, *County College of Morris*
Vanisa Sellers, *Ohio University*
Julie Stephens, *Central Missouri State University*
Brian Stiegler, *Salisbury State University*
Jason Summers, *University of Arkansas-Fayetteville*
Bruce Williams, *William Patterson University*
Elizabeth Willingham, *Baylor University*
Diane Wright, *Grand Valley State University*
Daniel Zalacaín, *Seton Hall University*

Plazas Second Edition

Special thanks to Judy Armen, Yolanda González from Valencia Community College, and Kim Faber from Oberlin College for their careful review of the *Plazas* program at the initial stages of this revision.

Ellen Abrams, *Northern Essex Community College*
Pilar Ara, *Pasadena City College*
Jon Aske, *Salem State College*
Frank Attoun, *College of the Desert*
Celestino Basile, *Northern Essex Community College*
Mara-Lee Bierman, *Rockland Community College*
Sherrie Bratcher, *New Mexico State University*
Ruth Budd, *Longwood College*
Piedad Burmaz, *California State University-Fullerton*
Elizabeth Cobb, *University of Alabama-Birmingham*
María Córdoba, *University of North Carolina-Greensboro*
Linda Crawford, *Salve Regina University*
Page Curry, *Bellarmine University*
Aaron Dziubinskyj, *DePauw University*
Love Ermentrout, *York Technical College*
J. César Félix-Brasdefer, *Indiana University*
Lillian Franklin, *Wittenberg University*
Don Gibbs, *Creighton University*

Andrew Gordon, *Mesa State College*
Terri A. Greenslade, *Guilford College*
Allan Hislop, *Northern Essex Community College*
Susan Jagendorf, *State University of New York-Cobleskill*
Steve Johnson, *Pellissippi State Technical Community College*
Michelle Johnson-Vela, *Texas A&M University-Kingsville*
Wendy Jones-Worden, *University of North Carolina-Greensboro*
Jennifer M. Leach, *Mount Saint Mary's College*
Benjamin Liu, *University of Connecticut*
Susan Linker, *High Point University*
Maria Luque-Eckrich, *DePauw University*
Olga Markof-Belaeff, *Oberlin College*
David McAlpine, *University of Arkansas-Little Rock*
Tim McGovern, *University of California-Santa Barbara*
Deanna Mihaly, *Emory and Henry College*
Don Miller, *California State University-Chico*
Lisa Nalbone, *University of Central Florida*
Fernando Palacios, *University of Alabama-Birmingham*

Leonardo Palacios, *University of Connecticut*
Osvaldo Pardo, *University of Connecticut*
Esperanza Román-Mendoza, *George Mason University*
Louise Rozier, *University of Arkansas-Fayetteville*
Jorge Sagastume, *Wittenberg University*
Keahi Salvador, *Leeward Community College*
Jaime Sánchez, *Volunteer State Community College*
Lourdes Sánchez-López, *University of Alabama-Birmingham*
Barbara Sawhill, *Oberlin College*
Theresa Ann Sears, *University of North Carolina-Greensboro*
Roger Simpson, *Clemson University*
Irwin Stern, *North Carolina State University*
Pamela Taylor, *University of North Carolina-Greensboro*
Guillermo Valencia, *Texas A&M University-Kingsville*
Roberto Vela-Córdova, *Texas A&M University-Kingsville*
Nancy Whitman, *Los Medanos College*
Richard Williams, *Benedict College*
Carol Jo Wilkerson, *Carson-Newman College*

Dear Student,

Spanish is quickly becoming a major second language of the United States. Although southern and costal states have seen dramatic increases in Spanish-speaking populations for years, the presence of Latino communities in every large city throughout the nation is now a reality. Spanish radio and television stations are multiplying and playing to huge audiences. Latino entertainers are soaring to the top of charts with smash hits and Spanish can be seen on road signs, menus and product literature. In the entertainment, leisure and travel industries, Spanish is more prevalent than ever before. Business people, teachers, civil servants, store clerks and especially emergency and hospital personnel are scrambling to keep up with am increasingly Spanish-speaking client base. Just recently peoples of Hispanic descent have become the largest minority group in the United States and are shaping social and political agendas in a profound way. Real-world incentives to learn Spanish are all around you. *Plazas* welcomes you to join a community of Spanish speakers not only in your class, but also in your neighborhood, work environment or travel destination. *Plazas* is based on the Five C's of Communication, Communities, Connections, Comparisons and Culture to ensure that your interaction with the Spanish-speaking world is dynamic and profound. In *Plazas* we not only introduce you to a language, but also to the people—their history, traditions and culture—who speak the language.

Learning Spanish successfully requires determination, good study habits and patience. You must commit yourself to learning the language every day. Mastery is the result of daily study and practice. Everything you learn relies, to a certain extent, on previous material. If you invest your time from the beginning, what you learn later will build naturally upon a solid foundation of understanding and competence.

We wish you the very best in your introduction to Spanish and welcome you to the communities of *Plazas.*

Robert Hershberger

Susan Navey-Davis

Guiomar Borrás A.

ESTADOS UNIDOS

Los Ángeles

San Diego

Tijuana   Mexicali

•Tucsón

Nogales

Ciudad Juárez

R. Grande

R. Bravo del Norte

R. Mississippi

•Austin

•San Antonio

Houston

Nuevo Laredo

BAJA CALIFORNIA

GOLFO DE CALIFORNIA

SIERRA MADRE OCCIDENTAL

MÉXICO

SIERRA MADRE ORIENTAL

•Monterrey

GOLFO DE MÉXICO

•Guadalajara

•Mérida

PENÍNSULA
DE
YUCATÁN

México

•Veracruz

•Taxco

Tikal

Belice

•Belmopán

BELICE

Acapulco

•Oaxaca

OCÉANO PACÍFICO

Copán

HON

Tegu

GUATEMALA

Quezaltenango

Guatemala

San Salvador

EL
SALVADOR

León

Pun

Cana

0	200	400	600	800 millas
0	200	400	600	800 kilómetros

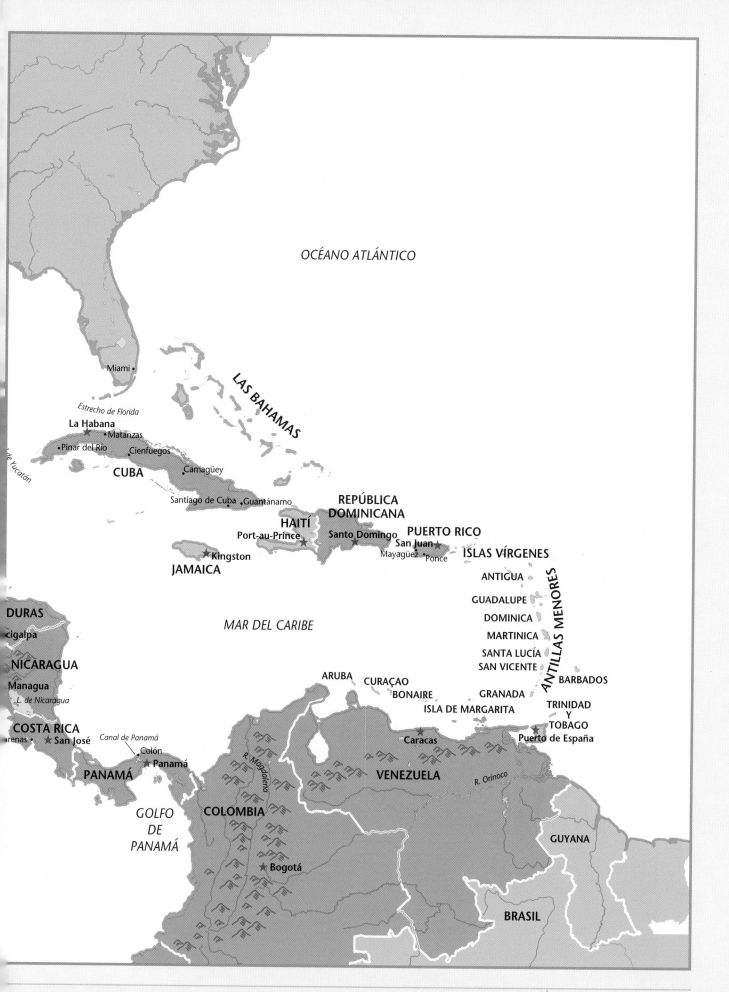

OCÉANO ATLÁNTICO

LAS BAHAMAS

Miami •

Estrecho de Florida

La Habana ★ • Matanzas
• Pinar del Río   • Cienfuegos

de Yucatán

CUBA   • Camagüey

Santiago de Cuba • Guantánamo

REPÚBLICA
DOMINICANA

HAITÍ

Port-au-Prince   Santo Domingo   PUERTO RICO
                                   San Juan ★
                                   Mayagüez • Ponce   ISLAS VÍRGENES

★ Kingston

JAMAICA

ANTIGUA

GUADALUPE

DOMINICA

DURAS

cigalpa   MAR DEL CARIBE   MARTINICA

                                              SANTA LUCÍA
NICARAGUA   SAN VICENTE

Managua   ARUBA   BARBADOS
  • L. de Nicaragua   CURAÇAO   GRANADA
                                BONAIRE
                                        ISLA DE MARGARITA   TRINIDAD
COSTA RICA   Y
arenas • ★ San José   Canal de Panamá   Caracas ★   TOBAGO
                            • Colón   Puerto de España ★
                          ★ Panamá

PANAMÁ   R. Magdalena   VENEZUELA   R. Orinoco

      GOLFO
       DE   COLOMBIA
     PANAMÁ   GUYANA

                            ★ Bogotá

                                                                      BRASIL

MAR CARIBE

Barranquilla
Cartagena
Maracaibo
Port of Spain
Caracas
TRINIDAD Y TOBAGO
R. Orinoco
Medellín
Georgetown
VENEZUELA
Manizales
GUYANA
Paramaribo
Bogotá
SURINAM
Cayenne
Cali
COLOMBIA
GUAYANA
FRANCESA

OCÉANO ATLÁNTICO

ECUADOR

Quito
Quayaquil
R. Amazo
Belem
ECUADOR
Manaus
Iquitos
PERÚ
R. Madeiro
Cajamarca
Recife

Machu Picchu
BRASIL
Lima
Ayacucho
Cuzco
Salvador
L.Titicaca
BOLIVIA
Brasilia
Arequipa
La Paz
Arica
Sucre
Belo Horizonte
Iquique
Potosí
Río de Janeiro
OCÉANO PACÍFICO
Antofagasta
PARAGUAY
São Paulo
Salta
Asunción
Santos
CHILE
Tucumán

R. Paraná
Porto Alegre
Córdoba
R. Uruguay
Mendoza
Rosario
Valparaíso
URUGUAY
Santiago
Buenos Aires
Montevideo
Concepción
La Plata
Río de la Plata
ARGENTINA

TRÓPICO DE CAPRICORNIO

Bahía Blanca

Puerto Montt

CORDILLERA DE LOS ANDES

ISLAS MALVINAS

| 0 | 200 | 400 | 600 | 800 millas |
| 0 | 200 | 400 | 600 | 800 kilómetros |

Punta Arenas
TIERRA DEL FUEGO
Estrecho de Magallanes
Cabo de Hornos

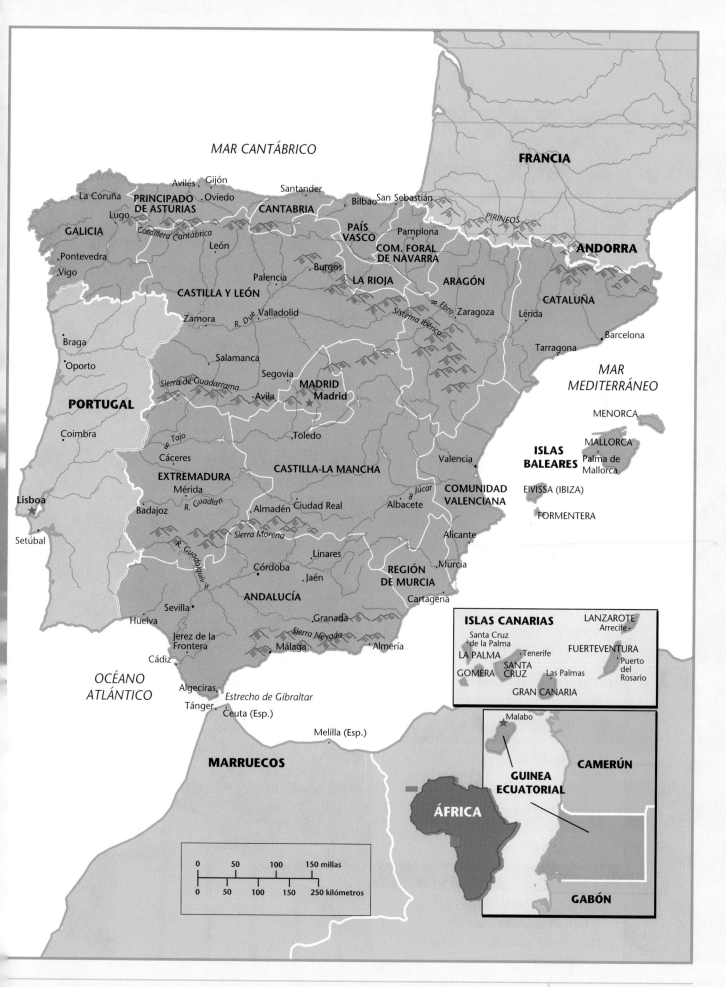

MAR CANTÁBRICO

FRANCIA

Avilés • Gijón
La Coruña • Santander
• Oviedo San Sebastián
PRINCIPADO Bilbao
DE ASTURIAS CANTABRIA
GALICIA Cordillera Cantábrica PAÍS PIRINEOS
Lugo VASCO Pamplona ANDORRA
León COM. FORAL
Pontevedra DE NAVARRA
Vigo Palencia Burgos ARAGÓN CATALUÑA
LA RIOJA
CASTILLA Y LEÓN R. Ebro Zaragoza Lérida
Zamora R. Due Valladolid Sistema Ibérico Barcelona
Braga Tarragona
Oporto Salamanca MAR
Segovia MEDITERRÁNEO
Sierra de Guadarrama MADRID
PORTUGAL Ávila Madrid MENORCA
Coimbra Toledo MALLORCA
Tajo ISLAS Palma de
Cáceres CASTILLA-LA MANCHA BALEARES Mallorca
EXTREMADURA Valencia
Mérida Júcar EIVISSA (IBIZA)
Lisboa R. Guadian Almadén Ciudad Real Albacete COMUNIDAD
Badajoz VALENCIANA FORMENTERA
Setúbal Sierra Morena Alicante
R. Guadalquivir Linares REGIÓN
Córdoba DE MURCIA
Jaén Murcia
Sevilla ANDALUCÍA Cartagena
Huelva Granada
Jerez de la Sierra Nevada Almería
Frontera Málaga
Cádiz

OCÉANO
ATLÁNTICO Algeciras Estrecho de Gibraltar
Tánger Ceuta (Esp.)

Melilla (Esp.)

MARRUECOS

ISLAS CANARIAS LANZAROTE
Santa Cruz Arrecife
de la Palma FUERTEVENTURA
LA PALMA Tenerife Puerto
SANTA Las Palmas del
GOMERA CRUZ Rosario
GRAN CANARIA

Malabo
CAMERÚN
GUINEA
ÁFRICA ECUATORIAL

GABÓN

0   50   100   150 millas
0 50 100 150   250 kilómetros

¡Mucho gusto!

Chapter Objectives

COMMUNICATIVE GOALS

In this chapter you will learn how to . . .

- Greet others, introduce yourself, and say good-bye
- Exchange personal information (origin, age, address, etc.)
- Identify quantities of objects
- Ask and answer questions

STRUCTURES

- Subject pronouns and the present tense of the verbs **ser** and **tener**
- The verb form **hay** and numbers 1–30
- Question words and inflection
- The Spanish alphabet

CULTURAL INFORMATION

- El lugar de encuentro: Las plazas
- ¿Ser informal o formal? ¿**Tú** o **usted**?
- El mundo hispanoamericano

A saludar y a conocer a la gente *(Greeting and meeting people)* In this section you will learn how to greet and say good-bye to people in Spanish in both formal and informal situations.

Una situación formal: entre un profesor y una estudiante *(A formal situation: between a professor and a student)*

Una situación informal: compañeros de clase *(An informal situation: classmates)*

Buenos días. Good morning.	**Encantada.** Nice to meet you. (women say this)
Buenas tardes. Good afternoon.	**Encantado.** Nice to meet you. (men say this)
Buenas noches. Good evening/night.	**Mucho gusto.** Nice to meet you. (men and women say this)
¡Hola! Hi! (informal)	**El gusto es mío.** The pleasure is mine. (men and women say this)

¿NOS ENTENDEMOS?

When you ask questions in Spanish, the voice rises on the last syllable of the last word in the question and falls on the syllable of the last word in a statement, for example:

¿Cómo está usted?

No hay más dinero.

¿NOS ENTENDEMOS?

Adiós carries a more definitive sense of *good-bye* than does **hasta luego**. Use **adiós** when you do not expect to see the other person(s) for a while, such as much later in the day or the following day.

Preguntas formales Formal questions

¿De dónde es usted? Where are you from?
¿Cómo está usted? How are you?
¿Cómo se llama usted? What is your name?
¿Y usted? And you?

Preguntas informales Informal questions

¿Cómo estás? How are you?
¿Cómo te llamas? What's your name?
¿De dónde eres? Where are you from?

¿Qué hay? What's new?
¿Qué tal? What's up?
¿Cómo te va? How's it going?

Respuestas Replies

Bastante bien. Pretty well.
Bien, gracias. Fine, thanks.
Más o menos / Así así. So-so.

(Muy) Bien. (Very) Well.
(Yo) Soy de... I'm from . . .
Me llamo... My name is . . .

Despedidas Farewells

Adiós. Good-bye.
Buenas noches. Good night.
Chao. Bye.
Hasta luego. See you later.

Hasta mañana. See you tomorrow.
Hasta pronto. See you soon.
Nos vemos. See you later.

CULTURA
The form **usted** is abbreviated as **Ud.** and used in formal situations with people whom you would address on a last-name basis. The abbreviation **Ud.** is pronounced just like **usted.**

CULTURA
The informal questions are used with classmates, friends, and other people whom you address on a first-name basis.

¿NOS ENTENDEMOS?
The expressions **nos vemos** and **chao** are used in informal situations with the expectation that you will see the other person(s) in the near future or the following day. In some countries such as Argentina, Chile, Colombia, and Venezuela people say **Chao** to express *good-bye*, due to the Italian immigration influences (**Ciao**) in these countries.

Palabras útiles

Para disculparse (*To excuse yourself*)

con permiso pardon me, excuse me (to ask permission to pass through)
disculpe pardon me (to formally ask for someone's forgiveness or to get someone's attention)
perdón pardon me, excuse me (to ask for someone's forgiveness)
por favor please

Títulos personales The following personal titles and their abbreviations are used in formal interactions between people. There is no standard Spanish equivalent for *Ms.;* use **señorita** or **señora,** as appropriate.

señor (Sr.) Mr., sir
señora (Sra.) Mrs., ma'am
señorita (Srta.) Miss

Palabras útiles are presented to help you enrich your personal vocabulary. The words here will help you interact in Spanish.

¡A PRACTICAR! *(Let's practice)*

P-1 | **Meter la pata *(To stick one's foot in one's mouth)*** Imagine that your friend is eager to practice his/her Spanish but makes mistakes by responding incorrectly to some of the expressions given below. Identify which responses are incorrect, then provide the correct response. Pay attention to whether the address is formal or informal.

> MODELO: ¿De dónde eres tú? *Me llamo Jessica.*
> *No es correcto. The student was asked where she was from and she responded with her name.*
> *She might have said, "Yo soy de Indiana."*

1. Mucho gusto. *Más o menos.*
2. ¿Cómo se llama usted? *Me llamo Jim.*
3. Hasta mañana. *¡Hola!*
4. ¡Hola! *¿Qué tal?*
5. Y tú, ¿qué tal? *Más o menos. ¿Y usted?*
6. Encantada. *Buenas noches.*

P-2 | **¿Qué dices? *(What do you say?)*** Match the situations on the left with an appropriate expression from the list on the right. Remember to distinguish between formal and informal situations.

1. You're introduced to Sra. Fuertes. _____
2. You're asking a child where he/she is from. _____
3. You're greeting a stranger on the way to class at 8:00 a.m. _____
4. You're saying good-bye to a friend going on vacation. _____
5. You're asking your mother's friend how she's doing. _____
6. You're saying hello to a friend. _____
7. You're leaving a party at a friend's house at 2:00 a.m. _____
8. You're asking an old man in the park what his name is. _____
9. You're walking to an afternoon class and you see your TA. _____

a. ¡Hola!
b. ¿De dónde eres?
c. Mucho gusto, señora.
d. ¿Cómo está usted?
e. ¡Buenos días!
f. ¡Adiós!
g. ¡Chao!
h. ¿Cómo se llama usted?
i. ¡Buenas tardes!
j. ¡Buenas noches!

EN VOZ ALTA *(Out loud)*

P-3 | **¡A conocernos! *(Let's get to know each other!)*** Use the following questions as a means of learning about other students in your class. Replace the italicized words to describe yourself. Practice changing roles several times and substitute other expressions for greetings and farewells.

With a greeting
E1: Hola.
E2: ¿Qué tal?

With the verb *llamarse*
E1: ¿Cómo te llamas?
E2: Me llamo *Jen.*

With the verb *ser*
E1: ¿De dónde eres?
E2: Soy de *Milwaukee.*
E1: ¿Eres estudiante?
E2: Sí, soy estudiante.

With the verb *estudiar*
E1: ¿Qué estudias? *(What do you study?)*
E2: Estudio español.

With the verb *estar*
E1: ¿Cómo estás?
E2: ¡Muy bien, gracias! / Más o menos.

With a farewell
E1: ¡Chao!
E2: ¡Hasta luego!

P-4 | **¡Buenos días, profesor(a)!** Working with a partner, decide how you would modify the expressions in activity **P-3** so that they would suit a formal conversation with your professor. Role-play the dialog with another student, with one acting as the student and the other as the professor.

El lugar de encuentro: Las plazas
(Place of meeting: The plazas)

PARA PENSAR

- Where do you meet your friends?
- Where do you get together with your family?
- What do you do or talk about when you meet them?

In the Spanish-speaking world, most of the big cities as well as small towns have their main plaza. At the plazas, older and younger people get together not only to talk about their families, or to celebrate

Antigovernment demonstration in Buenos Aires, Argentina

important dates such as independence day or a religious day, but also to talk about politics and economics in their countries. The plaza is a central meeting place and is an important part of life in all parts of the Spanish-speaking world.

Throughout the years, people have gathered in different plazas to protest the governments' economic policies, such as in the main plazas of Bogota, Colombia; Buenos Aires, Argentina; Montevideo, Uruguay; and Caracas, Venezuela, where lately, people join together with their pots and pans **(cacerolas)** in order to to make noise and express their frustration about the government and its inefficiency in improving the country's economy.

Also, people have congregated together at the main plazas to protest their governments' abuses toward human rights, such as in **La Plaza de Mayo** in Buenos Aires, Argentina, where mainly women have joined together since 1977 to protest the disappearance of their daughters, sons, sisters, brothers, and husbands.

In other important plazas such as the **Zócalo** in Mexico City, Mexico, people get together every year to celebrate with much enthusiasm on September 16 **(Grito de Dolores)**, which represents the first attempt by the Mexican people to obtain their independence from Spain in 1810.

In the Spanish-speaking world, spacious or tiny plazas, located in capitals or small towns, have always been the most important place for people to meet to talk about their families' affairs or to discuss their countries' economic and governmental policies.

PARA DISCUTIR

1. What do people celebrate in the plazas in Latin America?
2. What do people protest against in the plazas in Latin America?
3. What do people do in the parks and plazas in the United States?
4. Are there differences in the use of parks and plazas in the United States and in the Spanish-speaking world?

EN CONTEXTO (In context)

The following dialog describes the Ortega family's first meeting with Raquel, the new baby-sitter, at their home in Miami. Notice how Mr. Ortega and Raquel use the formal form of **usted** to address each other. However, when Raquel meets Mr. Ortega's daughter, María José, she talks to the child using the informal **tú** form, appropriate when addressing someone younger than the speaker.

CULTURA
According to the 2000 Census, Miami, Florida, has 2.68 million of the Spanish-speaking population as a result of large-scale immigration especially from Cuba, Puerto Rico, and the Dominican Republic. Millions of Spanish-speaking Americans also live in San Diego, Los Angeles, Phoenix, San Antonio, Chicago, and New York City.

CULTURA
La Paz, the capital city of Bolivia, is located at 12,001 feet above sea level in the altiplano (a high plateau region). It is the world's highest capital city and is nestled in a canyon. The center of the city's cultural life is the Plaza Murillo.

¿NOS ENTENDEMOS?
Nena or nene, particularly in Puerto Rico, is used when an adult wants to get a young person's attention.

Raquel:	**¡Buenas noches, señor!**
Sr. Ortega:	¡Buenas noches! **¿Es usted** la señorita Gandía?
Raquel:	Sí, soy yo (Yes, I am). **Me llamo** Raquel.
Sr. Ortega:	**Mucho gusto,** Raquel. Yo soy Ricardo Ortega.
Raquel:	Encantada, Señor Ortega.
Sr. Ortega:	**¿De dónde es usted?**
Raquel:	**Yo soy de** aquí (here)... de Miami. ¿Y ustedes?
Sr. Ortega:	Nosotros somos de La Paz, Bolivia. Llevamos **un** año aquí (We have been here for a year). ¿Y cómo es que usted habla tan bien (speak so well) el español?
Raquel:	Mi padre **es de Puerto Rico,** y en mi barrio (neighborhood) **hay** (there are) mucha gente (a lot of people) de allí (from there), de Cuba y de la República Dominicana.
Sr. Ortega:	Raquel, quiero presentarle a nuestra (our) hija, María José.
María José:	¡Hola!
Raquel:	**¡Hola,** María José! **¿Cómo estás?**
María José:	**Bien, gracias, ¿y usted?**
Raquel:	Muy bien, gracias. ¿Y **cuántos años tienes tú,** nena?
María José:	**Yo tengo nueve años.**
Raquel:	¡Dios mío! (Oh, my God!) ¿Sólo (Only) nueve años? Pareces mayor (You look older).

¿Comprendiste? (Did you understand?)

Decide whether the following statements are **cierto** (true) or **falso** (false). If the statement is false, change it to a true statement. The easiest way to do this is to negate the sentence by placing the word **no** in front of the verb. If the sentence is already negated, remove the **no** before the verb.

MODELO: Raquel es la madre de María José. (Raquel is María José's mother.)
Falso: Raquel no es la madre de María José.

1. El señor Ortega es boliviano.
2. Raquel es de Nueva York.
3. Raquel habla español muy bien.
4. El padre de Raquel es de Cuba.
5. Hay muchas personas hispanas en Florida.
6. María José tiene nueve años.

¿Ser informal o formal? ¿*Tú* o ***usted***?
(To be informal or formal?)

PARA PENSAR

- Do you use different forms to address older and younger persons in English?
- Do you talk the same way to your instructors as to your friends or classmates?

When Spanish speakers address one person, they express the word *you* in one of two ways: **tú** or **usted.** The following guidelines should be helpful to you:

- **Tú** is an informal form of addressing someone. In general, use **tú** with someone with whom you are on a first-name basis. For example, Spanish speakers use **tú** when addressing a relative, a close friend, a person of the same age or social position, a classmate, a small child, or a pet.

- **Usted** is used when speaking or writing to a person with a title such as **señora, señorita, doctor, profesora,** and so forth. Spanish speakers use **usted** when addressing a stranger, a casual acquaintance other than a child, a person much older than themselves, or a person in a formal position or a position of authority such as a supervisor, store clerk, or police officer. When you are unsure about whether to use **tú** or **usted,** it is wiser to use **usted.**

PARA DISCUTIR

1. Based on the information given above, how would you address the following people in Spanish? Write either **tú** or **usted** after each of the following phrases.
   a. your Spanish instructor
   b. your email friend from Guatemala
   c. Marisa Ramírez, a seven-year-old girl
   d. a waiter in a restaurant
   e. Dr. Guillermo Peraza, a friend's father
   f. an exchange student from Ecuador
   g. your supervisor at work
   h. your best friend from Venezuela
   i. a classmate you just met
   j. a distant relative you just met

2. Why do you think people address different people using various expressions in English?

3. Why do you think people use either **tú** or **usted** in Spanish?

4. Do you agree or disagree with the idea of addressing different people with different expressions?

For more information on the subject of the verb versus a subject pronoun, consult the Grammar Guide in the back of the book.

A *verb* is a word that expresses action (*run, jump,* etc.) or indicates a state of being (*is, seems,* etc.). The *subject* of the verb is either a *noun* or *pronoun* that identifies who does the action of a verb. Subjects that are nouns include names such as *Mary, Fred, Jerome,* and so forth. Subjects that are pronouns include words such as *you, I, we, they,* etc. Study the Spanish subject pronouns along with the present-tense forms of the verb **ser.**

ser *(to be)*

Singular		
yo	**soy**	*I am*
tú	**eres**	*you* (informal) *are*
usted (Ud.), él/ella	**es**	*you* (formal) *are, he/she is*
Plural		
nosotros(as)	**somos**	*we are*
vosotros(as)	**sois**	*you* (informal) *are*
ustedes (Uds.), ellos(as)	**son**	*you are, they are*

Note that in most of Spain, the plural form of **tú** is **vosotros** (referring to males only or to a mixed group of males and females) and **vosotras** (referring to females only). In Latin America, **ustedes** is the plural form for both **tú** and **usted.**

vosotras	*you are*			Alicia y Regina, **vosotras sois** muy sinceras.
		}	**sois**	*Alicia and Regina, you are very sincere.*
vosotros	*you are*			David y María, **vosotros sois** mis amigos.
				David and María, you are my friends.

¡A PRACTICAR!

P-5 **¿Sí o no?** Say whether you agree (**sí**) or disagree (**no**) with the following statements.

MODELOS: Penélope Cruz es actriz.
Sí. Penélope Cruz es actriz.

Penélope Cruz es profesora.
No. Penélope Cruz no es profesora.

1. Salma Hayek es elegante.
2. Ronaldo no es atlético.
3. Mis profesores son cómicos.
4. Marc Anthony es estudiante.
5. Mis amigas son independientes.
6. Mi papá es profesor.
7. Mi mamá es bailarina.
8. Yo soy sentimental.
9. ...

P-6 **¿Quiénes somos? ¿Quiénes son?** *(Who are we? Who are they?)* Complete the sentences below with correct verb form of the verb **ser**.

MODELO: Rudy Moreno *es* un cómico famoso.

1. Nosotros _____ estudiantes de español.
2. Tú _____ mi compañero(a) de clase.
3. Benicio del Toro y Antonio Banderas _____ dos actores famosos.
4. Harry Belafonte _____ un músico famoso.
5. Ustedes _____ de Costa Rica.
6. Ella _____ muy inteligente.
7. Yo _____ _____.
8. Carlos Fuentes _____ mexicano.

EN VOZ ALTA

P-7 **¿Quién entre nosotros?** *(Who among us?)* Working with a partner, form questions to ask your classmate, using the adjectives listed below. To ask a question in Spanish, place the verb before the adjective.

MODELO: cómica *(a woman)*
E1: ¿Es cómica Katie?
E2: *Sí, Katie es cómica.*
o *No, Katie no es cómica.*

1. atlético(a) *(your professor)*
2. sincero(a) *(you)*
3. extrovertidos *(two men)*
4. serios *(we)*
5. inteligentes *(a man and a woman)*
6. famosas *(two women)*

A useful Spanish verb form is **hay,** which means *there is* and *there are* (or *Is there . . . ?* and *Are there . . . ?* in questions). Use **hay** to indicate the existence of people, places, and things; **hay** may be followed by a singular or plural noun. Be careful not to confuse this verb form with the verb **ser,** which also means *to be* but does not express the idea of *there is / there are.*

¿Cuántas personas **hay** en tu clase de español?	*How many persons are there in your Spanish class?*
Hay una profesora y veintisiete estudiantes.	*There is a teacher and twenty-seven students.*

Los números del 0 al 30

0	cero	11	once	22	veintidós
1	uno	12	doce	23	veintitrés
2	dos	13	trece	24	veinticuatro
3	tres	14	catorce	25	veinticinco
4	cuatro	15	quince	26	veintiséis
5	cinco	16	dieciséis	27	veintisiete
6	seis	17	diecisiete	28	veintiocho
7	siete	18	dieciocho	29	veintinueve
8	ocho	19	diecinueve	30	treinta
9	nueve	20	veinte		
10	diez	21	veintiuno		

- Note that **uno** has three different forms.

  1. When counting, the form **uno** is used.

     Uno, dos, tres...   *One, two, three . . .*

  2. When preceeding a singular masculine noun, the **-o** is dropped to form **un (un señor, un chico).**

     Hay **un** profesor en la clase.   *There is a professor in the class.*

  3. Before a singular feminine noun, **una** is used **(una señora, una chica).**

     Hay **una** cafetería buena en esta universidad.   *There is one good cafeteria in this university.*

- The number **veintiuno** changes to **veintiún** before a plural masculine.

  Hay **veintiún** estudiantes.   *There are twenty-one students.*

- The numbers 16 to 19 and 21 to 29 can be written either as one word (e.g., **dieciséis**) or as three words (e.g., **diez y seis**). In most Spanish-speaking countries, people prefer to use the single word.

¡A PRACTICAR!

P-8 | **En la clase de español hay...** Fill in the blanks to complete the following. Notice that you use **hay** to show singular (*there is*) as well as plural (*there are*).

En mi clase de español, ___*hay*___ ___*veinte*___ estudiantes. _____

_____ chicas y ¡solamente (*only*) _____ chicos! _____ un(a) profesor, él/ella es muy simpático(a) (*nice*). _____ _____ escritorios (*desks*) y _____ pizarras (*chalkboards*).

P-9 | **¿Cuántos hay?** (***How many are there?***) State how many units there are of the following items.

MODELO: 18 casetes
Hay dieciocho casetes.

1. 11 raquetas de tenis
2. 1 auto
3. 5 libros (*books*)
4. 3 mochilas (*backpacks*)

5. 1 chica (*young woman*)
6. 13 teléfonos
7. 27 bicicletas
8. 30 puertas

P-10 | **Problemas de matemáticas** Do the following math problems with another student.

+ **más**   − **menos**

MODELOS: $2 + 2 = ?$ E1: *¿Cuántos son dos más dos?*
E2: *Dos más dos son cuatro.*

$3 − 1 = ?$ E1: *¿Cuántos son tres menos uno?*
E2: *Tres menos uno son dos.*

1. $3 + 3 = ¿?$
2. $8 − 3 = ¿?$
3. $11 + 4 = ¿?$
4. $16 + 10 = ¿?$
5. $6 − 2 = ¿?$
6. $7 + 3 = ¿?$
7. $14 + 5 = ¿?$
8. $25 − 11 = ¿?$

9. $4 + 2 = ¿?$
10. $9 − 1 = ¿?$
11. $15 − 4 = ¿?$
12. $22 + 7 = ¿?$
13. $6 + 1 = ¿?$
14. $7 − 4 = ¿?$
15. $16 − 3 = ¿?$
16. $30 − 9 = ¿?$

EN VOZ ALTA

P-11 | **¿Hay o no hay?** In pairs, answer these questions about your class. Follow the model, then switch roles.

MODELO: hombres (*men*)
—*¿Hay hombres en la clase?*
—*Sí. Hay doce hombres.*

1. mujeres (*women*)
2. hombres y mujeres
3. profesores
4. ...
5. ...

¿**Cómo?** How?

¿**Cuál(es)?** Which?

¿**Cuándo?** When?

¿**Cuántos(as)?** How many?

¿**De dónde?** From where?

¿**Dónde?** Where?

¿**Por qué?** Why?

¿**Qué?** What?

¿**Quién(es)?** Who?

As an English speaker, there are a few basic linguistic points to keep in mind when using Spanish question words.

¿**Cuál?** *(Which?)* is used far more frequently in Spanish than in English. It has the same meaning as *What?* when someone's name, address, or telephone number is being asked. When it refers to a plural noun, it becomes ¿**Cuáles?**

¿**Cuál** es tu nombre?	*What's your name?*
¿**Cuál** es tu número de teléfono?	*What's your telephone number?*
¿**Cuál** es tu dirección?	*What's your address?*
¿**Cuáles** son tus amigos?	*Which ones are your friends?*

¿**Quién?**, like ¿**Cuál?**, must be made plural when referring to a plural group of people.

¿**Quiénes** son tus padres?	*Who are your parents?*

¿**Cuántos(as)?** must agree in gender (masculine or feminine) with the noun it describes.

¿**Cuántos** hombres hay en la clase?	*How many men are in the class?*
¿**Cuántas** personas hay en tu familia?	*How many people are in your family?*

Notice that all question words carry accents. The accent indicates that the word is being used as an interrogative. For example, **que** without an accent means *that*. The word means *What?* only when it appears as ¿**Qué?**

¡A PRACTICAR!

P-12 **Preguntas** A friend of yours is doing a survey in a Spanish-speaking neighborhood. Help him fill in the missing question words. Are the survey questions addressed formally or informally?

MODELO: ¿_____*Cómo*_____ se llama usted?

1. ¿De _____ es usted?
2. ¿_____ es su *(your)* dirección *(address)*?
3. ¿_____ personas hay en su familia?
4. ¿_____ son sus padres?
5. ¿_____ es su número de teléfono?
6. ¿_____ es la fiesta *(party)*?
7. ¿_____ es Juan tan *(so)* curioso?
8. ¿_____ es ella?

EN VOZ ALTA

P-13 **Información personal** Circulate around your classroom to obtain the phone numbers and addresses of at least three different classmates. Be sure to use the appropriate mode of address (informal or formal).

MODELO: —¿Cuál es tu número de teléfono?
—Es el dos, veintinueve, quince, once (229-1511). ¿Y el tuyo? *(And yours?)*
—Es el cuatro, veinticinco, diez, trece (425–1013). ¿Cuál es tu dirección?
—Camino Linda Vista, número tres, cinco, cuatro, siete (3547); apartamento número once (11).

P-14 **¿Qué? ¿Cuántos? ¿Cómo?** Create questions in Spanish in order to find out personal information about two classmates. You want to get the following information:

- where they come from, their names,
- the names of their friends,
- their parents' names,
- their best friend's name, and so on.

Take turns asking each other the questions you come up with.

CULTURA

In most Spanish-speaking countries, telephone numbers have 7 digits, but they have only 5 or 6 in some areas. When expressing a telephone number with an uneven number of digits, it is common to begin with a single digit but express the remaining numbers in groups of two, as is shown in the model. If your telephone number contains numbers that you are not yet able to express in pairs, you may present each number individually, such as **dos, cuatro, uno, ocho, nueve, seis, cero** for 241-8960.

ESTRUCTURA II Telling age: the present tense of the verb *tener*

One of the uses of the verb **tener** (*to have*) is to express age in Spanish. Spanish speakers say they *have* _____ *years* rather than they *are* _____ *years old*. **Tener** is conjugated as follows:

tener (*to have*)

Singular		
yo	tengo	*I have*
tú	tienes	*you* (informal) *have*
usted, él/ella	tiene	*you* (formal) *have, he/she has*
Plural		
nosotros(as)	tenemos	*we have*
vosotros(as)	tenéis	*you* (informal) *have*
ustedes, ellos(as)	tienen	*you* (formal) *have, they have*

¡A PRACTICAR!

P-15 **Edades (*Ages*)** Indicate the age of the following people, using the verb **tener**.

MODELO: el profesor (30)
El profesor tiene treinta años.

1. Susana (25)
2. Lourdes (1)
3. Jorge y Héctor (19)
4. yo (_____)
5. mi amigo(a) _____ (_____)
6. mi amigo(a) _____ y yo (_____)

EN VOZ ALTA

P-16 **¿Cuántos años tienes? (*How old are you?*)** Ask a minimum of three classmates how old they are. Who is closer to your age? Don't forget to follow the model below. Then report your findings to the class.

MODELO: E1: ¿Cuántos años tienes?
E2: Tengo_____. ¿Y tú?
E1: _____

Encuentro cultural

El mundo hispanoamericano

PARA PENSAR

- Do you know what other languages have influenced the Spanish language?
- Do you know how many countries use Spanish as an official language? Do you know their names?
- What words do you know in Spanish that you use in English?

Spanish is the native language of over 400 million people. It is the main language of Spain, Mexico, Puerto Rico, Cuba, the Dominican Republic, and every Central American country except Belize, and all South American nations except the Guayanas and Brazil.

Spanish developed from Latin with influences from other languages such as German, Greek, Basque, and Arabic. It was also influenced by American languages such as Nahuatl in Mexico and Quechua in Bolivia, Peru, and Ecuador. In addition, diverse historical influences produced regional differences in spelling, pronunciation, and vocabulary of Spanish. These differences occur not only among the various Spanish-speaking countries, but also within those countries. For example, in most Spanish-speaking countries the words **carro, coche,** and **automóvil** all mean the same thing: *car.* On the other hand, if one wants to say *bus* in Spain, one says **autobús;** in Mexico, **camión;** in Cuba and Puerto Rico, **guagua** (which means *baby* in Chile and Peru); and in some Spanish-speaking portions of the United States, **bus.**

The fact that Spanish, like English, is still spoken and is always changing defines it as a living language, unlike Latin or Classical Greek. Spanish varies from country to country and region to region because it is a living language. Even though these differences exist, it is very rare that Spanish speakers from different places do not understand one another.

PARA DISCUTIR

1. Can you give examples of different words that mean the same thing in different Spanish-speaking countries?
2. What is the difference between a living language and a dead language? Explain. Why is Spanish described as a living language?
3. Do you know what other languages have influenced the English language? Can you give some examples?
4. Can you give examples of words that have the same or different meaning in the East and West coasts of the United States or in England or Australia?
5. Why do you think it is important to learn a second language, for instance, Spanish?

Población en julio de 2002

PARA PENSAR

- Do you know any of the man-made or natural wonders in South America?

- Why are there some countries that share the same colors in their flags?

- Which is the most populated South American country?

PARA DISCUTIR

Study the map and then answer the following questions.

1. Which country is the least populated of South America? What do you think is the reason for this?

2. What are the capitals of Argentina, Chile, and Paraguay?

3. What are the advantages of countries such as Colombia and Venezuela in relation to their location in South America?

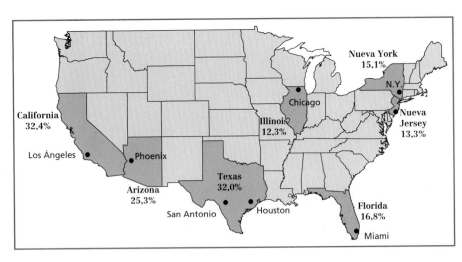

PARA PENSAR

- Do you know how many Spanish-speakers live in the United States? Can you estimate?

- Do you know in what states the Spanish-speaking population lives?

- Do you have friends that speak Spanish? Where do they live?

There are more than 26 million Spanish-speakers in the United States. They are the fastest growing minority group in the nation, with the largest concentration in California, Arizona, Texas, Colorado, Illinois, New York, New Jersey, and Florida.

PARA DISCUTIR

Study the map and then answer the following questions.

1. In what states is Spanish spoken in the United States?

2. In what states do you find the largest Spanish-speaking population? Why?

3. In what states do you find the least Hispanic concentration? Why?

4. Discuss the importance of learning Spanish after studying this map.

PARA PENSAR

- Do you know the name of the capital of Mexico?

- Have you met anybody from Mexico?

- Do you know in which Caribbean islands Spanish is spoken?

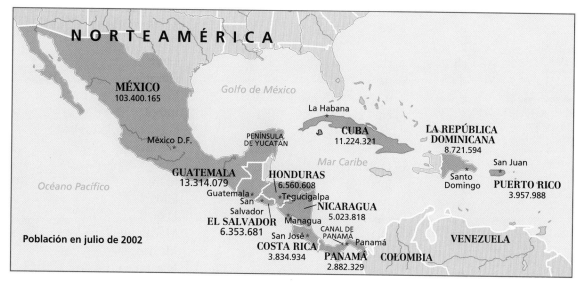

Mexico City, the capital of Mexico, has more than 25 million inhabitants in the greater metropolitan area, making it the world's largest city. The Yucatan Peninsula in Mexico is popular for its warm beaches and famous Mayan ruins. Cuba, Puerto Rico, and the Dominican Republic are three Caribbean islands that have a history of cooperation and confrontation with the United States.

PARA DISCUTIR

Study the map above and then answer the following questions.

1. What is the population of Mexico City? Would you like to live in a big city like Mexico City? Explain why or why not.

2. What is the capital of Panama? Why is Panama important to the rest of the world?

3. What are the capitals of the three Spanish-speaking Caribbean islands?

PARA PENSAR

- In what European country is Spanish spoken?

- What is the capital of this country?

- What countries form the Iberian Peninsula?

Although Spain occupies an important place in Hispanic culture, Spain's population represents only 12% of Hispanics worldwide. Spain makes up the largest part of the Iberian Peninsula along with Portugal. Spain's capital is Madrid, located in the center of the country. Lisbon is the capital of Portugal, where Portuguese is spoken.

PARA DISCUTIR

Study the map and then answer the following questions.

1. What is the capital of this European country where they speak Spanish?

2. What countries are bordering this country?

3. What is the population of this country?

4. What countries form the Iberian Peninsula?

5. Would you like to visit Spain? Why?

6. Discuss any experience you have had with a person from Spain.

EL ALFABETO EN ESPAÑOL *(The Spanish Alphabet)*

Track 1-3

The alphabet is also presented in the Lab Manual, where its pronunciation is practiced extensively. Note that some Spanish speakers will argue that there are only 28 letters, no longer considering **ch** and **ll** to be part of the alphabet.

The Spanish alphabet contains thirty letters:

a	a	América Central
b	be	Buenos Aires
c	ce	Costa Rica
ch	che	Chile
d	de	Durango
e	e	Ecuador
f	efe	fútbol
g	ge	Guatemala, Gibraltar
h	hache	Honduras
i	i (i latina)	isla
j	jota	Juárez
k	ka	kilo
l	ele	León
ll	elle	Manzanillo
m	eme	México
n	ene	Nicaragua
ñ	eñe	España
o	o	océano
p	pe	Paraguay
q	cu	Quito
r	ere	río Grande
rr	erre	Tierra del Fuego
s	ese	San José
t	te	Tegucigalpa
u	u	Uruguay
v	ve (ve chica, ve corta, uve)	Venezuela
w	doble ve (doble uve)	Washington
x	equis	Extremadura
y	i griega	Yucatán
z	zeta	Zaragoza

- All letters in the alphabet are feminine: **la a, la be, la ce,** etc.

- As opposed to the English alphabet, there are four more letters in the Spanish alphabet: **ch, ll, ñ,** and **rr.** In all dictionaries published prior to 1995, you will find separate sections for words beginning with **ch** and **ll** (**ñ** has always had its own section; **rr** is never found at the beginning of a word). Most dictionaries published after 1995 do not treat **ch** and **ll** separately.

- The letters **k** and **w** are not common and appear only in words of foreign origin, such as **karate** and **whiski.**

VOCABULARIO ESENCIAL

Cómo se saluda How to greet

Buenos días. Good morning.
Buenas tardes. Good afternoon.
Buenas noches. Good evening/night.

¡Hola! Hi! (informal)
¿Qué tal? What's up? (informal)
¿Qué hay? What's new? (informal)

¿Cómo estás? How are you? (informal)
¿Cómo está usted? How are you? (formal)

Cómo se contesta How to answer

Bastante bien. Pretty well.
Más o menos. / Así así. So-so.

(Muy) Bien. (Very) Well.
Bien, gracias. ¿Y usted? Fine, thanks. And you?

Me llamo... My name is . . .

Presentaciones Introductions

¿Cómo se llama usted? What's your name?
   (formal)
¿Cómo te llamas? What's your name?
   (informal)

¿Cuál es tu nombre? What's your name?
   (informal)
Me llamo... My name is . . .
El gusto es mío. The pleasure is mine.

Encantado(a). Nice to meet you.
Mucho gusto. Nice to meet you.
(Yo) Soy de... I'm from . . .

Cómo despedirse How to say good-bye

Adiós. Good-bye.
Buenas noches. Good night.
Chao. Bye. (informal)

Hasta luego. See you later.
Hasta mañana. See you tomorrow.
Hasta pronto. See you soon.

Nos vemos. See you later.

Los números del 0 al 30 Numbers from 0 to 30

cero zero
uno one
dos two
tres three
cuatro four
cinco five
seis six
siete seven
ocho eight

nueve nine
diez ten
once eleven
doce twelve
trece thirteen
catorce fourteen
quince fifteen
dieciséis sixteen
diecisiete seventeen

dieciocho eighteen
diecinueve nineteen
veinte twenty
veintiuno twenty-one
veintidós twenty-two
veintitrés twenty-three
veintiséis twenty-six
treinta thirty

Palabras interrogativas Question words

¿Cómo? How?
¿Cuál(es)? Which?
¿Cuándo? When?

¿Cuántos(as)? How many?
¿De dónde? From where?
¿Dónde? Where?

¿Por qué? Why?
¿Qué? What?
¿Quién(es)? Who?

Cómo se pide información How to ask for information

¿Cuál es tu nombre? What's your name?
   (informal)
¿Cuál es tu número de teléfono? What's your
   telephone number? (informal)
¿Cuál es tu dirección? What's your address?

¿De dónde es usted? Where are you from?
   (formal)
¿De dónde eres tú? Where are you from?
   (informal)

¿Cómo te llamas? What is your name?
   (informal)
¿Cómo te va? How's it going?

Verbos Verbs

ser to be

tener to have

Pronombres Pronouns

él he
ella she
ellas they
ellos they
nosotros(as) we

tú you (informal)
usted you (formal)
ustedes you (formal plural in Spain; formal and
   informal plural in Lat. Am.)

vosotros(as) you (informal plural in parts of
   Spain)
yo I

Expresiones idiomáticas Idiomatic expressions

hay there is / there are

¡Qué casualidad! What a coincidence!

1 En una clase de español:

Chapter Objectives

COMMUNICATIVE GOALS

In this chapter you will learn how to . . .

- Identify people and things in the classroom
- Indicate relationships and specify colors
- Describe everyday activities
- Talk about academic courses and university buildings
- Say what you like and don't like doing
- Tell time

STRUCTURES

- Definite and indefinite articles and how to make nouns plural (Gender of nouns)
- Present tense of regular **-ar** verbs
- **Me gusta** + *infinitive*

CULTURAL INFORMATION

- Hispanohablantes en los Estados Unidos
- La educación en Latinoamérica y España
- El sistema de 24 horas

Los Estados Unidos

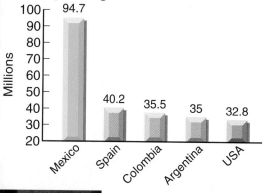

Population of Top Four Spanish-Speaking Countries and the U.S.

Millions

Mexico	94.7
Spain	40.2
Colombia	35.5
Argentina	35
USA	32.8

¡Bienvenidos a los EE.UU.!

In this video, you will learn about the native Spanish-speaking population in the major cities in the United States. After watching the video, answer the following questions:

1. Where do most native Spanish-speakers in the U.S. come from?

2. Which cities mentioned in the video boast a large native Spanish-speaking population?

3. What are some of the influences of Mexican culture in San Antonio?

4. Where are many native Spanish-speakers from in New York City?

5. Do you think it is important to know how to speak Spanish in the U.S.? Why yes or why not?

La Plaza de Rockafeller, Nueva York, Estados Unidos

VOCABULARIO En la clase

¿NOS ENTENDEMOS?

In Latin America, *computer* is either **la computadora** or **el computador**. In Spain, it is generally called **el ordenador**.

En la clase de la profesora Muñoz *(In Professor Muñoz's class)* In this section you will learn how to identify people and things in the classroom. How does Professor Muñoz's class compare to your own?

Otras cosas Other things

el dinero money
el examen exam
la lección lesson
la palabra word
la tarea homework

Otras personas Other people

el (la) amigo(a) friend
el (la) compañero(a) de cuarto roommate
el hombre man
la mujer woman
el (la) novio(a) boyfriend/girlfriend

Los colores Colors

¿NOS ENTENDEMOS?

The color brown has more than one name in Spanish. It can be **color café, castaño,** or **color pardo. Color café** tends to refer to the color of eyes, while **castaño** refers to hair color.

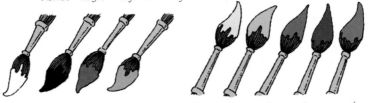

blanco   negro   rojo   anaranjado

amarillo   verde   azul   morado   marrón

Like other adjectives, colors must agree in gender and number with the noun they describe.

El papel es roj**o**.   Los papeles son roj**os**.

La mochila es roj**a**.   Las mochilas son roj**as**.

The colors **verde** and **azul** do not change when used with a feminine noun.

La pizarra es verde.   La mochila es azul.

Palabras útiles are presented to help you enrich your personal vocabulary. The terms provided here will help you talk about the people you interact with on campus.

Palabras útiles

el (la) bibliotecario(a) librarian
el (la) consejero(a) adviser
el decano dean

el (la) maestro(a) teacher
el (la) presidente/rector(a) de la universidad president of the university
el (la) secretario(a) secretary

¡A PRACTICAR!

1-1 **¿Cierto o falso?** Study the drawing of Professor Muñoz's classroom on page 24 and decide whether each of the following statements is true **(cierto)** or false **(falso).** If a statement is false, correct it.

MODELO: Hay doce mujeres en la clase.
Falso. Hay diez mujeres en la clase.

1. Hoy es martes.
2. La señorita Muñoz es profesora de francés.
3. Todos los estudiantes son hombres.
4. La mochila es verde.
5. Todos los estudiantes tienen el libro de texto.
6. Es una clase de matemáticas.
7. Hay una pluma anaranjada en el escritorio de la profesora.
8. Un chico escribe con un bolígrafo verde.

1-2 **¿De qué color es... ?** Match each of the following places or things to the color with which it is most generally associated.

1. _____ EE.UU. (los Estados Unidos de América)
2. _____ Sierra Club, Greenpeace
3. _____ los Bulls de Chicago
4. _____ Coca-Cola
5. _____ chocolate

a. rojo
b. rojo, azul, y blanco
c. rojo y negro
d. marrón
e. verde

1-3 **¿Cuántos hay en la clase?** Say how many of each of the following items appear in Professor Muñoz's classroon on page 24. Remember that **uno** changes to **una** before a singular, feminine noun and changes to **un** before a singular masculine noun.

MODELO: Hay __*quince*__ estudiante(s) en la clase.

1. Hay _____ tiza(s) en la clase.
2. Hay _____ mujer(es) en la clase.
3. Hay _____ hombre(s) en la clase.
4. Hay _____ luz (luces) en la clase.
5. Hay _____ mapa(s) en la clase.
6. Hay _____ cosas (*things*) en la pared (*wall*). Son: el reloj, _____,
   _____, _____.

EN VOZ ALTA

1-4 **¿Cuántos hay?** Working with two of your classmates, take turns asking about the quantity of each item listed below in your classroom. Remember to use **¿Cuántos... ?** for plural masculine nouns and **¿Cuántas... ?** for plural, feminine nouns.

> MODELO: Estudiantes
> E1: *¿Cuántos estudiantes hay en esta clase?*
> E2: *Hay quince estudiantes en la clase.*

1. cuadernos
2. lápices
3. bolígrafos azules
4. diccionarios
5. hombres

6. mujeres
7. profesores(as)
8. tizas
9. borradores
10. estudiantes inteligentes

1-5 **Cosas y colores** Ask a partner if he/she has the following items. If your partner has the item, he/she should state the color of the object. Your partner may also choose to identify another object.

> MODELO: un bolígrafo
> E1: *¿Tienes un bolígrafo?*
> E2: *Sí, tengo un bolígrafo. Mi bolígrafo es azul.*
> o E2: *No, no tengo un bolígrafo. Tengo un lápiz. Mi lápiz es rojo.*

1. una mochila
2. un diccionario
3. un lápiz

4. un cuaderno
5. una calculadora
6. una computadora

1-6 **La clase ideal** Working with a partner, design the ideal classroom. One person describes the room to the other person who draws it. The one who draws the classroom should explain the design to the class.

> MODELO: *En la clase ideal, hay muchos amigos, pero no hay profesor....*

1-7 **¿Estás de acuerdo? (Do you agree?)** Below is a list of ideal characteristics for people you know in and outside of class. Read each statement. If you agree with the statement, give an example of someone you know. If you disagree, indicate the characteristic that makes the statement true for you.

> MODELO: El profesor ideal es generoso.
> *Sí, para mí (for me) el profesor ideal es generoso. El profesor Jones es muy generoso.*
> o *No, para mí el profesor ideal no es generoso. El profesor ideal es inteligente.*

1. El amigo ideal es paciente.
2. La novia ideal es independiente.
3. El novio ideal es romántico.
4. El compañero de cuarto ideal es interesante.
5. La compañera de clase ideal es inteligente.
6. El estudiante ideal es honesto.

Text audio
Track 1-5

A na Guadalupe Camacho Ortega, a prospective student at the University of Chicago whose family plans to move to Illinois from Puerto Rico next year, is talking to Claudio Fuentes, a teaching assistant for Professor Muñoz. Ana is telling Claudio about her studies at the Universidad de San Juan.

Claudio:	¡Hola! Soy Claudio Fuentes. ¿Cómo te llamas?
Ana:	Ana Camacho. Mucho gusto.
Claudio:	El gusto es mío. ¿De dónde eres, Ana?
Ana:	Soy de Puerto Rico. Ahora *(Right now)* **estudio** *(I study)* en **la** universidad de San Juan. ¿Y tú?
Claudio:	Este... Originalmente soy de Mérida, Yucatán. Pero **estudio** *(I have been studying)* en esta universidad hace dos años. ¿Qué **estudias** allí *(there)* en Puerto Rico, Ana?
Ana:	**Estudio sicología, geografía, francés, alemán** e **inglés.**
Claudio:	Ah, eres estudiante de lenguas, ¿verdad?
Ana:	Sí. **Deseo** ser *(I want to be)* intérprete. Y tú, ¿qué **estudias** aquí en Chicago?
Claudio:	Yo **estudio literatura** y cultura latinoamericana. **Me gusta mucho.**
Ana:	¡Genial! ¿Hay muchos hispanohablantes *(Spanish speakers)* en tus clases?
Claudio:	Sí, hay varios *(several).* Algunos de ellos tienen dos **especialidades.** Ahora hay estudiantes que combinan el español con el inglés, la **computación,** la **administración de empresas,** con las **ciencias...**
Ana:	¡Parece que *(It appears that)* el español es muy popular!
Claudio:	¡Sí! Pues, la verdad es que *(the truth is that)* ahora hay muchas personas en los Estados Unidos que **hablan** *(that speak)* español. Los estudiantes que **toman** *(take)* clases de español aquí frecuentemente lo **usan** después *(use it later)* cuando **trabajan** *(they work)* en ciudades como aquí en Chicago, Miami, Nueva York, Phoenix o Los Ángeles. Por eso *(For this reason),* a ellos les gusta estudiar español en la universidad.

¿Comprendiste? *(Did you understand?)*

Indicate whether each of the following statements is true **(cierto)** or false **(falso).** If the statement is false, correct it.

1. Ana is a student at the University of Chicago.
2. Ana is from the Yucatan Peninsula.
3. Claudio studies Spanish history.
4. Ana studies science.
5. In the department there are only a few students who are native speakers.
6. Many students combine Spanish with other majors.
7. Many former students use their Spanish when working abroad.

CULTURA

Merida is the capital of the Mexican state of Yucatan, located 955 miles (1,537 kilometers) southeast of Mexico City in the Yucatan Peninsula. Merida's Plaza Mayor, also called Plaza de la Constitución, was built from rocks that were once used in Mayan temples.

¿NOS ENTENDEMOS?

The word **y** *(and)* becomes **e** before a word beginning with **i** or **hi.** The conjunction **o** *(or)* becomes **u** before a word beginning with **o** or **ho.** Both of these changes occur for pronunciation reasons. Note examples: **Hablo español e inglés. El padre e hijo son amables. ¿Te llamas Omar u Óscar? ¿Estudiamos mañana u hoy?**

¿NOS ENTENDEMOS?

In the same way that English speakers make the sound *Umm . . .* to indicate a pause in their train of thought, Spanish speakers make the sound **Este...** or use short words such as **pues** *(well).*

Encuentro cultural

El español en los Estados Unidos

PARA PENSAR

■ Originally, where is your family from? Do you know anything about that country / those countries?

■ Does your family celebrate or hold customs from other cultures? Name some customs.

Calle 8 en Miami, Florida

Entre los grupos hispanohablantes que hay en los Estados Unidos, el de los mexicanoamericanos es el más grande, porque representa un 60 por ciento del total de esta población. La mayoría *(majority)* de los hispanos de origen mexicano vive en los estados de Tejas, Nuevo México, California, Arizona e Illinois. Muchos mexicanoamericanos celebran *(celebrate)* sus fiestas en las plazas, como por ejemplo el Día de los Muertos *(Day of the Dead)* en noviembre *(November)*. En Los Ángeles, los hispanos celebran en los parques de Los Ángeles y en Santa Ana. También los mexicanoamericanos celebran el Día de la Independencia de España *(Independence Day from Spain)* el 16 de septiembre *(September)* en las principales plazas de los Estados Unidos.

Otro grupo relevante es el de los puertorriqueños que son ciudadanos norteamericanos porque Puerto Rico es un Estado Libre Asociado *(Commonwealth status)* de los Estados Unidos. Ellos celebran su Día de la Independencia el 4 de julio como en los Estados Unidos, en las diferentes plazas y con fuegos artificiales *(fireworks)*.

Hay otro grupo importante de hispanos, el de los cubanoamericanos en Miami, Florida, que viven *(live)* aquí desde la Revolución cubana *(Cuban Revolution)* en 1959. Los cubanos celebran sus fiestas y sus protestas en la Calle 8 de Miami. El Carnaval es muy famoso en la Calle 8 y también son las protestas contra *(against)* los gobiernos antidemocráticos de los países latinoamericanos.

En conclusión, uno de los lugares más importantes en la cultura hispana aquí en los Estados Unidos es el parque. Las personas hablan y conversan de los problemas sociales y políticos y de la vida de su familia en las plazas.

PARA DISCUTIR

1. What Spanish-speaking groups live in the United States?
2. What important holidays do Spanish speakers celebrate in the United States?
3. Where do many Spanish speakers get together to talk about their lives?
4. Where do you and your friends get together to talk? Why?

ESTRUCTURA I Talking about people, things, and concepts: definite and indefinite articles and how to make nouns plural

A noun names a person (**Ana, estudiante**), a place (**Mérida, ciudad**), a thing (**libro, computadora**), or a concept (**clase, español**). In Spanish, all nouns are classified as having a gender—either masculine or feminine. A noun is often preceded by a definite article, **el, la, los, las** *(the)*, or by an indefinite article, **un, una** *(a, an)*, **unos, unas** *(some)*. The words **un** and **una** can also mean *one*, depending on the context. Both definite and indefinite articles agree in number and gender with the nouns they modify.

el libro	*the book*	**las** mochilas	*the backpacks*
un libro	*a book*	**unas** mochilas	*some backpacks*

How to determine gender of nouns

1. In Spanish, nouns referring to males and most nouns ending in **-o** are masculine. Nouns referring to females and most nouns ending in **-a** are feminine. Definite and indefinite articles must match the gender (masculine or feminine) of the nouns they refer to.

   el/un amig**o**　　　　**la/una** amig**a**
   el/un escritori**o**　　　**la/una** bibliotec**a**

2. Most nouns ending in **-l** or **-r** are masculine, and most nouns ending in **-d** or **-ión** are feminine.

   el/un pape**l**　　　　　**la/una** universida**d**
   el/un borrado**r**　　　　**la/una** lecc**ión**

3. Some nouns do not conform to the rules stated above. One way to remember the gender of these nouns is to learn the definite articles and the nouns together, for example: **la clase, el día** *(day)*, **el mapa**, and **la mano** *(hand)*.

Many words that end in **-ma**, **-pa**, and **-ta** are masculine: **el problema** *(the problem)*, **el mapa, el sistema, el programa, el tema, el planeta**.

How to make nouns plural

In Spanish, all nouns are either singular or plural. Definite and indefinite articles (**el, la, los, las; un, una, unos, unas**) must match the number (singular or plural) of the nouns they refer to. To make Spanish nouns plural, add **-s** to nouns ending in a vowel, and **-es** to nouns ending in a consonant.

Singular	Plural	Singular	Plural
el amigo	**los** amigos	una clase	**unas** clases
la amiga	**las** amigas	un profesor	**unos** profesores
		una universidad	**unas** universidades

Here are two additional rules for making nouns plural:

1. For nouns ending in **-án, -és,** or **-ión,** drop the accent mark before adding **-es.**

   el/un alem**án**　　　　los/unos alem**anes**
   el/un japon**és**　　　　los/unos japon**eses**
   la/una lecc**ión**　　　　las/unas lecc**iones**

2. For nouns ending in **-z**, drop the **-z**, then add **-ces**.

   el/un lápi**z**　　　　　los/unos lápi**ces**

Spanish speakers do not consider nouns as being male or female (except when referring to people or animals). Therefore, the terms "masculine" and "feminine" are simply labels for classifying nouns.

¡A PRACTICAR!

1-8 | **¿El, la, los o las?** Supply the definite article for each noun below.

MODELO: ___*las*___ mochilas

1. _____ mapa
2. _____ universidad
3. _____ exámenes
4. _____ tarea
5. _____ bolígrafo
6. _____ lecciones
7. _____ compañero de clase
8. _____ salas de clase

1-9 | **¿Qué es? ¿Qué son?** Identify the following objects using the indefinite articles **un, una, unos,** or **unas.**

MODELO: Calendario
Es un calendario.

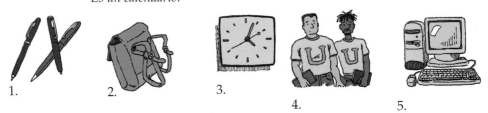

1.   2.   3.   4.   5.

1-10 | **¿Hay una profesora en la clase?** Use indefinite and definite articles together to complete the following statements.

MODELO: Hay ___*un*___ libro en ___*el*___ escritorio.

1. Hay _____ mujer en _____ silla.
2. Hay _____ diccionario en _____ clase.
3. Hay _____ plumas en _____ mochila.
4. Hay _____ cuadernos en _____ escritorio.

EN VOZ ALTA

1-11 | **Cuestionario: ¿Cuántos tienes?** Form the plural of each of the nouns below and then ask two of your classmates how many he/she has of each.

MODELO: libro
E1: *¿Cuántos libros tienes?*
E2: *Tengo tres libros de texto en la mochila.*

CUESTIONARIO

En esta clase

1. compañero(a) de clase _____
2. amigo(a) _____

Este semestre

3. compañero(a) de cuarto _____
4. profesor(a) _____
5. clase _____

En la mochila

6. libros _____
7. bolígrafo _____

En el cuarto

8. computadora _____
9. silla _____
10. televisor _____

VOCABULARIO Lenguas extranjeras, otras materias y lugares universitarios

In this section you will learn how to talk about foreign languages, other academic courses, and university buildings in Spanish.

Las lenguas extranjeras Foreign languages

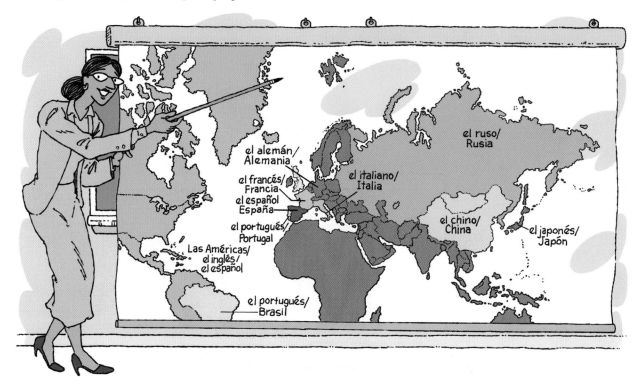

el alemán/Alemania
el francés/Francia
el español/España
el portugués/Portugal
Las Américas/el inglés/el español
el portugués/Brasil
el italiano/Italia
el ruso/Rusia
el chino/China
el japonés/Japón

Cursos y especializaciones Courses and majors

La música

Las matemáticas

La química

El teatro

La geografía

¿NOS ENTENDEMOS?
In many Spanish-speaking countries, the name for the language **el español** alternates with **el castellano**, or "Castillian Spanish." **El castellano** originated from the language spoken in north central Spain in the region of **Castilla.** It is one of the four main languages that are spoken in Spain. The other languages are Basque in the Basque region in the north, Catalan in Cataluña in the northeast, and Galician in Galicia in northwestern Spain.

Más cursos y especializaciones More courses and majors

la administración de empresas business administration
el arte art
la biología biology
las ciencias science
la computación computer science
el derecho law
la economía economics
la educación education
la filosofía philosophy
la física physics

la historia history
la ingeniería engineering
la literatura literature
la medicina medicine
los negocios business
la pintura painting
el periodismo journalism
la sicología psychology
la sociología sociology

¿NOS ENTENDEMOS?
It is not uncommon for Spanish speakers to shorten words. For example, la facultad becomes la facu, la universidad becomes la u, and el profesor becomes el profe.

Lugares y edificios universitarios University locations and buildings

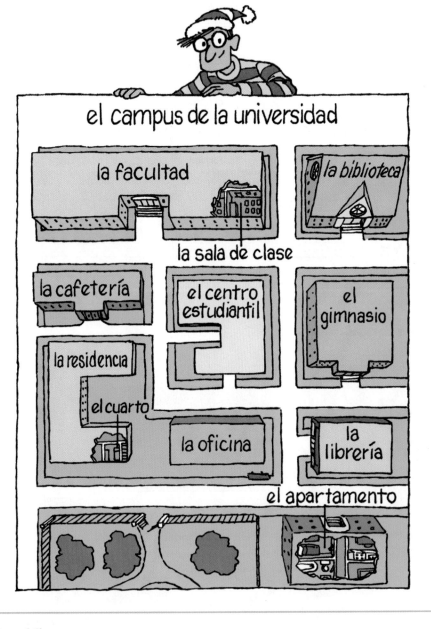

el campus de la universidad
la facultad
la biblioteca
la sala de clase
la cafetería
el centro estudiantil
el gimnasio
la residencia
el cuarto
la oficina
la librería
el apartamento

Palabras útiles are presented to help you enrich your personal vocabulary. The terms provided here will help you talk about your academic and personal interests.

Palabras útiles

la arquitectura architecture
el baile dance
la contabilidad accounting
la ecología ecology

la geología geology
las humanidades humanities
el turismo tourism
la zoología zoology

¡A PRACTICAR!

1-12 **¿Dónde... ?** Osvaldo is hiding in the buildings shown on the map on page 32. Identify the places where Osvaldo is doing the following activities.

> MODELO: Aquí tomo *(I have)* un café después de las clases.
> *en el centro estudiantil*

1. Aquí descanso *(I sleep)* después de las clases.
2. Aquí compro *(I buy)* mis libros de texto.
3. Aquí estudio *(I study)* para los exámenes.
4. Aquí hablo *(I speak)* con mis compañeros de clase y compro *(I buy)* comida.
5. Aquí toco *(I play)* la trompeta para los partidos de baloncesto *(basketball games).*

1-13 **¿Qué lengua habla?** *(What language does he/she speak?)* State where each of the following people is from and the native language he/she speaks **(él habla, ella habla).** Do you speak any other languages besides English and Spanish?

> MODELO: Antonio Banderas / España
> *Él es de España y habla español.*

1. Gerhard Schröder / Alemania
2. Marcel Marceau / Francia
3. Masao Miyoshi / Japón
4. Fernanda Montenegro / Brasil
5. Boris Yeltsin / Rusia
6. Giorgio Armani /Italia
7. Yo soy de _____ y hablo *(I speak)* _____, _____,...
8. Mis padres son de _____ y hablan *(they speak)* _____, _____,...

EN VOZ ALTA

1-14 **¿Cierto o falso?** Alternating with a classmate, make each of the following statements. If the statement your classmate makes is false, correct it.

> MODELO: E1: Estudiamos *(We study)* español en el gimnasio.
> E2: *No, es falso. Estudiamos español en la biblioteca.*

1. Hay libros de español en la sala de clase de ciencias.
2. Hay muchas copias de *Plazas* en la librería.
3. Hay comida buena en el centro estudiantil.
4. En nuestra universidad el departamento de matemáticas es grande.
5. Por la noche *(At night),* hay muchos estudiantes en la biblioteca.
6. En mi residencia, hablo francés con mis compañeros(as).

1-15 **En la librería** Imagine that you work in the campus bookstore and are helping Daniela and Fernando, two international students, find the textbooks they need for the courses they have jotted down. Of course, they've written their lists in Spanish! With a classmate in the role of either Daniela or Fernando, ask what general subject area each course is in just to make sure you read their lists correctly. Then, describe the book(s) they need including the title (in English), the color(s) of the book cover, and any other details you may wish to add.

> MODELO: Cálculo 130
> E1: *Es una clase de matemáticas, ¿verdad?*
> E2: *Sí, correcto.*
> E1: *El libro de texto se llama* Five Easy Steps to Calculus. *Es verde y azul. Tiene muchas fotos* (photographs) *bonitas.*

Fernando: Escritores británicos; Historia del pensamiento *(thought);* Fonética francesa; Sicología anormal; Revolución mexicana

Daniela: Economía y finanzas; Ecología acuática; Guitarra 1: clásica; Química orgánica; Estadística

Encuentro cultural

La educación en Latinoamérica y España

PARA PENSAR

- What is the school system like in your city or region?
- What do you remember most about your primary and/or secondary school years?

En el mundo hispano, la escuela primaria tiene varios nombres: escuela básica, escuela primaria o simplemente escuela o primaria, y son seis o siete años de estudios *(of studies)*.

La escuela secundaria también tiene varios nombres: liceo, bachillerato, instituto o secundaria, y son cinco o seis años de estudios.

Se llama colegio a una escuela privada donde hay primaria y secundaria. La palabra «colegio» es un cognado falso *(false cognate)* en inglés. La palabra *college* es universidad en español y son cinco años de estudios.

Después de terminar *(finish)* la primaria, los latinoamericanos y los españoles van a una escuela politécnica *(technical school)* o estudian en la secundaria. Después de terminar la secundaria, algunos *(some)* estudiantes estudian en la universidad.

La oposición *(competitive exam for school's or job's entrance)* es un examen muy difícil para entrar en una universidad pública o privada. La matrícula *(tuition)* es gratis *(free)* en muchas universidades públicas y por eso el examen es muy difícil. En las universidades, los estudiantes estudian una carrera *(major, field of study)* en un programa muy estructurado.

En Latinoamérica, no hay muchas residencias estudiantiles *(university dorms)* como en España o los Estados Unidos o Canadá. Por eso, los estudiantes viven en sus casas con sus padres, en **pensiones** *(boardinghouses)* o en casas particulares *(homes of people that rent rooms)*.

PARA DISCUTIR

1. What are the differences or similarities between the schooling years in the Spanish-speaking countries and the United States?
2. What are some of the differences or similarities among the Latin American countries, Spain, and the United States in relation to "college"?
3. Would you like to study in Spain or in Latin America? In what country would you like to study and why?

ESTRUCTURA II Describing everyday activities: present tense of regular *-ar* verbs

How to form the present tense

An infinitive is a nonpersonal (unconjugated) verb form, such as **hablar** *(to speak; to talk)*. Spanish infinitives end in either **-ar, -er,** or **-ir.** All Spanish infinitives have two parts: a stem **(habl-)** and an ending **(-ar).**

To form the present tense of Spanish verbs ending in **-ar,** drop the infinitive ending and add a personal ending to the stem.

hablar *(to speak; to talk)*

yo	habl**o**	*I speak*
tú	habl**as**	*you* (informal) *speak*
usted, él/ella	habl**a**	*you* (formal) *speak, he/she speaks*
nosotros(as)	habl**amos**	*we speak*
vosotros(as)	habl**áis**	*you* (informal) *speak*
ustedes, ellos/ellas	habl**an**	*you* (formal) *speak, they speak*

How to use the present tense

Spanish speakers use the present tense to express (1) what people do in a general sense, (2) what they're doing in a particular instance, (3) what they do habitually, and (4) what they intend to do at a later time. In this sense the present tense in Spanish is more flexible than in English.

(1) Anita estudia lenguas.	*Anita studies languages.*
(2) Anita estudia lenguas este semestre.	*Anita is studying languages this semester.*
(3) Ella estudia mucho por la noche.	*She studies a lot in the evening.*
(4) Mañana estudia con Laura.	*Tomorrow she's studying with Laura.*

In this chapter, you have already seen some **-ar** verbs in the **En contexto** section on page 27. Now study the following verbs with useful example phrases:

descansar por una hora	to rest for an hour	Yo descanso por una hora.
escuchar música	to listen to music	Tú escuchas música en tu cuarto *(room)*.
estudiar en la biblioteca	to study in the library	Él estudia español en la biblioteca.
llegar a la clase	to arrive at class	Ella llega a la clase de historia.
mandar cartas	to send letters	Usted manda cartas a su mamá.
regresar a casa	to return home	Vosotros regresáis a casa.
tomar clases/exámenes	to take classes/tests	Nosotros tomamos un examen mañana.
trabajar por la noche	to work at night	Ellos trabajan por la noche.

Here are some more common **-ar** verbs:

ayudar to help	**enseñar** to teach	**practicar** to practice
bailar to dance	**entrar** to enter	**preguntar** to ask
buscar to look for	**esperar** to hope; to expect	(a question)
caminar to walk	**llamar** to call; to phone	**terminar** to finish
cantar to sing	**mirar** to watch	**tocar** to touch; to play an
comprar to buy	**necesitar** to need	instrument
contestar to answer	**pagar** to pay	**usar** to use
desear to want, to wish	**pasar** to spend (time);	**viajar** to travel
dibujar to draw	to pass	**visitar** to visit

¡A PRACTICAR!

1-16 **¡Juan tiene una vida loca!** Juan's busy student life is described in the following paragraph. Conjugate the verbs in parentheses to agree with the subjects.

Yo soy Juan y yo tengo una vida loca. Mi compañero de cuarto, Miguel, y yo _____ (1. tomar) seis clases este semestre. Miguel también _____ (2. trabajar) quince horas a la semana (a week) en la biblioteca. Yo _____ (3. necesitar) más dinero pero no _____ (4. trabajar) porque (because) yo _____ (5. tocar) el saxofón para una banda de jazz. Dos días a la semana yo _____ (6. enseñar) español a unos chicos (kids) de la escuela primaria. ¡Ellos _____ (7. practicar) mucho! Por la noche, Miguel y yo _____ (8. estudiar), _____ (9. hablar) por teléfono con las novias o _____ (10. descansar). Los sábados yo _____ (11. bailar) en las fiestas (parties) con mi novia, Carmen. Los domingos mis padres y yo _____ (12. visitar) a la abuela y _____ (13. pasar) tiempo con la familia.

1-17 **La vida estudiantil (Student life)** Describe what the following people do, using appropriate phrases from the right column and conjugating the verbs correctly.

MODELO: nosotros   bailar en los fines de semana
Nosotros bailamos en los fines de semana.

1. mi amigo
2. yo
3. mi amiga _____
4. mis compañeros de clase
5. nosotros
6. el (la) profesor(a)
7. mis padres
8. ¿...?

desear tocar la guitarra
estudiar en su cuarto
mirar la televisión
descansar por la noche
regresar a la residencia después de la clase
pagar los libros de texto
cantar con la música del radio
escuchar la música de Marc Anthony
hablar por teléfono
comprar cuadernos en la librería

1-18 **La vida estudiantil (Student life) estadounidense e hispana** Describe what the following students do by conjugating the verbs in parentheses correctly.

MODELO: En 1999, los estudiantes hispanos _____*estudian*_____ (estudiar) más ciencias que en 1997.

1. En el 2001, el 11 por ciento de los estudiantes hispanos _____ (teminar) los estudios de la universidad.
2. En el 2001, el 28 por ciento de los estudiantes estadounidenses _____ (completar) los estudios de la universidad.
3. En el 2001, el 24 por ciento de las alumnas estadounidenses _____ (tomar) clases en la universidad y _____ (terminar) sus estudios.
4. En el 2000, el 3 por ciento de estudiantes hispanos del 8° grado/octavo grado (eighth grade) _____ (pasar) exámenes de matemáticas con excelentes notas.
5. En el 2000, el 87 por ciento de estudiantes estadounidenses del grado ocho _____ (pasar) exámenes de matemáticas con excelentes notas.
6. En el 2004, mis compañeros de clase y yo _____ (contestar) muchas preguntas en español.
7. En el 2004, tú _____ (trabajar) por la noche después de las clases.
8. En el 2004, el (la) profesor(a) _____ (enseñar) cinco clases de español todos los semestres.

EN VOZ ALTA

1-19 **Mi rutina diaria (My daily routine)** In pairs, read each of the following statements and decide whether it is **cierto** (*true*) or **falso** (*false*) for you. Correct false statements to make them true for you.

MODELO: Yo hablo mucho español en la clase.
E1: *Sí, yo hablo mucho español en la clase.*
E2: *Sí, yo también* (also) *hablo mucho español en la clase.*
o *No, no hablo mucho español en la clase.*

1. Yo descanso después de la clase.
2. Mis compañeros y yo estudiamos en la cafetería.
3. El (La) profesor(a) llega tarde a la clase.
4. En la clase, cantamos y bailamos.
5. Después de la clase mis compañeros regresan a casa.
6. Yo trabajo por la noche.
7. El (La) profesor(a) toca el piano en la clase.
8. Nosotros practicamos el vocabulario en la clase.
9. Yo tomo cinco clases este semestre.
10. Nosotros necesitamos estudiar mucho.

1-20 **Entrevista (Interview)** Ask a classmate about what he/she does around campus. Why is the **tú** form used in this activity?

1. ¿Estudias mucho en la biblioteca? ¿Qué estudias?
2. ¿Hablas por teléfono con personas en otras residencias? ¿Con quién hablas?
3. ¿Compras comida en el centro estudiantil? ¿Es buena la comida?
4. ¿Qué compras en la librería?
5. ¿Llegas a la universidad en auto, en autobús, en bicicleta, en motocicleta o a pie (on foot)?
6. Cuando regresas a tu cuarto, ¿estudias, trabajas o descansas?
7. ¿Practicas un deporte (sport) en el gimnasio?
8. ¿Tocas un instrumento?
9. ¿Miras muchos programas de televisión?
10. ¿Caminas mucho en el campus?

1-21 **Nuevos compañeros** In groups of three or four, discuss the following in Spanish.

- where you are from
- how many classes you are taking
- what subjects you are studying
- whether or not you work during school
- whether or not you study in the library

When you want to say you like doing something, use the construction **me gusta** + the infinitive form of the verb. For example, a Spanish speaker would say **Me gusta escuchar música** to mean *I like to listen to music*. To make this statement negative, place **no** before **me gusta: No me gusta escuchar música.** You will learn more about using the verb **gustar** to talk about likes and dislikes in **Capítulo 3.** Here are a few more examples:

Me gusta visitar la Plaza de Rockafeller en Nueva York.	*I like to visit Rockefeller Plaza in New York.*
Me gusta tocar el piano.	*I like to play the piano.*
No me gusta trabajar.	*I don't like to work.*
Me gusta escuchar a mi profesor(a).	*I like to listen to my professor.*

¡A PRACTICAR!

1-22 | **¡Me gusta! ¡No me gusta! (*I like to! I don't like to!*)** Indicate whether you like or dislike doing the following activities.

MODELO: estudiar en la biblioteca
Me gusta estudiar en la biblioteca. / No me gusta estudiar en la biblioteca.

1. hablar con mi compañero(a) de cuarto
2. escuchar a mis profesores
3. tomar exámenes
4. bailar en las fiestas
5. practicar deportes
6. descansar mucho
7. escuchar música clásica
8. pasar tiempo con mis amigos
9. caminar a mis clases
10. visitar la Plaza de Rockafeller en Nueva York

EN VOZ ALTA

1-23 | **Mis preferencias (*My preferences*)** Tell a classmate five things that you like to do and five things that you don't like to do.

MODELO: *Me gusta hablar por teléfono.*
No me gusta tomar exámenes.

Me gusta pescar *(to fish)* los sábados *(on Saturdays).*

ASÍ SE DICE Telling time and talking about the days of the week: *la hora y los días de la semana*

¿Qué hora es? *(What time is it?)* can be answered in three ways, depending on the time.

On the hour

Es la una.	*It's one o'clock.*
Son las siete.	*It's seven o'clock.*

On the quarter or the half-hour

Son las siete **y cuarto**.	*It's a quarter past seven.*
Son las siete **y media**.	*It's seven-thirty.*
Son las siete **menos cuarto**.	*It's a quarter till eight.*

Minutes before and after the hour

Es la una y diez.	*It's ten past one.*
Son las ocho menos diez.	*It's ten till eight.*

Other time expressions

a tiempo on time	**temprano** early
en punto on time	**la medianoche** midnight
ahora now	**el mediodía** noon
tarde tarde	

1. Use **es** to tell time between 12:31 and 1:30. Otherwise, use **son** because it refers to more than one hour (plural).

—¿Qué hora es?	*What time is it?*
—Es la una menos cuarto.	*It's 12:45 (a quarter till one).*
—No. Son las diez y veinte.	*No. It's 10:20.*

2. After a specific time, use **de la mañana** *(in the morning/a.m.)*, **de la tarde** *(in the afternoon/p.m.)*, or **de la noche** *(in the evening/p.m.)*.

Mi clase de computación es a las 9:00 **de la mañana** y mi clase de música es a las 2:00 **de la tarde**.	*My computer science class is at nine o'clock in the morning and my music class is at two o'clock in the afternoon.*

3. To ask or tell what time an event occurs, use the word **a**.

—¿**A** qué hora trabajas?	*What time do you work?*
—**A** las diez de la mañana.	*At ten o'clock in the morning.*

Los días de la semana

La agenda de Esther

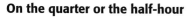

LUNES	MARTES	MIÉRCOLES	JUEVES	VIERNES	SÁBADO	DOMINGO
de la tarde	de la mañana	de la noche	de la mañana	de la noche	de la tarde	de la tarde
Tocar el violín 5:00 p.m.	biblioteca con Helen 11:45 a.m.	vólibol en el gimnasio 7:00 pm	trabajar en la librería 9:00 a.m.	fiesta 11:30 p.m.	descansar en el cuarto 1:00 p.m.	música en el centro estudiantil 5:15 p.m.

Otras expresiones

el día day	**todos los días** every day
la semana week	**hoy** today
el fin de semana weekend	**mañana** tomorrow

¡A PRACTICAR!

1-24 **¿Qué hora es?** Say the time for each of the clocks shown below.

1-25 **La vida de Esmeralda Santiago** Look at the page in the datebook of Esmeralda Santiago, prepared when she was a student at the prestigious New York High School for the Performing Arts. Form sentences about the many activities that she must complete, remembering to include a conjugated verb in each sentence.

> MODELO: lunes / Esmeralda / hablar con la profesora de historia / sala de clase / p.m.
> *El lunes Esmeralda habla con la profesora de historia en la sala de clase a las tres de la tarde.*

1. martes / Esmeralda y unos amigos / estudiar/ biblioteca / a.m.
2. miércoles / Esmeralda / terminar el proyecto de arte / el campus / p.m.
3. jueves / Esmeralda y su amiga Rosario / trabajar / librería / a.m.
4. viernes / Esmeralda y su familia / pasar tiempo / casa / p.m.
5. sábado / Esmeralda / ayudar a su mamá / casa/ p.m.
6. domingo / Esmeralda y su amigo David / escuchar música folklórica / centro estudiantil / p.m.

CULTURA

Esmeralda Santiago is a well-known writer of Puerto Rican descent. She moved to New York with her mother and ten younger brothers and sisters and worked hard to help her mother support the family while also excelling in her studies. She was admitted to the Performing Arts High School in New York and later to Harvard University, from which she graduated with high honors. Her most famous novel is *When I Was Puerto Rican* (**Cuando era puerto-rriqueña**), which she first wrote in English and then translated into Spanish.

EN VOZ ALTA

1-26 **Mis clases** Tell another student the days and hours of your classes. Follow the example below, and substitute your own class information for the words in **bold-face print.**

> MODELO: *Tengo clase de **biología** los **martes** y los **jueves**. La clase es a las **nueve de la mañana**.*

1-27 **Mi horario para la semana** Now expand upon the information you gave in the previous exercise to include the following information:

- when you arrive at school (days, times)
- your class schedule (classes, days, times)
- when you get home from school (days, times)
- something about your work (place, days, times)

Encuentro cultural

El sistema de 24 horas

PARA PENSAR

- Are you always on time to class or to other functions and activities?
- When you talk about time, do you use the 12- or the 24-hour system?

En varios países hispanos, el sistema de veinticuatro horas se usa *(is used)* en los horarios *(schedules)* de trenes, aviones y autobuses, programas de radio y televisión y también para celebraciones formales y oficiales. Para usar el sistema, se cuentan *(are counted)* las horas consecutivamente, comenzando por la medianoche.

Sistema oficial (24 horas)
10:00 diez (horas)
13:00 trece (horas)
23:00 veintitrés (horas)

Sistema informal (12 horas)
las diez de la mañana
la una de la tarde
las once de la noche

En España y en Latinoamérica, las citas de negocios *(job appointments),* las citas médicas, los servicios religiosos y los eventos deportivos comienzan a tiempo. Las cenas y las fiestas sociales comienzan de treinta minutos a una hora más tarde. Para llegar a la hora correcta a una cena o fiesta, pregunta «¿En punto?»

PARA DISCUTIR

1. When is the 24-hour system used in the Hispanic countries and in the United States?
2. Do you usually arrive on time to your classes, appointments, and celebrations?
3. Do you think it is a good characteristic to be punctual? Why?

¡A VER!

You are about to meet five young people who will be sharing a house in Puerto Rico. Throughout the Plazas video episodes, you will get to observe as the roommates interact, get to know each other, form friendships, and make plans for the future.

In this segment, the new roommates meet each other for the first time and explore their new home Hacienda Vista Alegre. You will learn where they are from, what they are studying, and a little bit about their personalities.

Expresiones útiles

The following are some new expressions you will hear in the video.

¡Bienvenida!	Welcome!
¿Cómo te va?	How's it going?
Qué aburrido ¿no?	How boring!
¡Ay... es una broma!	Oh, it's just a joke!

Antes de ver

Paso 1: What expressions have you learned to use to introduce yourself and greet others? What are the typical responses when you meet someone? Work with a classmate and greet each other in as many different ways as you can remember.

Paso 2: When you first meet someone, what are some of the other things that you are interested in learning about that person? Do you like to find out where they are from? Look at the photo of the five housemates and see if you can guess what country each one of them is from.

Paso 3: How about their interests and pastimes? Wouldn't you also like to know what each one studies? Work with a classmate to guess what each of the housemates studies.

Después de ver

Paso 1: Now you are ready to watch the video for the first time. As you do, pay attention to the phrases that the roommates use as they meet each other. When you hear one of the following expressions, place a check mark next to it under the name of the housemate who says it. When you were working on **Antes de ver, Paso 1**, did you and your classmate remember any phrases that are not on the chart?

	Javier	Alejandra	Antonio	Sofía	Valeria
Saludos					
Hola					
Me llamo					
Soy					
Mi nombre es					
Buenas tardes					
Qué tal					
Cómo te va					
Respuestas					
Mucho gusto					
Encantado					
Muy bien, gracias					

Paso 2: In **Antes de ver, Paso 2,** you tried to guess where each character was from. Now that you have seen the video, can you complete the statements below that each person might make about himself or herself? Use the word bank to help you.

Argentina	Colombia	cómico	España	hablar por teléfono
inteligente	medicina	Texas	tomar fotos	Venezuela

- Mi nombre es Alejandra. Soy de _____ y me gusta _____.
- Mi nombre es Valeria. Soy de _____ y me gusta _____.
- Mi nombre es Sofía. Soy de _____ y soy muy _____.
- Mi nombre es Antonio. Soy de _____ y soy muy _____.
- Mi nombre es Javier. Soy de _____ y estudio _____.

Paso 3: In **Antes de ver, Paso 3,** you and your classmate predicted what each housemate studies. Do you remember what they said? After you have watched the video a few times, see if you can match each roommate with his/her specialization:

Javier estudia   filología española

Antonio estudia   medicina

Sofía estudia   danza moderna

Valeria estudia   administración de empresas

Alejandra estudia   diseño

Were any of your predictions about the housemates correct?

¿Qué opinas tú?

Paso 1: Choose one of the housemates and imagine what a typical day might be like for him/her. What does he/she study? What does he/she do? Using vocabulary from this chapter, write at least 3 sentences about that person.

Paso 2: Now think about your typical day. What subjects do you study and what activities do you do? Write 3 sentences about yourself and your daily activities.

Paso 3: Working in groups of 3 or 4, compare your observations about the roommates and share the statements about yourself. Don't forget to begin by introducing yourself! Based on what you have discovered, would you want to be roommates

¡A LEER!

Strategy: Recognizing cognates

Cognates **(Cognados)** are words that belong to different languages but are identical or very similar to each other in spelling and meaning. There are many cognates in Spanish and English. Your ability to recognize them and guess their meaning will help you read Spanish more efficiently.

Paso 1: Skim the advertisement about English **(Inglés, su pasaporte para el futuro)** and write down as many cognates as you can find. Then write what you think each cognate means in English. Feel free to guess if you need to. Based on the cognates you have identified, what do you think is the purpose of the ad?

Paso 2: Read the ad again and answer the following questions.

INGLES
SU PASAPORTE PARA EL FUTURO.

Aprenda a mejorar en los EE.UU., Canadá o Inglaterra

Cursos intensivos para estudiantes, adultos y ejecutivos desde 2 semanas hasta un año.

- Escoja 20, 30, ó 40 lecciones por semanas.
- Grupos pequeños o individual, a todos niveles.
- Inglés especializado en su profesión.
- Hospedaje en dormitorios, hoteles o con familias.
- Altamente recomendado por referencia local

Para folletos e información favor de llamar a:
JEAN CORNELIUS LANGUAGE AND VACATION PROGRAMS

Tel. 723-9006 • 723-6796

INGLES para jóvenes 6-17 años en campamentos con deportes, actividades, cultura y excursiones en Inglaterra, Suiza, Canadá y EE.UU.

1. What is this advertisement about?
   a. getting a new passport
   b. traveling around the United States or Canada
   c. learning a new language, English
   d. spending time in England

2. This ad is aimed at . . .
   a. adults.
   b. children.
   c. professional people.
   d. adults, professional people, and children.

3. According to the ad, in which countries could people learn English?
   a. the United States
   b. Canada
   c. the United States, Canada, or England
   d. England

4. Write the Spanish equivalents for the following words.
   a. passport
   b. future
   c. courses
   d. intensive
   e. adults
   f. executives
   g. lessons
   h. groups
   i. profession
   j. culture

¡A ESCRIBIR!

Strategy: Organizing your ideas

A good way to improve your writing is to organize the ideas you want to express before you actually begin composing your document.

Task: Writing a short personal profile

Short personal profiles occur in many contexts such as newspapers, newsletters, and websites of companies, campus groups, and civic organizations. They are often used to introduce a new member of a group or to highlight a recent accomplishment of an individual. In this activity you will write a profile of a student at your university for the International Club newsletter.

Paso 1: Look at the chart below and familiarize yourself with the information about María Sánchez Pérez.

Nombre	María Sánchez Pérez	tu compañero(a) de clase	tú
Nación	Estados Unidos		
Lenguas	español e inglés		
Escuela	Universidad de Miami		
Cursos	francés, contabilidad, periodismo, economía		
Edad (Age)	diecinueve años		
Intereses	tocar el piano, escuchar y tocar música clásica, viajar		

Functions: Describing people; Introducing; Talking about the present
Vocabulary: Countries; Languages; Studies; Arts
Grammar: Verbs: **ser, tener;** Prepositions: **de;** Personal pronouns: **él, ella;** Articles: indefinite: **un, una;** Articles: definite: **el, la, los, las**

Paso 2: Now read the following description of María Sánchez Pérez. Note how the information in the chart above is used in this paragraph.

María Sánchez Pérez es de los Estados Unidos. Ella habla español e inglés. María tiene diecinueve años y es estudiante de la Universidad de Miami, en Florida. Estudia francés, contabilidad, periodismo y economía. Le gusta escuchar y tocar música clásica y ella toca el piano muy bien. También le gusta viajar.

Paso 3: Now interview a classmate to fill out the third column on the chart with information about him/her. Then write a similar descriptive paragraph about him/her.

Paso 4: Now fill out the chart with information about yourself. Then write a paragraph describing yourself.

Paso 5: Exchange both of your paragraphs with a classmate. Check over each other's work for mistakes and correct any mistakes that you find. Discuss the corrections and comments you made, and then return his/her paragraph. You may wish to share your paragraphs with other classmates, either by distributing them in class or by posting them on a class website.

¡A CONVERSAR!

Pronunciation focus: The vowels *a, e, i, o, u,* and the letters *h* and *ch*

The Spanish vowel system consists of five clear, short, distinct sounds with minimal variation in their pronunciation. They are pronounced as follows: **a,** close to the *a* in *father,* though a little more open; **e** like the *e* in *egg;* **i** like the *ee* in *see;* **o** like the *o* in *born;* and **u** like the *oo* in *moon.* Using clear, short, and distinct sounds for these and other vowels will help you achieve a more authentic accent as you speak Spanish. It is particularly challenging but very important to use correct Spanish pronunciation for the vowels in cognates (words that are the same or similar in Spanish and English). Practice the following sentences focusing on vowel sounds.

- ¿Cómo se llama el profesor?
- El libro es interesante.
- La economía es un curso difícil.
- Tengo la clase de inglés los lunes, miércoles y viernes a las 10:00.
- El lápiz es amarillo y la mochila es verde.
- Mañana es un día importante.
- El escritorio de la profesora es negro.

The letter **h** is the only silent letter in the Spanish alphabet; it is never pronounced. **Ch** is pronounced as in the English word *church.* Practice the following sentences, paying attention to the **h** and **ch** sounds.

- Elena habla chino.
- ¿A qué hora es la clase de historia?
- El hombre escucha música.
- Hay muchas mochilas en la clase.

Task: Introducing yourself and getting to know someone

Introducing yourself and initiating a conversation with a new acquaintance is a very important communicative task, and it is one that you can already accomplish at this point in your study of Spanish.

Paso 1: Look at the following list of steps that two people might use in an informal introductory conversation and, if necessary, look back through **Capítulo preliminar** and **Capítulo 1** to remind yourself of how to say everything you need to say in Spanish to complete those steps. Consider both questions that should be asked and answers that will be given.

1. Greet each other appropriately.
2. Introduce yourselves and shake hands.
3. Ask and tell each other where you are from.
4. Talk briefly about:
   a. your life at school (your courses, your instructors, etc.).
   b. your work or job (where you work, which days, your work schedule, etc.).
   c. several things you do and/or do not like to do (study, listen to music, travel, etc.).

Paso 2: Imagine that you are at a meeting of the International Club and are meeting many new students who speak Spanish. Work with a partner to role-play an introductory conversation, following the steps in **Paso 1.** Both you and your partner should ask and answer questions and learn as much about each other as possible. Remember to pay attention to pronunciation, concentrating on clear vowel sounds and correct pronunciation of **h** and **ch.**

Paso 3: Join another pair of students and expand your conversation. Share information that you learned about your partner and ask questions to learn more about the members of the new pair.

VOCABULARIO ESENCIAL

 Track 1-6

La gente People

el (la) amigo(a) friend
el (la) compañero(a) de clase classmate
el (la) compañero(a) de cuarto roommate

el (la) estudiante student
el hombre man
la mujer woman

el (la) novio(a) boyfriend/girlfriend
el (la) profesor(a) professor

Objetos en la clase Objects in the classroom

el bolígrafo ballpoint pen
el borrador eraser
la calculadora calculator
el calendario calendar
la computadora computer
el cuaderno notebook
el diccionario dictionary
el dinero money
el escritorio desk

el examen test
el lápiz pencil
la lección lesson
el libro (de texto) (text)book
la luz (las luces) light(s)
el mapa map
la mochila backpack
la palabra word
la pantalla screen

el papel paper
la pizarra chalkboard
la pluma fountain pen
el reloj watch
la silla chair
la tarea homework
la tiza chalk

Las lenguas extranjeras Foreign languages

el alemán German
el chino Chinese
el español Spanish

el francés French
el inglés English
el italiano Italian

el japonés Japanese
el portugués Portuguese
el ruso Russian

Cursos y especializaciones Courses and majors

la administración de empresas business administration
el arte art
la biología biology
las ciencias science
la computación computer science
el derecho law
la economía economics
la educación education

la física physics
la filosofía philosophy
la geografía geography
la historia history
la ingeniería engineering
el inglés english
la literatura literature
las matemáticas math

la medicina medicine
la música music
los negocios business
el periodismo journalism
la pintura painting
la química chemistry
la sicología psychology
la sociología sociology

Lugares y edificios universitarios University locations and buildings

el apartamento apartment
la biblioteca library
la cafetería cafeteria
el campus campus
el centro estudiantil student center

el cuarto room
la escuela school
el gimnasio gymnasium
la librería bookstore
la oficina office

la residencia dormitory
la sala de clase classroom
la universidad university

Verbos

ayudar to help
bailar to dance
(no) me gusta + *infinitive* I (don't) like + infinitive
bailar to dance
buscar to look for
caminar to walk
cantar to sing
comprar to buy
contestar to answer
descansar to rest
desear to want, wish
dibujar to draw

enseñar to teach
entrar to enter
escuchar (música) to listen (to music)
esperar to hope; to expect
estudiar to study
hablar to talk; to speak
llamar to call; to phone
llegar to arrive
mandar (cartas) to send (letters)
mirar to watch
necesitar to need
pagar to pay

pasar to spend (time)
practicar to practice
preguntar to ask (a question)
regresar (a casa) to return (home)
regresar to return
terminar to finish
tocar to touch; to play an instrument
tomar clases/exámenes to take classes/tests
trabajar to work
usar to use
viajar to travel
visitar to visit

Colores Colors

amarillo yellow
anaranjado orange
azul blue

blanco white
marrón brown
morado purple

negro black
rojo red
verde green

Artículos definidos Definite articles

el, la, los, las the

Artículos indefinidos Indefinite articles

un(a) a, an

unos(as) some

Los días de la semana Days of the week

el lunes Monday
el martes Tuesday
el miércoles Wednesday
el jueves Thursday
el viernes Friday

el sábado Saturday
el domingo Sunday
el día day
la semana week
el fin de semana weekend

todos los días every day
hoy today
mañana tomorrow
ahora now

La hora Time

el reloj clock
de (por) la mañana (tarde/noche) in the morning (afternoon/evening)

en punto on time
tarde/temprano/a tiempo early/late/on time
¿A qué hora... ? At what time . . . ?

¿Qué hora es? What time is it?
la medianoche midnight
el mediodía noon

En una reunión familiar:

Chapter Objectives

COMMUNICATIVE GOALS

In this chapter you will learn how to . . .

- Define and ask about family relationships
- Indicate ownership and possession
- Describe people and things
- Indicate nationality
- Express physical status
- Count from 30 to 100
- Describe daily activities at home or at school

STRUCTURES

- Possessive adjectives
- Possession with **de(l)**
- Common uses of the verb **ser**
- Agreement with descriptive adjectives
- Present tense of **-er** and **-ir** verbs
- Common uses of the verb **tener**

CULTURAL INFORMATION

- Los nombres y apellidos en español
- La familia hispana

México

ESTADOS UNIDOS MEXICANOS

Población: 100.349.766
Área: 1.958.201 kilómetros cuadrados (más de cinco veces el tamaño de Montana)
Capital: La Ciudad de México, Distrito Federal 20.000.000
Ciudades principales: Guadalajara, 3.908.000; Puebla, 2.800.000; Tijuana, 1.200.00; Monterrey, 1.100.000
Moneda: el peso
Lenguas: el español, las lenguas indígenas (el maya, el náhuatl y otros)

¡Bienvenidos a México!

In this video, you will learn about Mexico. After watching the video, answer the following questions:

1 Which countries does Mexico border?

2 What is another name for Mexico City?

3 What are some of the most popular places to visit in Mexico?

4 In what ways are Mexico and the U.S. connected?

5 Have you ever visited Mexico? Where did you go and why? If you've never been, what part of Mexico would you choose to visit and why?

Plaza del Zócalo, La Ciudad de México, México

El D.F. stands for *Distrito Federal* and is commonly used to refer to Mexico City.

La familia de Juan Carlos García Martínez In this section you will practice talking about family relationships by learning about Juan Carlos's family. Do you know of any families like Juan Carlos's that have relatives living in two or more countries?

Mi **padre** se llama Jorge y mi **madre** se llama Ana María. Papá es del DF y mamá de Los Ángeles. Mi **hermana** Juana es muy guapa. Nuestro **gato** se llama Tigre. Mis **abuelos** son muy simpáticos. Viven en una casa enorme. Mi **tío** Tomás es **soltero**. Mi **tía** Esperanza es una mujer **casada**. Gabriela, su **hija** y mi **prima**, tiene una **perra**, Lola.

Otros parientes Other relatives

el (la) esposo(a) husband/wife
el (la) cuñado(a) brother-in-law/sister-in-law
el (la) nieto(a) grandson/granddaughter
la nuera daughter-in-law
el (la) sobrino(a) nephew/niece
el (la) suegro(a) father-in-law/mother-in-law
el yerno son-in-law

Otras mascotas Other pets

el pájaro bird
el pez fish

Nombres Names

el apellido last name
el nombre first name

Palabras útiles are presented to help you enrich your personal vocabulary. The words here will help you talk about family relationships.

Palabras útiles

divorciado(a) divorced
el (la) hermanastro(a) stepbrother/stepsister
la madrastra stepmother
el padrastro stepfather
el (la) medio(a) hermano(a) half brother (sister)

el (la) padrino(a) godfather/godmother
separado(a) separated
soltero(a) single
viudo(a) widowed

¡A PRACTICAR!

2-1 **La familia de Juan Carlos** Complete the following sentences with the correct relationship based on the drawing on page 50.

> MODELO: Ana María es ___la esposa___ de Jorge.

1. Juan Carlos es _____ de Juana.
2. Soledad es _____ de Esperanza y Tomás.
3. Gabriela y Soledad son _____.
4. El esposo de Esperanza es _____ de Tomás.
5. Elena es _____ de la hija de Jorge y Ana.
6. La hija de Jorge y Ana es _____ de Esperanza.
7. Tomás es _____ de los hijos de Jorge y María.

2-2 **En otras palabras** Indicate the relationships between the family members listed below.

> MODELOS: yo / mi tía
> *Yo soy el (la) sobrino(a) de mi tía.*
>
> mis abuelos / mi padre
> *Mis abuelos son los padres de mi padre.*

1. mi hermano(a) / mis abuelos
2. mi hijo(a) / mi hermano(a)
3. mi madre / mi hijo(a)
4. mis primos / mi mamá
5. mi padre / mis abuelos

EN VOZ ALTA

2-3 **Adivinanzas (Riddles)** Ask a classmate the following questions, keeping in mind that some of them may be purely hypothetical. Then, add three questions of your own.

¿Quién es... ?

1. la madre de tu padre
2. el (la) hermano(a) de tu madre
3. las hijas de tus tíos
4. el (la) hijo(a) de tus padres
5. el hijo de mi hija

2-4 **Un árbol genealógico**

Primera parte Create your own family tree, real or imagined, based on the categories below. Be artistic if you'd like!

Mis abuelos

_____   _____   _____   _____

Mis tíos   **Mis padres**   **Mis tíos**
                 (papá)   **(mamá)**
_____   _____   _____   _____

Mis primos   **Mis hermanos**   **Yo**   **Mis primos**

_____   _____   _____   _____

_____

 Segunda parte Now describe your family relationships in Spanish to a partner. Your partner will then review your family tree with you before presenting it to the class.

Text audio
Track 1-7

EN CONTEXTO

R ead along as you listen to the following dialog describing Juan Carlos's reunion with his grandparents, Pedro and Elena, in Mexico. Juan Carlos and his sister, Juana, live in Los Angeles and are always eager to share their experiences in the United States with their grandparents.

Juan Carlos:	¡Hola, **abuelito**! ¡Hola, abuelita! ¿Cómo están? ¡Tengo muchas noticias (*news*) sobre mi vida en los Estados Unidos!
Elena:	¡Ay, qué bueno, Carlitos! Tenemos **tus** cartas (*letters*) y tus postales (*postcards*), pero deseamos tener más información.
Pedro:	Y ahora **vives** (*you live*) en un **barrio** (*neighborhood*) **nuevo.** ¿Tienes muchos amigos allí?
Juan Carlos:	Sí, abuelito. Tengo muchos compañeros, ¡y dos de ellos hablan español! Los padres de mis amigos mexicanos son del D.F. y **sus abuelos** viven aquí. Los **abuelos de mi amigo** Enrique **son muy simpáticos.**
Elena:	Entonces (*So*), ¡muchas personas tienen nietos en los Estados Unidos! ¿Y Juana? ¿Tiene amigas?
Juan Carlos:	Sí, por supuesto (*of course*). Hay una familia cubana que **vive** en la calle cuarenta y dos, y ellos tienen una hija de catorce años, la misma edad (*the same age*) que Juana.
Pedro:	¿Mi Juanita **tiene catorce años**? ¡Imposible!
Elena:	**Ves** (*You see*) como tu abuelo **vive** en el pasado, mi hijo. Él **cree** que los niños nunca crecen (*grow up*).

¿Comprendiste?

Based on the dialog, indicate whether each of the following statements is **cierto** or **falso.** If a statement is false, correct it.

1. Los abuelos no tienen información sobre la vida de Juan Carlos en los Estados Unidos.

2. Juan Carlos no tiene muchos amigos en el barrio nuevo.

3. Todos los amigos de Juan Carlos hablan español.

4. Juana tiene una amiga que habla español y es de México.

¿NOS ENTENDEMOS?
The forms **don** and **doña** are used before first names as titles of respect or affection (while maintaining formality), generally for addressing one's elders or superiors. Juan Carlos's grandparents, for example, might be addressed as **don Pedro** and **doña Elena. Don** means **de origen noble** and it was used when the Spaniards arrived in America in the 15th century to distinguish themselves from the original population. The term was later used to distinguish the owners of the land and the people who work that land.

¿NOS ENTENDEMOS?
Spanish speakers use the diminutive forms of certain nouns to express affection. Juan Carlos addresses his grandparents as **abuelito** and **abuelita** (literally, *little grandfather* and *little grandmother*). Another term of affection commonly used in Mexico as well as in other American countries is the contraction **m'hijo** or **m'hija** (from **mi hijo, mi hija**) to mean *my son, my daughter*.

ASÍ SE DICE Indicating ownership and possession: possession with *de(l)* and possessive adjectives

Possession with *de(l)*

One way English speakers express possession is to attach an *'s* to a noun. Spanish speakers show the same relationship by using **de** before the noun. Note that when using **de** + **el,** Spanish speakers form the contraction **del.**

Juana es la hermana **de** Juan Carlos.   *Juana is Juan Carlos's sister.*
El libro es **de la** tía Julia.   *The book is Aunt Julia's.*
Aquí está el perro **del** abuelo.   *Here's the grandfather's dog.*

Possessive adjectives

Another way to indicate relationships or ownership is to use *possessive adjectives*. In Spanish, possessive adjectives must match the number (singular or plural) and, in the cases of **nosotros** and **vosotros,** the gender (masculine or feminine) of the nouns they describe.

	Singular	Plural
my	**mi** abuelo	**mis** abuelos
your (informal)	**tu** gato	**tus** gatos
his, her, its, your (formal singular)	**su** familia	**sus** familias
our	**nuestro** hijo	**nuestros** hijos (masculine)
	nuestra hija	**nuestras** hijas (feminine)
your (informal)	**vuestro** primo	**vuestros** primos (masculine)
	vuestra prima	**vuestras** primas (feminine)
their, your (formal plural)	**su** madre	**sus** madres

¡A PRACTICAR!

2-5 **Cada uno con lo suyo (To each his own)** Members of Juan Carlos's family have strong prefences for certain colors. Use **del, de la, de las,** or **de los** to indicate to whom the following objects belong.

MODELO: la pluma azul
La pluma azul es del esposo de María.

| La nieta | La abuela | El esposo de Ana María | Los tíos de Juan Carlos | El gato de Juan Carlos |

CULTURA

Maximilian was born in Austria in 1832. He was the brother of the Austrian emperor, Franz Josef. He was a member of the house of Hapsburg, the oldest ruling European dynasty. He went to Mexico in 1864 with his wife Carlota to rule over a new empire in Mexico. He went there after President Benito Juarez had decided not to pay interest on foreign loans taken by previous governments. Therefore, France, Britain, and Spain decided to intervene to protect their investments. In 1861, Napoleon of France decided to invade Veracruz, Mexico. In 1862, the French faced a very strong resistance at Puebla and the Mexican army won the battle on May 5, 1862. This date is known as **Cinco de Mayo** and is a large, popular celebration here in the United States. After this battle, Napoleon decided to send the Austrian Archduke Maximilian to create a monarchy in Mexico. In 1867, Maximilian was executed in Queretaro, after the Juarez armies reconquered their country and occupied Mexico City.

1. La bicicleta amarilla _____.
2. Las computadoras azules _____.
3. El reloj negro y anaranjado _____.
4. Las mochilas rojas _____.
5. El coche verde _____.

2-6 **Las memorias de Maximiliano** Imagine you are listening to Maximilian, emperor of Mexico, describe his family and residence in Mexico. Complete the following paragraph with the indicated possessive adjective. Notice that the possessive forms agree in number and, in some cases, gender.

Yo tengo una familia pequeña. 1. _____ (*My*) padres y abuelos viven en Austria, pero 2. _____ (*our*) familia vive en México. 3. _____ (*My*) hermano, Francis Joseph, es emperador de Austria. 4. _____ (*His*) palacio es enorme. 5. _____ (*My*) palacio, en el parque de Chapultepec, también es grande y majestuoso. Es aquí donde mi esposa y yo pasamos la mayoría de 6. _____ (*our*) tiempo. El nombre de mi esposa es Marie-Charlotte-Amelie-Augustine-Victoire-Clementine-Leopoldine, pero para 7. _____ (*her*) amigas es Carlota. 8. _____ (*Her*) padre se llama Leopoldo I y él es rey de Bélgica. A veces la vida aquí es difícil para 9. _____ (*my*) esposa porque muchas de 10. _____ (*her*) amigas son de Francia, donde tenemos 11. _____ (*our*) castillo de Miramar.

EN VOZ ALTA

2-7 **¿Es tu libro o mi libro?** Working in groups of three or four, take turns role-playing a student suffering from temporary amnesia. When the forgetful student asks the others to whom an item in the classroom belongs, they respond in either the affirmative or negative. Use as many items as you can and consider whether you should use formal or informal possessive adjectives in this exercise.

> MODELOS: libro
> E1: *¿Es mi libro?*
> E2: *No, no es tu libro. Es el libro de David.*
>
> bolígrafos
> E1: *¿Son mis bolígrafos?*
> E2: *No, no son tus bolígrafos. Son los bolígrafos de Karen.*

1. la mochila
2. el reloj
3. los lápices
4. el escritorio
5. el cuaderno
6. las calculadoras
7. la clase de español
8. los diccionarios
9. los papeles

2-8 **Entrevista** Ask a classmate the following questions to learn more about his/her family and friends.

1. ¿Es grande tu familia? ¿De dónde son tus padres? ¿Viven otras personas con ellos en su casa? ¿Tienen tus padres mascotas en su casa? ¿Tienes hermanos o hermanas? ¿Desea tu familia visitar tu universidad? ¿Son largas o cortas las llamadas telefónicas *(telephone calls)* entre personas de tu familia?

2. ¿Son tus mejores amigos(as) de aquí? ¿Tienes amigos(as) en nuestra clase? ¿Son difíciles las clases de tus amigos? ¿Tienen tus amigos los mismos intereses que tú o son diferentes sus intereses?

Los nombres y apellidos en español

Teresa Ortega Ramos
Ricardo Castillo
Asesores Cáceres, España

E-mail: ramost@profbuild.com
E-mail: castillor@profbuild.com

Tel: 011.34.3.4667
Fax: 011.34.3.4668

PARA PENSAR

- Do you have traditional names in your family? What are they?
- Are these traditional names from your mother's or your father's side?

En la tradición hispana, los niños reciben más de un nombre, por ejemplo, María Rebeca, Tomás Enrique, Carlos Alberto. Algunas veces, los niños reciben el nombre del santo *(saint)* o de la santa *(female saint)* del día en que nacen *(they are born)*. Por ejemplo, el 25 de julio *(July)* es el día de Santiago Apóstol *(Saint James, patron saint of Spain);* por eso, el niño tiene el nombre de Santiago. A veces *(Sometimes)* los niños tienen el nombre de otro miembro de la familia y casi siempre *(almost always)* el primer hijo lleva el nombre de su papá.

Muchos hispanos tienen dos apellidos. El primero es el apellido del papá (padre) y el segundo *(second)* es el apellido de la mamá (madre): Lucila Palacios González.

A veces solamente se usa el apellido del padre (Palacios) y se usa la inicial del apellido de la madre (G.). Los dos apellidos se usan para propósitos legales *(legal purposes),* y se usa el apellido del padre para archivar *(file)* los documentos legales.

A veces, cuando una mujer se casa *(gets married),* ella usa el apellido de su esposo. Por ejemplo, si Lucila Palacios González se casa con Adán Griego, su nombre es Lucila Palacios de Griego. Muchas mujeres en el siglo XXI no usan el apellido de su esposo y usan solamente los apellidos de sus padres. Por ejemplo, en la tarjeta de presentación *(business card)* de los esposos Ricardo y Teresa Castillo, España, Teresa usa los apellidos de sus padres.

PARA DISCUTIR

1. Based on the information above, how would the following names appear in the phone book?
   a. Ana María Ross de Muñoz
   b. Juan Carlos Peraza Álvarez
   c. Mildred Berrizbeitia González
   d. Luis Ignacio Martínez Rodríguez
   e. Rafael Castro Ramírez
   f. Marta Mercedes Bazó de Monteverde
2. What last name do people use first in Latin America and Spain?
3. What last name do you use? Why?
4. What last name do you believe married women should use? Why?

ESTRUCTURA I Describing people and things: common uses of the verb *ser*

As you learned in **Capítulo preliminar,** the present tense of **ser** is formed as follows:

yo	soy	*I am*
tú	eres	*you* (informal) *are*
Ud., él/ella	es	*you* (formal) *are, he/she is*
nosotros(as)	somos	*we are*
vosotros(as)	sois	*you* (informal) *are*
Uds., ellos(as)	son	*you* (formal) *are, they are*

The verb **ser** *(to be)* is used:

1. to identify essential characteristics of people and things.

   Carlos Fuentes **es** inteligente
   y creativo.
   Sus libros **son** interesantes.

   *Carlos Fuentes is intelligent and
   creative.*
   His books are interesting.

2. to indicate profession or vocation.

   Carlos Fuentes **es** escritor.
   Yo **soy** músico.
   Tú **eres** doctora.

   Carlos Fuentes is a writer.
   I am a musician.
   You are a doctor.

3. to express nationality . . .

   Carlos Fuentes **es** mexicano.

   Carlos Fuentes is Mexican.

   . . . and origin with the preposition **de.**

   El Sr. Fuentes **es de** México.

   Mr. Fuentes is from Mexico.

4. to talk about time.

   Son las cinco.
   Es la una.

   It's five o'clock.
   It's one o'clock.

5. to talk about days of the week, months, and dates.

   Hoy **es** lunes.
   Mañana **es** el 4 de mayo.

   Today is Monday.
   Tomorrow is May 4.

¿NOS ENTENDEMOS?
In Spanish, adjectives of nationality are not capitalized. Example: **Hans es alemán.** *Hans is German.*

Note that the third-person plural form of **ser** is used to express time with the exception of one o'clock, which uses the third-person singular.

¡A PRACTICAR!

2-9 | **Matching** Choose the item on the right that best completes each statement on the left.

1. Yo soy de _____.
2. Son las _____.
3. Susana es _____.
4. Carlos es _____.
5. Hoy es _____.
6. Los exámenes de mi clase son _____.

a. difíciles
b. el Cinco de Mayo y celebramos la Batalla de Puebla
c. los Estados Unidos
d. maestro de español
e. dos de la tarde
f. simpática y sincera

2-10 | **Portraits of a civilization** Fill in the blanks with the appropriate form of **ser** to learn some interesting facts about Mexico. Remember to differentiate between formal and informal modes of address.

MODELO: *Juan es de Aguascalientes, México.*

1. Popocatépetl _____ un volcán activo cerca de la ciudad de México.
2. El emperador Maximiliano y su esposa _____ de Austria.
3. El Día de los Muertos _____ un día festivo muy importante para los mexicanos.
4. Vicente Fox _____ el presidente de México.
5. Vosotros _____ españoles, pero en México, en vez de usar **vosotros,** la forma correcta _____ ustedes.
6. Rocío y Memo _____ estudiantes en la Universidad Nacional Autónoma de México.
7. Ahora _____ las dos de la tarde, la hora de la siesta en México.
8. Las pirámides de Teotihuacán _____ de los aztecas.
9. El Zócalo _____ la plaza más grande y más conocida de México.
10. _____ la una. Para los méxicanos, la una _____ parte de la mañana.

EN VOZ ALTA

2-11 | **Una reunión familiar** Draw a picture of a scene from a family reunion. Each drawing should portray the five uses of **ser** explained in this section. Next describe the scene to your partner and ask at least two questions about your partner's drawing.

2-12 | **Una escena dramática** Working with a partner, compose a theatrical scene that represents an encounter between two students during the first day of Spanish class. Your dialog should contain all five uses of the verb **ser** presented in this section.

The words modeled above in the drawings are *adjectives* and are used to describe *nouns* or *pronouns*. In Spanish, descriptive adjectives must match the *gender* (masculine or feminine) and the *number* (singular or plural) of the noun or pronoun they describe.

How to match adjectives with their nouns

1. Spanish adjectives agree in number and gender with the nouns they modify. Adjectives ending in **-o** change to **-a** to indicate feminine gender and add an **-s** to indicate plural.

	Singular	Plural
Masculine	abuelo generoso	abuelos generosos
Feminine	abuela generosa	abuelas generosas

2. Adjectives ending in **-e** or in most consonants are invariable for gender. That is, they use the same form for the masculine and the feminine. For the plural of adjectives ending in **-e**, add **-s**. For the plural of adjectives ending in a consonant, add **-es**.

	Singular	Plural
Masculine	tío interesante	tíos interesantes
	hermano intelectual	hermanos intelectuales
Feminine	tía interesante	tías interesantes
	hermana intelectual	hermanas intelectuales

¿NOS ENTENDEMOS?
It is common for Mexicans to use the word **güero(a)** to describe someone who is blond. In some Central American countries, **canche** is the preferred term for *blond*. In Venezuela, blonds are referred to as **catire(a)**. In Colombia, blonds are referred to as **mono(a)**. The word **trigueño(a)** is also used for **moreno(a)**, and **pelirrojo** means red-haired.

Refer to the grammar index in the back of the book to learn more about the grammar terms appearing in italics.

3. Most adjectives of nationality ending in a consonant add **-a** for the feminine form. To form the plural, add **-es** to masculine adjectives and **-s** to feminine adjectives. Most adjectives that end in **-dor, -án, -ón,** and **-ín** also follow this pattern.

	Singular	Plural
Masculine	primo español	primos español**es**
	primo trabajador	primos trabajador**es**
	tío alemán	tíos aleman**es**
Feminine	prima español**a**	primas español**as**
	prima trabajador**a**	primas trabajador**as**
	tía aleman**a**	tías aleman**as**

Where to place adjectives

1. Most Spanish adjectives follow the nouns they describe.

La **música bonita** de los mariachis...　　*The mariachi's beautiful music . . .*
Son **personas simpáticas.**　　*They are nice people.*

2. Spanish adjectives of quantity precede the nouns they describe, as in English. Note that in Spanish, when the number *one* is used to quantify a singular masculine noun, speakers drop the **-o: un libro, un papel.**

Vicente Fox tiene **una** hija adoptada.　　*Vicente Fox has one adopted daughter.*
Yo tengo **cuatro** hermanos y　　*I have four brothers and two sisters.*
　　dos hermanas.

3. The adjectives **bueno** and **malo** can be placed before or after the noun they describe. When they come before a singular, masculine noun, the **-o** is dropped: **buen** and **mal.**

Rudy Moreno es un **buen** cómico.　　*Rudy Moreno is a good comedian.*
Rudy Moreno es un cómico **bueno.**

Alejandro Fernández no es un　　*Alejandro Fernández is not a bad man.*
　　mal hombre.
Alejandro Fernández no es un hombre **malo.**

Commonly used adjectives

cobarde coward	**rico(a)** rich
listo(a) smart, ready	**tacaño(a)** stingy
perezoso(a) lazy	**trabajador(a)** hard-working
pobre poor	**tonto(a)** silly, foolish

Cognates

Cognates are words of similar or identical spelling that share the same meaning between two languages.

artístico(a) artistic	**honesto(a)** honest	**paciente** patient
arrogante arrogant	**humilde** humble	**progresista** progressive
atlético(a) athletic	**indeciso(a)** indecisive	**rebelde** rebellious
bilingüe bilingual	**intelectual** intellectual	**reservado(a)** reserved
cómico(a) humorous	**inteligente** intelligent	**responsable** responsible
conservador(a) conservative	**intuitivo(a)** intuitive	**sincero(a)** sincere
dramático(a) dramatic	**irresponsable** irresponsible	**tímido(a)** timid
extrovertido(a) outgoing	**liberal** liberal	**tolerante** tolerant
generoso(a) generous	**moderno(a)** modern	**valiente** brave

The adjective **grande** can also be used before or after the noun it describes. When it precedes a singular noun (either masculine or feminine) it drops the -de to become **gran.** When **gran** precedes a noun, it takes on the figurative meaning of *great* or *impressive.* When **grande** follows a noun, it assumes its more literal meaning of *large* or *big.* For example, **Es una gran casa** *(It's a great house)* versus **Es una casa grande** *(It's a big house).*

¡A PRACTICAR!

2-13 **Descripciones de familiares y amigos** Choose from the adjectives you've learned in this section to describe what the following people are and are not like. Be sure the adjectives agree in gender and number with the nouns they describe. Compare your answers with those of a classmate.

MODELO: *Mi madre es trabajadora pero no es atlética.*

1. Mi mejor amigo(a) es...   pero no es...
2. Mis abuelos son...   pero no son...
3. Mis compañeros de clase son...   pero no son...
4. Mi padre es...   pero no es...
5. Los estudiantes en esta universidad son...   pero no son...
6. El (La) profesor(a) es...   pero no es...
7. Mi hermano(a) es...   pero no es...
8. Yo soy...   pero no soy...

2-14 **¿Cómo es/son?** Describe the following people, using descriptive adjectives and the appropriate form of the verb **ser.** Use adjectives that precede a noun in at least three of your sentences.

MODELO: Vicente Fox
Vicente Fox es alto, moreno y trabajador.

1. Roberto Durán
2. Thalía
3. Luis Miguel
4. mi profesor(a) de español
5. mis compañeros de clase
6. mi mejor amigo(a)
7. yo
8. mi familia y yo
9. mis padres
10. mis hermanos(as)

EN VOZ ALTA

2-15 **¿Quién puede ser? (Who could it be?)** Describe someone in the class for your classmates to identify.

MODELO: E1: *Es alta, delgada y atlética. Es morena.*
E2: *¿Es Michelle?*
E1: *¡Sí!*

2-16 **Personas ideales** Working with a partner, develop an ideal profile for the following people.

MODELO: El profesor ideal
E1: *Para mí (For me), el profesor ideal es inteligente, tolerante y paciente.*
E2: *Para mí, el profesor ideal es liberal, intelectual y un poco rebelde.*

1. el (la) compañero(a) de cuarto
2. los amigos
3. la abuela
4. los padres
5. el presidente
6. el (la) hermano(a)

Encuentro cultural
La familia hispana

PARA PENSAR

- Do you consider your family to be large or small? Why?
- What people do you consider part of your family?
- Do you visit your grandparents, aunts and uncles, or cousins frequently?

En la cultura hispana la unidad social más importante es la familia. La familia está formada por los padres, los hijos, los abuelos, los tíos, los primos, los sobrinos, los primos segundos *(second)* y terceros *(third)*. La familia también incluye *(includes)* a los padrinos: el padrino y la madrina. Los padrinos tienen la responsabilidad de ayudar a sus ahijados *(godchildren)* siempre, si los padres no pueden *(are not able)* ayudar a sus hijos espiritualmente *(spiritually)* o económicamente *(economically)*. Los padres siempre buscan a los padrinos perfectos para sus hijos. A veces, los padrinos tienen un alto rango social para ayudar a los ahijados a buscar una vida mejor.

Los familiares viven muy cerca para ayudar o esperar ayuda del resto de la familia. Toda la familia da ayuda material o emocional a la persona que la necesita. Muchas veces los abuelos viven con sus hijos para ayudar con la educación de sus nietos. Muy pocas veces *(rarely)* los abuelos viven en casa de ancianos *(nursing home)*. Los abuelos y los padrinos son una parte esencial dentro de la tradición familiar hispana.

PARA DISCUTIR

1. Do you have godparents? Do you visit them?
2. What is the godparents' "job" in Latin America or Spain?
3. What is the grandparents' "job" in Latin America or Spain?
4. Where do grandparents usually live in Latin America, Spain, and the United States? Why?
5. What do you think should be the grandparents' "job" in the United States?

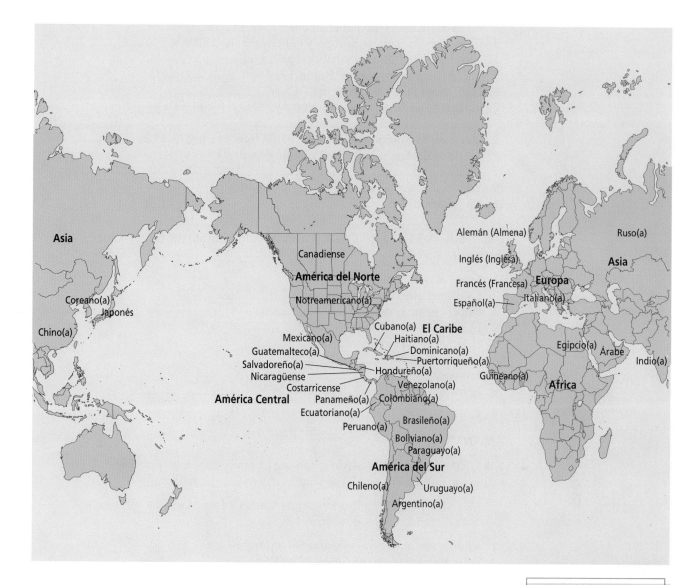

Asia

Canadiense

América del Norte

Notreamericano(a)

Coreano(a)
Japonés

Chino(a)

Cubano(a)   **El Caribe**

Mexicano(a)   Haitiano(a)

Guatemalteco(a)   Dominicano(a)

Salvadoreño(a)   Puertorriqueño(a)

Nicaragüense   Hondureño(a)

Costarricense

América Central   Panameño(a)   Colombiano(a)

Ecuatoriano(a)   Venezolano(a)

Peruano(a)   Brasileño(a)

Boliviano(a)

Paraguayo(a)

América del Sur

Chileno(a)   Uruguayo(a)

Argentino(a)

Alemán (Almena)   Ruso(a)

Inglés (Inglesa)   **Asia**

Francés (Francesa)   **Europa**

Español(a)   Italiano(a)

Egipcio(a)   Árabe

Guineano(a)   Indio(a)

África

¿NOS ENTENDEMOS?
Another way to say **costa-rricense** is **tico(a)**. **Puerto-rriqueños** are also known as **boricuas**. Spaniards from **Galicia**, the northwestern part of Spain, are called **gallegos**.

¡A PRACTICAR!

2-17 **Lenguas y nacionalidades** Identify the nationalities of the following people. In some cases there may be various possibilities.

1. Jorge es de América del Sur y habla portugués. Él es _____.
2. Zhou es de Asia y no habla japonés. Ella es _____.
3. Paquita y Mar son de Europa y hablan español. Ellas son _____.
4. Teresita es de San Juan y habla español. Ella es _____.
5. Tito y Florentina viven en Roma. Ellos son _____.
6. Hans es de Bon y habla alemán. Él es _____.
7. Margarita es de América del Norte y habla español. Ella es

   _____.
8. Pierre es de América del Norte y habla francés e inglés. Él es _____.
9. María es de América del Sur y habla español. Ella es

   _____.
10. Yo soy _____.
11. Mi profesor(a) es _____.

2-18 **Orígenes** Use adjectives of nationality to indicate the origins of the following items.

1. Sushi es una comida _____.
2. Las pirámides más famosas son _____.
3. Kimchi es una comida _____.
4. El BMW es un automóvil _____.
5. El tango es un baile _____.
6. Los burritos son _____.
7. Los espaguetis son _____.
8. El mejor *(The best)* café del mundo es _____.

EN VOZ ALTA

2-19 **¿De dónde es?** Take turns naming as many people as possible of a given nationality and have your partner state the nationality.

MODELO: E1: Gloria Estéfan, Andy García y José Martí
E2: *Ellos son cubanos.*

1. Vicente Fox y su esposa Marta Sahagún Jiménez
2. Sofía Vergara (película *Chasing Papi*), Shakira y Carlos Vives
3. Chelsea Clinton, Bárbara y Jenna Bush
4. Sammy Sosa y Pedro Martínez
5. ... ?

ESTRUCTURA II Describing daily activities at home or at school: present tense of *-er* and *-ir* verbs

In Spanish, in order to form the present tense of infinitives ending in **-er** and **-ir,** you need to add the appropriate personal ending to the stem.

	com + er *(to eat)*		viv + ir *(to live)*	
yo	com**o**	*I eat*	viv**o**	*I live*
tú	com**es**	*you (informal) eat*	viv**es**	*you (informal) live*
Ud., él/ella	com**e**	*you (formal) eat, he/she eats*	viv**e**	*you (formal) live, he/she lives*
nosotros(as)	com**emos**	*we eat*	viv**imos**	*we live*
vosotros(as)	com**éis**	*you (informal) eat*	viv**ís**	*you (informal) live*
Uds., ellos(as)	com**en**	*you (formal) eat, they eat*	viv**en**	*you (formal) live, they live*

The following are several useful **-er** and **-ir** verbs presented in sentences.

abrir	*to open*	Yo abr**o** la puerta para mi abuelo. *I open the door for my grandfather.*
aprender	*to learn*	Tú aprend**es** español. *You learn (are learning) Spanish.*
asistir a	*to attend*	Ella asist**e** a clase. *She attends class.*
beber	*to drink*	Ud. beb**e** mucho café. *You drink a lot of coffee.*
comprender	*to understand*	Él comprend**e** la tarea. *He understands the homework.*
creer	*to believe*	Nosotros cre**emos** en la importancia de nuestra familia. *We believe in our family's importance.*
deber	*ought to, must*	Vosotros deb**éis** hablar con mi primo. *You must talk to my cousin.*
escribir	*to write*	Ustedes escrib**en** cartas. *You write (are writing) letters.*
leer	*to read*	Ellos le**en** un libro. *They read a book.*
recibir	*to receive*	Yo recib**o** una tarjeta de mi sobrino. *I receive a card from my nephew.*
vender	*to sell*	¿Vend**es** tú mis libros? *Are you selling my books?*
vivir	*to live*	Viv**imos** con nuestros amigos. *We live with our friends.*

¿NOS ENTENDEMOS?
Deber is a special verb in Spanish that is used before other verbs to communicate the idea of obligation. In Spanish, as in English, when two verbs are used together the first is conjugated and the second appears in the infinitive form: Yo **debo ir** a la fiesta. *I should (must, ought to) go to the party.*

¡A PRACTICAR!

CULTURA
UNAM stands for **Universidad Nacional Autónoma de México.**

2-20 | **Mi compañero y yo** Complete the following sentences with the appropriate form of the **-er** and **-ir** verbs in parentheses to learn about Tomás's roommate at UNAM.

1. José, mi compañero de cuarto, y yo _____ (vivir) en un apartamento en la Colonia Roma.
2. Nosotros _____ (asistir a) la universidad de la UNAM en México.
3. Mi compañero _____ (ser) de Oaxaca del sur de México.
4. Todos los días él _____ (recibir) noticias *(news)* de su familia.
5. Su hermana _____ (escribir) mucho por correo electrónico *(e-mail).*
6. A veces yo _____ (leer) los mensajes *(messages)* de ella.
7. Por la mañana mi amigo _____ (abrir) sus cartas electrónicas.
8. Mis padres a veces _____ (escribir) cartas.
9. Ellos no _____ (comprender) la nueva tecnología.
10. Mi padre _____ (creer) que las computadoras son importantes, pero todavía no tiene computadora en casa.

2-21 | **Dos compañeros** Complete the following paragraph with the correct form of the verb. In a few cases you will use the infinitive. Several verbs will appear more than once.

asistir a	beber	comer
vivir	comprender	aprender

¡Hola! Me llamo Luisa. 1. _____ en el D.F. Soy estudiante de la UNAM, donde estudio para ser intérprete. 2. _____ mucho de la cultura y la lengua de los norteamericanos en mis clases. Yo 3. _____ clases con mi amigo Juan. Él es un compañero en la clase de inglés. Cuando nuestro profesor habla rápidamente en inglés, Juan no 4. _____ bien. Mi amigo estudia mucho pero el inglés es difícil. Juan y yo 5. _____ en la cafetería donde también 6. _____ café y 7. _____ sándwiches. Yo necesito 8. _____ en los Estados Unidos para 9. _____ más.

EN VOZ ALTA

2-22 | **Actividades diarias** Working with a partner, take turns forming questions, selecting items from each of the three columns.

MODELO: E1: *¿Beben café tus padres en casa?*
E2: *No, mis padres no beben café en casa, pero a veces beben café en el restaurante.*

¿Quién?	¿Qué?	¿Dónde?
nosotros	leer el periódico	en el cuarto
tu compañero(a)	comer	en casa
tú	aprender el vocabulario	en la cafetería
el (la) profesor(a)	beber café	en clase
tus padres	escribir cartas	en la biblioteca

2-23 | **Entrevista** Find out more about your classmate by asking him/her the following questions. Then report your findings to the rest of the class.

1. ¿Dónde vives ahora? ¿Con quién vives? ¿Cuál es tu dirección *(address)*?
2. ¿Aprendes mucho en tus clases? ¿Debes estudiar mucho?
3. En general, ¿eres un(a) estudiante bueno(a) o malo(a)?
4. ¿Lees mucho o poco? ¿Lees novelas, el periódico o páginas en Internet?
5. ¿Dónde comes? ¿Qué tipo de comida comes?

As you learned in **Capítulo preliminar,** the present tense of **tener** is formed as follows:

tener

yo	**tengo**	*I have*
tú	**tienes**	*you* (informal) *have*
usted, él/ella	**tiene**	*you* (formal) *have, he/she has*
nosotros(as)	**tenemos**	*we have*
vosotros(as)	**tenéis**	*you* (informal) *have*
ustedes, ellos(as)	**tienen**	*you* (formal) *have, they have*

Common uses of the verb *tener*

• The verb **tener** *(to have)* is frequently used to indicate possession.

—¿Cuántas hermanas **tienes**?　　*How many sisters do you have?*

—Yo **tengo** dos hermanas.　　*I have two sisters.*

—¿**Tienen** familia tus hermanas?　　*Do your sisters have families?*

—No, no **tienen** familia.　　*No, they don't have families.*

• Another common use of **tener** is to express age.

Mirta **tiene** solamente **dieciocho**　　*Mirta is only 18 years old and*
　años y Margarita **tiene veinte años.**　　*Margarita is 20 years old.*

• **Idiomatic expressions**

In addition to expressing age and possession, the verb **tener** is used in many idiomatic expressions:

tener éxito to be successful

tener hambre to be hungry

tener prisa to be in a hurry

tener razón to be right

tener sed to be thirsty

tener sueño to be tired/sleepy

¡A PRACTICAR!

2-24 **¿Qué tienes?** Provide the correct form of **tener** to complete each sentence.

MODELO: Yo ___*tengo*___ una mochila nueva.

1. Nosotros _____ una nueva profesora.
2. Ellos _____ el nuevo CD de Maná.
3. Roberto estudia mucho y _____ éxito en su clase de español.
4. Después de hacer ejercicio yo _____ sed.
5. Mi hermanita, Paqui, _____ nueve años.
6. Mi profesor siempre _____ razón.
7. ¡Tú siempre _____ sueño! Debes descansar más.
8. Yo _____ hambre. Yo quiero comer un taco.

CULTURA
Maná is a Mexican rock band.

2-25 **Una escena familiar (A family scene)** Complete the following dialog between Juan Carlos and his mother with the appropriate idiomatic expression with **tener.**

MODELO: Los padres de Juan Carlos siempre 1. ___*tienen éxito*___ con él cuando el tema es la comida.

Mamá: ¡Juan Carlos! Tu padre nos espera en el restaurante. ¡Nosotros 2. _____!

Juan Carlos: Ya voy, mamá. Pero es tan tarde y yo 3. _____.

Mamá: ¿No 4. _____? Tú debes comer algo. Y yo sé que tu padre 5. _____ después de su trabajo. Siempre bebe agua o un refresco.

Juan Carlos: Sí, quiero comer algo, mamá. 6. _____.

Mamá: Si vamos ahora, en quince minutos comes una hamburguesa en Sanborn's.

Juan Carlos: Muy bien, mamá. Tú 7. _____. Voy ahora mismo.

EN VOZ ALTA

2-26 **Conversemos** Ask the following questions of a partner and compare answers.

1. ¿Cuándo tienes sueño? ¿en clase o por la noche?
2. ¿Tienes razón con frecuencia? ¿En qué situaciones tienes razón?
3. ¿Cuándo tienes prisa? ¿Siempre llegas a tiempo a la clase?
4. ¿Tienes mucho éxito en tu vida? ¿Tienen éxito tus compañeros(as)?
5. ¿Tenemos clase mañana?
6. ¿Tenemos mucha tarea?
7. ¿Siempre tiene razón el (la) profesor(a)?
8. ¿Tienes hambre ahora?
9. ¿Cuándo tenemos vacaciones?

2-27 **¿Cuántos hermanos tienes?** Working with a partner, find out more about each other's family by asking questions with **tener.**

MODELO: E1: *¿Cuántos hermanos tienes?*
E2: *Yo tengo tres hermanos, una hermana y dos hermanos. Y tú, ¿tienes hermanos?*
E1: *Sí, yo tengo una hermana. Mi hermana se llama Carolina.*
E2: *¿Y cuántos años tiene Carolina?*
E1: *Ella tiene dieciocho años...*

ASÍ SE DICE Counting to 100: los números de 30 a 100

30 treinta	36 treinta y seis	60 sesenta
31 treinta y uno	37 treinta y siete	70 setenta
32 treinta y dos	38 treinta y ocho	80 ochenta
33 treinta y tres	39 treinta y nueve	90 noventa
34 treinta y cuatro	40 cuarenta	100 cien/ciento
35 treinta y cinco	50 cincuenta	

Note that the short form of **cien** is used before nouns and in counting. You will practice **ciento** later when you learn to count above one hundred.

cien libros *one hundred houses*
noventa y nueve, **cien** *ninety-nine, one hundred*

Numbers 30–90 always end in **-a**—**noventa, setenta**—and numbers 31–99 must be written as three words.

Remember, the numbers 16–29 are often written as one word: **dieciocho, veintitrés.**

¡A PRACTICAR!

2-28 **Problemas de matemáticas** Working with a partner, quiz each other over the following equations, taking turns reading the questions to one another.

+ y/más **− menos** **= son**

MODELOS $37 + 41 =$
E1: *¿Cuántos son treinta y siete **y (más)** cuarenta y uno?*
E2: *Treinta y siete **y** cuarenta y uno **son** setenta y ocho.*

$50 - 25 =$
E1: *¿Cuántos son cincuenta **menos** veinticinco?*
E2: *Cincuenta **menos** veinticinco son veinticinco.*

1. $15 + 15 =$ _____
2. $80 + 17 =$ _____
3. $77 - 22 =$ _____
4. $60 - 19 =$ _____
5. $59 + 7 =$ _____
6. $100 - 25 =$ _____
7. $22 + 24 =$ _____
8. $16 + 36 =$ _____
9. $99 - 10 =$ _____

EN VOZ ALTA

2-29 **¿Qué número es?** Working in groups of three or four, have one student think of a number between 30 and 100. The other students try to guess the number with hints from the first student, who will guide them with **más** *(more)* or **menos** *(less).* The first group to guess four numbers wins.

MODELO: E1: *¿Es cincuenta?*
E2: *No, no es cincuenta. Es menos.*
E3: *¿Es cuarenta?*
E2: *No, no es cuarenta. Es más.*
E1: *¿Es cuarenta y nueve?*
E2: *¡Sí! Tienes razón.*

¡A VER!

In this segment, the five housemates begin to settle in and get to know each other. After they share a little information about their families, you will learn some of the opinions they are forming about their new housemates. You will also begin to form your own opinions about each character as you watch them interact on a typical morning.

Expresiones útiles

The following are some new expressions you will hear in the video.

Hace un rato	A little while ago
Se trae un rollo	Has a big problem

Antes de ver

 Paso 1: Think about your immediate family. How many brothers and sisters do you have? What do they look like? Work with a classmate and describe your family and listen as he/she talks about his/hers. Are your families similar?

Paso 2: How would you describe the personalities of each of the following people? Write at least three adjectives for each one and then compare your list with that of a classmate. Did you both use any of the same adjectives? Be creative!

Mi mamá/padre _____

Mi hermano(a) _____

Mi profesor favorito _____

El Presidente _____

Mi mejor *(best)* **amigo(a)** _____

Now think about what you have already learned about the housemates in the video. What do you think they will say about each other? Discuss with a classmate the adjectives they might use to describe each other.

 Paso 3: What do you think a typical morning might be like at **Hacienda Vista Alegre.** Who would get up first in the morning? At what time? Who would take the longest to get ready? Work with four other classmates and role-play your imagined scenario.

Después de ver

Paso 1: Now that you have watched the video segment recall what each housemate said about his or her family and decide if the following statements are **cierto** *(true)* or **falso** *(false)* and correct those that are false. Then, think about the families you and your classmate described to each other in **Antes de ver, Paso 1.** Are your families anything like the families of the housemates?

1. Alejandra tiene dos gatos, Gitano y Lady. _____.

2. Javier tiene una hermana. _____.

3. La madre de Valeria es arquitecto. _____
_____

4. Valeria tiene dos hermanas que practican el modelaje. _____

5. La madre de Alejandra es alta y rubia. _____
_____

Paso 2: In **Antes de ver, Paso 2,** you and your classmate guessed the adjectives the housemates might use to describe each other. Were you correct? Read the descriptions below and see if you can remember who each housemates is describing.

Valeria   Alejandra   Sofía   Antonio

- Valeria: « _____ es atractivo, pero es también vanidoso.» « _____ y _____ son bonitas.»
- Alejandra: «_____ es muy linda y es una muchacha inteligente.»
- Sofía: «Creo que a _____ no le gusta su carrera para nada!»
- Antonio: «¡ _____ es guapísima!»

Paso 3: In **Antes de ver, Paso 3,** you predicted what a typical morning might be like at **Hacienda Vista Alegre.** Now that you have watched the video and know what actually happened, use the correct form of the verbs below to complete the paragraph. How accurate was the scenario that you and your classmates invented in

abrir	entrar	contestar	tener éxito	tener prisa
necesitar	ser	llamar	impaciente	treinta y cinco

Antes de ver, Paso 3?

1. _____ las ocho y 2. _____ de la mañana. Sofía 3. _____ porque ya es muy tarde, pero Valeria está en el baño. Todos 4. _____ usar el baño y se ponen muy 5. _____ con Valeria. Por fin, Antonio 6. _____ a Valeria. Ella no 7. _____, entonces Antonio 8. _____ la puerta, 9. _____ al baño y sorprende a Valeria. Su plan 10. _____. Valeria grita y sale del baño muy rápidamente.

¿Qué opinas tú?

Paso 1: Do you know anyone like the housemates? Maybe a family member or friend? Discuss with a classmate whether or not you know people like Valeria, Sofía, Alejandra, Antonio, and Javier.

Paso 2: Write a detailed description of each housemate from the video using your own opinions. Share your descriptions with a classmate and see if he/she can guess who you are describing. Share some of your descriptions with the class. Do your descriptions match those of other classmates?

¡A LEER!

Skimming and scanning

Two useful reading strategies are skimming and scanning. Skimming reading material is useful for quickly getting the gist or general idea of its content, and scanning is used to find specific information even in the same material.

Paso 1: Skim the following cards below to get a general understanding of what they are about. Then answer the following questions.

1. What type of presentation cards are these?
2. What is the purpose of these cards?
3. In what situation do you think you will receive one of these?

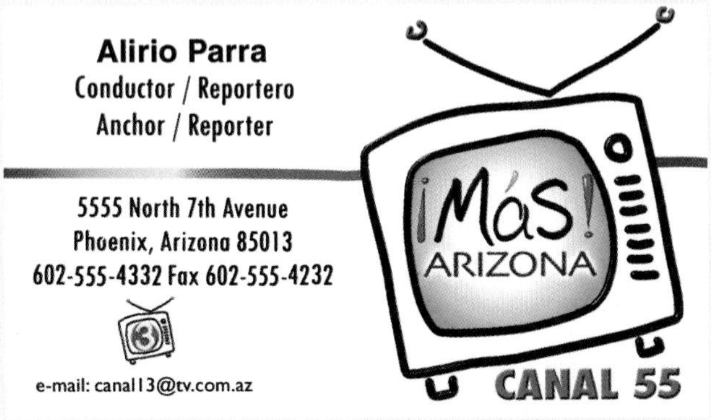

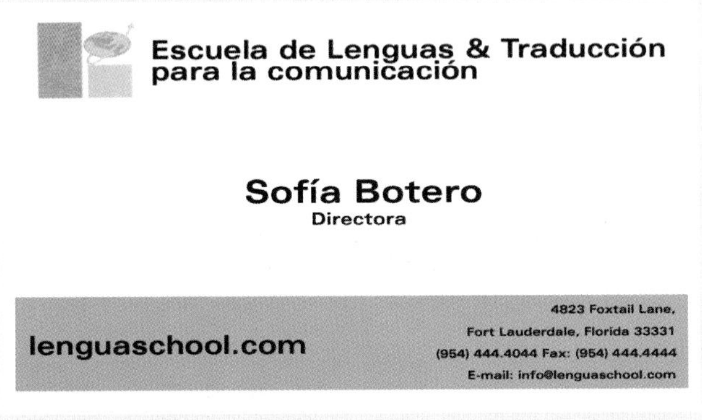

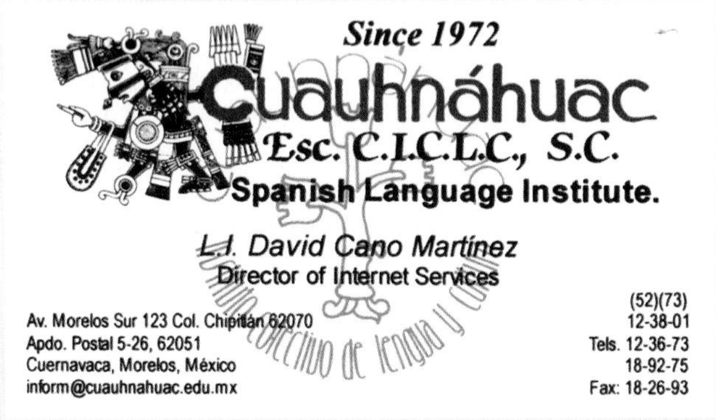

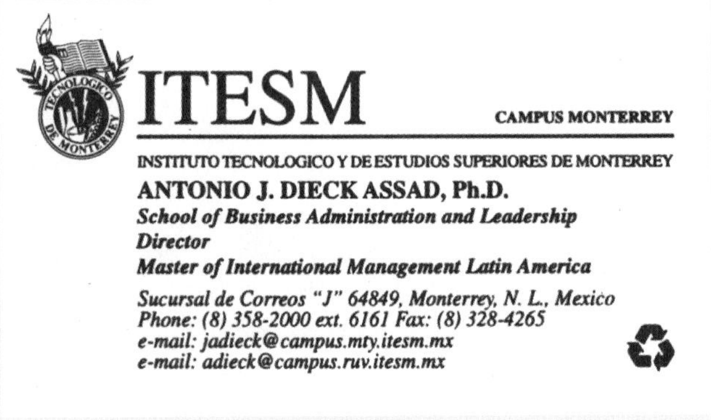

CULTURA
Notice how the phone numbers are written and are said in pairs and the address is shortened as **Av.** which means **avenida. Pte.** means **puente** (*bridge*).

Paso 2: Scan the cards and answer the following questions.

1. Who works in . . .
   a. Fort Lauderdale, Florida?
   b. Cuernavaca, Morelos, Mexico?
   c. Phoenix, Arizona?
   d. Monterrey, Mexico?
2. What is the position of Dr. Antonio J. Dieck Assad?
3. What is the position of Sofía Botero?
4. What is the position of Alirio Parra?
5. What is the phone number of the person who works in Cuernavaca, Mexico?
6. What is the Internet address of the Language Institute in Mexico?

¡A ESCRIBIR!

Strategy: Learning Spanish word order

Word order refers to the meaningful sequence of words in a sentence. The order of words in Spanish sentences differs somewhat from English word order. Some common rules of Spanish word order are:

- Definite and indefinite articles precede nouns.

  Los gatos y **los perros** son animales.
  Tengo **un gato** y **un perro.**

- Subjects usually precede their verbs in statements.

  Mi gato es negro.

- Subjects usually follow their verbs in questions.

  ¿**Tiene usted** animales en casa?

- Adjectives of quantity usually precede nouns.

  ¿**Cuántos animales** tienes en casa?

- Adjectives of description usually follow nouns.

  El **perro pardo** *(brown)* se llama Bandido.

- Possession is often expressed by using **de** with a noun.

  Tigre es **el gato de Sara.**

Task: Writing a family profile

Functions: Writing a letter (informal); Introducing; Describing people
Vocabulary: Family members; Numbers; Animals; Domestic; Colors; University
Grammar: Verbs: **ser, tener;** Possession with **de;** Adjectives: agreement, position

Family profiles may occur in many contexts. Some common contexts are informal letters of introduction such as ones written to a pen pal or a host family for a study abroad student; newsletters of organizations, civic groups, or religious groups; and websites of such organizations and groups or individuals. In this activity you will write a short family profile to include in a letter to a pen pal.

Paso 1: Unscramble the words in the following sentences. Then rewrite them in their correct sequence. Be sure to capitalize the first word of every sentence and to end each one with a period. Begin and end questions with appropriate question marks.

> MODELO: es Anita Camacho de México
> *Anita Camacho es de México.*

1. es Anita una universitaria estudiante
2. Carlos Suárez su clase compañero se llama de
3. Carlos un poco y Anita hablan de inglés
4. años tienen cuántos ellos ¿?
5. Carlos veintitrés tiene y tiene diecinueve Anita
6. tiene Anita hermanos ¿?
7. José padre el es Anita de
8. gato tiene un Anita
9. Pecas llama Anita se gato de el

Paso 2: Now work with a classmate. Compare your sentences and check for errors in word order, spelling, capitalization, and punctuation.

Paso 3: Imagine that you are Susana's new pen pal and that you are writing her a letter introducing yourself and your family. Describe your family as accurately as possible, including information such as names, ages, physical descriptions, personality traits, and favorite activities.

Paso 4: Share your letter with one or more classmates. Encourage your partner(s) to respond to what you have written and to ask questions about any information that is not clear.

¡A CONVERSAR!

Pronunciation focus: *r* and *rr; d*

In the middle of a word, the letter **r** in Spanish is pronounced with a single flap of the tongue on the ridge behind the upper front teeth, producing a sound similar to the English *tt* in *batter* or the *dd* in *ladder*. At the beginning of a word, **r** is pronounced like the Spanish **rr** with a sustained flapping of the tongue, known as "trilling."

There are two basic pronunciations for the Spanish **d;** context determines which one must be used. At the beginning of a sentence or phrase or after **l** or **n,** the **d** is articulated by pressing the front part of the tongue against the back of the upper teeth. A softer **d** is closer to the English *th* sound and occurs in the middle of a word unless the **d** is followed by **l** or **n.**

Practice the following sentences:

> Mi nombre es Roberto.
> Mi madre es muy trabajadora.
> Ricardo es costarricense; Ramona es puertorriqueña.
> ¿Dónde está San Diego?
> Mi primo desea descansar por una hora.

Task: Talking about your family

Think about how you described your family in the **¡A escribir!** section above as you work with a partner in this activity.

Paso 1: You may wish to review the family vocabulary and descriptive adjectives from **Capítulo 2,** activities from **Capítulo 1** and **Capítulo 2,** and the interrogative words from **Capítulo preliminar.** Imagine you are talking to a new friend or acquaintance and he/she wants to know about your family. Describe your family to your partner, making sure you include descriptive information about specific members of your family, such as where they live, their ages, and their favorite pastimes. Your partner should ask questions to clarify anything that he/she does not understand or to solicit more information.

Paso 2: Your partner will now describe his/her family to you, and you will ask questions as needed.

Paso 3: Each of you will describe your partner's family to another student or to the class. Include as much information as possible and respond to questions the other student asks.

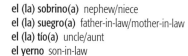
Miembros de la familia y otros parientes Members of the family and other relatives

el (la) abuelo(a) grandmother/grandfather
el apellido last name
el (la) cuñado(a) brother-in-law/sister-in-law
el (la) esposo(a) husband/wife
el (la) hermano(a) brother/sister
el (la) hijo(a) son/daughter

la madre (mamá) mother
el (la) nieto(a) grandson/granddaughter
el nombre first name
la nuera daughter-in-law
el padre (papá) father
el (la) primo(a) cousin

el (la) sobrino(a) nephew/niece
el (la) suegro(a) father-in-law/mother-in-law
el (la) tío(a) uncle/aunt
el yerno son-in-law

Las mascotas House pets

el gato cat
el pájaro bird

el perro dog
el pez fish

Adjetivos Adjectives

alto(a) tall
amable friendly
antipático(a) unpleasant
arrogante arrogant
artístico(a) artistic
atlético(a) athletic
bajo(a) short (height)
bilingüe bilingual
bonito(a) pretty
bueno(a) good
casado(a) married
cobarde coward
cómico(a) humorous
conservador(a) conservative
corto(a) short (length)
delgado(a) thin
dramático(a) dramatic
extrovertido(a) outgoing
feo(a) ugly
generoso(a) generous

gordo(a) fat
grande big
guapo(a) good-looking
honesto(a) honest
humilde humble
indeciso(a) indecisive
intelectual intellectual
inteligente intelligent
intuitivo(a) intuitive
irresponsable irresponsible
joven young
largo(a) long
liberal liberal
listo(a) smart, ready
malo(a) bad
moderno(a) modern
moreno(a) brunette
nuevo(a) new
paciente patient
pequeño(a) small

perezoso(a) lazy
pobre poor
progresista progressive
rebelde rebellious
reservado(a) reserved
responsable responsible
rico(a) rich
rubio(a) blonde
simpático(a) nice
sincero(a) sincere
soltero(a) single
tacaño(a) stingy
tímido(a) shy
tolerante tolerant
tonto(a) silly, foolish
trabajador(a) hard-working
valiente brave
viejo(a) old

Nacionalidades Nationalities

alemán(-ana) German
árabe Arab
argentino(a) Argentine
boliviano(a) Bolivian
brasileño(a) Brazilian
canadiense Canadian
chileno(a) Chilean
chino(a) Chinese
colombiano(a) Colombian
coreano(a) Korean
costarricense Costa Rican
cubano(a) Cuban

dominicano(a) Dominican (from the Dominican Republic)
egipcio(a) Egyptian
español(-a) Spanish
estadounidense from the United States
francés (-esa) French
guatemalteco(a) Guatemalan
haitiano(a) Haitian
hondureño(a) Honduran
indio(a) Indian
inglés (-esa) English
italiano(a) Italian

japonés (-esa) Japanese
mexicano(a) Mexican
nicaragüense Nicaraguan
norteamericano(a) North American
panameño(a) Panamanian
paraguayo(a) Paraguayan
peruano(a) Peruvian
puertorriqueño(a) Puerto Rican
ruso(a) Russian
salvadoreño(a) Salvadoran
uruguayo(a) Uruguayan
venezolano(a) Venezuelan

Verbos

abrir to open
aprender to learn
asistir a to attend
beber to drink
comer to eat
comprender to understand
creer to believe

deber ought to, must
escribir to write
leer to read
recibir to receive
ser to be
tener to have
    tener éxito to be successful

tener hambre to be hungry
tener prisa to be in a hurry
tener razón to be right
tener sed to be thirsty
tener sueño to be sleepy
vender to sell
vivir to live

Expresiones idiomáticas

¡Qué bueno! Wonderful!

por supuesto of course

Así que... So . . . (You mean to say that . . .)

El tiempo libre:

Chapter Objectives

COMMUNICATIVE GOALS

In this chapter you will learn how to . . .

- Describe leisure-time activities
- Express likes and dislikes
- Express plans and intentions
- Describe basic actions, places, and activities in town
- Talk about the months, seasons, and the weather.

STRUCTURES

- **Gustar** + *infinitive* and **gustar** + *nouns*
- **Ir a** + *destination* or *infinitive*
- Irregular **yo** verbs
- **Saber, conocer,** and the personal **a**

CULTURAL INFORMATION

- Los deportes en el mundo hispano
- El café en Colombia y en el mundo

Colombia

COLOMBIA

Población: 40.349.388
Área: 1.138.910 kilómetros
cuadrados, casi tres veces el tamaño
de Montana
Capital: Santa Fe de Bogotá,
6.540.400
Ciudades principales: Cali,
2.161.000; Medellín, 1.908.600;
Barranquilla, 1.273.000
Moneda: el peso
Lengua: el español

¡Bienvenidos a Colombia!

In this video, you will learn about
Colombia. After watching the video,
answer the following questions:

1 Where is Colombia?

2 What is the geography of Colombia like?

3 What are some of the main products that Colombia exports?

4 What are the names of some Colombian cities?

5 Would you like to visit Colombia? Why or why not?

La Plaza Bolívar, Bogotá, Colombia

In this section you will learn how to talk about sports and leisure-time activities.

esquiar

caminar por las montañas

jugar al tenis

levantar pesas

andar en bicicleta
(el ciclismo)

nadar (la natación)

montar a caballo

patinar en línea

correr

esquiar en el agua

pescar (la pesca)

Otras palabras deportivas Other sports words

el baloncesto basketball
el béisbol baseball
el campo de fútbol (de golf) football field (golf course)
el fútbol (americano) soccer (football)

ganar to win
el golf golf
el partido game
el vólibol volleyball

¿NOS ENTENDEMOS?
El baloncesto is also called **básquetbol** and *ball* can be called **el balón, la bola,** or **la pelota.**

Los pasatiempos Pastimes

bailar to dance
dar un paseo to go for a walk
hacer un picnic (planes, ejercicio) to go on a picnic
  (to make plans, to exercise)
ir... to go . . .
  a tomar un café to drink coffee
  a un bar to a bar
  a un club to a club
  a un concierto to a concert
  a una discoteca to a dance club
  a una fiesta to a party
  al cine to the movies
  de compras shopping

mirar la tele to watch TV
sacar fotos to take pictures
tocar la guitarra to play the guitar
tomar el sol to sunbathe
ver una película to watch a movie
visitar un museo to visit a museum

Palabras útiles are presented to help you enrich your personal vocabulary. The terms provided here will help you talk about leisure-time activities.

Palabras útiles

la bicicleta bicycle
la cámara camera
la cancha (de tenis) (tennis) court
los esquís (acuáticos) (water) skis
el estadio stadium
las gafas del sol sunglasses

el juego game
el (la) jugador(a) player
los palos de golf golf clubs
los patines (en línea) (in-line) skates
los zapatos de tenis tennis shoes (sneakers)

¡A PRACTICAR!

3-1 **Asociaciones** What activities do you associate with the following people?

MODELO: Carlos Vives
Ir a un concierto, tocar la guitarra, cantar, bailar

1. Felipe López
   (Timberwolves)
2. Peyton Manning
3. Mia Hamm
4. Shakira
5. Dave Matthews
6. Andre Agassi
7. Sammy Sosa
8. Tiger Woods
9. Gabrielle Reese
10. Lance Armstrong

CULTURA
Carlos Vives is a Colombian pop star, nominated for six Latin Grammys for his album *El amor de mi tierra* (The Love of My Land).

3-2 **¿En qué puedo servirle?** Imagine that you work in a sporting goods store and that you need to guess the activities or sports of your clients in order to send them to the appropriate section of the store. In a few cases there may be several possibilities.

MODELO: Un señor: Yo necesito un traje de baño.
¡Ah! Usted nada.
o *¡Ah! Usted practica natación.*

1. Dos chicos: Nosotros necesitamos una cámara.
2. Una chica: Necesito más pesas.
3. Dos señoras: ¿Dónde están los patines?
4. Una chica: Busco un casco *(helmet)* y riendas *(reins)*.
5. Dos chicos: ¿Hay zapatos de tenis en esta tienda?
6. Tu amiga: ¿Tienen gafas de sol?
7. Tu mamá: ¿Hay bicicletas a buenos precios?
8. Tus abuelos: Vamos a comprar otros esquís acuáticos.

EN VOZ ALTA

3-3 **Un fin de semana típico** Incorporate the items below in questions to ask a classmate about his/her weekend activities. Upon answering the questions, change the information in the questions so that it is true for you.

MODELO: tú / dar un paseo en el parque / los sábados
E1: *¿Das un paseo en el parque los sábados?*
E2: *Sí, doy un paseo en el parque los sábados con mi amiga Jill.*
o E2: *No, mis amigas y yo hacemos un picnic los sábados.*

1. tú / bailar en las fiestas / los viernes por la noche
2. tú y tu compañero(a) de cuarto / mirar la tele / los sábados por la tarde
3. tú y tu(s) amigo(a)(s) / tomar café / los sábados por la noche
4. tú / visitar un museo / los domingos por la mañana
5. tú / andar en bicicleta / los domingos por la tarde
6. tú y tus padres / tocar el piano y cantar / los domingos por la noche

¿NOS ENTENDEMOS?
To form **sí/no** questions, make your voice rise at the end of the questions. Another way is to invert the order of the subject and verb, in addition to making your voice rise at the end of the question:

¿Miguel regresa a las seis?

¿Regresa Miguel a las seis?

3-4 **Deportes favoritos** Ask another student the following questions about his/her favorite sport or pastime. Are there sports that you both share an interest in?

1. ¿Cuál es tu deporte favorito? ¿Qué deportes te gusta jugar? ¿Qué deportes te gusta mirar?
2. ¿Esquías? ¿Sí? ¿Dónde esquías? ¿Con quién esquías?
3. ¿Nadas bien o mal? ¿Dónde y con quién te gusta nadar? ¿Cuándo nadas?
4. ¿Pescas frecuentemente o no? ¿Dónde pescas?
5. ¿Montas a caballo? ¿Sí? ¿Es fácil o difícil montar a caballo? ¿Es más fácil montar a caballo o andar en bicicleta?
6. ¿Haces mucho o poco ejercicio? ¿Qué tipo *(kind)* de ejercicio haces? ¿Dónde haces ejercicio normalmente?

EN CONTEXTO

Three Colombian students, Catalina, Isabel, and Gerardo, are discussing plans for an upcoming party at Catalina's apartment in Cali, Colombia. As you read the following dialog, pay attention to the form of address used among the three friends.

¿NOS ENTENDEMOS?
It is common for Colombians to use the **usted** form even when addressing friends. The diminutive phrase of **un poquitico** (*a little bit*—derived from the Spanish phrase **un poco**) is also typical of Colombian speech. Most native speakers would use the word **poquito.** The word **chévere** *(fantastic, cool)* is used often in Colombia, Venezuela, and the Caribbean.

Sensible is a false cognate that means *sensitive* rather than *sensible.*

Gerardo:	¡Hola, Catalina! Isabel dice que usted **va a hacer una fiesta** este fin de semana.
Catalina:	¡Sí! Los invito a usted y a su hermano, Pepe. Ustedes tienen que venir.
Gerardo:	Mmm... ¿Cuándo es?
Catalina:	El sábado a las nueve en mi casa. Cuento con usted (*I'm counting on you*) para la música y con su hermano para **sacar fotos.**
Gerardo:	Bueno, **no sé.** No **toco la guitarra** mucho en estos días (*these days*) y...
Isabel:	¡Venga (*Come on!*), Gerardo! Va a ser una fiesta chévere, y usted nunca practica. ¡Es un maestro de la guitarra!
Gerardo:	Es un poquitico complicado. **Tengo** planes con una amiga para **ir a un club** el sábado. No sé si...
Catalina:	¡Pues! ¡Ella también puede venir (*She can come*) a pasar un buen rato (*a good time*) con nosotros!
Isabel:	**Vamos a bailar** mucho, y **yo sé** cómo **le gusta bailar a su hermano.**
Gerardo:	Bueno, acepto, pero mi compañera es muy sensible, y...
Catalina:	¡Ay! La mujer misteriosa de Gerardo debe ser muy especial.
Isabel:	¡Claro que sí! **Tú sabes,** Catalina, que todas las amigas de Gerardo son especiales.

¿Comprendiste?

Indicate whether the following are true or false. Change all false statements to true statements.

1. A Isabel le gusta sacar fotos.
2. Gerardo practica la guitarra todos los días.
3. La fiesta es el sábado por la noche en la casa de Catalina.
4. La amiga de Gerardo es muy tímida.
5. Gerardo no va a ir a la fiesta.

Encuentro cultural

Los deportes en el mundo hispano

PARA PENSAR

- Do you know any athletes from Spain or Latin America who play sports here in the United States? Can you name any Colombian athletes?

- Do you know what sports people play in Spain and Latin America?

Carlos Valderrama

El fútbol *(soccer)* y el béisbol son los deportes más populares en el mundo hispano. Los aficionados *(fans)* son muy apasionados y los deportes son una parte muy relevante en la vida de muchos países hispanos.

En España y en casi todos los países hispanos hay ligas profesionales *(professional leagues)* de fútbol. Así como *(Just like)* en los Estados Unidos, los jugadores hispanoamericanos son muy famosos y ganan mucho dinero. Por ejemplo, el brasileño Edson Nascimento Pelé y el argentino Diego Maradona son muy famosos dentro del mundo del fútbol y el colombiano Carlos Valderrama también, ya que ayuda a su equipo a clasificar por tercera (3ª) vez para la Copa Mundial de Fútbol.

El béisbol es también muy importante, especialmente en Cuba, Puerto Rico, Panamá, la República Dominicana y Venezuela. Los historiadores creen que el cubano Nemesio Guillot lleva el juego del béisbol a Cuba en 1866 después de estudiar en una universidad estadounidense. Algunos de los jugadores de béisbol que forman parte del Salón de la Fama *(Hall of Fame)* en los Estados Unidos son los cubanos Luis Tiant, Tony Oliva y Orlando Cepeda; los puertorriqueños Roberto Clemente y Roberto Alomar; el venezolano Luis Aparicio; los dominicanos Juan Marichal, Pedro Martínez y Sammy Sosa. Sammy Sosa compra boletos para los juegos de béisbol todos los domingos *(on Sundays)* y regala *(gives as a gift)* los boletos a los niños que no tienen dinero para ir a los juegos durante los fines de semana.

PARA DISCUTIR

1. What are the most popular sports in Spain and Latin America?

2. What are the names of some well-known athletes from Colombia, Argentina, Venezuela, etc.

3. Describe the fans in the Spanish-speaking world.

4. What does Sammy Sosa do every Sunday?

5. What sports do you like to play and which ones do you like to watch? Why?

—¿Qué **te gusta hacer**?	*What do you like to do?*
—**Me gusta correr.**	*I like to run (go running).*
—A mi papá **le gusta correr** también.	*My dad likes to run (go running), too.*
—Pero a mi madre y a mí, **nos gusta ir de compras.**	*But my mom and I like to go shopping.*
—Y a mi hermano, **le gusta el baloncesto.**	*And my brother likes basketball.*

To express likes and dislikes, Spanish speakers often use the verb **gustar** (*to be pleasing [to someone]*). The verb **gustar** can be used in two constructions: **gustar** + *infinitive* and **gustar** + *nouns*.

Gustar + infinitive

As you learned in **Capítulo 1,** the verb **gustar** can be used with infinitives to express that an activity or action is pleasing to someone. To express to whom an action or activity—talking, running, shopping—is pleasing, use one of the following pronouns with the verb form **gusta** plus an infinitive. Note that these indirect object pronouns below indicate *to whom* or *for whom* an action is pleasing.

me	*to me*	
te	*to you* (informal)	
le	*to you* (formal), *to him/her*	
nos	*to us*	+ **gusta** + infinitive
os	*to you* (informal, plural)	
les	*to you* (formal and informal, plural), *to them*	

Notice that in order to clarify or emphasize to whom something is pleasing, you can use the preposition **a** plus the person's (persons') name(s) or a pronoun. For instance, **a Catalina** and **a tus amigos** in the examples below are used to clarify to whom something is pleasing. However, **a ti, a mí,** and **a nosotros** are used for emphasis.

—¿**A Catalina le** gusta tomar el sol?	*Does Catalina like to sunbathe?*
—Sí. También **le** gusta nadar.	*Yes. She also likes to swim.*
—¿**A ti te** gusta nadar?	*Do you like to swim?*
—Sí, **me** gusta nadar mucho.	*Yes, I like to swim a lot.*
—¿**A tus amigos les** gusta tomar café?	*Do your friends like to drink coffee?*
—Sí, **les** gusta tomar café colombiano.	*Yes, they like to drink Colombian coffee.*
—¿**A ustedes les** gusta esquiar en el agua?	*Do you like to water ski?*
—Sí, **a nosotros nos** gusta.	*Yes, we do.*

Gustar + nouns

When you use **gustar** with nouns, its form changes depending on whether you are talking about one thing or more than one thing.

—A Carlos le **gusta** la piscina.	*Carlos likes the swimming pool.*
—A Carlos le **gustan** los deportes.	*Carlos likes sports.*

La piscina, in the first example, is singular, so you use the singular form of **gustar: gusta. Los deportes,** in the second example, is plural, so you use the plural form of the verb **gustar: gustan.** Note that with the **gustar** + *noun* construction, the noun is usually preceded by the definite article (**la** piscina, **los** deportes).

¡A PRACTICAR!

3-5 **Los fines de semana** Use **me, te, le, nos, os,** or **les** to complete the following statements describing the likes of Gerardo, Pepe, and their friends.

1. A ti _____ gusta sacar fotos.
2. A mí _____ gusta tocar la guitarra.
3. A Catalina e Isabel _____ gusta escuchar música.
4. A la familia de Isabel _____ gustan los patacones.
5. A un compañero de Pepe _____ gusta ir al cine con su novia.
6. A nosotros _____ gusta hacer fiestas los fines de semana.

> **CULTURA**
> **Patacones** are a Colombian dish made of fried plantains.

3-6 **Un niño difícil** Use the correct form of the verb **gustar** and the appropriate indirect object pronoun to complete the following dialog between a baby-sitter and a difficult child.

Niñera: ¿Pepito, *te gusta* mirar la tele?

Pepito: No. A mí no 1. _____ _____ los programas de esta noche.

Niñera: Pues, yo sé que a tu hermana 2. _____ _____ los dibujos animados *(cartoons)*.

Pepito: No es cierto. A mi hermana y a mí solamente 3. _____ _____ mirar las películas *(movies)* de horror.

Niñera: Entonces, ¿a ustedes 4. _____ _____ las canciones de Shakira? Yo tengo el nuevo CD de ella.

Pepito: No. No 5. _____ _____ escuchar música porque a mí no 6. _____ _____ cantar y a mi hermana no 7. _____ _____ bailar. Por eso no 8. _____ _____ la música.

> **CULTURA**
> Shakira Isabel Mebarak Ripoll is a Colombian singer of Latin-alternative folk-rock who exploded into the spotlight in 1996 with her third album, *Pies descalzos (Bare Feet)*. A single off that album, *"Estoy aquí" ("I Am Here")*, played on radio stations across Latin America. Her latest CD, *Laundry Service*, has been a success and "Whenever, Whatever" is recorded on it.

EN VOZ ALTA

3-7 **Preferencias personales** Ask a classmate about his/her family members' preferences for the following objects, persons, and activities. When necessary, use **a** + *pronoun* to specify the family members.

MODELO: el fútbol
   E1: *¿A tu papá, le gusta el fútbol?*
   E2: *Sí, le gusta el fútbol.*
   o E2: *No, no le gusta el fútbol. A mi papá le gusta el tenis.*

1. la música de Shakira
2. comer patacones
3. las películas románticas
4. el café colombiano
5. el fútbol americano
6. bailar

3-8 **¿Y a tus personas favoritas?** Ask another student what the following people like to do. The other student should choose from the list of activities in order to answer the questions.

ir de compras
patinar en línea con sus amigos
mirar la televisión
hacer ejercicio
andar en bicicleta

MODELO: a tu papá / jugar al tenis
   E1: *¿A tu papá le gusta jugar al tenis?*
   E2: *(No) Sí, (no) le gusta jugar al tenis.*

1. a ti
2. a tu mejor amigo(a)
3. a tu pareja ideal
4. a tu cantante favorito(a)
5. a tu actor (actriz) favorito(a)

3-9 **¿Qué te gusta hacer?** Write five sentences about pastimes you like to do alone. Next, write five sentences about things that you and your friends enjoy. Finally, compare your sentences to those of another classmate. Do you have a lot in common?

MODELO: *A mí me gusta escuchar música en mi cuarto. A mis amigos y a mí nos gustan las discotecas porque bailamos mucho...*

Siempre Verde, un pueblo colombiano In this section you will learn the names of places in a town. How does the imaginary town of **Siempre Verde** compare with your own?

la oficina de correos

el banco

el supermercado

la calle

el café

la piscina

la iglesia

el centro

la plaza

el museo

el parque

el mercado al aire libre

el cine

la tienda

el restaurante

el centro comercial

Palabras útiles are presented to help you enrich your personal vocabulary. The terms provided here will help you talk about the places in your city/town.

Palabras útiles

la carnicería butcher shop

la ferretería hardware store

la frutería fruit store

la gasolinera gas station

la joyería jewelry store

la papelería stationery store

la peluquería hair salon

la tienda de antigüedades (de música [de discos], de ropa) antiques (music, clothing) store

¡A PRACTICAR!

3-10 | **Asociaciones** What places do you associate with the following activities?

MODELO: estacionar *(to park)* el carro
la calle

1. ir de compras
2. rezar *(to pray)*
3. ir a tomar un café
4. comer
5. mandar cartas
6. ver una película
7. nadar
8. depositar dinero
9. reunirse *(to get together)* con amigos
10. jugar deportes

3-11 | **En mi pueblo hay... / no hay...** Form sentences to describe the place where you live or study.

MODELO: *En mi pueblo hay seis restaurante(s). Mi restaurante favorito se llama Marvin's.*

1. En mi pueblo hay _____ parques. Los más grandes se llama(n) _____, _____ y _____.
2. En mi pueblo hay _____ supermercados. Generalmente compro cosas en _____.
3. En mi pueblo hay _____ cafés. El café más popular es _____.
4. En mi pueblo hay _____ cine(s). Generalmente voy al cine _____.
5. Vivo en la calle _____.
6. En mi pueblo hay _____ piscina(s) pública(s).
7. En mi pueblo no hay _____, _____ ni _____.

EN VOZ ALTA

3-12 | **¿Te gusta el cine?** Ask a classmate whether he/she likes the following places in your town or city. If your classmate does like a particular place, ask what he/she does there.

MODELO: el café
E1: *¿Te gusta el café Maggie's?*
E2: *Sí, me gusta el café Maggie's.*
E1: *¿Qué haces en Maggie's?*
E2: *Hablo y tomo café con mis amigos.*

1. la plaza
2. el mercado
3. la tienda
4. el centro comericial
5. el centro
6. la oficina de correos
7. el restaurante
8. el banco
9. la discoteca
10. el museo

> **¿NOS ENTENDEMOS?**
> **El almacén** is another word for **la tienda**; it can sometimes mean *department store*, *warehouse*, or even *grocery store*, depending on the region.

3-13 | **Un estudio de mi pueblo** Ask a partner to identify the number of places in his/her town and then to indicate what places or buildings he/she feels are needed. Your partner should also express what kinds of buildings or places are not needed.

MODELO: *En mi pueblo hay seis bancos, tres cines, ocho restaurantes, dos parques y tres tiendas de video. Nosotros necesitamos un museo y una discoteca. No necesitamos (need) más restaurantes de comida china.*

ESTRUCTURA II Expressing plans with *ir: ir a +* destination, and *ir a +* infinitive

In this section, you will learn how to talk about future plans with the verb **ir** *(to go)*. First you will you learn how to conjugate the verb **ir** and then you will learn about two structures that you can use with this verb, **ir a +** *destination*, and **ir a +** *infinitive*, in order to express plans.

Present tense of the verb *ir* (to go)

The verb **ir** has the following irregular conjugation in the present tense:

yo	**voy**	*I go*
tú	**vas**	*you* (informal) *go*
Ud., él/ella	**va**	*you* (formal) *go, he/she goes*
nosotros(as)	**vamos**	*we go*
vosotros(as)	**vais**	*you* (informal) *go*
Uds., ellos(as)	**van**	*you* (formal and informal) *go, they go*

Ir a + destination

To tell where people are going, use a form of the verb **ir** plus the preposition **a,** followed by a destination.

—¿Adónde **van** Uds.?	*Where are you going?*
—**Voy a** la piscina.	*I'm going to the pool.*
—Y yo **voy al** parque.	*And I'm going to the park.*

In **Capítulo 2** you learned how to form the contraction **del** in talking about possessive constructions. Another common contraction in Spanish is **a + el = al,** as shown in the example **Yo voy *al* parque.** Note that the preposition **a** *(to)* combines with the definite article **el** *(the)* to form the word **al** *(to the).*

Ir a + infinitive

To express future plans, use a form of the verb **ir** plus the preposition **a,** followed by an infinitive.

—¿Qué **vas a hacer** ahora?	*What are you going to do now?*
—**Voy a jugar** al tenis.	*I'm going to play tennis.*

¡A PRACTICAR!

3-14 **Una invitación** Complete this conversation between two friends, Ana Margarita and Fernando. They are planning to go to a party with a group of students from the United States. Use **ir, voy, vas, va, vamos,** and **van.** After completing the dialog, practice the conversation with a classmate.

Ana Margarita: ¡Hola, Fernando! ¿Adónde 1. ___vas___ ahora?

Fernando: (Yo) 2. ___voy___ al cine. ¿Quieres (*Do yo want*) 3. ___ir___ conmigo?

Ana Margarita: No puedo (*I can't*). Mi hermana y yo 4. ___vamos___ al parque.

Fernando: ¿Qué 5. ___vas___ a hacer este fin de semana, Ana Margarita?

Ana Margarita: ¡(Yo) 6. ___voy___ a una fiesta! ¿Quieres 7. ___ir___?

Fernando: Bueno, gracias. ¿Quiénes 8. ___van___ con nosotros?

Ana Margarita: 9. ___van___ mi amiga Ramona y su novio Tomás. También un grupo de estudiantes de los Estados Unidos 10. ___va___ a ir.

Fernando: ¿11. ___vamos___ (nosotros) en auto o en metro?

Ana Margarita: En auto. La fiesta 12. ___va___ a ser en otra ciudad.

3-15 **¡Vamos a conocer Bogotá!** A group of students arrive in Bogota for the first time. Imagine that you are the professor and that you are explaining to Claire, a student, what the other students are going to do in the city. Use the contraction **al** as necessary.

MODELO: Megan / el Banco Nacional
Megan va al Banco Nacional.

1. Roger y Cindy / el parque Simón Bolívar
2. tú y Claire / el estadio El Campín
3. Mark / el concierto en la Plaza Bolívar
4. Janet y Meg / el Museo Nacional de Bogotá, Museo del Oro
5. nosotros / el Centro Histórico de Santa Fe de Bogotá
6. yo / el bar Shamua
7. las chicas del grupo / Iglesia de San Pedro Claver

CULTURA
Santa Fe de Bogotá is the capital of Colombia. Founded in 1538, this city of over 6 million inhabitants boasts a beautiful colonial center called La Candelaria. La Avenida Pepe Sierra is the heart of the nightlife in Bogota as it has many **clubes, bares,** and **discotecas.**

3-16 **¿Qué hacemos?** It's Saturday night, and you and your friends are deciding what to do. Write sentences with the construction **ir a** + *infinitive*.

MODELO: Juan / descansar en el cuarto
Juan va a descansar en el cuarto.

1. Helen y Claire / dar un paseo
2. nosotros / visitar los monumentos
3. Charlie / ir al cine
4. las chicas / bailar en la discoteca
5. los chicos / mirar el partido de fútbol en la tele
6. tú y Jason / sacar fotos
7. Uds. (Kevin and Mary) / tocar la guitarra en el parque
8. ¿yo?

EN VOZ ALTA

3-17 **¡A cenar con Luz Amelia!** You and a friend of yours want to invite Luz Amelia for lunch (**el almuerzo**) or dinner (**la cena**) and you are trying to determine the best time to do so. First study Luz Amelia's calendar below and write down where she normally goes each day. Then, based on her free time, you and your friend will decide when is the best time to invite her.

MODELO: E1: *¿El lunes?*
E2: *No. El lunes va a sus clases y después va al cine...*

El calendario semanal *(weekly)* de Luz Amelia

	lunes	martes	miércoles	jueves	viernes	sábado	domingo
10:00–12:00	Clases		Clases		Clases		Ir a la iglesia
12:00–13:00	Clases	Clases					
13:00–14:00				Ir al mercado			
14:00–15:00			Ir a la biblioteca		Ir a la piscina		Ir a la plaza con Miguel
15:00–16:00						Ir al museo	
16:00–17:00							
17:00–18:00		Ir al café con Lisa	Clases				
18:00–19:00	Ir al cine			Ir al parque con José	Ir al restaurante con María		
.....							

3-18 **Planes para un fin de semana** Using the subjects listed below, ask a classmate questions about activities for the next weekend. Choose a day for each subject listed.

el viernes por la tarde   el sábado por la noche
el sábado por la tarde   el domingo por la noche
el domingo por la tarde   el sábado por la mañana
el viernes por la noche   el domingo por la mañana

MODELO: tú / el viernes por la noche
E1: *¿Qué vas a hacer el viernes por la noche?*
E2: *Yo voy a ir al cine y, luego mis amigas y yo vamos a una fiesta.*

1. tú
2. tu compañero(a) de cuarto
3. tus padres
4. tú y tus amigo(a)s
5. tu profesor(a) de español
6. tus abuelos
7. tu hermano(a)

El café en Colombia y en el mundo

PARA PENSAR

- When do you drink coffee? How do you like your coffee?

- Do you go to cafés with your friends?

- Do you know why and how other people drink coffee around the world?

Un café con leche

En el siglo XXI, el café es una bebida universal. Después del petróleo *(oil)* y del turismo, el café es el producto comercial que mueve *(moves)* más dinero en el mercado mundial. Por ejemplo, el café colombiano se exporta a todas partes del mundo, ya que tiene un valor económico excelente y un valor cultural especial. El café está presente en las costumbres de muchos países en donde la gente toma café diariamente *(daily)*. En otros países millones de personas trabajan en la producción, industrialización y comercialización del café. Países como los Estados Unidos, Japón y Alemania son los consumidores más importantes del café.

Diferentes maneras de beber café en el mundo

- Los árabes usan canela *(cinnamon)* y clavos *(cloves)* para darle un sabor especial al café, y lo toman en tazas sin agarraderas *(cups without handles)*.

- Los griegos y los turcos hierven *(boil)* tres veces el café con azúcar *(sugar)* antes de servirle el café a una persona.

- Los estadounidenses inventaron *(invented)* el coffee break, o el descanso para tomar un café. Esta costumbre se usa ahora en todas las partes del mundo.

- En España y Latinoamérica se toma café con leche *(milk)* y azúcar para el desayuno, el almuerzo y especialmente para la merienda *(snack time)*.

- En países como Colombia, Cuba, Chile, Panamá y Venezuela hay diferentes tamaños de tazas *(cup sizes)* para tomar café. Hay tazas grandes para un café con leche grande y tazas pequeñas para un café con leche pequeño o para un café negro o tinto, como se llama en Colombia.

- El café colombiano es reconocido en todo el mundo. El 90 por ciento de los consumidores beben el café colombiano por su calidad *(quality)* y por su suavidad *(smoothness)*.

PARA DISCUTIR

1. What are the most important export products around the world?
2. Describe some of the ways people drink coffee in different parts of the world.
3. How is the Colombian coffee described above?
4. What kind of coffee do you like to drink (from Colombia, Costa Rica, Guatemala, Hawaii) or what kind would you like to try out? Why?

In this section you will learn how to use several verbs that describe basic actions. All the verbs given below have irregular **yo** forms but are otherwise regular in their present tense conjugations. These verbs are also useful in describing leisure-time activities.

Present tense of the verb **hacer**

The verb **hacer** *(to do; to make)* is a regular -**er** verb except for the **yo** form (**yo hago**). You have already seen the verb **hacer** used in this chapter to pose questions.

¿Qué **haces** en tu tiempo libre?	*What do you do in your free time?*
¿Qué **hacen** tus amigos durante los fines de semana?	*What do your friends do on the weekends?*

Hacer is conjugated as follows:

yo	hago	*I do*
tú	haces	*you* (informal) *do*
Ud., él/ella	hace	*you* (formal) *do, he/she does*
nosotros(as)	hacemos	*we do*
vosotros(as)	hacéis	*you* (informal) *do*
Uds., ellos(as)	hacen	*you* (formal and informal) *do, they do*

¿NOS ENTENDEMOS?
Some common idioms with hacer are **hacer un viaje, hacer planes, hacer una pregunta.**

There are several other Spanish verbs that, like **hacer,** have irregular **yo** forms only in the present tense.

conocer	*to know; to meet*	**conozco**	**Conozco** a Carlos Suárez.
dar	*to give*	**doy**	**Doy** una fiesta el viernes.
estar	*to be (location and health)*	**estoy**	**Estoy** en la discoteca. **Estoy** enfermo.
hacer	*to do; to make*	**hago**	**Hago** mucho ejercicio.
poner	*to put (on)*	**pongo**	**Pongo** música rock en casa.
saber	*to know (how)*	**sé**	**Sé** jugar bien al béisbol.
salir	*to leave; to go out*	**salgo**	**Salgo** todos los sábados.
traer	*to bring*	**traigo**	**Traigo** mis discos compactos después de la fiesta.
ver	*to see*	**veo**	**Veo** a mi profesora en la tienda.

The other present-tense forms of these verbs are regular with the small exception of **ver,** which does not carry an accent on the -**e** of the **vosotros(as)** form as other -**er** verbs do.

	hacer	estar	saber	conocer	dar	traer	ver	poner	salir
yo	hago	estoy	sé	conozco	doy	traigo	veo	pongo	salgo
tú	haces	estás	sabes	conoces	das	traes	ves	pones	sales
Ud., él/ella	hace	está	sabe	conoce	da	trae	ve	pone	sale
nosotros(as)	hacemos	estamos	sabemos	conocemos	damos	traemos	vemos	ponemos	salimos
vosotros(as)	hacéis	estáis	sabéis	conocéis	dais	traéis	veis	ponéis	salís
Uds., ellos(as)	hacen	están	saben	conocen	dan	traen	ven	ponen	salen

¡A PRACTICAR!

3-19 **Una carta de Bogotá** Claire is writing a letter in Spanish to her friend Ramón in the United States. Help her conjugate the verbs in parentheses.

> *Querido Ramón:*
>
> *¿Cómo estás? ¡Bogotá es increíble! La verdad es que aquí (here) (yo) 1. __salgo__ (salir) mucho con mis compañeros de clase por la ciudad, especialmente durante los fines de semana. Normalmente los sábados nosotros 2. __hacemos__ (hacer) muchas actividades juntos. A veces (Sometimes) 3. __vemos__ (ver) películas en el cine o en casa. Casi nunca (Almost never) Anne 4. __está__ (estar) en casa los sábados por la tarde porque 5. __sale__ (salir) con su novio, Juanjo. Pero por la noche todos 6. __estamos__ (estar) juntos para ir a fiestas. Por ejemplo, mañana una amiga colombiana, Luisa Gómez, 7. __da__ (dar) una fiesta en su casa. Yo 8. __sé__ (saber) que tú no 9. __conoces__ (conocer) a Luisa, pero es una chica muy simpática. En las fiestas yo normalmente llevo frutas y sándwiches y mis amigos llevan zumos y bebidas. Los domingos 10. __salimos__ (salir), pero generalmente (nosotros) 11. __estamos__ (estar) en la casa de un amigo o una amiga y 12. __ponemos__ (poner) música en la radio. Anne siempre 13. __pone__ (poner) música rock y yo siempre cambio de música y 14. __pongo__ (poner) jazz. Pues, durante la semana, en casa (yo) 15. __hago__ (hacer) mucho ejercicio. Anne nunca 16. __hace__ (hacer) ejercicio, pero ella 17. __pone__ (poner) música en la radio y habla conmigo (with me). Ahora yo 18. __estoy__ (estar) en casa y voy a descansar un poco.*
>
> *Abrazos,*
> *Claire*

3-20 **Juanita la buena y Juanito el malo** Juanita is a good girl and always **(siempre)** does what she should. Her brother, Juanito, however, never **(nunca)** follows his sister's example. Imagine that you are Juanita and write down what your brother Juanito does or doesn't do based on your actions.

MODELO: Yo *siempre* hago mi tarea, pero Juanito *nunca* hace su tarea.

1. Yo nunca veo la tele cuando necesito trabajar, pero Juanito...
2. Yo nunca pongo el estéreo muy alto (*very loud*), pero Juanito...
3. Yo siempre conozco a los estudiantes nuevos en clase, pero Juanito...
4. Yo sé jugar a muchos deportes, pero Juanito...
5. Yo hago ejercicio todos los días, pero Juanito...
6. Yo salgo solamente con mi novio los fines de semana, pero Juanito...
7. Yo nunca les doy mi número de teléfono a personas extrañas, pero Juanito...
8. Yo estoy en la biblioteca todos los fines de semana, pero Juanito...

EN VOZ ALTA

3-21 **¿Y tú?** Now, it is time to get to know some of your classmates a bit better. Form questions to ask them based on the statements in activity 3-20.

MODELO: E1: *¿Siempre ves la tele cuando tu compañero(a) necesita trabajar?*
E2: *No, yo nunca veo la tele cuando mi compañero(a) necesita trabajar.*

3-22 **Entrevista** In order to know what your classmate does during the weekend and to compare that with your activities, ask a classmate the following questions with the verbs **hacer, estar, saber, conocer, dar, traer, salir, poner,** and **ver.**

1. ¿Cuándo haces planes para el fin de semana? ¿Qué vas a hacer este fin de semana? ¿Vas a estar en casa o vas a salir? ¿Sales mucho durante la semana?
2. Cuando tienes una fiesta, ¿qué tipo de música pones? ¿Traen tus amigos comida (*food*) a la fiesta? ¿Saben tus padres que vas a tener una fiesta? ¿Sabe tu compañero(a) de cuarto? ¿Siempre conoces a todas las personas de la fiesta?
3. Cuando haces ejercicio, ¿sales de tu cuarto? ¿Ves videos cuando haces ejercicio? ¿Pones la tele o el estéreo cuando haces ejercicio?

ASÍ SE DICE Expressing knowledge and familiarity: *saber, conocer,* and the personal *a*

As you have seen earlier, the verbs **saber** and **conocer** both mean *to know,* and they have irregular **yo** forms (**sé/conozco**). These verbs represent two different kinds of knowledge, however.

Saber

Use the verb **saber** to express knowing something (information) or knowing how to do something.

—¿**Sabes jugar** al tenis?	*Do you know how to play tennis?*
—No, pero **sé jugar** al golf.	*No, but I know how to play golf.*
—¿**Sabes qué?** ¡Me gusta el golf!	*Do you know what? I like golf!*

Conocer

Use the verb **conocer** to express being acquainted with a person, place, or thing. Note that Spanish speakers use the preposition **a** immediately before a direct object that refers to a specific person or persons.

—¿**Conoces** Bogotá?	*Do you know Bogota?*
—No, pero **conozco** Cali.	*No, but I know Cali.*
—¿Quieres **conocer a** mi amiga?	*Do you want to meet my friend?*
—Ya **conozco a** tu amiga Luisa.	*I already know your friend Luisa.*

Note in the second example the use of the personal **a** with a direct object that is a person. The direct object of a verb is the person or thing that receives the action of the verb. For example, in the sentence *I know Carlos,* the direct object is **Carlos.** The personal **a,** which has no English equivalent, is usually used before each noun or pronoun; however, it is usually not used with the verb **tener** even when the direct object is a person.

Conozco **a** Carlos.	*I know Carlos.*
Conozco **a** Carlos y **a** Juan.	*I know Carlos and Juan.*
Carlos y Juan tienen muchos amigos.	*Carlos and Juan have many friends.*

¡A PRACTICAR!

3-23 | **¿*Saber* o *conocer*?** Decide whether to use **saber** or **conocer** to talk about the following people, places, and activities.

	Saber	Conocer
1. jugar al tenis	_____	_____
2. Cali	_____	_____
3. mi amigo José Alfredo	_____	_____
4. Fernando Botero	_____	_____
5. el arte de Botero	_____	_____
6. Juan Valdés	_____	_____
7. Barranquilla	_____	_____
8. Cartagena	_____	_____
9. bailar vallenato	_____	_____
10. hablar español	_____	_____
11. Gabriel García Márquez	_____	_____
12. andar en bicicleta	_____	_____

3-24 | **La *a* personal** When should you use the personal **a**? Decide whether or not you need to use the construction in the following sentences. Don't forget that **a** + **el** = **al**!

1. Yo no conozco _____ Bogotá.
2. Mis amigos conocen _____ mi hermano Pablo.
3. Joaquín conoce _____ la novia de Anne.
4. Julieta y Penélope conocen bien _____ la música de Carlos Vives.
5. ¿Conoces tú _____ el profesor de francés? ¡Es muy guapo!
6. ¿Tienes _____ muchos amigos en tu clase de español?

EN VOZ ALTA

3-25 | **¡Yo sé… ! ¡Yo conozco… !** Now, with a classmate, talk about your familiarity with the items of activity 3-23.

MODELO: jugar al tenis
E1: *Yo no sé jugar al tenis. ¿Sabes tú jugar al tenis?*
E2: *Sí, sé jugar al tenis.*
o E2: *No, no sé jugar al tenis.*

3-26 | **Entrevista** You are going to interview a classmate. You need to know who he/she knows, the places he/she is familiar with, and what things he/she knows how to do. Write four questions; then take turns answering.

MODELO: *¿Conoces Bogotá?*
¿Sabes esquiar?
¿Conoces al (a la) presidente de un país hispano?

CULTURA
Fernando Botero is one of Colombia's most famous artists. He is especially known for his satirical portraits of political, military, and religious figures who are portrayed as rotund and motionless.

CULTURA
Vallenato is a type of Colombian folk music, usually played on the accordion, that celebrates everyday events, passions, and village folklore. It originated in the Magdalena Grande area of northeastern Colombia. Carlos Vives, a Colombian musician, has become internationally famous for his **vallenato** sound.

CULTURA
Gabriel García Márquez is the most famous Colombian writer. He was a literature Nobel Prize recipient in 1982.

CULTURA
Cartagena and **Barranquilla** are two cities in the northern region of Colombia. These cities are famous for their beaches and their carnivals.

ASÍ SE DICE Talking about the months, seasons, and the weather

In this section you will learn how to talk about the months, seasons, and weather conditions.

Los doce meses y las cuatro estaciones

ENERO
L M M J V S D
1 2 3 4 5 6 7
8 9 10 11 12 13 14
15 16 17 18 19 20 21
22 23 24 25 26 27 28
29 30 31

FEBRERO
L M M J V S D
1 2 3 4
5 6 7 8 9 10 11
12 13 14 15 16 17 18
19 20 21 22 23 24 25
26 27 28

MARZO
L M M J V S D
1 2 3 4
5 6 7 8 9 10 11
12 13 14 15 16 17 18
19 20 21 22 23 24 25
26 27 28 29 30 31

ABRIL
L M M J V S D
1
2 3 4 5 6 7 8
9 10 11 12 13 14 15
16 17 18 19 20 21 22
23/30 24 25 26 27 28 29

MAYO
L M M J V S D
1 2 3 4 5 6
7 8 9 10 11 12 13
14 15 16 17 18 19 20
21 22 23 24 25 26 27
28 29 30 31

JUNIO
L M M J V S D
1 2 3
4 5 6 7 8 9 10
11 12 13 14 15 16 17
18 19 20 21 22 23 24
25 26 27 28 29 30

JULIO
L M M J V S D
1
2 3 4 5 6 7 8
9 10 11 12 13 14 15
16 17 18 19 20 21 22
23/30 24/31 25 26 27 28 29

AGOSTO
L M M J V S D
1 2 3 4 5
6 7 8 9 10 11 12
13 14 15 16 17 18 19
20 21 22 23 24 25 26
27 28 29 30 31

SEPTIEMBRE
L M M J V S D
1 2
3 4 5 6 7 8 9
10 11 12 13 14 15 16
17 18 19 20 21 22 23
24 25 26 27 28 29 30

OCTUBRE
L M M J V S D
1 2 3 4 5 6 7
8 9 10 11 12 13 14
15 16 17 18 19 20 21
22 23 24 25 26 27 28
29 30 31

NOVIEMBRE
L M M J V S D
1 2 3 4
5 6 7 8 9 10 11
12 13 14 15 16 17 18
19 20 21 22 23 24 25
26 27 28 29 30

DICIEMBRE
L M M J V S D
1 2
3 4 5 6 7 8 9
10 11 12 13 14 15 16
17 18 19 20 21 22 23
24/31 25 26 27 28 29 30

Las estaciones Seasons

el invierno winter
el otoño fall

la primavera spring
el verano summer

Expresiones de tiempo con *hacer* and *estar*

The verb **hacer** is used to talk about the weather in the following phrases.

hace buen tiempo the weather is nice
hace calor it's hot
hace frío it's cold

hace fresco it's chilly
hace sol it's sunny
hace viento it's windy

The verbs **llover** *(to rain)* and **nevar** *(to snow)* are used in the third person.

llueve it's raining

nieva it's snowing

The nouns derived from these verbs are:

la nieve snow

la lluvia rain

The verb **estar** is used to indicate whether the sky is overcast or clear.

está despejado it's clear

está nublado it's cloudy

¡A PRACTICAR!

3-27 Los días festivos (Holidays) Complete the following sentences with the appropriate months.

Los días festivos de Colombia

| 20/7 | Día de la Independencia | 1/11 | Día de Todos los Santos |
| 12/10 | Día de la raza | 8/12 | Fiesta de la Inmaculada Concepción |
---

1. El Día de Colón (*Columbus*) es el _____.
2. El Día de Acción de Gracias (*Thanksgiving*) es el _____.
3. El primer (*first*) día del año es el _____.
4. La Navidad (*Christmas*) es el _____.
5. El Día de San Valentín es el 14 de _____.
6. El Día de la Independencia de Colombia es el 20 de _____.
7. La fiesta de la Inmaculada Concepción es el 8 de _____.
8. Mi cumpleaños (*My birthday*) es el _____ de _____.

¿NOS ENTENDEMOS?
Usually in Latin America and Spain, the date is written differently from the United States. The day is presented first and the month is presented second. **20/7 La independencia de Colombia es el 20 de julio.**

3-28 ¿Qué tiempo hace? Look at the drawings and complete the statements.

En el _____ hace mucho _____ y a veces _____. El cielo (*sky*) está _____.

En el _____ hace _____ y _____. El cielo está _____.

En la _____ hace _____ y a veces _____.

En el _____ hace _____. Mi estación favorita es _____ porque _____. No me gusta _____ porque _____.

EN VOZ ALTA

3-29 ¿Qué fecha es? ¿En qué estación del año es? ¿Qué tiempo hace? State the following dates with a classmate. Next, identify the season and state the weather for that date for the area in which you live. Include a statement about your personal comfort level. Finally, mention what you typically like to do on that date.

MODELO: 13/4
Es el trece de abril. Es la primavera. En abril hace sol en Barranquilla. Me gusta dar paseos en la playa.

| 1. 22/12 | 3. 3/9 | 5. 29/8 | 7. 27/4 |
| 2. 25/7 | 4. 1/5 | 6. 7/10 | 8. hoy |

3-30 La realidad y la fantasía Working with a partner, identify what you generally like to do during the following periods and then what you must do for the next particular day.

MODELO: los sábados (*Saturdays in general*) / este sábado (*this Saturday*)
Generalmente me gusta descansar los sábados. Este sábado tengo que estudiar para mi clase de química.

1. los viernes por la noche / este viernes
2. los veranos / este verano
3. por la tarde / esta tarde
4. los días festivos / el próximo día festivo
5. por la mañana / esta mañana
6. los fines de semana / este fin de semana

¡A VER!

In this segment, the housemates are about to go on an excursion to Old San Juan. As they get ready, they talk about some of the things they like to do in their free time. When they arrive in the heart of Old San Juan, each person shares his or her plan for the day. Watch and see if the day turns out the way they expect it to!

Expresiones útiles

The following are some new expressions you will hear in the video.

Pensándolo bien...	Now that I think about it . . .
Estoy de acuerdo...	I agree . . .
No vale la pena...	It's not worth the trouble . . .
Es hora de vernos con los demás...	It's time to meet up with the others . . .

Antes de ver

 Paso 1: What types of activities do you like to do in your free time? Make a list of some of them and share it with a classmate. Do you have any pastimes in common? Now work with your classmate and guess what the housemates might like to do. Do you think you might have anything in common with them?

_____

_____

Paso 2: Imagine that you are one of the housemates in **Hacienda Vista Alegre** and that you are preparing to tour Old San Juan. Work with 3 or 4 classmates and discuss what you all are going to do during the excursion.

Después de ver

Paso 1: Now watch the video. As you do, listen for the different sports that each housemate likes to participate in or watch on television. Were any of your predictions from **Antes de ver, Paso 1,** correct? Read the statements below and fill in the blanks below with the appropriate activities based on what the housemates said in the video.

- A Javier le gusta _____, el alpinismo, el buceo, el esnórkeling y todas las actividades al aire libre.
- A Antonio le gusta ver el hockey sobre hielo por televisión y le gusta también _____ y _____.
- Sofía practica _____.
- A Alejandra no le gustan _____. Practica la danza y le gusta _____.
- Valeria practica _____ y _____.

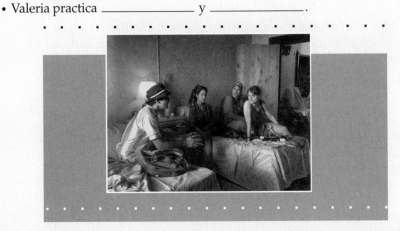

While they are discussing sports and other activities, Valeria uses the phrase **"Fui porrista en el colegio."** Based on what you know about her, do you think that means that she was a bowler, track & field star, or a cheerleader? _____

Paso 2: In **Antes de ver, Paso 2,** you and your classmates planned an excursion in Old San Juan. Were your plans anything like the plans the housemates made while they were gathered at the **Plaza**? Do you remember what each person said he or she was going to do? Based on the video, complete the following statements with the activity each of them originally had in mind.

- Alejandra va a _____.
- Sofía va _____.
- Valeria va _____.
- Antonio va _____.

Did all of the housemates do exactly what they originally planned to do? If not, how did what they actually did differ from what they said they were going to do?

Al final (At the end), *Valeria va* _____

_____

_____

_____

¿Qué opinas tú?

Paso 1: Imagine that you have a three-day weekend coming up. Work with 3 or 4 classmates and plan a trip based on the pastimes that you have in common. Where are you going to go? What activities are you going to do there? Don't forget to use your list from **Anter de ver, Paso 1.**

Paso 2: Now that you have learned more about Old San Juan from the video, what would you plan for each character to do on an excursion there? Work with a classmate to create a detailed itinerary for the day for each member of the group.

¡A LEER!

Strategy: Using context to predict content

Efficient readers use effective strategies for guessing the meaning of unfamiliar words and phrases in a reading selection. Some of these strategies are:

- Readers rely on what they already know about the reading topic (background information).
- Readers guess what the selection will be about (prediction).
- Readers will use the ideas they understand in the passage (context).

Paso 1: Background information

1. What do you know about Colombia's social and political situation?
2. Where have you read about Colombia?
3. Do you think the United States should help the situation in Colombia?

Paso 2: Prediction

1. Do you think the United States will physically intervene to solve the situation?
2. What do you think would be the outcome of this intervention?

Paso 3: Context

1. Skim the reading without stopping and try to understand the gist of the content.
   a. What is the opinion of the writer?
   b. Would you like to see another way to help the situation in Colombia?
2. Scan the article and complete the following tasks.
   a. Underline the words and phrases that indicate the author's favorable opinion or unfavorable opinion about the situation.
   b. How much money does Washington give to the Plan Colombia?

El Plan Colombia

Colombia va a usar desde ahora la ayuda monetaria y militar que los Estados Unidos da al Plan Colombia para luchar contra la guerrilla y los paramilitares, dice la primera ministra de Defensa (*the Chief Minister of Defense*) de Colombia, Martha Lucía Ramírez. La ministra dice que el presidente de los Estados Unidos, George W. Bush, firma una ley (*law*) que ayuda al presidente de Colombia, Álvaro Uribe, a usar la ayuda militar y los helicópteros del Plan Colombia para luchar contra los grupos irregulares (*subversive groups*) y el narcotráfico.

Un grupo de personas estadounidenses va a visitar Colombia para observar el uso de los recursos (*resources*) en la lucha contra el nar- cotráfico en el país. El Plan Colombia es una estrategia antidrogas (*against drugs*) con una inversión (*investment*) de 7.500 millones de dólares y de los que Washington da 1.300 millones principalmente para la ayuda militar. Se dice que la ayuda de los Estados Unidos es una esperanza (*hope*) para todo el pueblo colombiano que desea la paz (*peace*).

¡A ESCRIBIR!

Strategy: Combining sentences

Learning to combine simple sentences into more complex ones can help you improve your writing style immensely. In Spanish, there are several words you can use as connectors to combine sentences and phrases:

y	*and* (**y** becomes **e** before **i, hi**)
que	*that, which; who*
pero	*but*
o	*or* (**o** becomes **u** before **o** or **ho**)
porque	*because*

Paso 1: Read the following letter that Esther wrote to her pen pal in the United States about what she is doing during her summer vacation. Circle all of the connectors used in the following sentences.

Querida Kelly:

¿Qué tal? ¿Cómo estás?

De momento, estoy de vacaciones y tengo mucho tiempo libre. Me gusta practicar muchos deportes, como el tenis, la natación, el ciclismo y el baloncesto. Me gusta nadar todos los días pero cuando llueve, veo videos o miro la tele en casa. También paso mucho tiempo con mi amigo Carlos. Carlos tiene veintitrés años y es un chico muy simpático. Nos gusta salir por la noche los fines de semana e ir a las discotecas que están en el centro. Carlos conoce muy bien la ciudad. Nos gusta bailar y caminar por la ciudad. ¡Bogotá es preciosa!

Bueno, en pocos minutos van a llegar mis padres. Vamos al cine hoy porque deseamos ver una película.

Espero recibir tu carta pronto.

Tu amiga,

Esther

Paso 2: Now that you have seen how connectors were used in the above letter, combine the following sets of sentences, using **y, pero, que,** and **porque** appropriately.

> MODELOS: Estudio en la Universidad de Bogotá. Me gustan mis clases.
> *Estudio en la Universidad de Bogotá y me gustan mis clases.*
> Tengo muchos amigos. Son muy simpáticos.
> *Tengo muchos amigos que son muy simpáticos.*

1. Me gusta practicar deportes. No tengo mucho tiempo libre.
2. Mi amiga corre todos los días. Es muy atlética.
3. Deseo mirar un partido de fútbol en la tele. Necesito estudiar.
4. Tengo muchos amigos. Esquían en el invierno.

Task: Writing a letter to a friend

Paso 1: Using Esther's letter as a model, write a similar one telling a friend what you do in your free time. Be sure to include a description of several activities, and mention who (if anyone) you like to do these activities with and when you do them. Use connectors appropriately.

Paso 2: Work with one or more classmates, exchanging and reading one another's letters. This will give you an excellent opportunity to learn more about what some of your classmates like to do in their free time.

Functions: Writing a letter (informal); Describing people; Talking about the present
Vocabulary: Sports; Leisure; Board games; Family members; Animals; Domestic; University
Grammar: Verbs: **ser, tener, conocer, saber;** Verbs: Future with **ir;** Article: contractions **al, del**

¡A CONVERSAR!

Pronunciation focus: *i* and *u* before other vowels

The letter **i** (and **y**) placed before **a, e, o,** and **u** has a sound similar to the *y* sound in English words *yacht, yet, yoke,* and *you.* The letter **u** before **a, e, i/y,** and **o** has a sound similar to the *w* sound in *quit, quartz,* and *quench.* Practice the following sentences.

- En jun**io** y jul**io,** hay muchos conc**ie**rtos en el parque.
- C**ua**ndo ll**ue**ve, voy al centro comerc**ia**l o a un restaurante.
- N**ie**va mucho en el inv**ie**rno y hace v**ie**nto en la primavera.

Task: Discussing plans for leisure activities

Paso 1: Many factors affect our decisions about leisure activities. Each person has unique preferences; some people like to practice sports while others prefer less strenuous pursuits. The weather often affects what we feel like doing; one day may be better for going to the theater or for doing indoor activities, while another may be better for getting some exercise. Review the leisure activities from the **Capítulo 3** vocabulary, paying particular attention to the activities you most like to do. With a classmate, discuss in Spanish what you personally like to do during your free time in the following situations:

- when it's hot
- when it's raining
- when it's snowing
- when you are with a group of friends
- when you are with just one friend

Paso 2: Choose one of the situations from the list above and determine which activities both you and your partner prefer to do.

Paso 3: Join with several other students in your class to continue your discussion. Choose a situation and try to identify several activities that all members of the group wish to pursue.

VOCABULARIO ESENCIAL

Los deportes Sports

andar en bicicleta to ride a bike
caminar por las montañas to hike/walk in the mountains
el ciclismo cycling
correr to run

esquiar en el agua to water-ski
jugar (ue) al tenis to play tennis
levantar pesas to lift weights
montar a caballo to go horseback riding
nadar to swim

la natación swimming
patinar en línea to in-line skate
pescar to fish

Otras palabras deportivas Other sports words

el baloncesto basketball
el béisbol baseball
el campo de fútbol (de golf) football field (golf course)

el fútbol (americano) soccer (football)
ganar to win
el golf golf
el partido game

el vólibol volleyball

Los pasatiempos Pastimes

bailar to dance
dar un paseo to go for a walk
hacer un picnic (planes, ejercicio) to go on a picnic (to make plans, to exercise)
ir to go
  a tomar un café to drink coffee
  a un bar to a bar

a un club to a club
a un concierto to a concert
a una discoteca to a dance club
a una fiesta to a party
al cine to the movies
de compras shopping

mirar la tele to watch TV
sacar fotos to take pictures
tocar la guitarra to play the guitar
tomar el sol to sunbathe
visitar un museo to visit a museum

Los lugares en el pueblo Places in town

el banco bank
el café café
la calle street
el centro downtown
el centro comercial mall
el cine movie theater

la iglesia church
el mercado (al aire libre) (outdoor) market
el museo museum
la oficina de correos post office
el parque park
la piscina pool

la plaza plaza
el restaurante restaurante
el supermercado supermarket
la tienda store

Actividades y acciones Activities and actions

conocer to know; to meet
dar to give
estar to be (location and health)

hacer to do; to make
poner to put (on)
saber to know (how)

salir to leave; to go out
traer to bring
ver to see

Los meses del año Months of the year

enero January
febrero February
marzo March
abril April

mayo May
junio June
julio July
agosto August

septiembre September
octubre October
noviembre November
diciembre December

Las estaciones Seasons

el invierno winter
el otoño fall

la primavera spring
el verano summer

El tiempo Weather

está despejado it's clear
está nublado it's cloudy
hace buen tiempo it's nice out

hace calor it's hot
hace fresco it's cool
hace frío it's cold

hace sol it's sunny
hace viento it's windy
llueve it's raining

la lluvia rain
nieva it's snowing
la nieve snow

Expresiones idiomáticas Idiomatic expressions

chévere cool

Palabras que conectan Connecting words

a veces sometimes

nunca never

nunca más never again

siempre always

Lugar de encuentros

PLAZAS

REVISTA NO. 1

En esta edición vas a conocer a personas, lugares y aspectos culturales de los Estados Unidos, México y Colombia y vas a comparar tus ideas y opiniones con las de nuestros autores. Participa con nosotros y vas a ver que tenemos mucho en común.

- **Celebraciones hispanas en los Estados Unidos**
- **¿Necesitas 100.000 pesos? Tenemos un trabajo para ti.**
- **¿Sociable o tímido? Dos características de la nacionalidad mexicana**
- **Una nueva visión artística del pintor colombiano Fernando Botero**

Celebraciones hispanas en los Estados Unidos

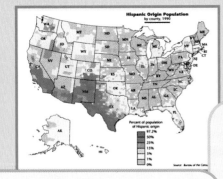

Nuestros 30 millones de vecinos *(neighbors)* latinos viven en muchas partes de los Estados Unidos. Hay grupos latinos en numerosas regiones del país y, aunque *(even though)* tienen en común el idioma, cada grupo conserva sus propias tradiciones. Los estados con una gran población de latinos son Arizona, California, Florida, Illinois, Nueva York y Texas. Vamos a examinar varios aspectos de la influencia latina en los Estados Unidos.

Celebrar la cultura hispana con los estudios

La Universidad de San Francisco tiene una oficina que se llama Center for Latino Studies in the Americas. Este centro ofrece un programa de estudios latinoamericanos. Los estudiantes tienen la oportunidad de tomar clases de política, cultura, literatura, economía y las diferentes olas *(waves)* de migración y religión en los Estados Unidos.

Este programa revela el interés que existe por la cultura latina en los Estados Unidos y por eso el centro celebra la cultura hispana con conciertos, lecturas *(readings)* de poesía, exposiciones de arte, charlas sobre temas históricos y contemporáneos, programas de radio —todo sobre la presencia de los latinos en los Estados Unidos y su relación con las Américas. Muchas universidades ofrecen un certificado o una especialización en estudios latinoamericanos.

- ■ **¿Qué programas similares tiene tu universidad?**
- ■ **¿Organiza tu universidad actividades relacionadas con las culturas latinas?**

- ■ **¿Qué porcentaje de la población en tu universidad es latina?**

En marzo en Miami y en abril en San Antonio

Si te gustan las grandes fiestas, el Festival de la Calle Ocho es para ti. Aproximadamente 1,2 millones de personas van al Festival de la Calle Ocho en Miami en marzo. Es posible escuchar música de más de 30 grupos musicales toda la tarde y toda la noche en este festival que ocupa un espacio de 27 cuadras *(street blocks)*.

Otra fiesta popular es la Fiesta de San Antonio, celebrada en abril en la magnífica ciudad tejana de San Antonio. La fiesta dura *(lasts)* diez días, con más de 150 eventos. Hay desfiles *(parades)* por la noche, conciertos, actividades deportivas, fuegos artificiales *(fireworks)* y, por supuesto, muy buena comida. Esta fiesta tiene su origen en el año 1891, en honor a los héroes que luchan por *(fight for)* la libertad de Texas. Esta fiesta reconoce la diversidad cultural de la ciudad. Más de 3,5 millones de personas participan en esta celebración, además de *(in addition to)* los 75.000 voluntarios que hacen posible estas actividades tan ricas en historia y cultura.

- ■ **¿Cómo comparas el Festival de la Calle Ocho con la Fiesta de San Antonio?**
- ■ **En la ciudad donde vives, ¿hay una cultura / varias culturas que tenga(n) celebraciones anuales? Describe estas celebraciones.**
- ■ **¿Cuáles son unas fiestas anuales que se celebran *(are celebrated)* en este país?**

¿Necesitas 100.000 pesos?
Tenemos un trabajo para ti.

Nuestra corresponsal, Silvia Jiménez, tiene una copia de la agenda del presidente de México. La fecha es el 23 de agosto y creemos que vas a aprender mucho sobre las actividades del presidente. ¿Deseas hacer este trabajo? Si respondes que sí, el salario que corresponde con el trabajo es 100.000 pesos, ¡por UN mes!

Y ahora tú...

Los editores aquí en *Plazas* tenemos una oportunidad para ti. ¡Necesitamos tu colaboración! El presidente tiene la tarde libre del día de su cumpleaños debido a *(due to)* la cancelación de un evento especial. Ahora, tú eres uno(a) de los asistentes que prepara el horario del presidente. ¿Qué planes preparas para el período de las 13:00 horas a las 18:00 horas? Si los consejeros políticos seleccionan tus planes, vas a recibir **100.000 pesos** y un viaje de diez días con todos los gastos pagados *(all-expenses-paid trip)* a las ciudades mexicanas más populares. ¡Buena suerte!

- ¿Te gusta ayudar a tus compañeros con sus planes de fin de semana?

- ¿Te gusta escribir tus planes en una agenda o en un *palm-pilot*?

- ¿Cómo celebras tu cumpleaños? ¿Con quiénes?

- ¿Te gustan las acciones del presidente de México con respecto a los Estados Unidos ahora?

Oficina del Presidente
Plaza Central
México D.F.

Recomendaciones de los consejeros políticos:
- Busca información biográfica del presidente de México en Internet.
- Considera las actividades típicas de nuestro presidente.
- Incluye una actividad divertida *(fun)* para su cumpleaños.
- Consulta un periódico mexicano para buscar noticias de actualidad o interesantes para ti.

MIÉRCOLES, 23 DE AGOSTO	
8:00	Hacer ejercicio en el gimnasio presidencial.
9:00	Tomar café con su esposa, leer el periódico y revisar los documentos del Tratado de Libre Comercio de Norteamérica (NAFTA).
10:00	Llegar a la oficina para una reunión *(meeting)* con los delegados de las Naciones Unidas.
13:00	Almorzar con los delegados de las Naciones Unidas. **(Cancelado)**
14:00	Asistir a la conferencia del Departamento de Educación sobre *(about)* la violencia en las escuelas públicas. **(Cancelado)**
16:00	Regresar a la oficina para firmar *(sign)* documentos y para practicar un discurso *(speech)* titulado «Las economías latinoamericanas: ¿Dónde está México?» El discurso es para la cumbre *(summit)* económica en Brasil a fin de mes. Van a participar en esta cumbre todos los presidentes de Latinoamérica. **(Cancelado)**
18:00	Hablar con los consejeros *(advisors)* políticos sobre el día de hoy y sobre los planes para mañana. **(Cancelado)**
19:00	Cenar *(Have dinner)* con su familia y celebrar su cumpleaños.

MÉXICO

Ciudad de México

¿Sociable o tímido?
Dos características de la nacionalidad mexicana

Octavio Paz (1914–1998), gran poeta y ensayista mexicano, recibió el Premio Nóbel de Literatura en 1990. Esta selección es de su ensayo sobre el perfil *(profile)* del mexicano, *El laberinto de la soledad* (1959):

«El solitario mexicano ama *(loves)* las fiestas y las reuniones públicas. Todo es ocasión para reunirse *(get together)*. Cualquier pretexto es bueno para interrumpir la marcha *(passing)* del tiempo y celebrar con festejos y ceremonias, hombres y acontecimientos *(events)*. Somos un pueblo ritual. Y esta tendencia beneficia a nuestra imaginación tanto como a nuestra sensibilidad, siempre afinadas y despiertas *(lively)*. El arte de la Fiesta, envilecido *(underappreciated)* en casi todas partes, se conserva intacto entre nosotros. En pocos lugares del mundo se puede vivir con un espectáculo parecido *(similar)* al de las grandes fiestas religiosas de México, con sus colores violentos, agrios y puros, sus danzas, ceremonias, fuegos de artificio *(fireworks)*, trajes insólitos *(unusual clothing)* y la inagotable *(endless)* cascada de sorpresas de los frutos dulces *(sweets)* y objetos que se venden esos días en plazas y mercados.»

¿Cierto o *falso?*

En la cultura mexicana hay muchas fiestas, celebraciones y ceremonias.

—

Los mexicanos dependen de su imaginación y de su sensibilidad cuando celebran.

—

Las fiestas religiosas no son muy importantes.

—

Una característica de las fiestas es la danza.

—

Los mexicanos compran frutos y otros objetos en las plazas.

■ ¿Es posible ser sociable y tímido a la vez *(at the same time)*?

■ Según Paz, ¿qué se vende en las plazas durante las celebraciones?

■ ¿Vas a las celebraciones mexicanas del 5 de mayo o del 16 de septiembre en los Estados Unidos? Describe estas celebraciones.

Una nueva visión artística del pintor colombiano Fernando Botero

Uno de los artistas colombianos contemporáneos más famosos: Fernando Botero

- Nace en 1932 en Medellín y comienza su carrera artística como ilustrador de un periódico a los diecisiete años. **1932**

- Viaja por *(throughout)* Colombia, Madrid, Nueva York, Los Ángeles y París.
- Tiene su primera *(first)* exposición en un museo, no en una galería, en 1979 en Washington, D.C. **1979**

- Después tiene numerosas exposiciones en museos de diferentes países como Colombia, Japón, Estados Unidos e Italia.
- En 1999 recibe una invitación de Florencia, Italia, para celebrar sus cincuenta años de artista con una exposición de pinturas y esculturas. **1999**

- Vive parte del año en París, Montecarlo, Nueva York e Italia.

uién es Fernando Botero?

rofesora, ¿quién es
o Botero?
SORA: Fernando Botero es
os pintores más famosos de
nérica y especialmente de
ia. Sus figuras son bastante
y...
, profesora, ¿por qué las
e Botero son grandes y

SORA: Bueno, Botero
sus figuras como
nosas», y no como gordas.
ELA: Profesora, ¿por qué el
a básicamente colores como
azul, el amarillo y el negro?
SORA: El artista
no usa los colores que no

cambian con la luz *(light)*. Para el pintor, los colores tienen que ser eternos y por eso usa los colores básicos o primarios.
LUIS: ¿Qué temas dibuja Botero?
PROFESORA: Él dibuja lo que tiene en la mente o en la inspiración. No usa modelos y tampoco usa **apuntes** *(notes)*. A veces dibuja sobre la realidad social y política de Colombia porque necesita regresar a su casa o a su país con la mente.
GRACIELA: Profesora, ¿regresa Botero a Colombia a menudo *(frequently)*?
PROFESORA: Bueno, va a regresar precisamente para abrir el museo Ciudad Botero en la ciudad de

Medellín. Para el artista es mejor dar sus obras de Picasso, Braque, Matisse, Miró, Monet y Renoir a Colombia que tener estas pinturas en casa.
LUIS: Botero no es solamente *(only)* un artista muy bueno, sino además una persona muy responsable y generosa.
JOSÉ: Gracias, profesora, por su entrevista.

◄ ¿Te gustan las obras de Botero? ¿Por qué sí o por qué no?

◄ ¿Qué colores y qué temas usa el artista?

◄ ¿Quién es tu artista favorito(a) y por qué?

Chapter Objectives

COMMUNICATIVE GOALS

In this chapter you will learn how to . . .

- Describe the features of your home or personal residence
- Talk about furniture and appliances
- Describe household chores
- Make commands
- State locations and describe feelings
- Describe actions in progress
- Count from 100 and higher

STRUCTURES

- Present tense of stem-changing verbs (o → **ue**, e → **ie**, e → **i**)
- More idioms with **tener**
- Affirmative **tú** commands
- **Estar** and the present progressive

CULTURAL INFORMATION

- Gaudí y su obra
- Viviendas en Latinoamérica y España

España

ESPAÑA

Población: 39.996.671
Área: 504.750 kilómetros
cuadrados, más o menos dos
veces el tamaño de Oregón
Capital: Madrid, 2.909.792
Ciudades principales: Barcelona,
1.623.542; Valencia, 752.909; Sevilla,
659.126; Zaragoza 586.219
Moneda: el euro
Lenguas: el español, el catalán,
el euskera (vasco), el gallego

¡Bienvenidos a España!

**En este video, vas a aprender sobre
las regiones y la arquitectura de
España. Después de ver el video,
contesta las siguientes preguntas:**

1 ¿Dónde está España y cuál es su capital?

2 ¿Cuántas Comunidades Autónomas existen en España?

3 Según el video, ¿cuáles son algunas de las Comunidades
   Autónomas y qué sabes de ellas?

4 Según el video, ¿cuáles son las regiones de España que
   tienen mucha influencia árabe en su arquitectura?

5 ¿Qué región española te gustaría (would you like) visitar?
   ¿Por qué?

La Plaza Mayor, Madrid, España

VOCABULARIO La casa

En la casa de doña Rosa In this section you will practice talking about household rooms and furniture. Are there any student houses on your campus? How do they compare with doña Rosa's?

¿NOS ENTENDEMOS?
La alcoba, el cuarto, la recámara, and la pieza are all synonyms for el dormitorio (which does not mean *dormitory*). In some parts of the Spanish-speaking world, el condominio means *apartment complex*, making the term somewhat of a false congnate.

¿NOS ENTENDEMOS?
La heladera and la nevera are two synonyms for el refrigerador.

Palabras útiles are presented to help you enrich your personal vocabulary. The terms provided here will help you talk about housing and household areas.

Palabras útiles

el apartamento / el departamento apartment
el balcón balcony
la chimenea fireplace, chimney
el coche / el carro car
el condominio condominium
el cuadro painting

el garaje garage
el hogar home
el techo roof
la terraza terrace
el tocador dresser
la vivienda housing

¡A PRACTICAR!

4-1 ¿Y dónde pongo los muebles nuevos? A doña Rosa le gusta ayudar a la gente a arreglar muebles. Ayúdala (*Help her*) a instalar los muebles (*furniture*) nuevos en la Casa de la Troya. Indica el cuarto adecuado para cada mueble.

La Casa de la Troya, Santiago de Compostela

CULTURA
La Casa de la Troya is Santiago de Compostela's most famous student residence. It provided lodging for students studying at the School of Medicine and is the birthplace of Santiago's most prestigious student musical group. Musical groups from different university schools are called **tunas** and feature talented musicians who dress up in medieval costumes to serenade young women.

MODELO: Usted debe poner el estante <u>*en el dormitorio.*</u>

1. Es lógico poner el sillón en _____.
2. Usted debe poner la cama y la cómoda en _____, ¿no?
3. El sofá debe estar en _____.
4. El refrigerador debe estar en _____.
5. ¿La ducha, la bañera, el inodoro y el lavabo? En _____, ¡por supuesto!
6. Es necesario poner la mesa y las sillas en _____.

4-2 ¿Qué hay en la Casa de la Troya? Describe los muebles y las otras cosas de cada (*each*) cuarto de la casa con la expresión verbal **hay...**

MODELO: El dormitorio
En el dormitorio hay <u>*un estante, un armario, una cómoda, una cama, un escritorio y una puerta.*</u>

1. la sala _____
2. el comedor _____
3. la cocina _____
   _____
4. el cuarto de baño _____

4-3 Y ¿qué hay en tu Casa? Completa las siguientes oraciones con los muebles y aparatos domésticos de tu casa o residencia.

MODELO: En el cuarto de baño hay *un lavabo, un inodoro, una bañera y unas toallas* (towels).

1. En mi casa hay _____ (#) dormitorios y _____ (#) cuartos de baño.
2. Hay _____ (#) puertas y _____ (#) ventanas.
3. En la cocina hay _____.
4. En el dormitorio hay _____.
5. En la sala hay _____.
6. En el comedor hay _____.
7. En el patio hay _____.
8. En el garaje hay _____.
9. ¿Tienes un jardín? ¿una piscina? ¿una chimenea? ¿una terraza?

4-4 En otras palabras Identifica los cuartos, los muebles o los electrodomésticos (*appliances*) que corresponden a las siguientes descripciones.

1. Es el cuarto donde la gente come.
2. Es un lugar subterráneo.
3. Es un mueble que usamos para escribir cartas o estudiar.
4. Conecta el primer piso al segundo piso.
5. Sirve para ver nuestra imagen.
6. Es donde preparamos la comida.
7. Se usa (*It is used*) para cocinar (*to cook*) la comida rápidamente.

EN VOZ ALTA

4-5 **Lugares preferidos** Habla con un(a) compañero(a) sobre las siguientes actividades. Dile en qué parte de la casa te gusta hacer estas actividades.

MODELO: leer libros
Me gusta leer libros en el dormitorio.

1. estudiar
2. comer con la familia
3. mirar la tele
4. comer solo(a)

5. hablar por teléfono
6. escuchar música
7. descansar
8. jugar a las cartas

4-6 **¡Es la casa de mis sueños!** Descríbele la casa de tus sueños *(dreams)* a un(a) compañero(a) de clase. Usa la imaginación e incluye algunos electrodomésticos.

MODELO: *La casa de mis sueños tiene tres pisos. En esta casa hay una cocina muy grande y un gimnasio en el sótano. También hay un jardín con plantas exóticas. En la cocina hay un horno de microondas...*

4-7 **Entrevista con la familia real española**
España es uno de los pocos países que tiene una familia real *(royal family)*. Juan Carlos I es el rey *(king)* y Sofía, su esposa, es la reina *(queen)*. Los reyes tienen tres hijos: Elena, Cristina y Felipe. Trabajando con un(a) compañero(a), imagina que una persona es o *(either)* Juan Carlos I o Sofía. El rey o la reina debe usar la imaginación para contestar las siguientes preguntas sobre el Palacio Real.

> **CULTURA**
> Spain is a parliamentary monarchy; the king is the official head of state and head of the armed forces, while the members of the two-chamber parliament, or **Cortes** in Spanish, are elected by the general public. The prime minister has to be unanimously elected by the members of the **Cortes**. The current prime minister of Spain is José María Aznar. Though the official residence of the king and his family is the Palacio Real, their actual residence is in the Palacio de la Zarzuela.

> **CULTURA**
> Elena and Cristina are married; Elena's husband is don Jaime de Marichalar and Cristina is married to don Iñaki Urdangarín. Felipe is planning to get married to Felicia Ortiz, a Spanish journalist.

El Palacio Real, planta principal

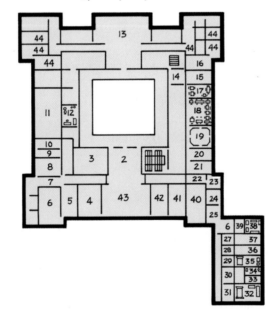

1   La gran escalera *(Grand staircase)*
12   La sala de música
17   El comedor menor
18   El comedor principal
19   La sala de los espejos
29   La biblioteca de la reina
32   El dormitorio de la reina
34   El cuarto de baño
38   La biblioteca principal
35   El dormitorio del rey

1. ¿Cómo es el Palacio Real? ¿Es grande? ¿elegante? ¿cómodo? ¿Cuántos dormitorios tiene? ¿Cuántos cuartos de baño hay en el palacio en la primera planta? ¿Por qué no tiene una cocina? ¿Hay un sótano en el palacio? ¿Hay muchas escaleras?
2. ¿A usted le gustaría *(Would you like)* vivir en el palacio? ¿Cuál es su cuarto favorito? Generalmente, ¿qué hace en este cuarto? ¿Cuál es el cuarto favorito de su esposo(a)?
3. ¿Quiere usted comprar muebles o electrodomésticos nuevos para algunos *(some)* cuartos? ¿Qué objetos busca usted y para qué cuartos?

EN CONTEXTO

Alberto, un estudiante de medicina de la Universidad de Santiago de Compostela, expresa sus opiniones sobre un apartamento desastroso que él ve con su amigo Francisco.

En la calle...

Alberto: Mmm... el césped no está cortado. Y las plantas en el patio **están muertas** (*dead*). **¡Tengo miedo** de entrar!

Francisco: ¡Hombre! **Espera** un momento para ver el interior. Seguro que **está mejor.**

En la sala...

Alberto: ¡Ay! ¡Dios mío! ¡Es un desastre el apartamento! Hay ropa por todos lados, y en el **sillón** hay un mogollón de libros.

Francisco: Deben ser estudiantes las personas que viven aquí. ¿**Quieres** ver la cocina?

En la cocina...

Alberto: ¡Qué barbaridad! Todos los platos **están sucios.** Y todavía no han quitado la **mesa** (*have not cleared the table*). Parece que nadie limpia aquí. Y para colmo (*And on top of that*), ¡una bolsa de basura en el **lavabo!**... No **puedo** imaginar cómo viven aquí.

Francisco: **Ten paciencia,** Alberto. ¿**Podemos** ver los dormitorios?

En el dormitorio...

Alberto: No veo la cama... Ah, allí está. Apenas **puedo** verla (*I can barely see it*) debajo de la ropa. Y ni siquiera (*not even*) un libro en el estante.

Francisco: Creo que **todos están en el sillón** en la sala. Bueno, Alberto,... **tienes razón.** El piso **está un poco desordenado** (*messy*). Pero **ven** conmigo para ver el cuarto de baño antes de (*before*) decidir.

En el cuarto de baño...

Alberto: Mira cómo está la **bañera**... y huele (*it smells*) mal aquí. No **puedo** vivir entre esta gente (*people*)... Los inquilinos (*tenants*) de este piso son unos sinvergüenzas (*shameless people*). Y la renta está super alta. **Prefiero** vivir al aire libre (*outdoors*). En fin, ya me voy... ¡No puedo más! (*I can't take anymore!*)

> **¿NOS ENTENDEMOS?**
> Spanish speakers say **¡Dios mío!** (*Oh my God!*) to express amazement in either a positive or negative context. **¡Qué barbaridad!** (*How atrocious!*) is reserved to express disgust and/or outrage. Among teens and young adults in Spain it's common in informal speech to use the adjective **mogollón** to mean *a lot*. Young Spaniards are also likely to use the adverb **super** to add emphasis to a quality or condition. In Spain the word **piso** is used to refer to an apartment instead of **apartamento.**

¿Comprendiste?

¿Cuáles son algunos de los problemas que Alberto encuentra con el apartamento? Escribe una lista de cuatro o cinco cosas que están mal.

MODELO: *El césped* no está cortado.

1. _____
2. _____
3. _____
4. _____

Encuentro cultural
Gaudí y su obra

La casa de Peralta de Antonio Gaudí

PARA PENSAR

- ¿Cómo es la arquitectura en tu ciudad?
- ¿Qué obra de arquitectura de este país te gusta más?
- ¿Sabes algo de Antonio Gaudí?

Antonio Gaudí y Cornet (1852–1926) se conoce como uno de los más prestigiosos y creativos arquitectos internacionales. Nace en *(He was born in)* Barcelona, España. Una de sus primeras obras es la Casa Vicens (1878–80) en Barcelona. Sus primeras obras tienen mucho éxito y por eso don Eusebio Güell, un hombre de negocios muy rico, le da dinero para construir *(to build)* el Palacio Güell (1885–89) y el Parque Güell (1900–14) con árboles *(trees)* de piedra *(stone)*, fuentes *(fountains)* con reptiles y mosaicos en concreto. Su obra maestra *(masterpiece)* es el Templo de la Sagrada Familia *(Church of the Holy Family)* que todavía sigue en obra y está en el centro de la ciudad de Barcelona.

La última obra de Gaudí es la Casa Milá (1905–07), que también se llama La Pedrera. El edificio tiene acceso al techo, donde la gente va de noche para ver la magnífica vista de la ciudad mientras toman una soda y escuchan música. La Pedrera tiene dos escaleras, siete chimeneas y está diseñada alrededor de dos patios. Las puertas, los muebles y los ascensores *(elevators)* muestran la dedicación de Gaudí en toda su obra. La Pedrera está abierta al público y hay muchas exhibiciones y eventos culturales continuamente.

PARA DISCUTIR

1. Nombra algunas obras de Gaudí.
2. Describe el Parque Güell.
3. Describe la Casa Milá o La Pedrera: ¿Dónde está? ¿Qué hace la gente en el techo de la Casa Milá? ¿Cuántas escaleras y chimeneas tiene?
4. ¿Te gusta el estilo de Gaudí? ¿Por qué sí o por qué no?

ESTRUCTURA I Describing household chores and other activities: present tense of stem-changing verbs (o → ue; e → ie; e → i)

In this section, you will learn how to conjugate verbs that change—either **o** to **ue**, **e** to **ie**, or **e** to **i**—in the stem of the verb. A stem is the part of an infinitive to which one adds personal endings. For example, the stem of **hablar** is **habl-**. The above-mentioned types of vowel changes occur in all stressed syllables. Since the stress does not fall on the stem in the **nosotros(as)** and **vosotros(as)** forms, there is no stem change.

The present tense of e → ie stem-changing verbs

Infinitive	comenzar (ie) (to begin)	pensar (ie) (to think)	querer (ie) (to want; to love)	preferir (ie) (to prefer)	tener (ie) (to have)	venir (ie) (to come)
Stem	comienz-	piens-	quier-	prefier-	tien-	vien-
	comienzo	pienso	quiero	prefiero	tengo	vengo
	comienzas	piensas	quieres	prefieres	tienes	vienes
	comienza	piensa	quiere	prefiere	tiene	viene
	comenzamos	pensamos	queremos	preferimos	tenemos	venimos
	comenzáis	pensáis	queréis	preferís	tenéis	venís
	comienzan	piensan	quieren	prefieren	tienen	vienen

Note that two verbs that have stem changes from **e** to **ie** have an irregular **yo** form. (stems: tien- and vien-). You have already learned the endings for **tener** in **Capítulo preliminar** and in **Capítulo 2**. The endings for **venir** are: **vengo, vienes, viene, venimos, venís, vienen.**

Other frequently used **e** to **ie** stem-changing verbs are:

regar (ie)	to water	entender (ie)	to understand
cerrar (ie)	to close	perder (ie)	to lose; to miss (a function)
empezar (ie)	to begin		

The present tense of o → ue stem-changing verbs

Infinitive	jugar (ue)* (to play)	almorzar (ue) (to have lunch)	poder (ue) (to be able)	volver (ue) (to return)	dormir (ue) (to sleep)
Stem	jueg-	almuerz-	pued-	vuelv-	duerm-
	juego	almuerzo	puedo	vuelvo	duermo
	juegas	almuerzas	puedes	vuelves	duermes
	juega	almuerza	puede	vuelve	duerme
	jugamos	almorzamos	podemos	volvemos	dormimos
	jugáis	almorzáis	podéis	volvéis	dormís
	juegan	almuerzan	pueden	vuelven	duermen

Jugar is the only **u** to **ue** stem-changing verb in Spanish.

The present tense of e → i stem-changing verbs

Infinitive	servir (i) (to serve)	pedir (i) (to ask for)	decir (i) (to say; to tell)
Stem	sirv-	pid-	dic-
	sirvo	pido	**digo** (the **yo** form of **decir** is irregular)
	sirves	pides	dices
	sirve	pide	dice
	servimos	pedimos	decimos
	servís	pedís	decís
	sirven	piden	dicen

¡A PRACTICAR!

4-8 **Entrevista con doña Rosa** Raquel Navarro es reportera. Ella quiere escribir un artículo sobre la gente de edad *(the elderly)*. En este momento ella está hablando *(is talking)* con doña Rosa. Completa su conversación, usando la forma correcta de los siguientes verbos: **comenzar, pensar, preferir, querer, tener, venir.**

Raquel:	Yo 1. _____ hablar con usted sobre su vida, doña Rosa. ¿Está bien?
Doña Rosa:	Por supuesto. ¿ 2. _____ nosotras con mi vida personal?
Raquel:	Muy bien. ¿ 3. _____ usted muchos hijos?
Doña Rosa:	Sí, 4. _____ cuatro. Dos de ellos viven aquí conmigo.
Raquel:	Y los otros... ¿5. _____ a verla frecuentemente?
Doña Rosa:	Bueno, no 6. _____ frecuentemente porque viven en Madrid.
Raquel:	Sé que los estudiantes la tienen muy ocupada. Pero ¿qué hace durante el día para divertirse?
Doña Rosa:	Me gusta mirar la tele. (Yo) 7. _____ ver telenovelas.
Raquel:	¿8. _____ usted una telenovela favorita, doña Rosa?
Doña Rosa:	Claro que sí, señorita. Se llama «Decepción y amor». El programa 9. _____ en una hora. ¿10. _____ verlo conmigo esta tarde?
Raquel:	Sí, gracias. Me gusta mucho este programa. ¡Qué guay! *(Cool!)* ¿Y qué 11. _____ usted de las telenovelas españolas, doña Rosa?
Doña Rosa:	Bueno, pues... me gustan mucho, pero mi hija 12. _____ las telenovelas norteamericanas porque son menos melodramáticas.

4-9 **¿Cierto o falso?** Ahora tienes que corregir *(correct)* algunos de los errores en el artículo de Raquel antes de publicarlo en el periódico *(newspaper)*. Si la oración es falsa, ¡corrígela!

MODELO: Doña Rosa: Yo tengo tres hijos.
     Es falso. Doña Rosa tiene cuatro hijos.

1. Doña Rosa: Mis hijos vienen a verme frecuentemente.
2. Raquel: Su hija la tiene muy ocupada.
3. Doña Rosa: Prefiero ver el noticiero *(news program)*.
4. Doña Rosa: No tengo un programa favorito.
5. Doña Rosa: Pienso que las telenovelas españolas son malas.
6. Doña Rosa: Nosotros preferimos ver telenovelas norteamericanas.

CULTURA
Pedro Almodóvar is one of Spain's most famous film-makers. He has directed over twelve films, including *All About My Mother*, which won an Academy Award for Best Foreign Language Film in 2000.

CULTURA
La calle Franco is one of the more popular streets for dining in Santiago de Compostela. The street is in the old part of the city where car traffic is prohibited and features numerous street musicians and other attractions.

4-10 **Planes para el sábado** Beti y su compañero, Tomás, dos estudiantes de medicina, están hablando de sus planes. Completa su conversación con la forma correcta de los siguientes verbos: **almorzar, dormir, jugar, poder** y **volver.**

Beti:	¿Por qué no 1. _____ (nosotros) al tenis esta tarde?
Tomás:	Yo no 2. _____ bien al tenis, Beti. Y después de mi accidente, no 3. _____ hacer mucho ejercicio por una semana.
Beti:	Pues, vamos a ir al cine. ¿Qué te parece? Nosotros 4. _____ ver la nueva película de Almodóvar.
Tomás:	Bien. Antes del cine, ¿ 5. _____ (nosotros) en la calle Franco? Conozco un restaurante nuevo.
Beti:	¡Perfecto! Y después de almorzar, nosotros 6. _____ a casa. Yo siempre 7. _____ la siesta.
Tomás:	¿Cómo? Tú 8. _____ dormir la siesta, si quieres, pero yo no.

EN VOZ ALTA

4-11 **¿Es verdad?** Con un(a) compañero(a) de clase, respondan a las siguientes observaciones. En este ejercicio se van a enfocar en los verbos **pedir, servir** y **decir.**

MODELOS: Tú siempre pides mucha comida en la cafetería.
No es verdad. Yo no pido mucha comida en la cafetería.

Tú y tus amigos siempre dicen la verdad.
Sí, es verdad. Nosotros siempre decimos la verdad.

1. Tú y tus amigos(as) siempre dicen cosas buenas sobre los profesores.
2. Tus amigos sirven comida exótica en las fiestas.
3. Tu profesor(a) de español pide la tarea.
4. Tú siempre dices cosas interesantes de tus compañeros de clase.
5. Tú siempre pides ayuda cuando no entiendes una cosa.
6. Vosotros pedís trabajos adicionales a los profesores.
7. Los restaurantes de la universidad sirven buena comida.

4-12 **Encuentra a alguien que...** Encuentra a alguien en tu clase que haga las siguientes cosas *(following things).* Con las siguientes frases, forma preguntas para tus compañeros(as) para saber si ellos(as) hacen o no hacen esas cosas.

MODELO: querer una casa con chimenea
E1: *¿Quieres una casa con chimenea?*
E2: *Sí, yo quiero una casa con chimenea.*

1. almorzar en la terraza
2. preferir una casa a un apartamento
3. pensar tener una fiesta en la casa de sus padres
4. poder preparar comida riquísima
5. tener que lavar los platos
6. pedir postres *(desserts)* en los restaurantes
7. decir cosas atrevidas *(bold)*
8. servir comida deliciosa en las fiestas

4-13 **Entrevista: Preguntas sobre la vivienda** Hazle las siguientes preguntas sobre su vivienda a un(a) compañero(a) de clase.

1. ¿Prefieres vivir en un apartamento, una casa o una residencia? ¿Almuerzas en casa *(at home)* o en una cafetería? ¿Vienen tus padres a verte con frecuencia?

2. ¿Cierras las ventanas de tu dormitorio por la noche? ¿Duermes bien cuando estás solo(a) en casa? ¿Pueden verte tus amigos a cualquier hora *(at any time)*?

3. ¿Tienes muchas fiestas en tu casa? ¿En qué cuarto prefieres estar con tus amigos en una fiesta? ¿Pierdes muchas fiestas porque tienes que estudiar? ¿Puedes dar fiestas en un patio o en un jardín? ¿A qué hora vuelves de una fiesta generalmente?

4. ¿Pierdes muchas cosas en tu dormitorio? ¿Puedes estudiar bien en tu dormitorio? ¿Duermes fácilmente en tu dormitorio? ¿Qué muebles tienes en tu dormitorio? ¿Qué electrodomésticos tienes?

You have already learned the conjugation of **tener** and several expressions that use the verb **tener.** Here you will learn some more expressions with **tener.**

Tener + nouns

As you learned in **Capítulo 2,** in certain cases you can use the stem-changing verb **tener** + noun to describe how people are feeling.

—¿**Tienes sueño,** mamá?   *Are you sleepy, Mom?*
—Sí, **tengo mucho sueño.**   *Yes, I'm very sleepy.*

Here are five more expressions you can use with **tener:**

tener calor *to be hot*   **tener miedo (de)** *to be afraid (of)*
tener celos *to be jealous*   **tener paciencia** *to be patient*
tener frío *to be cold*

Note that although Spanish speakers use **hacer** to say *it is cold* or *it is hot* (**hace frío, hace calor**), the verb **tener** is used with these two nouns when a person says *I am cold* (**Yo tengo frío.**) or *She is hot* (**Ella tiene calor.**).

Francisco **tiene paciencia** con su amigo Alberto.	*Francisco is patient with his friend Alberto.*
Alberto **tiene miedo de** entrar al apartamento.	*Alberto is afraid of entering the apartment.*
Mi novia **tiene celos** cuando hablo con otras chicas.	*My girlfriend is jealous when I speak to other young women.*
Tú **tienes calor** porque hace mucho sol y no hace viento.	*You are hot because it is very sunny and the wind is not blowing.*
Tomás y Margarita **tienen mucho frío** porque no tienen chaquetas.	*Tomás and Margarita are very cold because they don't have jackets.*

Tener ganas de + infinitive

When you want to say that you feel like doing something, use the expression **tener ganas de** + *infinitive*. Simply conjugate **tener** and use the infinitive form of the verb that expresses what you feel like doing.

Tienes ganas de pintar la casa?   *Do you feel like painting the house?*
Tenemos ganas de ver una película.   *We feel like watching a movie.*

Tener que + infinitive

The verb **tener** is also used in the construction **tener que** + *infinitive*, which means *to have to do something*. It is used in the same way as the verb **deber** (see **Capítulo 2),** but it carries a stronger sense of obligation. **Deber** normally carries the meaning of *should*, whereas **tener que** often means *must*. Note that both of these verb forms must be followed by an infinitive.

Yo deseo ir a la fiesta, pero yo   *I want to go to the party, but I have to*
tengo que estudiar.   *(must) study.*
Tenemos que ir a la discoteca.   *We have to (must) go to the disco.*
¡Hay muchos chicos guapos!   *There are a lot of cute guys!*

To express *very* with the **tener** expressions, use a form of the adjective **mucho,** which must match the gender (masculine or feminine) and number (singular or plural) of its noun, as in the example above.

¡A PRACTICAR!

4-14 **¿Qué tiene Juan?** Lee los escenarios y di lo que tiene o no tiene Juan.

tener celos	**tener frío**
tener calor	**tener paciencia**
tener miedo (de)	

MODELO: Hoy la temperatura es muy alta, hace mucho sol y Juan va a nadar.
Juan tiene calor.

1. Normalmente Juan puede esperar en la cola *(wait in line)* por horas.
   _____

2. Juan nunca viaja en avión. No le gustan las alturas *(heights)*.
   _____ de las alturas.

3. A Juan no le gusta el invierno porque hay mucha nieve y viento y tiene que llevar *(wear)* mucha ropa.
   En invierno _____.

4. A Juan no le importa si su novia sale con sus amigos los fines de semana.
   Juan no _____.

4-15 **En otras palabras** Usa una expresión con el verbo **tener** e indica qué tienen las siguientes personas.

MODELO: Mercedes: Yo quiero ir al cine.
Mercedes tiene ganas de ir al cine.

1. Manolo dice: Allí está Ramón hablando con mi novia.
2. Milagros y Maite dicen: Nosotras podemos esperar; no tenemos prisa.
3. Yo digo: ¡Ayyyy! ¡Un perro grande!
4. Tú dices: Yo quiero ir a la discoteca.

EN VOZ ALTA

4-16 **¿Qué haces cuando tienes... ?** Trabaja con un(a) compañero(a) de clase y forma preguntas usando expresiones con **tener.** Luego contesta las preguntas de la otra persona.

MODELO: E1: *¿Qué haces cuando tienes miedo por la noche?*
E2: *Cuando tengo miedo por la noche, yo cierro las ventanas.*

4-17 **En un campamento *(camp)*** Termina las siguientes oraciones con **tener que +** *infinitive* para indicar qué necesitan hacer los consejeros del campamento.

MODELO: los consejeros / descansar más los fines de semana
Los consejeros tienen que descansar más los fines de semana.

1. nosotros / nadar en la mañana
2. Vince y Stephen / jugar al tenis a las nueve
3. Wendy / patinar en línea por la tarde
4. Guadalupe / ver un video esta tarde
5. tú / hablar por teléfono con la Sra. Rogers
6. ¿yo?

4-18 **Preferencias y obligaciones** Trabajando con un(a) compañero(a) de clase, forma cinco oraciones *(sentences)* que expresen combinaciones de una cosa que tienes ganas de hacer y una cosa que tienes que hacer después.

MODELO: esta noche: *Yo tengo ganas de ir al cine, pero yo tengo que estudiar.*

1. hoy por la tarde: _____
2. esta noche: _____
3. mañana por la mañana: _____
4. este fin de semana: _____
5. en el verano: _____

LIMPIAR LA CASA

¡A PRACTICAR!

4-19 **¿Quién hace qué?** *(Who is doing what?)* Doña Rosa siempre ayuda a los estudiantes con los quehaceres domésticos. Completa las siguientes oraciones para identificar lo que cada uno hace en la casa.

1. Manuel y David: Nosotros _____ la mesa antes de comer.
2. Carlos _____ la mesa después de comer.
3. Doña Rosa y Marcos _____ los platos en la cocina.
4. Doña Rosa: Pepe, tú _____ la basura.
5. Manuel y David _____ la casa los fines de semana.
6. Ramón: Yo _____ el césped y _____ las plantas en junio, julio y agosto.
7. Los estudiantes _____ la cama todas las mañanas.
8. La hija de doña Rosa _____ la ropa y _____ el piso.
9. Si está de buen humor *(If she is in a good mood)*, doña Rosa _____ la aspiradora.

4-20 **¿Te ayudo?** Manuel siempre ayuda a su madre con los quehaceres en la casa, especialmente cuando hay mucho que hacer. ¿Qué tiene que hacer Manuel?

MODELO: La cama está desordenada *(messy)*.
Manuel tiene que hacer la cama.

1. Los platos están sucios *(dirty)*. *Manuel tiene que lavar los platos*
2. Hay mucha basura en la casa. *sacar la basura*
3. La ropa está arrugada *(wrinkled)*. *planchar la ropa*
4. La casa está sucia. *pasar la aspiradora*
5. El piso está sucio. *barrer el piso*
6. Las plantas necesitan agua. *regar las plantas*

EN VOZ ALTA

4-21 **¿Qué haces para limpiar la casa?** Pregúntale a un(a) compañero(a) de clase si hace los siguientes quehaceres. Si tu compañero(a) no hace el quehacer, debe indicar quién lo hace.

MODELO: sacar la basura
E1: *¿Sacas la basura?*
E2: *No, no saco la basura. Mi padre saca la basura.*

1. poner la mesa
2. lavar los platos
3. planchar la ropa
4 lavar la ropa
5. pasar la aspiradora
6 hacer la cama
7. cortar el césped
8. barrer el piso
9. regar las plantas

4-22 **Entrevista** Trabaja con un(a) compañero(a) de clase y hazle las siguientes preguntas sobre los quehaceres domésticos que él (ella) hace en casa.

1. ¿Tienes muchos quehaceres domésticos? ¿Cuáles son?
2. ¿Te gusta cocinar? ¿poner la mesa? ¿quitar la mesa? ¿lavar los platos?
3. ¿Qué hace(n) tu(s) hermanos(as)?
4. ¿Quién plancha la ropa en la familia? ¿Usas la lavadora y la secadora?
5. ¿Cuántas veces al mes limpias la casa? ¿el refrigerador?
6. ¿Tienes que cortar el césped?
7. ¿Quién riega las plantas en la familia?
8. ¿Tienes que barrer el piso? ¿el patio? ¿el garaje?

Encuentro cultural
Viviendas en Latinoamérica y España

PARA PENSAR

- ¿Vives en una ciudad grande o en un pueblo pequeño?
- ¿Es más común vivir en un apartamento o en una casa en tu ciudad?

Madrid

México

En Latinoamérica y España, las viviendas varían según el país, la región, el clima, la posición económica y el gusto de las personas. La arquitectura varía desde pequeñas casas coloniales hasta edificios de apartamentos muy altos, o desde condominios hasta casas de adobe o de cartón *(cardboard)*. En algunos países, los edificios altos tienen una forma de numerar los pisos que es diferente de la que usamos en los Estados Unidos. Lo que nosotros llamamos el primer piso *(floor),* ellos llaman la planta baja. Lo que nosotros llamamos el segundo piso, ellos llaman el primer piso.

Buenos Aires

Es difícil encontrar una casa típica del mundo hispano. El estilo de las casas depende de la región. Madrid, la capital de España, tiene casi 3 millones de habitantes. No hay mucho espacio, y por eso los apartamentos son las viviendas más comunes para mucha gente, así como en las ciudades grandes de los Estados Unidos.

PARA DISCUTIR

1. ¿Cómo es la arquitectura de las viviendas en Latinoamérica y España?
2. ¿Cuáles son las viviendas más comunes en las ciudades grandes de Latinoamérica y España?
3. ¿Dónde prefieres vivir tú? ¿en un apartamento o en una casa?

ESTRUCTURA II Expressing preferences and giving advice: affirmative *tú* commands

Spanish speakers use affirmative informal commands mainly to tell children, close friends, relatives, and pets to do something. You have already seen these commands in the direction lines of each exercise telling you **(tú)** what to do.

For most Spanish verbs, use the third-person singular (the **él/ella** verb forms) of the present indicative for the **tú** command form.

Espera un momento.	*Wait a minute.*
Pide un postre, si quieres.	*Order dessert, if you want to.*

Eight verbs have irregular affirmative **tú** commands.

decir: **di**	salir: **sal**
hacer: **haz**	ser: **sé**
ir: **ve**	tener: **ten**
poner: **pon**	venir: **ven**

—**Ven** conmigo para ver el piso.	*Come with me to see the apartment.*
—Sí, pero **ten** paciencia, Alberto.	*Yes, but be patient, Alberto.*
—**Pon** la dirección en el bolsillo, Francisco.	*Put the address in your pocket, Francisco.*
—**Dime** tus opiniones del piso.	*Give me your opinion about the apartment.*

Infinitive	3rd person present indicative	*tú* command	
hablar	habla	**habla** (tú)	*speak*
comer	come	**come** (tú)	*eat*
escribir	escribe	**escribe** (tú)	*write*
cerrar	cierra	**cierra** (tú)	*close*
dormir	duerme	**duerme** (tú)	*sleep*

In Spain, to form the informal **vosotros** command, replace the final **-r** in the infinitive with **-d**: hablar → hablad, comer → comed, escribir → escribid.

¡A PRACTICAR!

4-23 | **A sus órdenes, doña Rosa** Completa la siguiente conversación entre doña Rosa y los chicos de la casa, usando los mandatos informales de la lista. Puedes usar los verbos más de una vez.

ten	haz	riega	llama	ven	espera	quita	pon

Doña Rosa: ¡Chicos! Ya es tarde. Ayudadme a limpiar la casa. Tengo mucho que hacer.

Manuel: Ahora mismo, señora. Alberto, (1) _____ conmigo para lavar los platos.

Alberto: (2) _____ un minuto. Tengo que terminar la tarea.

Manuel: Alberto, (3) _____ la tarea después. La señora necesita nuestra ayuda ahora.

Alberto: ¿No me oyes, Manuel? (4) _____ paciencia. ¿No puedes esperar dos minutos?

Manuel: En dos minutos entonces. Te espero en el comedor.

Alberto: Muy bien. (5) _____ la mesa y te ayudo en la cocina con los platos.

Francisco: Manuel, ¿necesitas ayuda?

Manuel: ¡Sí! Gracias. (6) _____ los platos en el lavaplatos y luego (7) _____ las plantas en el patio. Antes de empezar, (8) _____ a Alberto. Él está un poco perezoso hoy.

4-24 | **Consejos para un nuevo estudiante** La supervisora le da algunos consejos (*advice*) a un nuevo estudiante de la casa. ¿Qué le dice ella al nuevo habitante de la casa? Contesta usando mandatos informales afirmativos.

MODELO: ayudar / con los quehaceres domésticos
Ayuda con los quehaceres domésticos.

1. tener / paciencia con los vecinos (*neighbors*)
2. barrer / el piso de tu dormitorio todas las semanas
3. estudiar / mucho
4. lavar / tu ropa los fines de semana
5. comer / a las horas establecidas
6. hacer / la cama todos los días
7. salir / para hacer ejercicio con los otros chicos
8. ir / al mercado los domingos por la mañana
9. dormir / la siesta
10. llamar / a tus padres todas las semanas

EN VOZ ALTA

4-25 | **¿Qué recomiendas?** Ahora un estudiante universitario de España te escribe una carta. Pide consejos para salir adelante (*get ahead*) en tu universidad en los Estados Unidos. Dale consejos para salir adelante en tu universidad. Trabaja con un(a) compañero(a) de clase para hacer una lista de mandatos afirmativos. Luego practica con el (la) otro(a) estudiante.

MODELO: *Come en la cafetería Hogate. ¡La comida en la otra es horrible!*

ESTRUCTURA III Talking about location, emotional and physical states, and actions in progress: the verb *estar*

The verb *to be* in English is translated in Spanish by either the verb **ser** or **estar**. As you learned in **Capítulo 2, ser** is used to identify essential or inherent characteristics, profession, nationality, origin, time, and dates. You learned the conjugation of **estar** in **Capítulo 3.** In this section you will learn three functions of the verb **estar.**

Location

To state the location of people and things, use **estar** + *preposition of location + location.*

Papá **está en** el comedor.	*Dad is in the dining room.*
La aspiradora está **detrás del** sofá **en** la sala.	*The vacuum cleaner is behind the sofa in the living room.*
La tarea **está encima de** la mesa **debajo del** libro de texto.	*The homework is on top of the table below the textbook.*

Prepositions of location often used with the verb **estar:**

al lado de	*next to, beside*	en	*in; on*
cerca de	*near*	encima de	*on top of*
con	*with*	entre	*between; among*
debajo de	*under, below*	lejos de	*far from*
delante de	*in front of*	sobre	*on; over*
detrás de	*behind*		

Emotional and physical states

To describe how people are feeling or the physical state of something, use **estar** + *adjective.*

¿Cómo **estás,** Elena?	*How are you, Elena?*
Estoy muy cansada, pero contenta.	*I'm very tired, but happy.*

Here are some adjectives commonly used with **estar** to describe emotional and physical states:

aburrido(a)	*bored*	limpio(a)	*clean*
contento(a)	*happy*	ocupado(a)	*busy*
desordenado(a)	*messy*	ordenado(a)	*neat*
emocionado(a)	*excited*	preocupado(a)	*worried*
enfermo(a)	*sick*	sucio(a)	*dirty*
enojado(a)	*angry*	triste	*sad*
furioso(a)	*furious*		

Note that **estar** can also be used with the adverbs **bien** and **mal.**

¿Cómo estás?	*How are you?*
Yo **estoy bien (mal).**	*I'm well (bad).*

Actions in progress

The **present progressive** tense is used to describe actions in progress. To form the present progressive, use a present tense form of **estar** plus a present participle, which is formed by adding **-ando** to the stem of **-ar** verbs and **-iendo** to the stem of **-er** and **-ir** verbs.

	{verb stem	+	progressive ending}	present participle
estoy				
estás				
está	estudi-		ando	estudiando *(studying)*
	com-		iendo	comiendo *(eating)*
estamos	escrib-		iendo	escribiendo *(writing)*
estáis				
están				

Two irregular present participles are **leyendo** *(reading)* and **trayendo** *(bringing)*. Verbs that end in **-ir** and have a stem change, such as the verbs **dormir, pedir,** and **servir,** change in the stem from **o** to **u** or **e** to **i** (forming **durmiendo, pidiendo,** and **sirviendo,** respectively).

While Spanish speakers often use the simple present tense to describe routine or habitual actions, they use the present progressive tense to describe what is happening right now—at this very moment. Compare the two examples.

Happens habitually

Generalmente, Lorena **come** con su familia en casa.

Generally, Lorena eats with her family at home.

Happening right now

Pero en este momento Lorena **está comiendo** en una cafetería.

But right now Lorena is eating in a cafeteria.

¡A PRACTICAR!

4-26 **¿Dónde está Oswaldo?** Usando la información a continuación, indica dónde están Oswaldo y su esposa Silvia. Varias respuestas son posibles.

MODELO: Silvia y Oswaldo almuerzan juntos.
Están en el comedor.

1. Oswaldo duerme profundamente *(deeply)*.
2. Silvia comienza a leer una novela.
3. Oswaldo piensa cortar el césped.
4. Silvia y Oswaldo juegan a las cartas.
5. Oswaldo empieza a cantar una canción.
6. Silvia y Oswaldo vuelven de su trabajo y cierran la puerta.
7. Oswaldo piensa en los ingredientes de una comida especial.
8. Oswaldo cierra con llave *(to lock)* el coche.

4-27 **Objetos de la casa** Ayuda a doña Rosa a buscar los siguientes objetos en la casa. Usa **estar** + *preposition* para indicarle dónde están las cosas que ella necesita encontrar.

MODELO: La aspiradora
La aspiradora está detrás del sillón en la sala.

1. la escoba (*the broom*)
2. los libros
3. el espejo
4. la ropa
5. el sofá
6. el gato (el reloj)

4-28 **¿Cómo está(n)?** Mira los siguientes dibujos y decide cómo están las personas. Usa la forma apropiada de los adjetivos de la lista y el verbo **estar.**

1. _____

2. _____

3. _____

4. _____

5. _____

6. _____

7. _____

8. _____

4-29 **¿Qué están haciendo?** Usa el presente progresivo (**estar** + *present participle*) para describir las acciones de estas personas.

> MODELO: Ramón / bailar
> *Ramón está bailando.*

1. Marta / cantar
2. nosotros / poner la mesa
3. los estudiantes / limpiar la casa
4. tú / dormir
5. Uds. / servir la comida
6. Beti y Tomás / pensar en los planes para el fin de semana
7. Carlos / quitar la mesa
8. la hija de doña María / planchar la ropa
9. yo / pasar la aspiradora
10. Miguel / leer el periódico

EN VOZ ALTA

4-30 **Situaciones y emociones** Trabajando con un(a) compañero(a) de clase, altérnense *(take turns)* identificando sus emociones en las siguientes situaciones, y expliquen por qué.

> MODELO: Cuando hace sol, estoy...
> *Cuando hace sol, estoy muy contento; me gusta mucho el sol.*

1. Cuando saco una mala nota *(bad grade)*, estoy...
2. Cuando tengo que hablar en español, estoy...
3. Cuando mi familia y yo limpiamos la casa todo el día, estamos...
4. Cuando mi hermano tiene que limpiar el cuarto de baño, está...
5. Cuando estoy con mis amigos, nosotros estamos...
6. Cuando mi compañero(a) pierde un documento en la computadora, está...
7. Cuando los estudiantes no tienen clase, están...
8. Cuando el (la) profesor(a) corrige *(corrects)* nuestros exámenes, está...

4-31 **La nueva estudiante** Helen, una chica de EE.UU., es una nueva estudiante. Hazle preguntas a ella con el verbo **estar** sobre los siguientes tópicos. Tu compañera va a ser Helen y debe contestar las preguntas. Túrnense.

> MODELO: sobre su estado emocional/físico
> E1: *¿Cómo estás?*
> E2: *Estoy bien, pero un poco cansada.*

1. sobre lo que ella está haciendo en Santiago
2. sobre sus planes académicos en Santiago
3. si ella trabaja en Santiago
4. si ella sabe si doña Rosa está en la casa
5. si ella sabe de las actividades de doña Rosa
6. si sus compañeras de cuarto estudian en este momento

4-32 **¡Actuemos!** En grupos de tres personas, túrnense actuando y adivinando varios quehaceres domésticos. Una persona hace pantomima y los otros del grupo preguntan sobre lo que está haciendo, usando el presente progresivo.

> MODELO: E1: *¿Estás lavando la ropa?*
> E2: *No, estoy en la cocina.*
> E3: *¿Estás lavando los platos?*
> E2: *¡Sí! Estoy lavando los platos porque están muy sucios.*

ASÍ SE DICE Counting from 100 and higher: los números de 100 a 1.000.000

100	cien (ciento + *número*)	600	seiscientos(as)
200	doscientos(as)	700	setecientos(as)
300	trescientos(as)	800	ochocientos(as)
400	cuatrocientos(as)	900	novecientos(as)
500	quinientos(as)	1.000	mil

1. The **y** never occurs directly after the number **ciento: ciento uno/a.**

2. The numbers 200–999 agree in gender with the nouns they modify: **doscientos libros,** but **doscientas pesetas.**

3. The word **mil,** which can mean *a thousand* or *one thousand,* is not usually used in the plural form. **Un millón** (*a million* or *one million*), however, has the plural form **millones,** in which the accent is dropped.

4. **Los números de más de 2.000** Use **mil** to express numbers over 1,000. For expressing hundreds of thousands, 200–900 must agree in gender with the nouns they modify.

2.000	dos mil
200.000	doscient**as** mil **personas**
300.055	trescient**os** mil cincuenta y cinco **estudiantes**
1.000.000	un millón

5. **La fecha** For expressing dates, the numbers 200–900 will be plural masculine to agree with the implied or stated masculine plural noun **años.**

1835	mil ochocientos treinta y cinco
1998	mil novecientos noventa y ocho
2009	dos mil nueve

   Use the preposition **de** to connect the day, month, and year.

   Nací (*I was born*) el 24 de junio **de** 1979.

6. Note that when writing numbers, Spanish uses a period where English uses a comma, and vice versa.

   | English: | $1,500.75 |
   | Spanish: | $1.500,75 |

   This is not the case when writing years. Years are written as follows:

   1999
   1969
   1492

Spain experienced a traumatic civil war between Republicans and Nationalists that raged between 1936 and 1939. This conflict left over a million dead and divided the country for several decades afterward.

Francisco Franco assumed dictatorial control of the country after the Civil War in 1939 and ruled until his death in 1975. After his death, King Juan Carlos introduced a democracy under a constitutional monarchy.

¿NOS ENTENDEMOS?
In January of 1999, Spain converted from the **peseta** (ESP) to the **euro** (EUR, the common currency of the European Common Market). Other countries that converted include Austria, Belgium, Finland, France, Germany, Ireland, Italy, Luxembourg, the Netherlands, Portugal, Greece, and the Vatican City. 1 euro = 166 pesetas = 87 cents.

CULTURA
Salvador Dalí (1904–1989) is most famous for his particular surrealist style, which features interior landscapes of the unconscious.
Diego Velázquez (1599–1660) was the official court painter for Philip IV. *Las Meninas,* featuring one of Philip's daughters posing for her portrait, is his most famous work.
Francisco Goya (1746–1828) was the court painter for King Fernando VII. *Duelo a garrotazos (Duel with Cudgels)* reflects a particularly violent moment in Spain's history.
Pablo Picasso (1881–1973) was one of the early innovators of cubism in Spain. *Guernica* is a national treasure of Spain depicting the horrors of modern warfare suffered by the inhabitants of Guernica, bombed by the Germans during the Spanish Civil War.

¡A PRACTICAR!

4-33 | **Eventos históricos de España** Para cada fecha histórica, escribe la fecha y luego dile la frase completa a un compañero(a) de clase.

MODELO: Barcelona hospedó los Juegos Olímpicos en 1992.
Barcelona hospedó los Juegos Olímpicos en mil novecientos noventa y dos.

1. Los romanos llegaron a España en el año 218 a. C. (antes de Cristo).
2. Los árabes invadieron desde África en el año 711 d. C. (después de Cristo).
3. Los Reyes Católicos, Fernando e Isabel, conquistaron Granada en 1492, el mismo año en que Cristobal Colón viajó a las Américas.
4. Miguel de Cervantes Saavedra publicó la primera parte de *Don Quijote de la Mancha* en 1605.
5. La Guerra Civil española empezó en 1936.
6. El príncipe Juan Carlos de Borbón fue nombrado sucesor de Franco en 1968.
7. El dictador Francisco Franco murió en 1975.
8. España entró en la Comunidad Económica Europea en 1986 y adoptó el euro en 1999.

4-34 | **Obras maestras** Doña Rosa busca algunas obras de arte para decorar su casa. Como eres vendedor(a) de arte, tienes que escribir los números del precio en euros para cada obra.

The Triangular Hour de Salvador Dalí

Las Meninas de Diego Velázquez

MODELO: *The Triangular Hour* de Salvador Dalí 87.329.200,00 EUR.
ochenta y siete millones trescientos veintinueve mil, doscientos euros.

1. *Las Meninas* de Diego de Velázquez 655.450.150,00 EUR.

Duelo a garrotazos de Francisco Goya

Guernica de Pablo Picasso

2. *Duelo a garrotazos* de Francisco Goya 25.745.285,00 EUR.

3. *Guernica* de Pablo Picasso 975.475.110,00 EUR.

EN VOZ ALTA

4-35 **¿Cómo se dice... en español?** Escribe los siguientes números y luego exprésalos a un(a) compañero(a) de clase.

> MODELO: la fundación de esta universidad
> *1825: mil ochocientos veinticinco*

1. la población de esta ciudad
2. el año de tu nacimiento
3. el número de estudiantes de esta universidad
4. la cantidad de dinero que querías *(you would like to)* tener en el banco
5. la población de la Ciudad de México
6. el número de días en el año
7. el número de cartas electrónicas que recibes en un año
8. 100 × (tu edad)
9. 1.000 × (el número de chicas en esta clase)
10. 1.000 × (el número de chicos en esta clase)

4-36 **¿Cuánto cuesta?** *(How much is it?)* Estás en Tecnolandia, una tienda de electrodomésticos en Santiago. Doña Rosa quiere unas cosas nuevas para la Casa de la Troya, y tú tienes que comprarlas. Tienes 240,00 euros para comprarlo todo. ¿Qué vas a comprar? ¿Puedes comprar todo lo que ella quiere? Habla con dos compañeros(as) de clase sobre qué van a comprar, qué no van a comprar y por qué.

> MODELO: *Yo compro la aspiradora por 117 euros, el microondas por 94,50, la tostadora por 15,50 y los dos despertadores por 9,00. Así gasto 236 euros. No puedo comprarlo todo.*

Doña Rosa quiere:

una aspiradora nueva
dos despertadores
una tostadora
un sillón
un refrigerador
un horno de microondas

Tecnolandia ofrece:

Aspiradora Kirby, 117 EUR.
Despertador Timex, 4,50 EUR.
Tostadora Krupps, 15,50 EUR.
Sillón Chico Flojo, 70 EUR.
Refrigerador Whirlpool, 205 EUR.
Microondas Sony, 94,50 EUR.

¡A VER!

En este segmento del video, los cinco compañeros de casa ya se conocen bien y están muy contentos en su nueva casa, la Hacienda Vista Alegre. Vas a ver varias escenas en la casa, incluso escenas del primer día en la Hacienda. Los jóvenes recuerdan (remember) las partes diferentes de la casa y cómo dividieron (how they divided) las habitaciones.

Expresiones útiles

The following are some new expressions you will hear in the video.

Si no les molesta	If it doesn't bother you all
Vale	Okay

Antes de ver

Paso 1: Con un(a) compañero(a) de clase y basándose en lo que ya saben *(know)* de la Hacienda Vista Alegre y usando su imaginación, descríbanla: ¿Cómo es la Hacienda? ¿Es grande o pequeña? ¿Tiene muchos muebles y electrodomésticos? Hagan *(Make)* una lista de los cuartos, muebles y electrodomésticos que recuerdan o que piensan que están en la Hacienda Vista Alegre.

Cuartos	**Muebles y electrodomésticos**
_____	_____
_____	_____
_____	_____
_____	_____
_____	_____
_____	_____

Paso 2: Los compañeros de casa tienen que dividir entre ellos las habitaciones. Adivina *(Guess)* cuántas habitaciones hay en la Hacienda Vista Alegre. En tu opinión, ¿quiénes deben compartir una habitación? Compara tus respuestas con las de un(a) compañero(a). ¿Están de acuerdo?

Paso 3: ¿Cómo te sientes *(How do you feel)* cuando haces los quehaceres domésticos y otras actividades? Lea los siguientes escenarios y escribe la emoción que es más apropiada para ti. Luego compara tus respuestas con las de un(a) compañero(a). ¿Tienen mucho en común?

Cuando barro el piso, estoy _____.
Si salgo con mis amigos, estoy _____.
Si tengo que lavar los platos, estoy _____.
Cuando juego al tenis, estoy _____.
Si miro un partido de fútbol en la televisión, estoy _____.
Cuando miro una telenovela, estoy _____.

Después de ver

Paso 1: Ahora sabes aún más *(even more)* sobre la casa. En **Antes de ver, Paso 1,** tu compañero(a) y tú escribieron *(wrote)* una lista de los cuartos, muebles y elecrodomésticos de la Hacienda Vista Alegre. ¿Falta algo? *(Is something missing?)* Corrige tu lista arriba y luego contesta las siguientes preguntas.

- ¿Cuántas habitaciones tiene la Hacienda Vista Alegre? _____
- ¿Cuántos baños tiene? _____
- ¿Dónde está la habitación de Antonio? _____
- ¿Qué muebles tiene la habitación de Alejandra? _____

Paso 2: En **Antes de ver, Paso 2,** adivinaste quiénes iban a compartir las habitaciones. ¿Tenías razón? *(Were you correct?)* Escribe los nombres de las personas que comparten las habitaciones.

* _____ y _____ comparten una habitación.
* _____ y _____ comparten una habitación.
* _____ tiene una habitación sola.

Paso 3: En **Antes de ver, Paso 3,** escribiste tus actitudes y emociones ante ciertos escenarios. Ahora piensa en las actitudes de los compañeros de casa en este segmento del video. Completa las siguientes oraciones con la emoción apropiada.

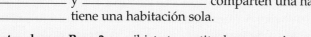

| contento | emocionado | enojado | triste |

* Sofía está _____ porque la habitación no tiene escritorio.
* Antonio está _____ porque le gusta molestar *(to bother)* a Valeria.
* Valeria está _____ con Antonio porque siempre hace bromas *(jokes around)*.
* Alejandra está _____ porque va a compartir el cuarto con Sofía.

¿Qué opinas tú?

Paso 1: Ahora que sabes cómo es la Hacienda Vista Alegre, piensa en tu Hacienda ideal. ¿Cuántas habitaciones tiene? ¿Tiene piscina? ¿Qué muebles hay? ¿Cómo son los cuartos? Escribe un párrafo para describir tu Hacienda ideal y luego comparte tu descripción con la de un(a) compañero(a). ¿Son similares sus casas ideales? ¿Qué aspectos tienen en común?

Paso 2: ¿Piensas que los compañeros de casa tienen muchos quehaceres domésticos? Con un(a) compañero(a), escriban una lista de los quehaceres domésticos que supuestamente tienen que hacer los jóvenes. Luego, decidan *(decide)* quién debe hacer cada quehacer doméstico y escriban su nombre al lado de la actividad en la lista.

Quehaceres domésticos	**¿Quién?**
_____	_____
_____	_____
_____	_____
_____	_____
_____	_____

Ahora imaginen que *(imagine that)* la Hacienda Vista Alegre está muy sucia y que Javier les dice a sus compañeros de casa lo que tienen que hacer para limpiarla. Usando su lista como guía, ayúdenlo a *(help him)* formar los mandatos para sus compañeros de casa.

¡Atención! ¡La casa está super sucia y tenemos que limpiarla! Yo voy a barrer el piso. Valeria, tú _____
Antonio, _____
y Sofía, _____
Alejandra, por favor _____

Paso 3: Imagina que vives en la Hacienda Vista Alegre con todo el grupo. ¿Te llevas bien *(Do you get along)* con los compañeros de casa? ¿Estás contento(a)? ¿Triste? ¿Enojado(a)? Completa las siguientes oraciones para indicar tus sentimientos. ¡Sé creativo(a)! *(Be creative!)*

* Yo estoy contento(a) cuando _____
* Yo estoy triste cuando _____
* Yo estoy enojado(a) cuando _____
* Yo estoy aburrido(a) cuando _____
* Yo estoy emocionado(a) cuando _____

¡A LEER!

Clustering words

Reading one word at a time is inefficient because it slows down your reading speed. Reading one word at a time can also lead to a great deal of frustration, as in many instances you will not know the meaning of every word in a given passage. It is more efficient to read meaningful groups of clusters of words.

Paso 1: Read the following ad to get the gist of its content.

70 m²

Un espacio integrado da vida a este apartamento, que tiene tres zonas prácticas: la sala de estar, el comedor y una cocina. También hay un dormitorio independiente. El equipo de decoradores de Estudio 48 hace la distribución del espacio y de los muebles. Los muebles pueden adaptarse a distintas situaciones y los materiales son duraderos y fáciles de limpiar. Los diseñadores utilizan colores brillantes que le dan a la casa una atmósfera funcional y limpia.

Paso 2: Based on what you read in the above ad, answer the following questions.

1. ¿Qué parte del apartamento no se menciona en el anuncio?
   a. la sala de estar   c. el comedor
   b. el garaje   d. la cocina
2. ¿Cómo son los materiales de los muebles?
   a. difíciles de limpiar   c. duraderos
   b. fáciles de limpiar   d. delicados
3. Los decoradores usan colores brillantes para la decoración.
   a. cierto   b. falso

Paso 3: Now reread the ad at your usual reading speed and try to pull out information you may have missed during the first reading. Concentrate on reading clusters of three words, as indicated by the red circles that appear in the body of the text. Then complete the following checklist.

Según el artículo, en el apartamento hay...

_____ un dormitorio independiente.

_____ un balcón.

_____ una chimenea.

_____ una atmósfera limpia y funcional.

Paso 4: Read the following ad, **"Concepto urbano,"** and circle clusters of words that appear in meaningful groups. Use the pictures provided for additional clues about the content of the passage.

Concepto urbano

El salón o sala de estar es la parte central del piso. Los decoradores hacen un espacio abierto con diferentes zonas, aprovechando al máximo la luz natural. El sofá tiene forma de ele (L), con una silla larga tapizada en algodón crudo. Frente a la sala de estar hay un ambiente que funciona como comedor y zona de trabajo. Santiago Nin de DM diseña la mesa y la librería pintadas con el mismo color de las paredes. La estantería tiene su propia luz y también tiene apliques instalados en la parte superior. Los jarrones son de cerámica mongol, de la Compañía Francesa de Oriente y de China. Las sillas de Philippe Starck se utilizan en el comedor y en la sala de estar y cierran la zona de reunión.

Paso 5: Read the previous ad again, making sure to pay attention to the word clusters you identified in **Paso 4.** Then, answer the following questions.

1. ¿Cuáles son los muebles más importantes del piso?
2. Describe el sofá.
3. ¿Dónde están los jarrones?
4. ¿Te gusta el «concepto urbano» de la sala? ¿Por qué?

¡A ESCRIBIR!

Strategy: Writing topic sentences

The first step in writing a well-structured paragraph is to formulate a clear, concise topic sentence. A good topic sentence has the following characteristics:

- It comes at the beginning of a paragraph.
- It states the main idea of the paragraph.
- It focuses on only one topic of interest.
- It makes a factual or personal statement.
- It is neither too general nor too specific.
- It attracts the attention of the reader.

 Paso 1: Below you will find five possible topic sentences for a paragraph a student has written about the house in which he lives in the north of Spain. Discuss the sentences with a classmate, focusing on the characteristics listed above.

1. Hay cuatro alcobas y dos baños en la casa.
2. La cocina no es muy grande pero tiene los electrodomésticos más importantes.
3. La casa, situada en una parte histórica de la ciudad, es el lugar ideal para un estudiante universitario.
4. El jardín es muy bonito porque los residentes de la casa riegan las plantas frecuentemente.

Paso 2: In your opinion, which is the best sentence to begin the paragraph? Why?

Task: Writing a property description

Functions: Writing an introduction; Describing objects
Vocabulary: House: bathroom, bedroom, furniture, kitchen, living room
Grammar: Verbs: **estar, tener;** Progressive tenses; Position of adjectives

Property descriptions often appear in several different contexts. Individuals who wish to sell or rent property provide them for prospective tenants and buyers. In addition, students may prepare written descriptions of their living quarters for friends and family members who live far away and are not able to see them. In this activity, you will prepare a property description. You may choose a real property or an imaginary one to describe.

Paso 1: Choose a property to describe. It may be your current house or apartment, one you know from the past, or one you hope to live in one day. Write a topic sentence for a paragraph describing the property, keeping in mind the characteristics listed above.

Paso 2: Write five or six sentences about the property, developing the idea stated in your topic sentence. If you have a photograph of the property or wish to prepare a sketch of it, you may want to submit it with your written description.

 Paso 3: Share your paragraph with a classmate and discuss how you might improve the topic sentence, focusing on the characteristics of a good topic sentence and its relationship to the rest of the paragraph. You may use the following checklist questions as a guide: Does the topic sentence . . .

1. come at the beginning of the paragraph?	___ yes	___ no
2. state the main idea of the paragraph?	___ yes	___ no
3. focus on only one topic of interest?	___ yes	___ no
4. make a factual or personal statement?	___ yes	___ no
5. seem neither too general nor too specific?	___ yes	___ no
6. attract the attention of the reader?	___ yes	___ no

Paso 4: Share your paragraph with several other class members. After you have read several descriptions, identify one or two properties that you find particularly interesting.

¡A CONVERSAR!

Pronunciation focus: *s, ce, ci,* and *z*

In most of the Spanish-speaking world, the pronunciation of **s, c** before **e** and **i,** and **z** is similar to but stronger than the English pronunciation of **s.** In most of peninsular Spain, the sound of **c** before **e** and **i** and of **z** is similar to the English *th.* Practice the following sentences.

Hay un sofá, dos sillones y una mesita en la sala.
Necesito sacar la basura, hacer la cama y pasar la aspiradora el sábado.
La clase comienza a las doce y diez.

Task: Describing the house of your dreams

Perhaps one day you will have the opportunity to build the house of your dreams, **el hogar de tus sueños.** It's never too early to start making plans! In this activity you will make some decisions about your dream house and compare your ideas with those of your classmates.

Paso 1: Make a list of at least five important characteristics of your dream house. Consider the following questions:

- ¿Qué tipo de residencia es?
- ¿Cuántos pisos tiene?
- ¿Cuántos cuartos tiene y qué son?
- ¿Cuáles son las otras características importantes?

Paso 2: Work with a partner and share your ideas about your dream house. Ask each other questions about the information presented and note the similarities and differences in your preferences. If you wish, prepare a sketch of your dream house and describe the sketch to your partner.

Paso 3: Form a group with two other students and continue sharing ideas about your ideal homes. Try to identify at least one characteristic that all the dream houses have in common. Also try to identify a unique feature in each dream house. If you wish, try to convince your classmates that the features you value most be included in their dream homes.

La casa The house

la alfombra carpet
la bañera bathtub
la cocina kitchen
el comedor dining room
el cuarto de baño bathroom
el dormitorio bedroom

la ducha shower
la escalera stairs
el inodoro toilet
el jardín garden
el lavabo bathroom sink
la pared wall

el piso floor
la puerta door
la sala living room
el sótano basement
la ventana window

Los muebles Furniture

el armario wardrobe, armoire, closet
la cama bed
la cómoda dresser
el escritorio desk

el espejo mirror
el estante bookshelf
la lámpara lamp
la mesa table

la mesita coffee (side) table
la silla chair
el sillón easy chair, arm chair
el sofá sofa, couch

Los electrodomésticos Appliances

la aspiradora vacuum cleaner
el despertador alarm clock
la estufa stove
el horno (de microondas) (microwave) oven

la lavadora washing machine
el lavaplatos dishwasher
la plancha iron
el refrigerador refrigerator

la secadora clothes dryer
la tostadora toaster

Los quehaceres domésticos Chores

barrer el piso to sweep the floor
cortar el césped to mow the lawn
hacer la cama to make one's bed
lavar (los platos, la ropa, las ventanas)
   to wash (dishes, clothes, windows)

limpiar la casa to clean the house
pasar la aspiradora to vacuum
planchar (la ropa) to iron (clothes)
poner la mesa to set the table

quitar la mesa to clear the table
regar (ie) las plantas to water the plants
sacar la basura to take out the garbage

Los números 100 y más Numbers 100 and higher

100 cien (ciento + *número*)
200 doscientos(as)
300 trescientos(as)
400 cuatrocientos(as)
500 quinientos(as)

600 seiscientos(as)
700 setecientos(as)
800 ochocientos(as)
900 novecientos(as)
1.000 mil

2.000 dos mil
20.000 veinte mil
200.000 doscientos(as) mil
1.000.000 un millón
2.000.000 dos millones

Adjetivos

aburrido(a) bored
contento(a) happy
desordenado(a) messy
emocionado(a) excited
enfermo(a) sick

enojado(a) angry
furioso(a) furious
limpio(a) clean
ocupado(a) busy
ordenado(a) neat, orderly

preocupado(a) worried
sucio(a) dirty
triste sad

Expresiones idiomáticas

tener calor to be hot
tener celos to be jealous
tener frío to be cold

tener ganas de to feel like (doing something)
tener miedo (de) to be afraid (of)
tener paciencia to be patient

tener que to have to (do something)

Verbos

almorzar (ue) to have lunch
cerrar (ie) to close
comenzar (ie) to begin
conseguir (i) to get, obtain
contar (ue) to count; to tell
costar (ue) to cost
empezar (ie) to begin
entender (ie) to understand

decir (i) to say; to tell
dormir (ue) to sleep
jugar (ue) to play
llover (ue) to rain
morir (ue) to die
pedir (i) to ask for
pensar (ie) to think
perder (ie) to lose; to miss (a function)

poder (ue) to be able
preferir (ie) to prefer
querer (ie) to want; to love
regar (ie) to water
seguir (i) to continue; to follow
servir (i) to serve
venir (ie) to come
volver (ue) to return

Preposiciones de lugar

al lado de next to, beside
cerca de near
con with
debajo de under, below

delante de in front of
detrás de behind
en in; on
encima de on top of

entre between; among
lejos de far from
sobre on; over

La salud:

Chapter Objectives

COMMUNICATIVE GOALS

In this chapter you will learn how to . . .

- Identify parts of the body
- Describe daily routines and hygienic practices
- Talk about what you have just finished doing
- Talk about illnesses and health conditions
- Describe people, things, and conditions
- Point out people and things

STRUCTURES

- Reflexive pronouns and present tense of reflexive verbs
- **Acabar de** + *infinitive*
- **Ser** vs. **estar**
- Demonstrative adjectives and pronouns

CULTURAL INFORMATION

- Bolivia y la salud
- Tradición de hierbas: Yerba mate en Paraguay y las hojas de coca en los Andes

Bolivia y Paraguay

BOLIVIA

Población: 8.300.463
Área: 1.098.580 kilómetros cuadrados, más o menos tres veces el tamaño de Montana
Capitales: La Paz (sede del gobierno), 810.300; Sucre (sede jurídica), 180.900
Ciudades principales: Santa Cruz, 1.089.400; El Alto, 766.100; Cochabamba, 558.500
Moneda: el dólar estadounidense
Lengua: el español, el quechua y el aymará (oficiales)

PARAGUAY

Población: 5.734.139
Área: 406.752 kilómetros cuadrados, el tamaño de California
Capital: Asunción, 569.800
Ciudades principales: Ciudad del Este, 234.000; Encarnación, 70.000; Villarrica, 83.000
Moneda: el guaraní
Lenguas: el español, el guaraní, el fronterizo (inoficial)

¡Bienvenidos a Bolivia!

En este video vas a aprender mucho sobre la cultura de Bolivia. Después de ver el video, contesta las siguientes preguntas.

1 ¿Dónde está Bolivia y cuál es su población?

2 ¿Cuál es la capital de Bolivia?

3 ¿Cuál es el porcentaje (%) de la población indígena en Bolivia?

4 ¿Cómo se llaman los diferentes grupos indígenas y qué impacto tienen en la cultura Boliviana?

5 ¿Te gustaría visitar Bolivia? ¿Por qué sí o por qué no?

La Plaza San Francisco,
La Paz, Bolivia

VOCABULARIO El cuerpo humano

CULTURA

Montero is a medium-size city in the tropical, lowland region of Bolivia, an hour north of Santa Cruz (Bolivia's second largest city). Montero is currently experiencing a large influx of people from surrounding rural areas who hope to improve their lives by migrating to the city.

En el centro de salud rural andino In this section you will learn how to talk about parts of the body by learning about Juan Carlos Guarabia and his work at the Andean Rural Health Center in Montero, Bolivia. Does your university sponsor trips to developing countries to assist with public health care?

¿NOS ENTENDEMOS?

Some useful expressions that name parts of the body are: **hablar hasta por los codos** (*to talk a lot*), **tener mucha cara** (*to have a lot of nerve*), **tomarse algo a pecho** (*to take something to heart*), **valer un ojo de la cara** (*to be worth an arm and a leg*), and **tomar el pelo** (*to pull somebody's leg*).

¿NOS ENTENDEMOS?

El cabello and **el pelo** are words that refer to hair. It is usually more polite to refer to **el cabello** when somebody is describing the hair.

Palabras útiles are presented to help you enrich your personal vocabulary. The terms provided here will help you talk about parts of the body.

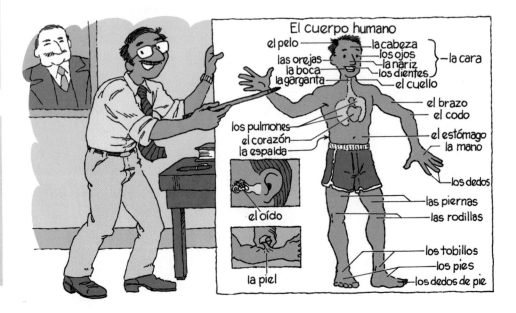

El cuerpo humano

el pelo — la cabeza
las orejas — los ojos
la boca — la nariz
la garganta — los dientes — la cara
el cuello
el brazo
el codo
los pulmones
el corazón
la espalda
el estómago
la mano
los dedos
las piernas
las rodillas
los tobillos
los pies
los dedos de pie
el oído
la piel

Palabras útiles

la cadera hip
las cejas eyebrows
el cerebro brain
el hueso bone
los labios lips
la lengua tongue
las mejillas cheeks
los músculos muscles
los muslos thighs
las pantorillas calves
el pecho chest
las pestañas eyelashes
las uñas fingernails

¡A PRACTICAR!

5-1 **¡No es lógico!** Identifica la palabra que no va con el grupo y explica por qué.

MODELO: los dedos, las manos, *los dientes*
Los dientes son parte de la cabeza; los dedos y las manos son parte del brazo.

1. la boca, la cabeza, el brazo
2. el corazón, el cabello, el estómago
3. los pulmones, la nariz, el oído
4. los dedos, las rodillas, los tobillos
5. la garganta, la cara, el estómago
6. las piernas, los pies, los codos, los dedos del pie/de los pies
7. el brazo, el codo, los dientes, las manos
8. los ojos, la boca, la espalda, las orejas, los dientes

5-2 **Asociaciones** ¿Qué parte del cuerpo asocias con las siguientes actividades?

MODELO: respirar
la nariz, la boca, los pulmones

1. hablar
2. comer
3. pensar
4. escribir
5. beber
6. caminar
7. escuchar
8. leer

5-3 **Anatomía 101** Tienes que darle una clase de anatomía a Juan Carlos, pero tu dibujo no tiene los nombres de las partes del cuerpo. Escribe los nombres en los espacios.

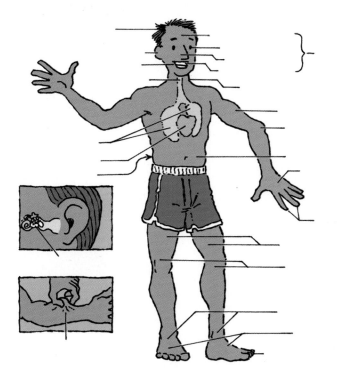

EN VOZ ALTA

5-4 **Retratos *(Portraits)* de un extraterrestre** Descríbele a un(a) compañero(a) las características físicas de un extraterrestre *(an alien)* mientras *(while)* tu compañero(a) lo dibuja. Después de dibujar, tu compañero(a) tiene que explicarte los atributos.

MODELO: *El extraterrestre tiene piernas cortas, pero dos brazos muy largos. Tiene pelo azul y largo. Tiene ojos anaranjados. La cara es pequeña pero la boca es grande. Tiene dos orejas enormes.*

EN CONTEXTO

La señora Mendoza y su hija Carolina están en una clínica, llenando (*filling out*) su historial clínico (*medical history*) y además están hablando con el doctor Chávez. Carolina piensa que está muy enferma.

Dr. Chávez:	¿Cómo **se siente** su hija hoy, señora Mendoza?
Sra. Mendoza:	Dice que **está muy mal** y que no puede asistir a la escuela. Hoy por la mañana (*This morning*) empiezan las clases y, es la primera vez (*first time*) que Carolina va solita (*all by herself*) a la escuela. Lleva tres días en cama mirando la tele. Generalmente **es** una niña muy **sana** (*healthy*).
Dr. Chávez:	Mmm... Carolina, **¿te duele el estómago?**
Carolina:	¡Ayyy! Sí, me duele mucho el estómago.
Dr. Chávez:	**¿Tienes fiebre?**
Sra. Mendoza:	Dice que sí, pero **acabo de tomarle la temperatura** y tiene 37 grados, o sea, normal.
Dr. Chávez:	Vamos a ver... ¿Tienes **dolor de cabeza?**
Carolina:	¡Sí! Y **tengo tos** (*cough*), y **estoy mareada** (*dizzy*) y... y... y **este lado** del cuerpo me duele mucho.
Dr. Chávez:	Parece que **estás muy grave,** Carolina. Tenemos que operarte inmediatamente. Creo que tienes la «escuelacitis». Es una condición del cerebro.
Carolina:	¿Una operación? ¿El cerebro? Pues... la verdad es que ahora me encuentro (*I'm feeling*) un poco mejor.

¿NOS ENTENDEMOS?

The expression **o sea** is frequently used in daily speech to provide further clarification, such as saying *I mean* or *in other words.*

¿NOS ENTENDEMOS?

Spanish speakers use the verb **llevar** (*to carry*) to indicate how long someone has been experiencing a condition, for example: **Carolina lleva tres días en cama. Llevar** is also used to indicate how long someone has been living in a certain place: **Nosotros lleva-mos dos años en Bolivia.** (*We've been living in Bolivia for two years.*)

¿Comprendiste?

Contesta las siguientes preguntas a base del diálogo.

1. ¿Está realmente enferma Carolina?
2. ¿Tiene síntomas verdaderos?
3. ¿Por qué recomienda una operación el doctor Chávez?
4. ¿Por qué se siente mejor Carolina al final?

Encuentro cultural

Bolivia y la salud

PARA PENSAR

- ¿Te gustan las montañas?
- ¿Qué montañas conoces?
- ¿Cómo te sientes cuando vas a las montañas?

La Paz, la capital de Bolivia, es la capital más alta del mundo, situada en la región del altiplano a 3.000 metros *(10,000 feet)* sobre el nivel del mar; por eso, las personas sufren de mareos *(dizziness)*. La severidad

La Paz, Bolivia

del mareo está relacionada con la altura, la rapidez de la subida *(climb)*, el esfuerzo físico *(physical exertion)* y la aclimatación. Los síntomas del mareo son: dolor de cabeza, insomnio, náuseas, debilidad *(weakness)* y jadeo *(panting)*. Estos síntomas pueden comenzar a las 48 horas después de subir y pueden desaparecer uno a siete días después de acostumbrarse *(get used to)* a la altura.

Para aclimatarse, es mejor subir *(to climb, go up)* a un nivel intermedio en intervalos de dos a cuatro días. Es importante descansar antes de seguir subiendo. Hay que beber mucho líquido y comer carbohidratos. Para el dolor de cabeza y la fiebre se puede tomar aspirina, pero las personas deben consultar con los médicos antes de tomar medicamentos especiales.

PARA DISCUTIR

1. ¿Cuál es la característica principal de la capital de Bolivia?
2. ¿Por qué la gente sufre de mareos?
3. ¿Cuáles son los síntomas del mareo?
4. ¿Qué puede hacer la gente para aclimatarse?
5. ¿Quieres visitar La Paz? ¿Por qué sí o por qué no?

A reflexive construction consists of a **reflexive pronoun** and a verb. In English, reflexive pronouns end in -*self* or -*selves*; for example: *myself, yourself, ourselves*. In Spanish, reflexive pronouns are used with some verbs (called **reflexive verbs**) that reflect the action back to the subject of a sentence, meaning that the subject of the verb also receives the action of the verb. In the following example, notice how Juan Carlos is both the subject and recipient of the action of getting himself up.

Subject Reflexive Pronoun Verb

Juan Carlos	**se**	levanta	a las ocho.
Juan Carlos	*gets (himself) up*		*at eight.*

Conjugating reflexive constructions

Reflexive verbs are identified by the pronoun **-se** attached to the end of the infinitive form of the verb. To conjugate these verbs, use a reflexive pronoun (e.g., **me**) with its corresponding verb form (e.g., **levanto**), according to the subject of the sentence (e.g., **yo**).

Reflexive infinitive: levantarse *(to get up)*

subject	reflexive pronoun + verb form	
yo	me levanto	*I get up*
tú	te levantas	*you* (informal) *get up*
Ud., él/ella	se levanta	*you* (formal) *get up, he/she gets up*
nosotros(as)	nos levantamos	*we get up*
vosotros(as)	os levantáis	*you* (informal) *get up*
Uds., ellos(as)	se levantan	*you* (formal and informal) *get up, they get up*

Note that when reflexive verbs are used with parts of the body or with articles of clothing, the definite article (**el, la, los, las**) precedes the noun, as shown in the following examples.

Juan Carlos se cepilla **los** dientes.	*Juan Carlos brushes his teeth.*
Sara está poniéndose **el** pijama.	*Sara is putting on her pajamas.*
Tomás va a lavarse **el** cabello.	*Tomás is going to wash his hair.*

Placing reflexive pronouns

- Place the pronoun in front of the conjugated verb.

Juan Carlos **se levanta** a las ocho.	*Juan Carlos gets up at eight.*

- When a reflexive verb is used as an infinitive or as a present participle, place the pronoun either before the conjugated verb (if there are two or more verbs used together) or attach it to the infinitive or to the present participle.

When a reflexive pronoun is attached to a present participle (e.g., **levantándose**), an accent mark is added to maintain the correct stress.

Sara **se va a levantar** pronto. or Sara **va a levantarse** pronto.	*Sara is going to get up soon.*
Sara **se está levantando** ahora. or Sara **está levantándose** ahora.	*Sara is getting up now.*

Reflexive vs. Nonreflexive verbs

When the action is performed on another person, a reflexive pronoun is not used. Compare these two examples:

Me despierto a las ocho.　　　　　*I wake up at eight o'clock.*
Despierto a mi mamá a las ocho.　　*I wake up my mom at eight.*

Verbos reflexivos de la rutina diaria y personal

acostarse (ue) to go to bed	**levantarse** to get up
afeitarse to shave	**maquillarse** to put on makeup
bañarse to take a bath	**peinarse** to comb one's hair
cepillarse los dientes to brush one's teeth	**pintarse** to put on makeup
cuidarse to take care (of oneself)	**ponerse (la ropa)** to put on (one's clothes)
despertarse (ie) to wake up	**quitarse (la ropa)** to take off (one's clothes)
dormirse (ue) to fall asleep	**secarse (el cuerpo)** to dry off (one's body)
ducharse to take a shower	**vestirse (i)** to get dressed
lavarse to wash up	

¡A PRACTICAR!

5-5　**Los domingos por la mañana** Completa las siguientes oraciones, usando las formas correctas de los verbos entre paréntesis y tu información personal.

MODELO: (afeitarse) Todos los días Juan Carlos ___se afeita___ pero yo nunca
　　　　　___me afeito.___

1. (levantarse) Los domingos Juan Carlos y Sara 1. _____ a las ocho, y Tomás, su hijo, 2. _____ a las nueve. Yo 3. _____ a las diez.
2. (cepillarse) Después, el esposo y la esposa siempre 1. _____ los dientes, pero a veces Tomás no 2. _____ los dientes. Y yo 3. _____.
3. (ducharse) Juan Carlos y Tomás se bañan en tina *(bathtub)*, pero Sara prefiere 1. _____. Yo prefiero 2. _____.
4. (vestirse) Juan Carlos y Sara 1. _____ elegantemente, y Tomás 2. _____ de jeans. Yo 3. _____ de... A veces, mis amigos y yo 4. _____ de...
5. (peinarse) Después, Juan Carlos y Sara 1. _____ bien, pero Tomás no 2. _____ porque es un poco perezoso. Y yo también (tampoco) 3. _____ bien.

5-6　**¡Qué mujer más ocupada!** Para comprender la vida diaria que tiene Sara durante la semana, completa las siguientes descripciones conjugando los verbos entre paréntesis. Nota que la primera descripción es de Sara y la segunda es de su esposo.

Sara:
　　Los días de trabajo Yo 1. _____ (despertarse) a las siete. Yo 2. _____ (levantarse) a las siete y cuarto. Primero, yo voy al baño, donde 3. _____ (ducharse) por diez minutos. Cuando tengo más tiempo, 4. _____ (bañarse) en la tina. Después, 5. _____ (secarse) bien todo el cuerpo y 6. _____ (peinarse).

Juan:
　　Entonces Sara 7. _____ (vestirse) elegantemente, 8. _____ (maquillarse) la cara y 9. _____ (ponerse) un poco de perfume. Después, desayuna y habla con nosotros. Luego ella 10. _____ (cepillarse) los dientes y sale de la casa. Ella camina al hospital, donde trabaja como enfermera. Sara trabaja por cinco horas hasta *(until)* la una de la tarde. Luego vuelve a casa. Ella 11. _____ (lavarse) las manos y almuerza con nosotros.

5-7 **Las actividades diarias de Tomás** Basándote en los dibujos, explícale a un(a) compañero(a) de clase lo que está haciendo Tomás en cada dibujo. Luego explícale lo que va a hacer mañana.

MODELOS: *Tomás está despertándose a las seis.*
o *Tomás se está despertando a las seis.*

Tomás se va a despertar mañana a las seis.
o *Tomás va a despertarse mañana a las seis.*

Primero   **Luego**   **Después**

1. _____ 2. _____ 3. _____
_____ _____ _____
_____ _____ _____
_____ _____ _____

Más tarde   **Finalmente**

4. _____ 5. _____
_____ _____
_____ _____
_____ _____

5-8   **Preferencias personales** Con un(a) compañero(a), comparen lo que hacen las siguientes personas los días de la semana con lo que hacen durante los fines de semana. Túrnense escogiendo *(choosing)* el sujeto que va con los verbos. Usen el pronombre reflexivo correcto.

yo
tú
mi mejor amigo(a) y yo
nuestro(a) profesor(a)
nuestro(a)s compañero(a)s de clase

MODELO: levantarse: *yo*
              Los días de la semana me levanto a las seis, pero los fines de semana,
              me levanto a las nueve.

1. peinarse
2. vestirse
3. ducharse
4. acostarse
5. dormirse

5-9   **Tus actividades diarias** Con un(a) compañero(a) de clase, contesten las siguientes preguntas.

1. ¿A qué hora te levantas normalmente? ¿Te levantas inmediatamente después de despertarte? ¿Te bañas en la tina o te duchas? ¿Prefieres bañarte por la mañana o por la noche? ¿Desayunas con tu compañero(a) de cuarto/casa? O si vives con tu familia, ¿desayunas con tu familia? ¿Siempre te cepillas los dientes después del desayuno?

2. Si eres mujer, ¿te maquillas todos los días? Si eres hombre, ¿te afeitas los fines de semana? ¿Te peinas durante el día, o solamente antes de salir?

3. ¿A qué hora almuerzas normalmente? ¿Duermes la siesta a veces después del almuerzo? De noche, ¿comes algo para la cena? ¿Ayudas a lavar los platos después? ¿A qué hora te gusta acostarte? Normalmente, ¿te duermes fácilmente? En general, ¿miras la tele o lees algún libro antes de dormir?

5-10   **Mis actividades diarias** Explícale tu rutina diaria a un(a) compañero(a) de clase. Tu compañero(a) debe dibujar tus actividades y usar el dibujo para explicarle las actividades a la clase.

ASÍ SE DICE Talking about things you have just finished doing: *acabar de* + infinitive

Acabar de + *infinitive* is a way speakers of Spanish talk about things that have just taken place without using the past tense. Literally, **acabar de** + *infinitive* means *to have just finished doing something.*

Juan Carlos **acaba de ver** a tres pacientes.
Juan Carlos has just seen three patients.

¡A PRACTICAR!

5-11 **Mamá, ¡acabo de hacerlo!** Tu mamá sugiere varias actividades para algunas personas en la familia. Dile que ya están hechas *(are done)*, usando **acabar de.**

MODELO: ¿Por qué no te bañas?
Yo me acabo de bañar.
o *Yo acabo de bañarme.*

1. ¿Por qué no se cepillan los dientes tú y tu hermana menor después del almuerzo?
2. ¿Por qué no se visten para la fiesta tus amigos?
3. ¿Por qué no se afeita tu padre?
4. ¿Por qué no tomas una siesta?
5. ¿Por qué no se peina tu mejor amiga?

5-12 **¡Adivina lo que acaba de hacer esa gente!** Las siguientes personas acaban de hacer algo. Tú y un(a) compañero(a) de clase tienen que adivinar lo que acaban de hacer, basándose en la información que tienen.

MODELO: Sara sale del baño. Tiene el cabello mojado *(wet).*
Sara acaba de bañarse.

1. Tomás se levanta de la cama.
2. Sarita y Tomás se levantan de la mesa. Son las ocho de la mañana.
3. Juan Carlos sale de su cuarto. Tiene puesta ropa elegante para una fiesta.
4. El doctor Chávez entra por la puerta de la clínica. Son las nueve de la mañana.
5. La señora Martínez sale del consultorio *(doctor's office)* del doctor Chávez.
6. Juan Carlos y Sara están en la cama y apagan la luz *(turn off the light).*

EN VOZ ALTA

5-13 **¿Quién acaba de... ?** Tienes dos minutos para buscar a alguien en la clase que acabe de hacer las siguientes cosas. Después de encontrar a alguien para cada categoría, pídele que firme *(sign)* tu lista. Al final del juego, cuéntales a tus compañeros(as) lo que acabas de saber.

MODELO: acabar de pasar dos horas estudiando
Tú: *Susie, ¿acabas de pasar dos horas estudiando?*
Susie: *Sí, acabo de pasar dos horas estudiando.* (Susie signs your paper.)
o Susie: *No, no acabo de pasar dos horas estudiando.* (Susie doesn't sign your paper and you look for someone else.)
Al final: *Susie acaba de estudiar dos horas. John y Heather acaban de levantarse tarde...*

Categorías

1. comer algo
2. cepillarse los dientes
3. llegar a clase de prisa
4. ver al doctor
5. tomar aspirina
6. tomar una ducha rápidamente *(quickly)*

VOCABULARIO La salud

En la clínica del Centro de Salud Rural Andino In this section you will learn how to talk about common illnesses and discuss treatments and remedies. In the drawing below, Dr. Carlos Dardo Chávez, the director of the clinic, is busy treating patients.

¿NOS ENTENDEMOS?
Unlike a medical doctor, a **curandero(a)** is a keeper of folkloric tradition while providing health-related consultations and remedies for various types of illnesses. A **curandero(a)** may provide psychological counseling and ritualistic motivation along with traditional herbal remedies, many of which have been used for centuries and some of which are now being employed in modern medicine.

Los problemas médicos

la alergia allergy
el catarro cold
congestionado(a) congested
el dolor de oídos (de cabeza) earache (headache)

la enfermedad illness
mareado(a) dizzy
el resfrío cold
el síntoma symptom

Verbos relacionados con la salud

doler (ue) (a alguien) to be painful (to someone)
enfermarse to get sick
estar enfermo(a) to be sick
estar resfriado(a) to have a cold
estar sano(a) to be healthy
estornudar to sneeze
examinar to examine
guardar cama to stay in bed
resfriarse to catch a cold
sentirse (bien/mal) to feel (good/bad)

tener dolor de cabeza to have a headache
tener escalofríos to have chills
tener fiebre to have a fever
tener gripe to have a cold
tener náuseas to be nauseous
tener tos to have a cough
tomarle la temperatura to take (someone's) temperature
toser to cough

The verb **doler** *(to hurt, be painful)* is used like the verb **gustar**, with indirect object pronouns (**me, te, le, nos, os,** and **les**) and only the third person singular and plural conjugations of the verb (**duele** and **duelen**). Rather than saying *my leg hurts,* Spanish speakers say *my leg is painful to me* (**me duele la pierna**). As with reflexive verbs, when one is using **doler** to talk about a body part, the definite articles (**el, la, los, las**) are used.

Palabras útiles

la ambulancia ambulance
el antiácido antacid
el diagnóstico diagnosis
la inyección shot

las lentillas/los lentes de contacto contact lenses
la radiografía X-ray
sala de urgencias/sala de emergencia emergency room
el tratamiento treatment

Palabras útiles are presented to help you enrich your personal vocabulary. The terms provided here will help you talk about health and health care.

¡A PRACTICAR!

5-14 **¿Qué recomiendas?** El doctor Chávez te explica algunos casos para ver lo que recomiendas para tratar *(treat)* cada enfermedad de la lista. Empareja cada enfermedad con el tratamiento *(treatment)* apropiado.

MODELO: Una persona que tiene *catarro* debe *tomar jarabe.*

Una persona que tiene...

1. fiebre
2. gripe
3. dolor de cabeza
4. tos
5. un problema grave
6. dolor de estómago
7. náuseas
8. escalofríos

debe...

tomar jarabe
descansar un poco
tomar Pepto-Bismol
tomar antibióticos
tomar aspirina
hablar con un(a) médico(a)
ir a una clínica
guardar cama

5-15 **¿Qué te duele?** Completa las siguientes oraciones con la forma correcta del verbo **doler** y el pronombre de objeto indirecto correspondiente.

MODELO: A Esteban ___le duele la mano.___

1. A mí le duelen los oídos

2. A Carolina y a Susi _____.

3. A ellos _____.

4. A ti _____.

5. A nosotros _____.

EN VOZ ALTA

5-16 **¿Qué haces para cuidarte?** Con un(a) compañero(a) de clase, haz preguntas sobre las siguientes enfermedades con las personas en el lado izquierdo. Túrnense recomendando un tratamiento para cada caso.

> MODELO: tú / tener tos
> E1: *¿Qué haces cuando tienes tos?*
> E2: *Yo tomo un jarabe para la tos y descanso más.*

tu mejor amigo(a)	estar congestionado(a)
tú	estar mareado(a)
tu compañero(a) de cuarto	enfermarse gravemente
tus padres	resfriarse
tu profesor(a)	sentirse mal
tú y tu compañero(a) de cuarto	tener dolor de estómago

5-17 **Conversación sobre la salud** Con un(a) compañero(a) de clase, habla de las siguientes preguntas sobre la salud.

1. ¿Qué haces cuando tienes catarro? ¿Tomas algún medicamento? ¿Tienes escalofríos cuando tienes un catarro?

2. ¿Tienes dolor de cabeza con mucha o poca frecuencia? ¿Qué haces cuando tienes dolor de cabeza? ¿Tomas aspirina?

3. ¿Qué haces cuando tienes náuseas? ¿Tomas Pepto-Bismol? ¿Te sientes mareado(a) a menudo? Si tienes náuseas, ¿guardas cama?

4. ¿Tienes un resfrío con más frecuencia en el verano o en el invierno? ¿Te da fiebre a veces? ¿Qué otros síntomas tienes cuando estás resfriado(a)? ¿Estornudas a veces? ¿Te da tos?

5. ¿Cómo te sientes hoy? ¿Te sientes bien, mal o más o menos? ¿Estás sano(a), o tienes una enfermedad? ¿Estás congestionado(a)? ¿Estás tomando algún medicamento?

5-18 **En la sala de urgencias** Habla con otro(a) estudiante: una persona es el (la) médico(a) y la otra persona es su paciente. El (La) paciente tuvo *(had)* un accidente y le duelen muchas partes de su cuerpo. El (La) médico(a) tiene que preguntarle qué le duele y recomendarle un tratamiento. Recuerda que entre doctor y paciente, normalmente se usa la forma de **usted.** Después, comparte el diálogo con la clase.

> MODELO: Médico(a): *¿Qué le duele?*
> Paciente: *Me duele el brazo, me duelen las piernas y me duele el cuello.*
> Médico(a): *Usted tiene que guardar cama por una semana y tomar pastillas para el dolor.*

ESTRUCTURA II Describing people, things, and conditions: *ser* vs. *estar*

As you have learned, the verbs **ser** and **estar** both mean *to be*, but they are used to express different kinds of information. In this section you will review the uses of **ser** and **estar**, two verbs that express the idea *to be* in English, and learn to better distinguish between the contexts for both verbs.

The verb **ser** often implies a fundamental quality or characteristic that describes or defines the essence of a person, thing, place, or idea. Use **ser** to express the following information:

• Identity	**Soy** el doctor Carlos Dardo Chávez. ¡Mucho gusto!
• Origin and nationality	**Soy** de Bolivia. **Soy** boliviano.
• Profession	El Dr. Chávez **es** médico.
• Characteristics of people and places	El doctor **es** alto e inteligente. La Paz, la capital de Bolivia, **es** una de las ciudades más altas del mundo.
• Possession	La clínica **es** de la comunidad.
• Time of day and dates	**Son** las dos de la tarde. **Es** sábado. **Es** el 24 de junio.
• Intentions	**Es** para ti, Sara. **Es** para tu cumpleaños.
• Impersonal statements	**Es** importante comer frutas y vegetales.
• Mathematical equations	Cinco más treinta **son** treinta y cinco.
• Location of events	La fiesta de los voluntarios de la clínica **es** en mi casa.

The verb **estar** often indicates a state or condition of a person, place, thing, or action at a given moment, which may be the result of a change or a deviation from the norm. Use **estar** to express the following information:

• Location of people	**Estoy** en casa.
• Location of things	La clínica **está** en Monteros.
• Location of places	Monteros **está** en Bolivia.
• Physical condition	**Estoy** cansado.
• Emotional condition	**Estoy** preocupada.
• Action in progress	**Estoy** trabajando.
• Weather expressions	**Está** despejado. **Está** lloviendo.

Ser and *estar* with adjectives

Ser and **estar** can be used with the same adjectives to communicate different ideas. In some cases, the choice of **ser** or **estar** can radically change the meaning of the sentence. Consider the following examples:

Ser	**Estar**
Carlos **es guapo.** *Carlos is handsome.* (*Carlos is a handsome man.*)	Carlos **está** muy **guapo** hoy. *Carlos looks unusally handsome today.*
Los voluntarios **son listos.** *The volunteers are smart.*	Los voluntarios **están listos.** *The volunteers are ready.*
Sara **es aburrida.** *Sara is boring.* (*Sara is a boring person.*)	Sara **está aburrida.** *Sara is bored.*
La fruta **es verde.** *The fruit is green (color).*	La fruta **está verde.** *The fruit is unripe.*

¿NOS ENTENDEMOS?

Marital status: The verbs **ser** and **estar** can be used to describe marital status. Most speakers use **ser** with **soltero(a)** and **viudo(a)**: **Grace es soltera y Roberto es viudo, hacen una buena pareja** (*they look good together*). **Soltero(a)** and **viudo(a)** are seen as defining the essence of a person. Most speakers use **estar** with **casado(a)**, since it is an adjective that comes from a verb; for example, **Sofía está casada con Manuel desde 2002 y están muy contentos.**

¡A PRACTICAR!

5-19 **Una visita a Bolivia: ¿*Ser* o *estar*?** Las personas que visitan Bolivia deben aprender un poco sobre el país antes de viajar allí. Indica si debes usar **ser** o **estar** para completar las siguientes oraciones de una guía turística sobre este país.

MODELO: Bolivia es / está un país de América del Sur.
Bolivia *es* un país de América del Sur.

1. La Paz es / está la capital de Bolivia.
2. La ciudad de La Paz es / está en la cordillera de los Andes.
3. La Paz es / está la ciudad más alta de América del Sur.
4. La ciudad de Cochabamba es / está al sureste *(southeast)* de La Paz.
5. El presidente de Bolivia es / está presidente durante cinco años.
6. El lago Titicaca, un lago muy importante entre Bolivia y Peru, es / está el lago navegable más alto del mundo.
7. Los turistas dicen que los bolivianos son / están muy simpáticos.
8. Es / Está necesario descansar más después de llegar al altiplano de Bolivia.
9. Muchos turistas en Bolivia son / están descansando ahora porque no están acostumbrados a la altura.
10. Hay muchos conciertos de música andina, la música típica de la región. Esta noche el concierto es / está en la ciudad de Santa Cruz.
11. Muchas personas no saben dónde son / están las ruinas de Tihuanaco, un sitio arqueológico cerca del lago Titicaca.
12. Esta guía turística es / está para las personas que van a visitar el país.

5-20 **La fiesta de los voluntarios** Completa la siguiente descripción y conversación con las formas correctas de los verbos **ser** y **estar**.

*Hoy 1. _____ sábado, 24 de junio. 2. _____ las dos de la tarde. Hace calor y
3. _____ lloviendo un poco. La temperatura 4. _____ a 26 grados centígrados. Juan
Carlos, su familia y unos amigos del Centro Salud Rural Andino 5. _____ comiendo
un pastel con Roberto, un voluntario de los Estados Unidos. La fiesta 6. _____ en su
apartamento. Roberto 7. _____ hablando con su amiga Rachel.*

Roberto:	Mmm. ¡Qué pastel más rico, Rachel!
Rachel:	¿Te gusta? 8. _____ tu pastel favorito.
Roberto:	Pero 9. _____ tan grande, Rachel.
Rachel:	Sí, cómo no. El pastel 10. _____ para muchas personas que 11. _____ aquí hoy.
Roberto:	Perdón, ¿dónde 12. _____ el Dr. Chávez?
Rachel:	Él 13. _____ durmiendo ahora, Roberto.
Roberto:	¿14. _____ enfermo?
Rachel:	No, él 15. _____ un poco cansado.
Roberto:	Él 16. _____ trabajando mucho en estos días.
Rachel:	Sí. Él 17. _____ muy dedicado.

EN VOZ ALTA

5-21 | **Datos personales** Con un(a) compañero(a) de clase, haz y contesta preguntas con los verbos **ser** y **estar** sobre los siguientes temas.

1. **La personalidad:** Ask about his/her personality in general and his/her emotional and physical state today.
2. **El pueblo:** Ask about his/her hometown, where it is, what it looks like, and whether it's big or small.
3. **La familia:** Ask about his/her family (size, ages, physical features, personalities).
4. **La fiesta ideal:** Ask about the date, the location, the time. For whom is the party?

5-22 | **Encuentra a alguien que...** Tienes dos minutos para buscar a una persona de tu clase para las siguientes categorías. Después de encontrar a alguien para cada categoría, pídele que firme tu lista. Al final del juego, cuéntales a tus compañeros(as) lo que acabas de saber. Ten cuidado con el uso de **ser** y **estar** en esta actividad.

MODELO: ser de Indiana
      Tú: *Brian, ¿eres de Indiana?*
      Brian: *Sí, soy de Indianápolis.* (Brian signs your paper.)
  o Brian: *No, no soy de Indiana. Yo soy de Colorado.* (Look for someone else for this category.)
      Al final: *Brian (no) es de Indiana... Cecilia está contenta... Bob es estudiante de medicina...*

1. estar enfermo(a)
2. ser una persona muy sana
3. estar contento(a)
4. ser estudiante de medicina
5. estar congestionado(a)
6. ser fumador(a) *(smoker)*

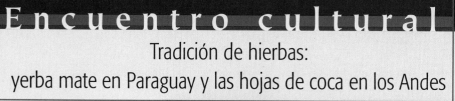

Tradición de hierbas:
yerba mate en Paraguay y las hojas de coca en los Andes

PARA PENSAR

- ¿Qué sabes de la hoja de coca o de la yerba mate?

- ¿En qué países de Sur América se usan estas hierbas?

- En tu familia, ¿alguien usa hierbas medicinales? ¿Para qué?

La coca es una planta de los países andinos. Los nativos del imperio Tahuantisuyo, de los países de Bolivia, Perú, Ecuador y el norte de Argentina, cultivan la planta antes de la llegada de los españoles. En los Andes no hay otra planta más apreciada por los indígenas que la coca. Las hojas *(leaves)* se usan en ritos religiosos y en la medicina folklórica de la región. Los indígenas no mastican las hojas por su sabor *(taste)*, sino *(rather)* por su efecto fisiológico y psicológico.

Los andinos usan las hojas de coca para aliviar el dolor de cabeza, el mareo y **el soroche.** Masticar la coca también sirve para aliviar el cansancio *(tiredness)*, el hambre y la sed. Por virtud de su profundo significado místico y espiritual en la religión, la cultura, la salud y el trabajo, la hoja de coca es un símbolo en la identidad del indígena andino.

Los indígenas de Paraguay y de Argentina usan la yerba mate desde antes de los conquistadores españoles al igual que las hojas de coca en los Andes. Los indígenas guaraníes (nombre de los indígenas de Paraguay) usan la yerba mate para aumentar la inmunidad, limpiar y desintoxicar la sangre, ayudar al sistema nervioso *(nervous system)*, restaurar *(to refresh)* el color joven del cabello, luchar *(to fight)* contra la fatiga, reducir *(to reduce)* el estrés y eliminar el insomnio. La yerba mate posee todos los minerales y las vitaminas necesarios para vivir con poca comida; por eso algunos gobiernos sudamericanos les enseñan a las madres de pocos recursos económicos *(economic resources)* a incluir la yerba mate en la dieta *(nutritional diet)* de los niños que van a la escuela primaria. Muchos voluntarios del Cuerpo de Paz *(Peace Corps)* observan casos en que muchas personas están con buena salud por muchos años aún en largos períodos de sequía *(dry seasons)* y hambre *(hunger)* solamente por beber grandes cantidades de yerba mate.

PARA DISCUTIR

1. ¿Cuáles son los países andinos donde se mastica la coca?
2. ¿Qué problemas médicos alivia la coca / la yerba mate?
3. ¿Qué significado tiene la coca en la cultura andina?
4. ¿Por qué es importante incluir la yerba mate en la dieta de los niños paraguayos?
5. ¿Se cultivan la hoja de coca u otro tipo de hierba en tu país? ¿Por qué sí o por qué no? ¿Estás de acuerdo con eso o no? ¿Por qué?

CULTURA

The Incan Empire was divided into four regions: Antisuyo, Collasuyo, Contisuyo, and Chinchasuyo.

CULTURA

El **soroche** is a Quechua word that means *altitude sickness*.

In this section you will learn how to specify people, places, things, and ideas.

Demonstrative adjectives

You can use demonstrative adjectives to point out a specific noun. Note that these adjectives must agree in gender (masculine or feminine) and number (singular or plural) with the noun to which they refer.

Singular	Plural
este(a) *this*	**estos(as)** *these*
ese(a) *that*	**esos(as)** *those*
aquel (aquella) *that (over there)*	**aquellos(as)** *those (over there)*

Note that in order to point out people, things, and places that are far from the speaker and from the person addressed and to indicate something from a long time ago, Spanish speakers use forms of the demonstrative adjective **aquel.** For example:

> **Este paciente** tiene dolor de estómago, **ese paciente** en la otra cama tiene fiebre y **aquel paciente** en la otra sala tiene náuseas. **Estos pacientes** que tenemos hoy no están tan enfermos como *(as sick as)* **aquellos pacientes** del mes pasado.

este historial clínico *this clinical history*	**estos historiales clínicos** *these clinical histories*
esta pastilla *this pill*	**estas pastillas** *these pills*
ese jarabe *that cough syrup*	**esos jarabes** *those cough syrups*
esa cama *that bed*	**esas camas** *those beds*
aquel doctor *that doctor*	**aquellos doctores** *those doctors*
aquella clínica *that clinic*	**aquellas clínicas** *those clinics*

Demonstrative pronouns

Demonstrative pronouns are used in place of nouns and must agree with them in gender (masculine or feminine) and number (singular or plural). These forms all carry accents to distinguish them from the demonstrative adjectives:

Singular	Plural
éste(a)	**éstos(as)**
ése(a)	**ésos(as)**
aquél (aquélla)	**aquéllos(as)**

—¿Quieres ir a esa farmacia?	*Do you want to go to that pharmacy?*
—Sí, a **ésa.**	*Yes, to that one.*
—¿Son tuyos aquellos libros?	*Are those books (over there) yours?*
—Sí, **aquéllos** son míos.	*Yes, those are mine.*

Neuter demonstrative pronouns

The words **esto** *(this)*, **eso** *(that)*, and **aquello** *(that over there)* can refer either to non-specific things that are not yet identified or to ideas that were already mentioned.

—¿Qué es **esto,** mamá?	*What's this, Mom?*
—Es un termómetro.	*It's a thermometer.*
—¿Sabes usar **eso,** papá?	*Do you know how to use that, Dad?*
—Sí, es fácil.	*Yes, it's easy.*

¡A PRACTICAR!

5-23 | **La clínica nueva de la Cruz Roja** El doctor Chávez está muy impresionado con la nueva clínica de la Cruz Roja y está mostrándoles el nuevo centro médico a los dos voluntarios del Cuerpo de Paz, Roberto y Rachel. Completa los comentarios, usando **este, esta, estos** o **estas** correctamente.

MODELO: **Dr. Chávez:** Amigos, entramos aquí, por _____*esta*_____ puerta.

Roberto: ¡Qué bonita! 1. _____ clínica tiene de todo.
Dr. Chávez: Sí, somos muy afortunados. Por fin la gente de 2. _____ barrio tiene un buen lugar para tratamientos médicos.
Rachel: ¿Y 3. _____ personas? ¿Todas vienen para consultas (*consultations*) hoy?
Dr. Chávez: Sí, en _____ días tenemos muchos pacientes porque hay un equipo (*team*) de médicos aquí de Italia. Y 4. _____ semana viene otro grupo de los Estados Unidos.
Roberto: ¿Cuánto tienen que pagar _____ personas por las consultas?
Dr. Chávez: _____ consultas no son totalmente gratis (*free*), pero solamente cobramos (*we charge*) según la capacidad (*according to the means*) de cada persona.

5-24 | **Para aclarar** Imagínate que estás en la librería de tu universidad comprando cosas para tus clases. Responde a las preguntas de modo positivo o negativo usando los adjetivos demostrativos **ese, esa, esos** o **esas.**

MODELO: ¿Quieres este libro?
Sí, quiero ese libro. o *No, no quiero ese libro.*

1. ¿Quieres estos bolígrafos?
2. ¿Necesitas estas mochilas?
3. ¿Te gusta ver este cuaderno?
4. ¿Compras este libro de texto?
5. ¿Buscas esta alfombra para tu cuarto?
6. ¿Estás aquí con estas personas?

5-25 | **Para aclarar más** Repite tus respuestas a las preguntas de la Actividad 5-24, pero ahora contesta las preguntas con los pronombres demostrativos de **ése, ésa, ésos** o **ésas.**

MODELO: ¿Quieres este libro?
Sí, quiero ése. o *No, no quiero ése.*

EN VOZ ALTA

5-26 | **Una venta (*sale*) en la clase** Trabajando con tres o cuatro compañeros(as) de clase, arreglen (*arrange*) las siguientes cosas en una mesa: dos libros, dos mochilas, dos bolígrafos y dos tareas de español. Una persona es el (la) vendedor(a) (*the seller*) y los otros son los clientes (*customers*). El (La) vendedor(a) y los clientes deben usar las formas correctas de los adjetivos o pronombres demostrativos de la conversación.

MODELO: E1: *¿Quieres comprar este libro?*
E2: *No, no quiero ese libro. Prefiero aquel libro.*
E1: *¿Ese libro?*
E2: *Sí, aquél.*

5-27 | **¿Conoces a aquel chico?** Trabajando con un(a) compañero(a) de clase, haz preguntas sobre los miembros de tu clase, usando adjetivos o pronombres demostrativos. Cada persona debe hacer cinco preguntas, y dos de ellas deben ser en la forma plural.

MODELO: E1: *¿Conoces a aquellos chicos?*
E2: *¿Esos chicos con la profesora?*
E1: *Sí, aquéllos.*
E2: *Sí, son Darius y Renault.*

¡A VER!

En este segmento del video, los compañeros de casa van a aprender un baile folklórico llamado la bomba puertorriqueña. Desafortunadamente, uno de ellos también sufre de un problema de salud.

Expresiones útiles

The following are some new expressions you will hear in the video.

¿Qué les parece?	How does that sound to you?
Me lastimé el tobillo	I hurt my ankle
De acuerdo	Okay
No me quedó otra opción	I didn't have any other choice

Antes de ver

Paso 1: ¿Tienes accidentes de vez en cuando *(every now and then)*? ¿Te lastimas *(Do you injure)* partes de tu cuerpo? Da algunos ejemplos de las partes del cuerpo que has lastimado *(that you have injured)* en el pasado.

Paso 2: Imagina que son las nueve de la noche y los compañeros de casa están para *(are about to)* acostarse. Adivina *(Guess)* todas las actividades que acaban de hacer durante el día. Completa las siguientes oraciones con lo que piensas que acaba de hacer cada uno de ellos.

Pienso que...

• Antonio acaba de _____.
• Alejandra acaba de _____.
• Sofía acaba de _____.
• Valeria acaba de _____.
• Javier acaba de _____.

Después de ver

Paso 1: En **Antes de ver, Paso 1**, pensaste en los accidentes y las partes del cuerpo que tú te has lastimado. Ahora, piensa en *(think about)* el accidente de Alejandra. Lee las siguientes oraciones y ponlas *(put them)* en órden cronológico según el video.

_____ Alejandra se lastima el tobillo y no puede bailar.
_____ Alejandra decide descansar, ¡pero solamente si puede salir con el instructor esa noche!
_____ Los jóvenes llegan al salón de baile.
_____ Valeria no quiere bailar y se sienta.
_____ El instructor dice que Alejandra no puede bailar más y que necesita descansar.
_____ Alejandra se jacta *(brags)* de ser la mejor bailarina de todo el grupo.
_____ Valeria tiene que bailar con Antonio.
_____ Alejandra se sienta y habla con el instructor sobre su dolor.
_____ El instructor explica los pasos del baile y los cuatro empiezan a bailar un poco.
_____ Alejandra dice que no le duele la rodilla, pero el pie le duele mucho. También dice que se rompió *(she broke)* la pierna hace un año *(a year ago)*.

Paso 2: En **Antes de ver, Paso 2**, adivinaste las actividades que acaban de hacer los compañeros de casa. Después de ver el video, sabes exactamente lo que los muchachos acaban de hacer hoy. Empareja las personas con las actividades que acaban de hacer.

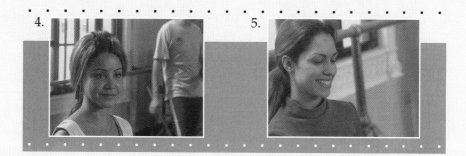

_____ No puedo bailar bien, pero acabo de aprender un poco.

_____ Yo acabo de divertirme mucho bailando con Sofía.

_____ Aunque el pie me duele mucho, estoy muy contenta porque acabo de salir con Víctor, el instructor de baile.

_____ Acabo de bailar con dos chicas muy guapas hoy.

_____ No me gusta bailar pero acabo de bailar con Antonio.

¿Qué opinas tú?

Paso 1: En este segmento, Alejandra no se siente bien porque le duele el pie. Ahora imagina que tú estás enfermo(a) y tu compañero(a) es el (la) médico(a). Describe tus síntomas a él/ella. ¿Tienes tos? ¿Estás mareado(a)? ¿Te duele algo? Luego, cambien de papel. ¡Sean creativos! *(Be creative!)*

Paso 2: ¿Qué piensas que los compañeros de casa hacen en un día típico? Escoge *(Choose)* uno(a) de los compañeros y escribe una lista de lo que normalmente hace durante el día. Por ejemplo, ¿se levanta tarde o temprano? ¿Se ducha o se baña? ¿Se viste muy casual o muy elegante? ¿Adónde va? Comparte tus respuestas con la clase. ¿Tienen mucho en común?

¡A LEER!

Strategy: Recognizing Spanish affixes

An affix is added to the beginning (prefix) or to the end (suffix) of a word stem to create a new word. Knowing the meaning of Spanish affixes can significantly increase your ability to read Spanish effectively.

Paso 1: Escribe el significado en inglés de los prefijos y los sufijos que siguen. Observa la lista de ejemplos para comprender el significado de cada afijo.

Español	Inglés	Ejemplos
Prefijos		
auto-	self-	**auto**control, **auto**defensa, **auto**estima
mono-	mono- (one)	**mono**lingüe, **mono**polio
mal-	bad, ill	**mal**tratar, **mal**estar
bi-	two, bi-	**bi**lingüe, **bi**cicleta, **bi**mestre
tri-	three, tri-	**tri**lingüe, **tri**ángulo, **tri**mestre
im-	not	**im**posible, **im**paciente, **im**parcial
in-	not	**in**necesario, **in**mortal, **in**creíble
Sufijos		
-mente	-ly	especial**mente**, rápida**mente**
-ado, -ada	-ed	ocup**ado**, motoriz**ado**, divorci**ada**
-oso, -osa	-ous	maravill**oso**, gener**oso**, fabul**osa**
-dad, -tad	-ty	oportuni**dad**, ciu**dad**, liber**tad**
-ción, -sión	-sion, -tion	conversa**ción**, ac**ción**, televi**sión**

Paso 2: Ahora, vas a leer un texto sobre la automedicación. Usa lo que sabes para contestar ¿Qué significa **la automedicación**? Escribe una definición en inglés y usa tus propias palabras.

Paso 3: Antes de leer el texto, piensa en tu propia experiencia e indica las respuestas que son verdaderas para ti.

¿Qué haces cuando te enfermas?

- ☐ Primero hablo con un(a) médico(a) y después él/ella me da una receta.
- ☐ Voy a la farmacia para comprar medicina.
- ☐ Le pido pastillas a un(a) amigo(a).
- ☐ Tomo una combinación de varias medicinas.
- ☐ Tomo la dosis (*dose*) necesaria de la medicina, según las instrucciones.

Paso 4: Ahora lee el texto. Usa lo que sabes sobre los afijos en español para comprender el texto.

1. Escribe el equivalente en inglés de las palabras que siguen.
   a. malestar
   b. anticoagulantes
   c. indicadas
   d. previamente
   e. peligroso
   f. combinación

2. Escribe los equivalentes en español de las expresiones que siguen.
   a. secondary effects
   b. dangerous combinations
   c. miniature adult

Nunca debes automedicarte más de cinco días seguidos: si siguen los síntomas, ve al médico.

Los cinco mandamientos de la automedicación:

1. Lee las instrucciones cuidadosamente.

Sigue las instrucciones cuidadosamente *(cautiously),* inclusive *(including)* la posología (el número de pastillas, de cápsulas, gotas, etc.). Tomar más pastillas no va a hacer al medicamento más eficaz *(efficient),* pero va a aumentar *(increase)* los efectos secundarios. Y es necesario tomar los medicamentos antes o después de las comidas, porque así se va a ayudar a curar *(cure)* la enfermedad *(illness).*

2. Sigue tratamientos a corto plazo.

El tratamiento no debe pasar más de cinco o siete días. Si siguen los síntomas, debes ir a ver al (a la) médico(a).

3. Ten cuidado con las combinaciones peligrosas.

No se deben mezclar *(to mix)* dos medicamentos distintos porque puede ser peligroso *(dangerous).* Una sustancia puede limitar o aumentar el efecto de otra medicina. Por ejemplo, los anticoagulantes junto con la aspirina aumentan *(increase)* el riesgo de hemorragia.

4. No debes medicar a los niños.

Un niño no es un adulto en miniatura y darle una medicina sin preguntarle al (a la) médico(a) puede ser muy peligroso y arriesgado, especialmente si el niño tiene seis años o menos. Siempre hay que darles a los niños medicina después de *(after)* consultar con el (la) médico(a).

5. Pídele consejo *(Ask for advice)* a tu farmacéutico.

No todos los remedios funcionan de la misma manera en todas las personas. El (La) farmacéutico(a) puede hacer el papel *(play the role)* de asesor(a), con respecto a los medicamentos.

¡A ESCRIBIR!

Strategy: Using a bilingual dictionary

A bilingual dictionary is a useful tool that, when used properly, can enhance the quality, complexity, and accuracy of your writing in Spanish. It is very important, however, that you learn to use it correctly. Here are some suggestions to help you use your bilingual dictionary properly.

1. When you look up the Spanish equivalent of an English word, you will often find several meanings for the same word, often appearing like this:

    cold: *n.* **frío, catarro, resfriado**
             adj. **frío**

2. In larger dictionaries, additional information may be given that will clarify meanings and uses.

    cold: *n.* **frío** *(low temperature);* **catarro** *(illness);* **resfriado** *(illness)*
             adj. frío

3. Pay attention to certain abbreviations in your dictionary that will tell you what type of word you have found. Notice the abbreviations *n.* and *adj.* in the examples above, indicating that the word is a noun or an adjective. Some of the more common abbreviations you will find are listed below. Their Spanish equivalents are in parentheses.

    n. noun (**sustantivo**)
    adj. adjective (**adjetivo**)
    adv. adverb (**adverbio**)
    conj. conjunction (**conjunción**)
    prep. preposition (**preposición**)
    v. verb (**verbo**)

4. Looking up a lot of different words in a bilingual dictionary when you are writing is inefficient. If you insist on looking up too many words as you write, you may become frustrated or feel like you want to give up altogether. It is wiser and faster to use the phrases you already know in Spanish as much as possible, rather than trying to translate too many new words you don't know from English to Spanish. You will learn more and more new words as you continue reading and listening to the language.

 Paso 1: Busca las siguientes palabras inglesas en tu diccionario bilingüe y escribe su equivalente en español en una hoja de papel.

1. wall (e.g., in a house)
2. to grade (e.g., to correct)
3. bank (e.g., of a river)

Paso 2: Indica si las palabras son sustantivos, verbos, adjetivos, adverbios, etcétera.

Paso 3: Compara tus respuestas con las de un(a) compañero(a) de clase. Si ustedes tienen preguntas, hablen con el (la) profesor(a).

Task: Writing a health report

Health reports may be written in a variety of situations and they may be official or unofficial, formal or quite informal. A physician or other health professional may ask a patient to complete a form that contains a narrative about the patient's current condition. Individuals may prepare health reports before they undertake new or strenuous activity such as participation in a sport. It is also common in personal correspondence to include an informal health report. You will now write a report of your own health that might be included in a letter to your parents or provided for a health care provider, coach, or other person who needs information about your current condition.

Paso 1: Prepara una lista de seis aspectos importantes de tu condición física actual *(current).* Puedes incluir aspectos positivos como: **Tengo mucha energía porque hago ejercicio regularmente,** y problemas como: **Me duele la cabeza cuando estudio mucho.**

Paso 2: Decide si tu estado físico es, en general, bueno o malo basándote en la información de **Paso 1.**

Paso 3: Escribe un informe de diez oraciones, explicando tu condición física e incluyendo la siguiente información.

- cuántos años tienes
- si tu condición es, en general, buena o mala
- un mínimo de cinco aspectos importantes de tu condición con los detalles *(details)* necesarios y adecuados

Paso 4: Cambia de papel con un(a) compañero(a) de clase. Lee el informe de tu compañero(a). Después, comenta con el (la) compañero(a) los aspectos positivos y negativos presentados en los informes y decide si uno(a) o los (las) dos necesita(n) hacer una cita con el (la) médico(a).

Functions: Describing health; Talking about the present
Vocabulary: Health: diseases and illnesses; Medicine
Grammar: Verbs: **ser & estar**

¡A CONVERSAR!

Pronunciation focus: *p* and *t*

The letters **p** and **t**, when placed at the beginning of a word, have a softer sound in Spanish than in English. In Spanish, the sounds are similar to the *p* in *spill* and the *t* in *still*. Practice these sentences:

- El paciente toma una pastilla porque tiene catarro.
- Me duelen los pies, las piernas y los pulmones cuando corro mucho.
- Tengo tos y necesito tomar jarabe.

Task: Discussing health conditions

Muchos estudiantes llevan una vida acelerada *(fast paced)* y difícil. Es importante considerar las actividades que una persona hace y el efecto que tienen en su salud. Trabaja con un(a) compañero(a) para considerar la siguiente información y para decidir si las actividades que tú haces te causan problemas a ti.

Paso 1: Preséntale a tu compañero(a) información sobre las actividades que haces en una semana típica y los efectos que tienen en tu estado físico. Por ejemplo: **Camino o corro a clase todos los días. Me duelen las piernas y los pies. Duermo solamente cinco o seis horas por noche. Frecuentemente me despierto con un dolor de cabeza y estoy cansado en clase.**

Paso 2: Escucha la información que tu compañero(a) presenta sobre sí mismo(a) *(him/herself)*.

Paso 3: Ofrécele consejos a tu compañero(a) sobre lo que debe hacer para reducir los efectos negativos en su salud. Por ejemplo: **Debes acostarte más temprano y dormir siete u ocho horas por noche.** Entonces, escucha los consejos que él/ella te presenta a ti.

Paso 4: Hablen sobre lo que ustedes van a hacer para mejorar *(improve)* la salud. Por ejemplo: **Voy a hacer ejercicio tres o cuatro veces a la semana y voy a dormir más.**

El cuerpo humano The human body

la boca mouth
los brazos arms
el cabello / el pelo hair
la cabeza head
la cara face
los codos elbows
el corazón heart
el cuello neck
los dedos fingers

los dedos del pie/de los pies toes
los dientes teeth
la espalda back
el estómago stomach
la garganta throat
las manos hands
la nariz nose
el oído inner ear
los ojos eyes

las orejas (outer) ears
la piel skin
las piernas legs
los pies feet
los pulmones lungs
las rodillas knees
los tobillos ankles

Verbos de la rutina diaria y personal Daily and personal routine verbs

acabar de + *infinitive* to have just (done
    something)
acostarse (ue) to go to bed
afeitarse to shave
bañarse (en la tina) to take a bath
cepillarse los dientes to brush one's teeth
cuidarse to take care (of oneself)

despertarse (ie) to wake up
dormirse (ue) to fall asleep
ducharse to take a shower
lavarse to wash up
levantarse to get up
maquillarse to put on makeup
peinarse to comb one's hair

pintarse to put on makeup
ponerse (la ropa) to put on (one's clothes)
quitarse (la ropa) to take off (one's clothes)
secarse (el cuerpo) to dry off (one's body)
vestirse (i) to get dressed

La salud Health

el antibiótico antibiotic
la aspirina aspirin
el (la) enfermero(a) nurse
la farmacia pharmacy
el jarabe cough syrup

la medicina medicine
el (la) médico(a) physician, doctor
el (la) paciente patient
la pastilla pill

la receta prescription
la sala de espera waiting room
la sala de urgencias/la sala de emergencia
    emergency room

Los problemas médicos Medical problems

la alergia allergy
el catarro cold
congestionado(a) congested

el dolor de oídos (de cabeza) earache
    (headache)
la enfermedad illness

mareado(a) dizzy
el resfrío cold
el síntoma symptom

Verbos relacionados con la salud Health-related verbs

dolerle (ue) (a alguien) to be painful (to
    someone)
enfermarse to get sick
estar enfermo(a) to be sick
estar resfriado(a) to have a cold
estar sano(a) to be healthy
estornudar to sneeze

examinar to examine
guardar cama to stay in bed
resfriarse to catch a cold
sentirse (bien/mal) to feel (good/bad)
tener dolor de cabeza to have a headache
tener escalofríos to have chills
tener fiebre to have a fever

tener gripe to have a cold / the flu
tener náuseas to be nauseous
tener tos to have a cough
tomarle la temperatura (a alguien) to take
    (someone's) temperature
toser to cough

¿Quieres comer conmigo esta noche?:

Chapter Objectives

COMMUNICATIVE GOALS

In this chapter you will learn how to . . .

- Talk about foods and beverages for breakfast, lunch, and dinner
- Make comparisons
- Order food in a restaurant
- Describe past events in detail

STRUCTURES

- Comparatives and superlatives
- Verbs regular in the preterite
- Verbs with stem and spelling changes in the preterite

CULTURAL INFORMATION

- La comida típica venezolana
- Los postres venezolanos

Venezuela

VENEZUELA

Población: 24.655.000
Área: 912.051 kilómetros
cuadrados, más de dos veces
el tamaño de California
Capital: Caracas, 5.000.000
Ciudades principales: Maracaibo,
1.249.700; Valencia, 903.600;
Barquisimeto, 625.500
Moneda: el bolívar
Lenguas: el español y 35 idiomas
indígenas

¡Bienvenidos a Venezuela!

**En este video, vas a aprender
mucho sobre Venezuela y su capital,
Caracas. Después de ver el video,
contesta las siguientes preguntas:**

1 ¿Cómo es la ciudad de Caracas?

2 ¿Puedes nombrar uno de los héroes de la historia venezolana que el video menciona? ¿Por qué es famoso?

3 ¿Qué sabes de la educación en Venezuela?

4 ¿Cuáles son algunas actividades típicas de los caraqueños
(las personas que viven en Caracas)? ¿Qué tipo de cafés
son muy populares en Caracas?

5 ¿Te gustaría visitar Caracas? ¿Por qué sí o por qué no?

La Plaza Bolívar,
Caracas, Venezuela

VOCABULARIO La comida

El menú del restaurante de doña Margarita In this section you will practice talking about foods by learning about doña Margarita's restaurant, El Criollito, on the east side of Caracas.

CULTURA
Venezuelan food, just like food from the Caribbean and other countries in South America, is known as **comida criolla** and features a mix of Spanish and Caribbean influences. For instance, in Maracaibo the "Café Trapos" is well known for its Pabellón—shredded meat served with fried plantain, black beans, and rice. In Caracas, "Café Cacique" is well known for its Parilla—marinated beef cooked over a grill. In Cumaná, "El Fogón de la Arepa" is well known for its Arepas—flat pancakes made from yellow corn flour, water, and salt. They are deep-fried or baked and are filled with butter, meat, or cheese, and in Ciudad Guayana the restaurant "La Llovizna" is well known for its empanadas—Spanish-style meat pastries.

¿NOS ENTENDEMOS?
There are four ways to order coffee in Venezuela: **un negrito** (black espresso coffee served in a demitasse), **un marroncito** (with a little milk added and served in a demi-tasse), **un marrón** (more coffee than milk and served in a coffee cup), and **café con leche** (less coffee and more hot milk added and served in a coffee cup). **La gaseosa** is another term for **el refresco**.

¿NOS ENTENDEMOS?
Various countries use different words for *banana*: **el plátano** in Spain and parts of Latin America such as Perú, **la banana/el banano** in some Latin American countries, **el guineo** in Puerto Rico, and **el cambur** in Venezuela.

Palabras útiles are presented to help you enrich your personal vocabulary. The words here will help you talk about dining at home and in restaurants.

El Criollito

Para empezar
las arepas (la especialidad de la casa)
la ensalada de la casa (lechuga, tomate, huevo duro)
la sopa de verduras
el pan (tostado)

To begin with
arepas (the house specialty)
house salad (lettuce, tomato, hard-boiled egg)
vegetable soup
bread (toast

Platos principales
La carne
la carne de res (bistec) con arroz y champiñones
las chuletas de cerdo en salsa de tomate
el sándwich de jamón y queso
el pavo con verduras
el pollo asado
la hamburguesa (con queso) y papas

Main dishes
Meats
beef (steak) with rice and mushrooms
pork chops in tomato sauce
ham and cheese sandwich
turkey with vegetables
roasted chicken
hamburger (cheeseburger) with french fries

Mariscos y pescado del día
la langosta
los camarones fritos
los calamares fritos

Shellfish and fish of the day
lobster
fried shrimp
fried calamari (squid)

Bebidas
el agua mineral con/sin gas
el café
la cerveza
el jugo de fruta
la leche
los refrescos
el té (helado)
el vino (blanco, tinto)

Beverages
carbonated/noncarbonated mineral water
coffee
beer
fruit juice
milk
soft drinks
(iced) tea
(white, red) wine

Postres
las frutas: manzana, naranja, banana
el flan casero
el helado

Desserts
fruit: apples, oranges, bananas
homemade caramel custard
ice cream

Las comidas Meals

almorzar (ue) to have (eat) lunch
el almuerzo lunch
la cena dinner, supper
cenar to have (eat) dinner (supper)
desayunar to have (eat) breakfast
el desayuno breakfast

Los condimentos Condiments

el aceite oil
el azúcar sugar
la mantequilla butter
la pimienta pepper
la sal salt
el vinagre vinegar

Palabras útiles

la copa goblet, wine glass
la cuchara spoon
el cuchillo knife
el mantel tablecloth
el pimentero pepper shaker
el plato plate

el salero salt shaker
la servilleta napkin
la taza cup
el tenedor fork
el vaso glass

¡A PRACTICAR!

6-1 **Un menú desorganizado** Doña Lupe está organizando el menú para su restaurante. Ayúdala a encontrar la comida que no forma parte del grupo. En cada número también indica lo que tienen en común los otros tres artículos *(items)*.

1. las chuletas, los camarones, el helado, el pescado
2. el vino tinto, el té, la cerveza, el vino blanco
3. el bistec, los calamares, la langosta, el pescado
4. el pavo, la carne de res, el pollo, el faisán *(pheasant)*
5. los champiñones, las papas, las manzanas, la lechuga
6. la mantequilla, el helado, el flan, las frutas
7. la sal, el azúcar, el aceite, los sándwiches

6-2 **¿Qué bebidas te gustan?** Escogiendo de la lista de bebidas a la derecha, completa las siguientes oraciones para expresar tus preferencias.

1. Para el desayuno, prefiero tomar...
2. Cuando estudio en casa, tomo...
3. Cuando tengo mucha sed, bebo...
4. Para el almuerzo, me gusta beber...
5. En las fiestas siempre tomo...
6. Los fines de semana me gusta tomar...
7. Para la cena prefiero beber...
8. Cuando estoy en el cine, tomo...

leche
café
té
vino tinto/blanco
agua mineral
jugo de naranja
un refresco
una cerveza

> **¿NOS ENTENDEMOS?**
> In Spain, **las papas** are referred to as **las patatas, jugo de naranja** is referred to also as **zumo de naranja** when people want to drink orange juice. In Puerto Rico, however, **jugo de naranja** is referred to as **jugo de china**.

EN VOZ ALTA

6-3 **Una invitación** Conversa con un(a) compañero(a) de clase para hacer planes para una comida durante el fin de semana. ¡Sé creativo(a)!

Estudiante A

1. Saluda a tu amigo(a).

3. Dile que no puedes aceptar su invitación. Habla de los planes que ya tienes.
5. Acepta la invitación. Dale las gracias a tu amigo(a). Pregúntale sobre la invitación.
7. Pregúntale si su familia va a estar en el almuerzo, o no.
9. Despídete.

Estudiante B

2. Contéstale a tu amigo(a) y pregúntale cómo está él/ella. Después invita a tu amigo(a) a un almuerzo en casa el sábado.
4. Reacciona a lo que dice tu amigo(a). Invítalo(la) al almuerzo otro día.
6. Responde a sus preguntas.
8. Contesta si tu familia va a estar en el almuerzo.
10. Responde.

6-4 **Entrevista** Pregúntale a otro(a) compañero(a) de clase sobre su rutina a la hora de comer. Después comparte esta información con la clase. ¿Tienen mucho en común tus compañeros de clase?

1. **el desayuno:** ¿A qué hora desayunas? ¿Desayunas solo(a) o con otras personas? ¿Qué prefieres tomar por la mañana, café, té, leche o jugo? ¿Qué te gusta comer para el desayuno?
2. **el almuerzo:** Normalmente, ¿dónde almuerzas? ¿Con quién te gusta almorzar? ¿A qué hora almuerzas? ¿Qué comes para el almuerzo?
3. **la cena:** Normalmente, ¿a qué hora cenas? ¿Cenas con tu familia, con otras personas o solo(a)? ¿Comes mucho o poco en la cena? Por ejemplo, ¿qué comes?

EN CONTEXTO

El siguiente diálogo tiene lugar *(takes place)* en el restaurante «El Criollito» de doña Margarita. Doña Margarita está sirviéndoles a sus primeros clientes, Rosa y Simón, y quiere servirles una cena perfecta.

Doña Margarita:	¡Bienvenidos al Criollito! ¿Quieren sentarse adentro o en la terraza?
Rosa:	En la terraza. ¡Las flores que tienen allí son muy bonitas!
Doña Margarita:	Gracias. Pasen por aquí, entonces.

*****

Doña Margarita:	¿Está bien? El mesero les trae el menú enseguida.
Simón:	¡Perfecto!

*****

El mesero:	¡Buenas noches! Aquí tienen el menú. ¿**Desean** *(Would you like)* tomar algo?
Rosa:	Para mí, **un jugo de naranja** con hielo.
Simón:	Y para mí, **una cerveza.** Me gusta **más** la cerveza **que** el jugo cuando hace un poquito de calor.
El mesero:	Muy bien. Seguro que quieren **unas arepas** para empezar, ¿no? ¡Son **las mejores de toda la ciudad**! Es la especialidad de la casa.
Simón:	**¡Cómo no!** *(Of course!)*

*****

El mesero:	Aquí están las arepas que **pidieron.**
Simón:	¡Están riquísimas!
Rosa:	¡Están para chuparse los dedos!
El mesero:	Están muy **frescas.** La cocinera **preparó** muchas esta mañana. ¿Quieren pedir algo del menú?
Rosa:	Sí. Vamos a ver. *(Let's see.)* **Yo quisiera los calamares fritos.** ¿Están frescos?
El mesero:	Sí, señora. **Recibimos los mariscos** esta mañana. Y los calamares son **los mejores del día.** Seguro que le van a gustar. ¿Y para el señor?
Simón:	Quisiera el bistec bien cocido *(well done)* con champiñones.
El mesero:	¿Algo más? ¿**Postre**? ¿**Café**?
Simón:	Un cafecito y **la cuenta, por favor.**
Rosa:	¿Por qué **pediste** la cuenta, mi amor? No nos mataría *(wouldn't kill us)* un postre de vez en cuando *(occasionally).*

¿NOS ENTENDEMOS?

The most common word for *waiter* or *waitress* in Spanish is **mesero(a).** In Spain, however, you will hear **camarero(a)** instead.

¿NOS ENTENDEMOS?

Spanish speakers use several expressions to indicate their enjoyment of a meal; for example: **¡Están para chuparse los dedos!** *(They're finger-licking good!)* and **¡Están riquísimas!** *(They're delicious!)* It is also quite common to use the diminutive form when requesting common beverages such as **un cafecito** *(coffee)* or **una cervecita** *(beer).* Also note that in Latin America, it is more appropriate to use **(yo) quisiera...** *(I would like—the past subjunctive form of the verb* **querer***)* when ordering food. In Spain, it is more common to use the more direct present-tense form **(yo) quiero...**

¿Comprendiste?

Identifica la frase del diálogo que corresponde a las siguientes oraciones *(sentences).*

> MODELO: Es por la tarde.
> *El mesero dice «¡Buenas tardes!»*

1. A Rosa le gusta sentarse en la terraza.
2. Rosa y Simón van a comer arepas.
3. Las arepas están muy sabrosas *(tasty)* y frescas.
4. Simón pide un plato del menú.
5. Rosa quiere comer postre.

Encuentro cultural

La comida típica venezolana

PARA PENSAR

- ¿Te gusta probar comidas de otros países? ¿Por qué sí o por qué no?
- ¿Probaste alguna vez las arepas o el pabellón criollo venezolano?
- En general, ¿qué ingredientes te gustan en las diferentes comidas?

Preparando arepas

El plato que mejor representa a Venezuela es el pabellón criollo. El pabellón criollo es el plato nacional del país y sus ingredientes son: las caraotas negras *(black beans)*, el arroz blanco, las tajadas *(slices)* de plátanos fritos y la carne mechada *(shredded meat)*.

Debido a que Venezuela tiene el mar Caribe en el norte, unos de los ingredientes más importantes para preparar las comidas son los mariscos. La sopa de chipichipi *(a thumbnail-size clam)* es muy apreciada y muy divertida de hacer. Los amigos se reúnen cerca de la playa y pasan muchas horas recogiendo *(picking up)* los chipichipis de la arena *(sand)*, mientras otras personas cortan los vegetales como las papas, las cebollas *(onions)*, los tomates y el ajo *(garlic)* y les ponen sal. Luego más tarde todos los amigos cocinan y comen la sopa de chipichipi juntos.

El pan de los venezolanos es la arepa. La arepa se prepara con harina de maíz *(corn flour)* y tiene la forma y el mismo tamaño que un *English muffin*. Las arepas se preparan al horno o fritas y se rellenan con queso, carne mechada, huevos fritos, jamón o mariscos. La más famosa y la más popular es la arepa que se llama «Reina Pepiada» *(Cool Queen)*; es rellena *(stuffed)* con una ensalada de pollo y aguacate *(avocado)*. Las arepas son tan populares que hay areperas por todas las ciudades venezolanas, como los restaurantes de hamburguesas en los Estados Unidos. Las areperas son un tipo de restaurante que se especializa en preparar arepas y son un lugar de reunión para los amigos después de las fiestas, ya que muchas de las areperas están abiertas durante todo el día y toda la noche.

> **¿NOS ENTENDEMOS?**
> The Spanish-speaking world has many words for *beans*, **las caraotas** in Venezuela, **los frijoles** in México.

Receta: Arepas

1. Mezcla (Mix) con las manos una taza de harina de maíz con 2 tazas de agua tibia (warm), sal y ½ cucharadita (teaspoon) de mantequilla.

2. Con las manos, amasa (knead) los ingredientes muy bien.

3. Toma un poco de masa y forma un English muffin.

4. Cocina (Cook) la arepa por los dos lados en una plancha caliente (hot grill).

5. Corta (Cut) la arepa por el medio y rellénala con tus ingredientes favoritos: queso, jamón, carne, etc.

PARA DISCUTIR

1. ¿Cómo se prepara el pabellón criollo venezolano?
2. ¿Por qué es divertido preparar la sopa de chipichipi?
3. ¿Cómo se prepara «el pan» de Venezuela?
4. ¿Cuál es para ti la comida típica de los Estados Unidos o la comida típica de tu región? ¿Qué ingredientes lleva o tiene?
5. ¿Preparas comidas con tus amigos? ¿Qué tipo de comida preparas y por qué?

In this section you will learn how to make comparative and superlative statements.

I. Comparative statements

English speakers make comparisons either by adding the ending **-er** to an adjective (e.g., *warmer*) or by using the words *more* or *less* with an adjective (e.g., *more interesting, less expensive*). Spanish speakers make comparisons in the following manner.

Comparisons of inequality

Use the preposition **de** *(than)* before a number; for example: Elena tiene **más de** diez amigos. *Elena has more than ten friends.*

• Use **más** *(more)* or **menos** *(less)* before an adjective, an adverb, or a noun, and **que** *(than)* after it.

más		adjective **(tímido)**	
	+	adverb **(pronto)**	+ que
menos		noun **(hambre)**	

—Sí. Creo que es **menos tímida que** su hermana y es **más impaciente.**	*Yes. I think she's less shy than her sister and she's more impatient.*
—Matilde quiere comer **más pronto que** su hermana Elena.	*Matilde wants to eat sooner than her sister Elena.*
—Posiblemente, pero hoy también Elena tiene **menos hambre que** Matilde.	*Possibly, but today Elena is also less hungry than Matilde.*

• Use **más que** or **menos que** after a verb form.

Lorena estudia mucho.	*Lorena studies a lot.*
Lorena estudia **más que** Roberto.	*Lorena studies more than Roberto.*

• Irregular comparatives

mejor(es)	*better*	peor(es)	*worse*
menor(es)	*younger*	mayor(es)	*older*

—El tiempo en Caracas es **mejor que** en Maracaibo.	*The weather in Caracas is better than in Maracaibo.*
—Sí, y la humedad en Maracaibo es **peor que** en Caracas.	*Yes, and the humidity in Maracaibo is worse than in Caracas.*
—Lorena y Roberto son **mayores que** Elena y Matilde, ¿verdad?	*Lorena and Roberto are older than Elena and Matilde, right?*
—Sí. Elena es **menor que** Roberto, y Lorena es **mayor que** su hermana Matilde.	*Yes. Elena is younger than Roberto, and Lorena is older than her sister Matilde.*

Comparisons of equality

- Use **tan** (*as*) before an adjective or an adverb and **como** (*as*) after it (the adjective or the adverb).

Note that **tan** can also be used by itself to show a great degree of a given quality; for example: ¡Qué día **tan** perfecto! *What a perfect day!*

		adjective (**nublado**)		
tan	+		+	como
		adverb (**frecuentemente**)		

—A veces está **tan** nublado en Caracas **como** en Maracaibo.

Sometimes it is as cloudy in Caracas as in Maracaibo.

—También no llueve **tan** frecuentemente en Maracaibo **como** en Mérida.

Also, it doesn't rain as frequently in Maracaibo as in Merida.

One can change a comparison of equality to one of inequality by using the word **no** before a verb; for example: **No** llueve **tanto** en Caracas **como** en Maracaibo. *It doesn't rain as much in Caracas as in Maracaibo.*

- Use **tanto(a)** (*as much*) or **tantos(as)** (*as many*) before a noun, and **como** (*as*) after it.

tanto (dinero)		
tanta (gente)		
	+ **como**	
tantos (días)		
tantas (fiestas)		

—¿Hace **tanto** calor en Puerto Ayacucho **como** en Ciudad Guayana?

Is it as hot in Puerto Ayacucho as in Ciudad Guayana?

—Sí. Y hay **tantas** tormentas en Puerto Ayacucho **como** en Ciudad Guayana.

Yes. And there are as many storms in Puerto Ayacucho as in Ciudad Guayana.

—¿Tiene Venezuela **tantos** días de sol **como** Ecuador?

Does Venezuela have as many sunny days as Ecuador?

—¡Sí! Pero Venezuela no tiene **tanta** lluvia **como** Ecuador.

Yes! But Venezuela does not have as much rain as Ecuador.

Tanto(s)/Tanta(s) can also be used without **como** to show a great amount of something; for example: ¡Hace **tanto** calor! *(It's so hot!)*

- To make comparisons of equality with verbs, use **tanto como** after the verb, followed by the person (or pronoun) that is being compared to the subject.

Estudias **tanto como** yo.

You study as much as I.

Estructura I   ciento setenta y tres   **173**

II. Superlative statements

English speakers single out someone or something from a group by adding the ending -est to an adjective (e.g., *warmest*) or by using the phrases *the most* or *the least* with an adjective (e.g., *the most elegant, the least expensive*). Spanish speakers form superlatives by using a definite article before the person or thing being compared + **más** *(most)* or **menos** *(least)* + an adjective. To introduce the group to which the person or thing is being compared (*the most/least . . . in the class/world/city*, etc.), the preposition **de** + a noun is used.

el (sobrino)		
la (familia)	más	
	+	+ *adjective* (+ **de** + *noun*)
los (amigos)	menos	
las (compañeras)		

—Estoy muy feliz.   *I'm very happy.*

—¿Por qué, doña Margarita?   *Why, doña Margarita?*

—Porque tengo **la familia más inteligente, el esposo más guapo, los amigos más generosos y el restaurante más popular de** Caracas.   *Because I have the most intelligent family, the most handsome husband, the most generous friends, and the most popular restaurant in Caracas.*

Irregular superlatives

el (la, los, las)	mejor(es)	*best*
el (la, los, las)	peor(es)	*worst*
el (la, los, las)	menor(es)	*youngest*
el (la, los, las)	mayor(es)	*oldest*

—¡El Criollito es **el mejor** restaurante **de** Caracas!   *El Criollito is the best restaurant in Caracas!*

—Sí. El otro, El Mesón, es **el peor** restaurante **de** Caracas.   *Yes. The other, El Mesón, is the worst restaurant in Caracas.*

—Elena es **la menor de** las niñas **de** Margarita y Jorge.   *Elena is the youngest of Margarita and Jorge's girls.*

—Matilde es **la mayor**.   *Matilde is the oldest.*

¡A PRACTICAR!

6-5 | **Comparaciones** Usando la información que sigue, haz comparaciones entre el restaurante de doña Margarita, El Criollito, y otro restaurante que se llama El Mesón y que es de don Paco. El Mesón queda en el Centro de Caracas y sirve las empanadas *(Spanish-style meat pastries)* que son las más populares de la ciudad. Usa **más, menos, mayor** o **menor.**

> MODELO: En El Criollito, la gente come arepas, que es la especialidad de la casa. En El Mesón, la gente come empanadas, que es la especialidad de la casa.
> *En El Criollito, la gente come más arepas que empanadas.*
> o *En El Mesón, la gente come menos arepas que en El Criollito.*

1. El Criollito es pequeño. El Mesón es grande.
2. El Mesón tiene 154 clientes. El Criollito tiene 49 clientes.
3. El Criollito tiene dos cocineros. El Mesón tiene seis cocineros.
4. El Mesón tiene quince mesas. El Criollito tiene nueve mesas.
5. En El Criollito, la comida es económica. En El Mesón, la comida es cara *(expensive).*
6. En El Criollito, hay pocos platos en el menú. En El Mesón, hay muchos platos en el menú.
7. En tu opinión, ¿cuál es el mejor restaurante? ¿Cuál es el peor restaurante?

6-6 | **Los intereses de Matilde y Elena** Matilde y Elena tienen muchos intereses en común. Completa las siguientes oraciones apropiadamente, usando **tan, tanto, tanta, tantos** o **tantas.**

> MODELO: Matilde es *tan* inteligente como Elena.

1. Matilde tiene _____ energía como Elena.
2. Matilde juega _____ como su hermana.
3. Elena hace _____ actividades como Matilde.
4. Y a Elena le gusta hacer _____ ejercicio como a Matilde.
5. Matilde juega al tenis _____ bien como Elena.
6. También Matilde está _____ contenta como Elena.
7. Elena tiene _____ amigos como Matilde.
8. A Elena le gusta ir al cine _____ como a Matilde.

6-7 | **¡La mejor comida de la ciudad!** Pensando en los restaurantes en tu ciudad, forma expresiones superlativas para describir los siguientes componentes con los adjetivos dados.

> MODELO: comida / picante
> *El restaurante con la comida más picante es La Charreada.*

1. los meseros / simpático
2. los precios / bajo
3. el ambiente / popular
4. el menú / variado
5. los platos / delicioso
6. En tu opinión, ¿cuál es el mejor restaurante de tu ciudad? ¿Cuál es el peor restaurante?

6-8 **Lo que me gusta hacer...** Usa las siguientes frases para describirle tus gustos y situaciones personales a un(a) compañero(a) de clase. Usa **más... que** o **tan... como** en cada oración. Después dile a la clase si tú y tu compañero(a) tienen mucho en común.

> MODELO: Me gusta nadar más (el invierno / el verano)
> *Me gusta nadar más en el invierno que en el verano. ¿Y a ti?*
> o *Me gusta nadar menos en el invierno que en el verano. ¿Y a ti?*
> o *Me gusta nadar más en el verano que en el invierno. ¿Y a ti?*

1. Me gusta caminar más (el invierno / el verano)
2. Me gusta dormir más (cuando hace frío / cuando hace calor)
3. Me gusta ducharme más frecuentemente (el verano / el invierno)
4. Me enfermo más (la primavera / el otoño)
5. Tengo más dolores de cabeza (durante el semestre / durante las vacaciones)
6. Tomo menos bebidas (cuando hace calor / cuando hace fresco)

6-9 **Dos cocineros y tú** Imagínate que quieres trabajar en el restaurante de doña Margarita. ¿Cómo te comparas con dos cocineros que ya trabajan allí? Vas a compararte con los dos cocineros, Pablo y Memo, para averiguar *(find out)* qué tienen Uds. en común. Vas a usar construcciones comparativas y construcciones superlativas.

Completa el cuadro *(table)* a continuación *(below)* y después usa la información para comparar a Pablo con su amigo Memo. Luego compárate con los dos. Hazle las preguntas a un(a) compañero(a) de clase.

> MODELOS: —¿Quién es más joven?
> —*Pablo es más joven que Memo.*
>
> —¿Eres tú menor o mayor que Memo?
> —*Soy menor que Memo; tengo veinte años.*

Persona	Edad	Horas de trabajo	Libros de recetas *(recipes)*	Intereses
Pablo	23	8 horas al día	5	libros, arte, conciertos
Memo	26	9 horas al día	5	fútbol, tenis, rap, fiestas
Tú				

1. ¿Quién es mayor? ¿Eres tú menor o mayor que Pablo? ¿Cuántos años tienes tú?
2. ¿Quién tiene más libros de recetas? ¿Tienes tú más o menos libros que Memo?
3. ¿Quién es más trabajador(a)? ¿Eres tú más o menos trabajador(a) que Memo?
4. ¿A quién le gusta más practicar deportes? ¿A qué deportes juegas tú? ¿Qué otros intereses tienes tú?
5. ¿Quién es la persona mayor de los tres? ¿la menor?

6-10 **¡Vamos a votar!** Usando el superlativo y según las categorías de la lista a continuación, escribe cuatro oraciones que describan a cuatro personas diferentes de tu universidad. Luego, lee tus oraciones en voz alta sin decir el nombre de la persona que describes. El resto de la clase tiene que adivinar de quién hablas.

> MODELO: *(El Profesor Rambo) es el profesor mayor de la universidad.*
> *(Amanda Manning) es la estudiante más generosa de la universidad.*

más contento(a)	más generoso(a)	el (la) mayor
menos tímido(a)	menos perezoso(a)	el (la) menor

En el restaurante El Criollito en Caracas In this section you will learn vocabulary and expressions associated with eating in a restaurant.

Adjetivos

caliente hot (temperature)
fresco(a) fresh
ligero(a) light (meal, food)
pesado(a) heavy (meal, food)
rico(a) delicious

Verbos

cocinar to cook
dejar una (buena) propina to leave a (good) tip
desear to wish; to want
pedir (i) to order (food)
picar to eat appetizers; to nibble
preparar to prepare
recomendar (ie) to recommend

Expresiones idiomáticas

¡Buen provecho! Enjoy your meal!
¡Cómo no! Of course!
Estoy a dieta. I'm on a diet.
Estoy satisfecho(a). I'm satisfied.
La cuenta, por favor. The check, please.
No puedo más. I can't (eat) any more.
¿Qué desean/quieren comer (beber)? What would you like to eat (to drink)?
¡Salud! Cheers!
Te invito. It's on me (my treat).
Yo quisiera... I would like . . .
¿Qué les gustaría? What would you like?

¿NOS ENTENDEMOS?

To decline second helpings of food, Spanish speakers say **Estoy satisfecho(a)** (*I am satisfied*) rather than *I'm full*, which would be considered rude in many Spanish-speaking countries. It is customary in Spanish-speaking countries to say **¡Buen provecho!** when others begin to eat.

¡A PRACTICAR!

6-11 **Impresiones de Pepe** Pepe, el mesero, siempre les sirve a don Fernando y a doña Olga cuando ellos vienen a comer al restaurante El Criollito. Completa el párrafo siguiente sobre tus impresiones de la pareja. Usa las siguientes frases, palabras y expresiones.

yo te invito	ensalada	agua mineral
¿qué desean?	propina	algo ligero
picar	menú	piden
está a dieta		

Hola. Yo llevo muchos años trabajando aquí en El Criollito. Conozco bien a don Fernando y a doña Olga —son clientes muy buenos. Siempre les pregunto a ellos: 1. «_qué desean_» Don Fernando siempre pide ver el 2. _menú_. Él siempre pide una cerveza Polar muy fría y 3. ~~picar~~ para 4. _algo ligero_. Les gustan mucho los mariscos —casi siempre 5. _piden_ langosta o pescado. Claro, ¡doña Margarita tiene el mejor pescado de Caracas! Como doña Olga es un poco gorda, siempre 6. _está a dieta_. Por eso, normalmente ella pide 7. _agua mineral_ para beber y una 8. _ensalada_ para comer con su plato principal. Realmente son unas personas especiales y muy románticas. Después de comer, don Fernando siempre, de broma (jokingly), le dice a su esposa: 9. «_yo le invito_, cariño». Ellos siempre dejan una buena 10. _propina_.

6-12 **Un mesero algo (a bit) confundido** Pepe, el mesero del restaurante de doña Margarita, está un poco confundido. Ayúdalo a poner en orden lógico las frases que les dice a los clientes.

10	Traigo la cuenta ahora mismo.	1	¡Buenas noches!
5	¿Qué quieren comer?	7	¡Buen provecho!
8	De postre hay fruta, torta de chocolate o quesillo.	9	¿Desean algo más?
6	¿Y para beber?	11	Gracias señores, y muy buenas noches.
2	¿Dos para cenar?	3	Aquí tienen el menú.
4	Les recomiendo los mariscos.		

EN VOZ ALTA

6-13 **Preguntas al (a la) mesero(a)** Haz preguntas con las siguientes palabras y luego hazle las preguntas a un(a) compañero(a) de clase. Tu compañero(a) tiene que contestar adecuadamente. Recuerda que los meseros y los clientes normalmente usan la forma de Ud. para conversar.

MODELO: el menú
E1: *¿Puedo ver el menú?*
E2: *Aquí está el menú.*

1. la especialidad de la casa
2. recomendar
3. refrescos
4. postre
5. la cuenta

6-14 **Escenas en un restaurante** Trabajando con un(a) compañero(a) de clase, hagan el papel de un(a) cliente y un(a) mesero(a) en un restaurante. Usen las expresiones que acaban de aprender y las comidas del menú en las páginas 168 y 177.

¿NOS ENTENDEMOS?
Here are some other expressions to talk about food: **¡Qué delicioso!** (How delicious!) and **¡Qué sabroso!** (How tasty!) While **caliente** means *hot*, it refers to the temperature of something, not to the weather. **Picante** means *hot*, as in *spicy*: **¡Qué picante!** (How spicy!)

¿NOS ENTENDEMOS?
La carta and **la lista** are other words for **el menú.**

Encuentro cultural

Los postres venezolanos

El flan o quesillo

La marquesa de chocolate

PARA PENSAR

■ ¿Cuál es tu postre favorito? ¿Cuáles son los ingredientes de este postre?

■ ¿Te gustan los postres muy dulces, con mucho azúcar o con poco azúcar?

■ ¿Conoces los ingredientes del flan español o quesillo? ¿Cómo se llama en Venezuela?

La cocina tradicional venezolana tiene muchos postres, dulces, pasteles o tortas. Uno de los ingredientes más importantes en la preparación de los postres es el azúcar o el papelón, que es azúcar sin refinar *(unrefined sugar)*. Los postres venezolanos son más económicos que los postres de otros países del mundo porque en ellos se usan muchas frutas, harinas y maíz, y todos los ingredientes son locales o del país.

Las personas de otros países, especialmente los europeos, creen que los postres venezolanos son más dulces que los postres de Europa. Hay varias razones para creer que los postres venezolanos son los más dulces:

• En los países tropicales se usa más el azúcar que en los países de clima templado para conservar los alimentos. El gusto de los venezolanos por el azúcar es mayor que en muchos de los otros países latinoamericanos.

• En la cocina venezolana se usa más el dulce debido a que las frutas son muy ácidas *(sour)* y necesitan más dulce para acabar con la acidez *(acidity)*.

• Algunas personas creen que los postres venezolanos son más dulces porque los trabajadores que llegan a Venezuela en el siglo XVI para trabajar en los campos o ingenios de caña de azúcar *(sugar plantations)* son las mismas personas que preparan los postres en las cocinas y por eso les ponen más azúcar a los postres.

En los dulces venezolanos, además de la influencia del uso del azúcar que viene de los africanos, también se nota la influencia de los postres españoles y de los postres franceses. Por ejemplo, el quesillo venezolano es parecido *(similar)* al flan español, el arroz con coco *(coconut rice)* es descendiente directo del arroz con leche español y la marquesa de chocolate o torta fría de chocolate desciende de la charlotte francesa. Los postres venezolanos son deliciosos y vale la pena *(it is worth)* probarlos siempre con una buena taza de café y un buen grupo de amigos.

PARA DISCUTIR

1. ¿Cuál es el ingrediente más importante en los postres venezolanos?

2. ¿Por qué los postres venezolanos son más dulces que los postres europeos?

3. ¿De dónde es tu postre favorito? ¿Tiene alguna influencia extranjera?

4. ¿A quién le recomiendas probar los postres venezolanos y por qué?

ESTRUCTURA II Describing past events: regular verbs and verbs with spelling changes in the preterite

Spanish speakers use the preterite tense to describe what occurred in the past.

Regular verbs in the preterite

Note the identical endings for -**er** and -**ir** verbs.

- To form the preterite for most Spanish verbs, add the following endings to the verb stem.

	hablar	comer	vivir
yo	habl**é**	com**í**	viv**í**
tú	habl**aste**	com**iste**	viv**iste**
Ud., él/ella	habl**ó**	com**ió**	viv**ió**
nosotros(as)	habl**amos**	com**imos**	viv**imos**
vosotros(as)	habl**asteis**	com**isteis**	viv**isteis**
Uds., ellos(as)	habl**aron**	com**ieron**	viv**ieron**

Mis padres **hablaron** en español con el mesero.

My parents spoke in Spanish with the waiter.

Ella **comió** mucho ayer.

She ate a lot yesterday.

- -**Ar** and -**er** stem-changing verbs in the present tense have no stem change in the preterite; use the same verb stem as you would for the **nosotros(as)** form.

pensar:	pens**é**, pens**aste**, pens**ó**, pens**amos**, pens**asteis**, pens**aron**
volver:	volv**í**, volv**iste**, volv**ió**, volv**imos**, volv**isteis**, volv**ieron**

Yo **pensé** mucho en doña Margarita.

I thought a lot about doña Margarita.

Volvió a casa a la 1:00.

She returned home at 1:00.

Verbs with spelling changes in the preterite

- Verbs ending in -**car**, -**gar**, and -**zar** have a spelling change in the **yo** form of the preterite tense.

c changes to **qu**	g changes to **gu**	z changes to **c**
tocar → to**qu**é	llegar → lle**gu**é	comenzar → comen**c**é

Yo **llegué** a las 2:00 y **almorcé** con su familia.

I arrived at 2:00 and had lunch with his family.

Toqué la guitarra y **saqué** unas fotos.

I played the guitar and took some photos.

Jugué a las cartas con toda la familia.

I played cards with the family.

- Verbs ending in **-er** and **-ir** that have a vowel before the infinitive ending require the following change in the **Ud./él/ella** and **Uds./ellos/ellas** forms of the preterite tense: the **e** or **i** between the two vowels changes to **y**.

	creer	leer	oír
Ud., él/ella	creyó	leyó	oyó
Uds., ellos(as)	creyeron	leyeron	oyeron

Margarita y su esposo Jorge **leyeron** un poco.	*Margarita and her husband Jorge read a bit.*
Jorge **oyó** algo raro en la calle.	*Jorge heard something strange in the street.*
Nadie le **creyó** su cuento.	*Nobody believed his story.*

Uses of the preterite

Spanish speakers use the preterite tense to express the beginning and completion of past actions, conditions, and events. Basically, the preterite is used to tell what did or did not happen or to tell what someone did or did not do. Observe the use of the preterite in the following paragraph.

Ayer Jorge **se despertó** un poco tarde porque no **oyó** su despertador.	*Yesterday, Jorge woke up a little late because he didn't hear his alarm clock.*
Margarita **llamó** a su esposo dos veces y finalmente él **se levantó.**	*Margarita called her husband two times and finally he got up.*
Luego Jorge **se duchó** y **desayunó** con sus dos hijas, Matilde y Elena.	*Then, Jorge showered and ate breakfast with his two daughters, Matilde and Elena.*

Here are some common expressions used to refer to the past:

anoche	*last night*
anteayer	*the day before yesterday*
ayer	*yesterday*
la semana / el mes / el año pasado(a)	*last week / month / year*

¡A PRACTICAR!

6-15 | **Cómo preparamos las arepas** Doña Olga explica cómo ella, su esposo Fernando y sus tres hijos, Alberto, Pedro y Óscar prepararon las arepas ayer. Escribe su historia con la siguiente información.

> MODELO: nosotros / entrar / a la cocina / para preparar arepas
> *Nosotros entramos a la cocina para preparar arepas.*

1. mi esposo Fernando / leer / la receta
2. yo / comenzar / a buscar los ingredientes
3. mi hijo Óscar / mezclar / la harina de maíz con agua
4. mis hijos Pedro y Alberto / formar / las arepas
5. nosotros / meter / las arepas / en el horno
6. Fernando / limpiar / la cocina
7. yo / sacar / todas las arepas
8. Óscar, Pedro y Alberto / comer / las arepas / rápidamente

6-16 | **Mi esposo y yo...** Doña Margarita recuerda unos momentos bien especiales para ella y su esposo. Ayúdala a contar estos momentos al completar las siguientes oraciones con las formas adecuadas en el pretérito.

1. yo / conocer / a Jorge en 1978
2. nosotros / comenzar a / salir inmediatamente
3. él / invitarme / a cenar en un restaurante elegante
4. después, nosotros / ver una película
5. él / decidir estudiar / ingeniería de sistemas en la Universidad Simón Bolívar
6. yo también / tomar / varias clases sobre negocios en la Universidad Metropolitana de Caracas y clases de cocina en la escuela de comida griega de Eduardo Castro
7. nosotros / casarse / en 1980
8. los padres de Jorge / comprar / un restaurante para nosotros
9. el restaurante / costar / mucho dinero
10. Jorge, Pepe el mesero y yo / abrir / el restaurante en el verano del 2000

6-17 | **Un secreto** Alberto, el hijo mayor de doña Olga y don Fernando, está secretamente enamorado de Matilde, la hija de doña Margarita. Una noche, él va con sus hermanos a la casa de Matilde y le dan una serenata. Usando los verbos de la lista, completa el siguiente párrafo en que Matilde describe lo que pasó.

creer *think*	oír *to hear*	invitar *invite*	despertarse *wake up*
apagar *turn off*	volver *to return*	recibir *recieve*	acostarse *go to bed*
cerrar *to close*	leer *read*	hablar *talk*	
llamar *call*	llegar *arrive*	cantar *sing*	

Anoche, yo 1. ~~desperté~~ *leí* un poco antes de dormir. A las 11:00, yo 2. *apagé* la luz y 3. *me acosté.* ¡Siempre estoy cansada después de trabajar en el restaurante con mamá! Una hora después, a las 12:00, 4. *me desperté.* Mi hermana Elena y yo 5. *oímos* algo fuera de la casa. Cuando yo 6. *llegué* a la ventana para mirar, ¡no lo 7. *creí* !

¡Óscar, Alberto y Pedro! Bueno. La semana pasada, yo 8. *recibí* un mensaje electrónico de Alberto en que él me hablaba de su amor por mí. Y ayer, él me 9. *llamó* por teléfono y me 10. *invitó* a cenar con él. ¡Ay, ay ay! ¡Yo no quiero ser la novia de Alberto! Pero anoche, él y sus dos hermanos me 11. *cantaron* una canción de amor. Elena y yo 12. *cerramos* la ventana y 13. *volvimos* a acostarnos. ¡Esos muchachos!

EN VOZ ALTA

6-18 | **Lo que yo hice** Dile a otro(a) compañero(a) de clase lo que tú hiciste (*you did*) la semana pasada. A continuación hay varias posibilidades que puedes usar si las necesitas. Luego comparte con la clase la información que tienes de tu compañero(a).

MODELO: levantarse tarde
Yo me levanté tarde.

1. **En el trabajo...**
   a. no trabajar mucho
   b. recibir un cheque
   c. hablar con mi jefe(a)
   d. conocer a otro(a) empleado(a)
   e. ¿...?

2. **En la universidad...**
   a. jugar a un deporte
   b. comer en la cafetería
   c. aprender mucho español
   d. tomar un examen difícil
   e. ¿...?

3. **En el restaurante...**
   a. decidir pedir algo para picar
   b. beber agua mineral
   c. comer pescado frito
   d. pagar la cuenta
   e. ¿...?

6-19 | **Ayer yo...** ¿Qué comió tu compañero(a) ayer? Pregúntale qué comió y después, cuéntale lo que tú comiste. Pide muchos detalles —no sólo de lo que comió, sino también con quién comió, cuánto, a qué hora, dónde, si lo preparó él/ella, etcétera.

MODELO: el desayuno
—*¿Qué comiste para el desayuno?*
—*Comí cereal con leche.*

1. el desayuno
2. el almuerzo
3. la cena

6-20 | **¿Quién... ?** Tienes dos minutos para buscar a alguien de tu clase que haya hecho (*has done*) las siguientes cosas. Después de encontrar a alguien para cada categoría, pídele que firme (*sign*) el espacio en blanco después de cada actividad. Al final, cuéntales a tus compañeros(as) de clase lo que acabas de saber.

MODELO: comer camarones ayer
Tú: *Bonnie, ¿comiste camarones ayer?*
Bonnie: *Sí, comí camarones ayer.* (Bonnie signs next to the activity.)
o *No, no comí camarones ayer.* (Bonnie doesn't sign and you look for someone else.)
Al final: *Bonnie comió camarones ayer...*

1. comer una hamburguesa anteayer: _____
2. oír música venezolana alguna vez: _____
3. leer un libro de recetas la semana pasada: _____
4. tocar la guitarra anoche: _____
5. llegar tarde a clase el mes pasado: _____
6. pagar la cuenta en un restaurante ayer: _____
7. comenzar a leer sobre las Cataratas del Salto Ángel la semana pasada: _____
8. preparar la receta de las arepas venezolanas: _____

CULTURA
James Ángel, a North American pilot saw the Salto Ángel in Canaima, Venezuela, in 1935, and reported the news for the first time to the authorities. This is the highest in the world with 979 meters height, and is fifteen times higher than the Niagara Falls, with the longest free waterfall in the world (807m).

ESTRUCTURA III Giving detailed description about past events: verbs with stem changes in the preterite

Spanish **-ir** verbs that have a stem change in the present tense also have a stem change in the third-person-singular and -plural forms (**Ud./él/ella** and **Uds./ellos[as]**) of the preterite. In these cases, **e** becomes **i,** and **o** becomes **u.** Remember, stem-changing **-ar** and **-er** verbs do not show stem changes in the preterite.

servir *(to serve)*			
Present		**Preterite**	
(i)		(i)	
sirvo	servimos	serví	servimos
sirves	servís	serviste	servisteis
sirve	sirven	sirvió	sirvieron

divertirse *(to have fun)*			
Present		**Preterite**	
(ie)		(i)	
me divierto	nos divertimos	me divertí	nos divertimos
te diviertes	os divertís	te divertiste	os divertisteis
se divierte	se divierten	se divirtió	se divirtieron

dormir *(to sleep)*			
Present		**Preterite**	
(ue)		(u)	
duermo	dormimos	dormí	dormimos
duermes	dormís	dormiste	dormisteis
duerme	duermen	durmió	durmieron

Here are other **-ir** stem-changing verbs that exhibit the same changes as the three verbs shown above. Many of these you have already learned. Note below that the first vowel in the parentheses indicates the stem change in the present tense, and the second vowel indicates the stem change in the preterite.

conseguir (i, i) *to get, obtain*
despedir(se) (i, i) (de) *to say good-bye (to)*
dormirse (ue, u) *to fall asleep*
morir(se) (ue, u) *to die*
pedir (i, i) *to request, order; to ask for*
preferir (ie, i) *to prefer*
reírse (i, i) *to laugh*
sentirse (ie, i) *to feel*
sonreír (i, i) *to smile*
sugerir (ie, i) *to suggest*
vestirse (i, i) *to get dressed*

The third-person forms of **reírse** undergo the following spelling simplification: **ri-ió** → **rió; ri-ieron** → **rieron.** The third-person forms of **sonreír** are simplified in the same manner as **reírse.**

¡A PRACTICAR!

6-21 Unas vacaciones para Julio Julio es el gerente (*manager*) del Restaurante del Lago en Maracaibo y normalmente va de vacaciones a Caracas, la capital. Él nos cuenta qué pasa en su viaje. Cambia las oraciones del presente al pasado para indicar lo que pasó en su último viaje.

> MODELO: Yo consigo un boleto (*ticket*) de avión para Caracas.
> *Conseguí un boleto de avión para Caracas.*

1. El día del viaje me despido de mis amigos.
2. Cuando llego al aeropuerto, los agentes me piden el boleto.
3. Al llegar a Caracas, prefiero ir a la Casa de Bolívar y al Capitolio Nacional primero.
4. Los empleados me sonríen cuando entro a la Galería de Arte Nacional.
5. También me divierto mucho en la Plaza Bolívar.
6. Varias personas me sugieren unas discotecas en el distrito Las Mercedes.
7. Me visto con chaqueta, pero sin corbata para ir a las discotecas.
8. Muchas personas en las discotecas se ríen.
9. Me siento cansado cuando vuelvo a mi hotel.
10. Me duermo muy rápido.

6-22 Una pequeña fiesta de doña Margarita y Jorge El sábado pasado doña Margarita y don Jorge hicieron una fiesta (*gave a party*) en su apartamento de Altamira en Caracas para celebrar su aniversario con unos amigos. Doña Margarita describe los preparativos y lo que pasó en la fiesta.

El sábado durante el día, nosotros 1. _____ (empezar) a prepararnos para la fiesta. Primero, Jorge y Elena limpiaron la casa. Mientras tanto (Meanwhile), yo fui (I went) a hacer las compras para la comida. En el mercado, yo 2. _____ (conseguir) unas comidas riquísimas. Dos dependientes (clerks) me 3. _____ (sugerir) empanadas de carne para picar en la fiesta.

A las 7:00, Jorge y yo nos duchamos, y luego 4. _____ (vestirse). Yo 5. _____ (vestirse) con un vestido largo, y Jorge 6. _____ (vestirse) elegantemente también. A las 9:30 de la noche llegaron los primeros invitados. Yo 7. _____ (servir) unas empanadas de carne y unas arepas de queso. Un señor 8. _____ (pedir) una cerveza, pero su esposa 9. _____ (preferir) tomar vino; Jorge les 10. _____ (servir) estas dos bebidas. Todos 11. _____ (divertirse) mucho en la fiesta. Cuando los invitados se fueron (left), Jorge y yo 12. _____ (acostarse) y 13. _____ (dormir) muy bien porque trabajamos mucho para dar esta fiesta.

CULTURA
These apartments are very nice because of their proximity to the Cerro of El Ávila. This hill protects the city of Caracas from the winds.

EN VOZ ALTA

6-23 Una cena memorable en un restaurante inovidable Pregúntale a un(a) compañero(a) de clase sobre una cena especial. Luego descríbele a la clase las experiencias de tu compañero(a).

1. ¿Dónde comiste? ¿Quiénes comieron contigo? ¿Qué pediste tú y qué pidieron las otras personas?
2. ¿Comiste en un restaurante comercial o en un restaurante pequeño? ¿A qué hora llegaste (llegaron Uds.) a tu (su) destino? ¿Se divirtieron tú y tus amigos? ¿Se rieron mucho durante la comida? ¿Pediste algo especial de postre?
3. ¿Después de cuánto tiempo volviste a casa? ¿A qué hora te acostaste cuando llegaste a casa? ¿Te sentiste contento(a) después de la cena? ¿Por qué sí o por qué no? ¿Te dormiste inmediatamente o no?

SÍNTESIS

¡A VER!

En este segmento del video, Valeria decide sorprender a los muchachos con una cena especial. Desafortunadamente, no tiene los resultados deseados.

Expresiones útiles

The following are some new expressions you will hear in the video.

A ver	Let's see
Yo ¿qué sé?	What do I know?
Se hace lo que se puede	One does what one can

Antes de ver

Paso 1: ¿Qué pasó la última vez que preparaste una cena especial para un(a) amigo(a) o pariente? ¿Te salió bien o mal? ¿A tu amigo(a) o pariente le gustó la sorpresa? Describe la experiencia a un(a) compañero(a).

Paso 2: ¿Te gusta cocinar? ¿Por qué? ¿Qué platos sabes preparar? ¿Prefieres las recetas con muchos ingredientes o pocos ingredientes? ¿Cocinas con frecuencia? Comparte tus respuestas con las de un(a) compañero(a). ¿Tienen mucho en común?

Después de ver

Paso 1: En **Antes de ver, Paso 1**, hablaste de la última vez que tú sorprendiste a un(a) amigo(a) o pariente con una cena especial. Ahora, según lo que acabas de ver en el video, completa el siguiente párrafo con el pretérito de los verbos apropiados de la lista para contar lo que pasó cuando Valeria intentó preparar algo típico mexicano para sorprenderle a Antonio.

comer	comprar	decidir	empezar	encontrar
leer	volver	quemarse	salir	

Un día, Valeria **1.** _____ sorprender a los muchachos con una cena típica mexicana. Alejandra y Valeria **2.** _____ libros de recetas y Alejandra **3.** _____ una receta para Chiles Rellenos al Horno. Las chicas **4.** _____ los ingredientes en el mercado, **5.** _____ a la Hacienda Vista Alegre, y Valeria **6.** _____ a cocinar. Desafortunadamente, ¡Valeria no es muy buena cocinera! Los chiles **7.** _____ y la cena fue (*was*) un desastre. Antonio **8.** _____ un poco, pero al final todos **9.** _____ a un restaurante.

Paso 2: En **Antes de ver, Paso 2**, hablaste con tu compañero(a) sobre los platos que sabes preparar. Ahora piensa en el plato que Valeria preparó en el video. ¿Cuáles son los ingredientes que usó? Mira la siguiente lista y pon una "X" para indicar los ingredientes que mencionó. Compara tus respuestas con las de un(a) compañero(a). ¿Se acordaron de todo?

Ingredientes para Chiles Rellenos al Horno

_____ chiles poblanos

_____ camarones

_____ aceite

_____ arroz blanco guisado

_____ crema

_____ vinagre

_____ cebollitas de cambray

_____ champiñones

_____ sal

_____ jamón

_____ caldillo de jitomate

_____ queso añejo

¿Qué opinas tú?

Paso 1: Con un(a) compañero(a), planea una cena sorpresa para un(a) amigo(a) especial. ¿Qué platos van a preparar? ¿Qué ingredientes van a tener que comprar? ¿Qué van a hacer para asegurar que no tengan *(don't have)* el mismo resultado que Valeria?

Paso 2: Ahora te toca a ti. *(Now it's your turn.)* ¿Cuál es tu cena ideal? Imagina que puedes pedir cualquier cosa *(anything)* sin preocuparte por el precio o la preparación. ¿Tienes un restaurante favorito adónde quieres ir o prefieres que alguien cocine algo en casa? ¿Pides algo para empezar? ¿Tienes un postre favorito? ¿Qué quieres beber? Comparte tu menú con la clase.

¡A LEER!

Strategy: Improving your reading efficiency: organizational features of a passage and skimming

Reading efficiently involves a great deal of guessing. By considering several organizational features of a passage, you can often make intelligent guesses about the content of the passage even before you begin reading it. You should use all the information available to you, including titles, subtitles (if any are present), and pictures, to help you get an idea of the topic of the reading. You should also skim over the passage before reading it in order to get the gist of the reading.

Oda al tomate

La calle se llenó de tomates,
mediodía,
verano,
la luz
se parte
en dos mitades (halves)
de tomate,
corre
por las calles (streets)
el jugo.
En diciembre
se desata (is untied)
el tomate,
invade
las cocinas,
entra por los almuerzos,
se sienta
reposado (quiet)
en los aparadores (shop windows)
entre los vasos (glasses),
las mantequilleras (butter plates),
los saleros (salt containers)
azules.
Tiene
luz propia,
majestad benigna.
Debemos, por desgracia,
asesinarlo:
se hunde (sinks into)
el cuchillo (knife)
en su pulpa viviente (alive pulp),
es una roja
víscera,
un sol
fresco,
profundo
inagotable,
llena las ensaladas
de Chile,
se casa alegremente
con la clara cebolla...
y para celebrarlo
se deja
caer
aceite,
hijo
esencial del olivo,
sobre sus hemisferios entreabiertos,
agrega (adds)

la pimienta
su fragancia,
la sal de su magnetismo:
son las bodas (wedding day)
del día
el perejil (parsley)
levanta
banderines (small flags)
las papas
hierven (boil) vigorosamente,
el asado
golpea con su aroma
en la puerta,
¡es hora!
¡vamos!
y sobre la mesa, en la cintura
del verano,
el tomate,
astro de tierra,
estrella
repetida
y fecunda (fruitful),
nos muestra
sus circunvalaciones,
sus canales,
la insigne plenitud
y la abundancia
sin hueso (bone),
sin coraza (armor),
sin escamas (fish scale) ni espinas (thorns),
nos entrega
el regalo
de su color fogoso (impetuous color)
y la totalidad de su frescura.

Pablo Neruda
(Odas elementales, 1954)

Paso 1: Read the title of the following poem.

¿Cuál es el tema de este poema?

Paso 2: Look at the accompanying image.

¿Qué hay en la foto?

Paso 3: Skim the poem to get the gist of it. Then complete the following sentences.

1. El tema principal del poema es...
   a. la cebolla.
   b. el tomate.
   c. el aceite.
   d. la sal.

2. El tomate es...
   a. una fruta sin importancia.
   b. una fruta con importancia.
   c. una fruta muy conocida.
   d. una fruta poco conocida.

3. El tomate y la cebolla se unen con...
   a. la sal y las papas.
   b. las papas y la pimienta.
   c. el aceite y la sal.
   d. la pimienta, la sal y el perejil.

Paso 4: Scan the poem for the information you need to answer the following questions.

1. Tres condimentos que menciona el autor son _____, _____ y _____.
2. En las ensaladas, el tomate se casa alegremente con _____.
3. El _____ se usa para poder ver la pulpa roja del tomate.
4. El _____ es el hijo del olivo.
5. El tomate nos entrega su color _____ y su _____.

Paso 5: ¿Qué impresión tienes de este poema? Explica tu respuesta.

Creo que el poema es... _____ _____ porque...

¡A ESCRIBIR!

Strategy: Adding details to a paragraph

In **Capítulo 4,** you learned how to write a topic sentence for a paragraph. The other sentences in the paragraph should contain details that develop the main idea stated in the topic sentence. The following procedure will help you develop a well-written paragraph in Spanish.

1. Write a topic sentence about a specific subject.
2. List some details that develop your topic sentence.
3. Cross out any details that are unrelated to the topic.
4. Number the remaining details in a clear, logical order.
5. Write the first draft of a paragraph based on your work.
6. Cross out any ideas that do not contribute to the topic.
7. Write the second draft of your paragraph as clearly as possible.

Paso 1: Lee la oración principal que sigue. Después, indica si cada oración de la lista de detalles está relacionada o no con la oración principal.

Oración principal: Mi restaurante favorito es Chez Claude.

Detalles:	**¿Oración relacionada?**	
El restaurante Chez Claude sirve comida francesa.	Sí	No
Mis amigos y yo comemos en casa a veces.	Sí	No
Chez Claude tiene muchos tipos de refrescos.	Sí	No
Los precios son altos, pero la comida es deliciosa.	Sí	No

Paso 2: Lee el párrafo siguiente. Vas a ver que el párrafo contiene unas ideas que no están relacionadas con la idea de la oración principal. Elimina la información que no sea importante. Para hacer el párrafo más corto, puedes combinar unas oraciones.

Mi restaurante favorito es Freddie's. Es un restaurante pequeño que sirve comida norteamericana. Mi madre siempre prepara la cena en casa a las 6:00. En Freddie's me gusta pedir sándwiches de jamón y queso. Las papas fritas siempre están muy ricas. A veces yo pido papas fritas en otros restaurantes también. Freddie's tiene muchos tipos de refrescos, licuados y otras bebidas deliciosas. La gente que trabaja en el restaurante es muy simpática y el servicio es muy bueno. Hay una tienda de ropa muy cerca a la que me gusta ir de compras. Por lo general, creo que Freddie's es un restaurante muy interesante. ¡Me gusta comer allí!

Task: Writing a restaurant review

You will now write a brief review of your favorite restaurant, being careful to include only pertinent details. Use the strategies you have practiced and follow the directions below.

Paso 1: ¿Cuál es tu restaurante favorito? Sigue los siete pasos anteriores *(above)* para escribir un párrafo en español sobre este restaurante.

Paso 2: Ahora trabaja con un(a) compañero(a) de clase. Uds. deben...

- eliminar los detalles que no estén relacionados con la oración principal.
- añadir *(add)* unos detalles, si es necesario.
- corregir los errores de vocabulario, de gramática o de ortografía *(spelling).*

Paso 3: Intercambia papeles con otros compañeros de clase. Lee los párrafos de varios otros estudiantes e identifica algunos restaurantes que quieras visitar.

Functions: Appreciating food; Describing objects; Stating a preference
Vocabulary: Food; Food: restaurant
Grammar: Verbs: **gustar, ser, tener;** Present tense of verbs

¡A CONVERSAR!

Pronunciation focus: *m*, *n*, and *ñ*

The Spanish **ñ** has a sound that does not exist in English; it is similar to *ny* in *canyon*. The letters **m** and **n** are pronounced the same in Spanish and English with one exception: the letter **n** before **p, b, v,** and **m** is pronounced like an *m*. Practice the following sentences:

- Me gusta comer calamares, camarones y jamón.
- En un restaurante elegante siempre pido un bistec con champiñones.

Task: Talking about your eating habits and food preferences

Si piensas compartir *(to share)* una casa o un apartamento con otras personas o si tienes planes para vivir con una familia en un programa de estudio al extranjero *(study abroad)*, puede ser necesario hablar de tus hábitos y tus preferencias en cuanto a *(in regard to)* la comida. Trabaja con un(a) compañero(a) de clase para hablar de este tema.

Paso 1: Describe lo que comes y cuándo comes en un día típico. Menciona también dónde comes en diferentes partes del día (en tu casa o apartamento, en una cafetería estudiantil, en un café o un restaurante, etc.). Presenta la información en orden cronológico, empezando por la mañana. Pregúntale a tu compañero(a) sobre sus hábitos.

Paso 2: Di si tú preparas la comida o si otra persona la prepara en las situaciones que acabas de describir. También di si te gusta cocinar o no y en qué situaciones cocinas. Pregúntale a tu compañero(a) si él/ella cocina. ¡También pregúntale si él/ella lava los platos!

Paso 3: Identifica algunas comidas que te gustan mucho y otras que no te gustan. Luego, hazle preguntas a tu compañero(a) sobre sus preferencias.

Paso 4: Decide si quieres compartir una casa o un apartamento con tu compañero(a), basándote en la información que Uds. presentaron en su conversación.

Las comidas Meals

el almuerzo lunch | **la cena** dinner, supper | **el desayuno** breakfast

Las bebidas Beverages

el agua (f.) **mineral con/sin gas**
carbonated/noncarbonated mineral water
el café coffee

la cerveza beer
el jugo de frutas fruit juice
la leche milk

el refresco soft drink
el té (helado) (iced) tea
el vino (blanco, tinto) (white, red) wine

Los platos principales Main dishes

el bistec steak
los calamares (fritos) (fried) squid
los camarones shrimp
la carne (de res) meat (beef)

la chuleta (de cerdo) (pork) chop
la hamburguesa hamburger
el jamón ham
la langosta lobster

los mariscos shellfish, seafood
el pavo turkey
el pescado fish
el pollo (asado) (roasted) chicken

Las frutas y los vegetales/las verduras Fruits and vegetables

la banana/el banano banana
los champiñones mushrooms
la lechuga lettuce

la manzana apple
la naranja orange
las papas (fritas) (french fried) potatoes

el tomate tomato

Otras comidas Other foods

el arroz rice
el champiñón mushroom
la ensalada salad

el huevo duro hard-boiled egg
el pan (tostado) (toasted) bread
el queso cheese

la salsa sauce
el sándwich sandwich
la sopa soup

Los condimentos Condiments

el aceite oil
el azúcar sugar

la mantequilla butter
la pimienta pepper

la sal salt
el vinagre vinegar

Los postres Desserts

el flan (casero) (homemade) caramel custard | **el helado** ice cream

El restaurante

el (la) camarero(a) waiter (waitress)
la cuenta check, bill

la especialidad de la casa house specialty
el menú menu

Adjetivos

caliente hot (temperature)
fresco(a) fresh

ligero(a) light (meal, food)
pesado(a) heavy (meal, food)

rico(a) delicious

Verbos

almorzar (ue) to have (eat) lunch
cenar to have (eat) supper (dinner)
cocinar to cook
dejar una (buena) propina to leave a (good) tip

desayunar to have (eat) breakfast
desear to wish; to want
pedir (i,i) to order (food)
picar to eat appetizers; to nibble

preparar to prepare
recomendar (ie) to recommend

Expresiones idiomáticas

¡Buen provecho! Enjoy your meal!
¡Cómo no! Of course!
Estoy a dieta. I'm on a diet.
Estoy satisfecho(a). I'm satisfied. I'm full.

La cuenta, por favor. The check, please.
No puedo (comer) más. I can't (eat) any more.
¿Qué desean/quieren comer (beber)? What
would you like to eat (to drink)?

¡Salud! Cheers!
Te invito. It's on me (my treat).
Yo quisiera... I would like . . .

Expresiones adverbiales de tiempo Temporal adverbial expressions

anoche last night
anteayer the day before yesterday

ayer yesterday

la semana / el mes / el año pasado(a) last
week / month / year

PLAZAS

En esta edición vas a conocer a lugares, negocios y aspectos sociales y culturales de España, Bolivia y Venezuela y vas a comparar tus ideas y opiniones con las de nuestros autores. Participa con nosotros y vas a ver que tenemos mucho en común.

- ¡Mi casa es su casa!
- Franquicias latinoamericanas en los Estados Unidos y en el mundo: Churro manía
- Curaméricas
- La casa de Bernarda Alba

Fuentes en el palacio de La Alhambra en Granada, España

¡Mi casa es su casa!

Las personas que visitan España ven una arquitectura bastante diversa de una región a otra. ¿Por qué hay tanta diversidad? En parte es porque la historia de España tiene una rica combinación de varias culturas. Una influencia principal es la influencia árabe en el sur de España, en la región que se llama Andalucía, por la invasión de los árabes, y su subsequiente *(subsequent)* ocupación desde el siglo VIII hasta el XV.

Los reyes de los diferentes grupos árabes vivieron en las ciudades de Granada, Córdoba y Sevilla, al sur de España, donde construyeron palacios hermosos y maravillosos.

Uno de los palacios más famosos españoles, y el mejor conservado, es La Alhambra, que se encuentra en la ciudad de Granada, el antiguo centro político y aristocrático musulmán al este de Andalucía. Con la construcción principal del palacio (1333–1391), los visitantes de hoy pueden apreciar esta residencia de la familia real *(royal)*. Las grandes salas con techos altos, los dormitorios y los cuartos de los sirvientes son sólo algunas partes del palacio que hoy se conservan. Además, el clima árido es una consideración en la construcción de estos palacios; por eso, las fuentes *(fountains)*, los baños, los patios interiores sombreados *(shaded)* y los extensos jardines sirven de ejemplo de cómo los reyes se adaptaron al calor tan intenso de Andalucía. La Alhambra es una verdadera joya *(gem)* de construcción y muestra la influencia árabe que la arquitectura española recibió en el pasado y que se puede seguir apreciando hoy.

Fuerte militar en La Alhambra, Granada, España

- ¿Dónde está La Alhambra?
- ¿Cómo es La Alhambra? Puedes buscar información sobre La Alhambra en Internet para hacer una descripción detallada de su arquitectura.
- ¿Cómo usaron la arquitectura los árabes para vivir con el calor?
- ¿Qué tipos de residencias existen para las personas de importancia histórica en los Estados Unidos? Describe estos lugares.
- ¿Qué influencias de otras culturas hay en la arquitectura en los Estados Unidos?

Churro manía
Una manía para chuparse los dedos

Rubio decidió invertir *(to invest)* todo su dinero en una tienda para vender churros y por esto todo el mundo le dijo «loco». En 1997, él abrió su primera tienda que ahora tiene mucho éxito *(success)* en Venezuela y en el mundo. Estos churros están rellenos de chocolate, dulce de leche, miel o tienen azúcar solamente.

Hay cuarenta tiendas de Churro Manía en Venezuela y ahora hay tiendas en Miami, Orlando, Tampa, Clearwater, St. Petersburg, Puerto Rico, España y Brasil. Las tiendas facturan 10 millones de dólares al año y las ganancias *(earnings)* son millonarias. Estas tiendas tienen mucho éxito aquí en los Estados Unidos porque hay 30 millones de hispanos y éstos son un mercado *(market)* natural para los productos latinos.

Los churros son un postre de masa *(dough)* cilíndrica con forma de estrella en las puntas *(ends)* con azúcar que tanto los españoles como los latinoamericanos comen para la merienda. Un joven venezolano, Ariel Acosta-

¿Dónde está **CHURRO MANÍA** en el mundo?

- ¿Qué tipo de franquicia discute el artículo?

- ¿Por qué tienen tanto éxito las franquicias hispanas en los Estados Unidos?

- ¿Te gustaría invertir tu dinero en una franquicia? ¿Qué tipo de franquicia?

- En grupos de cuatro personas, discutan una idea sobre una franquicia de comida y presenten sus ideas a la clase. Pueden considerar la siguiente información:
  - Tipo de comida
  - Logotipo *(logotype)*
  - Lugar donde van a abrir sus tiendas y por qué

Curaméricas

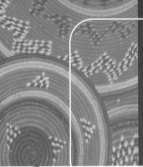

curaméricas
HOPE THROUGH HEALTH

HISTORY   OPPORTUNITIES   CONTACT
www.curamericas.org

20 YEARS

Henry Perry III y Alice Weldon, dos médicos de Carolina del Norte, fundaron Curaméricas en 1983. El objetivo principal de Curaméricas es reducir el número de enfermedades y muertes *(deaths)* en personas pobres o con pocos recursos económicos en países como Bolivia, Guatemala, Haití y México. Los médicos, enfermeros, enfermeras y voluntarios visitan todas las casas en una comunidad y estudian a las familias que tienen más riesgos *(risks)* de enfermedades.

En Bolivia, Curaméricas asistió a más de 75.000 mujeres, niños y familias en el Altiplano y en la región de Montero en los últimos años. Estas familias recibieron ayuda médica y educación médica de estas organizaciones. La combinación de la poca infraestructura y las difíciles condiciones de vida hacen de Bolivia uno de los países más pobres de Sur América. Muchas comunidades no tienen agua potable y las personas tienen que caminar un día completo para llegar a una clínica para ver a un(a) médico(a). Debido a la altitud y a una dieta no balanceada, las mujeres y niños mueren de pulmonía, diarrea y problemas del estómago. El programa de Curaméricas trabaja en más de 200 comunidades para enseñar a las personas a cuidarse de muchas enfermedades.

¿Cómo puedes ayudar a Curaméricas?

Puedes apoyar las diferentes organizaciones que trabajan desde los Estados Unidos.

Puedes trabajar como voluntario(a), o puedes hacer tus prácticas *(internship)* de medicina en uno de los países como Bolivia, Guatemala, Haití o México.

Puedes trabajar como embajador(a) *(ambassador)* para los programas de Curaméricas.

Puedes mandar medicinas a los diferentes países.

- ¿Tienes ganas de trabajar como voluntario(a)?
- ¿Qué trabajo deseas hacer como voluntario(a)?
- ¿En qué país deseas trabajar como voluntario(a)? ¿Por qué?

La casa de Bernarda Alba

Uno de los más conocidos poetas y dramaturgos españoles del siglo XX es
Federico García Lorca (1898–1936). Estudió en Granada y en Madrid.
Viajó por toda España, por los Estados Unidos y la América del Sur. Es autor
de numerosos poemas y obras teatrales. Es famoso por su lirismo y su
preocupación *(concern)* por la muerte y por el conflicto humano.

Uno de sus dramas más populares y su última creación dramática se titula
La casa de Bernarda Alba. Se trata de *(It's about)* la vida solitaria de una
viuda y sus hijas, que siempre están en casa bajo el estricto control de la
madre, Bernarda Alba. Lorca describe con sencillez *(simplicity)* el escenario
(stage) de los tres actos.

Acto primero

<u>Habitación blanquísima</u> del interior de la casa
de Bernarda.

Muros gruesos. Puertas en arco con cortinas
de yute *(jute fabric)*. Sillas de anea *(rush, used for
chair seats)*. Cuadros con paisajes *(landscapes)*
inverosímiles de ninfas o reyes de leyenda.
Es verano. Un gran silencio umbroso *(shadowed)*
se extiende por la escena. Al levantarse el
telón *(curtain)*, está la escena sola.

La casa de Bernarda Alba

Acto segundo

<u>Habitación blanca</u> del interior
de la casa de Bernarda. Las
puertas de la izquierda dan
a los dormitorios. Las hijas de
Bernarda están sentadas en
sillas bajas cosiendo *(sewing)*.

Acto tercero

Cuatro <u>paredes blancas
ligeramente</u> *(slightly)*
<u>azuladas</u> del patio
interior de la casa de
Bernarda. Es de noche.
El decorado ha de ser
(should be) una perfecta simplicidad. Las puertas
iluminadas por la luz de los interiores dan un tenue
fulgor (esplendor delicado) a la escena. En el centro,
una mesa con un quinqué *(oil lamp)*, donde están
comiendo Bernarda y sus hijas. La Poncia las sirve.
... Al levantarse el telón hay un gran silencio,
interrumpido por el ruido de los platos y los
cubiertos.

- ¿Qué tipo de ambiente *(atmosphere)* crea Lorca con las descripciones de la casa y sus habitaciones?

- ¿Cuál crees que es la importancia de la luz y de los colores en este drama? ¿Por qué crees que Lorca los menciona?

- ¿Qué representa la descripción de los colores «blanquísimo», «blanco» y «blanco ligeramente azulado»?

- En grupos de tres personas, describan la casa donde quieren vivir.

7

De compras:

Chapter Objectives

COMMUNICATIVE GOALS

In this chapter you will learn how to . . .

- Talk about shopping for clothing
- Make emphatic statements about possession
- Talk about singular and/or completed events in the past
- Make selections and talk about sizes and other shopping preferences
- Describe ongoing and habitual actions in the past

STRUCTURES

- Stressed possessives
- Verbs irregular in the preterite
- Direct object pronouns
- Imperfect tense

CULTURAL INFORMATION

- De compras en Buenos Aires
- El tango argentino

Argentina

ARGENTINA

Población: 37.384.816
Área: 2.779.221 kilómetros cuadrados, cuatro veces el tamaño de Texas
Capital: Buenos Aires, 11.624.000
Ciudades principales: Córdoba, 1.434.900; Rosario, 1.229.800; Mendoza, 957.400; Tucumán, 774.500
Moneda: el peso
Lenguas: el español, el italiano (no es oficial)
Exportación: aceites vegetales, electricidad, cereales, carne de res, vehículos, uvas, tabaco

¡Bienvenidos a Argentina!

En este vídeo, vas a aprender de la cultura de Argentina. Después de ver el vídeo, contesta las siguientes preguntas:

1 ¿Dónde está Argentina?

2 ¿Cómo es la capital de Buenos Aires y cuál es su apodo (nickname)?

3 ¿Qué es el tango?

4 Según el video, ¿en qué aspecto es el campo muy distinto de la ciudad? ¿Quién es el «gaucho», cuál es su trabajo y qué representa?

5 Si vas a Argentina, ¿adónde te gustaría ir? ¿a la ciudad o al campo? ¿Por qué?

La Plaza del Congreso, Buenos Aires, Argentina

VOCABULARIO La ropa

CULTURA

Argentina is especially famous for its leather goods: jackets, handbags, gloves, wallets, and shoes. Stores specializing in leather can be found in all of Argentina's major cities: Buenos Aires, Mendoza, Córdoba, San Juan, and Rosario, to name a few. In the south, San Carlos de Bariloche is known for its woolen goods. In the province of Salta, one can find unique **ponchos de Guemes.** The legacy of the **gaucho** (the Argentine cowboy of the Pampas region) has also had a lasting influence on contemporary Argentine clothing styles.

¿NOS ENTENDEMOS?

In Argentina, a skirt is called **la pollera** instead of **la falda;** a jacket is called **la campera** instead of **la chaqueta;** a sweatshirt is called **el buzo** and **las camisetas** are called **las remeras.** It is important to note that in the major cities people do not wear shorts when walking around the city; people wear shorts only at the beach or cities that are located close to shore. Another term for **la cartera** in Argentina is **la billetera** or for a coin purse **el monedero;** and a woman's purse is sometimes referred to as **la cartera. Los lentes** and **los anteojos** are synonyms for **las gafas.**

¿NOS ENTENDEMOS?

Notice that in Spain and Argentina, people say **a cuadros** as well as **a lunares** and **a rayas.**

La ropa de última moda en Buenos Aires In this section you will learn how to talk about clothing and related accessories by looking at pages from a fashion magazine. What kinds of clothing are fashionable for people today? Do you think fashions in Spanish-speaking countries are ahead of or behind styles currently popular in the United States?

Para chicas y chicos este otoño

¡Mamá y papá están de moda!

...o en la lluvia

En la playa...

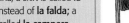

Estilos y telas Styles and fabrics

de (a) cuadros plaid
de (a) lunares polka-dotted
de (a) rayas striped
es de... it's made of . . .
  algodón cotton
  cuero leather
  lana wool
  seda silk

Palabras útiles are presented to help you enrich your personal vocabulary. The words here will help you talk about clothing and accessories.

Palabras útiles

el bosillo pocket
el botón button
el cierre / la cremallera zipper
llevar to wear
la prenda article of clothing

el smoking tuxedo
las yuntas / los gemelos cufflinks
los zapatos de tenis tennis shoes, athletic shoes
los zapatos de tacón (alto) high heels

¡A PRACTICAR!

7-1 **¿Para hombres o mujeres?** Decide si los siguientes artículos se asocian más con los hombres, las mujeres o ambos *(both):* los hombres y las mujeres. Luego, trata de encontrar una persona en la clase que lleve los mismos artículos de ropa.

MODELO: la bufanda
Es para los hombres y las mujeres. Soledad lleva (wears) *una bufanda.*

1. la blusa
2. la camisa
3. las botas
4. pantalones de lana

5. la mini-falda
6. los guantes
7. los calcetines

8. las medias
9. los aretes
10. la corbata

7-2 **Asociaciones** ¿Cuál es la palabra que no va con las otras?

1. la cartera, la bolsa, el abrigo, el anillo
2. la chaqueta, los pantalones cortos, la camiseta, el suéter
3. el sombrero, las medias, los zapatos, las sandalias
4. el traje, el vestido, el cinturón, la corbata
5. los guantes, el traje de baño, el impermeable, el abrigo

EN VOZ ALTA

7-3 **Tus preferencias** Con un(a) compañero(a), hablen de sus preferencias. Después de contestar tus preguntas, él/ella va a preguntarte sobre las tuyas.

MODELO: botas negras de cuero / zapatos de tenis
E1: *¿Qué prefieres tú, unas botas negras de cuero o unos zapatos de tenis?*
E2: *Mmm, yo prefiero unas botas negras. No me gustan mucho los zapatos de tenis. ¿Y tú?...*

1. bufanda de cuadros / bufanda de lana
2. sombrero de cowboy / gorra de béisbol
3. mini-falda / falda larga
4. guantes de seda / guantes de algodón
5. abrigo de lana / chaqueta de esquiar
6. pantalones de cuero / los vaqueros
7. traje o vestido formal / ropa cómoda *(comfortable)*
8. pantalones cortos / pantalones largos

7-4 **La ropa y el clima** Pregúntale a otro(a) compañero(a) sobre qué ropa se necesita para las siguientes situaciones. ¿Están de acuerdo?

1. Es octubre, hace sol y no hace viento. Tú y dos amigos quieren caminar por la ciudad de Buenos Aires. ¿Qué ropa van a ponerse?
2. Tú y tu mejor amigo(a) piensan ir de vacaciones a Mar del Plata por dos semanas en enero cuando hace buen tiempo allí. ¿Qué ropa van a llevar?
3. Una amiga te invita a esquiar en Bariloche por cinco días. Tú aceptas la invitación y ahora tienes que decidir qué ropa vas a llevar.

7-5 **Estoy pensando en una persona** Un(a) estudiante va a pensar en otro(a) estudiante sin revelar quién es. Los otros estudiantes tienen que averiguar *(find out)* la identidad de la persona, haciendo preguntas de tipo **sí** o **no.**

MODELO: E1: *¿Lleva esta persona botas de cuero?*
E2: *No, no lleva botas de cuero.*
E3: *¿Lleva esta persona zapatos de tenis?*
E2: *Sí, esta persona lleva zapatos de tenis.*
E3: *¿Es Raymond?*
E2: *Sí, es él.*

CULTURA
October is generally a month of pleasant weather in Buenos Aires since it is springtime in the southern hemisphere. In Buenos Aires and other cities of Latin America, attire is less casual than it is in most U.S. cities.

CULTURA
Mar del Plata is a beachside resort about 250 miles south of Buenos Aires. It is one of Argentina's largest tourist attractions and receives over 6 million visitors each year.

CULTURA
San Carlos de Bariloche is known as the **Suiza de las Américas** *(Switzerland of the Americas)* as it is a mountain town rich with European influences and winter attractions, especially skiing.

Text audio
Track 1–17

EN CONTEXTO

Hoy es sábado, 18 de diciembre. Julio y Silvia Sepúlveda y su hijo están en un almacén (tienda) en la calle Florida en Buenos Aires. Silvia está probándose *(is trying on)* un vestido blanco que quiere llevar para una fiesta que ella y su esposo van a dar la semana que viene. Julio está esperándola con su hijo, Juan Carlos.

CULTURA
La calle Florida is a pedestrian-only street that features many boutiques and shops.

Silvia:	¿Qué te parece este vestido, Julio? **¿Cómo me queda?** *(How does it look on me?)*
Julio:	¡Me gusta mucho! **Te queda muy bien.** Estás muy elegante.
Silvia:	Gracias. Me gusta este color porque va bien con las joyas *(jewelry)*.
Julio:	Pero, ¿qué joyas?
Silvia:	Las **mías.** Las que me diste *(you gave me)* para mi cumpleaños. Creo que el vestido va a ser perfecto para nuestra fiesta, ¿verdad?
Julio:	¡Claro que sí! ¿Recuerdas la fiesta tan estupenda que **dieron** *(gave)* Jorge y Hortensia el año pasado cuando **hacía tanto frío y llovía?**
Silvia:	Nunca voy a **olvidarla.** ¡Cómo nos divertimos!, ¿no? Comimos tantas cosas ricas y conocimos a tanta gente.
Julio:	Sí, sí. La fiesta fue *(was)* fabulosa. Bueno, ahora voy a **pagar** el vestido con mi **tarjeta de crédito.** ¿Cuánto **cuesta,** Silvia?
Silvia:	Menos de 100 pesos. Es un buen precio, ¿no crees, Julio?
Julio:	Pues... creo que sí. Oye, Silvia, tenemos que volver a la zapatería *(shoe store)* para **cambiar** estos zapatos que le compramos a Juan Carlos la semana pasada. **Le quedan un poco grandes.**
Silvia:	Bueno. Y después vamos a casa porque Juan Carlos tiene hambre y estoy cansada de tanta actividad.

¿NOS ENTENDEMOS?
In Spanish the meaning of some verbs includes the preposition *for.* Verbs that exhibit this feature are **buscar** *(to look for),* **pedir** *(to ask for),* and **esperar** *(to wait for).* For the verb **pagar,** the inclusion of the preposition depends on whether or not there is mention of the price. For example, Silvia **paga el vestido** *(pays for the dress)* versus Silvia **paga 100 pesos por el vestido** *(pays 100 pesos for the dress).*

¿NOS ENTENDEMOS?
The **vosotros(as)** form that is used in Spain could be recognized by the other Spanish-speaking population, but it is not actively used. The form of **ustedes** is used formally and informally as the plural of *you.* In Argentina and other countries in Central America, **vos** is used as another form of **tú.** When **vos** is used with present-tense verbs, it is conjugated differently: for **-ar** verbs, add **-ás: Vos habl*ás* español como un argentino(a);** for **-er** verbs, add **-és: Vos com*és* parrillada argentina todos los fines de semana;** and for **-ir** verbs, add **-ís: ¿Vos decid*ís* estudiar en Buenos Aires o en Córdoba?** The irregular verb **ser** has an irregular form for **vos** also: **Vos sois muy inteligente.**

¿Comprendiste?
Contesta las siguientes preguntas a base del diálogo.

1. ¿Dónde están los Sepúlveda en este momento?
2. ¿Qué están haciendo allí?
3. Y después, ¿qué van a hacer?
4. ¿Qué compró Silvia?
5. ¿De qué color es su vestido?
6. ¿Qué puedes comprar en una zapatería?
7. ¿Dónde va a ser la fiesta?
8. ¿Son los zapatos de Juan Carlos viejos o nuevos?

Encuentro cultural

De compras en Buenos Aires

PARA PENSAR

- ¿Hay vecindades o barrios en tu ciudad que tienen especializadas?
- ¿Hay ferias de arte en mercados al aire libre en tu ciudad?
- ¿Te gusta visitar las ferias de arte al aire libre?

centro comercial

En Buenos Aires hay todo tipo de tiendas. Desde lujosos *(luxurious)* centros comerciales, boutiques o tiendas especializadas hasta mercados al aire libre, donde se venden antigüedades *(antiques)* y ropa de cuero o piel. Muchas de las tiendas de cuero están situadas en las mismas fábricas *(factories)*. Así, las personas pueden comprar los artículos de cuero del color, del tamaño o de la forma que deseen, o hechos a la medida *(made to order)*, en solamente uno o dos días. También, hay en Buenos Aires los grandes centros comerciales donde están situadas desde tiendas internacionales hasta tiendas con gusto local. Todos los centros comerciales tienen restaurantes y cafés para comer y descansar después de ir de compras. Algunos de estos centros comerciales son: Alto Palermo, Alto Avelleda, El Centro de Diseño de Buenos Aires, Harrod's, Plaza Liniers y Unicentro.

Por todas partes de la ciudad, se encuentran tiendas especializadas o boutiques donde se puede comprar pinturas, joyas, ponchos y artículos de cuero y de lana. Los mercados o ferias al aire libre se abren los domingos, y la feria más famosa es la Feria de las Antigüedades en el barrio de San Pedro Telmo, que funciona en la Plaza Dorrego. La Feria de San Pedro Telmo comenzó en 1970, cuando se reunieron por primera vez en la Plaza Dorrego un pequeño grupo de vecinos *(neighbors)* para vender sus cosas viejas el día domingo. Así comenzó una tradición en la Plaza Dorrego que hoy en día reúne a 270 vendedores; cada uno tiene un pequeño puesto *(stand)* donde vende sus antigüedades. Estos puestos son muy exclusivos y difíciles de conseguir y hay que llenar *(fulfill)* varios requisitos antes de poder vender en este lugar. Algunos de los requisitos son: obtener los puestos por sorteo *(raffle);* vender objetos de antes de los años sesenta y hay que trabajar durante todo el día del domingo. Esta plaza es un buen lugar para ir a conversar y discutir de política y de economía con los amigos, así como también para mirar y comprar objetos que representan la cultura de los habitantes de Buenos Aires en Argentina.

PARA DISCUTIR

1. ¿Qué tipo de tiendas hay en Buenos Aires, Argentina?
2. ¿Dónde puede comprar la gente artículos de cuero o piel?
3. ¿Qué ventajas *(advantages)* hay en comprar cuero en las fábricas?
4. ¿Cuándo y cómo comenzó la feria de San Pedro Telmo en la Plaza Dorrego?
5. ¿Deseas ir de compras en Buenos Aires? ¿Por qué sí o por qué no?
6. ¿Qué tipo de ferias hay en tu ciudad o estado?
7. ¿Qué producto se vende en tu estado que es muy famoso en otros lugares?

Possessives are used to express ownership. In **Capítulo 2** you learned how to indicate possession by using **de (El vestido es *de* Silvia)** and by using unstressed possessive adjectives: **mi(s), tu(s), su(s), nuestro(a)(s), vuestro(a)(s), su(s).** In English, we place emphasis on the possessive by using intonation (*This is **my** dress*) or by using the form *of mine, of his, of hers,* etc. In Spanish, emphasis is placed on the possessive by using the stressed forms, identified below:

mío(a)(s)	*my, (of) mine*
tuyo(a)(s)	*your, (of) yours*
suyo(a)(s)	*your, of yours; his, (of) his; her, (of) hers; its, (of) its*
nuestro(a)(s)	*our, (of) ours*
vuestro(a)(s)	*your, (of) yours*
suyo(a)(s)	*your, (of) yours; their, (of) theirs; his, (of) his; her, (of) hers; its, (of) its*

Stressed possessive adjectives

The stressed possessive adjective must come after the noun and, like most other adjectives, agree in number and gender.

Unstressed:	Éstos son mis guantes.	*These are my gloves.*
Stressed:	Éstos son guantes **míos.**	*These are my gloves.*
		These gloves are mine.

Unstressed:	Es su blusa.	*It's her blouse.*
Stressed:	Es una blusa **suya.**	*It's her blouse.*
		It's a blouse of hers.

Stressed possessive pronouns

Stressed possessives often function as pronouns, substituting for the omitted noun. When used as a pronoun, stressed possessives are preceded by a definite or indefinite article.

Silvia no tiene chaqueta.	*Silvia doesn't have a jacket.*
Le doy **la mía.**	*I'll give her mine.*

Mi camiseta está sucia.	*My shirt is dirty.*
Préstame **una tuya.**	*Lend me one of yours.*

Note that with **ser** the article is omitted unless there is a choice between items.

Este sombrero **es mío.**

but

Este sombrero **es el mío** y ése **es el tuyo.**

¡A PRACTICAR!

7-6 **¿A quién le pertenece (belong)?** Llena los espacios con la forma correcta del pronombre posesivo enfático.

MODELO: Es mi falda. Es *mía.*

1. Son los zapatos de Tamara. Son _____
2. Es la corbata de Sebastián. Es _____
3. Son tus pantalones. Son _____
4. Es mi chaqueta. Es _____
5. Son las sandalias de Mauricio. Son _____
6. Son nuestros trajes. Son _____

7-7 **Confusión en la lavandería** Dos chicos acaban de lavar la ropa y tienen que separar las prendas *(articles)* de ropa. Utiliza la forma correcta del adjetivo o del pronombre posesivo entre paréntesis.

Daniel: Esos pantalones no son _____ *(mine)* —son _____ *(yours).*

Tomás: ¡Imposible! Son muy grandes. Son de Óscar. Son _____ *(his).*

Daniel: Y esa camiseta, ¿también es _____ *(his)?*

Tomás: No, esa camiseta es _____ *(mine).*

Daniel: ¡Ay! Me olvidé de separar estos vaqueros de la blusa blanca de mi hermana. ¡Mira la blusa _____ *(hers)!*

Tomás: No importa. Mi hermana le puede prestar _____ *(hers)* para la fiesta esta noche.

EN VOZ ALTA

7-8 **¿De quién son... ?** Con un(a) compañero(a) de clase, contesten las siguientes preguntas sobre de quién son estas cosas que encontramos en nuestro salón de clase en un día de invierno. En sus respuestas usen el pronombre posesivo correcto.

MODELO: E1: ¿Éstos son mis guantes?
E2: *Sí, son los tuyos.*
o *No, no son los tuyos. Son los míos.*

1. ¿Éste es mi libro?
2. ¿Éstos son nuestros lápices?
3. ¿Éstos son nuestros cuadernos?
4. ¿Éstos son sus abrigos?
5. ¿Éstas son sus gafas de sol (de Uds.)? ¿(de ellos)?
6. ¿Ésta es mi bufanda?
7. ¿Éste es tu impermeable?
8. ¿Éste es su sombrero (de él)?

7-9 **¿Es tuya?** Basándote en el vocabulario de este capítulo que ya sabes, hazles ocho preguntas a dos compañeros(as) de clase sobre las prendas de ropa que encuentres *(you may find)* en la clase.

MODELO: E1: *Jason, ese abrigo, ¿es tuyo?*
E2: *No, no es mío. Es de mi compañero de cuarto. Es un abrigo suyo.*

As you know, Spanish speakers use the preterite tense to express the beginning and ending/completion of past actions, conditions and events. Some Spanish verbs have irregular verb stems in the preterite and their endings have no accent marks.

dar:	di, diste, dio, dimos, disteis, dieron
hacer:	hice, hiciste, hizo, hicimos, hicisteis, hicieron
ir:	fui, fuiste, fue, fuimos, fuisteis, fueron
poder:	pude, pudiste, pudo, pudimos, pudisteis, pudieron
poner:	puse, pusiste, puso, pusimos, pusisteis, pusieron
saber:	supe, supiste, supo, supimos, supisteis, supieron
querer:	quise, quisiste, quiso, quisimos, quisisteis, quisieron
venir:	vine, viniste, vino, vinimos, vinisteis, vinieron
estar:	estuve, estuviste, estuvo, estuvimos, estuvisteis, estuvieron
tener:	tuve tuviste tuvo tuvimos tuvisteis tuvieron
decir:	dije, dijiste, dijo, dijimos, dijisteis, dijeron
traer:	traje, trajiste, trajo, trajimos, trajisteis, trajeron
ser:	fui, fuiste, fue, fuimos, fuisteis, fueron

Note the spelling change from **c** to **z** in the **Ud./él/ella** form.

Note that the preterite stems of **decir** and **traer** end in **-j**. With these two verbs, the **-i** is dropped in the **Uds./ellos/ellas** form to become **dijeron** and **trajeron**, respectively.

Mi familia **vino** a visitarme ayer.	*My family came to visit me yesterday.*
La semana pasada **hicimos** muchas compras.	*Last week we did a lot of shopping.*

- Note that the preterite forms for **ir** and **ser** are identical; context clarifies their meaning in a sentence.

Fui dependiente por un día.	*I was a salesclerk for a day.*
Fui a la tienda de ropa ayer.	*I went to the clothing store yesterday.*

Andar also follows this pattern: anduve, anduviste, anduvo, anduvimos, anduvisteis, anduvieron.

- Also note that **poder, poner, saber, querer, venir, estar,** and **tener** share the same endings:

pud-	-e
pus-	-iste
sup-	-o
quis-	-imos
vin-	-isteis
estuv-	-ieron
tuv-	

- The preterite of **hay** is **hubo.**

—**Hubo** un robo hoy en esta tienda.	*There was a robbery today in that store.*
—¿Qué pasó?	*What happened?*
—No sé, pero **hubo** policías para hacer la investigación toda la mañana.	*I don't know, but there were police officers to do the investigation all morning.*

¡A PRACTICAR!

7-10 | De compras Silvia fue de compras un sábado con su amiga Andrea. Conjuga los verbos entre paréntesis para saber adónde fue de compras Silvia. Silvia se levantó temprano...

1. Ella _tuvo_ (tener) que ir de compras para buscarle un regalo de cumpleaños a su esposo.
2. Ella _dijo_ (decir) a su esposo que iba (*she was going*) a visitar a una amiga.
3. Silvia y su amiga Andrea _fueron_ (ir) a la calle Florida.
4. Silvia _trajo_ (traer) las tarjetas de crédito para hacer compras en Argentina.
5. Las dos amigas _fueron_ (ir) a la tienda más lujosa de Buenos Aires.
6. Ellas _tuvieron_ (tener) mucha suerte porque todas las prendas estaban rebajadas.
7. Las dos _pusieron_ (ponerse) muy emocionadas.
8. Las dependientes _fueron_ (ser) muy simpáticas con ellas.
9. Silvia _pudo_ (poder) pagar con sus tarjetas de crédito.
10. Silvia _tuvo_ (tener) que mostrar otra tarjeta de crédito para revisar su crédito.

7-11 | ¡Qué generoso es Julio! Julio, el esposo de Silvia, se enteró de (*found out about*) las compras de su esposa aquella misma noche. Él nos cuenta cómo lo supo y qué le regaló Silvia a él. Completa el siguiente párrafo con la forma correcta del pretérito de los infinitivos entre paréntesis.

Ayer por la noche yo me 1. ___di___ (dar) cuenta que mi esposa Silvia había ido de compras con su amiga Andrea. Por la mañana, ella no me 2. ___dijo___ (decir) lo de las compras. Ella salió a las 9:00 de la mañana. Primero, ella y Andrea 3. ___fueron___ (ir) a la calle Florida, donde las dos compraron zapatos nuevos. Después, ellas tomaron un café en la Recoleta. En la Recoleta, ellas entraron a muchas tiendas muy caras y encontraron un regalo de cumpleaños para mí y vestidos nuevos y regalos para su familia. Menos mal que Silvia usó su tarjeta de crédito para esas compras. Cuando ella 4. ___vino___ (venir) a casa anoche, me contó lo de sus compras: «Lo siento, Julio, pero 5. ¡___hubo___ (haber) unas rebajas fantásticas en la Recoleta, y Andrea y yo no 6. ___pudimos___ (poder) resistir la tentación de comprar!» Ella me 7. ___hizo___ (hacer) un regalo muy bonito —¡una cartera de cuero! Yo le 8. ___di___ (dar) un beso muy fuerte a mi esposa. Nosotros 9. ___tuvimos___ (tener) una cena deliciosa de pizza a la piedra con nuestro hijo Juan Carlos. La noche 10. ___fue___ (ser) muy buena. Todos nos acostamos contentos a las 10:00 de la noche.

CULTURA

Pizza a la piedra is a very popular dish in Buenos Aires. The pizza is cooked with the crust directly on a stone surface over a wood fire, which makes the crust have a more crispy consistency than when baked on a pan. A famous **pizzería** in the microcenter of Buenos Aires is called **Los Inmortales.**

EN VOZ ALTA

7-12 | **Entrevista: Una fiesta estupenda** Quieres saber más de tu compañero(a) de clase. Haz preguntas con los verbos entre paréntesis para hacérselas a tu compañero(a) sobre varios detalles de una fiesta especial. ¿Tienen muchos de los detalles en común?

> MODELO: cuándo (ir)
> E1: *¿Cuándo fuiste a una fiesta estupenda?*
> E2: *Fui el fin de semana pasado.*

1. tipo de celebración (ser) (fiesta de cumpleaños, etc.)
2. dónde (ser)
3. hora de la llegada de los invitados (ir)
4. tu llegada (llegar)
5. cuántos invitados (estar)
6. regalos (dar)
7. nuevos amigos (poder conocer)
8. actividades (hacer)
9. una sorpresa (haber)
10. impresión (hacerte)

7-13 | **De compras... (Shopping . . .)** Descríbele a un(a) compañero(a) de clase una experiencia que ocurrió cuando fuiste al centro comercial Alto Palermo en la Avenida Santa Fe de Buenos Aires. Considera las siguientes preguntas en tu historia. ¡Sé creativo(a)!

- ¿Adónde y con quién fuiste?
- ¿Llevaste las tarjetas de crédito?
- ¿Qué compraste? Y ¿por qué compraste eso?
- ¿Cuánto costó (costaron)?
- ¿Pudiste encontrar alguna oferta o ganga *(bargain)*?
- ¿Hiciste algún regalo con lo que compraste?
- ¿Qué más hiciste allí?
- ¿Estuviste contento(a) con tus compras?
- ¿Hablaste de tus compras con tus padres / tu novio(a) / tu esposo(a)?

VOCABULARIO De compras

En las tiendas de la Recoleta In this section you will practice vocabulary for shopping and expressions by learning more about one of the most famous shopping areas in Buenos Aires.

Sustantivos

el **cheque** check
el (la) **dependiente** salesclerk
el **descuento** discount
el **efectivo** cash
la **liquidación** sale (Lat. Am.), reduction (in price)
el **número** shoe size

la **oferta** sale (Lat. Am.)
el... **por ciento** percent
la **rebaja** sale (Spain), reduction (in price)
la **talla** size (clothing)
la **tarjeta de crédito** credit card

Verbos

cambiar to change
costar (ue) to cost
gastar to spend (money)
hacer juego con to match
llevar to wear; to carry
mostrar (ue) to show

pagar to pay (for)
ponerse to put on
probarse (ue) to try on
quedarle (a uno) to fit (someone)
rebajar to reduce (in price)
usar to wear; to use

Adjetivos

barato(a) inexpensive, cheap
caro(a) expensive

grande big
pequeño(a) small

Expresiones idiomáticas

¿Cómo me queda? How does it look/fit me?
¿Cuánto le debo? How much do I owe you?
¡Es una ganga! It's a bargain!

¡Está de (última) moda! It's the latest style!
¡Me quedan muy pequeños! They're too small!

CULTURA
In Buenos Aires the most luxurious boutiques can be found in the Recoleta neighborhood. Other popular shopping areas in Buenos Aires are the **calle Florida, Alto Palermo,** and **Galerías Pacífico.** The **avenida Santa Fe** also offers boutiques with very elegant clothing and accessories.

¿NOS ENTENDEMOS?
Spanish sometimes "borrows" words from English. For example, in Buenos Aires another way to say **Está de moda** is to say **Está fashion.**

¡A PRACTICAR!

7-14 | **¡Es una ganga!** A Silvia le fue muy bien en las tiendas de la Recoleta. Termina los siguientes párrafos con las palabras de cada lista.

hace juego	por ciento	descuentos	rebajas	queda
talla	probarse	de última moda	cara	

Cuando Silvia vio unas 1. _____ en su tienda favorita, no pudo resistir y entró. ¡Había (There were) 2. _____ de hasta el 20 3. _____! Silvia decidió 4. _____ una blusa 5. _____. La dependiente le dijo «Es su 6. _____, señora. La blusa le 7. _____ divinamente. Además, la blusa 8. _____ con los pantalones que lleva.» «Me gusta mucho,» dijo Silvia. «¿Es muy 9. _____?»

Cuánto le debo	efectivo	tarjeta de crédito	rebajamos
cuesta	gastar	estilos	

La dependiente le respondió, «No. Hoy nosotros 10. _____ todas las prendas que ve en esta sección. La blusa le 11. _____ 30 pesos. Tenemos otros 12. _____, pero son más caros.» Entonces Silvia le dijo: «No puedo 13. _____ más de 30 pesos. Voy a llevar la blusa.» «¿Algo más?», le preguntó la dependiente. «No», dijo Silvia. «¿14. _____ por la blusa?» La dependiente pensó un segundo y luego añadió, «Si usted paga en 15. _____, le puedo bajar el precio un poquito más.» «Lo siento», dijo Silvia. «Creo que tengo que pagar con 16. _____. No tengo suficiente en efectivo.»

EN VOZ ALTA

7-15 | **¡Me encanta esta chaqueta anaranjada!** Estás de compras con Rolanda, una persona de muy mal gusto. Ella te sugiere muchas cosas, y tú tienes que decirle a ella (¡sin insultarla!) que no te gustan. Usa excusas como **es demasiado caro(a), me queda grande/chico/mal, no es mi color, no está de moda, no hace juego con mi...** ¡Trata de usar una excusa diferente cada vez! Tu compañero(a) hace el papel de Rolanda.

> MODELO: una chaqueta anaranjada
> Rolanda: ¿Por qué no compras esta chaqueta anaranjada?
> Tú: *Bueno, realmente no es mi color.*

1. un bikini de lunares talla 1
2. unas gafas de sol rojas
3. unos zapatos verdes
4. una corbata de color amarillo fuerte
5. un traje morado de poliéster talla 60
6. una camisa roja y amarilla
7. unas medias de rayas
8. un sombrero de cowboy
9. una mini-falda muy corta
10. unas botas de piel de cocodrilo

LAS TALLAS DE ROPA

CULTURA

Sizes in European and in some Latin American countries run on an entirely different scale. In this case a 36 would be equivalent to a woman's size 8.

DAMAS

Vestidos / Trajes

Sistema norteamericano	6	8	10	12	14	16	18	20
Sistema europeo	34	36	38	40	42	44	46	48

Calcetines / Pantimedias

Sistema norteamericano	8	8½	9	9½	10	10½
Sistema europeo	0	1	2	3	4	5

Zapatos

Sistema norteamericano	6	6½	7	8	8½	9
Sistema europeo	36	37	38	38½	39	40

CABALLEROS

Trajes / Abrigos

Sistema norteamericano	36	38	40	42	44	46
Sistema europeo	46	48	50	52	54	56

Camisas

Sistema norteamericano	14	14½	15	15½	16	16½	17	17½	18
Sistema europeo	36	37	38	39	41	42	43	44	45

Zapatos

Sistema norteamericano	5	6	7	8	8½	9	9½	10	11
Sistema europeo	37½	38	39½	40	41	42	43	44	46

7-16 **En una tienda de ropa** Habla con otro(a) campañero(a): una persona es el (la) dependiente y la otra persona es su cliente.

Dependiente

1. Greet your customer.
3. Ask how you can help.
5. Inquire about size(s) using the chart above.
7. Find the correct size(s).
9. Ask about form of payment.
11. End the conversation.

Cliente

2. Answer appropriately.
4. Say what you want to try on.
6. Respond to the question(s).
8. Decide whether or not to buy.
10. State method of payment.
12. Respond appropriately.

7-17 **Situaciones difíciles** Con un(a) compañero(a), interpreten las siguientes situaciones. Intenten usar expresiones que estudiaron en esta sección.

ESTUDIANTE 1: Vas a una fiesta formal con uno(a) de tus mejores(as) amigos(as). Quieres vestirte formalmente porque te gusta la ropa elegante y quieres dar una buena impresión en la fiesta. Llama a tu amigo(a) para convencerlo(la) que él/ella necesita vestirse tan elegantemente como tú.

ESTUDIANTE 2: Eres una persona relajada e informal. Te gusta vestirte siempre cómodamente y no te gusta gastar mucho dinero, especialmente en ropa de última moda. Comunícale estos sentimientos a tu amigo(a) cuando te llame por teléfono.

ESTUDIANTE 1: Tu amigo(a) está probándose un traje o vestido horrible para la ceremonia de graduación de la universidad. Quieres ser cortés, pero necesitas convencerlo(la) que él/ella no debe comprarlo. Usa muchos argumentos.

ESTUDIANTE 2: Vas a comprar un traje o un vestido para la ceremonia de graduación de la universidad. Tienes gustos excéntricos y por fin encontraste algo de lunares que te encanta. Vas a comprarlo a pesar de *(in spite of)* lo que piensan otras personas.

Verbos útiles: quedarle bien (mal), hacer juego con

Encuentro cultural

El tango argentino

PARA PENSAR

■ ¿Conoces el tango argentino?

■ ¿Sabes bailar algún baile típico de tu región, o sabes bailes especiales? ¿Cómo se llama(n)? ¿Te gusta bailar estos bailes?

Una pareja bailando tango.

Es difícil hablar de Argentina sin mencionar el tango. Para bailar bien el tango, hay que tener mucho corazón. Pero, para encontrar el corazón del tango, hay que aprender todas las reglas básicas. El patrón *(pattern)* más básico del tango es la caminata *(the walk)*. Algunos otros pasos *(dance steps)* de este baile argentino son el paseo *(the stroll)*, la cadencia, la caza *(the chase)* y la cunita *(the cradle, or rock step)*.

Lo más complicado del tango es el ritmo. En el tango los movimientos de la mujer deben ocurrir muy rápido después de los del hombre. Los pasos de la mujer son precisos y parecen ser sin esfuerzo *(effortless)*. Todos los impulsos de la mujer son dirigidos por el hombre con gestos e indicaciones sutiles con la mano derecha que descansa en la espalda de la mujer.

El tango es hermoso cuando dos personas pueden integrar la pasión y el drama en el baile. El tango toma tiempo y sentimiento y no es necesario tener talento acrobático. Este baile argentino apareció en 1911, y la canción más famosa del tango es «La comparsita». Para el año 1924, el tango era *(was)* sin duda el baile más popular de Buenos Aires, y es hoy el baile nacional de Argentina. El cantante más famoso de tango es Carlos Gardel (1890–1935), quien además hizo muchas películas para Paramount Pictures en las que cantó tango, como, por ejemplo, *Espérame* (1933, *Wait for Me*), *Cuesta abajo* (1934, *Downhill*), *El Tango en Broadway* (1934, *The Tango on Broadway*). Gardel murió en un accidente de avión en 1935 y todavía hoy en día la gente visita su tumba *(tomb)* en Buenos Aires, porque lo consideran el dios del tango.

PARA DISCUTIR

1. ¿Cuántos patrones básicos del tango puedes nombrar?
2. ¿Qué es necesario para bailar el tango?
3. ¿Cuál es la canción más famosa del tango?
4. ¿Quién es el cantante de tango más famoso de Argentina?
5. ¿Qué tumba de cantantes visita la gente en los Estados Unidos?
6. ¿Te gustaría aprender a bailar el tango? ¿Por qué?

ESTRUCTURA II Simplifying expressions: direct object pronouns

In this section you will learn how to simplify expressions by substituting direct objects with direct object pronouns.

Direct object pronouns

All sentences have a subject and a verb. Many sentences also have an object that receives the action of the verb. For example, in the sentence below, the direct object (**la blusa**) receives the action of the verb (**compró**) performed by the subject (**Silvia**).

Subject	Verb	Direct Object
	↓	↓ ↓
Silvia	compró	la blusa.
Silvia	*bought*	*the blouse.*

The direct object of a sentence is usually a person or a thing and it answers the question *whom?* or *what?* in relation to the sentence's subject and verb.

Julio llamó a **su mamá.**   *Whom did he call? (his mom)*

Silvia compró **la blusa.**   *What did she buy? (a blouse)*

In Spanish, as in English, a direct object pronoun may be used in place of a direct object noun.

Singular	Plural
me *me*	**nos** *us*
te *you* (informal)	**os** *you* (informal)
lo *you* (formal); *him; it* (masculine)	**los** *you* (formal); *them* (masculine)
la *you* (formal); *her; it* (feminine)	**las** *you* (formal); *them* (feminine)

Julio llamó a **su mamá.**   Él **la** llamó.
Julio called his mother.   *He called her.*

Silvia compró **las blusas.**   Ella **las** compró.
Silvia bought the blouses.   *She bought them.*

In the preceding sentences, the direct object pronouns **la** and **las** replace the direct object nouns **mamá** and **las blusas,** respectively. In the following example, see how **los** replaces **los Reynosa, lo** replaces **el suéter,** and **las** replaces **las sandalias.**

—Julio, ¿conoces a **los Reynosa?**   *Julio, do you know the Reynosas?*
—Sí, **los** conozco.   *Yes, I know them.*

—Silvia, ¿lavaste mi **suéter?**   *Silvia, did you wash my sweater?*
—No, no **lo** lavé.   *No, I didn't wash it.*

—Papá, ¿dónde están mis **sandalias?**   *Dad, where are my sandals?*
—**Las** tengo aquí.   *I have them here.*

Placement of the direct object pronouns

- Place the pronoun in front of the conjugated verb.

—¿Cambiaste los pantalones, Julio?　　*Did you exchange the pants, Julio?*
—Sí, **los cambié** anoche.　　*Yes, I exchanged them last night.*

- In negative sentences, place the **no** in front of the pronoun.

—¿Me llamaste, Silvia?　　*Did you call me, Silvia?*
—No, Julio. N**o te** llamé.　　*No, Julio. I did not call you.*

When the direct object pronoun is used with an infinitive or a present participle, place it either before the conjugated verb or attach it to the infinitive or the present participle. (A written accent is needed to retain the stressed vowel of a present participle when a direct object pronoun is attached to it.)

<table>
<tr><td>**Lo voy** a llamar mañana.</td><td rowspan="2">}</td><td rowspan="2">*I'm going to call him tomorrow.*</td></tr>
<tr><td>**Voy a llamarlo** mañana.</td></tr>
<tr><td>**Lo estoy llamando** ahora.</td><td rowspan="2">}</td><td rowspan="2">*I'm calling him now.*</td></tr>
<tr><td>**Estoy llamándolo** ahora.</td></tr>
</table>

Note that the direct object pronoun **lo** can be used to stand for actions or ideas in general.

—Julio, compré tres nuevas blusas.　　*Julio, I bought three new blouses.*
—¡No puedo creer**lo**!　　*I can't believe it! (it = the fact that Silvia bought three new blouses)*

> With reflexive verbs in the infinitive form, the direct object pronoun is placed after the reflexive pronoun at the end of the verb. For example: **Voy a probarme el suéter. Voy a probármelo.** Affirmative commands also require that the direct object pronoun be attached to the verb. You will learn more about commands and placement of pronouns in **Capítulos 8 and 11.**

¡A PRACTICAR!

7-18 | **El asistente de Julio** Julio está trabajando en la tienda con su nuevo asistente, Rogelio. Están hablando de dónde poner la nueva ropa que acaba de llegar. Completa las conversaciones con los pronombres **lo, la, los** o **las.**

MODELO: —Julio, ¿va a poner los pantalones de lana aquí?
　　　　—No, voy a poner*los* allí.

1. —Julio, ¿usted vendió la última blusa de seda?
　—Sí, __la__ vendí ayer.
2. —Rogelio, ¿terminó con las cuentas de ayer?
　—Pues... no, Julio. Yo estoy haciéndo__las__ ahora.
3. —Julio, ¿encontró los nuevos suéteres de algodón?
　—No, todavía estoy buscándo__los__.
　—Yo creo que __los__ puse allí, al lado de los trajes de baño.
4. —Julio, mañana tengo que llevar a mi hermano al hospital. No puedo venir a trabajar hasta mediodía.
　—¡Yo no __lo__ creo! ¡Ud. no tiene hermanos!

7-19 | **Conversaciones domésticas** Completa los siguientes diálogos con el pronombre correcto.

En casa

Silvia: ¿Conoces a Ramón Sarmiento, Julio?

Julio: Pues... sí, ____lo____ conozco un poco. ¿Por qué?

Silvia: Porque Ramón y su esposa ____nos____ (a nosotros) invitaron a una fiesta.

Julio: ¿____nos____ (a nosotros) invitaron? Mmm... ____los____ conocimos el año pasado, ¿no?

Silvia: Sí, en una fiesta, pero nunca ____los____ visitamos. ¿Vamos a la fiesta?

Julio: Sí, cómo no. Vamos.

Silvia: Pues, si vamos, ¡me voy a comprar aquel vestido rojo que encontré ayer en la Recoleta! ¿Qué te parece, Julio?

Julio: Me parece muy bien mi amor, cómprate____lo____.

En la fiesta

Silvia: Gracias por tu invitación, Ramón. ____la____ recibimos la semana pasada.

Ramón: De nada, Silvia. ¿Conocen ustedes a mis hijas?

Julio: Pues... Creo que sí ____los____ conocemos.

Ramón: Bueno, ésta es Angelina y ésta es Berta.

Berta: Mucho gusto.

Silvia: Berta, ¿no ____me____ recuerdas? Soy la señora Sepúlveda. ____te____ conocí hace un año.

Berta: Ah, sí, señora Sepúlveda. Ahora ____la____ recuerdo. ¿Cómo está?

EN VOZ ALTA

7-20 | **¿Qué quieres?** Tu compañero(a) va a ofrecerte las siguientes cosas. Responde, indicando si quieres comprar el objeto o no, sustituyendo el sustantivo (*noun*) por el pronombre (*pronoun*) correcto. ¿Tienen mucho en común?

MODELO: las camisetas
     E1: *¿Quieres comprar las camisetas?*
     E2: *Sí, las quiero comprar.*
  o E2: *Sí, quiero comprarlas.*
  o E2: *No, no las quiero comprar.*
  o E2: *No, no quiero comprarlas.*

1. el abrigo
2. las corbatas de seda
3. la chaqueta de cuero
4. el suéter de algodón
5. las medias de seda
6. las gafas de sol negras
7. los zapatos de tenis Adidas
8. la blusa de Versace

Spanish speakers use the imperfect tense to describe past actions, conditions, and events that were in progress or that occurred habitually or repeatedly.

To form the imperfect, add the following endings to the verb stem. Note the identical endings for **-er** and **-ir** verbs.

Verbs regular in the imperfect

	jugar	hacer	divertirse
yo	jugaba	hacía	me divertía
tú	jugabas	hacías	te divertías
Ud., él/ella	jugaba	hacía	se divertía
nosotros(as)	jugábamos	hacíamos	nos divertíamos
vosotros(as)	jugabais	hacíais	os divertíais
Uds., ellos(as)	jugaban	hacían	se divertían

Note that only three Spanish verbs are irregular in the imperfect:

	ir	ser	ver
yo	iba	era	veía
tú	ibas	eras	veías
Ud., él/ella	iba	era	veía
nosotros(as)	íbamos	éramos	veíamos
vosotros(as)	ibais	erais	veíais
Uds., ellos(as)	iban	eran	veían

—¿**Ibas** mucho de compras cuando **eras** niña?

—Sí, y mi familia y yo **comprábamos** mucha ropa.

Did you use to go shopping a lot when you were a little girl?

Yes, and my family and I used to buy lots of clothes.

The imperfect tense of **hay** is **había.**

—¿**Había** muchas personas enfrente del Palacio del Congreso?

—Sí, Silvia. **Había** mucha gente.

Were there a lot of people in front of the Palacio del Congreso?

Yes, Silvia. There were many people.

CULTURA

The **Palacio del Congreso** is a majestic structure located in the **Plaza del Congreso.** The palace was completed in 1906 and is a major tourist attraction for those visiting Buenos Aires.

Talking about the past: the preterite and the imperfect

The preterite

You have learned that Spanish speakers use the preterite tense to describe the beginning or completion of past actions, conditions, and events. For example, notice how Silvia uses the preterite to tell what happened at her home this morning.

Esta mañana mi despertador **sonó** a las 7:00 como siempre. **Me levanté, fui** al baño, **me duché** y **me vestí.** Luego **desperté** a Juan Carlos y **preparé** el desayuno. **Comimos** fruta y pan tostado y **tomamos** café. Después, **nos lavamos** los dientes y **salimos** de casa. **Fuimos** en colectivo al centro.	*This morning my alarm went off at 7:00 as always. I got up, went to the bathroom, showered, and got dressed. Then, I woke up Juan Carlos and prepared breakfast. We ate fruit and toast, and we drank coffee. Next, we brushed our teeth and left the house. We went downtown by bus.*

CULTURA

The easiest and most common way of getting around Buenos Aires is by buses called **colectivos.**

The imperfect

- Spanish speakers use the imperfect tense to express actions, conditions, and events that were in progress at some focused point in the past. For example, notice how Silvia uses the imperfect tense to tell what was going on when she got off the bus with her son.

Cuando nos bajamos del colectivo, **hacía** un poco de frío y **llovía.** Juan Carlos no **quería** ir de compras conmigo porque todavía **estaba** cansado.	*When we got off the bus, it was a little cold and it was raining. Juan Carlos didn't want to go shopping with me because he was still tired.*

- Spanish speakers also use the imperfect to describe actions, conditions, and events that occurred habitually or repeatedly in the past. Notice how Silvia uses the imperfect to describe how her life was when she was a girl.

Cuando **era** niña, todo **era** diferente de lo que es ahora. Yo **tenía** menos responsabilidades y creo que **era** más feliz. Todos los sábados **me levantaba** tarde porque no **había** mucho que hacer en casa. Luego **iba** a la cocina, me **servía** un vaso de leche y **miraba** la tele. Por la tarde mis amigas y yo **jugábamos** juntas.	*When I was a child, everything was different than it is now. I had fewer responsibilities and I think I was happier. Every Saturday I would get up late because there wasn't much to do at home. Then, I would go to the kitchen, I would serve myself a glass of milk, and I would watch TV. In the afternoon my friends and I would play together.*

- Note that the imperfect tense can be translated in different ways, depending on the context. For example, read the following paragraph and notice the English meaning of the forms in parentheses.

De niña yo **vivía** (*I lived*) en un pueblo cerca de Buenos Aires. Los sábados mi mamá y yo **íbamos** (*used to go*) de compras a la calle Florida donde **mirábamos** (*we would look at*) muchas cosas en las tiendas. Todos los domingos, cuando **caminábamos** (*we were walking*) por el barrio de San Pedro, veíamos (*we used to see*) la feria de antigüedades en la Plaza Dorrego.

¡A PRACTICAR!

7-21 **Querido abuelo** Cambia los verbos de la siguiente lista al imperfecto para completar el primer párrafo de una carta que Silvia le escribió a su abuelo.

ir	estar	poder	llamar
tener	escribir	querer	trabajar

¿Cómo estás, abuelito? Yo 1. _____ escribirte antes pero no lo pude hacer porque
2. _____ tantos quehaceres aquí en casa para prepararnos para la fiesta. Julio, Juan
Carlos y mi trabajo me ocupan casi todo el tiempo. Ayer Julio 3. _____ preguntándome
sobre ti y le dije que 4. _____ a escribirte muy pronto. Recuerdo que te 5. _____
cartas y que te 6. _____ por teléfono más frecuentemente cuando no 7. _____
tanto como ahora.

7-22 **Silvia de niña** Silvia está contándole a Juan Carlos algunas cosas que ella hacía de niña. ¿Qué le dice a su hijo?

MODELO: yo / jugar con mis amigos
Yo jugaba con mis amigos.

1. mi familia y yo / vivir en una estancia veinte kilómetros al norte de Buenos Aires
2. (nosotros) no / tener auto, pero / tener muchos caballos
3. tu abuelo / ser agricultor; también / comprar y / vender caballos
4. mi mamá / trabajar en casa
5. mis dos hermanos y yo / divertirse mucho; / andar en bicicleta / montar a caballo e / ir a jugar en diferentes lugares
6. (nosotros) nunca / aburrirse porque / haber muchas cosas que hacer
7. antes de acostarnos por la noche mi mamá leer o / contar historias sobre cuando ella / ser niña
8. a veces, mi papá / tocar el acordeón y nos / cantar tangos y viejas canciones italianas
9. yo / querer mucho a mis padres y muchas veces les / decir que (yo) no / poder vivir sin ellos

CULTURA

An **estancia** is a farm or ranch in Argentina. Cattle ranching is very common in the center of the country; sheep ranching is more common in the south. Horses are very important animals on many ranches.

CULTURA

Around the turn of the twentieth century, many Italians immigrated to Argentina. People of Italian descent still make up a large portion of the Argentine population.

7-23 **¿Pretérito o imperfecto?** Julio está conversando con Juan Carlos en la sala sobre cómo llegaron a vivir en Buenos Aires. Completa su conversación, indicando los verbos correctos entre paréntesis.

Juan Carlos: Papá, ¿dónde (vivieron/vivían) tú y mamá después de casarse?

Julio: (Vivimos/Vivíamos) por un año y medio con mis padres cerca de Buenos Aires porque no (tuvimos/teníamos) mucho dinero.

Juan Carlos: ¿Qué tipo de trabajo (hiciste/hacías), papi?

Julio: (Trabajé/Trabajaba) como dependiente en un almacén. (Vendí/Vendía) zapatos allí. Nosotros (ganamos/ganábamos) poco dinero, pero (fue/era) suficiente para vivir.

Juan Carlos: ¿Cuándo (vinieron/venían) ustedes a vivir aquí en Buenos Aires?

Julio: Dos meses después de que (naciste/nacías), hijo.

Juan Carlos: ¿(Fue/Era) en diciembre?

Julio: Sí. Luego, tú, mamá y yo (pasamos/pasábamos) la Navidad (*Christmas*) juntos en esta casa. ¿Recuerdas eso?

Juan Carlos: ¿Cómo voy a recordar si solamente (tuve/tenía) cuatro meses?

EN VOZ ALTA

7-24 | **¿Qué hacías?** Dile a un(a) compañero(a) las actividades que tú hacías cuando eras más joven. ¿Hacían Uds. las mismas cosas?

MODELO: Cuando vivía en... yo...
Cuando vivía en Vermont, yo compraba ropa para esquiar.

1. Cuando tenía quince años, mi familia...
2. Cuando estudiaba en..., yo...
3. Vivía en... cuando mis hermanos...
4. Compraba ropa... cuando nosotros...
5. Me gustaba... cuando tenía...

7-25 | **Cuando yo tenía diez años...** Trabajando con un(a) compañero(a) de clase, terminen las siguientes oraciones con la información adecuada sobre su niñez *(childhood)*. Luego, comparen sus respuestas con las de otros compañeros. ¿Tienen mucho en común?

1. Cuando yo tenía diez años, mi familia y yo vivíamos en...
2. Nuestra casa (apartamento) era...
3. Mi papá trabajaba en... y mi mamá...
4. En general, mis padres...
5. Yo me divertía mucho. Por ejemplo...
6. Yo tenía un(a) amigo(a), que se llamaba...
7. A veces, él/ella... y yo...
8. También nosotros...

7-26 | **Entrevista** Hazle estas preguntas a un(a) compañero(a) de clase.

1. **La familia:** ¿Dónde y con quién vivías cuando tenías seis años? ¿Cuántos hermanos tenías? ¿Quién era el menor? ¿y el mayor? ¿Qué tipo de trabajo hacía tu papá? ¿y tu mamá? ¿Dónde? ¿Cuándo visitabas a tus tíos y a tus abuelos? ¿Qué otras cosas hacías con tu familia?

2. **Las posesiones:** De niño(a), ¿tenías una bicicleta? (¿Sí? ¿De qué color era?) ¿Tenías un perro o un gato? (¿Sí? ¿Cómo se llamaba?) ¿Qué otras cosas tenías? ¿Qué era la cosa más importante que tenías?

3. **Los amigos:** ¿Tenías muchos o pocos amigos en la escuela primaria? ¿Cómo te divertías con ellos? ¿Cómo se llamaba tu mejor amigo(a) en la escuela secundaria? ¿Dónde vivía? ¿Qué hacían ustedes juntos(as)? ¿Tenías novio(a)? (¿Sí? ¿Cómo se llamaba? ¿Cómo era él/ella?)

4. **Los pasatiempos:** De adolescente, ¿cómo pasabas el tiempo cuando no estudiabas o trabajabas? ¿Practicabas algún deporte? ¿Cuál? ¿Con qué frecuencia ibas al cine? ¿Qué tipo de películas veías? ¿Qué programas de televisión mirabas? ¿Qué otras cosas hacías para divertirte?

¡A VER!

En este segmento del video, Sofía y Alejandra hablan de la moda mientras se preparan para un día en la playa y Antonio y Javier se visten en ropa especial. También, vas a ver escenas de todos los compañeros de casa vestidos de varias maneras.

Expresiones útiles

The following are some new expressions you will hear in the video.

Desde que salí del colegio	Since I graduated from high school
Ya pasó de moda	It's out of style
Playeras de algodón	Cotton t-shirts
Como digas	Whatever you say

Antes de ver

Paso 1: ¿Qué tipo de ropa crees que tiene la mayoría de las mujeres? ¿Y la mayoría de los hombres? Nombra todo tipo de ropa que pueda llevar una mujer y un hombre y luego compara tus listas con las de un(a) compañero(a). ¿Están de acuerdo?

Las mujeres   **Los hombres**

_____   _____

_____   _____

_____   _____

_____   _____

_____   _____

_____   _____

Paso 2: ¿Cuál es tu estilo personal en cuanto a *(with regard to)* la moda? ¿Te consideras tradicional o moderno(a)? ¿Te gusta llevar ropa de última moda? Compara tus respuestas con las de un(a) compañero(a). ¿Tienen el mismo estilo de vestirse o son diferentes?

Después de ver

Paso 1: En **Antes de ver, Paso 1,** nombraste los diferentes artículos de ropa que pueda llevar un hombre y una mujer. Ahora, mira las fotos y describe con mucho detalle lo que lleva cada uno de los compañeros de casa. ¿Llevan algo que no tienes en tus listas de **Antes de ver, Paso 1?**

Valeria lleva _____

Sofía lleva _____

Javier lleva _____

Alejandra lleva _____

Antonio lleva _____

Paso 2: En **Antes de ver, Paso 2,** tu compañero(a) y tú hablaron de su estilo personal en cuanto a la moda. Ahora, según lo que viste en el video describe el estilo personal de las tres compañeras en la Hacienda Vista Alegre, Alejandra, Sofía, y Valeria. Luego compara tus descripciones con las de un(a) compañero(a). ¿Están de acuerdo?

Sofía: _____

Alejandra: _____

Valeria: _____

¿Qué opinas tú?

Paso 1: En el video, Alejandra dijo que Sofía tenía que ir de compras. ¿Y tú? ¿Qué ropa nueva quieres y/o necesitas comprar? ¡No te preocupes por el dinero! Luego compara tu lista con la de un(a) compañero(a). ¿Necesitan las mismas cosas?

Paso 2: En cuanto al estilo personal y la ropa que usas, ¿a quién te pareces más? ¿a Valeria? ¿a Antonio? ¿a cuál de los compañeros del video? Comparte con la clase tu respuesta y justifícala. ¿Cuál es el estilo personal más popular en tu clase?

¡A LEER!

Strategy: Using background knowledge to anticipate content

The better you can anticipate what you will read, the more easily you will be able to understand the main ideas in reading a passage. In addition to looking at the pictures, titles, and subtitles that accompany a text, you should also think about what you already know about the topic.

Paso 1: Antes de leer el siguiente texto, observa lo siguiente.

1. **la foto**
   a. ¿Quiénes son estas personas?
   b. ¿Qué prendas de ropa llevan?
   c. ¿Cuál es la estación del año según la foto?

2. **el título**
   a. ¿Qué ideas asocias con la estación del año mencionada en el título?
   b. El verbo alterar es sinónimo de cambiar *(change).* Según el título, ¿qué está cambiando?

Paso 2: El texto que vas a leer es sobre la moda. Antes de leer, piensa en lo que ya sabes sobre la moda.

1. ¿Cuáles son los estilos y telas más populares hoy en día?
2. ¿Cuáles son los colores más populares?
3. ¿Cuáles son las tiendas de ropa más populares?

Paso 3: Antes de leer el texto, lee las preguntas que siguen. Después, lee el texto y contesta las preguntas.

1. ¿Cómo se describen los tres estilos principales mencionados en el texto? Llena el cuadro que sigue con algunas palabras y expresiones.

el sport urbano	el cyberchic	el neohippy

2. Según el texto, ¿cuáles son los tejidos (las telas) más populares? ¿Cuáles son los colores más populares?
3. Entre los tres estilos que se describen en el texto, ¿cuál prefieres tú? ¿Por qué?

La primavera la moda altera
Todo lo que se llevará esta próxima temporada

Durante décadas, la moda masculina y femenina no parecían guardar conexión. Sin embargo, en los últimos años, los diseños se han aproximado lo justo en cuanto a tendencias –si no en formas, sí en estilos, colores y tejidos.

En la próxima temporada primavera-verano, esa relación va a ser evidente por el paralelismo entre los guardarropas de estilos de ambos sexos.

En términos generales, se puede hablar de una tendencia clara hacia un corte sencillo, muy estructurado, con preferencia de tejido sobre la forma, que se ha plasmado en las pasarelas a través de tres estilos: el sport urbano, el cyberchic y el neohippy.

El primero, inspirado principalmente en las prendas técnicas deportivas y en las náuticas, se llevará la palma.

Triunfan los combinados de blanco y negro, los ácidos naranja y amarillo.

El segundo –resultado de la ciencia ficción y la eclosión tecnológica que define el siglo– es una apuesta clara por las formas atrevidas, los tejidos de aspecto técnico y las fibras artificiales. Se aleja, no obstante, de la visión apocalíptica de los diseños futuristas de otros tiempos y adquiere un aspecto más sofisticado.

Por último, el neohippy representa la vuelta a lo natural, lo rústico y lo étnico y una recuperación de materiales y fibras nobles. Esta tendencia se presenta como vía formal de escape frente a una sociedad que se imagina dominada por las máquinas, y responde a las nuevas filosofías de humanización de la persona.

En la misma línea, los diseñadores han trabajado con fibras naturales y artificiales. Ambas se mezclan y es el resultado final –después de tratadas– lo que hace que adopten un aspecto u otro, también con aspectos brillantes y tornasolados. Al mismo tiempo, la piel, el algodón, el lino y la seda vuelven a primera línea.

En colores, el blanco desplaza al gris. Su mezcla más exitosa es con el negro.

Y frente a los tonos neutros, llegan los ácidos, jugosos como el naranja o el amarillo, que se combinan con otros tan poco sutiles –aunque sí muy atractivos– como el fucsia, los jades e, incluso, los ultravioletas.

¡A ESCRIBIR!

Strategy: Editing your writing

Editing your written work is an important skill to master when learning a foreign language. You should plan on editing what you write several times. When checking your compositions, consider the following areas.

1. **Content**
   a. Is the title of your composition captivating? Would it cause readers to want to read further?
   b. Is the information you wrote pertinent to the established topic?
   c. Is your composition interesting? Does it capture reader interest?

2. **Organization**
   a. Does each paragraph in the composition have a clearly identifiable main idea?
   b. Do the details in each paragraph relate to a single idea?
   c. Are the sentences in the paragraph ordered in a logical sequence?
   d. Is the order of the paragraphs correct in your composition?

3. **Cohesion and style**
   a. Does your composition as a whole communicate what you are trying to convey?
   b. Does your composition "flow" easily and smoothly from beginning to end?
   c. Are there transitions between the different paragraphs you included in your composition?

4. **Style and accuracy**
   a. Have you chosen the precise vocabulary words you need to express your ideas?
   b. Are there grammatical errors in your composition (i.e., subject-verb agreement, adjective-noun agreement, errors with verb forms or irregular verbs, etc.)
   c. Are there spelling errors in your composition (including capitalization, accentuation, and punctuation)?

If you consider these factors as you edit your written work, the overall quality of your compositions can increase drastically!

Task: Simple reporting in the past

Simple reporting in the past occurs in a variety of contexts and focuses on the narration of a series of events. You may encounter this sort of reporting in brief newspaper or magazine articles and in informal as well as more formal correspondence. You will now prepare a short report about a recent shopping trip following the steps below and focusing on completed actions such as where you went and what you did during your outing.

Functions: Talking about past events; Talking about recent events
Vocabulary: Clothing; Fabrics; Colors; Stores and products
Grammar: Verbs: irregular preterite, regular preterite; Personal pronouns: direct, indirect

Paso 1: Antes de escribir, piensa en la última vez que fuiste de compras para buscar ropa. Contesta las siguientes preguntas.

- ¿Adónde fuiste de compras? (¿Cómo se llama el centro comercial o cómo se llaman las tiendas?)
- ¿Fuiste solo(a) o con otra persona?
- ¿A qué hora llegaste a la primera tienda?
- ¿Fuiste a otras tiendas?
- ¿Qué artículo(s) de ropa compraste? ¿Dónde compraste el artículo o los artículos?
- ¿Cuánto dinero gastaste en las compras que hiciste?
- ¿Cuánto tiempo pasaste en las compras?
- ¿Qué hiciste después?

Paso 2: Ahora, escribe una composición breve (de dos o tres párrafos) sobre esta excursión. En tu composición, incluye la información que usaste para contestar las preguntas en **Paso 1.**

Paso 3: Ahora, tienes que corregir tu composición. Usa las preguntas de la sección anterior (partes 1, 2, 3 y 4 de *Editing your writing*) como guía de corrección.

Paso 4: Intercambia papeles con un(a) compañero(a) de clase. Cada persona debe usar la sección de arriba para evaluar la composición de su compañero(a). Si hay partes de las composiciones que necesiten corrección, cada persona debe hacer los cambios necesarios.

¡A CONVERSAR!

Pronunciation focus: *c* and *qu; l, ll,* and *y*

The letter **c** before any consonant except **h** or before the vowels **a, o, u,** and the letters **qu** before **e** or **i** are represented by the sound [k], a sound similar to the English *k* but without a puff of air. Practice these sentences.

• Quiero comprar una corbata, unos calcetines y una cartera de cuero.
• ¿Cómo me queda?

The single **l** sound in Spanish resembles the **l** sound in English. The **ll** is pronounced like the **y** in most of the Spanish-speaking world. This sound is like the *y* in the English word *yellow*. In most of Argentina this sound is like the *z* in the English word *azure* or like the *s* in the Enlgish word *Asia*. Practice these sentences.

• Me gustan los pantalones de lana, pero no los tienen en mi talla.
• Prefiero la falda de rayas, no el vestido de lunares.

Task: Discussing shopping for clothes

Antes de ir a la universidad por primera vez o de volver para un nuevo semestre, muchos estudiantes van de compras para buscar ropa. Ahora vas a hablar con otro(a) estudiante sobre lo que quieres comprar antes del próximo semestre.

Paso 1: Identifica los meses del próximo semestre y el tiempo que hace en esos meses en la región donde vives. Menciona algunas actividades que vas a hacer durante el semestre. Después menciona varios artículos de ropa que vas a necesitar.

Paso 2: Comenta sobre los artículos importantes que ya tienes y que no necesitas comprar.

Paso 3: Nombra algunos artículos que necesitas comprar y describe los artículos con muchos detalles *(details).* Menciona los colores, las telas y los estilos que prefieres.

Paso 4: Habla de las tiendas adonde quieres ir y lo que quieres comprar en cada tienda. Incluye información sobre los precios que esperas pagar y cómo vas a pagar las cosas que vas a comprar.

Paso 5: Habla con tu compañero(a) sobre cómo son similares y cómo son diferentes sus planes para ir de compras antes del nuevo semestre.

La ropa Clothing

el abrigo overcoat	el cinturón belt	las sandalias sandals
la blusa blouse	la corbata necktie	el sombrero hat
las botas boots	la falda skirt	el suéter sweater
la bufanda scarf	la gorra de béisbol baseball cap	el traje suit
los calcetines socks	los guantes gloves	el traje de baño swimsuit
la camisa shirt	el impermeable raincoat	los vaqueros jeans
la camiseta T-shirt	los jeans blue jeans	el vestido dress
el chaleco vest	las medias stockings	los zapatos shoes
la chaqueta jacket	los pantalones (cortos) pants (shorts)	

Los accesorios Accessories

el anillo ring	el collar necklace	el reloj watch
los aretes earrings	las gafas de sol sunglasses	el sombrero hat
la bolsa purse, bag	el paraguas umbrella	
la cartera wallet, purse	la pulsera bracelet	

De compras Shopping

el cheque check	la liquidación sale (Lat. Am.), reduction (in price)	el... por ciento percent
el (la) dependiente salesclerk		la rebaja sale (Spain), reduction (in price)
el descuento discount	el número shoe size	la talla size (clothing)
el efectivo cash	la oferta sale (Lat. Am.)	la tarjeta de crédito credit card

Verbos

cambiar to change	llevar to wear; to carry	probarse (ue) to try on
costar (ue) to cost	mostrar (ue) to show	quedarle (a uno) to fit (someone)
gastar to spend (money)	pagar to pay (for)	rebajar to reduce (in price)
hacer juego con to match	ponerse to put on	usar to wear; to use

Estilos y telas Styles and fabrics

de (a) cuadros plaid	es de... it's made of . . .
de (a) lunares polka-dotted	algodón cotton
de (a) rayas striped	cuero leather
	lana wool
	seda silk

Adjetivos

barato(a) inexpensive, cheap	grande big, large
caro(a) expensive	pequeño(a) small

Expresiones idiomáticas

¿Cómo me queda? How does it look/fit me?	ir de compras to go shopping	un par de... a pair of . . .
¿Cuánto le debo? How much do I owe you?	¡Me quedan muy pequeños! They're too small!	Vamos a ver. Let's see.
¡Es una ganga! It's a bargain!	pagar en efectivo (con cheque) to pay in cash (by check)	
¡Está de última moda! It's the latest style!		

Fiestas y vacaciones:

Chapter Objectives

COMMUNICATIVE GOALS

In this chapter you will learn how to . . .

- Talk about holidays, events, and activities at the beach and in the countryside
- Describe changes in emotion
- Inquire and provide information about people and events
- Narrate in the past
- State indefinite ideas and quantities
- Talk about periods of time since an event took place

STRUCTURES

- Preterite vs. imperfect
- Affirmative and negative expressions
- **Hace** and **hace que**

CULTURAL INFORMATION

- Chichicastenango
- Arzobispo Óscar Arnulfo Romero

Guatemala y El Salvador

GUATEMALA

Población: 12.974.361
Área: 108.890 kilómetros cuadrados, un poco más pequeño que Tennessee
Capital: Guatemala, 1.053.100
Ciudades principales: Mixo, 268.300; Villa Nueva, 129.600, Quezaltenango, 115.900
Moneda: el quetzal y el dólar estadounidense
Lenguas: el español y más de veinte idiomas indígenas

EL SALVADOR

Población: 6.237.662
Área: 21.040 kilómetros cuadrados, un poco menos grande que Massachusetts
Capital: San Salvador, 516.700
Ciudades principales: Soyaoango, 324.800; Santa Ana, 162.700; Mejicanos, 152.900
Moneda: el colón y el dólar estadounidense
Lenguas: el español y el nahua

¡Bienvenidos a Guatemala!

En este video, vas a aprender de la geografía y cultura de Guatemala. Después de ver el video, contesta las siguientes preguntas:

1. ¿Dónde está Guatemala y cómo es la naturaleza del país?

2. ¿Cuál es un ejemplo de los contrastes que existen en Guatemala?

3. Según el video, ¿cuál es el papel (*role*) de Guatemala en la cultura maya?

4. ¿Cómo celebran los guatemaltecos las fiestas religiosas? ¿Cómo se disfrazan?

5. ¿Te gustaría visitar Guatemala? ¿Por qué sí o por qué no?

La Plaza San Salvador, San Salvador, El Salvador

225

CULTURA
The people of Santo Tomás de Chichicastenango combine ancient Mayan beliefs with a Christian ideology in their celebration of the Winter Solstice, the shortest day of the year. In the Northern Hemisphere, this event takes place on December 21. In this small Guatemalan village, the inhabitants celebrate the day of their patron saint with processions and dances. The festivities of the day are also directed to the pagan Sun god who is honored in order that he continue to bless the town with light and warmth.

¿NOS ENTENDEMOS?
Generally, when people toast in Spanish they say ¡Salud! In Spain, however, it is common to say ¡Salud, amor y pesetas, y tiempo para gozarlos! *(Health, love, and money, and time to enjoy them!)* Another word for **la fiesta** and **la celebración** is **el festejo**, which comes from the verb **festejar** *(to celebrate).*

¿NOS ENTENDEMOS?
Un(a) fiestero(a) is *a partygoing person* while **un(a) aguafiestas** is *a party pooper.* Note also that the word **desfile** is most often used for a political or social parade, while the word **procesión** is used for a religious parade or celebration.

CULTURA
Pascua can mean *Easter, Passover,* and *Christmas. Easter* is sometimes referred to as **la Pascua Florida** while *Christmas* is referred to as **la Pascua Navideña.**

CULTURA
Semana Santa is Guatemala's largest celebration, featuring processions and celebrations throughout the country.

Palabras útiles are presented to help you enrich your personal vocabulary. The terms provided here will help you talk about holidays and celebrations.

Celebrando el Día de Santo Tomás en Chichicastenango, Guatemala In this section you will learn how to talk about parties and celebrations while learning about the festivities surrounding a Mayan holiday in a small, Guatemalan mountain town.

Verbos

cumplir años to have a birthday
dar (hacer) una fiesta to give a party
olvidar to forget
pasarlo bien (mal) to have a good (bad) time
ponerse + adjective to become, (to get) + adjective

portarse bien (mal) to behave well (poorly)
reaccionar to react
recordar (ue) to remember
reunirse con to get together with

Sustantivos

el cumpleaños birthday

el día feriado holiday

Expresiones idiomáticas

¡Felicitaciones! Congratulations!
Me pongo contento/avergonzado/molesto I become happy/embarrassed /annoyed

Palabras útiles
Días festivos del mundo hispánico

el Cinco de Mayo Cinco de Mayo
el Día de la Raza Columbus Day
el Día de los Muertos Day of the Dead
el Día de los Reyes Magos Day of the Magi (Three Kings)
el Día de Todos los Santos All Saints' Day (November 2)
el Día del Santo Saint's Day (the saint after whom one is named)

la Pascua Easter, Passover, Christmas
la Navidad Christmas
la Noche Vieja New Year's Eve
la Nochebuena Christmas Eve
la Semana Santa Holy Week

¡A PRACTICAR!

8-1 **Un cumpleaños** Selecciona la palabra adecuada/lógica para completar las siguientes oraciones.

1. Ayer fue el disfraz / ~~cumpleaños~~ de Tomás.
2. Hubo una fiesta de ~~sorpresa~~ / anfitriona con todos sus amigos y parientes.
3. Vinieron muchos brindis / ~~invitados~~ a la fiesta.
4. Sus parientes le dieron ~~regalos~~ / velas.
5. Su esposa le preparó un día feriado / ~~pastel~~ de cumpleaños muy grande con muchas ~~velas~~ / celebraciones.
6. Su esposa Marta y su amiga Tulia fueron las ~~anfitrionas~~ / procesiones de la fiesta.
7. La hermana de Tomás, Claudia, les ofreció cohetes / ~~entremeses~~ a los invitados que tenían hambre.
8. Los niños pequeños se ~~portaron~~ / recordaron bien durante la fiesta.
9. Todos los invitados lo pasaron ~~bien~~ / lo pasaron mal en esa máscara/ ~~celebración~~.

8-2 **¡Una fiesta sorpresa para Tomás!** Este año Tomás cumplió treinta años. Describe los preparativos (*preparations*) que hizo su esposa para la fiesta sorpresa. No te olvides usar los verbos en el pretérito donde sea necesario.

llorar	hacer un brindis	reunirse
disfrazarse	cumplir años	reaccionar
asustarse	dar una fiesta	recordar
celebrar	divertirse	gritar

Este año mi esposa Marta 1. _dio una fiesta_ para mi cumpleaños. Todos mis amigos 2. _se reunían_ afuera de mi casa y me 3. _gritaron_, «¡Feliz cumpleaños!» Después, encendieron unos cohetes, una tradición de Guatemala. Una niña 4. _se asustó_ por el ruido y 5. _lloró_. Más tarde, mi mejor amigo Rodrigo 6. _hizo una brindis_ y luego nos contó la «Leyenda de la niña flor». Mi esposa Marta 7. _reaccionó_ de una manera muy sentimental —ella 8. _recordó_ su quinceañera, un cumpleaños muy especial para ella. A las 12:00 de la noche, mi amigo Rodrigo y su esposa Claudia 9. _se disfrazaron_ de un matrimonio muy viejo para hacernos imaginar nuestra vida del futuro. Después, mi esposa sirvió un pastel con velas. Mis amigos me obligaron comer un poquito antes de servirlo. Normalmente, no me gusta mucho 10. _cumplir años_, pero este año nosotros 11. _celebramos_ con mucho entusiasmo y todos nosotros 12. _nos divertimos_ muchísimo.

CULTURA
Guatemala has a strong oral tradition, and it is not uncommon for stories to be shared at family gatherings. **La leyenda de la niña flor** is a Mayan legend that Miguel Ángel Asturias included in his collection of Mayan legends and folklore entitled *Leyendas de Guatemala*.

CULTURA
The **quinceañera**—a girl's 15th birthday—marks a girl's passage into womanhood. Though this tradition is more commonly associated with Mexico, it is also an important ritual in Guatemala.

CULTURA
Like North Americans, Guatemalans celebrate birthdays with cakes and candles. It is customary for the birthday celebrant to take a bite of cake before serving it to the rest of the party.

EN VOZ ALTA

8-3 | **Mi día feriado favorito** Con un(a) compañero(a) de clase, hablen sobre su día feriado favorito. Luego, compartan con la clase esta información. ¿Cuál es el día feriado favorito para la clase?

1. ¿Cuál es tu día feriado favorito? ¿Por qué?
2. ¿Cómo celebras esta ocasión especial? ¿Das una fiesta en tu casa? ¿Vas a algún lugar por la noche?
3. ¿Preparas una comida o bebida especial?
4. ¿Te emocionas con esta fiesta especial?
5. ¿Qué hiciste el año pasado para celebrar ese día? ¿Recibiste algunos regalos ese día? ¿Diste algunos regalos?

8-4 | **Una mujer cínica** Esperanza, una amiga de Marta, es muy cínica con respecto a *(with regard to)* las fiestas de familia. Habla con dos compañeros(as) de clase para ver si son ciertas o falsas las opiniones de ella, según Uds.

MODELO: Es mejor acostarse temprano en la Noche Vieja.
  E1: *No es cierto. Nosotros siempre nos acostamos tarde en la Noche Vieja.*
  E2: *Es cierto. Mi familia se acuesta antes de la medianoche.*
  E3: *En mi familia, depende del año. Este año nos acostamos tarde pero el año pasado nos acostamos temprano.*

1. Siempre recibo regalos raros o inútiles.
2. La época de la Navidad puede ser un poco deprimente *(depressing)*.
3. No me gusta ir de compras en las tiendas antes de las fiestas de diciembre.
4. Recibo cartas de personas que quieren decirme mucho sobre el éxito de todos los miembros de su familia.
5. Las fiestas son una invención de Hallmark para ganar dinero.
6. Hay demasiados días festivos.
7. No recuerdo un cumpleaños divertido.
8. Mis amigos nunca reaccionan como quiero cuando abren mis regalos.

8-5 | **¿Cómo te pones?** Dile a un(a) compañero(a) de clase cómo reaccionas en las siguientes situaciones.

MODELO: Estás en una fiesta y tu novio(a) está bailando con otra persona.
  Me pongo furioso(a) con él (ella).

1. Das una fiesta y los invitados comen toda la comida en media hora.
2. Es tu cumpleaños y tus amigos te hacen una fiesta sorpresa.
3. Estás en una fiesta y los invitados no se ríen, no se sonríen y hablan muy poco.
4. Estás en una fiesta y te cae una bebida en tu camisa/vestido.
5. No recuerdas que hoy es el cumpleaños de tu mejor amigo(a).
6. Estás en una fiesta hablando y conversando y alguien apaga las luces.

Text audio
Track 2–2

CULTURA
Quezaltenango is a small city located west of Guatemala City in the mountainous region of the country.

Bienvenida, la madre de Tomás, decidió visitar a su hijo y a su esposa en Chichicastenango sin avisar *(without warning)*. Presta atención al uso del pretérito y del imperfecto.

Ayer fue domingo, 20 de diciembre. **Eran las 11:40 de la mañana;** la temperatura en Chichicastenango **estaba a 14 grados centígrados** y **llovía.** Marta **estaba duchándose** y Tomás **se estaba vistiendo** porque muy pronto **iban a ir** a la iglesia. De repente *(Suddenly)*, **sonó el teléfono** y Tomás **fue a contestarlo.**

—¿Bueno?

—¡Hola, hijo! Habla tu mamá.

—Mamá, ¿cómo estás?

—Bien, bien. Acabo de llegar de Quezaltenango. Estoy aquí en la estación de autobuses.

—¡Mamá! ¿Estás aquí en Chichicastenango?

—Sí, hijo. Decidí venir a última hora *(at the last minute)*. **Hace seis meses que** no los veo.

—¡Qué bueno, mamá! Voy a la estación a...

—No, mi hijo. Puedo ir a tu casa en taxi porque vives muy lejos de la estación y tengo mucho equipaje.

—Bueno. Entonces te esperamos aquí en casa, ¿eh?

—Sí, sí. Nos vemos pronto. Hasta luego, hijo.

—Hasta luego, mamá.

Bienvenida **salió** de la estación con su maleta, **encontró** un taxi y se subió *(and she got in)*. Luego ella le **dio** al taxista la dirección de la casa de Marta y Tomás. **Mientras** Bienvenida y el taxista **iban** a la casa, **conversaban** sobre el mal tiempo, pero el taxista **estaba tan cansado** que casi *(almost)* **se durmió** dos veces.

De repente, ¡pum! El taxi **chocó** con *(crashed into)* un autobús que **venía** de otra calle y los dos vehículos pararon *(stopped)* inmediatamente. El taxista **estaba tan cansado** que **no vio** el autobús. Afortunadamente, **nadie se lastimó,** pero Bienvenida estaba nerviosa.

Dos horas más tarde, el taxi **llegó** finalmente a la casa de Marta y Tomás, quienes **esperaban** a Bienvenida en la puerta. Ella **salió** del taxi y todos **se saludaron** con abrazos y besos. Bienvenida estaba muy asustada y nerviosa pero cuando vio a Marta y a Tomás se puso muy contenta.

¿Comprendiste?

Indica si las siguientes oraciones son ciertas o falsas. Si la oración es falsa, ¡corrígela!

1. Hacía mal tiempo el día en que llegó Bienvenida.
2. Bienvenida causó el accidente entre el taxi y el autobús.
3. Bienvenida llegó rápidamente a la casa de su hijo.
4. Ella llegó en verano.
5. La madre de Tomás no tenía miedo de nada.
6. Tomás se puso triste cuando su mamá lo llamó.

Chichicastenango

PARA PENSAR

■ En otros **Encuentros culturales,** vemos cómo las plazas son un punto de reunión para hablar de la salud de la familia, de la política, de la economía en los diferentes países o para vender objetos viejos como en la Plaza Dorrego en Buenos Aires. ¿Qué más pasa en las plazas? ¿Qué pasa en las plazas de tu ciudad o región?

■ ¿Tienen ustedes *farmer's market* (mercado) algunos días de la semana en tu ciudad?

■ ¿Pueden describir la foto de la Iglesia de Santo Tomás de Chichicastenango?

Iglesia Santo Tomás de Chichicastenango

Chichicastenango es un pueblo blanco y pequeño que está a solamente 140 km. (87 millas) de la Ciudad de Guatemala y se conoce por el mercado que se lleva a cabo *(takes place)* todos los jueves y domingos. Este pueblo es un centro de comercio muy importante para los indígenas mayas del altiplano occidental *(western highlands)*. Hoy en día este mercado es tan grande y tan importante para los indígenas que la plaza principal y la escalera de la Iglesia de Santo Tomás se llenan de gente que viene a vender sus productos de todas partes de Guatemala. El mercado está muy bien organizado; cada persona se coloca en su lugar tradicional para vender sus productos, como piezas de cerámica, condimentos, plantas medicinales, copal (que es el incienso maya), frutas, vegetales y animales. En la parte central de la plaza están los comedores donde la gente puede comer comida típica de todas las regiones.

En la Iglesia de Santo Tomás se celebran una mezcla de ritos católicos y paganos. En las escaleras de la iglesia la gente ora *(pray)* y quema *(burn)* incienso de copal. Una vez dentro de la iglesia, ofrecen velas y flores a las almas *(souls)* de los muertos, mientras oran a los santos de toda clase de fuerzas naturales.

En Chichicastenango también está el Monasterio de Santo Domingo, el lugar donde encontraron el *Popol Vuh,* el libro sagrado *(sacred)* de los mayas donde se cuenta el origen del mundo y de la vida.

PARA DISCUTIR

1. ¿Adónde van los indígenas a vender sus productos en Guatemala?
2. ¿Por qué es importante este lugar para los indígenas?
3. ¿Cómo está organizado el mercado?
4. ¿Qué y cómo celebra la gente en la Iglesia de Santo Tomás?
5. ¿Quieres conocer algún lugar similar a Chichicastenango? ¿Por qué sí o por qué no?

ASÍ SE DICE Inquiring and providing information about people and events: interrogative words

Throughout *Plazas* you have been using interrogative words to ask for information about people and events. Below is a summary of interrogative words and examples of their uses.

1. To ask *where* somone is going, use **¿Adónde?** If you are asking about the location of some thing, person, or place, use **¿Dónde?** If you are asking where somone is from, use **¿De dónde?**

¿Adónde? *Where (to)?*	**¿Adónde** vas? *Where are you going?*
¿Dónde? *Where?*	**¿Dónde** está el centro del pueblo? *Where is the center of town?*
¿De dónde? *From where?*	**¿De dónde** eres tú? *Where are you from?*

2. To ask *what* a person or thing is like, or *how* something is done, use **¿Cómo?**

¿Cómo es Miguel? *What is Miguel like?*	**¿Cómo** lo hiciste? *How did you do it?*

3. To ask *when* something is taking place, use **¿Cuándo?** To ask specifically at what time an event takes place, use **¿A qué hora?**

¿A qué hora es la fiesta? *What time is the party?*	**¿Cuándo** es la fiesta? *When is the party?*

4. To ask *How much?* or *How many?* use a form of **¿Cuánto?** When a form of **¿Cuánto?** precedes a noun, it must agree in number and in gender.

¿Cuántos entremeses sirvieron? *How many hors d'oeuvres did they serve?*	**¿Cuántas personas** vienen a la fiesta? *How many people are coming to the party?*

5. To ask *who* does something, use **¿Quién?** if you are asking about one person or **¿Quiénes?** if you are asking about more than one person. To ask *Whose?* use **¿De quién?** or **¿De quiénes?** if you are asking about more than one person.

¿Quién es ella? *Who is she?*	**¿De quién** es la fiesta? *Whose party is it?*

6. To ask *Why?* use **¿Por qué?** To ask *What for?* use **¿Para qué?**

¿Por qué quieres ir a las montañas? *Why do you want to go to the mountains?*	**¿Para qué** tienes los cohetes? *Why do you have the rockets?*

7. To ask *What?* or *Which?* use **¿Qué?** or **¿Cuál?**

¿Qué quieres comer? *What do you want to eat?*	**¿Cuál** es tu plato favorito? *What is your favorite dish?*

Note that **¿Cuál(es)?** is used much more frequently than the English *Which?* and can mean both *What?* and *Which?* **¿Cuál(es)?** cannot be used when the next word in the question is a noun. In such cases, **¿Qué?** must be used.

¿Qué libro quieres?	*Which book do you want?*
¿Cuál de los dos libros quieres?	*Which of the two books would you like?*
¿Cuál es la fecha?	*What is the date?*
¿Qué hora es?	*What time is it?*

As you can see, the choice of whether to use **¿Qué?** or **¿Cuál?** depends on the syntax of the question. Use **¿Qué?** before a verb to ask for a definition or explanation.

¿Qué quieres?	*What do you want?*
¿Qué es el *Popol Vuh*?	*What is the Popol Vuh?*
¿Qué es esto?	*What is this?*

¡A PRACTICAR!

8-6 **Preguntas de un turista** Dos turistas están hablando sobre lugares en o cerca del centro histórico de la Ciudad de Guatemala. Un turista le hace muchas preguntas al otro. Indica la palabra interrogativa correcta para completar cada pregunta.

1. ¿De dónde / Dónde está el mejor hotel en la Ciudad de Guatemala?
   —Está en el centro histórico y es el Hotel Pan American.

2. ¿Cómo / Cuándo son los cuartos en ese hotel?
   —Son grandes. También hay unas suites.

3. ¿Cuánto / Cuántas cuesta el alojamiento *(lodging)* en el hotel?
   —Un cuarto cuesta alrededor de 100 dólares por noche.

4. ¿Con quiénes / Cuántas personas comparten tu cuarto?
   —Mi amiga Sara y yo compartimos el cuarto.

5. ¿Qué / Quiénes van con nosotros a la discoteca Casbah esta noche?
   —Mis nuevos amigos que conocí en el Parque Central van con nosotros.

6. ¿Dónde / Quién es tu amiga que sabe tanto sobre marimba?
   —Mi amiga Luisa es experta en marimba.

7. ¿A qué / Adónde hora vas al centro histórico para ver la Plaza Mayor de la Constitución?
   —Vamos a las once de la mañana.

8. ¿Para qué / Por qué no quieres ir con nosotros al Palacio Nacional?
   —Porque prefiero ir al mercado.

9. ¿Cuál / Qué es tu monumento favorito en la Ciudad de Guatemala?
   —El monumento que más me gusta es la Catedral Metropolitana.

10. ¿Dónde / Adónde vas en las próximas vacaciones con tu familia?
    —¿   ?

8-7 **¿Qué o cuál(es)?** Selecciona la palabra correcta y luego hazle la pregunta a un(a) compañero(a) de clase.

1. ¿_____ es el amor?
2. ¿_____ es tu grupo de música favorito?
3. ¿_____ clase tienes después de esta clase?
4. ¿_____ son los videos más recientes que viste en las últimas tres semanas?
5. ¿_____ es el Internet?
6. ¿_____ es tu número de teléfono?
7. ¿_____ residencia estudiantil vives?
8. ¿_____ es la capital de El Salvador?
9. ¿_____ ciudad es la capital de Guatemala?

EN VOZ ALTA

8-8 **¿Cuándo es la fiesta?** Habla con un(a) compañero(a) de clase. Una persona va a inventar detalles sobre una fiesta y la otra persona va a hacerle todas las preguntas posibles sobre esa fiesta.

CULTURA
The Casbah is a popular destination for young people in the old part of Guatemala City.

CULTURA
The **marimba** is the national instrument of Guatemala and has indigenous origins. It resembles a large xylophone with pipes of varying lengths under the keys.

ESTRUCTURA I Narrating in the past: the preterite vs. the imperfect

The preterite vs. the imperfect tense

The choice of using the preterite tense or imperfect tense is not arbitrary. The choice depends on how a speaker or writer views the past actions, conditions, and events that he/she describes.

The following parameters may be used to distinguish between the use of the preterite and imperfect tenses:

Preterite	Imperfect
• **single, completed action (what someone did or didn't do)** Marta **dio** una fiesta de sorpresa para su marido con amigos especiales. *Marta gave a surprise party for her husband with special friends.*	• **habitual action or event (expresses the idea in English of something you *used to do* or *would always do* in the past)** Tomás y Marta siempre **celebraban** los cumpleaños. *Tomás and Marta always celebrated (used to celebrate) birthdays.*
• **highlighted, main action** Tomás **llegó** a casa y **entró.** *Tomás arrived at home and went in.*	• **background action or description that sets the stage for preterite action (including time, location, mood, age, weather, and physical and emotional states)** La noche de la fiesta **hacía** buen tiempo y Marta **estaba** muy contenta. *The night of the party the weather was nice and Marta was very happy.*
• **beginning or end of an event** A las 11:00 de la noche **empezó** a llover. *At 11:00 at night, it began to rain.*	• **middle of an event or emphasis on indefinite continuation of event** En la fiesta algunos de los invitados **hablaban** mientras otros **comían.** *At the party, some of the guests were talking while others were eating.*
• **action that interrupts another action or event** Cuando Tomás **entró** en la sala... *When Tomás entered the room . . .*	• **ongoing event or action in the past that is interrupted** ...los invitados **cantaban.** *...the guests were singing.*
	• **past actions, conditions, and events that were anticipated or planned** **Queríamos** quedarnos un día más en Guatemala pero no **teníamos** dinero. *We wanted to stay another day in Guatemala but we didn´t have the money.*
• **The preterite is often used with verbs associated with time expressions such as *ayer, anteayer, anoche, una vez, dos veces, el mes pasado,* and *de repente* (suddenly).** El mes pasado, **fuimos** a Guatemala. *Last month we went to Guatemala.*	• **The imperfect is often used with time such as *todos los días, cada semana, siempre, frecuentemente, de niño(a),* and *de joven.*** **Todos los veranos** mi esposa y yo **íbamos** de vacaciones a un país extranjero. *Every summer my wife and I would go on vacation to a foreign country*

To describe two simultaneous actions that were occurring in the past, Spanish speakers often use **mientras** *(while)* to join the two clauses in the imperfect tense.

To describe an ongoing action in the imperfect that is interrupted by an event in the preterite, Spanish speakers often use the word **cuando** to introduce the preterite action.

When the verb **ir** is used in the imperfect with the preposition **a** + *infinitive,* it translates as *was/were going to do something.* The implication is usually that something happened later that prevented the intended action from taking place. For example, **Yo iba a mirar la tele, pero un amigo me llamó pidiéndome ayuda.** *(I was going to watch TV, but a friend called asking for help.)*

Verbs that refer to states or conditions

Verbs that normally refer to states or conditions (**saber, querer, tener, poder**) take on a special meaning in the preterite.

Preterite		Imperfect	
supe	*I found out*	sabía	*I knew*
quise	*I wanted to* (and did)	quería	*I wanted to* (outcome undetermined)
pude	*I was able to* (and did)	podía	*I was able to* (outcome undetermined)
tuve que	*I had to* (and did)	tenía que	*I had to* (outcome undetermined)
tuve	*I got, received*	tenía	*I had* (in my possession)

The preterite and imperfect tenses together

Spanish speakers often use the preterite and imperfect together to describe past experiences within the framework of the time they occurred. The following paragraph exemplifies many of the uses of the two tenses in the context of a single paragraph.

CULTURA

El Salvador is the small country to the south of Guatemala and is one of its major trading partners. It boasts a varied landscape including beaches on the Pacific coast, mountains and volcanoes in the center and north, and the famous **el bosque El Imposible** *(Impossible Forest)*. Salvadorans refer to themselves as **guanacos.**

El segundo día de las vacaciones en El Salvador, **eran** las 2:15 de la tarde: Tomás y Marta **tenían** mucha hambre. Por eso, **fueron** al restaurante Torremolinos. Marta le **preguntó** a su marido si ellos **podían** sentarse en la terraza como lo **hacían** siempre cuando **almorzaban** allí. Tomás le **dijo** al camarero que su esposa **quería** sentarse en la terraza porque a ella **le gustaba** el papagayo que **tenían** allí. Tomás y Marta **hablaban** sobre los acontecimientos de aquel día cuando **vino** el camarero con los entremeses.

*On the second day of the trip in El Salvador, it **was** 2:15 in the afternoon: Tomás and Marta **were** very hungry. So, they **went** to the restaurant Torremolinos. Marta **asked** her husband if they **could** sit on the terrace as they **used to** when they **ate lunch** there. Tomás **told** the waiter that his wife **wanted** to sit on the terrace because she **liked** the papagayo they had out there. Tomás and Marta **were talking** about the events of that day when the waiter **came** with the appetizers.*

¡A PRACTICAR!

8-9 | **La fiesta de mamá** Decide si las siguientes oraciones en inglés requieren (*require*) el pretérito, el imperfecto o ambos (*both*) para describir las fiestas de cumpleaños en casa. Explica por qué es necesario usar cada forma que selecciones.

1. Our family used to celebrate all our birthdays together. *imperfecto*
2. My mother would always make a cake for our birthdays. *imperfecto*
3. When I was ten, my Aunt Jeanie had a big party for my mother. *pretérito / imperfecto*
4. It was a nice day, and we were all very excited. *imperfecto*
5. We were all having a good time when my aunt brought in a large birthday cake. *imperfecto / pretérito*
6. My mom began to cry. *pretérito*
7. It was a wonderful party. *preterito*

8-10 | **La primera cita de Tomás y Marta** Lee el siguiente párrafo una vez y luego selecciona el pretérito o el imperfecto, según el contexto.

Marta 1. *estaba* / estuvo leyendo un libro en su apartamento cuando Tomás la 2. llamaba / *llamó* por teléfono. Tomás le 3. preguntaba / *preguntó* si 4. *quería* / quiso ir al parque cerca de la Plaza San Salvador con él. Marta le 5. decía / *dijo* que sí, aunque 6. *tenía* / tuvo mucho que leer para la semana próxima.

Tomás 7. venía / *vino* a las 3:00 y los dos 8. salían / *salieron* juntos al parque. Mientras ellos 9. *caminaban* / caminaron, los dos se 10. *hablaban* / hablaron cariñosamente. Los dos 11. *se sentían* / se sintieron muy contentos porque 12. *hacía* / hizo buen tiempo y 13. *era* / fue sábado. ¡No 14. *tenían* / tuvieron que levantarse temprano el día siguiente! En el parque ellos 15. se sentaban / *se sentaron* en un banco y 16. miraban / *miraron* a la gente por un rato. Cuando ellos 17. *observaban* / observaron a una pareja vieja en otro banco, un señor se les 18. acercaba / *acercó* con unos globos grandísimos. El señor les 19. explicaba / *explicó* que él los 20. *vendió* / vendía en el parque todos los sábados. Tomás le 21. compraba / *compró* uno a Marta y los dos 22. se reían / *se rieron*.

Ahora contesta las siguientes preguntas sobre la primera cita de Tomás y Marta.

1. ¿Qué hacía Marta cuando Tomás la llamó?
2. ¿Qué le preguntó Tomás?
3. ¿Qué tenía que hacer Marta para la semana próxima?
4. ¿A qué hora fue Tomás al apartamento?
5. ¿Por qué se sentían contentos Tomás y Marta en el parque?
6. ¿Qué hicieron ellos en el parque?
7. ¿Por qué se les acercó un señor en el parque?

> **CULTURA**
> The Plaza San Salvador was built in honor of Dr. José Matías Delgado, the father of Independence in Central America.

8-11 | **Preparativos para una fiesta de cumpleaños** Decide qué tiempo verbal —pretérito o imperfecto— es necesario para completar las siguientes oraciones. Después, pon el verbo en el forma correcta. Recuerda que los verbos **tener, saber, querer** y **poder** tienen significados diferentes en el pretérito y el imperfecto.

MODELO: Ayer cuando Tomás llegó a casa, él ___*supo*___ (saber) que había una fiesta para su cumpleaños.

1. Ayer antes de la fiesta yo __*tuve*__ (tener) que limpiar la casa. Lo hice. Yo __*sabía*__ (saber) que __*iba*__ (ir) a tener muchos invitados.
2. Ayer por la tarde nosotros __*supimos*__ (saber) que los primos de Tomás __*querían*__ (querer) venir a la fiesta pero no __*pudieron*__ (poder).
3. El año pasado, nosotros __*tuvimos*__ (tener) que hacer planes con más tiempo porque __*queríamos*__ (querer) tener mucha gente para la celebración.

EN VOZ ALTA

8-12 **Ocasiones memorables** Hazle las siguientes preguntas a un(a) compañero(a) de clase y luego comparen sus respuestas. ¿Tienen mucho en común?

1. ¿Cuándo fue la primera vez que le enviaste una tarjeta *(card)* a una persona para el Día de San Valentín? ¿Cómo reaccionó la persona? ¿Cómo te sentías en aquel momento? ¿Recibiste alguna vez flores de otra persona?

2. Cuando eras joven, ¿qué hacías para celebrar el Día de Acción de Gracias *(Thanksgiving)*? ¿Comías mucho pavo?

3. ¿Cuál fue el cumpleaños más memorable para ti? ¿Con quién lo celebraste? ¿Recibiste algunos regalos especiales? ¿Lo pasaste muy bien?

4. ¿Ibas a la iglesia para la Pascua cuando eras joven?

5. ¿Gritaste «¡Feliz año nuevo!» el año pasado a la medianoche de la Noche Vieja? ¿Qué hacías cuando el reloj dio las 12:00?

8-13 **Entrevista: La niñez y la juventud** Hazle a otro(a) compañero(a) las siguientes preguntas sobre experiencias y relaciones de la juventud.

1. **Su niñez:** ¿De dónde eres originalmente? ¿Por cuánto tiempo viviste allí? ¿Te gustaba vivir allí? ¿Por qué? ¿Qué cosas no te gustaban allí? ¿Vivías en una casa o en un apartamento? ¿Cómo era? ¿Tenías pocos o muchos amigos? ¿Cómo eran? ¿Cuántos años tenías cuando asististe *(attended)* a la escuela por primera vez? ¿Tenías miedo? ¿Cómo se llamaba la escuela? ¿Cómo celebrabas tus cumpleaños cuando eras niño(a)? Durante tu niñez, ¿qué actividades hacías?

2. **Su adolescencia:** ¿Cuántos años tenías cuando comenzaste clases en la secundaria? ¿Cómo se llamaba la escuela y dónde estaba? ¿Dónde vivías? ¿Tenías novio(a) cuando eras adolescente? (¿Sí? Háblame de él/ella, por favor.) ¿Te llevabas bien con tus hermanos en esta época? Cuando eras adolescente, ¿qué hacías los fines de semana? ¿Adónde iban de vacaciones tú y tu familia? ¿Veías mucho a tus abuelos?

8-14 **Había una vez *(Once upon a time)*...** Forma un grupo con dos o tres compañeros(as) de clase. Luego una persona comienza con la siguiente oración: **Había una vez unos estudiantes que querían planear una celebración memorable para el fin del semestre.** Las otras personas del grupo se turnan para continuar el cuento lógicamente hasta su desenlace. Usa la imaginación y el vocabulario de este capítulo para contar la historia de estos estudiantes.

VOCABULARIO La playa y el campo

De vacaciones... In this section you will learn vocabulary and expressions to talk about outdoor activities at the beach and in the countryside.

¿NOS ENTENDEMOS?

Hacer esnórquel is also known as **el buceo de superficie** in some Spanish-speaking countries. In some countries, like Puerto Rico, **el balneario** means *public beach* instead of *beach resort*.

- el balneario
- correr las olas
- la playa
- la costa
- el océano/el mar
- bucear
- pasear en velero
- hacer esnórquel
- pescar
- el lago
- el río
- hacer camping
- caminar por las montañas
- pasear en canoa
- hacer una parrillada
- broncearse/tomar el sol
- la crema bronceadora

¡A PRACTICAR!

8-15 **¿Qué hace esta gente?** Mira los dibujos a continuación y describe lo que estas personas hacen en la playa o en el campo. Usa el vocabulario que acabas de aprender.

MODELO:

Tomás

Tomás corre las olas.

1. nosotros

2. José Carlos y Eva

3. tú

4. Eva

5. Marta

6. Lucho

CULTURA
Guatemala has 27 active volcanos. Tajumulco is the highest volcano in all of Central America.

CULTURA
Both **el Río Dulce** and **el Lago de Izabal** are popular tourist destinations. **El Lago de Izabal** is the country's largest lake.

CULTURA
Tikal is an ancient Mayan ruin.

CULTURA
The beach of **Puerto de San José** is located 108 miles from Guatemala City in the town of Escuintla. The beaches of the Pacific coast in Guatemala are of black sand and open directly to the ocean, making them ideal for surfers.

8-16 | **Asociaciones y preferencias** Para saber un poco más de la geografía variada de Guatemala y para apreciar los lugares más famosos, haz la siguiente actividad. Puedes consultar un mapa del país si quieres.

Parte I Selecciona la palabra que no vaya con el resto del grupo y explica por qué.

1. el océano Pacífico, las montañas (o el volcán Tajumulco), el Río Dulce, el Lago de Izabal
2. hacer camping en Tikal, hacer una parrillada, caminar por las montañas, bucear en la costa del Caribe
3. el balneario, la playa del Puerto de San José, caminar por las montañas, la costa
4. pasear en canoa, broncearse, tomar el sol en la playa, la crema bronceadora

Parte II Entre cada grupo de palabras arriba, selecciona la palabra o expresión que te guste más y explica por qué.

Parte III Ahora, según las respuestas en las secciones anteriores, dile a un(a) compañero(a) de clase lo que harías tú si fueras (*if you went*) de vacaciones a Guatemala.

EN VOZ ALTA

8-17 | **Problemas y soluciones** Conversa con otro(a) compañero(a). El estudiante 1 es un(a) cliente en el balneario Hotel Playa de Tesoro y el estudiante 2 es el (la) director(a) de actividades para el balneario. El (La) director(a) debe ofrecer una solución lógica a los problemas del (de la) cliente. Luego, cambien de papel y hagan otra conversación.

MODELO: E1: No me gusta nadar en el mar.
E2: *Usted puede nadar en nuestra piscina.*

1. Quiero ir a la playa, pero no tengo traje de baño.
2. Tengo hambre y quiero comer unas pupusas.
3. No sé bucear, pero quiero ver cómo es por debajo del mar.
4. Quiero aprender a bucear, pero no sé adónde ir.
5. Siempre tengo miedo de broncearme mucho cuando voy a la playa.
6. Me gusta pasear en canoa, pero no quiero ir solo(a).
7. Quiero jugar al vólibol en la playa, pero no tengo una pelota ni conozco a nadie aquí.

8-18 | **¡A pasarlo bien!** Trabaja con otro(a) compañero(a). Imagínense que ustedes van a pasar un fin de semana en un balneario o en el campo. Primero, hagan una lista de las actividades que ustedes van a hacer en ese lugar el sábado y el domingo. Luego hagan una lista de todo lo que ustedes van a llevar. Traten de (*Try to*) usar el vocabulario de este capítulo y del **Capítulo 3.** Al terminar, explíquenle el itinerario a la clase.

MODELO: **Actividades**   **Cosas para llevar**
sacar fotos   *una cámara*
tomar el sol   *un traje de baño*
comer mariscos   *200 dólares*

Arzobispo Óscar Arnulfo Romero

PARA PENSAR

- ¿Sabes quién fue el arzobispo Óscar Arnulfo Romero?

- ¿Qué es una guerra civil? ¿Conoces un país que haya tenido *(has had)* una guerra civil o que tenga *(has)* ahora una guerra civil?

Arzobispo Óscar Arnulfo Romero

Durante los años 1981 y 1992 en El Salvador existió una gran violencia que se transformó en una guerra civil *(civil war)* entre los trabajadores, los campesinos del país y las fuerzas militares que querían mantener su poder político, social y económico. El arzobispo *(archbishop)* Romero comenzó a luchar por los derechos humanos *(human rights)* y denunció a los que abusaban de los derechos civiles de la gente más débil. Al arzobispo se le consideraba «la voz de la gente que no tenía voz» porque luchaba contra las injusticias sociales.

Por haber luchado en favor de los derechos humanos fue asesinado el 24 de marzo de 1980 cuando estaba diciendo la misa en una iglesia al oeste de la ciudad capital, San Salvador. Nunca se supo quién asesinó al arzobispo Romero, según la respuesta oficial.

En 1997, la iglesia católica salvadoreña puso los papeles del arzobispo Romero ante El Vaticano para declararlo «santo». Aunque el proceso es muy largo, los representantes de la Iglesia de El Salvador piensan que el arzobispo Romero va a ser declarado santo en un futuro próximo.

PARA DISCUTIR

1. ¿Qué pasó en El Salvador durante la guerra civil?

2. ¿Por qué luchaba el arzobispo Óscar Arnulfo Romero?

3. Expliquen la frase que describe al arzobispo Romero: «la voz de la gente que no tenía voz».

4. Algunas personas comparan al arzobispo Romero con el defensor de los derechos civiles *(civil rights defender)* norteamericano Martín Luther King. ¿Qué piensan de esta comparación?

5. ¿Qué les parece a ustedes la lucha por los derechos humanos? ¿Es importante hoy en día?

ESTRUCTURA II Stating indefinite ideas and quantities: affirmative and negative expressions

Below are some useful affirmative and negative expressions.

algo *something, anything*	**nada** *nothing, not anything, at all*
alguien *somebody, anybody*	**nadie** *nobody, no one*
algún, alguno(a) *some, any*	**ningún, ninguno(a)** *none, not any*
o... o *either . . . or*	**ni... ni** *neither . . . nor*
siempre *always*	**nunca** *never*
también *also, too*	**tampoco** *neither, not either*

In Spanish, a negative sentence always has at least one negative word before the conjugated verb. Sometimes there are several negative words in one sentence.

—¿Quieres beber **algo** antes del masaje, Marta?

Do you want to drink something before your massage, Marta?

—**No, no** quiero **nada**, gracias.

No, I don't want anything, thank you.

—¿Hay **alguien** con el masajista ahora?

Is there someone with the massage therapist now?

—**No, no** hay **nadie**, **ni** con el masajista, **ni** con el entrenador.

No, there's no one, neither with the massage therapist nor with the trainer.

• If a negative word precedes the conjugated verb, the negative word **no** is omitted.

no + *verb* + *negative word*	*negative word* + *verb*
No viene nadie conmigo a nadar.	**Nadie viene** conmigo a nadar.
Nobody is coming with me to swim.	

no + *verb* + *negative word*	*negative word* + *verb*
No voy nunca al gimnasio.	**Nunca voy** al gimnasio.
I never go to the gym.	

• The words **algún, alguno, alguna, algunos**, and **algunas** are adjectives; use **algún** before a masculine singular noun.

—¿Hay **algún** traje de baño para mí, Marta?

Is there any swimsuit for me, Marta?

—No, pero tengo **algunos** zapatos de tenis para ti.

No, but I have some tennis shoes for you.

—¿Hay **algún** restaurante en este pueblo?

Is there not a restaurant in this town?

Note that the plural forms **ningunos** and **ningunas** are not used often; instead, use the singular form, and use **ningún** before a masculine singular noun.

—¿Cuántos campos de fútbol hay aquí?	*How many soccer fields are there here?*
—No hay **ningún** campo de fútbol aquí.	*There aren't any soccer fields here.*
—¿A qué hora viene mi entrenador?	*What time is my trainer coming?*
—No tengo **ninguna** idea sobre esto, Tomás.	*I have no idea about this matter, Tomás.*
—¿Cuántas piscinas tiene el balneario?	*How many swimming pools does the resort have?*
—No tiene **ninguna**.	*It doesn´t have any.*

- Express *neither / not either* with a subject pronoun (**yo, tú, usted, él, ella,** etc.) + **tampoco.**

—Nunca voy al gimnasio.	*I never go to the gym.*
—Yo **tampoco.**	*Me neither.*

- Place **ni** before a noun or a verb to express the idea of *neither . . . nor.*

—¿Quieres ir a correr o a levantar pesas?	*Do you want to go running or lift weights?*
—No quiero **ni** ir a correr **ni** a levantar pesas.	*I want neither to go running nor to lift weights.*

Ningunos and ningunas are used only with nouns that always come in pairs or are always plural. For example: ¿Hay algunos zapatos de tenis para mí? No, no hay ningunos. *(Are there any tennis shoes for me? No, there aren't any.)* Other nouns that always come in pairs or are always plural are **guantes, calcetines, medias, pantalones,** and **vacaciones.**

¿NOS ENTENDEMOS?
Spanish speakers will often say **No tengo la menor idea/ni idea** *(I don't have the slightest idea)* to emphatically express that they don't know the answer.

¡A PRACTICAR!

8-19 **Ideas opuestas** Forma una oración con el significado opuesto sustituyendo las palabras afirmativas con palabras negativas.

> MODELO: Yo siempre voy con mi familia de vacaciones.
> *Yo nunca voy con mi familia de vacaciones.*

1. Hay algunos libros sobre turismo en El Salvador en la tienda del hotel.
2. Alguien en el balneario sabe correr las olas.
3. Tomás quiere bucear también.
4. Marta tiene algo para su esposo en la playa.
5. Rita quiere bucear o hacer esnórquel.
6. Siempre es divertido pasear en velero.

8-20 **Entre esposos en el balenario** Completa las dos conversaciones siguientes, usando **algo, nada, alguien, nadie, o... o, ni... ni, también, tampoco, siempre** y **nunca.**

—Tomás, voy al supermercado porque no hay casi 1. _____ en el refrigerador en nuestra habitación. ¿Quieres comer 2. _____ especial esta noche?
—No, gracias, Marta. No quiero comer 3. _____ porque comí mucho en el almuerzo.
—Pero, ¿qué te pasa, Tomás?
—4. _____. Es que no tengo hambre, Marta.
—Bueno. Hasta luego.
(Más tarde...)
—¡Hola, Tomás! Conocí a 5. _____ en el supermercado cerca del balneario. Y 6. _____ es una persona que te conoce a ti.
—Ah, ¿sí? Debe ser 7. _____ un amigo 8. _____ un compañero de trabajo. ¿Quién es?
—Bueno, no es 9. _____ un amigo 10. _____ un compañero tuyo. Se llama Lucía.
—¿Cómo? ¿Lucía? No conozco a 11. _____ con ese nombre, ni tengo muchas amigas 12. _____.
—¿No? Pues, ella me dijo que fue tu novia.
—¿Mi novia? Marta, 13. _____ estás inventando cosas.
—Yo 14. _____ invento historias sobre tu vida. ¿No recuerdas a Lucía? Era tu novia cuando ella tenía catorce años.
—Ah sí, ahora recuerdo, era muy amable conmigo y con mi mamá.

8-21 **Enfrente del hotel Playa de Tesoro** Completa la siguiente conversación, usando **algún, alguna, algunos, algunas, ningún, ninguna** y **ninguno.**

—Perdón, estoy buscando la piscina pública.
—¿Cómo? No hay 1. _____ por aquí, señor.
—2. _____ amigos me dijeron que hay una piscina pública cerca de un mercado.
—No. No hay 3. _____ mercado por aquí. Hay una piscina, pero es privada. La piscina pública está lejos.
—¿Está abierta o cerrada?
—No tengo 4. _____ idea sobre eso, señor.
—¿Hay 5. _____ teléfono aquí que funciona?
—No, aquí no hay 6. _____.
—Muchas gracias.
—De nada.

EN VOZ ALTA

8-22 | **De mal humor** Tú estás de mal humor hoy y, por eso, siempre le contestas negativamente a tu compañero(a) que te hace preguntas con los siguientes elementos. ¡Ojo! Tu compañero(a) necesita añadir palabras para formar una pregunta completa.

> MODELO: ¿ir con alguien al cine esta noche? (nadie)
> E1: *¿Quieres ir con alguien al cine esta noche?*
> E2: *No, no quiero ir con nadie al cine esta noche.*

1. ¿hacer la tarea?
2. ¿estudiar con otra persona en la clase?
3. ¿correr las olas o esquiar en el agua?
4. ¿hacer ejercicio?
5. ¿hacer algo hoy?
6. ¿nadar en la piscina?

8-23 | **De vacaciones** Hazle las siguientes preguntas a un(a) compañero(a) de clase.

1. ¿Celebran algunos amigos tuyos el Cinco de Mayo? ¿Hay alguna otra fiesta latina que prefieras celebrar?

2. ¿Prefieres ir a una fiesta con alguien? Generalmente, ¿llevas alguna cosa a la fiesta?

3. ¿Quieres ir a Chichicastenango algún día? ¿Hay algún lugar en Guatemala que prefieras visitar?

4. ¿Prefieres viajar a la playa o a las montañas, cuando no tienes nada que hacer para tus clases? Cuando tienes algo que hacer, ¿prefieres ir a algún sitio especial? ¿Lees tú algunos libros cuando estás de vacaciones?

Hace + period of time + *que*

The verb construction **hace** + period of time + **que** is used to talk about how long an event or condition has been taking place or how long it has been since an event or condition took place.

• **Hace** + period of time + **que** + present tense

To indicate how long something has been happening, Spanish speakers use the construction **hace** + period of time + **que** + present tense.

Hace seis años que vivo en San Salvador.   *I've been living in San Salvador for six years.*

• **Hace** + period of time + **que** + preterite tense

To express how long ago an action or state occurred, Spanish speakers use the verb form **hace** + period of time + **que** + preterite tense.

Hace un año que se mudaron.   *They moved a year ago.*
(Se mudaron hace un año.)

¿Cuánto tiempo hace que... ?

Note that in order to ask about either (1) a period of time that continues into the present or (2) the amount of time since an event took place, you need to use the following model: **¿Cuánto tiempo hace que...?** The only feature that distinguishes the first scenario from the second is the choice of the present tense versus the past tense. Note the different implications for the following questions:

—**¿Cuánto tiempo hace que estudias** medicina?
How long have you been studying medicine? (You continue to study or be a student.)

—**Hace tres años que estudio** medicina.
I have been studying medicine for three years.

—**¿Cuánto tiempo hace que estudiaste** medicina?
How long has it been since you studied medicine? (You are no longer studying medicine.)

—**Hace dos años que estudié** medicina.
It has been two years since I studied medicine.

¡A PRACTICAR!

8-24 **¿Cuánto tiempo hace que... ?** Completa las siguientes oraciones con el período de tiempo adecuado y la conjugación correcta del verbo en el presente.

MODELO: Hace __un año__ que yo __estudio__ (estudiar) español.

1. Hace _3 años_ que mi compañero(a) de cuarto y yo _vivimos_ (vivir) juntos.
2. Hace _____ que yo no _____ (vivir) con mis padres.
3. Hace _____ que el (la) profesor(a) _____ (enseñar) en esta universidad.
4. Hace _____ que nosotros _____ (practicar) español en esta sala.
5. Hace _____ que esta universidad _____ (ofrecer) clases.
6. Hace _____ que yo _____ (leer) novelas.

8-25 **Hechos memorables** ¿Cuánto tiempo hace que los siguientes acontecimientos (events) ocurrieron en el pasado?

MODELO: yo / ir a la universidad por primera vez
Hace tres años que yo fui a la universidad por primera vez.

1. yo / conocer a mi mejor amigo(a) _Hace conoce_
2. mis amigos(as) / invitarme a una fiesta _me invitaron_
3. el nuevo milenio / empezar _empezo_
4. mis amigos(as) y yo / disfrazarse para una celebración _se disfrazamos_
5. mi novio(a) / comprarme un regalo de cumpleaños _me compra_
6. yo / venir a la universidad para estudiar _yo vene_ _Hace un día_
7. mis amigos(as) y yo / ponernos ropa elegante para una fiesta _Hace un semana nos repusimos_
8. mis padres / ir de vacaciones _fueron_

EN VOZ ALTA

8-26 **¿Hace cuánto tiempo que... ?** Pregúntale a un(a) compañero(a) de clase hace cuánto tiempo que hace o que hizo las siguientes cosas. Luego comparen sus respuestas. ¿Tienen mucho en común?

MODELO: estar con tu novio(a)
E1: *¿Hace cuánto tiempo que estás con tu novio(a)?*
E2: *Hace seis meses que estoy con mi novio(a).*
o E1: *¿Hace cuánto tiempo que estuviste con tu novio(a)?*
E2: *Hace dos semanas que estuve con mi novio(a). Nosotros dejamos de salir.* (We broke up.)

1. vivir en esta ciudad
2. conocer a tu mejor amigo(a)
3. visitar otro país
4. ir a un balneario
5. estudiar español _Hace un día_
6. ir a la biblioteca

8-27 **Entrevista** Haz preguntas para hacerle a otro(a) compañero(a), usando **¿Cuánto tiempo hace que...?** para pedir información sobre las siguientes actividades. Debes hacer dos preguntas adicionales sobre cada actividad. Luego comparen sus respuestas. ¿Tienen mucho en común?

MODELO: hacer esnórquel
—*¿Cuánto tiempo hace que hiciste esnórquel? ¿Dónde lo hiciste? ¿Te divertiste?*
—*Hace tres años que yo hice esnórquel. Lo hice en Florida y me gustó mucho.*

1. dar una fiesta
2. asustarse
3. llorar
4. caminar por las montañas
5. pasarlo bien
6. hacer una parrillada

¡A VER!

En este segmento del video, vas a ver un flashback y aprender más del día de la lección de baile. ¿Recuerdas aquel día? Fue un día muy especial para Valeria que estaba muy triste al principio porque todos sus amigos se olvidaron de su cumpleaños.

Expresiones útiles

The following are some new expressions you will hear in the video.

No lo tomes tan a pecho	Don't take it so hard
Un bizcocho	A cake
Ni tan siquiera	Not even

Antes de ver

 Paso 1: Normalmente, ¿qué hace la gente para celebrar el cumpleaños? ¿Tiene reuniones, fiestas y qué comida se sirve típicamente? Habla con un(a) compañero(a) de clase sobre los diferentes tipos de celebraciones de cumpleaños.

 Paso 2: Algunas veces, hay ciertas circunstancias y los cumpleaños u otras celebraciones no resultan en días felices/festivos. ¿Conoces a alguien que se puso triste el día de su cumpleaños? ¿Qué pasó? ¿Cambió su estado de ánimo a lo largo del día? ¿Por qué sí o por qué no? Cuéntale este acontecimiento a un(a) compañero(a).

Después de ver

Paso 1: En **Antes de ver, Paso 1**, hablaste con un(a) compañero(a) sobre las diferentes maneras en que la gente celebra el cumpleaños. En el video, Valeria y Alejandra también hablaron de cómo celebraban el cumpleaños cuando eran niñas y parece que tenían experiencias diferentes. Lee los siguientes recuerdos y conjuga el verbo en el imperfecto. Luego indica si el comentario corresponde a Valeria o a Alejandra.

Valeria	Alejandra	
_____	_____	Mis padres siempre me _____ (**hacer**) una fiesta muy grande.
_____	_____	Mi mamá me _____ (**celebrar**) una fiesta de cumpleaños con mis compañeros de escuela.
_____	_____	Mi mamá me _____ (**traer**) un bizcocho de cumpleaños, refrescos y helados a la escuela.
_____	_____	Mi papá siempre me _____ (**llevar**) un ramo de flores a mi cuarto.
_____	_____	Mi mamá me _____ (**preparar**) mi comida favorita.

Paso 2: En **Antes de ver, Paso 2**, tu compañero(a) y tú hablaron de personas que no tuvieron buenas experiencias durante su cumpleaños. Según el video, al principio Valeria no está tampoco el día de su cumpleaños. Pero, ¿cambió su estado de ánimo al final? ¿Cómo? Lee las siguientes oraciones sobre el cumpleaños de Valeria e indica si son ciertas o falsas. Corrige las oraciones falsas.

- Muchos amigos la llamaron. _____
- No recibió ningún correo electrónico. _____
- No tenía pastel de cumpleaños. _____
- Cumplió 26 años. _____
- Habló con Sofía sobre las fiestas de cumpleaños que tenía cuando era niña.
  _____
- Su puso feliz mientras bailaba con Antonio, Javier y Sofía. _____
- Los compañeros de casa la sorprendieron con un regalo de cumpleaños después del baile. _____
- Alejandra le entregó un disco compacto de música cubana. _____
  _____
- Javier le regaló un ramo de flores. _____
- Sofía le invitó a cenar. _____
- Al final Valeria se divirtió mucho el día de su cumpleaños. _____

¿Qué opinas tú?

Paso 1: ¿Cuál fue el mejor día de cumpleaños que has tenido? ¿Cómo lo celebraste? ¿Con quiénes? ¿Hiciste alguna actividad especial? Piensa en todos los detalles. Describe este cumpleaños tan especial a un(a) compañero(a) y escucha mientras te describe su mejor cumpleaños. ¿Son similares sus experiencias? ¿Tienen mucho en común?

Paso 2: ¿Qué tipo de cosa puede afectar el estado de ánimo de una persona durante una situación festiva? ¿La enfermedad de un pariente? ¿Unas noticias muy buenas o malas? Trabaja con un(a) compañero(a) y nombren al menos cinco cosas (positivas y negativas) que puedan afectar y cambiar el estado de ánimo durante un día especial.

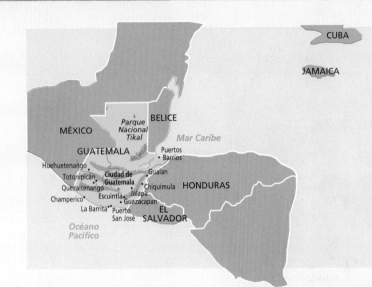

Map labels:
CUBA
JAMAICA
MÉXICO
Parque Nacional Tikal
BELICE
Mar Caribe
GUATEMALA
Puertos Barrios
Huehuetenango
Totonicapán
Ciudad de Guatemala
Gualan
Quezaltenango
Chiquimula
HONDURAS
Champerico
Escuintla
Jalapa
Guazacapan
La Barrita
Puerto San José
EL SALVADOR
Océano Pacífico

¡A LEER!

Strategy: Guessing meaning from word roots

Up to this point, you have learned a large number of new Spanish words. You are also able to recognize a large number of cognates, even if these words are new to you. Using this knowledge, you can guess the meaning of even more new Spanish words if you know the meaning of their roots. For example, in this chapter you learned the word **sorpresa;** based on your knowledge of this word, what would you guess that the verb **sorprender** means?

Words like **sorpresa** and **sorprender** that have the same root (e.g., **sorpr-**) are called "word families" because such words are closely related to one another.

Now look at the following list of words; these new words have the same word root as some of the new vocabulary items you learned in this chapter (refer to the vocabulary list at the end of the chapter if necessary). Can you guess the meanings of these new words based on the word root they contain?

_____ 1. asustado(a)　　a. memento, souvenir
_____ 2. campamento　　b. good-bye, farewell
_____ 3. el recuerdo　　c. scared, frightened
_____ 4. la despedida　　d. camp, campsite

Paso 1: Antes de leer el artículo sobre «Guía del viajero», contesta las siguientes preguntas.

1. Mira el mapa, la foto, el título y los subtítulos de la siguiente lectura. ¿Qué tipo de información crees que contiene este artículo?
2. Consulta el mapa de nuevo. ¿Qué subtítulos se refieren a los nombres de regiones geográficas (e.g., ciudades, lagos, montañas, regiones, etc.) en Guatemala? Escribe una lista de estos nombres.

Paso 2: Identifica las palabras que contienen la misma **raíz** (*word root*). ¿Qué significan estas palabras?

_____ 1. la altitud　　a. traído
_____ 2. viajar　　b. cercano
_____ 3. pervivir　　c. pueblo
_____ 4. traer　　d. altura
_____ 5. cerca　　e. vivir
_____ 6. población　　f. baños
_____ 7. bañarse　　g. viajero

Paso 3: Ahora, lee el artículo con cuidado. Luego, contesta las siguientes preguntas.

1. Según el artículo, ¿aproximadamente cuántos dialectos indígenas se hablan en Guatemala?
2. ¿Qué documentación es necesaria para viajar a Guatemala?
3. ¿Qué tipo de museo es el Museo Popol Vuh en la capital de Guatemala?
4. ¿Cómo se llama la ciudad más importante en la zona central del altiplano?
5. ¿Dónde está el Castillo de San Felipe?
6. ¿Qué tipos de cosas puede comprar un viajero en Guatemala?

Paso 4: De los sitios y ciudades descritos en el artículo, ¿cuáles te gustaría visitar? ¿Cuáles te parecen más importantes? ¿Por qué?

Guía del Viajero

Guatemala

SITUACIÓN

Se trata del país más septentrional de América Central. Limita al Norte y al Oeste con México, al Noroeste con Belice y al Este con Honduras y El Salvador. Tiene una costa atlántica de 117 kms. y un litoral pacífico de 332. Ocupa un área de 131.800 kms², dos veces la superficie de Suiza.

POBLACIÓN

La mitad de los ocho millones de habitantes del país pertenecen a los más de 20 grupos indígenas descendientes de los antiguos mayas. En la capital, la más grande de América Central, viven 1.300.000 habitantes.

IDIOMA

Aunque el español es el oficial, se hablan alrededor de 28 dialectos indígenas entre los que destacan el quiché, cakchiquel, kekchí y el mam.

DOCUMENTACIÓN

Sólo el pasaporte **en regla.**

QUÉ SE DEBE VER

GUATEMALA, CAPITAL Y ALREDEDORES

En la ciudad merece la pena visitar tres museos: el de *Arqueología y Etnología,* en Finca La Aurora, zona 13. El *Museo Ixchel,* del traje indígena, en la 4ª avenida 16–27, zona 10. Y el *Museo Popol Vuh,* de arte maya colonial, en la avenida de la Reforma 8–60, sexto piso, zona 9. En la llamada zona 1: destaca la plaza Mayor, donde está la Catedral, el Palacio Nacional, el pintoresco Mercado Central. En la zona 2, el Parque Minerva, zona residencial, y el «mapa en relieve» del país a gran escala.

A unos 25 kms. de la capital: *el lago Amatitlán.* Hay una vista panorámica excepcional desde el Parque de las Naciones Unidas. El volcán Pacaya, junto al pueblo de San Vicente Pacaya, con sus con-

tinuas erupciones constituye todo un espectáculo.

La ciudad de Antigua, declarada por la UNESCO Monumento de las Américas, conserva magníficos edificios del siglo XVI y XVIII. Es famosa su Semana Santa.

EL LAGO AMATITLÁN

A unos 25 kms. de la ciudad de Guatemala es, según muchos, uno de los lagos más hermosos del mundo. Doce pueblos indígenas habitan en sus **orillas,** destacando Panajachel, centro turístico de la región, y las **aldeas** de Santiago Amatitlán, Santa Catarina Palopó y San Pedro La Laguna. Es muy interesante asistir al día de mercado en Sololá, en la parte alta del lago.

QUETZALTENANGO

En la zona central del altiplano destaca Quetzaltenango, la segunda ciudad en importancia del país, a más de 2.300 metros de altura. Cerca está la aldea de *Zunil,* y *Fuentes Georginas,* ambas con baños termales y antiguas iglesias coloniales. *Salcajá,* es la cuna del jaspe y en *Totonicapán* se pueden comprar coloridos **huipiles** bordados con flores. Son también famosas las **mantas** y **alfombras** de lana, hechas a mano, de *Momostenango.* A 10 kms. de Quetzaltenango se encuentra uno de los mercados más auténticos y típicos donde pervive el trueque: *San Francisco el Alto.*

EL QUICHÉ

Este Departamento es famoso por la población de *Chichicastenango* y su mercado de los jueves y domingos, que reúne artesanías de todo el país. En el cerro cercano de Pascual Abaj (O Turkaj) se realizan ritos perhistóricos mayas. Hacia el Norte se halla *Santa Cruz del Quiché,* la capital de este Departamento. En las afueras se encuentran las ruinas de *Utatlán,* última capital de los mayas quichés.

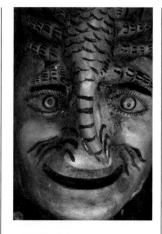

HUEHUETENANGO

La sierra de los Cuchumatanes alcanza aquí los 4.000 metros de altitud. En medio de valles y abruptas quebradas están las aldeas de *Todos Santos Cuchumatán* y *San Mateo Ixtatán,* famosas por sus **tejidos,** tradicionales y rituales mayas. En el área denominada triángulo ixil, merece la pena conocer los pueblos indígenas de *Nebaj, Chajul y Cotzal,* detenidos en el tiempo.

LA RUTA MAYA

En la selva del Petén se ocultan las ruinas más impresionantes de la civilización maya, *Tikal.* Desde el aeropuerto de Santa Elena se llega en unos 45 minutos al Parque Nacional del Petén. Se necesitan mínimo dos días para visitar este centro religioso, sus pirámides, palacios, amplias avenidas, juegos de pelota y el Museo de Tikal.

Otras ruinas son las de *Uaxactún,* 25 kms. al Norte de Tikal, por un camino casi intransitable en época de lluvias. El pueblecito de *Sayaxché,* 61 kms. al Sudoeste de *Flores,* es la base para visitar las ruinas mayas del Sudoeste del Petén. Los yacimientos más interesantes son *El Ceibal* a 17 kms. de Sayaxché. A lo largo del río de la Pasión hay otros sitios arqueológicos para los más aventureros

como *Aguateca, Dos Pilas* y *Tamarindito,* cerca del lago Petexbatún.

LAGO IZABAL

Situado al Noroeste de la carretera del Atlántico, destaca en él el Castillo de San Felipe, que data de 1652, construido para defenderse de los piratas.

EL CARIBE

La ciudad de Livingstone está habitada por los descendientes de los esclavos traídos desde África. Pintoresco lugar de cocoteros y casas pintadas de chillones colores. Excursiones por el río Dulce, a la reserva *Natural de Chocón-Machacas.* Y a los *Siete Altares,* cataratas y pozas a lo largo de la Bahía de Amatique.

QUÉ COMPRAR

Lo más famoso de Guatemala son sus textiles, hechos de forma artesanal en los telares primitivos de cintura o palitos. Los huipiles o camisas bordadas de las indígenas son la prenda más llamativa y colorista. Los más bonitos son los de las aldeas de San Antonio Aguas Calientes, Santa María de Jesús, Santiago Atitlán y los de Nebaj de Chajul. Son conocidos los chalés jaspeados de Salcajá o Totonicapán, y las cintas bordadas del pelo de Aguacatán. Los sacos o bolsos de hombre de Sololá y los pantalones bordados con aves de Santiago Atitlán o San Pedro la Laguna.

Hay también máscaras muy originales de la Danza del Venado o la Conquista que se venden en el mercado de Chichicastenango. En la capital se puede comprar artesanía de todo tipo: huipiles, joyas de jade y plata, tallas de madera, máscaras en el Mercado Central (detrás de la Catedral).

---

en regla in order
orillas banks
aldeas villages
huipiles huipils (traditional embroidered dresses)
mantas blankets
alfombras rugs
tejidos textiles

¡A ESCRIBIR!

Strategy: Writing a summary

A good summary tells the reader the most important information about an event. The following is a list of important data that one should include in a summary.

- An interesting title or topic sentence
- Description of the setting: when and where the action took place, who was involved, any special conditions that were in existence
- What made the situation interesting or unique
- What actions took place, expected or unexpected
- How the event or situation ended or was resolved

Lee el siguiente resumen de una celebración memorable. Después, indica si la narración contiene los elementos importantes para un resumen.

El 21 de diciembre fue un día memorable para mí el año pasado. Estaba en Guatemala, pasando unos días con mis primos que vivían en la capital. La mañana del 21 decidimos ir al pueblo de Chichicastenango para la celebración del Día de Santo Tomás, el santo patrón del pueblo. Eran las diez de la mañana cuando salimos de la capital en el coche de mi primo. Cuando llegamos a Chichicastenango, mucha gente estaba en las calles. Vimos a una amiga de mi primo y pudimos ayudarla con los últimos preparativos para la procesión. La procesión empezó unos minutos después y me puse muy contenta cuando vi a los adultos y los niños que lo pasaban maravillosamente bien en esta celebración. Más tarde comimos mucha comida típica de la región y bailamos por muchas horas. Tuvimos que volver a la capital antes del fin de la gran celebración y me sentía un poco triste pero también estaba contenta porque había participado (had participated) en una de las celebraciones más importantes de ese país.

¿Tiene la narración...

	Sí	No
• un título o una oración introductoria?	_____	_____
• información sobre dónde y cuándo ocurrió la acción?	_____	_____
• información sobre los participantes?	_____	_____
• explicación de elementos únicos de la situación?	_____	_____
• información sobre lo que las personas hicieron?	_____	_____
• una conclusión o una resolución?	_____	_____

Task: Writing a summary of an important event

Summaries of past events occur in a variety of contexts such as in newspapers or magazines or in letters written by participants to friends and family who may be interested in the event. The writer must present sufficient detail to capture and keep the interest of the reader but must not overwhelm the reader with unnecessary information. Follow the steps outlined below to prepare a summary of an important event in which you took part.

Paso 1: Piensa en una celebración que quieres describir en forma escrita. Trata de recordar detalles importantes, como el día o la fecha de la celebración, las preparaciones, las personas, las actividades, los problemas, si había algunos, y la conclusión de la celebración.

Paso 2: Escribe un resumen de la celebración, contestando las siguientes preguntas.

1. ¿Qué día era o cuál era la fecha? ¿Qué hora era?
2. ¿Qué tiempo hacía?
3. ¿Dónde estabas tú? ¿Dónde estaban las otras personas? ¿Qué hacían todos?
4. ¿Cómo estaban las personas? ¿Por qué?
5. ¿Qué pasó en la celebración? ¿Qué hizo una persona o qué hicieron varias personas? ¿Qué hiciste tú? Menciona varias actividades e incluye información sobre cuándo ocurrieron si puedes.
6. ¿Ocurrió algo especialmente interesante?
7. ¿Cómo y cuándo terminó la celebración?
8. ¿Lo pasaste bien? Explica.

Paso 3: Lee la información que acabas de escribir y prepara un título o una oración de introducción para el resumen. Después, lee el resumen otra vez y haz las correcciones necesarias en el contenido, la organización, la gramática y la ortografía *(spelling)*.

Paso 4: Intercambia papeles con un(a) compañero(a) de clase. Lee el resumen de él/ella y después hazle preguntas sobre su resumen y, contesta las preguntas que tenga *(may have)* sobre el tuyo.

Functions: Writing about past events; Writing about theme, plot, or scene
Vocabulary: Family members; Religious holidays; Time expressions
Grammar: Verbs: Preterite & Imperfect

¡A CONVERSAR!

Pronunciation focus: *x*

The letter **x** rarely occurs at the beginning of a word in Spanish but when it does, it is pronounced like an **s.** Between vowels it is pronounced like the English *x,* but before a consonant it is pronounced more like an **s.** In Mexico, the **x** sounds like a **j,** as in the word **México.** Practice the following sentences:

- Pasé unas vacaciones excelentes en México.
- Para tener éxito en la clase, tienes que leer el libro de texto.

Task: Discussing a recent vacation

A todos nos gusta recordar y hablar de nuestras vacaciones. Ahora vas a conversar con un(a) compañero(a) sobre unas vacaciones que pasaste en la playa, en el campo o en las montañas. Uds. van a comparar las vacaciones y las actividades que hicieron.

Paso 1: Dile a tu compañero(a) adónde fuiste y pregúntale adónde fue él/ella. Describe el lugar que visitaste, diciéndole cómo era (bonito, tranquilo, etc.) y qué tenía (olas grandes, árboles, lugares para caminar, etc.). Pregúntale si el lugar que visitó era igual o diferente.

Paso 2: Conversa sobre las actividades que hiciste. Incluye tanta información como sea posible (dónde y cuándo hiciste cada actividad, si la hiciste solo[a] o con otra[s] persona[s], si te gustó o si te asustaste, si estabas contento[a], nervioso[a], etc.). Compara tus experiencias con las de tu compañero(a).

Paso 3: Decide si quieres visitar el lugar que tu compañero(a) visitó y explica por qué sí o por qué no. Después, pregúntale si él/ella quiere ir al lugar que tú visitaste.

Fiestas y celebraciones Holidays and celebrations

Verbos

asustarse *to get frightened*
celebrar *to celebrate*
cumplir años *to have a birthday*
dar (hacer) una fiesta *to give a party*
disfrazarse *to wear a costume*

gritar *to shout*
hacer un brindis *to make a toast*
llorar *to cry*
olvidar *to forget*
pasarlo bien (mal) *to have a good (bad) time*

ponerse + *adjective* *to become (get)* + adjective
portarse bien (mal) *to behave well (poorly)*
reaccionar *to react*
recordar (ue) *to remember*
reunirse con *to get together with*

Sustantivos

el anfitrión *host*
la anfitriona *hostess*
el brindis *toast*
la celebración *celebration*
los cohetes *rockets*
el cumpleaños *birthday*

el día feriado *holiday*
el disfraz *costume*
los entremeses *hors d'oeuvres*
la fiesta (sorpresa) *(surprise) party*
el (la) invitado(a) *guest*
la máscara *mask*

el pastel *cake*
la procesión *religious parade*
los regalos *gifts*
las velas *candles*

La playa y el campo The beach and the country

Sustantivos

el balneario *beach resort*
la costa *coast*
la crema bronceadora *suntan lotion*

el lago *lake*
el mar *sea*

el océano *ocean*
el río *river*

Pasatiempos

broncearse (tomar el sol) *to get a suntan*
bucear *to scuba dive*
caminar por las montañas *to hike in the mountains*

correr las olas *to surf*
hacer camping *to go camping*
hacer esnórquel *to snorkel*
hacer una parrillada *to have a cookout*

pasear en canoa/velero *to go canoeing/sailing*
pescar *to fish*

Expresiones afirmativas

algo *something, anything*
alguien *somebody, someone, anybody, anyone*

algún, alguno(a) *some, any*
o... o *either . . . or*

siempre *always*
también *also, too*

Expresiones negativas

nada *nothing, not anything, at all*
nadie *nobody, no one*

ningún, ninguno(a) *none, not any*
ni... ni *neither . . . nor*

nunca *never*
tampoco *neither, not either*

Palabras interrogativas

¿A qué hora? *At what time?*
¿Adónde? *Where (to)?*
¿Cómo? *How?*
¿Cuál(es)? *What? Which one(s)?*
¿Cuándo? *When?*

¿Cuánto(a)? *How much?*
¿Cuántos(as)? *How many?*
¿Dónde? *Where?*
¿De dónde? *From where?*
¿De quién(es)? *Whose?*

¿Para qué? *For what purpose?*
¿Por qué? *Why?*
¿Qué? *What? Which?*
¿Quién(es)? *Who?*

Expresiones idiomáticas

¡Felicitaciones! *Congratulations!*
Me pongo contento/avergonzado/molesto.
   I get happy/embarrassed/annoyed.

De viaje por el Caribe:

Chapter Objectives

COMMUNICATIVE GOALS

In this chapter you will learn how to . . .

- Talk about air travel, other types of transportation, and lodging
- Simplify expressions with indirect and double object pronouns
- Talk about getting around in the city
- Give directions and express desires
- Make informal requests

STRUCTURES

- Indirect object pronouns
- Double object pronouns
- Prepositions and adverbs of location
- Formal and negative **tú** commands

CULTURAL INFORMATION

- La República Dominicana: Santo Domingo, la primera ciudad de las Américas
- Cuba: Escuela Latinoamericana de Ciencias Médicas
- Puerto Rico: Estado Libre Asociado

La República Dominicana, Cuba y Puerto Rico

CUBA

Población: 11.637.600
Área: 110.992 kilómetros cuadrados, casi del tamaño de Pennsylvania
Capital: La Habana, 2.312.100
Ciudades principales: Santiago de Cuba, 534.600; Camagüey, 342.900; Holguín, 305.000
Moneda: el peso cubano
Lengua: el español

PUERTO RICO

Población: 3.808.610
Área: 8.897 kilómetros cuadrados
Capital: San Juan, 425.900
Ciudades principales: Bayamón, 205.400; Carolina, 169.800; Ponce, 156.500
Moneda: el dólar estadounidense
Lenguas: el español y el inglés

LA REPÚBLICA DOMINICANA

Población: 8.582.477
Área: 48.308 kilómetros cuadrados, del tamaño de New Hampshire y Vermont juntos
Capital: Santo Domingo, 2.006.200
Ciudades principales: Santiago, 446.800; La Romana, 177.800; San Pedro de Macorís, 154.800
Moneda: el dólar estadounidense
Lenguas: el español y el inglés

¡Bienvenidos a Cuba!

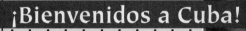

En este vídeo, vas a aprender mucho sobre Cuba y su cultura. Después de ver el vídeo, contesta las siguientes preguntas:

1 ¿Dónde está Cuba? Y, ¿cuál es su capital?

2 ¿Cuáles son algunos de los cultivos principales de Cuba?

3 ¿Qué sabes del gobierno cubano? ¿Sabes quién es el líder de Cuba?

4 ¿Cómo es La Habana? ¿Qué medios de transporte emplean (use) los habaneros? ¿Cuáles son las zonas turísticas más populares de la ciudad?

5 ¿Te gustaría visitar Cuba? ¿Por qué sí o por qué no?

La Plaza de Armas,
Viejo San Juan, Puerto Rico

En el aeropuerto las Américas In this section, you will learn vocabulary and expressions used for traveling by airplane. The drawing below represents a typical scene in main airports like the one in the Dominican Republic.

EL AEROPUERTO

la inmigración
LA LLEGADA
la aduana
PUERTA 5
la maleta
LA SALIDA
PUERTAS 1-4
el equipaje (de mano)
el control de seguridad
el horario
AGE...
la agencia de viajes
la agente de viajes

EL AVIÓN
la sección de fumar
la asistente de vuelo
el pasaporte
el pasillo
la ventanilla
el asiento
la pasajera

CULTURA

Santo Domingo is the capital city of the Dominican Republic. The international airport is called **Las Américas,** and it is about 20 minutes east of Santo Domingo.

Sustantivos

el boleto (billete) de ida one-way ticket	**el viaje** trip
el boleto (billete) de ida y vuelta round-trip ticket	**el vuelo (sin escala)** (nonstop) flight

¿NOS ENTENDEMOS?

In addition to **el (la) asistente de vuelo,** the word **la azafata** is also used to refer to a female flight attendant.

Verbos

abordar to board	**ir en avión** to go by plane
bajar(se) (de) to get off	**pasar por** to go through
facturar el equipaje to check the luggage	**recoger** to pick up, claim
hacer escala (en) to make a stop (on a flight) (in)	**viajar** to travel
hacer la(s) maleta(s) to pack one's suitcase(s)	

¿NOS ENTENDEMOS?

While a *passenger* is **un(a) pasajero(a),** a *traveler* is **un(a) viajero(a).**

Expresiones idiomáticas

¡Bienvenido(a)! Welcome!	**¡Buen viaje! / ¡Feliz viaje!** Have a nice trip!

Palabras útiles are presented to help you enrich your personal vocabulary. The words here will help you talk about air travel.

Palabras útiles

abrocharse el cinturón de seguridad to buckle the seatbelt	**la demora** delay
la aerolínea airline	**despegar** to take off
aterrizar to land	**el (la) piloto** pilot
la cabina cabin	**procedente de** arriving from
con destino a departing for	**la salida de emergencia** emergency exit

¡A PRACTICAR!

9-1 **Definiciones** Lee cada frase y luego identifica su definición.

1. la gente que paga para viajar en avión ____
2. el lugar en que se aborda el avión ____
3. la lista de los días y las horas de vuelos ____
4. el documento para poder entrar en otro país ____
5. el asiento desde el cual se puede ver hacia afuera ____
6. el equipaje que se factura ____
7. el lugar donde se mira lo que hay en las maletas ____
8. la tienda donde se compran los boletos de avión ____
9. el boleto que se compra cuando uno no quiere volver ____
10. lo que uno les dice a los amigos antes de viajar ____

a. de ida
b. la aduana
c. la puerta de la salida
d. el horario
e. las maletas
f. ¡Buen viaje!
g. el pasaporte
h. los pasajeros
i. el asiento de ventanilla
j. la agencia de viajes

9-2 **Un viaje en avión a Santo Domingo** Teresita, una mujer puertorriqueña, hizo un viaje a Santo Domingo para visitar a unos familiares el verano pasado. Pon sus acciones en un orden lógico.

___ Pasó por la aduana. *customs*
___ Se bajó del avión. *get off the plane*
___ Facturó el equipaje. *check your luggage*
___ Abordó el avión con destino a Santo Domingo. *board the plane*
___ Fue a la agencia de viajes. *book flight*
___ Compró un boleto de ida y vuelta. *round trip ticket*
___ Hizo las maletas. *pack your suitcase*
___ Recibió una invitación de sus parientes en Santo Domingo. *receive invitation*
___ Buscó su asiento de ventanilla. *sit near window*
___ Recogió su equipaje. *pick up luggage*
___ Pasó por el control de seguridad. *metal detector*

9-3 **Nuestra luna de miel** Teresita y su esposo, Manny, fueron a La Habana para pasar su luna de miel. Escoge de las siguientes palabras para completar el párrafo.

agente de viajes	salida	viaje
equipaje de mano	asiento de pasillo	hacer escala
inmigración	vuelo sin escalas	ir en avión
llegada	agente de la aerolínea	Bienvenidos

El mes pasado, Manny y yo fuimos a La Habana, Cuba, para nuestra luna de miel. No queríamos ir en barco, preferíamos 1. _____. Nuestro 2. _____ nos reservó un 3. _____ en la aerolínea Cubana. Yo estaba contenta porque a mí no me gusta 4. _____. Tampoco me gusta mirar afuera del avión cuando vuelo, así que yo pedí el 5. _____. Antes de la 6. _____ del vuelo, le enseñamos el pasaporte y el boleto a un 7. _____. No teníamos muchas maletas, pero Manny llevó 8. _____ con las cosas más necesarias. Durante el vuelo, esperamos con mucha emoción la 9. _____ a Cuba. Al llegar a La Habana, el piloto anunció «¡10. _____ a Cuba!» Tuvimos que pasar por la 11. _____, pero fue fácil. Total, nuestra luna de miel en La Habana fue el mejor 12. _____ de mi vida.

CULTURA

In December of 1999, the first charter flight in more than 30 years left New York for Havana, Cuba. During most of the Castro regime, travel to Cuba for American citizens has been extremely limited. As of December 1999, it became legal for some people to go to Cuba from the U.S.—citizens with familial relations in Cuba, researchers, students, and medical personnel. Today, an increasing number of U.S. citizens are able to visit Cuba.

CULTURA

Cubana: Empresa Consolidada de Aviación is the national airline of Cuba.

¿NOS ENTENDEMOS?

In Latin America, the words **boleto** and **billete** are used to talk about an airplane ticket. In Spain it is more common to use **el pasaje**, which is also used in Latin America.

EN VOZ ALTA

9-4 | **¿Qué opinas?** Léele las siguientes oraciones a un(a) compañero(a), que debe decirte si está de acuerdo o no, y por qué. ¿Tienen mucho en común?

MODELO: E1: Es mejor pedir un vuelo sin escalas que con escalas.
E2: *Estoy de acuerdo.*
E1: *¿Por qué?*
E2: *Porque los pasajeros llegan más rápidamente.*

1. Es mejor sentarse en la ventanilla que en el pasillo de un avión.
2. Es difícil viajar en avión con un bebé o con un niño pequeño.
3. Es buena idea llevar poco equipaje cuando se viaja en avión.
4. Es preferible pagar un boleto de avión antes de viajar que después de viajar.
5. Es importante sentarse cerca de una puerta de emergencia en el avión.
6. Es más interesante sentarse en la sección de clase turística que en primera clase.

9-5 | **Entrevista** Pregúntale a un(a) compañero(a) lo siguiente sobre sus hábitos y preferencias de viaje. Luego, añadan *(add)* sus propias preguntas, usando el vocabulario nuevo. Prepárense para compartir esta información con la clase.

1. ¿Tienes pasaporte? ¿Sí? ¿Cuándo sacaste tu pasaporte? o ¿No? ¿Piensas sacar un pasaporte algún día? ¿Por qué?
2. ¿A qué países viajaste en los últimos cuatro años? ¿Cuál es tu país favorito? ¿Qué países quieres visitar algún día? ¿Por qué?
3. Normalmente, ¿llevas mucho o poco equipaje cuando viajas?
4. ¿Cuándo fue la última vez que viajaste en avión? ¿Adónde fuiste? ¿Por qué fuiste a ese lugar?
5. ¿Prefieres sentarte en el pasillo o al lado de la ventanilla cuando viajas en avión? ¿Por qué?

9-6 | **En el aeropuerto** Haz esta actividad con otros(as) dos compañeros(as). Dos personas son pasajeros en el aeropuerto, y la otra persona es el (la) agente de la aerolínea.

Agente

1. Greet your passengers.
3. Find out where they are going.
5. Ask for their tickets and passport.
7. Ask their seating preference (window/aisle).
9. Answer the question, then check in their luggage.
11. Respond, then say where they should board the airplane.
13. Explain, then return their travel documents.
15. Respond, then wish them a good trip.
17. Say good-bye.

Pasajeros

2. Respond appropriately.
4. Answer the question.
6. Do what the agent asks and say something appropriate.
8. Answer, then ask if your plane will leave on time.
10. Ask how the weather is at your destination.
12. Ask for directions to your departure gate.
14. Ask what time it is. Express appreciation.
16. Express your appreciation.
18. Answer appropriately.

EN CONTEXTO

Sharon y su amiga Kate son estudiantes de la Universidad Internacional de la Florida en Miami, donde han estudiado español por tres años. Ahora ellas están de vacaciones en Santo Domingo visitando la Ciudad Colonial. Lo que sigue es una parte del diario que grabó Sharon en su grabadora.

CULTURA
The Dominican Republic was the first European colony of the New World. Its capital, Santo Domingo, is home to the first Spanish fortresses, hospitals, and churches. It is also the site of the first colonial cathedral and university.

27 de junio

Kate y yo fuimos al Hotel Montesinos. Cuando llegamos aquí anoche, estábamos tan cansadas que nos acostamos inmediatamente. Esta mañana caminamos por la ciudad colonial y vimos algunas plazas e iglesias coloniales. En una librería **cerca de** La Plaza de Armas compramos tarjetas postales para **mandarles a nuestros padres y amigos.** Luego tomamos un autobús al Fuerte del Ángulo, desde donde vimos el puerto. Yo saqué una foto de Kate **enfrente de** la fortaleza y **se la mandé** por correo electrónico a un amigo que tenemos, llamado Rodrigo Enrique. Después, Kate me dijo otra vez, «**No te olvides** de enviarles la foto a los miembros de mi familia también». Yo le respondí, «¡**No me pidas** más este favor si no puedes recordar las direcciones del correo electrónico!» En la Plaza de la Hispanidad conocí a Eduardo Pérez, a su esposa Gabriela y a sus dos hijas. **Se los presenté a Kate** cuando ella volvió de la Plaza España de hacer algunas compras. Ellos nos invitaron a su casa.

28 de junio

Esta mañana visitamos muchas iglesias, como la Capilla de Nuestra Señora de los Remedios. Por la tarde, fuimos al mercado de artesanías en el Parque Colón para comprar algunos recuerdos. Yo compré un anillo y unos aretes, y **se los di a Kate.** Luego, ella **me compró un sombrero** y una camiseta muy bonita. Allí en el parque conocimos a Juan Ochoa Valderrama y a José Hernández Lillo, que son empleados del Museo Casas Reales. Juan tiene veintitrés años y José tiene veinte. Ellos nos invitaron a tomar café en un pequeño restaurante, donde charlamos por dos horas. Antes de irse, Juan nos invitó a una fiesta en su casa. Hemos estado en Santo Domingo solamente dos días y ya tenemos seis amigos. ¡Qué simpáticos son los dominicanos!

¿Comprendiste?

Contesta las siguientes preguntas basándote en la lectura.

1. Según **En contexto,** ¿cuáles son algunos sitios de interés turístico que ofrece Santo Domingo?
2. ¿Cuáles son los lugares que Sharon y Kate visitaron durante su visita en Santo Domingo y las actividades que ellas hicieron allí? Haz una lista, siguiendo el modelo.

MODELO: **Lugares** **Actividades**
Hotel Montesinos *Durmieron en ese hotel.*
una librería *Compraron tarjetas postales allí.*

3. ¿Por qué se puso Sharon un poco enojada con Kate?
4. Imagínate que tú estás en Santo Domingo ahora. De las cosas que Sharon y Kate vieron e hicieron en esta isla, ¿cuáles te gustaría ver y hacer?
5. ¿Qué impresiones tienes de Kate y Sharon?

Encuentro cultural

La República Dominicana: Santo Domingo, la primera ciudad de las Américas

PARA PENSAR

- ¿Existe la presencia de varias culturas en las tradiciones de tu ciudad o región?
- ¿Puedes describir las diferentes culturas que hay dentro de la cultura norteamericana?
- ¿Conoces algún lugar en los Estados Unidos declarado Patrimonio de la Humanidad?

CULTURA

Santo Domingo has been declared "World Cultural Heritage" by UNESCO in 1992 due to its rich colonial architecture. Some sites that have been declared "World Heritage" by UNESCO in the United States are Mesa Verde, 1978; Yellowstone, 1978; Grand Canyon National Park, 1979; Pueblo de Taos, 1992; Carlsbad Caverns National Park, 1995.

Parque Colón. Santo Domingo, República Dominicana

Varias culturas forman el carácter del pueblo dominicano. De los indígenas llamados taínos, que quiere decir «gente amable», todavía se usan sus medicinas y su comida tradicional al igual que varias palabras de su lengua tales como *hamaca* y *tabaco*. Éstos fueron los habitantes que le dieron la bienvenida a Cristóbal Colón en 1492. De los conquistadores españoles, se mantiene en la isla la lengua y la religión católica. De los esclavos africanos que llegaron en el siglo XVI para trabajar en la industria del azúcar, todavía se mantienen su fe y su religión, su arte y especialmente su música. Y de las tropas norteamericanas que estuvieron en la República Dominicana varias veces de 1916 a 1924 y más tarde en 1966, se mantiene el amor por el béisbol.

La ciudad capital, Santo Domingo, fue fundada entre 1494 y 1498 por Bartolomé Colón, hermano de Cristóbal Colón. Esta ciudad sirvió como ejemplo de construcción para las otras ciudades en las Américas. En el sector colonial los edificios más importantes eran: la Fortaleza Ozama, que fue la primera construcción militar del Nuevo Mundo *(New World);* el primer hospital de San Nicolás de Bari; y el Monasterio de San Francisco.

En 1521 se construyó la primera catedral de las Américas, y en 1538 se fundó la primera universidad de América con el nombre de Santo Tomás de Aquino. Esta universidad fue un centro intelectual muy importante que le dio a Santo Domingo el nombre de Atenas del Nuevo Mundo.

En 1992, la UNESCO declaró la Zona Colonial de la ciudad de Santo Domingo Patrimonio de la Humanidad *(World Heritage Site)* por todas las bellezas arquitectónicas e históricas que tiene que ofrecer la ciudad al mundo.

PARA DISCUTIR

1. ¿Qué culturas influyen en el carácter de la gente en la República Dominicana?
2. ¿Cuál es una contribución importante de cada cultura que está presente en la isla?
3. ¿Por qué fue importante la ciudad de Santo Domingo para el resto de las Américas?
4. ¿Por qué se declaró Patrimonio de la Humanidad a la ciudad de Santo Domingo?
5. ¿Hay influencia dominicana en los Estados Unidos? ¿Dónde y cuáles son estas influencias?
6. ¿Te gustaría visitar la ciudad de Santo Domingo? ¿Por qué sí o por qué no?

ESTRUCTURA I Simplifying expressions: indirect object pronouns

The concept of indirect objects

All sentences have a subject and a verb. As you learned in **Capítulo 7,** many sentences also have a direct object or a pronoun that replaces the direct object (the direct object pronoun).

Subject	Verb	Direct Object	Subject	D.O.P.	Verb
↓	↓	↓	↓	↓	↓
Manny	compró	**un boleto.**	Manny	**lo**	compró.
Manny	*bought*	*a ticket.*	*Manny bought it.*		

Note below that some sentences also have an indirect object.

Subject	Indirect Object Pronoun	Verb	Direct Object	Indirect Object
↓	↓	↓	↓	↓
Manny	le	compró	un boleto	**a su esposa.**
Manny bought a ticket for his wife.				

Indirect objects (and their respective pronouns) refer to people already mentioned as indirect objects; that is, the pronoun tells *to whom* or *for whom* the action of the verb is performed.

To whom did he give the tickets?

Manny **le** dio los boletos **a su esposa.**	*Manny gave the tickets to his wife.*
Él **le** dio los boletos.	*He gave the tickets to her.*

For whom did she buy the souvenirs?

Teri **les** compró recuerdos **a sus hermanos.**	*Teri bought souvenirs for her brothers.*
Ella **les** compró los recuerdos.	*She bought the souvenirs for them.*

Indirect object pronouns

In the sentences above, the indirect object pronouns **le** and **les** replace the indirect object nouns **esposa** and **hermanos,** respectively.

Singular		Plural	
me	*to/for me*	nos	*to/for us*
te	*to/for you* (informal)	os	*to/for you* (informal in Spain)
le	*to/for you* (formal), *him, her*	les	*to/for you* (formal in Spain), *them*

- Note that indirect object pronouns are placed in the same positions as direct object pronouns.

1. Place the pronoun in front of the conjugated verb.

—¿Marta **te dio** esa maleta?   *Did Marta give you that suitcase?*
—Sí. También **me compró** estos   *Yes. She also bought me these hats.*
sombreros.

2. In negative sentences, place the **no** in front of the pronoun.

—Le di el boleto a mi esposo.   *I gave my husband the ticket.*
—¿Por qué **no nos** diste uno?   *Why didn't you give us one?*

3. When the pronoun is used with an infinitive, a present participle, or an affirmative command, either place it before the conjugated verb or attach it to the infinitive, the present participle, or the command.

Le voy a escribir.   ⎫
Voy a escribir**le.**   ⎬   *I'm going to write to him.*

Le estoy escribiendo ahora. ⎫
Estoy escribiéndo**le** ahora. ⎬   *I'm writing to him now.*

¡Escríb**ele** ahora!   *Write to him now!*

> A written accent is needed to mark the stressed vowel of a present participle or an affirmative command when an indirect object pronoun is attached to it.

- Also note that since **le** and **les** can have different meanings, you may add the expressions **a él, a ella, a usted, a ellos, a ellas,** or **a ustedes** to the sentence for clarification or emphasis.

For clarification

—¿**Le** prometiste el viaje **a él**   *Did you promise the trip to him*
o a ella?   *or her?*
—**Le** prometí el viaje **a ella**.   *I promised the trip to her.*

For emphasis

—¿**A quién** le está comprando   *For whom are you buying this*
este recuerdo?   *souvenir?*
—Estoy comprándole este recuerdo   *I'm buying this souvenir for you.*
a usted.

- Indirect object pronouns are normally used with the verbs **dar** (*to give*) and **decir** (*to say; to tell*). Other verbs that frequently employ indirect object pronouns are:

escribir *to write*
explicar *to explain*
hablar *to speak*
mandar *to send*
ofrecer (zc) *to offer*
pedir (i, i) *to request; to ask for*
preguntar *to ask a question*
prestar *to lend*
prometer *to promise*
recomendar (ie) *to recommend*
regalar *to give (as a gift)*
servir (i, i) *to serve*

> The **yo** form of **ofrecer** is **ofrezco**.

¡A PRACTICAR!

9-7 **De viaje por el Caribe** Imagínate que vas de viaje por las islas del Caribe y quieres describir lo que haces allá. Llena los espacios en blanco, usando el pronombre de objeto indirecto correcto.

MODELO: Yo ___les___ escribo postales del Caribe. (a mis padres)

1. Yo ___le___ hago muchas preguntas al agente de viajes sobre Santo Domingo. (a él)
2. Él ___me___ recomienda visitar la Fortaleza Ozama que fue la primera construcción militar de América. (a mí)
3. Yo ___te___ prometo comprar cosas típicas como guayaberas dominicanas, cubanas y puertorriqueñas. (a ti)
4. En el Café Merengue en Santo Domingo, mi amigo José ___le___ pidió plátanos fritos con chuletas de cochino y huevos fritos, que es un plato típico. (al mesero)
5. Los padres de mis compañeros de viaje ___les___ piden fotos de La Habana. (a sus hijos)
6. En Cuba, el botones del hotel ___nos___ recomienda comer helado en el Café Coppelia en La Habana. (a nosotros)
7. En el Hotel Nacional en La Habana, el mesero ___me___ sirve mojitos cubanos, que es una de las bebidas típicas de Cuba. (a mí)
8. De regreso en casa, mis amigos ___me___ piden ayuda con los edificios coloniales que deben visitar en Santo Domingo y los restaurantes en La Habana. (a mí)
9. Yo ___les___ ofrezco ayuda con sus planes para visitar San Felipe del Morro, la fortaleza famosa de Puerto Rico. (a mis amigos)
10. Mis compañeros de viaje y yo ___les___ escribimos mensajes electrónicos para darles las gracias. (a nuestros amigos caribeños)

9-8 **En una tienda en el aeropuerto** Teri y Manny deciden a última hora comprarle un recuerdo de Cuba al hermano de Teri. Llena los espacios en blanco, conjugando los verbos entre paréntesis (si es necesario) y colocando (*placing*) el pronombre de objeto indirecto en el lugar correcto.

MODELO: **Dependiente:** ¿Puedo _____ayudarles_____ (ayudar/les)?

Dependiente: Hola, ¿en qué puedo 1. _____ (servir/les)?

Teri: Queremos 2. _____ (comprar/le) un regalo a mi hermano.

Dependiente: Bien. ¿Qué tipo de regalo 3. _____ (buscar/le)?

Teri: Pues, a mi hermano y a mí 4. _____ (gustar/nos) mucho la ropa.

Dependiente: ¿Ropa? ¿Qué tipo de ropa 5. _____ (gustar/les) a Uds., por ejemplo?

Teri: Bueno, el año pasado él 6. _____ (regalar/me) un sombrero típico de Perú y ahora quiero 7. _____ (dar/le) a él un sombrero típico cubano.

Manny: Y a mí 8. _____ (gustar/me) mucho las guayaberas. Teri, ¿no quieres _____ (dar/le) a tu hermano una guayabera como ésta?

Teri: Mmm, es verdad que necesito 9. _____ (hacer/te) un regalo de boda a ti todavía. ¿Por qué no 10. _____ (comprar/te) esa guayabera a ti? Pero creo que a mi hermano 11. _____ (ir a gustar/le) más el sombrero.

Dependiente: Comprendo. Bueno, ¿a Ud. 12. _____ (gustar/le) éste?

Teri: ¡Sí! Él 13. _____ (ir a decir/nos), «¡Muchas gracias!» ¿Puedo 14. _____ (probar/me) el sombrero? Mi esposo puede 15. _____ (regalar/me) uno también.

Manny: Y tú 16. _____ (poder/me) regalar la guayabera, ¿no?

CULTURA
A **guayabera** is a typical dress shirt worn by men in the Caribbean. They are usually made of lightweight material due to the hot weather and have four pockets embroidered on the front. Today, they come in different colors as well.

CULTURA
A **mojito cubano** is a Cuban drink made with rum, sugar, and mint leaves. Supposedly, it was the writer Ernest Hemingway's preferred drink during his stay in Cuba.

CULTURA
The largest fort in the Caribbean, San Felipe del Morro, was built in the 16th century. Additional construction took place in the 18th century, and a recent restoration was completed in 1992. It stands 140 feet above sea level and has served to protect the tiny island of Puerto Rico.

9-9 **¡Ayúdanos!** Teri y Manny están muy cansados después de su luna de miel y te piden ayuda. Explica lo que tú haces por ellos, y lo que ellos hacen por ti, usando el pronombre de objeto indirecto correcto.

MODELO: (a ellos) hacer las reservas para el vuelo
Les hago las reservas para el vuelo.

1. (a Teri) bajar las maletas *le bajo*
2. (a ellos) llamar un taxi *les llamo*
3. (a Manny) prestar dinero para el taxi *le presto*
4. (a Teri) ofrecer ayuda con las maletas en el aeropuerto *le ofrezco*
5. (a ellos) ayudar a facturar el equipaje *les ayudo*
6. (al agente) preguntar el horario *le pregunto*
7. (a Teri y Manny) prometer escribir una carta *les prometo*
8. (a mí) Manny y Teri regalar un recuerdo de La Habana *me regalan*
9. (a nosotros) Teri dar un beso *nos da*
10. (a Manny) decir «Buen viaje» *le digo*
11. (a mí) Manny y Teri dar una guayabera cubana por mi ayuda *me dan*
12. (a nosotros) Manny comprar Coca-Cola a todos *nos compra*

EN VOZ ALTA

9-10 **Un esposo ansioso** En el aeropuerto Manny está preocupado con todos los detalles *(details)* del viaje, pero Teri le explica que ella ya *(already)* hizo varias cosas. Así que Manny puede estar más tranquilo. ¿Cómo responde Teri a las preocupaciones de Manny? Túrnense haciendo los papeles de Teri y Manny.

MODELO: —¿Les compramos los regalos a nuestros amigos?
—*Ya les compramos regalos ayer. Les compramos los dibujos.
¿No te acuerdas?*

1. ¡Ay! Me olvidé de confirmarles el vuelo a nuestros amigos.
2. ¡Caramba! Yo quería comprarme una camiseta de Cuba.
3. También quería comprarme una caja de puros de aquí.
4. ¿Le preguntaste al agente si está a tiempo el vuelo?
5. Tenemos que mandarle una tarjeta postal a mi abuelo.
6. Tenemos que explicarle al agente de vuelos que llevamos mucho equipaje.

9-11 **Escenas en la clase** Vamos a describir las actividades de las personas en nuestra clase. Por eso, con un(a) compañero(a), hagan preguntas sobre estas actividades, usando pronombres de objeto indirecto. ¡Sean *(Be)* creativos!

MODELO: la profesora
E1: *¿Qué le dice la profesora a Juan?*
E2: *Le dice que no debe llegar tarde a la clase.*

Verbos útiles: contestar, decir, escribir, explicar, hacer, ofrecer, pedir, preguntar

1. el (la) profesor(a)
2. nosotros
3. ellos
4. tú
5. él
6. ella

9-12 **Preguntas personales** Hazle las siguientes preguntas sobre su vida personal a uno(a) de tus compañeros. Túrnense contestándose las preguntas.

Tus amigos ¿Les hablas a tus amigos sobre tu vida personal? ¿Te ayudan tus amigos con algunos problemas? ¿Les ayudas a ellos con sus problemas? ¿Cuándo fue la última vez que un amigo te hizo un favor? ¿Les prestas dinero a tus amigos? ¿Por qué sí o por qué no?

Tus padres ¿Les haces muchos favores a tus padres? ¿Ellos te hacen favores a ti? ¿Qué tipo de favores? ¿Te escriben cartas o correos electrónicos de vez en cuando? ¿Les escribes a ellos? ¿Te hicieron una visita de sorpresa alguna vez? ¿Qué pasó?

Cuba: Escuela Latinoamericana de Ciencias Médicas

PARA PENSAR

- ¿Conoces a alguien de Cuba?

- ¿Qué piensas de las relaciones que los Estados Unidos tienen con Cuba?

- ¿Qué opinas del sistema de estudios médicos en los Estados Unidos?

José Azel/AURORA

La salud pública y la medicina en Cuba es una prioridad universal y completamente gratis *(free)* del gobierno cubano para sus ciudadanos. Aunque Cuba sufre *(suffers)* un bloqueo económico por parte de los Estados Unidos, Cuba ofrece un número de becas *(scholarships)* de medicina para estudiantes estadounidenses ya que tiene el sistema de salud pública más impresionante del mundo:

- El país gradúa a 200 nuevos médicos todos los años.
- La mortalidad infantil *(infant mortality)* es menor que en muchas ciudades de los Estados Unidos.
- El Ministro de Salud mantiene clínicas con un(a) doctor(a) y un(a) enfermero(a) por cada 120 familias.

En septiembre del año 2000, en la Iglesia de Riverside en Nueva York, el gobernante cubano Fidel Castro les ofreció 250 becas a personas de pocos recursos económicos *(economic resources)* de los Estados Unidos para estudiar medicina en la Escuela Latinoamericana de Ciencias Médicas en La Habana, Cuba. Los estudiantes que reciben estas becas van a tener que trabajar en las comunidades más necesitadas aquí en los Estados Unidos después de graduarse.

La Escuela Latinoamericana de Ciencias Médicas tiene 28 edificios con 80 salones de clases, 37 laboratorios, dormitorios y enfermerías *(infirmaries)*. La escuela tiene 3.500 estudiantes de 23 países diferentes de Latinoamérica, el Caribe y África. El programa de estudios comienza con un curso de preparación de seis meses, doce semanas de español intensivo y seis años de estudios rigurosos en esta escuela y en las otras veintiuna escuelas de medicina del país. Las actividades extracurriculares incluyen arte, deporte, cine, viajes a la playa y actividades en la «Casa de la Cultura» donde los estudiantes que representan los diferentes grupos étnicos comparten aspectos de su propia cultura. Con este sistema de becas, Cuba ayuda a los estados más pobres y más necesitados de los Estados Unidos.

PARA DISCUTIR

1. ¿Qué le ofrece el gobierno cubano a sus ciudadanos con respecto a la salud pública?
2. ¿A quién le ofreció becas para estudiar medicina el gobierno cubano?
3. ¿Qué incluye el programa de estudios de medicina?
4. Basándote en lo que tú sabes de la educación de los médicos en los Estados Unidos, ¿puedes identificar unas diferencias entre la educación de los médicos en Cuba y los de los Estados Unidos?
5. ¿Te gustaría estudiar en Cuba? ¿Qué te gustaría estudiar y por qué?

ESTRUCTURA II Simplifying expressions: double object pronouns

Sometimes you may want to use both direct and indirect object pronouns together in the same sentence. In this case, note that indirect object pronouns always precede direct object pronouns.

Indirect before direct		
me		
te		lo
le (se)		la
nos	+	los
os		las
les (se)		

- In the examples below, notice that the indirect object pronouns **le** and **les** always change to **se** when they are used together with the direct object pronouns **lo, la, los,** and **las.**

Teri **le** compró **un regalo a su hermano.**	*Teri bought a gift for her brother.*
Se lo compró ayer en el aeropuerto.	*She bought it for him yesterday in the airport.*
También **le** compró **una camiseta a su madre.**	*She also bought a shirt for her mother.*
Teri **se la** compró en una tienda en el centro.	*Teri bought it for her in a store downtown.*

- Also note that in a sentence with an infinitive or a present participle, pronouns may be placed before conjugated verbs or attached to the infinitive or present participle.

Teri quiere comprar**le** un sombrero a Humberto.	*Teri wants to buy Humberto a hat.*
Se lo va a comprar hoy. ⎫ Va a comprár**selo** hoy. ⎭	*She´s going to buy it for him today.*
Se lo está comprando ahora. ⎫ Está comprándo**selo** ahora. ⎭	*She is buying it for him now.*

- In the case of affirmative commands, the pronouns must be attached to the command form. Note that when two pronouns are attached, an accent mark is written over the stressed vowel.

Teri, cómpra**selo** en esa tienda.	*Teri, buy it for him in that store.*

¡A PRACTICAR!

9-13 **¿Qué hicieron Manny y Teri en Cuba?** Para saber lo que hicieron Manny y Teri en Cuba, lee las siguientes preguntas. Subraya el objeto directo y haz un círculo alrededor del objeto indirecto. Después, sustitúyelos con los pronombres de objeto directo e indirecto necesarios para hacer la oración más corta.

MODELO: ¿Les venden los agentes de viaje los boletos a los turistas?
        Sí, *se los* venden.

1. ¿Le explicó Manny a Teri los detalles del viaje?
   Sí, _____se_____ _____los_____ explicó.
2. ¿Les trajo Teri los famosos puros *(cigars)* de Cuba a sus hermanos?
   No, no _____se_____ _____los_____ trajo.
3. ¿Le compró Teri una guayabera cubana a Manny?
   Sí, _____se_____ _____la_____ compró.
4. ¿Teri y Manny nos trajeron un recuerdo a nosotros?
   Sí, _____nos_____ _____lo_____ trajeron.
5. ¿Les trajo Manny dos botellas de ron a sus amigos?
   Sí, _____se_____ _____las_____ trajo.
6. ¿Manny va a prestarte a ti su nueva guayabera?
   No, no _____me_____ _____la_____ va a prestar.

9-14 **La mandona *(bossy one)*** Teri está muy nerviosa con los preparativos de su viaje, y por eso se pone muy mandona con Manny. Para cada situación, cambia el verbo a un mandato *(command)* de **tú.** Sustituye los objetos directos e indirectos con los pronombres necesarios.

MODELO: mandar la carta a mi mamá   *¡Mándasela!*

1. plancharme la blusa   planchármela
2. servirnos el desayuno   servírnoslo
3. mandar el dinero a Visa   mándaselo
4. prepararte las maletas (de Manny)   prepártelas
5. dar comida a los perros   dásela
6. comprar una maleta nueva para mí   cómpramela

EN VOZ ALTA

9-15 **Preguntas y preguntas...** La madre de Manny le hace preguntas sobre el viaje. Una persona va a leer las preguntas de la madre y la otra persona va a indicar cómo responde Manny a las preguntas, usando pronombres de objeto directo e indirecto. ¡Sé *(Be)* creativo(a) con las explicaciones!

MODELO: ¿Compraste un regalo para tu padre?
        Sí, mamá, se lo compré porque...   o   No, mamá, no se lo compré porque...

1. ¿Trajiste las fotos de La Habana para mí?
2. ¿Le diste las gracias al recepcionista del hotel?
3. ¿Nos hiciste una reserva en el hotel para nosotros para el año que viene?
4. ¿Le regalaste las guayaberas a la familia de Teri?
5. ¿Tienes el recuerdo del viaje para mí?
6. ¿Te trajo Teri tu pasaporte?

9-16 **Entrevista** Hazle las siguientes preguntas a un(a) compañero(a). Intenta usar pronombres de objeto directo e indirecto cuando sea posible.

1. Cuando necesitas dinero para un viaje, ¿a quiénes se lo pides? (¿Y te lo dan?) Y tus padres, ¿te dan mucho o poco dinero? ¿Se lo pides con mucha o con poca frecuencia?
2. Cuando vas de viaje, ¿a quiénes les compras regalos? ¿Qué cosas les compras? ¿A quiénes les compraste regalos la última vez que viajaste?
3. ¿Te gusta escribirles cartas a tus amigos si estás de viaje? ¿Mandas cartas o tarjetas postales? ¿Alguien te escribe a ti? ¿Cuándo fue la última vez que escribiste una tarjeta postal? ¿A quién se la escribiste, y por qué?

En el hotel nacional de Cuba, La Habana In this section you will learn vocabulary and expressions associated with lodging by observing scenes from Teri and Manny's honeymoon in La Habana.

CULTURA

The monetary unit in Cuba is the Cuban peso, but as a tourist you cannot spend this currency. The tourist facilities on the island accept only U.S. dollars. One dollar is worth about 210,000 Cuban pesos.

Sustantivos

la cama sencilla (doble) single (double) bed
la recepción front desk
la reserva reservation

Adjetivos

arreglado(a) neat, tidy
cómodo(a) comfortable
limpio(a) clean
privado(a) private
sucio(a) dirty

Verbos

quedarse to stay
quejarse (de) to complain (about)
registrarse to register

Palabras útiles are presented to help you enrich your personal vocabulary. The words here will help you talk about visits to hotels.

¿NOS ENTENDEMOS?

In Latin America, one asks for **un cuarto** in a hotel. In Spain it is more common to call a hotel room **una habitación.**

Palabras útiles

la antena parabólica satellite television dish
la caja fuerte security box
el centro de negocios business center
las comodidades ammenities, features
la sala de conferencias / para banquetes conference/banquet room
el servicio de habitación (cuarto) room service

¡A PRACTICAR!

9-17 ¿Cierto o falso? Según lo que aprendiste del viaje de Teri y Manny, indica si las siguientes oraciones son ciertas o falsas. Si la oración es falsa, corrígela para que sea cierta.

MODELO: Teri y Manny piden dos cuartos para dos personas.
Es falso. Piden un cuarto para dos personas.

1. Teri y Manny no necesitan un baño privado.
2. El cuarto tiene aire acondicionado porque es un hotel de cuatro estrellas.
3. El cuarto cuesta 100 dólares al día.
4. Hay otro cuarto más barato en el segundo piso.
5. Para llegar a su cuarto, Teri y Manny tienen que subir la escalera.
6. El cuarto no estaba arreglado cuando Teri y Manny entraron.

9-18 Definiciones Busca las palabras de la lista del vocabulario que correspondan con las definiciones a continuación. Luego compara tu lista con la de un(a) compañero(a) de clase. ¿Están de acuerdo?

MODELO: Nosotros dormimos en esta cosa. *la cama*

1. Es una cama para una persona.
2. Entramos en esto para subir o bajar.
3. En este lugar uno se registra.
4. Es un baño que no hay que compartir con otros.
5. Es una máquina que enfría el cuarto.
6. Es un hotel muy lujoso *(luxurious)*.
7. Es un objeto de metal que abre la puerta.
8. Cuando nadie limpia el cuarto, el cuarto está...

EN VOZ ALTA

9-19 ¡Bienvenido a La Habana! Habla con un(a) compañero(a) de clase. Imagínense que una persona es el (la) cliente que busca una habitación en un hotel, y la otra es el (la) recepcionista.

Cliente

1. Greet the receptionist.
3. Ask for a single room with a private bath.
5. Find out how much the room costs.
7. Ask about the hotel facilities.
9. Describe the kind of room you want.
11. Express your appreciation.

Recepcionista

2. Return the greeting.
4. Ask how many days he/she is going to stay.
6. Inform your guest about your various room rates.
8. Answer your guest's questions.
10. Respond, then say the number and floor of the room.
12. Respond, then say something to make your guest feel welcome.

9-20 Situaciones Lee cada problema. Luego habla con un(a) compañero(a) de clase sobre la mejor solución para resolverlo. Luego compartan su solución con la clase. ¿Cuál es la solución más común en la clase?

1. Tú y tu amigo(a) acaban de llegar al aeropuerto de José Martí en La Habana, Cuba. Ustedes hablan con un agente de viajes para que les ayude a encontrar un cuarto barato en la ciudad. El agente les informa que el cuarto más barato cuesta 40 dólares al día, pero ustedes no quieren pagar más de 25 dólares. Son las 10:00 de la noche y ustedes están muy cansados.
2. Después de entrar a su cuarto de hotel, ustedes se duchan, miran las noticias de la televisión y luego se acuestan. A las 3:00 de la mañana un ruido tremendo los despierta. Una pareja en otro cuarto comienza a hablar muy alto y ustedes no pueden dormir.

ASÍ SE DICE Giving directions: prepositions of location, adverbs, and relevant expressions

CULTURA
Puerto Rico is a common-wealth of the United States. Puerto Ricans are U.S. citizens but do not have the right to vote in national elections, as they do not pay federal taxes.

In this section, you will learn how to ask for and give street directions. Look at the map below and read the accompanying description of El Viejo San Juan in Puerto Rico with the prepositions of place highlighted.

El mapa

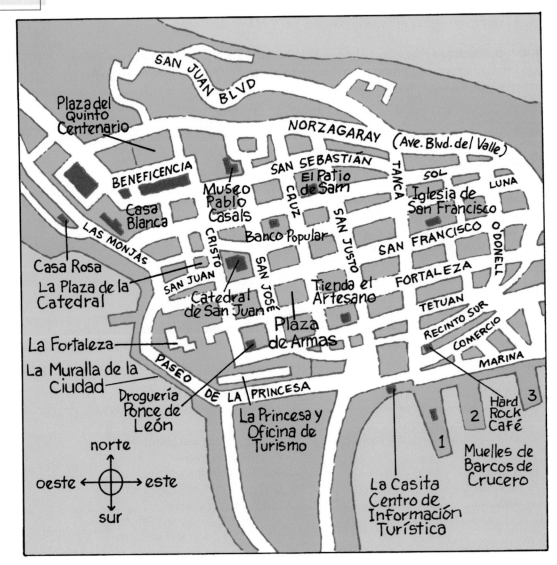

¿NOS ENTENDEMOS?
There are two ways to say *map* in Spanish: **el plano** and **el mapa.**

La Plaza de Armas está en el centro de la ciudad. **Hacia** *(Toward)* el **sur** de la ciudad el Paseo de la Princesa está **detrás de** *(behind)* la Muralla de la Ciudad *(City Wall)*. En el **norte** de la ciudad el restaurante el Patio de Sam está **entre** *(between)* las Calles San Justo y Cruz. Los Muelles de Barcos de Crucero están **enfrente de** *(across from)* la Calle Marina. La Plaza de la Catedral está **a la izquierda de** *(on the left of)* la Catedral de San Juan. La Catedral de San Juan está **a la derecha de** *(on the right of)* la Plaza de la Catedral. El mar está **al lado de** *(next to)* los Muelles de Barcos de Crucero. El Museo Pablo Casals está **cerca del** *(near the)* Patio de Sam. San Juan Bulevard está **delante de** *(in front of)* la Calle Norzagaray. El aeropuerto está **lejos de** *(far from)* la ciudad.

Asking for directions

In the following dialog, Manny asks for directions from the Plaza de Armas to the Casa Blanca.

Manny:	**Perdón,** ¿dónde está la Casa Blanca?	*Excuse me, where is the Casa Blanca?*
Señor:	Está en la calle Monjas. **Suba tres cuadras** en la calle San José. **Doble** en la calle Sol, **cruce** la calle y **siga derecho.**	*It's on Monjas Street. Go up three blocks on San José Street. Turn on Sol Street, cross the street, and continue straight ahead.*
Manny:	¿Eso es **hacia** el **este,** verdad?	*That is going toward the east, right?*
Señor:	No, es **hacia** el **oeste.**	*No, it's toward the west.*
Manny:	Muchísimas gracias.	*Thank you very much.*

Suba, doble, cruce, and siga are formal commands that you will be learning later in this chapter.

¿NOS ENTENDEMOS?

In Spain, it is more common to say **recto** (*straight ahead*), whereas in Latin America, **derecho** is more commonly used. Likewise in Spain, it is more common to say **la manzana,** instead of **la cuadra,** for *block.* Also, in some countries in Latin America, when you say that someone is studying **derecho,** it means the person is studying law.

The following are additional words and phrases related to talking about location and giving directions:

Otros lugares Other places

la estación de trenes train station
el puerto port
la terminal de autobuses bus station

Adverbios

cerca near
demasiado too much
hasta up to, until
lejos far (away)

Verbos

cruzar to cross
doblar to turn
ir... to go . . .
parar(se) to stop
seguir (i, i) to continue
subir(se) (a) to go up

Modos de transporte

a pie on foot
en autobús by bus
en barco by boat
en bicicleta by bike
en coche by car
en metro by subway
en taxi by taxi
en tren by train

¡A PRACTICAR!

9-21 | **Opuestos** Indica lo opuesto de cada palabra indicada.

MODELO: a la izquierda
a la derecha

1. norte
2. lejos de

3. delante de
4. detrás de

5. oeste
6. entre

9-22 | **Lugares y transporte** Usa una palabra del vocabulario para completar las siguientes oraciones. Luego compara tus respuestas con las de un(a) compañero(a). ¿Están de acuerdo?

1. Tengo mucha prisa; no quiero tomar el autobús y no tengo tiempo para ir a pie. Voy a pedir un _____.
2. Compré ayer un boleto para el tren que sale a las 5:00. ¿Dónde está la _____?
3. No sé dónde está la estación, pero tengo aquí un _____ de la ciudad. Podemos mirarlo, si quieres.
4. Voy del Viejo San Juan a Ponce en autobús. Pero no sé dónde está el _____.
5. Uy, hay mucho tráfico. Yo quiero cruzar la ciudad bajo de tierra —voy _____.

CULTURA
Ponce is the second-largest city in Puerto Rico and is a popular tourist destination.

9-23 | **¿Te acuerdas?** Con un(a) compañero(a), llenen los espacios en blanco con las preposiciones correctas para describir La Plaza de Armas.

La Plaza de Armas está en el centro de la ciudad. 1. _____ (Toward) el sur de la ciudad el Paseo de la Princesa está 2. _____ (behind) la muralla de la ciudad (city wall). En el norte de la ciudad el Patio de Sam está 3. _____ (between) las Calles San Justo y Cruz.

Los Muelles de Barcos de Crucero están 4. _____ (across from) la calle Marina. La Plaza de la Catedral está 5. _____ (on the left of) la Catedral de San Juan. La Catedral de San Juan está 6. _____ (on the right of) la Plaza de la Catedral. El mar está 7. _____ (next to) los Muelles de Barcos de Crucero. El Museo Pablo Casals está 8. _____ (near the) Patio de Sam. San Juan Bulevard está 9. _____ (in front of) la Calle Norzagaray. El aeropuerto está 10. _____ (far from) la ciudad.

EN VOZ ALTA

9-24 | **¿Dónde está?** Trabajas en una oficina de turismo en el Viejo San Juan, y tienes que indicarle a un(a) compañero(a) de clase dónde están los siguientes lugares en el mapa de la página 270. Usa **al lado de, cerca de, delante de, detrás de, enfrente de, entre** y **lejos de**.

MODELO: el aeropuerto
El aeropuerto está lejos del centro de la ciudad.

1. la Plaza del Quinto
2. el Patio de Sam
3. el Banco Popular
4. la droguería Ponce

5. la Catedral de San Juan
6. la Calle San Francisco
7. el Museo Pablo Casals
8. la Fortaleza

¿NOS ENTENDEMOS?
The most common words for *bus* in Spanish are **el autobús** and **el bus.** In Puerto Rico, however, buses are called **las guaguas;** in Argentina and El Salvador, **los colectivos;** in Mexico, **los camiones;** and in other countries like Cuba, the terms **el ómnibus** and **el microbús** are common. In some countries the terms **el trolebús** and **el tranvía** are still used. **Un camello** *(camel)* is what Cubans call a bus that is mounted on the bed of a truck and used as public transportation.

9-25 | **En esta ciudad** Pregúntale a un(a) compañero(a) dónde están varios lugares en la ciudad o pueblo donde estudias.

MODELO: ¿Dónde está la Iglesia Gobin?
Está al lado de East College, en la Calle Locust.

Encuentro cultural

Puerto Rico: Estado Libre Asociado

PARA PENSAR

- ¿Conoces la isla de Puerto Rico?
- ¿Qué piensas de un país con dos lenguas oficiales?
- ¿Qué sabes de la situación política de Puerto Rico?

Puerto Rico es una isla *(island)* muy pequeña. Tiene solamente 158 kilómetros de largo y 58 kilómetros de ancho, y es una de las áreas más densamente pobladas del mundo. Puerto Rico tiene casi 4 millones de habitantes. El primer idioma de la isla es el español, pero como es oficialmente una parte de los Estados Unidos, también se habla inglés. En 1993, el español y el inglés se declararon como los idiomas oficiales de la isla. Es el único país de habla hispana que tiene el inglés como lengua oficial.

Puerto Rico es una mezcla de lo muy nuevo y lo muy viejo. Tiene cosas de la vida de los Estados Unidos y al mismo tiempo conserva las influencias formales de lo español. El Viejo San Juan, un barrio de la ciudad San Juan, es uno de los barrios coloniales mejor conservados de las Américas. El barrio está casi totalmente rodeado *(surrounded)* de murallas de piedra *(stone walls)* construidas por los españoles.

Puerto Rico es un Estado Libre Asociado *(commonwealth)* de los Estados Unidos. Los puertorriqueños no pueden votar en la elecciones presidenciales de los Estados Unidos. Los puertorriqueños han podido votar para elegir *(elect)* a su propio gobernador(a) desde 1948. El (La) gobernador(a) está en su trabajo por cuatro años y se encarga de cumplir y hacer cumplir las leyes en Puerto Rico. La isla está dividida políticamente: muchas personas quieren ver a Puerto Rico libre, otras personas quieren ver a Puerto Rico como el estado número 51 de la unión y la mayoría quiere que Puerto Rico siga siendo un Estado Libre Asociado de los Estados Unidos.

> **¿NOS ENTENDEMOS?**
> **Puertorriqueños** sometimes refer to themselves as **boricuas.** This term comes from the Taino name for the island, *Borinquen.*

PARA DISCUTIR

1. ¿Cuáles son las lenguas oficiales de Puerto Rico? ¿Cómo es Puerto Rico especial en ese sentido?
2. ¿Pueden describir el Viejo San Juan?
3. ¿Cuál es la situación política de Puerto Rico hoy en día? ¿Cómo está dividida la isla políticamente?
4. ¿Crees que Puerto Rico debe ser un Estado Libre Asociado, otro estado de los Estados Unidos o debe ser un país libre? Discute tu opinión.
5. ¿Te gustaría visitar esta isla? ¿Por qué sí o por qué no?

ESTRUCTURA III: Giving directions and expressing desires: formal and negative *tú* commands

In **Capítulo 4** you learned how to form familiar affirmative commands. In this section you will learn how to form affirmative and negative formal commands and negative **tú** commands.

I. Formal commands

When we give advice to others or ask them to do something, we often use commands such as *Take bus No. 25* and *Give me your address*. Spanish speakers use formal commands when they address people as **usted** or **ustedes.**

To form formal commands for most Spanish verbs, drop the **-o** ending from the present-tense **yo** form and add the following endings to the verb stem:

-e/-en for -**ar** verbs;
-a/-an for -**er** and -**ir** verbs.

To form the negative, simply place **no** before the verb.

	Infinitive	Present-tense *yo* form	usted	ustedes
-ar verbs	hablar	hablo	(no) hable	(no) hablen
-er verbs	volver	vuelvo	(no) vuelva	(no) vuelvan
-ir verbs	venir	vengo	(no) venga	(no) vengan

Vengan a San Juan a visitarme pronto.   *Come to San Juan to visit me soon.*
No olvide mi dirección.   *Don't forget my address.*

- Note that verbs ending in **-car, -gar,** and **-zar** have a spelling change: the **c** changes to **qu, g** changes to **gu,** and **z** changes to **c,** respectively.

Infinitive	Present-tense *yo* form	usted	ustedes
sacar	saco	saque	saquen
llegar	llego	llegue	lleguen
comenzar	comienzo	comience	comiencen

Saque una foto del parque.   *Take a picture of the park.*
Lleguen a tiempo, por favor.   *Arrive on time, please.*
No comience a caminar todavía.   *Don't start walking yet.*

- Several irregular verbs vary from the pattern above.

Infinitive	usted	ustedes
dar	dé	den
estar	esté	estén
ir	vaya	vayan
saber	sepa	sepan
ser	sea	sean

Sean buenos estudiantes.   *Be good students.*
Vaya al banco.   *Go to the bank.*

- In affirmative commands, attach reflexive and object pronouns to the end of the command, thus forming one word. If the command has three or more syllables, write an accent mark over the stressed vowel. In negative commands, place the pronouns separately in front of the verb.

Póngase el abrigo.	*Put on your overcoat.*
No se lo ponga.	*Don't put it on.*
Cómprelo ahora.	*Buy it now.*
No lo compre mañana.	*Don't buy it tomorrow.*

II. Negative *tú* commands

Formation of negative informal commands

In **Capítulo 4** you learned how to form affirmative informal commands. To form negative informal commands, you'll be using the same strategy as you would to form either affirmative or negative formal commands.

As you recall from the section above, to form both affirmative and negative formal commands for most Spanish verbs, you drop the **-o** ending from the present-tense **yo** form and add the following endings to the verb stem: **-e/-en** for **-ar** verbs; **-a/-an** for **-er** and **-ir** verbs. Remember that there are also spelling changes for verbs ending in **-car, -gar,** and **-zar** and that there are irregular verbs such as **dar, estar, ir, saber,** and **ser.**

The chart below, demonstrating all the command forms for the verbs **hablar, comer, vivir, dormir,** and **ir,** graphically illustrates the similarities among the negative informal command forms and all the formal command forms.

Infinitive	Informal command *(tú/vosotros)*		Formal command *(Ud./Uds.)*	
	(+)	(−)	(+)	(−)
hablar	habla	no hables	hable	no hable
	hablad	no habléis	hablen	no hablen
comer	come	no comas	coma	no coma
	comed	no comáis	coman	no coman
vivir	vive	no vivas	viva	no viva
	vivid	no viváis	vivan	no vivan
dormir	duerme	no duermas	duerma	no duerma
	dormid	no durmáis	duerman	no duerman
ir	ve	no vayas	vaya	no vaya
	id	no vayáis	vayan	no vayan

As you can see from the chart above, only the affirmative informal commands (**habla/hablad, come/comed, vive/vivid, duerme/dormid,** and **ve/id**) deviate from the endings used in the remaining command forms.

Note that as with negative formal commands, place reflexive or object pronouns before the negated verb.

—No **te** olvides de escribirme.	*Don't forget to write me.*
—No **le** hables.	*Don't talk to him.*
—¿Debo llamarte?	*Should I call you?*
—No, no **me** llames.	*No, don't call me.*

¡A PRACTICAR!

9-26 **Consejos para el hermano de Manny** El hermano de Manny va a San Juan a visitar a la pareja. Con el infinitivo dado, forma mandatos negativos informales que Manny le ofrece a su hermano.

1. No _digas_ (decir) tonterías (silly things) en la aduana.
2. No _fumes_ (fumar) en el avión.
3. No _hables_ (hablar) demasiado con la azafata en el avión.
4. No _comas_ (comer) en el aeropuerto.
5. No _te duermas_ (dormirte) en el autobús.
6. No _contestes_ (contestar) el teléfono en inglés.
7. No _cenes_ (cenar) antes de las 9:00 de la noche.
8. No _hagas_ (hacer) muchas preguntas sobre la habitación en el hotel.

9-27 **Entre amigos** Manny está hablando por teléfono con Jorge, un amigo que quiere visitarlo con su esposa. Manny está dándoles instrucciones para llegar en autobús a su apartamento. Completa la siguiente conversación con las formas correctas de los verbos entre paréntesis para formar mandatos formales.

—Primero, 1. _salgan_ (salir) ustedes de su hotel. Luego 2. _caminen_ (caminar) dos cuadras a la derecha hasta la Calle Fonseca. Allí 3. _doble_ (doblar) a la izquierda y 4. _vayan_ (ir) una cuadra más hasta la Calle de Plata.

—Hasta la Calle de Plata, ¿dices, Manny?

—Sí, Jorge. Luego 5. _vayan_ (ir) ustedes al otro lado de esa calle y 6. _esperen_ (esperar) el autobús número 32.

—¿El autobús 32, Manny?

—Correcto, amigo. 7. _tómenlo_ (Tomar/lo) hasta la Avenida Buena Vista. 8. _bájense_ (Bajarse) allí en esa avenida.

—¿Cómo sabemos dónde está la Avenida Buena Vista?

—Bueno, 9. _pregúntenle_ (preguntar/le) ustedes al chófer del autobús. 10. _Díganle_ (Decir/le) que quieren bajarse en la Avenida Buena Vista. Pues, 11. _bájense_ (bajarse) allí y 12. _cambien_ (cambiar) a otro autobús... al número 19. 13. _súbanse_ (Subirse) a ese autobús y 14. _tómenlo_ (tomar/lo) hasta la Calle San Juan.

—¿Está lejos esa calle?

—No, Jorge. Está a como siete cuadras más o menos. 15. _sepan_ (Saber) Uds. que no es muy difícil. Entonces 16. _seguan_ (seguir) ustedes derecho hasta la Calle San Juan. Luego 17. _salgan_ (salir) del autobús y en esa esquina los espero. ¿Qué te parece?

—Pues, es un poco complicado. Pero nos vemos pronto.

—Claro que sí. Hasta luego, Jorge.

9-28 | **Consejos para turistas en Santo Domingo** Completa los mandatos de un guía de turistas para la ciudad de Santo Domingo, usando mandatos formales o informales, según lo indicado.

MODELOS: (ustedes) caminar para ver todo lo que ofrece la ciudad
Caminen para ver todo lo que ofrece la ciudad.

(tú) caminar para ver todo lo que ofrece la ciudad
Camina para ver todo lo que ofrece la ciudad.

1. (tú) salir temprano del hotel ~~Sal~~
2. (usted) ir a un mercado cercano ~~Vaya~~
3. (tú) no sacar fotos sin pedir permiso ~~saca, no saques~~
4. (tú) descansar un poco por la tarde ~~descan, no descanes~~
5. (ustedes) no subirse a un autobús sin saber la ruta ~~no se subanse subanse~~
6. (usted) no andar en bicicleta; es muy peligroso ~~no ande~~
7. (tú) pararse para las procesiones ~~parte, parese, no te paras~~
8. (usted) no cruzar las calles sin mirar en las dos direcciones ~~no cruce~~
9. (ustedes) ser buenos con la gente de la ciudad, y ellos los van a tratar bien a Uds. ~~sean~~

EN VOZ ALTA

9-29 | **Sugerencias** Manny y Teri te explican cómo se sienten. Dales sugerencias en forma de mandatos. Primero haz el ejercicio con mandatos informales para cada situación. Luego compara tus sugerencias con las de otro(a) compañero(a). ¿Tienen mucho en común? Luego, hazlo otra vez, usando las formas **Ud.** o **Uds.**

MODELO: Yo estoy cansado de caminar y tomar el autobús.
¡Toma un taxi entonces!
o *¡Tome Ud. un taxi entonces!*

1. Yo tengo muchas ganas de comer comida china.
2. Queremos quedarnos en un hotel lujoso.
3. Necesito cambiar dinero. ¿Dónde está el banco?
4. Tengo ganas de beber algo.
5. Necesito comprar regalos para mi familia.
6. Necesitamos confirmar nuestro vuelo.
7. No sabemos cómo agradecerle a Ud.

9-30 | **Un agente de turismo** Trabajen en grupos de tres personas. Una persona es un(a) agente de turismo. Los otros estudiantes van a presentarle una situación que contiene una necesidad o un problema que tienen. El (La) agente entonces va a ofrecerles consejos en forma de mandatos. Hagan el ejercicio primero, usando mandatos formales y luego repítanlo con mandatos informales.

MODELO: E1: *No puedo descansar* (to rest) *en mi habitación.*
E2: *Busque/Busca otro hotel.*
E3: *Mi compañero de cuarto y yo nunca podemos desayunar antes de salir por la mañana.*
E2: *Levántense más temprano.*

You can soften commands to make them sound more like requests than demands, by using **usted** or **ustedes** after the command form or by adding **por favor: Pasen ustedes por aquí,** or **Pasen por aquí, por favor.** *(Come this way, please.)* **No hable usted tan rápido.** or **No hable tan rápido, por favor.** *(Don't speak so fast, please.)* When you want people to do something, but you wish to say so tactfully, ask a question or make a simple statement with reference to your wish rather than using a direct command. For example, suppose you are a dinner guest at a friend's house. The dining room is uncomfortably hot, and you want a window opened or the air conditioner turned on. You might say **Hace un poco de calor, ¿no?**

¡A VER!

En este segmento del video, Valeria, Antonio, y Javier están en la ciudad de San Juan. Valeria va de compras mientras Javier y Antonio visitan una agencia de viajes.

Expresiones útiles

Las siguientes son expresiones nuevas que vas a escuchar en el video.

Me doy cuenta de	I realize
Será que le duele la mano	Her hand probably hurts
Algo no salió bien	Something didn't go well

Antes de ver

 Paso 1: ¿Te gusta viajar? ¿Quieres visitar muchos lugares exóticos? Haz una lista de los lugares que quieres visitar en los próximos cinco años. Incluye el modo de transporte que vas a usar para esos viajes. Luego compara tu lista con la lista de un(a) compañero(a). ¿Tienen mucho en común?

MODELO: *Primero quiero volar en avión al norte de España...*

Paso 2: ¿Qué pasó la última vez que te perdiste en una ciudad o en otro lugar desconocido? Cuéntale a un(a) compañero(a) exactamente lo que pasó. ¿Quién te ayudó? ¿Qué hizo para ayudarte? ¿Te explicó cómo llegar a un lugar específico? ¿Cómo llegaste?

Después de ver

Paso 1: En **Antes de ver, Paso 1**, tu compañero(a) y tú hablaron de los viajes que van a hacer en el futuro. En el video, Javier también habló de sus planes para un viaje. Lee las siguientes oraciones y pon el número apropiado en el espacio previsto para indicar el orden cronológico de los planes de Javier.

_____ Pienso recorrer la costa pacífica de Costa Rica en bicicleta.

_____ Voy a visitar Belice, Honduras, y Costa Rica.

_____ Voy a tomar un tren a Macchu Picchu.

_____ Voy a tomar un avión a Centroamérica.

_____ Voy a tomar un avión a Cuzco.

Paso 2: En **Antes de ver, Paso 2**, tu compañero(a) y tú hablaron de lo que pasó la última vez que se perdieron. En el video viste que Valeria se perdió también en San Juan mientras iba de compras y tuvo que pedirle ayuda a una señora. Ahora imagínate que tú eres la persona que la está ayudando. Completa tu conversación con Valeria al poner los verbos en la forma correcta del mandato formal.

Valeria: Señora, ¿qué hago para llegar a la Plaza de la Rogativa?

La señora: No 1. _____ **(preocuparse)**, es muy fácil. De esta esquina, 2. _____ **(caminar)** tres cuadras. De allí, 3. _____ **(doblar)** a la izquierda y 4. _____ **(seguir)** tres cuadras más.

Valeria: Gracias.

¿Qué opinas tú?

Paso 1: Ahora, escoge uno de los viajes que quieres hacer que aparece en **Antes de ver, Paso 1**. Imagínate que estás en una agencia de viajes, tal como Javier lo hizo, y que tu compañero(a) es el (la) agente. Hazle preguntas al (a la) agente sobre el itinerario, modo de transporte, alojamiento, etc. Luego, presenta tu itinerario a la clase.

Paso 2: Como ya sabes, no es una buena experiencia perderse en un lugar desconocido. ¿Cómo puedes ayudar a los nuevos estudiantes para que ellos no se pierdan cuando llegan a tu universidad? Trabaja con dos compañeros(as) de clase y preparen un guía para que los nuevos estudiantes de tu universidad no se pierdan (*don't get lost*). Su guía debe incluir cinco mandatos sobre lo que uno debe hacer para no perderse y cinco mandatos sobre lo que uno no debe hacer cuando se pierda (*when he/she gets lost*).

¡A LEER!

Strategy: Using format clues

Printed material often contains different kinds of cues that can help you skim, scan, and guess meaning. For example, some words and phrases appear in large, boldface, or italic print to attract the reader's attention; some words are repeated several times to persuade the reader; and other words appear together with a graphic design to help the reader remember a particular concept.

Paso 1: Lee la lectura rápidamente y contesta las preguntas generales que siguen.

1. ¿Cuál es el país que se menciona en la lectura?
2. ¿Cuál es la capital de esta isla?
3. La lectura presenta cierta información organizada en cuatro secciones, sobre la capital. ¿Cómo se llaman estas cuatro secciones?

Paso 2: Lee la lectura otra vez y contesta las preguntas específicas que siguen.

1. Según el título de la lectura, ¿por qué se conoce La Habana por sus noches «calientes»?
   a. la falta de aire acondicionado
   b. el clima del Caribe
   c. la cantidad de turistas que visitan La Habana

2. Según la lectura, ¿dónde se encuentran los jóvenes roqueros y los iniciados de la santería?
   a. en Varadero
   b. en el barrio del Vedado
   c. en la Calle Empedrado

3. De los dos hoteles, ¿cuál es el más barato?

NOCHES 'CALIENTES' EN LA HABANA

Aunque la capital cubana no está en su mejor momento, la afluencia de miles de turistas cada verano eleva la temperatura de la ciudad.

Ver El ambiente de la Rampa, en el barrio del Vedado, donde jóvenes con aspecto rockero se cruzan con 'iyawós' o iniciados en santería, al lado de la mítica heladería Copelia, cuyo surtido es francamente escaso. Las noches son del Malecón, imán de la juventud.

Comer La Bodeguita del Medio (Empedrado, 207), la más famosa taberna criolla (se come por unas 3.500 ptas). En Los Doce Apóstoles, al lado del Castillo del Morro, se goza de la mejor vista de La Habana.

Salir En Varadero, La Salsa (Península de Cauama) o La Bamba (Av. de las Américas, km 3,5). Discotecas, las del Hotel Comodore y el Copacabana. Ambiente 'gay' en Giovanni (Habana Vieja) y Kirachi (Vedado).

Dormir Copacabana (C. Primera, más de 15.000 ptas). Vedado (Calle 0, unas 7.500 ptas). Precio: 100.000 ptas, con Iberia. Turismo de Cuba: 91 411 30 97.

La deteriorada Habana Vieja aún conserva su encanto.

¡A ESCRIBIR!

Strategy: Using commands to give directions

If you're traveling in a Spanish-speaking country or city, chances are you might need to ask for directions. In addition, you might even have to give directions! The most important element of explaining to someone how to get from one place to another is accuracy. If you explain your directions clearly and concisely, people will be able to follow them easily.

Here are six basic requirements for giving directions to a place:

1. Choose the easiest route.
2. Be very clear in your directions.
3. Give the directions in chronological order.
4. Use linking expressions such as **Primero..., Luego..., Después de eso..., Entonces..., Usted debe..., Después...,** and **Finalmente...**
5. Identify clearly visible landmarks such as:

la avenida avenue	**el cruce de caminos** intersection
el bulevar boulevard	**el edificio** building
la calle street	**el letrero** sign
el camino road	**el puente** bridge
la colina hill	**el semáforo** traffic light

6. When possible, include a sketch of the route.

MODELO: *Para llegar a mi casa desde el aeropuerto, siga estas indicaciones. Primero, siga la calle del aeropuerto hasta la salida. Doble a la derecha y siga por el Bulevar Glenwood dos kilómetros hasta el primer semáforo, donde hay un cruce de caminos. Entonces, doble a la izquierda y siga por el Camino Parkers Mill dos kilómetros (pasando debajo de un puente) hasta la Calle Lane Allen. En esa calle, doble a la derecha y siga otros dos kilómetros hasta el segundo semáforo. Después, doble a la izquierda en el Camino Beacon Hill y siga derecho medio kilómetro hasta el Camino Normandy. Doble a la izquierda y vaya a la cuarta casa a la derecha. Allí vivo yo, y ¡allí tiene su casa!*

Task: Giving directions from the airport to your house or a hotel

Paso 1: Vas a escribir una composición en que le explicas a un viajero hispanoha-blante cómo ir del aeropuerto de tu ciudad hasta tu residencia o hasta un hotel de tu ciudad. Antes de empezar, vuelve a leer los seis puntos y el párrafo anterior.

Paso 2: Dibuja un mapa de la ruta para usar, mientras escribes las direcciones.

Paso 3: Siguiendo el modelo anterior, e incluyendo los seis puntos, escribe un párrafo. Emplea mandatos formales.

Paso 4: Repasa y corrige tu composición. Puedes consultar la siguiente lista:

____ easiest route	____ visible landmarks	____ clear directions
____ correct punctuation	____ chronological order	____ correct grammar
____ linking expressions	____ correct spelling	

Paso 5: Trabaja con un(a) compañero(a) de clase. Intercambien sus composiciones, pero no compartan los mapas que dibujaron. Cada persona debe leer la composición de la otra persona y dibujar un mapa de la ruta explicada. Si ustedes encuentran errores o problemas en las composiciones, hagan las correcciones y después hablen sobre los cambios.

Functions: Asking for and giving directions; Linking ideas; Expressing distance; Expressing location
Vocabulary: City; Directions and distance; Means of transportation; Metric systems and measurements
Grammar: Verbs: imperative: **usted(es)**, **ser** and **estar**, **tener** and **haber**

¡A CONVERSAR!

Pronunciation focus: *j* and *g*

The Spanish **j** has a sound somewhat like the *h* in *hill* but harder. The **g** before an **e** or **i** is pronounced like the **j** in **Juan.** In all other cases, the **g** is pronounced like the English *g* in *go.* Practice the following sentences:

- La oficina del agente de viajes está lejos de aquí.
- El cuarto está arreglado antes de la llegada de los viajeros.

Task: Discussing travel plans

Muchas personas viajan de los Estados Unidos al Caribe y es posible que tú viajes allí un día. Ahora vas a conversar con un(a) amigo(a) sobre los planes para un viaje al Caribe.

Paso 1: Empieza por hablar del medio de transporte que prefieres, avión o barco. Explica tu preferencia. Después, compara y contrasta el viaje en avión con el viaje en barco.

Paso 2: Después, habla del hotel que quieres visitar. Menciona las comodidades *(amenities)* que consideras importantes. Indica si prefieres estar en el centro de una ciudad o cerca de la playa.

Paso 3: Habla de los medios de transporte que piensas usar durante tu viaje, indicando en qué circunstancias cada uno es adecuado.

Paso 4: Termina la conversación expresando tus preferencias para actividades durante la visita al Caribe.

Viajar en avión Airplane travel

Sustantivos

la aduana customs
la agencia de viajes travel agency
el (la) agente de la aerolínea airline agent
el (la) agente de viajes travel agent
el asiento seat
el (la) asistente de vuelo flight attendant
el avión plane
el boleto (billete) de ida one-way ticket
el boleto (billete) de ida y vuelta round-trip
  ticket

el control de seguridad security
el equipaje (de mano) (carry-on) baggage,
  luggage
el horario schedule
la inmigración Immigration; passport control
la llegada arrival
la maleta suitcase
el (la) pasajero(a) passenger
el pasaporte passport
el pasillo aisle

la puerta gate
la salida departure
la ventanilla airplane window
el viaje trip
el vuelo (sin escala) (nonstop) flight

Verbos

abordar to board
bajar(se) (de) to get off
facturar el equipaje to check the luggage

hacer escala (en) to make a stop (on a flight) (in)
hacer la(s) maleta(s) to pack one's suitcase(s)
ir en avión to go by plane

pasar por to go through
recoger to pick up, claim
viajar to travel

Expresiones idiomáticas

¡Bienvenido(a)! Welcome!

¡Buen viaje! Have a nice trip!

Perdón. Excuse me.

El hotel The hotel

Sustantivos

el aire acondicionado air-conditioning
el ascensor elevator
la cama sencilla (doble) single (double) bed

el cuarto room
el hotel de cuatro estrellas four-star hotel
la llave key

la recepción front desk
el (la) recepcionista receptionist
la reserva reservation

Adjetivos

arreglado(a) neat, tidy
cómodo(a) comfortable

limpio(a) clean
privado(a) private

sucio(a) dirty

Verbos

registrarse to register

quedarse to stay

quejarse (de) to complain (about)

Indicaciones Directions

a la derecha de to the right of
a la izquierda de to the left of
al lado de next to
cerca de near
delante de in front of

derecho straight
detrás de behind
enfrente de across from
entre between
el este east

hacia toward
lejos de far from
el norte north
el oeste west
el sur south

Otros lugares de la ciudad y el transporte Other places in the city and transportation

Sustantivos

la cuadra city block
la estación de trenes train station

el puerto port

la terminal de autobuses bus station

Adverbios

cerca near
demasiado too much

hasta up to, until

lejos far (away)

Verbos

cruzar to cross
doblar to turn

ir... to go . . .
  a pie on foot
  en autobús by bus
  en barco by boat
  en bicicleta by bike
  en coche by car

  en metro by subway
  en taxi by taxi
  en tren by train
parar(se) to stop
seguir (i, i) to continue
subir to go up

PLAZAS

En esta edición, vas a leer sobre las diferentes experiencias de un grupo de estudiantes que pasó el semestre de la primavera en el mar para visitar y conocer diferentes países de Latinoamérica. Los estudiantes salieron del puerto de Miami, Florida. Como parte de sus tareas, los estudiantes tuvieron que escribir un diario, narrando y describiendo las experiencias que más les gustaron o impresionaron de sus visitas a estos lugares. Ésta es la revista publicada por la universidad de este grupo, en que aparecen las experiencias de los estudiantes: *Vivir y contar:*

- **La magia de los magos**
- **Experiencias en Santo Domingo, República Dominicana y La Habana, Cuba**
- **Gigante salvadoreño durmiente**
- **Mar del Plata, Argentina**

Desde Puerto Rico, Cristóbal Banik describe el Día de los Reyes Magos que se celebra con una gran fiesta en Puerto Rico y también en España.

- ¿Cuándo compras regalos a tu familia y tus amigos?

- ¿Qué días festivos celebran tú y tu familia? Describe lo que hacen durante ese día.

- ¿Celebran tú y tu familia algún día religioso? ¿Qué día celebran y cómo lo celebran?

- En grupos de tres personas, escojan *(choose)* uno de los días festivos del mundo hispano que aparecen en la página 226 y preparen un informe breve sobre cuándo y cómo se celebra este día. Si ustedes celebran ese día en su casa, expliquen cómo lo celebran y si las actividades que hacen son similares o diferentes a las de la celebración hispana.

VIVIR Y CONTAR

La magia de los magos

6 de enero

Hoy acabo de regresar de la casa de Marisol Coriano, una estudiante de la Universidad de Puerto Rico. Su familia me invitó a pasar el Día de los Reyes Magos en su casa. En Puerto Rico y en España, los niños y los adultos celebran este día con mucha alegría. Como yo no conocía esta fiesta, Marisol me explicó el origen de esta tradición. Los Tres Reyes Magos vinieron del Oriente para adorar al Niño Jesús y de regalo le trajeron incienso *(incense)*, oro *(gold)* y mirra *(myrrh)*. Los Tres Reyes se llamaban Melchor, Gaspar y Baltasar. Melchor era un hombre mayor de barba blanca, Gaspar era un joven rubio y Baltasar era un hombre de raza negra y tenía barba también. Se cree que la diversidad en las razas se usó en la historia para simbolizar la universalidad del cristianismo.

Como es la tradición, en casa de Marisol, había muchos regalos por la mañana para imitar la generosidad que estos magos tuvieron con el Niño Jesús. En preparación a la llegada de los Reyes Magos, los hermanitos de Marisol pusieron hierba *(grass)* para los camellos *(camels)* de los Reyes anoche y así los camellos pudieron comer antes de seguir para la próxima casa. Sus hermanitos se levantaron muy temprano esta mañana para ver los regalos que les dejaron los Reyes. ¡Qué sorpresa! ¡Los camellos se habían comido *(had eaten)* toda la hierba! Por supuesto, este día no fue sólo para los niños. Los adultos también se hicieron regalos y todos lo pasamos muy bien. Aunque ésta fue la primera vez que celebré este día feriado, la celebración me mostró la importancia que las tradiciones tienen para la familia hispana.

San Juan

PUERTO RICO

VIEQUES

At 8.4"

Experiencias en Santo Domingo, República Dominicana y La Habana, Cuba

Después de pasar varios días en Puerto Rico, la próxima parada llevó a los estudiantes a Santo Domingo en la República Dominicana y luego a La Habana en Cuba. Sofía Botherus y David Hatch describen sus experiencias en las islas del Caribe.

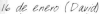

... enero (Sofía)

Después de Puerto Rico, nuestro siguiente puerto fue en ...to Domingo, República Dominicana. Lo que más me impresionó de ...to Domingo fue su Ciudad Colonial, el número de parques y plazas ...hay en la ciudad y su comida sencilla pero con tanto sabor. Me ...stó mucho el palacio del virrey (viceroy) don Diego Colón, que era el ...jo de Cristóbal Colón. Don Diego Colón y su esposa María de Toledo ...ueron los primeros virreyes de América. El palacio fue remodelado y ...hora es un museo donde se pueden ver piezas (pieces) valiosas ...(valuable) de otros palacios españoles de los siglos XIV, XV y XVI. Al ...visitar este palacio, podemos imaginarnos cómo eran la vida y las costumbres de esos siglos.

En frente del palacio está la Plaza España, donde hay muchos cafés al aire libre y excelentes restaurantes de comida típica dominicana. Aquí nos sentamos a hablar y a ver pasar la gente; la comida estuvo excelente. En el Café Merengue comimos plátanos fritos, que son como las bananas pero más grande en tamaño y mucho sabor con chuletas de cochino, salami frito y huevos fritos. También alguien pidió "mangú" que está hecho de plátanos verdes hervidos (boiled) machucados (mashed) con leche, especias, queso. Algunas personas cocinan los plátanos con cebolla. Según la dueña del restaurante, éste es un plato típico dominicano. A mí me encanta cocinar y por eso pido recetas de cocina en cualquier restaurante o lugar que visitamos.

Al final de esta calle llena de cafés y restaurantes, está la Calle de Las Damas, que se llama así porque durante la colonia las damas de la virreína María de Toledo paseaban por esta calle para que los hombres del virrey las vieran y pudieran hablar con ellas. Era una costumbre muy interesante; en vez de conocer a los muchachos en la universidad, en las fiestas o en el gimnasio como hacemos hoy en día, las mujeres de aquellos siglos salían a caminar.

16 de enero (David)

Llegamos a La Habana y estoy muy emocionado de estar aquí después de leer tanto sobre Cuba. La Habana es la segunda ciudad del Caribe en extensión, y el centro de todas las actividades en Cuba. Lo bello de La Habana es que sus edificios siguen igual a cuando fueron construidos (were built) hace 100 años. La ciudad tiene un aire de los años 50 o 60 y todavía se ven automóviles estadounidenses de esos años por las calles.

Hay muchas actividades por las noches en la ciudad: cines, teatros, cabarets, clubs y muchos bares de música de jazz, salsa, mambo, etc. Uno de los lugares que más me gustó fue el bar llamado La Bodeguita del Medio, cerca de la Plaza de la Catedral donde personalidades como Ernest Hemingway, Harry Belafonte, Nat King Cole y Salvador Allende dejaron su autógrafo en las paredes del bar.

También, me gustó muchísimo La Habana Vieja, que fue declarada por la UNESCO «Patrimonio de la Humanidad» en 1982. Muchos de los edificios son ahora museos y hay tantas iglesias, castillos y monumentos revolucionarios para ver que nadie puede aburrirse por un momento. Algunos lugares inolvidables (unforgettable) para mí fueron la Plaza de la Catedral, que durante los fines de semana se convierte en un mercado al aire libre, y las torres de la Catedral de San Cristóbal de La Habana que cuidan la plaza. Cerca se encuentra el Castillo de la Real Fuerza, que es uno de los castillos más viejos de América.

Después de mucho caminar visitamos la Habana Central, donde se encuentra el Capitolio Nacional, que es ahora la casa de la Academia Cubana de las Ciencias. Cerca del lugar se encuentra una de las industrias de puros o habanos (cigars) más viejas de Cuba, donde trabajan 400 personas que enrollan (roll) los puros a mano. Una tarde fuimos a comer helado en la famosa heladería Coppelia, donde se filmó la película Fresas y chocolate (Strawberry and Chocolate), para luego ir a visitar el famoso Hotel Nacional de Cuba y el Riviera, hoteles que fueron construidos por la mafia de los Estados Unidos durante los años 50. Es increíble como la historia de La Habana ha estado tan relacionada con la historia de los Estados Unidos por estos años.

- ¿Te gustaría conocer La Habana o San Juan de Puerto Rico? ¿Por qué sí o por qué no?

- ¿Qué tipo de monumentos te gusta visitar cuando vas de viajes?

- ¿Qué tipo de comida te gusta probar?

Gigante salvadoreño durmiente

Después de visitar Guatemala, los estudiantes fueron de excursión por El Salvador, donde pudieron apreciar la belleza natural y majestuosa de los lugares que visitaron. El lugar que más le impresionó a Jarv Campbell fue la ciudad de Santa Ana y la excursión al volcán Izalco. Así describe Jarv sus experiencias en El Salvador:

La visita a la ciudad de Santa Ana fue impresionante, debido al volcán Izalco, que forma parte de la cadena volcánica *(volcanic chain)* de la América Central y estuvo activo desde 1770 hasta 1958. En esa época era llamado «el faro *(lighthouse)* del Pacífico». Como me gustó tanto el volcán y su historia, comencé a investigar y encontré que la escritora Claribel Alegría (1924), que es nicaragüense pero que vivió muchos años en El Salvador, describió así la fuerza de este volcán:

San Salvador
★
EL SALVADOR

- ¿Cómo expresa Alegría el tono nostálgico del poema?

- ¿Parece realista o artística esta descripción? Explica.

- ¿Cómo utiliza los colores la autora? ¿Qué significan los colores?

- ¿En qué aspectos es similar esta descripción a una descripción de la naturaleza de tu ciudad o pueblo? ¿En qué aspectos es diferente?

CLARIBEL ALEGRÍA

FLORES DEL VOLCÁN

Catorce volcanes se levantan
en mi país memoria
en mi país mito
que día a día invento.
Catorce volcanes de follaje *(foliage)* y piedra *(stone)*
donde nubes *(clouds)* extrañas se detienen
y a veces el chillido *(screech)*
de un pájaro extraviado *(lost bird)*.
¿Quién dijo que era verde mi país?
es más rojo
es más gris
es más violento:
el Izalco que ruge *(roars)*
exigiendo *(demanding)* más vidas.
Los eternos chacmol
que recogen la sangre
y los que beben sangre *(blood)*
del chacmol
y los huérfanos *(orphans)* grises
y el volcán babeando *(slavering)*
toda esa lava incandescente
y el guerrillero muerto
y los mil rostros *(faces)* traicionados
y los niños que miran para contar la historia.

✵

Un mes más tarde, los estudiantes llegaron a la costa de Argentina y visitaron una ciudad que se llama Mar del Plata, donde la gente de Buenos Aires y de Montevideo va a pasar sus vacaciones de verano en diciembre, enero y febrero. Aquí tenemos las impresiones de Maricarmen Trujillo.

- **¿Recuerdas por qué el verano es en diciembre, enero y febrero en Argentina?**

- **¿En qué deportes acuáticos participas?**

- **Si no te gusta comer carne, ¿qué haces en Argentina?**

- **¿Qué te gustaría hacer en Mar del Plata?**

ARGENTINA

Buenos Aires

Mar del Plata

Villa Geisell

Mar del Plata, Argentina

25 de marzo

En marzo llegamos a la costa del Océano Atlántico, a uno de los balnearios sudamericanos más famosos de América del Sur en Argentina, Mar del Plata. De tantas actividades que podíamos hacer, algunos de nosotros decidimos hacer esnórquel, David y Sofía decidieron pasear en velero. Nos pusimos mucha crema bronceadora porque sabíamos que íbamos a pasar casi todo el día en el sol.

Además de todas estas actividades acuáticas, la ciudad de Mar del Plata ofrece para los visitantes calles peatonales *(pedestrian streets)* con muchas tiendas y restaurantes, galerías y un casino. Y la vida nocturna *(night life)*… ¡Es bárbara *(awesome)*! Aunque estábamos muy cansados después de un día con tantas actividades, no nos queríamos perder la vida nocturna en Mar del Plata. Empezamos con una parrillada en el

restaurante que estaba enfrente del casino. Al comer la parrillada, nos dimos cuenta de lo importante que es la carne dentro de la cultura argentina. Los meseros traen a la mesa la carne en unos pinchos *(skewers)* muy largos y sirven cualquier tipo de carne todas las veces que uno lo pida. Si eres vegetariano(a), prepárate a comer en restaurantes italianos y no en restaurantes argentinos. Luego, seguimos a un lugar que se llama Los Alfajores para bailar y hablar toda la noche; aquí conocimos a muchos argentinos y uruguayos. ¡Nuestros días en Mar del Plata fueron regios *(great)*!

Las relaciones sentimentales:

Chapter Objectives

COMMUNICATIVE GOALS

In this chapter you will learn how to . . .

- Talk about relationships and courtship
- Describe recent actions, events, and conditions
- Describe reciprocal actions
- Talk about receptions and banquets
- Qualify actions

STRUCTURES

- Present perfect
- Reciprocal constructions with **se, nos,** and **os**
- Adverbs and adverbial expressions of time and sequencing of events
- Relative pronouns

CULTURAL INFORMATION

- Los novios en los países hispanoamericanos
- Las bodas en el mundo hispano

Honduras y Nicaragua

HONDURAS

Población: 6.406.052
Área: 112.090 kilómetros cuadrados, un poco más grande que Tennessee
Capital: Tegucigalpa, 1.127.600
Ciudades principales: San Pedro, 469.100; La Ceiba, 108.900, El Progreso, 106.000
Moneda: el lempira
Lengua: el español y varias lenguas indígenas

NICARAGUA

Población: 4.918.393
Área: 129.494 kilómetros cuadrados, un poco menos grande que Nueva York
Capital: Managua, 1.068.500
Ciudades principales: León, 153.200; Chinandega, 120.400; Masaya, 110.000
Moneda: el córdoba oro
Lenguas: el español y algunas lenguas indígenas

¡Bienvenidos a Nicaragua!

En este video, vas a aprender mucho sobre Nicaragua. Después de ver el video, contesta las siguientes preguntas:

1 ¿Dónde está Nicaragua y cuál es su capital?

2 ¿Cuál es el centro intelectual de Nicaragua y quién fue Rubén Darío?

3 ¿Qué sabes de la ciudad de Managua?

4 ¿Qué pasó en Nicaragua durante los años setenta?

5 ¿Qué parte de Nicaragua te gustaría conocer más? ¿Por qué?

Una plaza sin nombre, Tegucigalpa, Honduras

El noviazgo de Francisco Morazán y Celia Herrera In this section you will learn vocabulary associated with courtship and marriage and how to talk about intimate relationships by following an imagined version of the courtship of Francisco Morazán and his wife, Celia Herrera de Morazán.

Cuando se conocieron, fue **el amor a primera vista.**

Se llevaron bien durante **la primera cita.**

Se declaron **su amor.**

Un año después de **enamorarse,** decidieron **casarse.**

En **la boda los novios se besaban** mientras las madres **se abrazaban** y los padres **se daban la mano.**

Los invitados **tiraron** arroz cuando **los recién casados** salían de la iglesia para **su luna de miel.**

CULTURA

Francisco Morazán (1792–1842), a Honduran soldier and statesman, is considered a national hero of Honduras. Morazán was the guiding force behind the Central American Federation (1823–1839), which united Costa Rica, El Salvador, Guatemala, Honduras, and Nicaragua. Disputes between liberals and conservatives and among the five national groups finally broke up the federation in 1839. Morazán was also president of Costa Rica for a few months before he was assassinated in 1842.

Sustantivos

la amistad friendship
el cariño affection
el compromiso engagement
el divorcio divorce
la flor flower
el matrimonio marriage
el noviazgo courtship
el ramo bouquet
la separación separation
la vida life

Verbos

amar to love
divorciarse (de) to get divorced (from)
querer to love
romper (con) to break up (with)
salir (con) to go out (with)
separarse (de) to separate (from)

¡A PRACTICAR!

10-1   **Etapas de un amor fracasado (failed)** No todas las parejas tienen el mismo éxito que Francisco y Celia. Pon los siguientes eventos de un amor fracasado en un orden lógico.

_____ el compromiso
_____ el divorcio
_____ la separación
_____ la amistad
_____ el matrimonio
_____ el noviazgo

¿NOS ENTENDEMOS?
Some other ways of talking about romantic breakups are **dejar a alguien** and **cortar con alguien**. You can also say that a relationship ended by stating the following: **Se acabó (terminó) la relación.** *(The relationship has ended.)*

10-2   **Definiciones** Busca la palabra de la lista a la derecha que vaya con la definición a la izquierda. Luego compara tus definiciones con las de un(a) compañero(a) de clase. ¿Están de acuerdo?

1. _____ cuando dos personas empiezan a quererse
2. _____ tener una boda
3. _____ hacer planes con otra persona para salir o hacer algo a una hora determinada
4. _____ cuando dos personas se enamoran la primera vez que se ven
5. _____ tener mucho amor por alguien es como tenerle mucho _____
6. _____ cuando dos personas nunca pelean y se divierten mucho juntas
7. _____ una muestra de amor con los labios
8. _____ una muestra de amor con los brazos
9. _____ cuando dos personas se casan, prometen pasar toda _____ juntas
10. _____ cuando dos personas siempre pelean y no les gusta estar juntas
11. _____ lo que los invitados hacen con el arroz después de la boda
12. _____ cuando las personas de una pareja deciden no seguir juntas
13. _____ tener una persona en la vida con quien ir al cine, a fiestas, etcétera, sin estar casados
14. _____ cuando una pareja casada se separa legalmente para terminar su matrimonio para siempre
15. _____ dos verbos que indican el amor
16. _____ una manera de saludar a una persona con la mano

a. separarse
b. casarse
c. llevarse bien
d. darse la mano
e. amar
f. divorciarse
g. romper con alguien
h. querer
i. tirar
j. abrazarse
k. besarse
l. llevarse mal
m. enamorarse
n. el amor a primera vista
o. la cita
p. la vida
q. cariño
r. salir con alguien

10-3   **Preparaciones para una boda** Completa el párrafo con palabras y frases adecuadas de la lista. Luego compara tu párrafo con el de un(a) compañero(a). ¿Están de acuerdo?

flores   luna de miel   novia   recién casados   boda   ramo   novio

Normalmente, las preparaciones para una 1. _____ consumen mucho tiempo y mucha energía. Primero, la 2. _____ tiene que comprar su vestido. También ella pide las 3. _____ a una florería, así como el 4. _____ que ella va a llevar al altar de la iglesia. El 5. _____ compra un traje nuevo o puede alquilar un smoking (tuxedo). Finalmente, los novios planean la 6. _____, según el dinero que tengan (may have). A veces, los 7. _____ van a otro país, pero frecuentemente lo pasan bien cerca de su ciudad o pueblo.

EN VOZ ALTA

10-4 **Una boda memorable** Descríbele a un(a) compañero(a) de clase una boda memorable a la que tú asististe. En tu descripción, debes contestar las siguientes preguntas.

1. ¿Cómo se llamaban los novios?
2. ¿Cuándo y dónde fue la boda?
3. ¿Qué tiempo hacía ese día?
4. ¿Quiénes estuvieron allí?
5. ¿Con quién fuiste tú a la boda?
6. ¿A qué hora comenzó la ceremonia?
7. ¿Qué pasó después de esa ceremonia?
8. ¿Qué comieron los novios y sus invitados?
9. ¿Qué cosa interesante pasó en la recepción?
10. ¿Dónde pasaron los novios su luna de miel?

10-5 **Entrevista** Hazle a otro(a) compañero(a) las siguientes preguntas sobre el matrimonio y comparen sus respuestas para ver si tienen mucho en común.

1. ¿Eres soltero(a) o estás casado(a)? ~~soy soltero~~
2. Si eres soltero(a), ¿tienes novio(a) ahora? Si estás casado(a), ¿cuándo y dónde te casaste? ~~se tengo un novio~~
3. Para ti, ¿es importante casarse en nuestra sociedad? ¿Por qué? ~~no es important~~
4. Para ti, ¿qué es una familia? En tu opinión, ¿qué futuro tiene la familia en nuestra sociedad? ~~una familia, poco fa~~
5. ¿Por qué hay tanto divorcio en nuestro país? ~~se 1~~
6. ¿Qué se puede hacer para tener éxito en el matrimonio?
7. Para ti, ¿cuál es el lugar ideal para casarse?
8. ¿Cuál es el lugar ideal para pasar una luna de miel?

10-6 **Encuesta (Survey)...** Busca a una persona en tu clase para cada una de las siguientes descripciones. Pon la firma (signature) de las personas en el lugar indicado. Al final, comparte tus respuestas con las de los otros compañeros de clase para ver cuál es el resultado y qué es lo que cree la mayoría (majority) de tu clase.

MODELO: Estoy casado(a).
E1: *¿Estás casada?*
E2: *Sí, estoy casada. Y tú, ¿estás casado?*
E1: *No, no estoy casado.* (E2 signs E1's paper.)

Firma

1. Estoy casado(a). — *Oscar*
2. Tengo novio(a). — *Diael*
3. No quiero casarme nunca. — *Teeny*
4. Me gusta salir, pero no tengo ganas de tener una relación seria.
5. No creo en el matrimonio. — *Doris*
6. No creo en el divorcio.
7. Pienso que la idea de la familia está cambiando en los Estados Unidos.
8. Quiero (Tuve) una boda grande. — *lll*

Resultados: *La mayoría de los estudiantes de la clase...*

¿NOS ENTENDEMOS?
El (La) **amigo(a)** and el (la) **novio(a)** are two Spanish words that do not have an exact English equivalent. **Amigo(a)** is used for *friend*. **Novio(a)** is used for *boyfriend* or *girlfriend*, and is also used when two people are very close to getting married. **Prometido(a)** is *fiancé/fiancée*. The verb **comprometerse** is used to indicate that two people have promised to marry each other. El (La) **amigovio(a)** is a slang term comprised of the words **amigo(a)** and **novio(a)** to mean a little more than just friends. In Chile, the word **el (la) pololo(a)** can be used to say *boyfriend/girlfriend*, as can the word **el (la) enamorado(a)** in Ecuador.

Text audio
Track 2-6

El 14 de marzo Munci Pujol, **la novia** de Jorge Goytisolo, recibió una invitación de su amigo Felipe. Luego Munci llamó por teléfono a Jorge.

Jorge:	Aló.
Munci:	Hola, Jorge, ¿cómo estás?
Jorge:	Bien, mi **amor.** ¿Qué tal?
Munci:	Muy bien. Oye, Jorge, ¿sabes qué? **He recibido** (*I have received*) muy buenas noticias de mi amigo Felipe Vega. **Se va a casar** el próximo mes con Marisol Flores.
Jorge:	¡No me digas! ¿Es la mujer **con quien** (*with whom*) estuvo Felipe en el cine la semana pasada?
Munci:	Sí, la misma (*the same one*). Él me **ha hablado** (*He has spoken to me*) mucho de ella. Parece muy simpática. Según él, ellos **se quieren** (*they love each other*) **locamente.**
Jorge:	¿Cuándo es **la boda**?
Munci:	**Han decidido** casarse el 16 de abril en la Iglesia de San Jacinto. Es la iglesia que está enfrente del restaurante El Alba. ¿Quieres ir a la boda conmigo?
Jorge:	Pues, claro que sí, Munci. ¡Muchas gracias! Pero, ¿sabes qué? Nunca **he asistido** (*I have attended*) a una boda.
Munci:	No importa. Yo te lo explico todo (*I'll explain everything to you*). Vamos a pasarlo bien. Bueno, ahora voy a llamar a Felipe para felicitarlo. Chao, Jorge.
Jorge:	Chao, Munci.

¿Comprendiste?

Contesta las siguientes preguntas en oraciones completas.

1. ¿Cuál es el tema principal de este diálogo?
2. ¿Cuál sería un título adecuado para el diálogo?
3. ¿Por qué llamó Munci a su novio?
4. ¿Conoce Jorge a Marisol? ¿Por qué sí, o por qué no?
5. ¿Están muy enamorados Felipe y Marisol?
6. ¿Va a ser la primera vez que Jorge va a una boda?

> **¿NOS ENTENDEMOS?**
> Spanish speakers use many terms of endearment, for example, **mi amor, mi amorcito(a), mi vida, viejo(a), querido(a), cielo, corazón, corazoncito.**

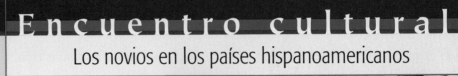

Encuentro cultural

Los novios en los países hispanoamericanos

PARA PENSAR

- Por lo general, ¿a qué edad salen en parejas los jóvenes de tu país?

- ¿Qué beneficios hay en salir en grupo?

- Cuando tú estabas en la escuela secundaria, ¿salías en grupo con tus amigos? ¿Qué hacían tú y tus amigos juntos? ¿Salías en pareja?

Las costumbres tradicionales de salir en pareja están cambiando rápidamente en Latinoamérica y en España pero, por lo general, todavía son distintas de las costumbres norteamericanas. Por ejemplo, los jóvenes hispanos comienzan a salir en grupo alrededor de los catorce años. Ellos salen juntos al cine, a fiestas, a la playa y a eventos deportivos. Generalmente, los jóvenes hispanos comienzan a salir en parejas a una edad mayor que la de la mayoría de los jóvenes norteamericanos, y aún así las salidas *(going out)* son más estrictas. A veces, ya a los dieciocho o diecinueve años, salen en pareja. Todavía en algunos países de Latinoamérica, algunas muchachas al salir en pareja van acompañadas de un chaperón o una chaperona. En Latinoamérica y en España, como en muchas otras culturas, algunos jóvenes prefieren una unión libre. En algunos casos, el costo de un matrimonio es mucho, y la anulación es difícil de obtener, especialmente por la Iglesia católica.

PARA DISCUTIR

1. ¿Adónde van los jóvenes hispanos cuando salen en grupo a los catorce o quince años?
2. ¿Cuántos años tienen cuando comienzan a salir en parejas?
3. ¿Por qué algunos jóvenes prefieren vivir en una unión libre?
4. ¿Qué te gustaría hacer a ti con respecto al noviazgo y al matrimonio?

ESTRUCTURA I Describing recent actions, events, and conditions: the present perfect tense

Spanish speakers use the present perfect indicative tense to describe what has and has not happened recently. Unlike the preterite tense, which is used to make time-specific references to either the beginning or end of an action or event in the past, the present perfect merely establishes the fact that an action has taken place some-time in the past before the present. The emphasis is placed on the fact that the action took place, not *when* it took place. Consider the following examples:

Present perfect	Yo **he comido.**	*I have eaten.*
		(past action with no specific reference to time)
Preterite	Yo **comí** a las 7:00.	*I ate at 7:00.*
		(past action with specific reference to time)

How to form the present perfect

Use the present-tense forms of the auxiliary verb **haber** *(to have)* with the past participle of a verb.

Present of *haber* + past participle:

yo	**he** *I have*	
tú	**has** *you* (inf.) *have*	
Ud., él/ella	**ha** *you* (form.) *have, he/she has*	**hablado** *spoken*
nosotros(as)	**hemos** *we have*	**comido** *eaten*
vosotros(as)	**habéis** *you have*	**vivido** *lived*
Uds., ellos(as)	**han** *you have, they have*	

How to form past participles

• **Regular past participles**

Add **-ado** to the stem of **-ar** verbs, and **-ido** to the stem of **-er** and **-ir** verbs.

Infinitive -ar verb	Past participle stem + -ado	Infinitive -er/-ir verb	Past participle stem + -ido
habl-ar	habl**ado** *spoken*	com-er	com**ido** *eaten*
pens-ar	pens**ado** *thought*	viv-ir	viv**ido** *lived*
lleg-ar	lleg**ado** *arrived*	dorm-ir	dorm**ido** *slept*

—¿**Has hablado** con el novio de Ana?	*Have you spoken to Ana´s boyfriend?*
—No, pero ellos **han ido** a la casa de mi hermano antes.	*No, but they have come to my brother´s house before.*
—¿Y Uds. todavía no se **han conocido**?	*And you still haven´t met each other?*
—No, pero creo que él **ha vivido** en Tegucigalpa por muchos años.	*No, but I believe he has lived in Tegucigalpa for many years.*

Note that several **-er** and **-ir** verbs have an accent mark on the **í** of their past participles.

leer	leído *read*	traer	traído *brought*
creer	creído *believed*	reír	reído *laughed*

—Te **he traído** un regalo, Celia.	*I've brought a gift for you, Celia.*
—¿Qué me **has traído,** mi amor?	*What have you brought me, my love?*
—Un ramo de flores.	*A bouquet of flowers.*

- **Irregular past participles**

Other verbs have irregular past participles. Here are some of the most common ones.

Infinitive	Past participle	Infinitive	Past participle
abrir	**abierto** *opened*	morir	**muerto** *died*
decir	**dicho** *said; told*	poner	**puesto** *put*
escribir	**escrito** *written*	ver	**visto** *seen*
hacer	**hecho** *done; made*	volver	**vuelto** *returned*

—¿Qué **han hecho** ustedes hoy?   *What have you done today?*

—**Hemos visto** una película.   *We have seen a movie.*

—**He escrito** algunas cartas.   *I have written some letters.*

¡A PRACTICAR!

10-7 **En una terraza en las islas Bahías, Honduras** Completa la siguiente conversación durante la luna de miel de Francisco y Celia con la forma correcta de **haber: he, has, ha, hemos** o **han.**

Camarero: ¿1. _____ estado Uds. en estas islas antes?

Celia: Sí, señor. Nosotros 2. _____ venido aquí antes.

Camarero: ¿3. _____ comido en este restaurante antes?

Francisco: Sí, señor. Nosotros 4. _____ comido aquí antes.

Camarero: Oiga, señora, ¿5. _____ visto nuestras flores en la terraza?

Celia: Sí, sí. Yo las 6. _____ visto. Y nosotros 7. _____ decidido pasar la tarde entre las flores.

Francisco: Mejor dicho, tú 8. _____ decidido venir aquí, Celia.

Celia: Sí, Francisco. Pero también nosotros 9. _____ comido bien aquí otras veces.

Francisco: ¡Tienes razón, amorcito, corazón!

10-8 **Una situación complicada... el amor de un perro** Clementina, una niña de diez años, ha encontrado un perro en la calle. Ahora ella lo quiere mucho y por eso intenta explicárselo a sus padres. Completa las siguientes conversaciones entre dos padres y su hija, usando los participios de los verbos indicados.

1. ver / escribir / hacer / encontrar

   Padre: ¿Qué has _____ hoy, hija?

   Clementina: He _____ algunas cartas y he _____ este perrito en la calle.

   Padre: ¡Ay! ¿Qué has _____? ¿Lo ha _____ tu madre?

2. morir / jugar / dar / querer

   Clementina: Papá, creo que el perro ha _____.

   Padre: No, está durmiendo. Tú le has _____ muchas galletas.

   Madre: Ella ha _____ mucho con el perrito hoy, ¿verdad?

   Padre: Sí, porque ha _____ estar con él.

3. abrir / decir / poner / comer / volver

   Padre: ¿Qué tienes en la mano, hija?

   Clementina: Más galletas. El perro ya se ha _____ las otras. He _____ una caja nueva.

   Madre: ¿Qué te hemos _____, hija? El perrito no quiere más.

   Padre: Sí, niña. Nos has _____ en una situación difícil. ¿Qué van a decirles los dueños si su perro no ha _____ a su casa esta tarde?

CULTURA

Las islas Bahías are located off the Caribbean coast in Honduras and are a very popular tourist destination. There are three main islands in the group, and the government of Honduras has established somewhat strict laws to protect the environment there. They suffered devastating damage from Hurricane Mitch in 1998.

10-9 **Mis queridos amigos...** Celia está escribiéndoles a sus amigos sobre algunas actividades que Francisco y ella han hecho en las islas Bahías. ¿Qué les dice en su carta?

MODELO: Yo ___*he hecho*___ (hacer) mucho ejercicio aquí.

Yo 1. _____ (nadar) en la piscina del hotel y 2. _____ (jugar) al tenis con Francisco. Él 3. _____ (montar) en bicicleta dos veces esta semana. Desafortunadamente yo no 4. _____ (comprar) muchas cosas aquí porque no 5. _____ (ir) a ninguna tienda. (Yo) 6. _____ (querer) descansar solamente.

Francisco y yo 7. _____ (divertirse) mucho. Esta tarde 8. _____ (almorzar) en un buen restaurante y 9. _____ (pasar) toda la tarde en una terraza magnífica. En la terraza de este restaurante 10. _____ (ver) unas flores estupendas y yo 11. _____ (leer) el periódico. El camarero nos 12. _____ (traer) mucha comida. Pienso que él 13. _____ (creer) que teníamos mucha hambre. Nosotros 14. _____ (reírse) mucho. En total, lo 15. _____ (pasar) muy bien aquí en esta ciudad maravillosa.

EN VOZ ALTA

10-10 **Recientemente...** Basándote en *(Based on)* las siguientes situaciones, debes componer preguntas para hacérselas a un(a) compañero(a) de clase. Tú y tu compañero(a), ¿tienen mucho en común?

MODELO: tu clase de español / tu profesor
E1: *¿Qué ha hecho recientemente tu profesor en la clase de español?*
E2: *El profesor (no) nos ha dado un examen.*

1. tus clases / tú
2. la residencia / tus amigos y tú
3. la biblioteca / tu mejor amigo y su novia
4. tu casa / tú y los miembros de tu familia
5. tu trabajo / tus compañeros de trabajo

10-11 **¿Qué has hecho?** Trabajen en parejas haciendo y contestando las siguientes preguntas. Comparen sus respuestas y compartan *(share)* la información que ya saben sobre los tópicos.

1. ¿Has visto fotos de Managua, la capital de Nicaragua? ¿Has visto fotos de Tegucigalpa, la capital hondureña? ¿Has visto fotos de las capitales de otros países hispanos? ¿Has visitado la capital de un país hispano?
2. ¿Has leído la poesía de Rubén Darío, Ernesto Cardenal, Gioconda Belli o de otro poeta nicaragüense? ¿Has escrito poesía?
3. ¿Has visto un episodio del programa *Baywatch* con el actor nicaragüense José Solano? ¿Has visto este programa muchas veces? ¿Qué piensas del programa?
4. ¿Has comido muchos plátanos o bananas de Honduras y Nicaragua? ¿Has bebido mucho café?
5. ¿Qué has aprendido de la civilzación maya? ¿Qué has aprendido de las ruinas de Copán, un sitio maya que está al oeste de Honduras?

10-12 **¡Adivinen Uds.!** Cada estudiante de tu clase de español va a escribir en un papel una acción que él (ella) ha hecho recientemente. Luego van a formar grupos de cinco o seis personas. Mientras cada persona muestra *(shows)* con gestos (pantomima) lo que escribió una persona del grupo, los otros compañeros del grupo tratan de *(try to)* adivinarlo; luego esa persona dice si los otros lo adivinaron bien o no.

MODELO: E1: Un(a) estudiante lee un periódico.
E2: *¿Has leído un periódico?*
E1: *¡Sí! ¡Excelente!*

CULTURA 7-11
Managua and Tegucigalpa are both cities of just over 1 million inhabitants. Managua is located in the lowlands of western Nicaragua, on the southern shore of Lake Managua. Tegucigalpa is located in a valley at an altitude of about 3,000 feet, giving it an ideal climate.

CULTURA 7-11
Nicaragua is known as **"la tierra de los poetas"** because it has produced an impressive number of outstanding poets such as Rubén Darío from the late 19th and early 20th centuries and the contemporary poets Ernesto Cardenal and Gioconda Belli.

CULTURA 7-11
José Solano was the first Latino actor to appear on the popular television show *Baywatch*, playing the part of lifeguard Manny Gutiérrez.

CULTURA 7-11
Bananas have been cultivated in Central America since the 19th century and are a principal product of the region. They are eaten raw or cooked, depending on the variety.

CULTURA 7-11
Coffee is another important crop from Honduras, Nicaragua, and other Central American countries.

CULTURA 7-11
The Mayan civilization, dating from 1500 BC and flourishing between 600 and 900 AD, was located in the present-day countries of Mexico, Guatemala, Belize, and Honduras. It is known for achievements in mathematics, astronomy, and architecture.

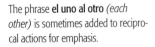

ASÍ SE DICE Describing reciprocal actions: reciprocal constructions with *se, nos,* and *os*

The phrase **el uno al otro** *(each other)* is sometimes added to reciprocal actions for emphasis.

Spanish speakers express the idea of *each other* or *one another* with the plural reflexive pronouns **se, nos,** and **os.** Verbs that are not normally reflexive are frequently used to express reciprocal actions. Consider the following examples:

Osvaldo y Lola **se miran** el uno al otro.	*Osvaldo and Lola look at each other.*
Mi novia y yo **nos besamos.**	*My girlfriend and I kiss each other.*
¿**Se conocen?**	*Do you (they) know one another?*

¡A PRACTICAR!

10-13 **Amor a primera vista...** Completa las siguientes frases para terminar la historia de amor entre Alicia y Emilio a quien conoció en un café. Ojo con el uso del pretérito.

MODELO: Alicia y Emilio / conocerse / en un café
Alicia y Emilio se conocieron en un café.

1. Alicia y Emilio / verse / una tarde de julio en un café
2. no hablarse / pero / ellos mirarse profundamente
3. inmediatamente / la muchacha y el muchacho / enamorarse
4. ellos / abrazarse / y / besarse / aquella tarde
5. Pronto Alicia explicó a sus padres: «Emilio y yo / enamorarse» ...Fue un amor a primera vista...

10-14 **¿La pareja ideal?** Indica si estás de acuerdo con las siguientes cualidades de la pareja ideal. Si no estás de acuerdo, explica por qué. Luego compara tu razonamiento *(reasoning)* con el de un(a) compañero(a) de clase. ¿Piensan igual?

MODELO: Ellos nunca se miran a los ojos cuando se hablan.
No es una cualidad de la pareja ideal, porque dos personas de una pareja ideal siempre se miran cuando se hablan.

1. Ellos se comunican todas sus ideas y opiniones.
2. Ellos se ayudan con problemas difíciles.
3. Ellos siempre se dicen la verdad.
4. Ellos no se contradicen *(contradict one another)* con frecuencia.
5. A veces se besan en público.
6. Se enamoraron a primera vista.
7. Nunca se separan cuando van juntos a una fiesta.
8. Se casan después de un noviazgo largo.

EN VOZ ALTA

10-15 **Mis relaciones sentimentales** Haz preguntas con las siguientes frases para hacérselas a un(a) compañero(a) de clase sobre sus relaciones sentimentales.

MODELO: tú y tus amigos / verse frecuentemente
E1: *¿Se ven tú y tus amigos frecuentemente?*
E2: *Sí, nos vemos frecuentemente los fines de semana.*

1. tú y tus padres / hablarse por teléfono una vez a la semana
2. tú y tu mejor amigo(a) / escribirse durante las vacaciones
3. tú y tus abuelos / conocerse muy bien; respetarse
4. tú y tus hermanos / ayudarse con problemas económicos
5. tú y tu compañero(a) de cuarto / hablarse sinceramente
6. tú y tu novio(a) / mirarse cariñosamente; quererse
7. tú y tus compañeros de clase / darse la mano en clase
8. ¿...?

VOCABULARIO La recepción

La recepción de Rubén y Rafaela en Managua, Nicaragua In this section you will practice vocabulary used to describe receptions and banquets.

Carolina, an historian and a true romantic, decided to investigate the event. While she was reading, she started to imagine what happened. Below are the scenes she imagined from the wedding reception of Rubén Darío, Nicaragua's most famous literary talent, and his bride, Rafaela Contreras, in the National Palace in Managua in 1890.

CULTURA
Managua is the capital and largest city of Nicaragua. It is located in the western central part of the country along the southern shore of Lake Managua. It was chosen to be the capital of Nicaragua in 1857 in order to resolve a dispute over the location of the capital between the then larger cities of Granada and León.

Todas las personas importantes de Managua **asistieron a la recepción** para Rubén y Rafaela.

Los invitados felicitaban a la **pareja** mientras entraban a la sala. Más tarde el presidente del país le hizo un brindis especial.

La recepción de **la pareja tuvo lugar** en una sala en el Palacio Nacional.

El banquete era elegante con todos los invitados **vestidos de gala. La orquesta** de la ciudad tocó para la celebración.

Rafaela tiró el ramo de flores y una chica de veinte años lo **agarró.** Todos **aplaudieron.**

Rubén tenía celos de un viejo amigo de Rafaela que la **acompañaba** durante una buena parte de la noche. Cuando Rafaela bailaba con su amigo, Rubén les interrumpió y así **terminó** la celebración.

CULTURA
Rubén Darío is Nicaragua's most famous poet. He is credited with introducing **el modernismo,** an innovative poetic aesthetic, to European intellectual circles at the end of the 19th century. He was born in Metapa, Nicaragua, in 1867 and his original name was Félix Rubén García.

¡A PRACTICAR!

10-16 **¿En qué palabra estoy pensando?** Busca la palabra adecuada del nuevo vocabulario que vaya con cada definición a continuación.

1. dos palabras que se refieren a la fiesta que se da después de una boda
2. un grupo de dos personas
3. el grupo musical que toca en fiestas o en conciertos
4. con ropa elegante
5. Los _____ se refiere a la gente que va a una boda o a otro evento.

10-17 **La perspectiva de un músico** Félix, un miembro de la orquesta que tocó para los recién casados, narra la historia de la recepción. Usa los siguientes verbos para terminar su relato, escogiendo entre el pretérito o el imperfecto.

terminar   asistir a   felicitar   tener lugar   aplaudir   acompañar   agarrar

Más de 300 personas 1. _____ la recepción para Rubén y Rafaela. La celebración 2. _____ en el elegante Palacio Nacional. Nosotros, los músicos, 3. _____ a un cantante en una canción de amor cuando los novios entraron. Todos los invitados 4. _____ con alegría. El presidente los 5. _____ con un brindis. Una chica joven 6. _____ el ramo de flores que Rafaela tiró. La fiesta 7. _____ bruscamente cuando Rubén y Rafaela se fueron de la recepción.

EN VOZ ALTA

10-18 **Planes, planes y planes** Felipe y Gabriela están organizando la recepción para su boda y siempre hay un poquitín de desacuerdo. Con un(a) compañero(a), hagan los papeles de Felipe y Gabriela y hablen de los planes para la fiesta. Hagan preguntas con la información dada. ¡Sean creativos!

MODELO: Fecha
           Felipe: *¿Cuándo quieres tener la recepción?*
           o   *Para ti, ¿cuál es la fecha ideal para la recepción?*
           Gabriela: *Yo quiero tener la recepción el día de la boda.*
           Felipe: *¡Ay que no, mi amor! Yo prefiero tenerla el próximo día.*

Preguntas de Felipe	Respuestas de Gabriela	Desacuerdo de Felipe
el lugar	sala de baile, Palacio Nacional	....
el número de invitados	50 personas	....
la cena	cena de cinco platos: mariscos, carne, ensalada, queso y postre; vino blanco y vino tinto o rojo	....
el tipo de ropa	ropa muy formal y elegante	....
el tipo de música	merengue	....
su primer baile	¡Baile!	....
tirar arroz	no tirar arroz	....

10-19 **Entrevista** Con un(a) compañero(a) de clase, contesten las siguientes preguntas sobre las bodas para ver si tienen mucho en común.

1. ¿Estás casado(a)? Si no, ¿piensas casarte algún día? ¿Cómo vas a celebrar? Si estás casado(a), ¿cómo celebraste la boda? ¿Hubo una fiesta grande? ¿Quién fue a tu boda? ¿Qué llevaste tú? ¿Qué llevaron los invitados?
2. ¿Fuiste a una boda alguna vez? ¿De quién? ¿Lo pasaste bien? ¿Hubo mucha gente? ¿Qué tipo de ropa se vistieron los invitados? ¿Dónde se celebró la boda?
3. ¿Fuiste alguna vez a una recepción o un banquete para celebrar una boda? ¿Hubo una orquesta? ¿un baile? ¿Cómo trataron los invitados a los novios? ¿Les tiraron mucho arroz? ¿Bailaron juntos los novios?

Encuentro cultural
Las bodas en el mundo hispano

PARA PENSAR

- ¿Qué impresiones tienes de las bodas en el mundo hispano? ¿Cómo son las bodas norteamericanas?

- Qué te parece mejor, ¿los noviazgos cortos o los largos? ¿Cuáles son las ventajas y las desventajas de estos tipos de noviazgos?

Cuando dos novios piensan casarse, es posible estar comprometidos *(engaged)* por varios meses o años mientras los novios trabajan y ahorran dinero para alquilar un apartamento y comprar muebles. Muchas veces, las personas posponen la boda hasta terminar sus estudios universitarios. Es común que el novio le pida la mano de su novia al padre de ella. Si éste está de acuerdo *(agrees)*, las dos familias comienzan a planear juntas la boda. Muchos matrimonios en Latinoamérica y en España consisten en dos ceremonias oficiales, una civil y otra religiosa. A veces, la ceremonia civil tiene lugar en la casa de la novia o del novio, y participan en ella algunos familiares y amigos íntimos de las dos familias. Un(a) juez *(judge)* casa a los novios, leyendo palabras de un texto oficial. Después de que prometen cumplir *(they promise to honor)* con todas las responsabilidades del matrimonio, los novios están casados oficialmente. Luego ellos y sus testigos *(witnesses)* firman *(sign)* los documentos correspondientes.

Después de la boda civil, los novios celebran la boda religiosa que tradicionalmente es la ceremonia más importante para los novios y sus familiares. A esta celebración asisten muchos más invitados y algunas veces se celebra en un lugar más grande como en una casa de fiestas donde hay comida, bebidas y música. Esta celebración puede durar entre cinco o seis horas durante la tarde o la noche. Después de esta celebración, los novios se despiden y se van para su luna de miel.

PARA DISCUTIR

1. ¿Por qué dura mucho el noviazgo en los países hispanos?
2. ¿Pueden describir las dos ceremonias que hay en una boda hispana?
3. ¿Cómo son las bodas norteamericanas en comparación con las hispanas?
4. ¿Qué opinas sobre la idea de tener dos ceremonias y por qué?

Adverbs

An adverb is a word that modifies a verb, an adjective, or another adverb. It may describe *how, when, where, why,* or *how much.* You already know many adverbs such as **muy, ayer, siempre, después, mucho, bien, mal, tarde, temprano, mejor,** and **peor.**

- To form most Spanish adverbs, add **-mente** (*-ly*) to an adjective.

| natural | **naturalmente** | *naturally* |
| frecuente | **frecuentemente** | *frequently* |

- If an adjective ends in **-o,** change the **-o** to **-a,** then add **-mente.**

| perfecto | **perfectamente** | *perfectly* |

- If an adjective has an accent mark, the adverb retains it.

| fácil | **fácilmente** | *easily* |
| rápido | **rápidamente** | *rapidly* |

Note that adverbs modifying a verb are generally placed immediately after the verb, whereas adverbs modifying adjectives or other adverbs are placed directly before them.

| Ellos salieron **rápidamente** de la sala. | *They left the room quickly.* |
| Rubén estaba **muy** enojado. | *Rubén was very mad.* |

Adverbial expressions of time and sequencing of events

In previous chapters, you learned many of the following adverbs and adverbial expressions with their English equivalents.

- Use the following adverbs to express how often something is done.

a veces *sometimes*	**nunca** *never*
cada día (semana, mes, etc.) *each day* (*week, month, etc.*)	**otra vez** *again*
(casi) siempre *(almost) always*	**solamente** *only, just*
dos (tres, etc.) veces *twice* (*three times, etc.*)	**todos los años (días, meses, etc.)** *every year (day, month, etc.)*
muchas veces *very often*	**una vez** *once*

—Hablo con mi novio **todos los días.**   *I talk to my boyfriend every day.*
—**Siempre** voy con él al cine los fines de semana.   *I always go to the movies with him on the weekend.*

- Use the following adverbs to express the order of events.

después *afterward*	**finalmente** *finally*	**por fin** *at last, finally*
entonces *then; so*	**luego** *then*	**primero** *first*

—¿Adónde vamos **primero,** mi amor?   *Where are we going first, my love?*
—Al cine. **Luego** a la discoteca.   *To the movies. Then to the disco.*
—¿Y **después**?   *And afterward?*
—Volvemos a casa.   *We're going back home.*

¡A PRACTICAR!

10-20 **Más impresiones de la recepción** Vamos a describir lo que vimos en la celebración imaginada por Carolina, y para darle más énfasis a las siguientes impresiones, convierte el adjetivo en adverbio, y luego incorpóralo en la oración.

MODELO: fabuloso / Rafaela estaba vestido
fabulosamente / Rafaela se vestía fabulosamente.

1. puntual / El carruaje nupcial llegó a la recepción
2. fácil / La chica agarró el ramo de flores
3. constante / La orquesta tocaba
4. estupendo / Rafaela y su amigo bailaban
5. inmediato / Rubén se puso enojado
6. tranquilo / El amigo de Rafaela le habló a Rubén
7. paciente / Rafaela intentó calmar a su esposo
8. total / Los invitados estaban sorprendidos
9. rápido / La recepción terminó
10. inmediato / Rafaela y Rubén se fueron

10-21 **Hablando del amor** Completa las siguientes oraciones con la siguiente lista de adverbios.

nunca	muchas veces	una vez	dos veces	a veces
siempre	cada	otra vez	solamente	todos los días (años)

1. Me gusta mucho ser soltero(a). Yo no quiero casarme _____.
2. Algunas personas famosas se han casado _____.
3. El matrimonio puede ser muy aburrido. Las parejas hablan de lo mismo _____, y van de vacaciones al mismo lugar _____.
4. Mi amiga todavía quiere a su viejo amigo. Le habla _____ día por teléfono.
5. Mi novio es muy celoso. Cuando él me ve a mí hablando con otros hombres, él _____ se pone furioso.
6. ¿Qué tal la primera cita con Carolina? ¿Quieres salir con ella _____?
7. Si salgo con alguien _____ una vez, generalmente no conozco bien a la persona.
8. ¿Es el amor una cosa que ocurre solamente _____ en la vida?
9. _____ es posible enamorarse de alguna persona al conocerla, pero no es muy probable.
10. _____ es importante decirle a la persona que uno la quiere, que es maravillosa.

10-22 **Un fracaso amoroso** Luis Eduardo cuenta de una relación amorosa que terminó mal para él. Pon el relato en orden. Después, vuelve a contar la historia y añade palabras como **primero, un día, entonces, después, finalmente, por fin** y **luego** para hacerla más completa.

_____ Me fui corriendo de su casa. Me puse muy triste —¡yo quería casarme con esta chica!

_____ ¡La encontré en los brazos de mi hermano, Raúl!

_____ La invité a cenar conmigo.

_____ Después de salir con ella por algunas semanas, yo me enamoré seriamente de ella.

_____ Un día, salí temprano del trabajo, y me paré en su casa para sorprenderla.

_____ Conocí a Raquel, la mujer más guapa del mundo, el año pasado.

_____ Después de comer, fuimos a tomar un café y hablamos toda la noche.

_____ Decidí romper con ella para siempre.

_____ Empezamos a salir todas las noches.

EN VOZ ALTA

10-23 **¿Cómo haces esas cosas?** Con un(a) compañero(a), busquen el adverbio que corresponda con las palabras a continuación para describir cómo hacen Uds. las siguientes cosas. **¡Ojo!** Algunas de las palabras no requieren cambios —ya son adverbios.

MODELO: jugar con niños pequeños
E1: *¿Cómo juegas con niños pequeños?*
E2: *Juego pacientemente con niños pequeños. ¿Y tú?*
E1: *Yo juego mal con niños pequeños; no me gustan los niños.*

natural	paciente	mejor
frecuente	mal	fácil
bien	tarde	peor
perfecto	rápido	

1. hablar con gente del sexo opuesto
2. conducir
3. hablar español
4. estudiar para mis clases
5. tocar el piano
6. bailar

10-24 **Actividades familiares** Cuéntale a otro(a) compañero(a) algunas actividades que hacen tus parientes. Escoge un elemento de cada una de las tres columnas para hacer tus oraciones.

MODELO: *Mi papá me llama por teléfono frecuentemente.*

¿Quién(es)?	¿Qué hace(n)?	¿Con qué frecuencia?
mi papá (mamá)	venir a visitarme	a veces
mi tío(a)	escribirme una carta	casi todos los meses
mi esposo(a)	llamarme por teléfono	una vez al día
mi novio(a)	darme un regalo bonito	frecuentemente
mi hermano(a)	jugar al béisbol (golf)	todos los años
mi(s) _____	ir de compras (al cine)	todos los fines de semana

¿NOS ENTENDEMOS?
Married couples are referred to as **el matrimonio**. Some Spanish-speaking countries use the word **el matrimonio**, rather than the more common words **la boda** or **el casamiento**, for *wedding*.

ESTRUCTURA II Using the Spanish equivalents of *who, whom, that,* and *which:* relative pronouns

Relative pronouns are used in joining two clauses together. There are four primary relative pronouns in English: *who, whom, that,* and *which.* Their Spanish equivalents are words you already know.

que	refers to people and things
quien	refers only to people
lo que	refers to an entire idea, concept, or situation

¿Quién es el hombre **que** hablaba contigo? ↑ ↑ **(first clause)** **(second clause)**	*Who is the man who was talking with you?*
Ella es la mujer **con quien** yo bailaba. ↑ ↑ **(first clause)** **(second clause)**	*She is the woman with whom I was dancing.*
No sabemos **lo que** él hizo en la fiesta. ↑ ↑ **(first clause)** **(second clause)**	*We don't know what he did at the party.*

- Note that in distinguishing between the use of the relative pronouns **que** or **quien,** both of which can be used to refer to people, Spanish speakers use **quien** *(who/whom)* only when it is preceded by a preposition or when it functions as an indirect object of the sentence. Compare the following examples:

Es una mujer **que** tiene muchos amigos.	*She is a woman who has many friends.*
Es la mujer **con quien** yo bailaba. (**quien** preceded by the preposition **con**)	*She is the woman with whom I was dancing.*
Es la mujer **a quien** yo le di el regalo. (**quien** as the indirect object pronoun in this sentence)	*She is the woman to whom I gave the gift.*

- Also notice that the relative pronouns **que** and **quien** carry accents when they are used in interrogative or exclamatory sentences.

¿Con **quién** sales ahora?	*Whom are you going out with now?*
¡**Qué** mujer tan interesante!	*What an interesting woman!*

- **Lo que** at the beginning of a sentence translates into English as *what* or *the thing that.*

Lo que me gusta de la clase es la cultura.	*What (The thing that) I like about the class is the culture.*

¡A PRACTICAR!

10-25 **Una mujer misteriosa** Usa el pronombre relativo adecuado para completar las siguientes oraciones.

1. ¿Quién es la mujer _____ lleva el vestido azul?

2. Creo que es la mujer con _____ Ramón hablaba el otro día.

3. Me gustan las mujeres _____ tienen ese aire misterioso.

4. Dicen que es la mujer _____ se divorció de Juan Medellín porque él no era muy fiel.

5. ¡_____ dicen es mentira! Juan salía con una chica _____ era la amiga de esa mujer.

6. ¿ _____ dices? Él me dijo que siempre le fue fiel a la mujer con _____ se casó.

10-26 **La civilización maya** Usa el pronombre relativo adecuado para completar el siguiente párrafo que describe la civilización de los mayas.

La civilización maya, _____ se desarrolló en México, Guatemala, Belice, El Salvador y Honduras, era una civilización muy avanzada. Esta civilización tuvo su mayor desarrollo en los años 300 a 900 después de Cristo. _____ _____ distinguió a esta civilización fue su arquitectura. Construyeron pirámides de piedra _____ servían para celebraciones religiosas, templos y esculturas. Además, los mayas fueron grandes matemáticos y astrólogos _____ explicaron sus descubrimientos con su escritura de símbolos o jeroglíficos. En el siglo XVI, los españoles conquistaron esta civilización y hoy en día, los descendientes (descendants) de los mayas _____ viven en estos países todavía tienen y conservan algunas de sus tradiciones culturales.

EN VOZ ALTA

10-27 | **Lo que necesitamos es amor** Completa las siguientes preguntas con **que, lo que** o **quien.** Después, contéstalas con un(a) compañero(a) de clase para expresar sus opiniones personales. ¿Tienen mucho en común?

MODELO: E1: ¿Tu mejor amiga es la persona ____*que*____ sabe más de ti?
E2: *Sí, mi mejor amiga sabe todos mis secretos.*
o E2: *No, yo le cuento más a mi mamá que a mi mejor amiga.*

1. ¿Es el matrimonio _____ da felicidad en la vida?

2. ¿El divorcio es _____ está destruyendo nuestra sociedad?

3. ¿Te quieres casar con una persona _____ tiene los mismos gustos que tú?

4. ¿Con _____ quieres compartir tus secretos más íntimos?

5. ¿_____ es la persona que menos quieres en el mundo? ¿Por qué?

10-28 | **La pareja ideal** ¿Cómo es la pareja ideal? Con un(a) compañero(a) de clase, completa las siguientes oraciones para describir la pareja ideal.

MODELO: Dos personas que...
Dos personas que se comunican mucho son la pareja ideal.

1. El amor que...
2. El matrimonio es lo que...
3. La persona con quien...
4. El amor a primera vista es lo que...
5. La amistad que...
6. La pareja ideal que...

¡A VER!

En este segmento del video, Valeria y Antonio hablan sobre las relaciones sentimentales. Los dos han tenido malas experiencias amorosas y parece que se sienten mejor al compartir esta información. A ver si los buenos amigos pueden llegar a ser algo más...

Expresiones útiles

Las siguientes son expresiones nuevas que vas a escuchar en el video.

Es el colmo	It's an outrage
Puedo hacerte compañía	I can keep you company

Antes de ver

Paso 1: Con un(a) compañero(a) expresen su opinión sobre lo siguiente: ¿Creen que los hombres y las mujeres pueden ser amigos? ¿De qué hablan los amigos del sexo opuesto? ¿Hablan de las relaciones sentimentales que han tenido? ¿Creen que los amigos pueden llegar a ser novios? ¿Por qué sí o por qué no?

Paso 2: Las relaciones sentimentales no son fáciles y a veces se rompen. Haz una lista de varias posibles causas del fracaso *(failure)* de una relación sentimental. Compara tu lista con la de un(a) compañero(a). ¿Piensan igual *(Do you think alike)*?

Después de ver

Paso 1: En **Antes de ver, Paso 1**, tu compañero(a) y tú expresaron opiniones sobre las relaciones sentimentales. En el video, viste también los principios de una relación sentimental entre Valeria y Antonio. Pon las siguientes oraciones en orden cronológico para contar exactamente lo que pasó. Luego no te olvides añadir en el espacio previsto las expresiones adverbiales apropiadas de la caja abajo.

después	**entonces**	**finalmente**	**luego**	**primero**

_____ _____ , los dos decidieron cenar juntos y pasear por la playa.

_____ _____ Antonio preguntó si se sentía bien y Valeria explicó por qué la relación con César terminó.

_____ _____ , Valeria dijo que se sentía muy sola y Antonio respondió que no debía sentirse así y ofreció acompañarla esa noche.

_____ _____ Valeria estaba hablando con su ex novio César por teléfono cuando descubrió que Antonio estaba escuchando la conversación. Colgó con César y empezó a gritar a Antonio.

_____ _____ Antonio contó lo que pasó con su ex novia Raquel y cómo ella se enamoró de su mejor amigo Rubén. A pesar de eso, Antonio perdonó a los dos.

Paso 2: Piensa en el comportamiento de Antonio y Valeria durante este segmento del video e indica si las siguientes oraciones son ciertas o falsas. No te olvides corregir las oraciones falsas.

- Antonio y Valeria se miran mientras se hablan sobre sus ex-novios. _____
- Se besan apasionadamente en la playa. _____
- Se escuchan mientras caminan en la playa. _____
- Se abrazan en la playa. _____

¿Qué opinas tú?

Paso 1: Escoge uno de los temas abajo y escribe un párrafo. Incluye información sobre lo que pasó primero, segundo, luego, etc., a lo largo de esa relación personal. Luego, comparte tu experiencia con la de un(a) compañero(a). ¿Han tenido experiencias similares? ¿Las cosas han progresado en el mismo orden? ¿Por qué crees que hay diferencias?

- Cuando conocí a mi mejor amigo(a)
- Cuando conocí a mi novio(a)/esposo(a)

Paso 2: Cada persona es bien distinta en cuanto a las relaciones sentimentales. ¿Cómo eres tú? ¿Cuáles son algunas de las actividades que has hecho a lo largo de tus relaciones?¿Has hablado por teléfono mucho con tu novio(a)? ¿Has planeado un fin de semana romántico? ¿Qué es lo que no has hecho? Haz una lista de tres cosas que has hecho y tres cosas que no has hecho y luego compara tu lista con la de un(a) compañero(a). ¿Tienen mucho en común?

CULTURA

Este evento social se lleva a cabo en el Casino Sampedrano, que está situado en San Pedro Sula, Honduras. Aunque tiene el nombre del casino, es solamente un centro social.

¡A LEER!

Strategy: Summarizing a reading pasaje

Summarizing in English a reading passage that you have read in Spanish can help you synthesize its most important ideas. Some guidelines for writing this type of summary are as follows:

- Underline the main ideas in the reading passage.
- Circle the key words and phrases in the passage.
- Write the summary of the passage in your own words.
- Do not include your personal reactions to the summary.
- Avoid the following common errors in writing a summary:
  too long/short
  too many details
  main ideas not expressed
  key ideas not emphasized
  wrong key ideas

LA PRENSA On the Web   Home   Ediciones anteriores

Sociales   17 de febrero de 1998

PORTADA

Casino Sampedrano exalta a "Novios del año"

La pareja conformada por Marco Tulio Crespo y Rosario de Crespo, exaltados "Novios del año" por el Casino Sampedrano.

NACIONALES

El matrimonio conformado por Marco Tulio Crespo y Rosario Pineda de Crespo fueron exaltados "Novios del año", en el marco de una romántica velada que tuvo lugar el sábado por la noche en el Casino Sampedrano.

ECONOMICAS

Anualmente el Consejo Administrativo de este centro social elige a una pareja que reúna numerosas cualidades y sea ejemplo de matrimonio en la sociedad, con el propósito de dedicarles la Fiesta de San Valentín.

CENTRO AMERICA

Don Marco Tulio y doña Rosario cumplieron 25 años de vida matrimonial, durante la cual han procreado a sus tres hijos: Marco Tulio, Rosario María y María José.

DEPORTES

La pareja aconseja a los nuevos matrimonios que sólo la comprensión, perseverancia, condescendencia y sobre todo el amor puede lograr la felicidad y la armonía familiar.

OPINION

Agregó, que el matrimonio es una institución que fortalece la estabilidad de cualquier persona y que además contribuye al desarrollo del país, pues es injusto ver a tanta madre soltera debido a la paternidad irresponsabilidad.

Don Marco Tulio y doña Rosario fueron finamente atendidos y recibieron varias muestras de cariño y admiración de parte de los asistentes y regalos sorpresas.

SOCIALES

Decenas de parejas de la sociedad sampedrana calorizaron esta festividad, quienes bailaron hasta altas de la madrugada y degustaron una exquisita cena a base de ensalada verde, ensalada cupido, filete con salsa dorada, surich de pollo, vegetales, arroz y papas al perejil, también unos deliciosos postres y finas bebidas.

Paso 1: Lee la **reseña social** (*social write-up*) y subraya las ideas principales.

Paso 2: Lee la reseña social una vez más. Luego marca con un círculo alrededor de las palabras y las expresiones clave.

Paso 3: Escribe las ideas principales.

Paso 4: Escribe un resumen de este artículo.

Paso 5: Lee la reseña social rápidamente y busca la información necesaria para completar las siguientes oraciones.

1. Don Marco Tulio y doña Rosario fueron nombrados los _____ el sábado por la noche en el Casino Sampedrano.
2. En la fiesta de San Valentín los administradores de este centro social escogen a _____, ejemplo de un buen _____ de la sociedad de San Pedro Sula.
3. Don Marco Tulio y doña Rosario cumplieron _____ de vida matrimonial y tienen _____ hijos.
4. El matrimonio es una institución que contribuye a _____ de una persona y al desarrollo de un país.
5. Las parejas bailaron hasta la madrugada y disfrutaron de una cena a base de _____ y _____.

Paso 6: Reacciones personales

1. ¿Qué te parece la idea de hacer una celebración para una pareja que tenga mucho tiempo de casada?
2. ¿Estás de acuerdo con **los consejos** (*advice*) que dan los señores Crespo sobre el matrimonio cuando dicen que la comprensión, la perseverancia y el amor son los elementos para un buen matrimonio? ¿Piensas que hay otros elementos importantes? ¿Cuáles son estos elementos?
3. ¿Crees que es importante el matrimonio para tener una buena sociedad?

¡A ESCRIBIR!

Strategy: Using expressions of frequency in descriptions of activities

Descriptive paragraphs occur in many contexts. They are often found in works of fiction such as novels and short stories but they also appear in newspaper articles, advertising materials, educational publications, and personal letters. A descriptive paragraph contains sentences that describe people, places, things, and/or events. In this chapter we will focus on describing events. To express how often events take place or how often you or others do something, you can use adverbs of frequency such as the following:

a veces	sometimes
cada año	each year
dos veces a la semana	twice a week
muchas veces	often
nunca	never
raras veces	rarely, infrequently
siempre	always
todos los días	every day
una vez al mes	once a month

You can also modify these expressions to express a wide variety of time frames: **dos veces al mes, tres veces a la semana, cada mes,** and so on.

Ahora, lee el siguiente párrafo y pon un círculo alrededor de los adverbios que expresan la frecuencia de una actividad.

Mi esposo Antonio y yo nos queremos mucho y tratamos de pasar mucho tiempo juntos. Cada día de la semana desayunamos juntos antes de ir al trabajo. No podemos cenar juntos todas las noches a causa del trabajo, pero una vez a la semana salimos a un restaurante para comer y para charlar. Muchas veces vamos a un restaurante cerca de nuestra casa, pero una vez condujimos a la playa y cenamos allí. Tenemos que limpiar la casa y hacer otros quehaceres durante el fin de semana, pero siempre pasamos un poco de tiempo juntos divirtiéndonos. Cada año planeamos un viaje especial para celebrar nuestro aniversario. Nunca quiero olvidar la importancia del tiempo que pasamos juntos.

Task: Writing a descriptive paragraph

Paso 1: Ahora, vas a escribir un párrafo para describir unas actividades que tú haces con tu familia o con otras personas importantes en tu vida. Para empezar, identifca a las personas que vas a incluir en la composición. Después, escribe una lista de actividades que tú haces con esas personas. Incluye un mínimo de ocho actividades.

Paso 2: Indica con qué frecuencia haces cada actividad en la lista. Puedes referirte a la lista de palabras y expresiones anterior.

Paso 3: Escribe un párrafo bien planeado en el cual describas las actividades que haces, las personas con quienes las haces y la frecuencia de cada actividad. Puedes organizar el párrafo basándote en las actividades o en las personas que hacen las actividades contigo.

Paso 4: Intercambia papeles con un(a) compañero(a) de clase. Lee el párrafo de la otra persona para ver si ha incluido la información necesaria en su composición. Si es necesario hacer algunos cambios, hazlos.

Paso 5: Habla con tu compañero(a) sobre las actividades que cada persona ha incluido en su composición y la frecuencia identificada para cada actividad. Comparen y contrasten Uds. las actividades que hacen y la frecuencia con que las hacen.

Functions: Expressing time relationships; Linking ideas; Talking about habitual actions
Vocabulary: Family members; Leisure; Time expressions
Grammar: Adverbs; Adverb types

¡A CONVERSAR!

Pronunciation focus: Review of pronunciation of vowels

The **a** in Spanish sounds like the English *a* in the word *craft*. The Spanish **e** sounds like the English *e* in the word *get*. The Spanish **i** is pronounced approximately like the English *i* in *machine*. The Spanish **o** is pronounced like the English *o* in *born,* and the Spanish **u** is pronounced like the English *oo* in *choose*. Practice these sentences.

- Mañana es el día de la boda de mi mejor amiga.
- Me gustan las flores en este ramo.
- No he visto las fotos de la luna de miel de mis padres.

Task: Discussing a wedding

El día de una boda es un día muy importante para los novios, su familia y sus amigos. Cada boda es única, pero la mayoría de las bodas tiene algunos aspectos en común. Ahora vas a conversar con un(a) amigo(a) sobre una boda. Puede ser una boda a la que asististe, una boda que viste en una película o en un programa de televisión o tu propia *(own)* boda.

Paso 1: Empieza por decirle a tu compañero(a) los datos básicos de la boda. Contesta las siguientes preguntas.

- ¿Cuándo fue?
- ¿Quiénes se casaron?
- ¿Dónde tuvo lugar la boda?
- ¿Quiénes asistieron a la boda?
- ¿Cómo fue? ¿Lo pasaron bien los invitados?

Paso 2: Añade otros detalles que consideres importantes. Puedes contestar las siguientes preguntas o escoger otra información.

- ¿Cómo fue la recepción? ¿Hubo una banda? ¿Bailaron los invitados?
- ¿Qué comida sirvieron? ¿Cómo estuvo la comida?
- ¿Cómo estaban vestidos los novios? ¿Y los invitados?
- ¿Hubo otro aspecto importante o divertido de la boda?

Paso 3: Cambia de papel con tu compañero(a) y habla sobre otra boda. Incluye tanta información y tantos detalles como sea posible.

Paso 4: Concluye con una presentación de opiniones y preferencias sobre estas bodas y las bodas en general.

Las relaciones sentimentales Relationships

Sustantivos

la amistad friendship	**el divorcio** divorce	**el novio** groom
el amor love	**la flor** flower	**el ramo** bouquet
la boda wedding	**la luna de miel** honeymoon	**los recién casados** newlyweds
el cariño affection	**el matrimonio** marriage	**la separación** separation
la cita date *(social)*	**el noviazgo** courtship	**la vida** life
el compromiso engagement	**la novia** bride	

Verbos

abrazar(se) to hug (each other)	**divorciarse (de)** to get divorced (from)	**romper (con)** to break up (with)
amar to love	**enamorarse (de)** to fall in love (with)	**salir (con)** to go out (with)
besar(se) to kiss (each other)	**llevarse bien (mal) (con)** to get along well (poorly) (with)	**separarse (de)** to separate (from)
casarse (con) to get married, marry	**querer** to love	**tirar** to throw
darse la mano to shake hands		

La recepción

Sustantivos

el banquete banquet	**la orquesta** band	**la pareja** couple
los invitados guests		

Verbos

acompañar to accompany	**asistir (a)** to attend *(a function)*	**tener lugar** to take place
agarrar to catch	**felicitar** to congratulate	**terminar** to end
aplaudir to applaud	**hacer un brindis** to make a toast	

Adverbios

a veces sometimes	**finalmente** finally	**primero** first
cada día (semana, etc.) each day (week, etc.)	**luego** then	**solamente** only, just
(casi) siempre (almost) always	**muchas veces** very often	**todos los años (días, meses, etc.)** every year (day, month, etc.)
después afterward	**nunca** never	
dos (tres, etc.) veces twice (three times, etc.)	**otra vez** again	**una vez** once
entonces then; so	**por fin** at last, finally	

Participios pasados

abierto opened	**hecho** done; made	**visto** seen
dicho said; told	**muerto** died	**vuelto** returned
escrito written	**puesto** put	

Expresiones idiomáticas

a primera vista at first sight	**vestido(a) de gala** dressed elegantly

El mundo del trabajo:

Chapter Objectives

COMMUNICATIVE GOALS

In this chapter you will learn how to . . .

- Talk about professions, the office, and work-related activities
- Make statements about motives, intentions, and periods of time
- Describe the job hunt, benefits, and personal finances
- Express subjectivity and uncertainty
- Express desires and intentions

STRUCTURES

- **Por** and **para**
- Subjunctive mood and impersonal expressions with the subjunctive
- Formation of the present subjunctive and statements of volition

CULTURAL INFORMATION

- El Canal de Panamá
- Protocolo en los negocios del mundo hispanohablante

Panamá

PANAMÁ

Población: 13.183.978

Área: 41.283.560
kilómetros cuadrados, más o menos
del tamaño de Nevada

Capital: Panamá, 1.017.600

Ciudades principales: David, 79.100;
La Chorrea, 56.900; Colón, 42.900

Moneda: el balboa y el dólar
estadounidense

Lenguas: el español y el inglés

¡Bienvenidos a Panamá!

**En este vídeo, vas a aprender de
Panamá. Después de ver el video,
contesta las siguientes preguntas:**

1 ¿Dónde está Panamá?

2 Según el video, ¿qué es el Canal de Panamá y por qué es
conocido internacionalmente?

3 ¿Cuáles son algunos otros atractivos que ofrece al mundo
el país de Panamá?

4 Según el video, ¿cómo se llama la fiesta que todo
panameño espera con anticipación? ¿en qué consiste?

5 ¿Te gustaría hacer un viaje a Panamá? ¿Por qué sí o por
qué no?

La Plaza del Monumento
Francés, la Ciudad de Panamá,
Panamá

315

CULTURA

Panama is one of the most strategically located countries in Central America. As early as the sixteenth century, the idea of building a canal in Panama to connect the Atlantic and Pacific oceans was debated. After declaring its independence from Spain in 1821, Panama became part of la Gran Colombia, a territory comprised of what is today known as Ecuador, Colombia, and Venezuela. Motivated by interest in ratifying a treaty that would allow the Panama Canal to be built, the United States helped Panama gain its independence from Colombia in 1903.

En una oficina de Panamá In this section you will learn to talk about professions in the working world.

¿NOS ENTENDEMOS?

The Spanish language is constantly changing to accommodate the entrance of women into professions previously dominated by men. Some job titles are modified by **la mujer;** for example, **la mujer policía.** Note that while it was once acceptable, in some places, to change **el presidente** into **la presidenta,** many feminists insisted on keeping the original form of the word **presidente** and modifying it only with the feminine article **la:** for example, **el (la) presidente, el (la) médico** or **el (la) jefe.**

¿NOS ENTENDEMOS?

Don't confuse the following words: **la policía** (police), **la póliza** (insurance policy), and **la política** (politics; policy).

Palabras útiles are presented to help you enrich your personal vocabulary. The words here will help you talk about jobs and professions.

Más profesiones

el (la) **abogado(a)** lawyer
el (la) **arquitecto(a)** architect
el (la) **carpintero(a)** carpenter
el (la) **contador(a)** accountant
el (la) **empleado(a)** employee
el (la) **gerente** manager
el (la) **jefe** boss

el (la) **maestro(a)** teacher
el (la) **obrero(a)** worker, laborer
el (la) **periodista** journalist
el (la) **programador(a)** programmer
el (la) **traductor(a)** translator
el (la) **veterinario(a)** veterinarian

Palabras útiles

el (la) **accionista** stockbroker
el (la) **analista de sistemas** systems analyst
el (la) **bombero(a)** firefighter
el (la) **cajero(a)** cashier
el (la) **comerciante** merchant
el (la) **criado(a)** servant; maid
el (la) **electricista** electrician
el (la) **intérprete** interpreter
el (la) **mecánico(a)** mechanic
el (la) **ranchero(a)** rancher
el (la) **reportero(a)** reporter
el (la mujer) **soldado** soldier
el (la) **técnico** technician
el (la) **vendedor(a)** salesperson

¡A PRACTICAR!

11-1 | **¿A quién vas a llamar?** Tú trabajas para una agencia de empleos en la Ciudad de Panamá y estás tratando de identificar las profesiones que tus clientes buscan. Lee las siguientes descripciones y decide cuál de las profesiones mejor corresponde a cada situación.

> MODELO: hombre / preparar comida en el Restaurante Las Palmas
> *un cocinero*

1. mujer / enseñar a chicas activas en la escuela Nuestra Señora de las Lágrimas *la maestra*
2. mujer / sacar fotos de la boda de nuestra querida hija, Alejandra *la fotógrafa*
3. hombre o mujer / escribir documentos legales *la mujer de negocios o abogado*
4. mujer / recibir y contar dinero de nuestros clientes en el Banco Central *el banquero*
5. hombre / ayudar en el diseño *(design)* de un nuevo centro comercial *el ingeniero*
6. mujer / ayudar a nuestros clientes con problemas emocionales *el siquiatra*
7. mujer / escribir artículos cortos sobre la moda para *La Prensa* *la periodista*
8. mujer / supervisar un departamento de una compañía *el jefe o gerente*
9. hombre / ayudar con las finanzas de una gran corporación *el contador*
10. mujer / construir un nuevo cuarto en una residencia personal *el arquitecto o carpinero*

CULTURA
La Prensa is a daily newspaper in Panama with one of the highest circulation numbers in the country.

11-2 | **¡Una niñera *(nanny)* desesperada!** Tu amiga Dora está cuidando a los dos hijos de su hermana Susana. Te llama pidiendo consejos para las siguientes situaciones. ¿A quién debe llamar Dora?

1. ¡El lavabo de la cocina está atascado *(clogged)* y hay agua por todos lados! *el plomero*
2. ¡Miguelito acaba de romperse dos dientes! *el dentista*
3. ¡Tomás me cortó el pelo cuando me dormí en el sofá! *la peluquera*
4. ¡Miguelito le dio una patada *(kicked)* a la computadora y ahora no funciona! *el programador o técnico*
5. ¡Tomás se robó unos juguetes de una tienda y el gerente está aquí y está muy enojado! *la policía*
6. ¡Los niños le dieron chocolate al perrito!
7. ¡Tomás y Miguelito tienen hambre y yo quemé la cena!
8. ¡Las instrucciones para el televisor solamente están en francés!

EN VOZ ALTA

11-3 **Impresiones del mundo del trabajo** Dale tus impresiones de las siguientes profesiones a un(a) compañero(a) de clase, escogiendo de la siguiente lista de adjetivos. Explica tu respuesta. Puedes modificar los adjetivos con adverbios como **muy, un poco** y **demasiado**. ¿Tienes mucho en común con tu compañero(a)?

> MODELO: el hombre (la mujer) de negocios
> E1: *Yo creo que ser hombre (mujer) de negocios es aburrido.*
> E2: *Pues, yo pienso que ser hombre (mujer) de negocios es interesante. Los hombres (Las mujeres) de negocios siempre viajan y ganan mucho dinero. Yo quiero ser hombre (mujer) de negocios algún día.*

interesante/aburrido   creativo/rutinario
peligroso/seguro   variado/monótono
flexible/rígido   divertido/aburrido
exigente/fácil   prestigioso/ordinario

1. el (la) veterinario(a)
2. el (la) obrero(a)
3. el (la) peluquero(a)
4. el (la) periodista
5. el (la) maestro(a)
6. el (la) abogado(a)

11-4 **Entrevista** Trabajando con dos compañeros(as) de clase, háganse las siguientes preguntas sobre las profesiones.

1. ¿Tienes un trabajo ahora? ¿Qué haces? ¿Cuántas horas a la semana trabajas?
2. Cuando te gradúes de la universidad, ¿qué quieres hacer? ¿Por qué? ¿Qué clases te dan preparación para tus planes en el futuro?
3. ¿Cuáles son las profesiones más populares entre tus amigos?
4. ¿Cuáles son las carreras de mayor prestigio en nuestra sociedad? ¿de menor prestigio? ¿Hay alguna profesión que te guste pero que no vas a hacer porque no es prestigiosa?
5. Pensando en los miembros de tu clase, ¿cuáles son las profesiones más adecuadas para algunos de ellos?

11-5 **Encuesta** En grupos de cuatro o cinco personas, háganse las siguientes preguntas. Comparen sus respuestas para después compartirlas con toda la clase.

> MODELO: *En nuestro grupo, hay dos personas que quieren ser abogados, una que quiere ser ingeniera y una que quiere ser mujer de negocios. Tres de nosotros queremos trabajar en una compañía pequeña, y una persona quiere trabajar por su cuenta. Pensamos que la profesión más peligrosa es la de policía. La profesión más aburrida para nosotros es la de contador(a). A todos nosotros nos importa ganar mucho dinero. El trabajo más lucrativo es el de abogado(a).*

1. ¿Qué profesión te interesa para después de la universidad?
2. ¿Quieres trabajar en una compañía pequeña, una compañía grande, por tu cuenta *(for yourself)*, para el gobierno o... ?
3. ¿Qué trabajo te parece el más peligroso de todos?
4. ¿Qué trabajo te parece el más aburrido de todos?
5. ¿Te importa ganar mucho dinero en el trabajo? En tu opinión, ¿cuál es el trabajo más lucrativo?

Text audio
Track 2-8

Julián Darío está solicitando un puesto *(applying for a job)* en una oficina de abogados. Lo que sigue es parte de la entrevista con Carlos Infante Garrido, el jefe de la empresa.

Carlos: Buenos días, Julián. Siéntate.

Julián: Gracias, Sr. Garrido. Ud. es muy amable.

Carlos: Gracias a ti, Julián, por venir *(for coming)* a charlar con nosotros. Tienes un currículum *(résumé)* fabuloso **para un hombre tan joven.**

Julián: Pues, he tenido algunas oportunidades buenas.

Carlos: No seas tan modesto. Tienes todas las cualidades que esperamos de un abogado que trabaja para nosotros. ¿Y quieres trabajar **para nosotros**?

Julián: ¡Sí, señor! **Espero que Uds. me ofrezcan** el puesto, ya que yo tengo mucho con lo que puedo contribuir a su bufete *(law office)* de **abogados**.

Carlos: ¡No te preocupes *(Don't worry)*, Julián! La verdad es que no habíamos encontrado a la persona adecuada todavía. **Quiero que nuestros abogados tengan** suficientes responsabilidades y que **sean** dedicados, honestos y, sobre todo, muy profesionales con los clientes.

Julián: Pues, le puedo asegurar con respecto a *(with regard to)* estas cualidades. **Por ejemplo,** que soy muy trabajador, me gusta tener responsabilidades y...

Carlos: Ya lo sé, Julián. Tu currículum lo dice todo. ¡No me digas más! *(Say no more!)* El puesto es tuyo, si lo quieres.

> **CULTURA**
> Note how Carlos uses **tú** to address a subordinate while Julián uses **Ud.**, a sign of respect in addressing a superior. It is important to remember to use **Ud.** in business situations.

¿Comprendiste?

Contesta las siguientes preguntas con oraciones completas.

1. ¿Por qué está tan impresionado el jefe, Carlos, con Julián?
2. ¿Por qué piensa Carlos que Julián es modesto?
3. ¿Hay otros candidatos que Carlos esté considerando?
4. Para Carlos, ¿qué atributos son importantes para los abogados que trabajan en su bufete u oficina de abogados?
5. ¿Cree Julián que él puede hacer el trabajo?
6. ¿Cómo termina la entrevista? ¿Recibe Julián el puesto?
7. ¿Piensas tú que Carlos debe hacerle más preguntas a Julián?

El Canal de Panamá

La esclusa de Gatún, Canal de Panamá

Barco de crucero o de turista cruzando el Canal de Panamá

PARA PENSAR

- ¿Conoces los nombres de algunos canales famosos?
- ¿Para qué sirven los canales?
- ¿Por qué crees que es necesario el Canal de Panamá?

El primero que pensó en abrir un paso por el Istmo de Panamá para unir los dos océanos fue Vasco Núñez de Balboa en 1513. En 1870 el gobierno francés y el gobierno estadounidense comenzaron a discutir la construcción de un canal para ayudar al transporte mundial. El costo *(expense)* económico para la construcción del canal del gobierno de los Estados Unidos con el gobierno de Francia fue de 639 millones de dólares. Más de 80.000 trabajaron en esta obra, donde murieron 30.000 personas; les tomó 34 años a los dos gobiernos terminar el canal. Finalmente, los Estados Unidos terminaron la construcción en 1914 y el 15 de agosto del mismo año cruzó el primer barco oficial de carga *(cargo ship)* americano llamado el *SS Ancon.*

El canal está situado en el punto más angosto *(narrow)* entre el Océano Pacífico y el Atlántico. El canal es la única vía de comunicación hoy día que conecta los dos océanos. Esta ruta es la más económica en cuanto al *(with regard to)* dinero y al tiempo necesarios para transportar mercancía y productos de un lado al otro de las Américas.

El canal es la fuente de trabajo más importante para la economía panameña, ya que le da al gobierno una gran cantidad de contratos, trabajos e ingresos. La economía del país se concentra en el área urbana central de Panamá que rodea *(surrounds)* el canal. En 1977, el presidente de los Estados Unidos, Jimmy Carter y el presidente de Panamá, Omar Torrijos, firmaron un acuerdo, donde el gobierno de los Estados Unidos le daba los derechos de la administración del canal al gobierno panameño el 31 de diciembre de 1999. Desde entonces, Panamá administra el canal y con muchísimo éxito.

PARA DISCUTIR

1. ¿Quiénes pensaron a través de la historia en construir un canal entre los dos océanos?
2. ¿Cuántos años tomó la construcción del canal y cuándo se abrió el canal al mundo?
3. ¿Por qué ayuda a la economía mundial el uso del canal?
4. Para ti, ¿quién crees que debería administrar el canal, Panamá, los Estados Unidos o los dos países juntos? ¿Por qué?

ESTRUCTURA I Making statements about motives, intentions, and periods of time: *por* vs. *para*

Uses of *por*

You may have noticed that the prepositions **por** and **para** have different uses and meanings. The preposition **por** has a wider range of uses than **para.** In general, **por** conveys the underlying idea of a cause, reason, or source behind an action.

1. **Duration of time** *(for, in, during)*

   —¿**Por** cuánto tiempo viviste en Panamá?

   (For) How long did you live in Panama?

   —Viví allí **por** más de tres años.

   I lived there for more than three years.

   —¿Trabajas en la clínica todo el día?

   Do you work in the clinic all day?

   —Sí, **por** la mañana y **por** la tarde.

   Yes, during the morning and during the afternoon.

2. **Motion** *(through, along)*

   —¿Quieres caminar conmigo **por** la oficina para conocer a la gente?

   Would you like to walk through the office with me to meet the people?

3. **General area** *(around)*

   —Perdón, ¿hay una fotocopiadora **por** aquí?

   Excuse me, is there a copy machine around here?

   —Sí, señora. Hay una **por** allí.

   Yes, ma'am. There is one over there.

4. **In exchange** *(for)*

   —¿Desea cambiar esta máquina de escribir?

   Would you like to exchange this typewriter?

   —Sí, **por** una computadora, por favor.

   Yes, for a computer, please.

5. **Value or cost** *(for)*

   —¿Cuánto pagaste **por** los servicios del abogado?

   How much did you pay for the lawyer's services?

   —Le pagué $500 **por** su tiempo.

   I paid him $500 for his time.

6. **In place of** *(for)*

   —Yo no sabía que trabajas aquí, Tomás.

   I didn't know you work here, Tomás.

   —Trabajo **por** Juan, que está muy enfermo.

   I'm working for (substituting for) Juan, who is very ill.

7. **Gratitude** *(for)*

   —Gracias **por** toda su ayuda, Sr. Navarro.

   Thanks for all your help, Mr. Navarro.

   —De nada. ¡Buena suerte con el proyecto!

   You're welcome. Good luck with the project!

8. **On behalf of** *(for)*

   —Hola, Miguel. Vengo a verte **por** parte de mis hijos.

   Hello, Miguel. I've come to see you on behalf of my kids.

9. **Mistaken identity** *(for)*

   —En Panamá me tomaron **por** canadiense.

   In Panama, they took me for a Canadian.

   —¿Sabes qué? ¡Me tomaron **por** mexicana!

   You know what? They took me for a Mexican!

10. **Unit of measurement** *(by, per)*

—La secretaria escribe más de sesenta palabras **por** minuto.

The secretary writes more than sixty words per minute.

11. **Reason** *(because of)*

—¡Hombre, viniste muy tarde a la oficina!

Wow, you arrived late at the office!

—Llegué tarde **por** el tráfico tan tremendo.

I arrived late because of all the terrible traffic.

12. **Purpose** *(for, after)* followed by noun

—¿Vas a la oficina **por** tu cheque?

Are you going to the office for your check?

—Sí, y después voy a la tienda **por** comida.

Yes, and afterward I'm going to the store for some food.

13. **Idiomatic expressions**

Por favor. *Please.*

¡Por Dios! *¡Oh my God!*

Por eso... *That's why . . .*

Por casualidad... *By the way . . .*

¡Por supuesto! *Of course!*

Por ejemplo *For example*

Uses of *para*

In general, **para** conveys the underlying idea of purpose (goal), use, and destination.

1. **Recipient** *(for)*

—Estos papeles son **para** la jefe.

These papers are for the boss.

2. **Employment** *(for)*

—¿**Para** quién trabajas ahora?

For whom do you work now?

—Trabajo **para** mi papá en su oficina.

I work for my father in his office.

3. **Specific time** *(by, for)*

—¿**Para** cuándo necesita el dinero, señora?

(By) When do you need the money, ma'am?

—Lo necesito **para** el próximo sábado.

I need it by (for) next Saturday.

4. **Destination** *(to, for)*

—¿**Para** dónde sales mañana por la tarde?

(To) Where are you going tomorrow afternoon?

—Salgo **para** la costa.

I'm leaving for the coast.

5. **Purpose** *(in order to)* + infinitive

—¿Por qué estudias español?

Why do you study Spanish?

—Lo estudio **para** hablar con mis clientes.

I study it in order to speak with my clients.

6. **Member of a group** *(for)*

—**Para** un chico de diez años, él es muy responsable.

For a ten-year-old, he is very responsible.

7. **To show one's opinion** *(for)*

—**Para** Elena, es mejor trabajar por la mañana.

For Elena, it is better to work in the morning.

—**Para** mí, el peluquero tiene un trabajo fascinante.

For me (In my opinion), the hairstylist has a fascinating job.

¡A PRACTICAR!

11-6 **¿Por o para?** Escoge entre **por** o **para** para completar las siguientes oraciones y explica por qué. Luego, hazle las preguntas a un(a) compañero(a) de clase.

1. ¿Vives por / para trabajar o trabajas por / para vivir?
2. ¿Prefieres trabajar por / para la mañana o por / para la tarde?
3. ¿Pasas por / para el campus universitario todos los días?
4. ¿Vas a trabajar por / para una compañía multinacional o por / para una compañía pequeña?
5. Por / Para ti, ¿cuál es la profesión menos agradable?
6. ¿Trabajaste alguna vez por / para una persona que estuviera (*was*) enferma?
7. ¿Por / Para cuánto tiempo has estudiado en esta universidad?
8. ¿Cuánto pagaste por / para tus libros este semestre?
9. ¿Por / Para dónde vas al final del semestre?
10. ¿Por / Para cuándo necesitas entregar tu próximo trabajo escrito?

11-7 **¿Qué sabes de los indios cunas?** Escoge entre **por** o **para,** a fin de (*in order to*) completar las siguiente narración sobre un grupo indígena de Panamá.

1. Los indios cunas han vivido en la isla de San Blas por / para varios siglos.
2. Ellos hacen tapices llamados «molas» por / para vender. Estos tapices son hechos por las mujeres.
3. Los indios cunas tienen canciones por / para curar enfermedades de la mente.
4. Los indios cunas usan la naturaleza por / para explicar los fenómenos positivos o negativos relacionados con el ser humano.

11-8 **Una encuesta** Elena va al Banco Central. Una empleada le hace algunas preguntas. Con un(a) compañero(a), completen la conversación, usando las preposiciones **por** o **para** en el diálogo. Luego, actúen la escena para la clase.

Empleada

1. ¿_____ qué viene Ud. aquí, señora?
3. ¿_____ qué decidió Ud. venir aquí ahora por la mañana?
5. Generalmente, ¿cuándo viene aquí _____ usar nuestros servicios?
7. ¿Cuánto paga _____ los servicios de este banco?
9. ¿Le parece razonable?
11. ¡Muy bien! _____ casualidad, ¿conoce Ud. a nuestra cajera, Susana?
13. ¡Ah! _____ eso se parecen tanto. Permítame una última pregunta, _____ favor: ¿Qué impresión tiene Ud. del Banco Central?
15. Gracias _____ su cooperación.

Elena

2. _____ servicio rápido y porque es muy conveniente.
4. _____ depositar dinero.
6. Los sábados _____ la mañana.
8. Quince balboas _____ mes.
10. Sí, _____ mí está muy bien. Y voy a abrir otra cuenta (*account*) _____ mi hija en un año.
12. Sí, alguien me tomó _____ ella el otro día. ¡Ja, ja! Ella es mi hermana.
14. _____ mí, es un banco fabuloso.
16. De nada, señora.

> **CULTURA**
> The **balboa** is the official monetary unit of Panama. It is roughly equivalent to the U.S. dollar. In fact, the Panamanian government makes only coins for smaller amounts than the balboa and circulates paper dollars issued by the U.S. government—this is a manner of maintaining the balboa's stability on a level more or less equal to the U.S. dollar at all times.

EN VOZ ALTA

11-9 **¿Qué sabes tú de Panamá?** Con otro(a) estudiante, hagan una conversación, usando la siguiente información. Estudiante 1 tiene unas preguntas sobre Panamá. Estudiante 2 tiene una lista de información sobre Panamá, y tiene que buscar la respuesta para cada pregunta. Noten el uso de **por** y **para** en las preguntas y en las respuestas.

CULTURA
El Canal de Panamá, or the Panama Canal, was first put into use in 1914. The United States controlled and ran the canal during the entire twentieth century. On December 31, 1999, the canal was officially handed over to Panama. During the last years of U.S. control, as much as 93% of the workforce running the canal was Panamanian. Thus, the transfer was quite smooth. The Panama Canal affords travel by sea from the Atlantic to the Pacific oceans (or vice versa) without having to go around the entire continent of South America—thus saving thousands of miles and unnecessary time at sea for ocean transport.

CULTURA
La Panamericana, or the Panamerican Highway, is a highway that begins at Fairbanks, Alaska, and continues almost without interruption down to Tierra del Fuego in Argentina. There is only one area where this highway could not be built: the highway is missing a stretch of about 150 kilometers between Panama and Colombia. This break in the road is called the Darien Gap.

CULTURA
La Zona Libre de Colón, or the Colon Free Trade Zone, is located in Colon. It is an enclosed commercial park where companies can import and export goods—normally on a wholesale level—without great governmental interference and without having to pay international duties. Colon is a port city located at the entrance of the Panama Canal on the Caribbean coast. It is also famous for its bazaars, beautiful beaches, and colonial Spanish fortress.

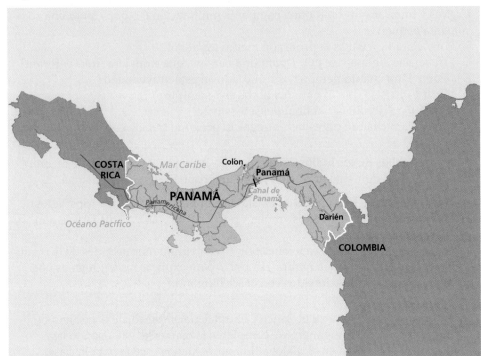

Estudiante 1

1. ¿Hay que pasar **por** otros países **para** llegar de los Estados Unidos a Panamá?
2. ¿Hay un sitio **por** donde los barcos pueden pasar del Océano Atlántico al Pacífico en Panamá?
3. **Para** los turistas, ¿hay playas bonitas en Panamá?
4. ¿Hay algún lugar especial **para** hacer compras?
5. ¿Se puede viajar **por** Panamá en autobús?
6. ¿Pasa la Panamericana **por** Panamá?

Estudiante 2

a. El Canal de Panamá es el único sitio **por** donde los barcos pueden pasar del Océano Atlántico al Pacífico.
b. **Para** llegar de los Estados Unidos a Panamá, hay que pasar **por** México y **por** toda Centroamérica.
c. La Panamericana cruza casi todo el país de Panamá, excepto **por** 150 kilómetros de la región de Darién, donde es imposible construir carreteras.
d. La Zona Libre de Colón es un lugar especial **para** mayoristas *(wholesalers)* donde no hay impuestos de importación.
e. Panamá tiene un sistema bastante bueno de autobuses **para** viajar alrededor del país.
f. La Isla Taboga es un lugar histórico de Panamá que tiene una playa muy bonita. Hay varias playas en el país, y también muchos lugares históricos.

VOCABULARIO La oficina, el trabajo y la búsqueda de un puesto

Solicitando un puesto en la oficina de Infante Garrido y Garrido: Abogados In this section you will learn how to talk about a typical office environment and work-related activities. You will also learn words and expressions related to the job search.

Sustantivos

los beneficios benefits
la empresa corporation; business
la entrevista interview

el puesto job, position
el salario/sueldo salary
la solicitud application (form)

Verbos

contratar to hire
dejar to quit
despedir (i, i) to fire
imprimir to print
jubilarse to retire
llenar to fill out (a form)
renunciar to resign
reunirse to meet

Expresiones idiomáticas

de tiempo completo/parcial full-time/part-time
llamar por teléfono to make a phone call
pedir un aumento to ask for a raise
solicitar un puesto to apply for a job

> **¿NOS ENTENDEMOS?**
> The following words can be useful when filling out a job application in Spanish: **la letra de molde** (print), **el estado civil** (marital status), **actual** (current, present), **el sueldo mensual** (monthly salary), **el puesto desempeñado** (position held).

¡A PRACTICAR!

11-10 **Emparejar** Empareja la definición de la derecha que mejor corresponda a cada una de las palabras o frases de la izquierda.

1. _____ jubilarse
2. _____ de tiempo completo
3. _____ la solicitud
4. _____ solicitar un puesto
5. _____ la impresora
6. _____ imprimir
7. _____ despedir

a. trabajar desde las 8:00 hasta las 5:00 todos los días
b. producir un documento escrito de una computadora
c. algo que se conecta con la computadora
d. dejar de trabajar después de muchos años
e. el formulario que entregas con el currículum
f. eliminar una persona de la empresa
g. buscar un trabajo nuevo

11-11 **Un día en la vida de Sofía** Sofía es la secretaria de la oficina de Infante Garrido y Garrido. Completa la historia a continuación con las palabras de la lista para describir un día en su trabajo. En algunos casos vas a tener que conjugar los verbos.

imprimir
reunirse
llenar
correo electrónico
llamar por teléfono
pedir un aumento
puesto

sala de conferencias
renunciar
tiempo parcial
beneficios
candidato
fax

Yo tengo un 1. _____ en la oficina de Infante Garrido y Garrido. Aunque el sueldo no es muy alto, los 2. _____ que me dan son buenos. ¡El problema es que me dan demasiado que hacer! Tengo que contestar cuando alguien 3. _____. Paso mucho tiempo trabajando con el 4. _____ cuando la gente manda documentos urgentes. También, yo tengo que contestar los mensajes que vienen en la computadora por 5. _____. A veces necesito 6. _____ los mensajes para mi jefe porque él no sabe usar la computadora. A veces, me hacen 7. _____ formularios muy importantes, y me pongo nerviosa. Estoy cansada de trabajar tanto; estoy pensando 8. _____ si no encontramos a alguien más para ayudarme. Buscamos un 9. _____ para un puesto de 10. _____ para ayudarme por la mañana. Además, los jefes de la oficina van a 11. _____ en la 12. _____ para hablar de mí esta tarde —yo les acabo de 13. _____ de sueldo. ¡A ver qué pasa!

El caso de un empleado despedido Escogiendo de la lista de palabras, completa la siguiente narrativa sobre el nuevo empleado de Infante Garrido y Garrido. En algunos casos, vas a tener que conjugar los verbos.

¿NOS ENTENDEMOS?

The words **la empresa, la compañía,** and **el negocio** often can be used interchangeably to mean *business.* The word *job* may be expressed as **el trabajo** or **el puesto** while **la colocación** or **la plaza** may be used in more formal language.

sueldo   dejar   jubilarse

contratar   proyectos   informe

fotocopiadora   entrevista   empresa

despedir   currículum   computadora

reunión

La oficina de Infante Garrido y Garrido 1. _____ a Julián Darío el año pasado. Julián tenía un 2. _____ impresionante y le cayó muy bien a Carlos durante la 3. _____. Por eso, Carlos le ofreció un 4. _____ muy bueno y una 5. _____ nueva. Julián los aceptó y él y su esposa se mudaron a la Ciudad de Panamá para poder estar más cerca de la 6. _____. Durante el primer mes el jefe estaba muy contento con el trabajo de Julián. Carlos pensó que por fin podía 7. _____ sin preocupaciones.

    Los problemas empezaron el segundo mes cuando Julián faltó a una 8. _____ importante y empezó a entregar documentos tarde. Además, dejaba documentos importantes en la 9. _____ y en dos ocasiones no firmó testamentos (*wills*). Además, Carlos encontró el 10. _____ anual, que él había escrito sobre los 11. _____ del año pasado, en la basura de Julián.

    Carlos lo 12. _____ al día siguiente. Julián le dijo que él iba a 13. _____ el puesto de todos modos (*anyway*).

EN VOZ ALTA

Adivinanzas Con un(a) compañero(a), túrnense describiendo las palabras en la lista sin usar la misma palabra. Tu compañero(a) tiene que adivinar (*guess*) la palabra que estás describiendo.

> MODELO: el currículum
> E1: *Es un papel en que un(a) candidato(a) escribe todos los trabajos que él o ella ha tenido. Un(a) candidato(a) les da este papel a las compañías donde quiere trabajar.*
> E2: *¿Es el currículum?*
> E1: *¡Sí!*

E1

los beneficios

la fotocopiadora

el fax

la sala de conferencias

E2

despedir

un trabajo de tiempo completo

pedir un aumento

la entrevista

11-14 **Para solicitar un puesto** Con un(a) compañero(a) de clase, hablen de lo que se necesita para conseguir un trabajo. Después, hagan una lista de los pasos *(steps)*. Usen las sugerencias a continuación para sacar ideas. **¡OJO!** Las sugerencias no están en orden —es necesario cambiarlas un poco para tu lista.

MODELO: 1. *Es necesario preparar un currículum para describir tu experiencia de trabajo.*
2. *Hay que buscar una compañía interesante para ti.*
3. *Tienes que escribirle una carta al jefe de la compañía.*
4. ...

- preparar el currículum
- hacer preguntas sobre la empresa, el puesto y el sueldo
- contestar un anuncio en el periódico
- celebrar
- ir a la oficina
- llenar una solicitud

- pedir cartas de recomendación y referencias personales
- comprar un traje/vestido nuevo
- conocer a los otros empleados
- presentarse al jefe y contestar preguntas
- levantarse temprano y vestirse cuidadosamente

11-15 **La entrevista** Con un(a) compañero(a), hagan una entrevista de trabajo entre un(a) candidato(a) y el (la) jefe de Infante Garrido y Garrido. A la izquierda, hay una lista de información para el (la) candidato(a). A la derecha hay información para el (la) jefe. Formen preguntas y respuestas con la información.

El (La) candidato(a)

Información sobre ti:
Tienes mucha experiencia.
Has trabajado tres años en una oficina.
Nunca vienes tarde al trabajo.
Nunca pides días de vacaciones.
¿ ?

Tú quieres saber si la compañía...

ofrece un buen sueldo.
es una compañía con buena reputación.

ofrece beneficios.

tiene un puesto disponible *(available)* de tiempo completo.

El final de la entrevista:
Decide si el trabajo te interesa o no.

Explica al (a la) jefe tus razones.

El (La) jefe

Quieres saber si el (la) candidato(a)...
tiene experiencia.
tiene más de dos años de experiencia.
es responsable, confiable.
necesita mucho tiempo libre.
¿ ?

Información sobre la compañía / el puesto:
El puesto paga $800 al mes.
La compañía tiene más de cuarenta años de experiencia.
La compañía tiene un buen plan de seguro médico.
Buscamos a alguien para un puesto de tiempo parcial.

El final de la entrevista:
Decide si el (la) candidato(a) te interesa o no.

Ofrécele el trabajo si quieres, o explícale por qué no le quieres ofrecer el trabajo.

Encuentro cultural

Protocolo en los negocios del mundo hispanohablante

PARA PENSAR

- ¿Cómo te gusta que te llamen en tu trabajo, por tu apellido o por tu nombre?
- ¿Cuáles son para ustedes algunas normas de cortesía y respeto dentro del mundo de los negocios?

Saludos en el mundo de negocios hispano

Muchas veces las interacciones personales entre los hispanos en el mundo de los negocios son más formales que en los Estados Unidos. Muchas veces en los Estados Unidos, las personas llaman a sus clientes por el primer nombre; esto no pasa en el mundo hispanohablante porque puede ser interpretado como una falta de respeto *(lack of respect)*. Es más común llamar a los colegas o clientes por su título y apellido. Por ejemplo, a la gerente general de una compañía, la señorita Rosario González, es más común llamarla «Srta. González» que «Rosario».

Los colegas se saludan al principio del día y se despiden al final de la tarde con frases más formales como «Buenos días», «Hasta mañana». Estas frases también se usan con los clientes.

Muchas reuniones de negocios comienzan y terminan con un apretón de manos *(handshake)*. La distancia que la gente mantiene entre sí es generalmente menor que la distancia que la gente mantiene en los Estados Unidos, especialmente en una conversación animada. Muchas veces en una conversación una persona le puede tocar levemente *(lightly)* el brazo a la otra persona mientras conversan.

La jerarquía *(hierarchy)* en los negocios hispanos está bien definida. Los subordinados generalmente saludan al (a la) director(a) o al (a la) gerente general usando su título y su apellido, y lo (la) tratan de **Ud.** aunque muchas veces el (la) gerente use **tú** con los subordinados. Los colegas del mismo nivel pueden usar **tú** o **Ud.**, dependiendo de la diferencia de edad y el grado de familiaridad entre ellos. Algunos(as) jefes tratan a sus empleados de Ud. como un medio para mantener el respeto y distancia en el ambiente de trabajo.

PARA DISCUTIR

1. ¿Cómo tratan los directores o gerentes a sus clientes o subordinados en el mundo hispano de negocios?
2. ¿Cómo se saludan generalmente?
3. ¿Cuál es la distancia entre los participantes en una conversación dinámica?
4. ¿Cuáles son las diferencias más importantes en el trato entre los empleados en los Estados Unidos y el mundo hispanohablante?

ESTRUCTURA II Expressing subjectivity and uncertainty: the subjunctive mood

Thus far in *Plazas* you have been learning the indicative mood of the present and past tenses. The indicative mood is used to state facts and ask questions objectively. A second mood exists in Spanish called the subjunctive mood. The subjunctive is used to express more subjective concepts as well as to make statements about wishes, wants, and emotions. The subjunctive is also used to express doubt, uncertainty, or negation. You will learn more about the subjunctive mood in **Estructura III** of **Capítulo 11**. The formation of the subjunctive follows the same procedure as that of formal commands. For now, you should at least be able to recognize the subjunctive mood and have a basic understanding of why the subjunctive is used. Here are a few examples of the subjunctive mood and the contexts that require it:

volition/influence	Yo quiero que tú **vayas** a la reunión. *I want you to go to the meeting.*
emotion	Siento que el empleado no **reciba** un aumento. *I'm sorry the employee does not receive a raise.*
doubt	Ella duda que Ramón **termine** el proyecto hoy. *She doubts that Ramon will finish the project today.*
negation/denial	No es cierto que Pedro **sepa** usar el fax. *It's not certain that Pedro knows how to use the fax.*

¡A PRACTICAR!

11-16 **Reconocer el subjuntivo** Mira las siguientes oraciones y explica por qué usan el subjuntivo (*volition, emotion, doubt, or negation*). Subraya el verbo en subjuntivo en cada caso.

1. Estoy contento de que tengamos que vivir en Panamá.
2. Me alegro de que hagamos muchos viajes por el país.
3. Quiero que tú y yo vayamos a las playas en el Océano Atlántico y en el Océano Pacífico.
4. Dudo que en la ciudad de Darién haga más fresco que en la Ciudad de Panamá.
5. No es que la ciudad de Colón no me guste, sino que prefiero la playa.
6. No creo que los turistas no quieran pasear por el canal.
7. Mis padres desean que nosotros visitemos las esclusas (*locks*) del Canal de Panamá.
8. El gobierno estadounidense desea que el gobierno panameño administre muy bien el canal.

EN VOZ ALTA

11-17 **Consejos para Javier** Javier ha aceptado un nuevo puesto y sus amigos le ofrecen muchos consejos (*advice*). Lee las siguientes oraciones e indica si estás de acuerdo (*you agree*) o no con los consejos.

MODELO: Es importante que un(a) nuevo(a) empleado(a) llegue a la oficina temprano.
Estoy de acuerdo. Es importante que un(a) nuevo(a) empleado(a) llegue a la oficina temprano.
o *No estoy de acuerdo. No es importante que un(a) nuevo(a) empleado(a) llegue a la oficina temprano. Es importante que llegue a tiempo.*

1. Recomiendo que un(a) nuevo(a) empleado(a) conozca a muchas personas en el lugar donde trabaja.
2. Es necesario que todas las personas sepan usar la computadora.
3. No es probable que una persona reciba un aumento después de sólo un mes.
4. Es importante que un(a) jefe hable con sus empleados regularmente.

VOCABULARIO Las finanzas personales

En el Banco Nacional de Panamá In this section you will learn how to talk about your personal finances.

¿NOS ENTENDEMOS?
Another way to say **la factura** (*bill*) is **la cuenta.** Note that **la factura** is also used for *invoice.*

Sustantivos

la cuenta corriente checking account
la cuenta de ahorros savings account
el préstamo loan

Verbos

ahorrar to save
pagar to pay
a plazos in installments
en efectivo in cash
prestar to loan
rebotar to bounce (a check)

Palabras útiles

el cargo charge
el cheque de viajero traveler's check
el gasto expense
la hipoteca mortgage
el recibo receipt
la tarjeta de cajero automático ATM card
la tarjeta de cheque check card
transferir (ie, i) (fondos) to transfer (funds)

Palabras útiles are presented to help you enrich your personal vocabulary. The words here will help you talk about your personal finances.

¡A PRACTICAR!

11-18 **Definiciones** Empareja cada una de las palabras a continuación con su definición.

a. pagar en efectivo
b. pagar a plazos
c. depositar
d. pedir dinero prestado
e. el cajero automático

f. pagar las cuentas
g. el cheque
h. ahorrar
i. préstamo
j. la tarjeta de crédito

1. _____ Es un papel pequeño que usas para pagar algo. No es dinero, pero representa dinero de tu cuenta.

2. _____ Es cuando tú no gastas tu dinero, sino que (*but rather*) lo pones en el banco para usar otro día.

3. _____ Es algo plástico que usas para pagar en tiendas y restaurantes. Si no pagas la cuenta cada mes, tienes que pagar mucho interés.

4. _____ Es el acto de poner dinero en el banco.

5. _____ Cada mes mandas cheques por correo para pagar la electricidad, tus tarjetas de crédito, el gas, etc.

6. _____ Eso es lo que haces si pagas poco a poco por algo, por ejemplo, si compras una bicicleta y pagas $50 por mes durante seis meses en vez de pagar $300 inmediatamente.

7. _____ Es una máquina del banco que puedes usar para sacar dinero de tu cuenta las veinticuatro horas del día.

8. _____ Muchos estudiantes tienen que pedir uno para estudiar.

9. _____ Eso es cuando no usas crédito o un cheque para pagar, sino dólares, balboas, pesetas, etc.

10. _____ Si tienes una deuda y no tienes como pagarla, puedes ___.

11-19 **¿Qué hago con tanto dinero?** La mamá de Dora acaba de ganarse la lotería. Dora le da consejos sobre lo que debe hacer con el dinero que se ganó. Completa su conversación con las siguientes palabras.

sacar   presupuesto   cuenta corriente   cuenta de ahorros   prestar

Mamá: Dora, ¡no sé qué hacer con tanto dinero! Quiero abrir una 1. _____, así voy a poder escribir muchos cheques sin preocupaciones.

Dora: Bueno, mamá, está bien, pero también quieres ahorrar parte de tu dinero, ¿no? ¿Por qué no abres una 2. _____ también?

Mamá: Pero, hija, si es necesario, ¿puedo 3. _____ dinero de esa cuenta?

Dora: Claro, mamá. ¿Sabes cuánto dinero usas cada semana? Debes tener un plan. Tú necesitas hacer un 4. _____ que incluya todos tus gastos.

Mamá: Gracias por tu ayuda, hija.

Dora: De nada, mamá. Quiero lo mejor para ti. A propósito, ¿me podrías 5. _____ unas balboas para el alquiler?

EN VOZ ALTA

11-20 | **Entrevista** Habla con un(a) compañero(a) de clase sobre las siguientes preguntas. ¿Quién tiene más éxito con las finanzas personales?

1. ¿Les prestas dinero a tus amigos con frecuencia? ¿Cuánto dinero le(s) prestaste la última vez? ¿La persona te devolvió el dinero? Cuando sales con tus amigos(as), ¿quién paga la cuenta generalmente?

2. ¿Tienes un presupuesto mensual (*monthly*)? ¿Tienes el dinero suficiente al final del mes? ¿Cuánto dinero necesitas para actividades de diversión todas las semanas?

3. ¿Tienes un trabajo? ¿Quieren tus padres que pagues parte de la matrícula para la universidad? ¿Pediste algunos préstamos?

4. ¿Tienes algunas tarjetas de crédito? ¿Usas las tarjetas solamente para urgencias o con más frecuencia? ¿Puedes pagar todo el monto de tu tarjeta al final del mes? ¿Cuándo fue la última vez que pagaste con tarjeta de crédito?

11-21 | **Situaciones en el banco** Trabajando con un(a) compañero(a) de clase, inventen un diálogo para una de las siguientes situaciones. Usen el nuevo vocabulario de este capítulo. ¡Sean creativos!

1. Quieres abrir una cuenta corriente en el banco, pero solamente tienes $20 para abrirla.

2. Según el banco, tienes $100 menos de lo que tú pensabas en tu cuenta de ahorros. Crees que es un error por parte del banco.

3. Perdiste tu tarjeta de cajero automático. Quieres saber si alguien la usó para sacar dinero de tu cuenta.

ESTRUCTURA III Expressing desires and intentions: the present subjunctive with statements of volition

In **Estructura II** you learned that the present tense has both an indicative mood and a subjunctive mood. Thus far, you have used the present indicative to state facts, describe conditions, express actions, and ask questions. In this section you will learn more about the subjunctive mood and how Spanish speakers use it to express what they want others to do.

As you recall, the most common use of the subjunctive mood is for influence—in the form of wanting, hoping, demanding, preferring, recommending, and prohibiting: the first subject/verb combination (clause) of a sentence influences the second subject/verb combination. Note that, with few exceptions, the subjunctive appears only in dependent clauses.

Carlos **quiere que José trabaje** más.   *Carlos wants José to work more.*

In the example above, the first clause **(Carlos quiere...)** causes the subjunctive in the second (dependent) clause **(...que José trabaje)** because the first clause is a statement of *causing* or *volition*. This is the type of subjunctive situation you'll be practicing later in this section.

I. The present subjunctive verb forms

To form the present subjunctive of most verbs, drop the **-o** from the present indicative **yo** form, then add the endings shown. Note that it is the same procedure as the one that you would use to form formal and negative informal commands

	-ar **lavarse**	**-er** **hacer**	**-ir** **escribir**
yo	me lav**e**	hag**a**	escrib**a**
tú	te lav**es**	hag**as**	escrib**as**
Ud., él, ella	se lav**e**	hag**a**	escrib**a**
nosotros(as)	nos lav**emos**	hag**amos**	escrib**amos**
vosotros(as)	os lav**éis**	hag**áis**	escrib**áis**
Uds., ellos(as)	se lav**en**	hag**an**	escrib**an**

Note that the stem of verbs that end in **-car, -gar,** and **-zar** have a spelling change to maintain pronunciation.

yo recommend

sacar (c → qu)	**llegar (g → gu)**	**comenzar (z → c)**
sa**que**	lle**gue**	comien**ce**
sa**ques**	lle**gues**	comien**ces**
sa**que**	lle**gue**	comien**ce**
sa**quemos**	lle**guemos**	comen**cemos**
sa**quéis**	lle**guéis**	comen**céis**
sa**quen**	lle**guen**	comien**cen**

—¿Quieres que yo **saque** los documentos?   *Do you want me to take out the documents?*

—Sí, recomiendo que **comencemos** ahora.   *Yes, I recommend that we begin now.*

Also note that stem-changing verbs that end in **-ar** and **-er** have the same stem changes (**ie, ue**) in the present indicative and in the present subjunctive. Pay special attention to the **nosotros** and **vosotros** forms.

pensar (e → ie)		poder (o → ue)	
Present Indicative	Present Subjunctive	Present Indicative	Present Subjunctive
pienso	piense	puedo	pueda
piensas	pienses	puedes	puedas
piensa	piense	puede	pueda
pensamos	pensemos	podemos	podamos
pensáis	penséis	podéis	podáis
piensan	piensen	pueden	puedan

—¿Qué te dijo la jefe?   *What did the boss tell you?*

—Ella insiste en que yo **vuelva** a Colón.   *She insists that I return to Colón.*

Stem-changing verbs that end in **-ir** have the same stem changes (**ie, ue**) in the present indicative and in the present subjunctive. However, the **nosotros** and **vosotros** forms have a stem change (**e** to **i, o** to **u**) in the present subjunctive.

divertirse (ie)		dormir (ue)	
Present Indicative	Present Subjunctive	Present Indicative	Present Subjunctive
me divierto	me divierta	duermo	duerma
te diviertes	te diviertas	duermes	duermas
se divierte	se divierta	duerme	duerma
nos divertimos	nos divirtamos	dormimos	durmamos
os divertís	os divirtáis	dormís	durmáis
se divierten	se diviertan	duermen	duerman

—Espero que **te diviertas** en la Isla Taboga.   *I hope you have fun on Taboga Island.*

The verbs **pedir** and **servir** have the same stem change (**e** to **i**) in the present indicative and in the present subjunctive. The **nosotros** and **vosotros** forms have an additional stem change (**e** to **i**) in the present subjunctive.

pedir (i)		servir (i)	
Present Indicative	**Present Subjunctive**	**Present Indicative**	**Present Subjunctive**
pido	pida	sirvo	sirva
pides	pidas	sirves	sirvas
pide	pida	sirve	sirva
pedimos	pidamos	servimos	sirvamos
pedís	pidáis	servís	sirváis
piden	pidan	sirven	sirvan

—Deseo que **sirvamos** a los clientes con respeto.

I want us to serve the clients with respect.

—¿Quieres que yo **pida** una reunión con los empleados?

Do you want me to request a meeting with the employees?

Some verbs have irregular forms in the present subjunctive because their stems are not based on the **yo** form of the present indicative.

dar	estar	ir	saber	ser
dé	esté	vaya	sepa	sea
des	estés	vayas	sepas	seas
dé	esté	vaya	sepa	sea
demos	estemos	vayamos	sepamos	seamos
deis	estéis	vayáis	sepáis	seáis
den	estén	vayan	sepan	sean

—¿Permites que le **dé** yo el número de la oficina en Panamá?

Do you permit me to give him the number of the office in Panama?

—Sí. Y quiero que él **sepa** el número en Colón también.

Yes. And I want him to know the number in Colon also.

The subjunctive form of **hay** is **haya**, which is invariable.

Espero que **haya** muchos candidatos para el puesto.

I hope that there are many candidates for the position.

II. The use of the present subjunctive with verbs of volition

The examples given in the previous section demonstrate several common verbs of volition that cause the subjunctive to be used in the dependent clause. These verbs include the following:

desear	*to wish; to want*
insistir en	*to insist*
mandar	*to command*
pedir (i, i)	*to request*
permitir	*to permit*
preferir (ie, i)	*to prefer*
prohibir	*to prohibit, forbid*
querer (ie)	*to want*
recomendar (ie)	*to recommend*

A verb of volition is followed by a verb in the subjunctive when the subject of the dependent clause is different from that of the independent clause. The two clauses are linked together by the word **que** *(that)*.

	Change of subject
(Carlos) quiere que	(José) trabaje más.
Independent clause	Dependent clause

In sentences that have no change of subject, an infinitive—not the subjunctive—follows the verb of volition. Compare the following sentences.

No change of subject	**Change of subject**
José prefiere trabajar ahora.	Carlos prefiere que José trabaje ahora.
José prefers to work now.	Carlos prefers that José work now.

Place pronouns before conjugated verbs in the present subjunctive.

—Deseamos que **te diviertas.**	*We want you to have fun.*
—Y yo insisto en que **me escribas.**	*And I insist that you write to me.*
—¿Quieres mi dirección?	*Do you want my address?*
—Sí, recomiendo que **me la des** ahora.	*Yes, I recommend that you give it to me now.*

¡A PRACTICAR!

11-22 **¿Qué quiere mi jefe?** ¿Qué dice José sobre lo que quiere el jefe de él y de los otros empleados? Termina cada oración con un verbo adecuado de la lista.

llegue   conteste   termine   dé   llame

Mi jefe quiere que yo...

1. _____dé_____ informes mensuales (*monthly*).
2. _____llegue_____ a tiempo a la oficina.
3. _____llame_____ a mis clientes por teléfono todas las semanas.
4. _____termine_____ mi trabajo antes de salir de la oficina.
5. _____conteste_____ el correo electrónico.

nos comuniquemos   no hablemos   tengamos   nos vistamos

Mi jefe prefiere que nosotros...

6. _____tengamos_____ reuniones cortas.
7. _____nos vistamos_____ de una manera profesional.
8. _____no hablemos_____ de nuestros proyectos fuera de la oficina.
9. _____nos comuniquemos_____ mucho entre nosotros.

imprima   no trabaje   haga

Mi jefe recomienda que Sofía...

10. _____haga_____ las fotocopias.
11. _____imprima_____ todos los documentos antes de las reuniones.
12. _____no trabaje_____ durante los fines de semana.

11-23 **Consejos para Dora** Dora tiene una hermana, Susana, que trabaja en un banco. Susana le da consejos a su hermana sobre las finanzas personales. Completa la historia con la forma correcta del verbo entre paréntesis.

Dora, yo quiero que tú 1. _____abras_____ (abrir) una cuenta de ahorros. No quiero que tú y tu esposo 2. _____sigan_____ (seguir) con tantos problemas económicos. Insisto en que tú 3. _____dejes_____ (dejar) de pagar a plazos cuando compras cosas. Prefiero que tú me 4. _____pidas_____ (pedir) prestado el dinero, o sugiero que no 5. _____compres_____ (comprar) cosas tan caras. Te recomiendo que tú 6. _____enseñes_____ (enseñar) a tu hijo a ahorrar más dinero. No queremos que él 7. _____tenga_____ (tener) problemas luego con el dinero. Espero que todos Uds. 8. _____sepan_____ (saber) que estas ideas son buenas para Uds.

11-24 **Mi trabajo en la universidad** Forma oraciones completas con las siguientes palabras. Nota que a veces tienes que usar el infinitivo en la segunda cláusula.

MODELO: mis padres / prohibir / yo / trabajar / la semana
Mis padres prohíben que yo trabaje durante la semana.

1. el consejero / recomendar / los estudiantes / no hablar por teléfono / sus amigos
2. mi jefe / pedir / yo / no usar / la fotocopiadora / asuntos personales
3. los profesores / esperar / los gerentes / dar / a nosotros / un sueldo bueno
4. yo / querer / aprender / mis experiencias
5. nosotros / preferir / no trabajar / los sábados
6. la profesora / insistir / nosotros / estudiar / antes / salir para el trabajo
7. yo / desear / encontrar / trabajo / tiempo completo
8. mi madre / recomendar / yo / buscar / trabajo / tiempo parcial

EN VOZ ALTA

11-25 Mamá siempre sabe más Tu mamá te quiere dar muchos consejos sobre tus finanzas personales. Explícale a un(a) compañero(a) lo que tu mamá quiere que hagas, según la información a continuación. Usa los verbos de voluntad para comenzar las oraciones: **desear, insistir en, mandar, pedir, permitir, preferir, prohibir, querer, recomendar.**

to send
to commande

mi mama prefere

1. ahorrar más dinero
2. pagar las cuentas a tiempo
3. dejar de comprar a plazos
4. pedir préstamos para la universidad
sirvos 5. servir comida barata para mis fiestas
6. llegar temprano para mi trabajo
7. dar un poco de dinero a la caridad (charity) todas las semanas
8. ir a los cajeros automáticos para sacar dinero
9. saber ahorrar bien mi dinero
10. ser inteligente con los asuntos de las finanzas personales

11-26 Aspiraciones ¿Qué aspiraciones tienes en cuanto al dinero? Contesta las siguientes preguntas y después compara tus respuestas con las de un(a) compañero(a) de clase. ¿Tienen mucho en común? Noten que pueden usar las sugerencias a continuación o usar otros verbos de voluntad.

1. ¿Quieres mejorar tu posición económica? ¿Cómo quieres hacerlo?
   Yo quiero... Espero...

2. ¿Qué consejos les da tu madre a ti y a tus hermanos sobre el dinero?
   Mi mamá quiere que nosotros... Ella desea que nosotros... Ella no quiere que nosotros...

3. ¿Qué le dices tú a tu novio(a) o esposo(a) sobre el dinero?
   Yo le mando que él/ella... Yo le recomiendo que él/ella... Yo le prohíbo que él/ella...

4. ¿Qué le dices tú a tu compañero(a) de clase en cuanto a sus finanzas personales?
   Yo deseo que él/ella... Yo recomiendo que él/ella...

5. ¿Qué les dice un contador a sus clientes sobre las finanzas personales?
   Yo recomiendo que Uds.... Yo insisto en que Uds....

11-27 ¿Qué dices tú? Con un(a) compañero(a), hablen de lo que les gusta y sobre lo que es importante para Uds. en un trabajo. Túrnense, recomendando trabajos y explicando por qué.

MODELO: E1: *Me gustan las matemáticas y quiero trabajar con dinero.*
E2: *Recomiendo que seas contador(a) porque los contadores tienen que entender mucho de matemáticas.*

¡A VER!

En este segmento del video, Sofía y Javier hablan sobre sus carreras futuras. Sofía tiene un secreto que comparte con Javier que lo inspira realizar sus propios planes.

Expresiones útiles

Las siguientes son expresiones nuevas que vas a escuchar en el video.

Se me ocurrió	It occurred to me
Vida cotidiana	Daily life
No me atrevo	I don't dare
Ya veremos	We'll see

Antes de ver

Paso 1: Con un(a) compañero(a) hablen de sus planes para el futuro. ¿Tienen una especialización en la universidad? ¿Cómo seleccionan sus cursos cada semestre? ¿Sus amigos o sus padres tienen mucha influencia en cuanto a la selección de cursos?

Paso 2: Con un(a) compañero(a) expresen su opinión sobre lo siguiente: ¿Creen que es necesario planear cada aspecto de su vida o es mejor ser espontáneo? ¿Creen que las cosas buenas pasan sin esfuerzo ninguno o hay que intervenir? Justifiquen sus respuestas. ¿Tienen mucho en común?

Después de ver

Paso 1: En **Antes de ver, Paso 1**, tu compañero(a) y tú hablaron de sus planes futuros. Ahora para contar lo que pasa en la vida de Sofía y de Javier y sus planes, completa el siguiente párrafo con la forma apropiada de los verbos entre paréntesis. ¡Ojo con el uso del presente del subjuntivo!

Sofía busca un apartamento porque desea _____ **(quedarse)** en Puerto Rico más tiempo. Quiere _____ **(escribir)** un libro sobre la cultura, el arte, la historia y la vida cotidiana en Puerto Rico. Le pide a Javier que no _____ **(decir)** su secreto a nadie. Javier también tiene un sueño para su futuro. Él quiere _____ **(tener)** su propia agencia de ecoturismo y deportes de aventura, pero su padre manda que _____ **(ser)** un médico. Sofía le recomienda que Javier no _____ **(abandonar)** su deseo. Le sugiere que _____ **(hacer)** un plan muy preciso, y que lo _____ **(presentar)** a su padre.

Paso 2: En **Antes de ver, Paso 2**, tu compañero(a) y tú hablaron de la necesidad o no de hacer planes. Para Sofía y Javier, es muy importante planear bien. Completa el siguiente párrafo con **por** o **para** para contar qué piensan hacer Sofía y Javier.

Sofía quiere vivir en Puerto Rico _____ un año. Si quiere pagar _____ un apartamento, necesita encontrar un trabajo muy pronto. _____ eso, piensa que puede trabajar _____ la universidad y dar clases de literatura o de gramática. Javier no quiere estudiar medicina y lo hace solamente _____ su padre. Después de hablar con Sofía, decide luchar _____ su propio sueño de tener una agencia de deportes de aventura _____ los turistas. _____ lograr esa meta, tiene que decidir adónde quiere ir y exactamente lo que va a hacer. Cuando ya sabe todos los detalles, _____ supuesto, tiene que hablar con su padre _____ explicar la situación.

¿Qué opinas tú?

Paso 1: Sofía tiene un plan muy difícil, pero ha decidido luchar por ello. Javier tiene un sueño pero está en conflicto con el de su padre. ¿Con quién te identificas más? ¿Con Javier o con Sofía o con ninguno de los dos? Habla con un(a) compañero(a) y explícale tus respuestas.

Paso 2: Habla con un(a) compañero(a) sobre lo que necesitas hacer o no hacer para realizar tus sueños futuros. Justifiquen sus planes e ideas.

¡A LEER!

Strategy: Guessing unfamiliar words and phrases

When you read a passage in English and come to an unfamiliar word or phrase, you probably try to guess its meaning from context or skip over it and continue reading. When learners of Spanish as a foreign language read any type of passages in Spanish, they will likely encounter a number of unfamiliar vocabulary items. However, if you can transfer your ability to guess word meaning from context over to Spanish, your reading comprehension will increase significantly, as will your reading speed.

Take a few minutes to skim the following business etiquette passage. After skimming it, complete the following exercises. While reading the passage, try to incorporate as many of the reading strategies you have learned up to this point as you can!

Paso 1: Lee la siguientes normas de cortesía dentro del mundo de los negocios en Panamá y en Latinoamérica. Luego usa el contexto para determinar el significado de las siguientes palabras y expresiones.

_____ 1. ruda
_____ 2. mala educación
_____ 3. furiosa
_____ 4. la puntualidad
_____ 5. rango

a. mad, furious
b. on time, punctuality
c. rank, class, position
d. rude, unpolished
e. ill-mannered

Etiqueta en el mundo de los negocios en Panamá

– Generalmente los saludos al comienzo de una conversación entre los latinoamericanos es larga y las personas se preguntan cómo está la salud, la familia, los viajes de negocios y los amigos. Si una persona no toma el tiempo suficiente para hacer estas preguntas y comienza hablar de negocios rápidamente, se considera una persona **ruda** y sin buena educación.

– Toser o bostezar (*yawning*) en público se considera de **mala educación.** Siempre cubra su boca al toser o bostezar.

– Tampoco es recomendable comer en público.

– Nunca ponga sus manos en sus caderas (*hips*) ya que se considera que la persona está **furiosa.**

– **La puntualidad** es muy importante en las reuniones de negocios especialmente si usted es extranjero(a). Si lo (la) invitan a una fiesta no llegue a tiempo, llegue media hora a una hora más tarde.

– Si visita Panamá, estudie la cultura y la historia del país y la historia del canal de Panamá. No discuta el hecho de que esta sociedad está muy «americanizada» y no se refiera a los estadounidenses como «americanos(as)» ya que todos los (las) ciudadanos(as) de Norte, Centro y Sur América son americanos(as).

– Los panameños creen en el valor interno de cada persona y no hacen distinción en la clase social de las personas. Por eso es muy importante no hablar del **rango** de una persona o criticarla en público.

– Los panameños así como los latinoamericanos son muy hospitalarios e invitan siempre a sus casas para cenar. La cena es entre las 7:00 y las 9:00 de la noche. Pero al mismo tiempo, una persona nunca debe presentarse en casa de la persona con la que hace negocios sin antes llamar por teléfono para avisar.

Paso 2: Ahora, vuelve a leer las reglas de cortesía en los negocios y luego contesta las siguientes preguntas.

1. ¿Qué es importante saber sobre Panamá? ¿Se puede usar el término «americanos(as)» para referirse a los estadounidenses? ¿Por qué sí o no?
2. ¿Cuándo es importante la puntualidad en Panamá o en Latinoamérica?
3. ¿Qué se considera mala educación en Latinoamérica?

Paso 3: Ahora contesta las siguientes preguntas.

1. ¿Cuáles son algunas diferencias en la puntualidad entre los Estados Unidos y Latinoamérica?
2. ¿Qué piensas sobre el hecho de que no se puede toser, bostezar o comer en público o visitar a las personas con las que uno hace negocios sin llamar anteriormente? ¿Cuáles son las diferencias con los Estados Unidos?

¡A ESCRIBIR!

Strategy: Writing from an idea map

An idea map is a tool for organizing your ideas before you begin developing them in a composition. In this section you are going to write a job description with the aid of an idea map. You may write a description of your dream job or you may write a job description such as the ones that appear in newspapers or on job-search websites. Using an idea map will help you organize your thoughts about this topic before you write about it.

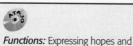

Functions: Expressing hopes and aspirations; Expressing intention
Vocabulary: Professions, trades, working conditions
Grammar: Verbs: present; Verbs: subjunctive

Paso 1: Escribe el nombre de la profesión o del oficio que vas a describir. Dibuja un círculo alrededor de esta(s) palabra(s).

Paso 2: Escribe unas palabras o ideas relacionadas a este tema. Estas ideas son los detalles que apoyan *(support)* la idea principal, en este caso la profesión que vas a describir. Dibuja unos círculos alrededor de estas ideas y escribe líneas para conectar los círculos de una manera que te parece lógica. Puedes seguir el siguiente modelo:

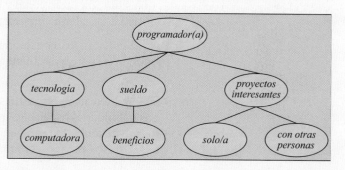

Paso 3: Basándote en el mapa que has dibujado, haz una lista de frases sobre el tema principal que puedas incluir en un párrafo. Al escribir las frases, debes considerar las siguientes preguntas.

1. ¿Al lector le va a interesar la información?
2. ¿Tienes bastante información para un párrafo?
3. ¿Puedes limitar la información a sólo un párrafo?

Task: Writing a job description

Paso 1: Ahora vas a escribir una descripción de un puesto. Tienes que decidir si quieres describir el empleo de tus sueños o si quieres hacer una descripción de un puesto para publicar en un periódico o en la red. Después de tomar una decisión, escribe la primera oración de tu descripción.

Paso 2: Refiérete al mapa que has dibujado para desarrollar las ideas necesarias para el resto de tu descripción. Escribe unas siete u ocho oraciones en que describas claramente las responsabilidades del puesto y el salario que la persona que hace el trabajo va a recibir. Usa el tiempo presente para describir el empleo.

Se busca programador(a) para trabajar en una empresa financiera. El candidato (La candidata) debe tener un título en computación o un mínimo de cinco años de experiencia como programador(a) profesional. Para tener éxito en este puesto, es esencial conocer la tecnología más reciente. El puesto es de tiempo completo y es necesario trabajar por la noche de vez en cuando. La persona debe tener la habilidad de trabajar solo(a) en algunos proyectos y de colaborar con nuestros otros programadores en algunos proyectos muy grandes. Es recomendable que tenga experiencia en el entrenamiento y la supervisión de nuevos empleados. Se ofrece buen salario y buenos beneficios, los cuales se pueden discutir en la entrevista con la directora de la empresa. Las personas que tengan interés en este puesto deben enviar el currículum por fax al 929-555-0040.

Paso 3: Intercambia papeles con un(a) compañero(a) de clase. Lee el párrafo de la otra persona para ver si ha incluido la información necesaria en su composición. Si ha omitido algo, infórmaselo. Entonces, habla con él o ella sobre el puesto que ha descrito. Indica si te interesa o no te interesa y explica por qué sí o por qué no.

¡A CONVERSAR!

Task: Practicing for a job interview

Muchas personas tienen que participar en una entrevista para un trabajo y muchas se ponen muy nerviosas en esta situación. Es posible que tú tengas que hablar español en una entrevista algún día y que si te encuentras en esa situación, es muy probable que te sientas muy preocupado(a). Ahora vas a trabajar con un(a) compañero(a) de clase para practicar para este tipo de encuentro.

Paso 1: Una persona va a ser el (la) candidato(a) y la otra persona va a ser el (la) jefe. Después de algunos minutos, Uds. deben cambiar papeles. Recuerden Uds. que ésta es una situación profesional y formal y que deben emplear la forma de Ud. en sus conversaciones. Para empezar, identifiquen el puesto que el (la) candidato(a) solicita.

Paso 2: El (La) jefe debe hacerle algunas preguntas al (a la) candidato(a). Puede preguntarle sobre lo siguiente:

• Su educación
• Su experiencia en otros puestos
• Las habilidades especiales que tiene
• El tipo de ambiente *(environment)* en el cual prefiere trabajar
• Sus aspiraciones para el futuro

Paso 3: El (La) candidato(a) debe contestar las preguntas y después puede hacerle algunas preguntas al (a la) jefe. Puede incluir lo siguiente:

• Las responsabilidades del puesto
• Información sobre la empresa
• La oportunidad de ascender *(be promoted)*
• El sueldo y los beneficios

Paso 4: El (La) jefe debe decidir si quiere emplear al (a la) candidato(a) y, el (la) candidato(a) debe decidir si tiene interés en el puesto. Después, cambien de papel y practiquen otra entrevista.

Las profesiones y los oficios Professions

Sustantivos

el (la) abogado(a) lawyer	el (la) fotógrafo(a) photographer	el (la) peluquero(a) hairstylist
el (la) arquitecto(a) architect	el (la) gerente manager	el (la) periodista journalist
el (la) banquero(a) banker	el hombre (la mujer) de negocios	el (la) plomero(a) plumber
el (la) carpintero(a) carpenter	businessperson	el policía (la mujer policía) police officer
el (la) cocinero(a) cook, chef	el (la) ingeniero(a) engineer	el (la) programador(a) programmer
el (la) contador(a) accountant	el (la) jefe boss	el (la) siquiatra psychiatrist
el (la) dentista dentist	el (la) maestro(a) teacher	el (la) traductor(a) translator
el (la) empleado(a) employee	el (la) obrero(a) worker; laborer	el (la) veterinario(a) veterinarian

La oficina, el trabajo y la búsqueda de trabajo The office, work, and the job hunt

Sustantivos

los beneficios benefits	la entrevista interview	el puesto job, position
el (la) candidato(a) candidate, applicant	el fax fax machine	la reunión meeting
la computadora computer	la fotocopiadora photocopier	la sala de conferencias conference room
el correo electrónico email	la impresora printer	el salario / el sueldo salary
el currículum résumé	el informe report	la solicitud application (form)
la empresa corporation; business	el proyecto project	

Verbos

contratar to hire	jubilarse to retire	renunciar to resign
dejar to quit	llamar por teléfono to make a phone call	reunirse to meet
despedir (i, i) to fire	llenar to fill out (a form)	solicitar un puesto to apply for a job
imprimir to print	pedir un aumento to ask for a raise	

Expresiones idiomáticas

de tiempo completo full-time	de tiempo parcial part-time

Las finanzas personales Personal finances

Sustantivos

el cajero automático ATM	la cuenta de ahorros savings account	el presupuesto budget
el cheque check	la factura bill; invoice	la tarjeta de crédito credit card
la cuenta corriente checking account	el préstamo loan	

Verbos

ahorrar to save	pagar en efectivo to pay in cash	rebotar to bounce (a check)
depositar to deposit (money)	pedir prestado to borrow	sacar to withdraw (money)
pagar a plazos to pay in installments	prestar to loan	

El medio ambiente:

Chapter Objectives

COMMUNICATIVE GOALS

In this chapter you will learn how to . . .

- Talk about rural and urban locales and associated activities and problems
- Express emotion and opinions
- Talk about the conservation and exploitation of natural resources
- Hypothesize and express doubts and uncertainty
- Talk about a nature preserve, animals, and endangered species

STRUCTURES

- Subjunctive following verbs of emotion, impersonal expressions, and **ojalá**
- Subjunctive to state uncertain, doubtful, or hypothetical situations

CULTURAL INFORMATION

- Costa Rica: Puros ingredientes naturales
- Costa Rica: Estación biológica La Selva

Costa Rica

COSTA RICA

Población: 3.773.057
Área: 51.000 kilómetros
cuadrados, un poco más
pequeño que West Virginia
Capital: San José, 351.700
Ciudades principales: Limón,
64.200; Alajuela, 54.600;
Puntarenas, 47.200
Moneda: el colón
Lengua: el español

¡Bienvenidos a Costa Rica!

En este video, vas a aprender de
Costa Rica. Después de ver el video,
contesta las siguientes preguntas:

1 ¿Cómo es la naturaleza de Costa Rica? ¿Cuáles son algunos
de los atractivos naturales del país?

2 Según el video ¿qué hacen los costarricenses para
proteger la naturaleza? ¿Por qué es necesario?

3 ¿Por qué tradición cultural es conocido el pueblo de Sarchí?
¿Qué sabes de esta tradición?

4 ¿Qué es la Finca de Mariposas? ¿Qué se puede hacer allí?

5 ¿Te gustaría ayudar a proteger la riqueza natural de Costa
Rica u otra parte del mundo? ¿Por qué sí o por qué no?

La Plaza de la Basílica de
Nuestra Señora de los Ángeles,
Cartago, Costa Rica

347

VOCABULARIO La geografía rural y urbana

CULTURA
Golfito is a small port town of 14,000 inhabitants located on the southern tip of Costa Rica. The town is almost entirely surrounded by lush, forested hills. Golfito is world famous for sport fishing and its natural beauty. Golfito developed into a major port in the 1930s when the United Fruit Company set up operations there along the Pacific Coast.

CULTURA
San José is the capital city of Costa Rica. San José lies in the mountainous center of the country. Population estimates range from 300,000 to a million inhabitants, depending on which suburbs are included. The city is subject to frequent earthquakes because of its location in a zone of tectonic activity.

CULTURA
Since gaining its independence from Spain in 1821, Costa Rica has been one of Latin America's long-standing democracies. After an armed conflict in 1948, Costa Rica abolished the army to ensure democratic rule.

¿NOS ENTENDEMOS?
La cascada is another word for a small catarata.

Palabras útiles are presented to help you enrich your personal vocabulary. The words here will help you talk about rural geography.

Golfito y San José, Costa Rica In this section you will learn how to talk about rural and urban areas and the associated activities and problems.

Sustantivos

la naturaleza nature
la sobrepoblación overpopulation
el transporte público   public transportation

Verbos

cultivar to cultivate, grow (plants)
llevar una vida tranquila to lead a peaceful life
regar (ie) to irrigate; to water
sembrar (ie) to plant

Adjetivos

acelerado(a) accelerated
bello(a) beautiful
denso(a) dense
tranquilo(a) tranquil, peaceful

Palabras útiles

el árbol tree
la frontera border
el paisaje landscape
el llano plain
el valle valley
el volcán volcano

¡A PRACTICAR!

12-1 Asociaciones ¿Con qué se asocian las siguientes palabras? Empareja cada palabra o frase de la primera columna con la palabra o frase más lógica de la segunda columna.

1. _f_ el bosque
2. _d_ bello
3. _j_ las cataratas
4. _h_ el campesino
5. _b_ denso
6. _c_ sembrar, cultivar
7. _i_ el transporte público
8. _k_ la selva
9. _e_ tranquilo
10. _g_ el rascacielos
11. _a_ la metrópolis

a. la Ciudad de México, Tokio, Nueva York
b. con muchas plantas y vegetación
c. Johnny Appleseed
d. bonito
e. pacífico, sin ruido
f. Caperucita Roja (*Little Red Riding Hood*)
g. el edificio Empire State
h. una persona del campo
i. el autobús, el tren, el metro
j. Niágara, Iguazú, el Salto Ángel
k. Tarzán

12-2 La llegada a San José Termina la historia de Mario escogiendo la palabra adecuada.

1. Cuando Mario llegó a (la metrópolis / el arroyo) de San José, se dio cuenta de que la vida era mucho más (tranquila / acelerada) de lo que él había experimentado (*had experienced*) en el campo.
2. Había mucho (arroyo / tráfico) en las (carreteras / colinas), y no estaba acostumbrado al ruido causado por los coches.
3. Miró los grandes (campesinos / rascacielos) y pensó en los hermosos árboles del bosque que él había abandonado (*had abandoned*).
4. Miró la (basura / finca) en las calles y el humo (*smoke*) de las fábricas y pensó en la tierra limpia y pura de su finca.
5. ¡Y cuánta gente! Seguro que la (selva / sobrepoblación) era la fuente (*source*) de los problemas (urbanos / densos), pensó Mario.

12-3 Érase una vez... Completa la siguiente historia sobre la vida rural de Mario, un campesino tico, usando las palabras de la lista.

regar	tierra	arroyo	selva	cultivaba
agricultor	finca	colinas	llevaba una vida tranquila	

Érase una vez un 1. _____ joven y trabajador que cultivaba una porción (piece) de 2. _____ en la 3. _____ tropical de Costa Rica. El hombre industrioso se llamaba Mario y 4. _____ muchos plátanos todos los años. No tenía que 5. _____ las plantas porque llovía muchísimo en aquella región. Mario 6. _____ y exitosa. Había un lago en su 7. _____ donde él pescaba durante los fines de semana. También corría un 8. _____ muy bonito entre unas verdes 9. _____ donde él descansaba después de trabajar. A pesar de la belleza de su finca, Mario sufría de la soledad del lugar. Por eso un día decidió vender su propiedad e irse para la ciudad para encontrar un trabajo en el centro urbano de San José.

CULTURA 12-3
Throughout the late nineteenth and the entire twentieth centuries, there has been mass movement in Latin America from the countryside to urban centers. This population shift is due in part to industrialization in the cities, where many jobs have become available, as well as to a decline in the world market for small-scale production of farm produce.

¿NOS ENTENDEMOS?
Tico(a) is another way to say **costarricense**. It is the affectionate name to describe people from Costa Rica.

¿NOS ENTENDEMOS?
While **la finca** is understood throughout most of the Spanish-speaking world to mean *farm*, some regions use other terms. In Mexico, **el rancho** is used to mean *ranch* or *farm*. **La hacienda** is also used in Mexico and in other Latin American countries to mean *farm*, usually with an estate manor on it; it is also called **la estancia** in Argentina. **La granja** is commonly used in Spain to refer to small family farms, while **la chacra** is used in countries such as Costa Rica.

EN VOZ ALTA

12-4 | **Opiniones** Completa las siguientes oraciones con el vocabulario de esta sección para expresarle tus opiniones sobre las siguientes ideas a un(a) compañero(a) de clase.

MODELO: Trabajar en una finca (no) es fácil porque... *es necesario levantarse muy temprano todos los días. Hay mucho trabajo físico, y uno se cansa fácilmente.*

1. (No) Me gusta vivir en la ciudad porque...
2. La vida rural (no) es atractiva para mí porque...
3. Lo que más me impresiona de la metrópolis es/son...
4. Cuando voy al campo, prefiero estar en... porque...
5. La última vez que estuve en una ciudad grande vi...
6. La última vez que estuve en un parque natural había...

12-5 | **Los problemas de mi pueblo** Trabajando con un(a) compañero(a) de clase, pongan los siguientes temas en orden de mayor a menor importancia con referencia al pueblo donde Uds. viven. Después de establecer los problemas más importantes, indiquen lo que recomiendan para resolver tres de ellos. ¿Cuáles son los temas que no son problemáticos en su pueblo?

MODELO: el tráfico
El tráfico en nuestra ciudad es un problema muy grande. Recomendamos que más gente camine o ande en bicicleta en vez de ir en coche. También sugerimos que las personas vayan juntas (together) al trabajo en vez de una sola persona en cada coche.

> **¿NOS ENTENDEMOS?**
> Note that in English, the word *people* is plural while its Spanish equivalent, **la gente,** is singular. When you want to express *people* in the sense of *nation* or *national group,* use the term **el pueblo.**

1. el transporte público
2. el ruido
3. la basura
4. la sobrepoblación
5. las fábricas
6. las metrópolis
7. los rascacielos

12-6 | **Entrevista** Con un(a) compañero(a) de clase, háganse preguntas sobre los siguientes temas. Luego, compartan su información con la clase. ¿Tienen Uds. mucho en común?

1. ¿Has pasado tiempo en una ciudad grande? ¿Cuándo? ¿Qué ciudad? ¿Te gustó? ¿Qué hiciste allá? ¿Cómo se compara esa ciudad con el lugar donde vives?

2. ¿Has pasado tiempo en el campo? ¿Cuándo? ¿Con quién? ¿Te gustó? ¿Es muy diferente del lugar donde vives? ¿Qué hiciste allá?

3. ¿Cómo es el lugar donde vives tú? ¿Es más rural o más urbano? ¿Quieres vivir en una ciudad grande algún día? O, ¿prefieres el campo o un pueblo más pequeño? ¿Cuáles son las ventajas de vivir en una ciudad grande? ¿Cuáles son las ventajas (*advantages*) de vivir en el campo?

Text audio
Track 2-10

Rona y Luis Grandinetti son hermanos pero tienen ideas muy diferentes sobre el lugar ideal donde quieren vivir en el futuro.

Rona: Luis, ¿no te molesta **el tráfico** de San José? No entiendo por qué te gusta tanto esta ciudad.

Luis: No me molesta para nada. **Me gusta que las calles estén llenas** de gente y de actividad.

Rona: Pues, te digo que **prefiero que vivamos** en otro lugar. Quiero vivir en un pueblo pequeño cerca del mar, **un lugar que tenga aire puro** y un medio ambiente sano.

Luis: La vida del campo es bella, pero no tiene ni las oportunidades ni los servicios de una ciudad grande. Con tu afán *(desire)* de ir al cine todos los fines de semana, **yo dudo que la vida rural sea tan atractiva** como piensas tú.

Rona: ¿Y cómo sabes tú? No has pasado mucho tiempo en el campo. Hiciste camping una vez, ¿y ya eres experto? Y no tengo que ir al cine todos los fines de semana.

Luis: Así que, ¿quieres ser **campesina**? ¿Quieres vivir con los **monos** *(monkeys)* y los insectos? ¿Y si ves una **culebra** *(snake)*?

Rona: ¡Ay! **Ojalá que (I wish that) fueras (you were) más sensible.** No quiero vivir en la selva. Solamente quiero llevar una vida tranquila. Necesito vivir en **un sitio donde no haya tanto ruido,** ni **contaminación,** ni **rasca-cielos,** ni **carreteras.**

Luis: Pues, **es importante que decidas** de una vez. El mes pasado estabas convencida de que querías vivir en Tokio, y ahora empiezas con estas fantasías de la vida rural.

Rona: **Es mejor tener ilusiones.** Tú no puedes imaginarte la vida fuera de tu cuarto.

¿Comprendiste?

Contesta las siguientes preguntas en oraciones completas.

1. ¿Por qué no está contenta Rona?
2. Según Luis, ¿cuáles son algunas ventajas *(advantages)* de vivir en la ciudad?
3. ¿Sabe Luis mucho de la vida rural?
4. Según Rona, ¿cuál es el lugar ideal para ella?
5. ¿Por qué sospechamos *(do we suspect)* que Rona es un poco indecisa?

Encuentro cultural

Costa Rica: puros ingredientes naturales

Montañas cerca del Parque
Monteverde, Costa Rica

Volcán Arenal, San José,
Costa Rica

Excursión por el tope
de los árboles

PARA PENSAR

- ¿En tu región hay algún parque nacional? ¿Puedes describirlo?

- ¿Quién debe tener la responsabilidad de cuidar los animales y las plantas en tu región o en el país?
¿Por qué?

CULTURA

El quetzal is one of the most beautifully colored birds with a three-foot-long tail. It means "freedom" for the Mayans.

Costa Rica es un país situado en América Central; tiene 51.010 km cuadrados (19.653 millas cuadradas) y más de 3,8 millones de habitantes. Su paisaje es muy variado, lo cual quiere decir que tiene una biodiversidad maravillosa. Hay montañas, costas, ríos, volcanes y varios tipos de bosques y selvas tropicales, donde viven más de 700.000 especies de flora y fauna. Hay más de 2.000 variedades de orquídeas *(orchids)* y cientos de especies de insectos, incluyendo una cantidad de tipos de mariposas *(butterflies)* que viven en los ecosistemas del país. También hay mamíferos *(mammals)* interesantes como el perezoso con tres dedos *(three-toed sloth)* y diversos tipos de aves, como el quetzal.

Como en muchos países en vías de desarrollo *(developing countries),* la fuente de ingreso *(source of income)* más importante de Costa Rica era la agricultura. Eso significaba talar *(to cut down)* árboles para cultivar la tierra. En una época la deforestación llegó a ser un problema ambiental tan grave del país, que puso en peligro de extinción a muchas especies de flora y fauna. Afortunadamente, el gobierno de Costa Rica reconoció el problema y comenzó una campaña de reforestación y cuidado de la naturaleza.

En 1970, el gobierno costarricense estableció un sistema de parques nacionales con el fin de proteger las áreas de vida silvestre del país. Hoy en día, el 28 por ciento del país se encuentra protegido contra la destrucción del ecosistema. Hay reservas biológicas, refugios naturales y parques nacionales y los esfuerzos del gobierno han llegado a tal punto que el ecoturismo es ahora la fuente de ingreso más importante del país. Así, se asegura el bienestar del ser humano y también de la fauna y la flora.

PARA DISCUTIR

1. ¿Qué plantas, qué mamíferos, insectos y aves hay en Costa Rica que sean interesantes para el ecosistema?
2. Según el texto, ¿cuál era el problema más grave en Costa Rica?
3. ¿Cómo resolvió el gobierno costarricense este problema?
4. ¿Crees que es necesario establecer áreas para proteger la fauna y la flora?
5. ¿Cómo protege el gobierno estadounidense las áreas naturales importantes del país?
6. ¿Crees que el ecoturismo ha ayudado o beneficiado a Costa Rica o a los Estados Unidos? ¿Cómo?

ESTRUCTURA I Expressing emotion and opinions: subjunctive following verbs of emotion, impersonal expressions, and *ojalá*

In the previous chapter, you learned how to use the present subjunctive to express wishes, intentions, preferences, advice, suggestions, and recommendations. Spanish speakers also use verbs of emotion with the subjunctive to express their emotions and opinions.

I. Verbs of emotion and impersonal expressions

The list below contains verbs of emotion for expressing feelings and impersonal expressions for expressing opinions.

Verbs of emotion	Impersonal expressions
alegrarse (de) to be glad	**es bueno (malo)** it's good (bad)
esperar to hope	**es importante** it's important
gustar to like	**es (im)posible** it's (im)possible
molestar to bother	**es lógico** it's logical
preocuparse (de) (por)	**es mejor** it's better
to worry (about)	**es necesario** it's necessary
quejarse (de) to complain (about)	**es ridículo** it's ridiculous
sentir (ie) to be sorry	**es una lástima** it's a shame
sorprender to surprise	
tener miedo de to be afraid of	

The impersonal expressions **es obvio que, es cierto que, es seguro que,** and **es verdad que** do not cause the subjunctive in the subordinate clause because of their strong affirmative meanings: *Es obvio* que Mario *tiene* mejores oportunidades en la ciudad.

Use these above verbs and impersonal expressions exactly as you did with the verb **querer** and other verbs of volition.

One subject	**Change of subject**
Mario **espera encontrar** una vida mejor.	Mario **espera que la ciudad ofrezca** una vida mejor.
Mario hopes to find a better life.	*Mario hopes that the city offers a better life.*
Es importante tener un trabajo bueno.	**Es importante que Mario tenga** un trabajo bueno.
It's important to have a good job.	*It's important that Mario have a good job.*

II. Ojalá

You have learned that one way to express your desires and hopes is to use verbs like **querer, desear,** and **esperar.** Another way to express those feelings is to use the expression **ojalá (que)** with the subjunctive. This expression has several English equivalents including *let's hope that, I hope that,* and *if only,* all of which refer to some pending, unrealized action in the future. Note that **ojalá (que)** is always followed by the subjunctive, whether there is a change of subject or only one subject. The word **que** is often used after **ojalá** in writing, but it is usually omitted in conversation.

ojalá (que) + subjunctive

Ojalá lo pases bien en Costa Rica.	*I hope you have a good time in Costa Rica.*
Ojalá haga buen tiempo allá.	*Let's hope the weather is good there.*
Ojalá que recibas esta carta.	*I hope you receive this letter.*

¡A PRACTICAR!

12-7 | **Entre hermanos** Completa la siguiente conversación entre Rona y Luis Grandinetti, dos jóvenes de la ciudad, usando la forma correcta del verbo entre paréntesis.

Rona: Es una lástima que no te 1. (gustar / guste) pasar más tiempo al aire libre. Es bueno que 2. (disfrutar / disfrutes) de la naturaleza para relajarte *(relax)*.

Luis: No me gusta que 3. (criticarme / me critiques) por lo que hago en mi tiempo libre. ¿Necesito 4. (decirte / te diga) lo que tú debes hacer? Siento que no me 5. (comprender / comprendas), Rona.

Rona: Te comprendo perfectamente. Es lógico que no te 6. (gustar / guste) la naturaleza. Siempre estás mirando la tele.

12-8 | **Dos hermanos** Completa las siguientes oraciones para conocer un poco mejor a Luis y a Rona.

MODELO: Rona tiene quince años. Es mejor que ella *vaya a fiestas / exprese sus opiniones* (ir a fiestas / expresar sus opiniones).

1. A Rona no le gusta ver los programas deportivos. Es posible que ella _____ (no ser deportista / no practicar ningún deporte / preferir escuchar discos compactos / pasar mucho tiempo hablando por teléfono).
2. Rona es una estudiante excelente en el colegio, donde tiene muchos amigos. Es bueno que ella _____ (estudiar todos los días / tocar el piano / tener muchos amigos / ser una chica popular).
3. A veces, Luis y su hermana Rona tienen conflictos. Es lógico que ellos _____ (no siempre estar de acuerdo / discutir mucho en casa / expresar sus opiniones / darse consejos con cariño).

12-9 | **Ojalá que en Costa Rica...** Haz oraciones completas usando la información de Costa Rica con las frases a continuación y la forma correcta del verbo en el subjuntivo.

1. ojalá que / el volcán activo Irazú nunca hacer erupción *(eruption)*
2. ojalá que / el río San Juan, / que separa Costa Rica de Nicaragua por el norte, / no estar contaminado
3. ojalá que / llover mucho en la estación de lluvias / de mayo a diciembre
4. ojalá que / la gente / poder ver / las tortugas en la playa Parismina de la costa del Atlántico
5. ojalá que / el gobierno costarricense / cuidar / la fauna y la flora / por medio de reservas y parques naturales

EN VOZ ALTA

12-10 | **¡Ojalá!** Usando la expresión **ojalá,** descríbele a un(a) compañero(a) de clase diez deseos que quieres realizar dentro de tres años. Luego, cambien de papel.

> MODELO: E1: *Ojalá que yo encuentre trabajo.*
> E2: *Ojalá que yo pueda vivir en Hawai.*

12-11 | **¿Qué te parece?** Primero, escribe tus opiniones positivas y negativas sobre la posibilidad de vivir en una ciudad grande. Luego léele tus opiniones a un(a) compañero(a), que debe reaccionar positiva o negativamente.

> MODELO: E1: *Es mejor que vivas en la ciudad porque hay más oportunidades culturales.*
> E2: *No estoy de acuerdo. Solamente los ricos tienen acceso a los eventos culturales.*

Opiniones positivas

1. Me alegro de (que)...
2. Es bueno (que)...
3. Es mejor (que)...
4. No es malo (que)...
5. Me gusta (que)...
6. Es importante (que)...
7. Espero (que)...

Opiniones negativas

8. No me gusta (que)...
9. Me sorprende (que)..
10. Me molesta (que)...
11. Es malo (que)...
12. Es ridículo (que)...
13. Es terrible (que)...
14. Es una lástima (que)...

12-12 | **Tus opiniones** Escribe tus reacciones ante los siguientes temas. Luego forma un grupo con otros dos o tres compañeros y discutan sus opiniones sobre estos temas.

> MODELO: En la ciudad: la sobrepoblación
> E1: *Es necesario que tengamos familias más pequeñas.*
> E2: *No estoy de acuerdo. Ojalá que los padres tengan la libertad de tener familias grandes.*

1. En la ciudad: el tráfico
2. En el campo: las tierras para cultivar
3. En la ciudad: las oportunidades
4. En el campo: la tranquilidad
5. En la ciudad: muchos servicios
6. En el campo: poca gente, nada que hacer como diversión
7. En la ciudad: eventos culturales
8. En el campo: la naturaleza, los animales y las plantas

12-13 | **Un debate** Formen grupos de cuatro personas. Dos del grupo tienen que hacer una lista de las ventajas de vivir en una ciudad. Los otros dos tienen que escribir una lista de las ventajas de vivir en el campo. Después, hagan un debate entre las dos parejas del grupo.

La destrucción y la conservación del medio ambiente In this section you will learn how to talk about the destruction and the conservation of the environment.

¿NOS ENTENDEMOS?
While the verb **reciclar** means *to recycle,* **el reciclaje** is *recycling.* Although recycling is not as widespread a practice in the Spanish-speaking world as in other countries, awareness and participation are growing. Costa Rica leads Latin America in its recycling efforts.

Sustantivos

la capa de ozono ozone layer
el desarrollo development
la ecología ecology
la escasez lack, shortage

la extincíon extinction
el medio ambiente environment
la naturaleza nature
el petróleo petroleum

Verbos

acabar to run out
contaminar to pollute
desarrollar to develop
destruir to destroy
explotar to exploit

proteger to protect
recoger to pick up
reforestar to reforest
resolver (ue) to solve, resolve

Adjetivos

contaminado(a) polluted
destruido(a) destroyed
puro(a) pure

Expresión idiomática

¡No arroje basura! Don't litter!

¡A PRACTICAR!

12-14 | **Definiciones** Empareja cada palabra o frase con su definición.

1. ___ acabar
2. ___ resolver
3. ___ explotar
4. ___ el aire
5. ___ la capa de ozono
6. ___ el desarrollo
7. ___ puro

a. encontrar la solución de un problema
b. no contaminado
c. construcción de nuevos edificios
d. usar todo lo que hay de algo
e. aprovecharse de algo, usarlo sin pagar el precio
f. una parte de la atmósfera que se está destruyendo
g. lo que respiramos

12-15 | **Un chico muy malcriado** Jorge, un niño muy malcriado *(spoiled)*, no entiende nada de la preocupación con el medio ambiente. Él habla de sus opiniones sobre la ecología. Escoge las palabras a continuación para completar sus pensamientos.

destruir   naturaleza   conservar   petróleo   energía solar
contaminación   reciclar   arrojar   ecología   recursos naturales

Yo no comprendo nada de las preocupaciones sobre la 1. _____. Yo sé que yo no debo 2. _____ basura en el suelo, pero a veces no hay dónde ponerla. No veo por qué necesitamos 3. _____ el papel y otras cosas. Tampoco me gusta la idea de usar la energía del sol, o la 4. _____, para las casas. Yo no creo que vayamos a 5. _____ el medio ambiente. La 6. _____ siempre ha existido (has existed). Tenemos muchos 7. _____ como el aire, el agua y el 8. _____ No tengo ganas de 9. _____ nada. Yo sé que el mundo puede sobrevivir. ¿Para qué preocuparme por la 10. _____?

12-16 | **Consejos...** Termina los siguientes consejos que tus padres o familiares te dan con respecto a problemas del medio ambiente. Luego compara tus respuestas con las de tu compañero(a). ¿Tienen mucho en común?

MODELO: la naturaleza: Es recomendable que...
         Es recomendable que conservemos la naturaleza.

1. el agua: Es necesario que...
2. las latas *(cans)* de aluminio: Es mejor que...
3. la basura: Es importante que...
4. los periódicos *(newspapers)*: Es lógico que...
5. la capa de ozono: Es importante que...

EN VOZ ALTA

12-17 | **¿Por el bien o mal del medio ambiente?** A continuación hay una lista de palabras asociadas con el medio ambiente. En grupos de tres o cuatro estudiantes, dividan la lista en dos columnas. La primera columna debe tener las palabras que se asocian con los problemas del medio ambiente. La segunda columna debe incorporar palabras que sugieren modos de ayudar el medio ambiente. Luego, miren los dos grupos de palabras que escogieron. Hablen de por qué algunos términos son buenos o malos para el medio ambiente.

> MODELO: E1: *La deforestación es mala para el medio ambiente porque significa la destrucción de selvas y bosques.*
> E2: *Mi grupo seleccionó reforestar como algo bueno para el medio ambiente porque puede salvar bosques y selvas.*

1. recoger basura
2. reforestar
3. el desperdicio
4. la destrucción
5. proteger
6. la escasez de los recursos naturales
7. reciclar aluminio
8. conservar
9. proteger
10. el desarrollo
11. la energía solar
12. contaminar

12-18 | **Prioridades** Imagínate que eres el (la) presidente de los Estados Unidos y tus consejeros te dan una lista de medidas *(measures)* posibles que tienes que evaluar. Indica la urgencia de cada situación con las siguientes letras: necesidad **(N)**, prioridad **(P)**, importante pero no urgente **(I)**, no es importante **(NI).** Puedes marcar solamente tres cosas como **necesidades.** Luego, explícales tus decisiones a dos de tus consejeros (miembros de tu clase). Ellos deben persuadirte de que cambies de opinión si no están de acuerdo.

> MODELO: prohibir el uso de coches privados
> *(P) Yo creo que es necesario que prohibamos el uso de coches privados. Pienso que todo el mundo debe usar el transporte público para evitar la contaminación.*

1. poner multas *(fines)* a los individuos que arrojan basura en las carreteras
2. acabar con la destrucción de la capa de ozono
3. reducir los desperdicios de los centros urbanos
4. desarrollar la energía solar
5. controlar mejor la contaminación de los ríos
6. evitar *(to avoid)* el consumo de los recursos naturales
7. sembrar más árboles en los centros urbanos
8. hacer leyes *(laws)* más estrictas para proteger la ecología de las selvas tropicales

12-19 | **Entrevista** Hazle las siguientes preguntas a un(a) compañero(a) de clase y comparen sus respuestas. ¿Tienen mucho en común?

1. En tu opinión, ¿cuál es el problema ecológico más grave que tenemos ahora? ¿Es posible que encontremos una solución para este problema? ¿Haces algo para aliviar este problema?
2. ¿Qué haces para conservar nuestros recursos naturales? ¿Reciclas? ¿Andas en bicicleta o vas a pie para gastar menos gasolina? ¿Bajas el termostato en invierno o usas menos el aire acondicionado en verano?
3. ¿Depende nuestra sociedad demasiado del petróleo? ¿Es posible tener desarrollo económico y conservar energía a la vez? ¿En qué sentido es la crisis ecológica un problema de dimensiones internacionales? ¿Qué debemos enseñarles a nuestros hijos para que no tengan los mismos problemas que nosotros?

Costa Rica: Estación biológica La Selva

Automris panima, Costa Rica

Sapo flecha venenoso,
La Selva Estación Biológica, Costa Rica

PARA PENSAR

- ¿Cuántas estaciones hay donde vives?

- ¿Cómo es la fauna y la flora de tu región y cómo las protege el gobierno?

- ¿Hay estaciones de estudios científicos para tu universidad o escuela en algún país del mundo?

En Costa Rica existen varias estaciones biológicas importantes como, por ejemplo, Palo Verde, Las Cruces y la Estación de La Selva. En 1954, la doctora Leslie Holdridge estableció un arboretum de más de 1.000 árboles para experimentar con plantas y estudiar cómo utilizar mejor los recursos naturales en la Estación La Selva. En 1968, la Organización de Estudios Tropicales adquirió la estación como un centro privado de estudios y de investigación científica. Esta organización está formada por 65 facultades (*departments*) de biología de universidades de Costa Rica, los Estados Unidos, Latinoamérica y de Australia que actualmente estudian el equilibrio (*balance*) del medio ambiente. Esta estación es uno de los lugares más importantes para investigar la selva nubosa tropical (*rain forest*). Hay más de 240 trabajos científicos escritos sobre esta región.

En esta estación hay más de 5.000 especies diferentes de plantas, más de 700 especies de árboles, hay animales de gran tamaño como jaguares y pumas, más de 400 especies de aves y 60 diferentes especies de murciélagos (*bats*) para estudiar e investigar. Este lugar sirve de laboratorio vivo y por eso los estudiantes e investigadores tienen la facilidad de usar dos laboratorios bien equipados, entre ellos uno analítico, donde se puede trabajar en un ambiente con aire acondicionado y otro con el equipo básico necesario. Para las referencias espaciales se usa el Sistema de Información Geográfica (SIG) y la estación tiene correo electrónico e Internet.

La Selva puede recibir confortablemente a unas ochenta personas, en habitaciones y cabinas para seis personas cada una. El comedor central puede servir a cien personas diariamente. También hay un taller que sirve para suplir (*supply*) las necesidades de mantenimiento de la estación y las necesidades de los investigadores. Los servicios que ofrece la estación, además de la ventaja de tener el Parque Nacional Braulio Carrillo muy cerca, hacen de La Selva un lugar ideal para investigar diferentes ecosistemas.

PARA DISCUTIR

1. ¿Cómo comenzó la estación biológica de La Selva?

2. ¿Qué hace la Organización de Estudios Tropicales? ¿Cómo está formada?

3. ¿Qué facilidades tiene esta estación para los estudiantes y científicos?

4. ¿Te gustaría estudiar o trabajar por un semestre en una estación biológica? ¿Por qué sí o por qué no?

5. ¿Crees que deben haber más estaciones biológicas como las de Costa Rica en el mundo?

ESTRUCTURA II Expressing doubts, uncertainty, and hypothesizing: the subjunctive with verbs, expressions of uncertainty, and adjective clauses

I. Present subjunctive following verbs and expressions of doubt and uncertainty

Spanish speakers also use the subjunctive mood to express doubt, uncertainty, disbelief, nonexistence, and indefiniteness. You can use the following verbs and expressions to communicate uncertainty; they are used like those shown in **Estructura I**.

dudar *to doubt*

> **Dudo** que Rona **conserve** energía.

> *I doubt that Rona conserves energy.*

es dudoso *it's doubtful*

> **Es dudoso** que **haya** mucha agua pura.

> *It's doubtful that there is much pure water.*

no creer *not to believe*

> **No creo** que **salvemos el planeta.**

> *I don't believe that we will save the planet.*

no es cierto *it's uncertain*

> **No es cierto** que **tengamos** suficientes recursos naturales.

> *It's not true that we have enough natural resources.*

Although the subjunctive is not used after the impersonal expression **es cierto que,** it is required after the negative form because it expresses doubt. The verb **pensar** also requires the subjunctive when it is negated.

no estar seguro(a) (de) *to be uncertain*

> **No estoy seguro(a) de** que **ayude** el reciclaje.

> *I'm not sure that recycling helps.*

no pensar *to not think*

> **No pienso** que **debamos seguir** así.

> *I don't think that we should continue like this.*

II. Present subjunctive following adjective clauses that express hypothetical situations

Spanish speakers use the indicative mood after **que** to refer to people and things they are *certain about* and *believe to be true*. Consider the following example:

> Me llamo Rona Grandinetti. Vivo en San José, una ciudad grande. **Sé** que el aire **está** contaminado aquí. **Creo** que **hay** demasiados autos que contaminan el aire. **No dudo** que **necesitamos** más transporte público.
>
> *Rona tells us that she lives in San José, a large city. She also knows that the air is polluted there, caused by too many cars in the city. She has no doubt that San José needs more public transportation.*

Since Rona knows these facts or feels certain about them, she uses verbs in the indicative after **que.**

Spanish speakers use the subjunctive mood after **que** when they describe hypothetical people, places, things, or conditions, or when they do not believe that they exist at all. These types of structures are called *adjective clauses* because they qualify the preceding noun. In the following example, **una ciudad** is qualified by the clause **que sea tan bonita como Golfito.** Note that this particular use of the indicative or the subjunctive does not depend on the concept conveyed by the verb in the independent clause.

> Quiero vivir en **una ciudad que sea** tan bonita como Golfito. **Busco una ciudad que no tenga** mucha gente y **que esté** cerca del mar.
>
> *Now Rona tells us about an idealized city that she is searching for. The city must have certain qualifications such as being in a beautiful location, not having a lot of people, and being near the sea. Since it is indefinite or uncertain that Rona will find such a city, she uses the subjunctive after* **que.**

¡OJO! Use the **a personal** before a direct object that refers to a specific person (in the indicative). If the person referred to is not specified, however, omit the **a personal**, except before **alguien, nadie, alguno,** and **ninguno.** ¿Conoces **a alguien** que vaya a la conferencia? (a + **alguien**) Conozco **a María Cristina** que es estudiante. (a + *specific person*) *But:* Necesito **un amigo** que vaya conmigo. (omit a + *nonspecific person*)

¡A PRACTICAR!

12-20 | Una conversación entre Luis y Rona Luis y Rona quieren ir con su familia a un parque nacional durante sus vacaciones. Usando el verbo adecuado entre paréntesis, completa la siguiente conversación para saber qué parque escogen.

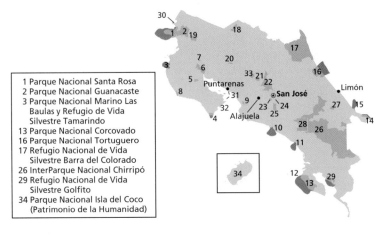

1 Parque Nacional Santa Rosa
2 Parque Nacional Guanacaste
3 Parque Nacional Marino Las Baulas y Refugio de Vida Silvestre Tamarindo
13 Parque Nacional Corcovado
16 Parque Nacional Tortuguero
17 Refugio Nacional de Vida Silvestre Barra del Colorado
26 InterParque Nacional Chirripó
29 Refugio Nacional de Vida Silvestre Golfito
34 Parque Nacional Isla del Coco (Patrimonio de la Humanidad)

Rona: Creo que 1. (debemos / debamos) visitar el Parque Nacional Tortuguero.

Luis: Pues, sé que se 2. (encuentra / encuentre) en la costa caribeña al norte de nuestro país, pero no estoy seguro (de) que ese parque 3. (tiene / tenga) flora y fauna especialmente interesante.

Rona: ¿Dudas que las tortugas verdes 4. (son / sean) interesantes? Seis de las ocho especies marinas de tortugas del mundo viven en Tortuguero.

Luis: ¿De veras? Ahora pienso que 5. (podemos / podamos) aprender mucho si vamos allá. ¿Cuándo salimos para ese parque?

Rona: Espera un momentito. Tenemos que considerar otra posibilidad. Mi profesor de biología piensa que la Reserva Biológica Bosque Nuboso Monteverde 6. (es / sea) el lugar natural más interesante de Costa Rica. Tiene una variedad enorme de flora y fauna. Él dice que las orquídeas son bellísimas y los jaguares son muy impresionantes. ¿No crees que este parque 7. (merece / merezca) consideración?

Luis: Pues, claro que sí. Pero dudo que (8) (podemos / podamos) visitar dos parques este año. Debemos ir a Tortuguero ahora y planear una visita a Monteverde en el futuro.

12-21 | Unas vacaciones ecológicas El año pasado Rona y Luis fueron a Golfito para participar en un proyecto de conservación ecológica en el Parque Nacional Piedras Blancas. Se quedaron en un hotel donde se quejaron un poco de algunas cosas que encontraron. ¿Qué le dijeron al recepcionista?

MODELO: ¿hay un cuarto / tener dos camas?
E1: *¿Hay un cuarto que tenga dos camas?*
E2: *Sí, hay un cuarto que tiene dos camas.*
o *No, no hay un cuarto que tenga dos camas.*

Antes de ver el cuarto

1. ¿no tiene Ud. otros cuartos / costar un poco menos?
2. ¿puede Ud. darnos un cuarto / estar en el tercer piso?
3. ¿es posible darnos un cuarto / tener una vista al bosque?
4. ¿hay alguien / poder ayudarnos con las maletas?

Después de ver el cuarto

5. deseamos un cuarto / no ser tan feo como ése
6. buscamos un empleado / poder darnos más toallas
7. queremos otro cuarto con una ducha / funcionar mejor

CULTURA
In addition to marine turtles, manatees and crocodiles live under protection in Tortuguero.

CULTURA
Monteverde is a privately funded park that includes more than 100 species of mammals, 400 species of birds, 120 species of reptiles and amphibians, and more than 2,500 species of plants.

CULTURA
The Piedras Blancas National Park was established in 1991 in an effort to preserve one of the last unprotected lowland tropical rainforests on the Pacific coast of Central America. Before the declaration of the park, deforestation was taking place, causing irreversible damage to the Esquinas Forest. While logging has ceased almost completely, some of the land in the park still belongs to private owners who can legally request logging permits until that land is all owned by the national parks system.

12-22 **Dos amigos** Con un(a) compañero(a), completa las siguientes conversaciones entre Luis y su amigo Jorge, como en el modelo.

> MODELO: Luis: mis padres creen / (yo) reciclar mucho
> Jorge: ¿Cómo? no creo / (tú) reciclar mucho porque...
> Luis: *Mis padres creen que reciclo mucho.*
> Jorge: *¿Cómo? No creo que recicles mucho porque eres perezoso.*

1. Jorge: creo / ir (yo) a participar en el proyecto de conservación
   Luis: dudo / (tú) participar porque...
   Jorge: no creo / (tú) tienes razón porque...
2. Jorge: quiero / tú y yo volver a Golfito en mayo
   Luis: es dudoso / (nosotros) volver porque...
3. Jorge: mis padres creen / (yo) ser perezoso
   Luis: no dudo / (tú) ser perezoso porque...
4. Luis: Rona no está segura / sus amigos querer participar en el proyecto
   Jorge: no hay duda / ellos querer participar porque...

EN VOZ ALTA

12-23 **La ciudad ideal** Descríbele a un(a) compañero(a) de clase cinco atributos de tu ciudad ideal, utilizando el vocabulario de este capítulo.

> MODELO: *Quiero vivir en una ciudad donde no haya contaminación, que tenga un buen sistema de transporte público y que sea bonita.*

12-24 **¿Qué crees tú?** Descríbele tus ideas sobre los siguientes temas a un(a) compañero(a) y hablen de sus respuestas. Expresen sus creencias con las siguientes frases: **Creo que... Dudo que... No creo que... Es dudoso que... Estoy seguro(a) de que... Es obvio que...** , etcétera.

> MODELO: la ecología
> *Creo que la ecología es muy importante.*
> o *No creo que la ecología sea importante.*

1. el aire y el agua
2. el reciclaje
3. los recursos naturales
4. la deforestación
5. la capa de ozono
6. el universo
7. el medio ambiente
8. la construcción de carreteras grandes
9. ¿ ?

12-25 **El futuro incierto** No hay nada más incierto que el futuro, pero es importante hacer planes. Habla con un(a) compañero(a) de clase sobre tus ambiciones. ¿Tienen mucho en común?

> MODELO: *Algún día quiero vivir en un lugar que esté cerca del mar...*

1. Algún día quiero vivir en un lugar que...
2. Para vivir allí sé que..., pero dudo que...
3. No estoy seguro(a) que... en ese lugar, pero creo que...
4. En ese lugar, hay...
5. Por eso, estoy seguro(a) de que...

VOCABULARIO Los animales y el refugio natural

CULTURA

The Golfito Reserve is in a wilderness area with a lot of rain. The forest is very thick, with species that are similar to those within the Osa Peninsula. Many animals such as butterflies, toucans, monkeys, scarlet macaws, tapirs, parrots, boas, sloths, and jaguars call the reserve home. The reserve is important for the conservation of the water supply for the city of Golfito.

CULTURA

A large variety of birds and snakes are to be found in the lush woods of Golfito, Costa Rica. Though rare, coral snakes and vipers live in the forest and their bites can be life-threatening. The vipers grow to more than six feet long and are characterized by a triangular head.

¿NOS ENTENDEMOS?

La víbora and la serpiente are synonyms for la culebra.

En la reserva biológica de Golfito In this section you will learn about animals on a wildlife reserve.

Las especies en peligro de extinción

Palabras útiles are presented to help you enrich your personal vocabulary. The words here will help you talk about animals on a wildlife reserve.

Palabras útiles

el **búho** owl
el **caimán** alligator
el **camello** camel
la **cebra** zebra
el **ciervo** deer
el **elefante** elephant
el **gorila** gorilla
el **hipopótamo** hippopotamus
el **león** lion

el **lobo** wolf
el **oso** bear
la **pantera** panther
la **rana** frog
el **rinoceronte** rhinoceros
el **tigre** tiger
la **tortuga** turtle
el **zorro** fox

¡A PRACTICAR!

12-26 ¿Dónde viven los animales? En grupos de tres o cuatro, hablen de dónde viven los siguientes animales —en el agua, los árboles, la tierra o el aire. Más de una respuesta puede ser correcta.

1. la culebra
2. el mono
3. el pájaro
4. el jaguar
5. el cocodrilo
6. la mariposa
7. los murciélagos
8. el sapo
9. las hormigas

12-27 Ricardo, el guardaparques Ricky ha trabajado en numerosas reservas naturales en Costa Rica; por eso él conoce muchos tipos de animales. Completa la historia a continuación con las siguientes palabras para terminar la historia de Ricardo.

culebra	en peligro de extinción	especies	naturalistas
murciélagos	jaguar	guardaparques	cocodrilos
pájaros	monos	hormigas	sapo

¡Hola! Me llamo Ricardo, y he trabajado como 1. _____ en muchas reservas biológicas de Costa Rica. En las reservas ecológicas hay muchas 2. _____ de plantas y animales diferentes. Mi trabajo siempre ha sido muy interesante, porque me gusta mucho la naturaleza.

He visto 3. _____ que vuelan en el cielo. En Costa Rica, el pájaro más espectacular es el quetzal. En los árboles, viven muchos 4. _____ con cara blanca que juegan colgándose de las ramas (hanging from the branches). En el agua, a veces hay 5. _____ verdes y peligrosos. Pero no son muy comunes. Éstos fácilmente se confunden con los caimanes americanos. También, he tenido la oportunidad de ver muchos animales que están 6. _____. Cuando me mantengo el silencio, he podido ver a veces al rey de la selva latinoamericana, el 7. _____. Una vez, vi un anfibio (amphibian) que hoy ha desaparecido, se llama 8. «el _____ dorado». También hay muchos 9. _____ que solamente vuelan de noche, cazando insectos y frutas. Siempre he tenido cuidado de no pisar (to step on) una 10. _____ venenosa (poisonous), como «la víbora de árbol». Éstas prefieren los árboles, pero se encuentran a veces sobre la tierra. Son de un verde brillante con dos rayas laterales amarillas. ¡Son muy peligrosas! Finalmente, hay muchos insectos que viven en la selva, como las 11. _____. Muchas veces, tenemos 12. _____ que vienen a visitar las reservas para estudiar los animales y las plantas. ¡Me fascina mi trabajo!

> **CULTURA**
> Costa Rica has 136 species of snakes. Of these, only 18 are venomous.

EN VOZ ALTA

12-28 Yo estoy pensando en un animal... Un miembro de la clase va a escoger un animal de la lista de vocabulario. Los otros estudiantes solamente pueden hacer preguntas de **sí** o **no** para adivinar el animal. La persona que adivine correctamente toma el siguiente turno.

MODELO: E1: *¿Vive en el agua?*
E2: *No. Pero a veces anda por el agua.*
E3: *¿Es un animal peligroso?*

E1: *Sí. Puede ser muy peligroso.*
E2: *¿Es una culebra?*
E1: *¡Sí!*

12-29 ¡Peligro de extinción! Los siguientes animales están en peligro de extinción. En grupos de tres personas, hablen de lo que podemos hacer para salvar estos animales. Por ejemplo, ¿podemos controlar el número de otros animales que sean sus depredatores? ¿Podemos tratar de criarlos (raise them) en una reserva o en un parque zoológico? Traten también de adivinar por qué están en peligro.

Después, busquen información en Internet o en una enciclopedia para averiguar sobre sus adivinanzas.

1. el gorila
2. el oso panda
3. el tigre de Bengala
4. el cocodrilo
5. el elefante
6. el jaguar

SÍNTESIS

¡A VER!

En este segmento del video, el grupo participa en una actividad en el mar que es muy popular para los turistas. Sin embargo, a pesar de su popularidad, no se disfrutan todos los compañeros de esta actividad.

Expresiones útiles

Las siguientes son expresiones nuevas que vas a escuchar en el video.

Zarpar   To cast off
Chiquilla   Little one

Antes de ver

Paso 1: Con un(a) compañero(a) hagan una lista de algunas actividades que los turistas pueden hacer en Puerto Rico. Luego elijan las actividades que les gustan más.

Paso 2: Con un(a) compañero(a) respondan a las siguientes preguntas para ver quién de Uds. conoce más gente que se disfruta de las actividades del mar.

- ¿Quién conoce a alguien que no sepa nadar?
- ¿Quién conoce a alguien que vaya al esnórkeling con frecuencia?
- ¿Quién conoce a alguien que sepa bucear?
- ¿Quién conoce a alguien a quien le guste pescar en el mar?

Después de ver

Paso 1: En **Antes de ver, Paso 1**, tu compañero(a) y tú hicieron una lista de las actividades que los turistas pueden hacer en Puerto Rico. En el video, viste que la actividad que los compañeros hicieron fue esnórkeling. Completa el siguiente párrafo con la forma apropiada del presente del indicativo o del subjuntivo de los verbos entre paréntesis para contar algunos de los detalles de esta experiencia de los compañeros de casa.

En general, Javier se alegra de que todos los compañeros _____ **(ir)** al esnórkeling en Puerto Rico. Cuando llegan a la marina, todos abordan el bote y se preparan para la actividad. El guía les da el equipo e insiste en que _____ **(agarrar)** las máscaras cuando brincan del bote. Valeria no participa porque no sabe nadar y tiene miedo del agua. Alejandra se preocupa porque no _____ **(poder)** respirar bien con la máscara al principio. Sin embargo, luego se acostumbra. Sofía no vive cerca del mar, y por eso es lógico que no _____ **(estar)** acostumbrada a estar en un barco. Antonio dice que el esnórkeling _____ **(ser)** una experiencia que nunca va a olvidar y los otros compañeros están de acuerdo.

Paso 2: En **Antes de ver, Paso 2**, tu compañero(a) y tú hablaron de gente conocida que hace actividades del mar. Ahora, piensa en los compañeros de casa y sus actividades en este segmento del video. Completa las siguientes oraciones con la forma apropiada del presente del indicativo o del subjuntivo de los verbos entre paréntesis. Luego decide si las oraciones son ciertas o falsas. Corrige las oraciones falsas.

• Hay una persona en el grupo que no _____ **(saber)** nadar. _____

• No hay nadie que no _____ **(ir)** al esnórkeling. _____

• Hay dos personas que _____ **(brincar)** de cabeza (*dive head first*) del bote. _____

• Hay cuatro personas que _____ **(divertirse)** mucho en la playa. _____

¿Qué opinas tú?

Paso 1: A Valeria no le gustó la idea de esnórkeling en el segmento del video porque no sabe nadar y tiene miedo del agua. Trabaja con un(a) compañero(a) y planea otra actividad al aire libre en Puerto Rico que creen que todos los compañeros (incluso Valeria) van a disfrutar. Justifiquen la selección de la actividad que proponen a la clase.

Paso 2: Quieres saber qué tipo de actividades acuáticas son muy populares en tu clase. Habla con tus compañeros de clase para poder responder a las siguientes preguntas:

¿Hay alguien en la clase que...

• sepa bucear?
• no pueda nadar?
• haga esnórkeling con frecuencia?
• practique la pesca en el mar?
• ¿ ?

Luego usa las siguientes oraciones para presentar los resultados de tu encuesta a la clase:

Hay _____ personas que _____ , y _____ personas que _____ .
No hay nadie que _____ .
En mi clase, parece que una actividad acuática bien popular es la de _____ .

¡A LEER!

Strategy: Understanding the writer's perspective

In many cases, you can use information you know about the author, his/her background, or his/her previous work to give you some perspective on the reading. Often this information can be useful in interpreting themes or messages that the author is attempting to convey via literature. Fortunately, many literary works (novels, collections of short stories, collections of poems, etc.) contain an introduction that gives at least some biographical information about the author, and in many cases provides some insight into the nature of the author's literary production.

For example, consider the following short story, written by the well-known Costa Rican female writer Carmen Naranjo. A short biography is provided. Does this introduction to the author provide you with information you can use to interpret the short story that follows?

Paso 1: Lee la siguiente biografía de la autora Carmen Naranjo y contesta las siguientes preguntas.

1. ¿Dónde nació la autora? ¿Dónde vive ahora?
2. ¿Qué tipos de trabajo ha tenido la autora?
3. Al leer los títulos (*titles*) de sus obras, ¿qué tipo de literatura escribe?

- **Carmen Naranjo** nació el 30 de enero de 1928 en Cartago, Costa Rica.
- Estudió la escuela primaria en la Escuela República del Perú. Luego la secundaria en el Bachiller del Colegio Superior de Señoritas en 1946. Estudió en la Facultad de Ciencias y Letras de la Universidad de Costa Rica, donde obtuvo el título de licenciada en filología (*Bachelor in philology*). Luego, siguió cursos de posgrado (*Master's*) en la Universidad Autónoma de México y en la Escuela de Letras de la Universidad de Iowa, en Estados Unidos.
- La autora ha trabajado como experta de las Naciones Unidas y en la Organización de Estados Americanos en El Salvador, la República Dominicana, México y los Estados Unidos. Además, ella ha dirigido los programas Regionales del Fondo para la Infancia de las Naciones Unidas UNICEF, y ha sido coordinadora técnico-administrativa del Instituto Centroamericano de Administración Pública ICAP.
- Ha sido embajadora de Costa Rica en Israel, ministra de Cultura, presidenta del Consejo Nacional de Educación Física y directora del Museo de Arte Costarricense, entre otras funciones.
- Ella ha ganado todos los premios literarios en Costa Rica: entre otros, el Premio Nacional Magón (1986) y Aquileo J. Echeverría de novela en dos ocasiones (1966 y 1971). Además, la Universidad de Santo Domingo (República Dominicana) le confirió un doctorado honoris causa (1991), y el gobierno de Chile, la Medalla Gabriela Mistral (1996).
- La autora tiene más de 31 textos de varios géneros: poesía, ensayo, cuento y novela. Algunas de sus obras han sido traducidas al inglés, al hebreo, al yugoslavo y al griego. Entre sus obras están:

América	*Las relaciones públicas en las instituciones de seguridad social*
Canción de la ternura	
Hacia tu isla	*Idioma del invierno*
En el círculo de los pronombres	*Hoy es un largo día*
Misa a oscuras	*Diario de una multitud*
Camino al mediodía	*Por las páginas de la Biblia y los caminos de Israel*
Memorias de un hombre palabra	
Los girasoles perdidos	*Mi guerrilla*
Responso para el niño Juan Manuel	*Cinco temas en busca de un pensador*

- Ahora vive en medio de los árboles frutales en su oasis de Tambor de Alajuela, Costa Rica.

Paso 2: Ahora, lee el fragmento del cuento *Responso para el niño Juan Manuel* por Naranjo. Luego organiza los acontecimientos de acuerdo con la historia. En esta historia la escritora explora la frustación humana, el aislamiento, el abandono y la soledad. Usando el diálogo y el monólogo interior, el viejo muestra la soledad que le rodea...

_____ El señor trabaja arreglando jardines.

_____ Al principio, al viejo le gusta vivir en casas pequeñas, vacías porque parecen acogedoras.

_____ El viejo aburre a las personas con sus cuentos.

_____ La única credencial del viejo es su honradez.

_____ En las casas pequeñas, la persona es sólo un ser extraño.

Responso para el niño Juan Manuel

– Estaba pensando en algún tema de interés para conversar. Debe estar aburrido de tanto silencio...

– Nunca me aburro *(get bored)*, los viejos tenemos esa cualidad. Lo malo es que aburrimos a los demás...

– ¿En qué trabaja?

– Hago todo lo que es posible hacer a mi edad. Arreglo jardines, cuido casas, trabajo de guardia *(guard)*. Últimamente no he podido encontrar un trabajo fijo. Mi única credencial es la honradez *(honesty)* y no me dan oportunidad de probarla.

– ¿Cuida casas vacías?... ¿Qué se siente al vivir en una casa vacía?

– Se sienten muchas cosas, claro esto depende del tipo de casa. Las casas grandes, por ejemplo, nunca parecen del todo vacías. Las casas pequeñas resultan acogedoras *(cozy)* al principio, pero luego lo llenan a uno de inquietudes incómodas, para recordarle que no es su sitio, es sólo un extraño entre las paredes.

– He hablado mucho. Ése es el problema de los silenciosos. Se les pide una opinión y se exceden. Sin embargo, veo en sus caras una cordialidad que no había antes, los gestos de estos dos señores se han suavizado.

Paso 3: Después de leer el cuento, contesta las siguientes preguntas.

1. En tu opinión, ¿cuál es el tema principal del cuento?

2. ¿Qué comentario hace Naranjo acerca de la relación de los viejos cuando buscan un trabajo?

3. ¿Qué piensas de la honradez como parte de tu currículum cuando vas a buscar un trabajo?

4. ¿Qué tipos de trabajos has hecho? ¿Has cuidado casas alguna vez? ¿Te gustó ese trabajo?

5. ¿Qué relación existe entre el cuento *Responso para el niño Juan Manuel* y la forma en que vive la autora?

¡A ESCRIBIR!

Strategy: Making your writing persuasive

Writers often try to convince readers to understand or adopt particular points of view. Persuasive writing is used by writers of editorials, by political figures, and often by professionals such as attorneys, medical personnel, educators, and reviewers or critics. In this section you will write an essay in which you try to convince your reader of your point of view regarding a particular environmental issue. The following words and phrases will allow you to connect your ideas in this type of composition.

To express opinions . . .
creo que I believe
pienso que I think
en mi opinión in my opinion

To support opinions . . .
primero first
una razón one reason
por ejemplo for example

To show contrast . . .
pero but
aunque although
por otro lado on the other hand

To summarize . . .
por eso therefore
finalmente finally
en conclusión in conclusion

Task: Writing a persuasive essay

Paso 1: Formula tu opinión sobre uno de los temas que siguen.

- El mejor lugar para vivir (en el campo, en la ciudad, etc.)

- El mejor medio de transporte (el coche, la bicicleta, el autobús, el tren, etc.)

- El problema global más grave (la contaminación del aire, la sobrepoblación, la destrucción de las selvas tropicales, etc.)

- La mejor manera de resolver los problemas del medio ambiente (controlar la contaminación de los ríos, reciclar, desarrollar energía solar, etc.)

- El mejor lugar para los animales (en estado silvestre *(in the wild)* o en un refugio natural)

Functions: Persuading; Expressing an opinion; Agreeing and disagreeing; Comparing and contrasting
Vocabulary: Animals; Automobile; Geography; Means of transportation
Grammar: Verbs: present; Verbs: subjunctive

Paso 2: Escribe un ensayo en el cual des tu opinión sobre el tema que hayas escogido. Debes mencionar dos razones con detalles que apoyan tu posición. Al final, escribe una conclusión. Tu ensayo debe tener cuatro párrafos. Puedes seguir el esbozo *(outline)* y el modelo que siguen, los cuales tratan de este tema: **El mejor medio de transporte.**

I. Introducción (tu opinión sobre el tema)
El mejor medio de transporte es el autobús.

II. Primera razón a favor de tu opinión
Hay menos coches en la carretera cuando la gente viaja en autobús.
Viajar en autobús ayuda a reducir la contaminación del aire.

III. Segunda razón a favor de tu opinión
Una persona puede leer y descansar mientras viaja en autobús.
El autobús reduce el estrés de los pasajeros.

IV. Conclusión
Todos deben viajar en autobús.

MODELO:

> Creo que el mejor medio de transporte es el autobús. El autobús tiene varios aspectos positivos.
>
> Una razón es que el autobús nos ayuda a conservar el medio ambiente. Cuando la gente viaja en autobús, no tiene que usar el coche. Si hay menos coches en la carretera, hay menos contaminación del aire. Por eso, el autobús no contamina el medio ambiente tanto como los coches.
>
> Otra razón es que el autobús es mejor para el bienestar de las personas. Por ejemplo, una persona puede leer y descansar mientras viaja en autobús. Esto reduce el estrés de los pasajeros.
>
> En conclusión, pienso que el autobús es el mejor medio de transporte. Es bueno para el medio ambiente y para los pasajeros.

Paso 3: Intercambia papeles con un(a) compañero(a) de clase. Lee el ensayo de la otra persona para ver si tiene los elementos necesarios y para ver si presenta la opinión claramente. Si la otra persona necesita hacer algunos cambios, habla con él/ella sobre los cambios que recomiendas. También dile si estás de acuerdo con su opinión o no.

¡A CONVERSAR!

Task: Talking about environmental issues

Es cierto que el medio ambiente es un tópico de mucha importancia en el mundo moderno. Algunas personas se preocupan por los efectos de la contaminación, la sobrepoblación, el desarrollo y la destrucción de la capa de ozono. Otras personas no se preocupan tanto, pero casi todos reconocen que éste es un tema que provoca mucha discusión. Ahora vas a tratar sobre este tópico.

Paso 1: Habla con un(a) compañero(a) de clase acerca de los problemas ambientales que existen en el mundo contemporáneo. Debes hacerle las preguntas que siguen.

- ¿Te preocupas poco o mucho por los problemas del medio ambiente? Explica tu respuesta.
- ¿Qué problemas te molestan más? ¿Por qué?
- En tu opinión, ¿qué responsabilidades tenemos para conservar los recursos naturales?

Paso 2: Entonces, cambien de papel y continúen la conversación.

Paso 3: Formen grupos de cuatro para comparar y contrastar las respuestas de los varios miembros del grupo.

La geografía rural y urbana Rural and urban geography

Sustantivos

el (la) agricultor(a) farmer
el arroyo stream
la basura trash
el bosque forest
el (la) campesino(a) farm worker, peasant
la carretera highway

la catarata waterfall
la colina hill
la fábrica factory
la finca farm
la metrópolis metropolis
el rascacielos skyscraper

el ruido noise
la selva jungle
la sobrepoblación overpopulation
la tierra land, earth
el tráfico traffic
el transporte público public transportation

Verbos

cultivar to cultivate; to grow (plants)
llevar una vida tranquila to lead a peaceful life

regar (ie) to irrigate; to water

sembrar (ie) to plant

Adjetivos

acelerado(a) accelerated
bello(a) beautiful

denso(a) dense

tranquilo(a) tranquil, peaceful

Conservación y explotación Conservation and exploitation

Sustantivos

el aire air
la capa de ozono ozone layer
la contaminación pollution
el desarrollo development
el desperdicio waste

la destrucción destruction
la ecología ecology
la energía solar solar energy
la escasez lack, shortage
el medio ambiente environment

la naturaleza nature
el petróleo petroleum
los recursos naturales natural resources

Verbos

acabar to run out
conservar to conserve
construir to construct
contaminar to pollute

desarrollar to develop
destruir to destroy
explotar to exploit
proteger to protect

reciclar to recycle
recoger to pick up
reforestar to reforest
resolver (ue) to solve, resolve

Adjetivos

contaminado(a) polluted

destruido(a) destroyed

puro(a) pure

Expresiones idiomáticas

¡No arroje basura! Don't litter!

Los animales y el refugio natural Animals and the wildlife preserve

Sustantivos

el cocodrilo crocodile
la culebra snake
las especies species
el guardaparques park ranger

las hormigas ants
el jaguar jaguar
la mariposa butterfly
el mono monkey

los murciélagos bats
el (la) naturalista naturalist
el pájaro bird
el sapo toad

Expresiones idiomáticas

en peligro de extinción in danger of extinction

PLAZAS

En esta edición vas a conocer a personas importantes de la política y del mundo artístico. Vas a conocer también lugares y aspectos culturales y económicos de países centroamericanos como Nicaragua, Honduras, Costa Rica y Panamá. Luego vas a comparar tus ideas y opiniones con las de tus compañeros de clase y nuestros editores. Participa con nosotros y vas a ver que tenemos mucho en común.

- Fundación Violeta Barrios de Chamorro
- En Honduras hay trabajo para el verano
- Costa Rica: Recursos naturales para pagar la deuda externa
- Rubén Blades: Cuando una carrera no es suficiente...

Fundación Violeta Barrios de Chamorro

Violeta Barrios de Chamorro (1929) fue la primera mujer elegida presidenta en un país centroamericano (Nicaragua, 1990–1997), y hoy en día a través de la Fundación que lleva su nombre sigue trabajando para programas y proyectos en tres diferentes líneas de acción:

1. «Educación por la paz, la democracia y la reconciliación de la familia nicaragüense».
2. «Consolidar y defender la libertad de expresión y apoyar el periodismo nacional».
3. Disminuir la pobreza.

Doña Violeta antes de ser Presidenta de Nicaragua fue la directora del Diario La Prensa en nombre/honor a su esposo Pedro Joaquín Chamorro quien murió asesinado *(was assassinated)* el 10 de enero de 1978 por ser un periodista muy valiente *(courageous)* que criticaba las políticas corruptas de la familia Somoza.

- ¿Quién es Violeta Barrios de Chamorro?
- ¿Por qué la familia de la Sra. Chamorro estuvo dividida por muchos años?
- ¿Cuál es la misión de la Fundación Violeta Barrios de Chamorro?
- El Presidente John F. Kennedy (1917–1963) dijo: «No preguntes lo que tu país puede hacer por ti, sino lo que tú puedes hacer por tu país». ¿Tiene esta afirmación relación con lo que dice la expresidenta Violeta B. de Chamorro: «...las tareas del desarrollo no deben ser únicamente responsabilidad de los gobiernos, sino de los ciudadanos...»? ¿Qué piensan tú y tus compañeros acerca del papel del gobierno y de la empresa privada en el desarrollo *(development)* de nuestro país? Den ejemplos.
- ¿Ha estado tu familia dividida políticamente alguna vez? Explica.

Home
Misión y líneas de acción
Constitución y Estatutos
Actualidad
Documentos
Contáctenos
Pedro Joaquín Ch.

¿Qué es la Fundación Violeta Barrios de Chamorro?

La expresidenta de Nicaragua piensa que las tareas del desarrollo no deben ser únicamente responsabilidad de los gobiernos, sino que los ciudadanos *(citizens)* deben y pueden contribuir a la solución de los problemas con la ayuda de las empresas privadas *(private companies)* y desde la sociedad civil.

Con esta visión, la Sra. Chamorro creó *(founded)* la Fundación Violeta Barrios de Chamorro, que es una organización de carácter nacional e internacional, independiente de la política que tiene como objetivo utilizar las experiencias de la expresidenta para establecer la paz y facilitar, desde la sociedad civil, iniciativas con alto rendimiento *(high return)* para la inversión *(investment)* en los pueblos del país con más necesidades.

Los programas de la Fundación Violeta Barrios de Chamorro intentan darles una oportunidad a todos y, por eso tratan de crear diferentes programas de enseñanza para personas con diferentes necesidades sociales.

La Fundación Violeta Barrios de Chamorro tiene un capital mínimo, aportado por los hijos de la Sra. Chamorro, Pedro Joaquín, Claudia,

Cristina y Carlos Fernando y por la propia expresidenta. Por medio de esta Fundación la familia se ha unido nuevamente, después de haber estado dividida políticamente por muchos años y un hijo de la Presidenta Pedro Joaquín trabajó en las fuerzas militares en contra *(against)* del nuevo gobierno socialista que se formó en 1980. Cristina desde el Diario La Prensa se opuso al régimen socialista mientras que los otros hijos menores, Carlos Fernando y Claudia, formaban parte del gobierno sandinista. La Sra. Chamorro quiere dar el ejemplo con su familia a toda Nicaragua de que todo el mundo se puede unir para luchar por una unión nacional. Así, la misión de la Fundación Violeta Barrios de Chamorro se puede definir de la siguiente manera:

«Contribuir a preservar una Cultura de Reconciliación, Paz y Democracia a través de la educación, la libertad de expresión y acciones para disminuir la pobreza en los sectores más desprotegidos *(unprotected)*.»

En Honduras hay trabajo para el verano

En un periódico digital de Honduras hay las siguientes descripciones de diferentes empresas donde puedes hacer unas prácticas o pasantías *(internships)* durante el verano y así practicar español. Lee con cuidado las diferentes descripciones y decide luego cuál de los trabajos deseas. Los sueldos son negociables, de acuerdo con la experiencia del (de la) candidato(a).

PANADERÍA Y PASTELERÍA SAN MIGUEL

Panadería y pastelería, franquicia internacional, pasteles de bodas, aniversarios y compromisos *(engagements)*

Para obtener un empleo: Para trabajar en la Panadería y Pastelería San Miguel, la persona debe ser amable con los clientes, limpia y organizada, honesta, puntual y tener algunos conocimientos de repostería.

Dirección: Food-Court Mall Multi Plaza
San Pedro Sula

Teléfono: (504) 555-1987

Contacto: Sra. Cristina Camacho

Servicio de Rey

Nosotros alquilamos todo lo que usted y su familia necesitan para sus cumpleaños, compromisos, bodas, aniversarios de bodas y fiestas de graduación.

PARA OBTENER UN EMPLEO:
Para trabajar en nuestra compañía, la persona interesada debe ser animada, creativa para poder ofrecerles a nuestros clientes diferentes menús de comida, **arreglos florales** *(floral arrangements)*, diferentes colores para **manteles** *(tablecloths);* también debe gustarle trabajar con diferentes tipos de personas, ser puntual y muy organizada.

DIRECCIÓN: 7 Calle, 14 y 15 ave. S.O. (Sur oeste) No. 100 Barrio Suyapa
San Pedro Sula

TELÉFONO: (504) 555-8939

CONTACTO: Sr. Cristóbal Mendoza

- ¿Qué puesto te gustaría solicitar? ¿Por qué?

- ¿Qué sueldo recomiendas para los candidatos?

- ¿Cuáles son las características que se necesitan para estos trabajos?

- ¿Qué cualidades tienes tú y para qué trabajo vas a solicitar empleo? ¿Por qué?

Correo Expreso

Servicio de courier de un día entre los Estados Unidos y los centros de negocios más importantes de Centro América, como Tegucigalpa, Honduras; Managua, Nicaragua; San José, Costa Rica; Ciudad de Panamá, Panamá. Más de 20 años de experiencia en esta región.

Para obtener un empleo: Para trabajar en esta empresa, la persona debe ser responsable, puntual, organizada, amable y paciente con los clientes, y querer trabajar de 8 a 10 horas diarias, inclusive los sábados. Si está interesado(a), por favor escribir a la siguiente dirección:

E-mail: salesperson@courier.hn.com

2003 **A17**

Costa Rica: Recursos naturales para pagar la deuda externa

Volcán Poas en San José, Costa Rica

- ■ ¿Te parece una buena solución el de usar «deuda por naturaleza» para resolver el problema de la deuda nacional de un país? ¿Por qué sí o por qué no?

- ■ ¿Qué futuro ves para nuestro planeta en términos del medio ambiente?

- ■ ¿Qué es importante que hagamos para cuidar el medio ambiente del lugar donde vives?

- ■ ¿Eres parte del problema o parte de la solución para la protección del medio ambiente? ¿Cómo?

La tierra en Costa Rica está protegida *(is protected)* gracias a uno de los planes de conservación más ambiciosos de América Central. El gobierno costarricense protege más del 28% del territorio nacional en forma de parques nacionales. Costa Rica ha sido el primer país en participar en el programa llamado «deuda por naturaleza» *(debt-for-nature swaps)*. Este programa cancela parte de la deuda nacional a cambio de *(in exchange for)* la protección de una cantidad específica de tierra de la destrucción ambiental *(environmental degradation)*. En un esfuerzo por mejorar su economía, Costa Rica ha desarrollado también la industria del turismo ecológico para cuidar y proteger el ambiente de los daños de los turistas. Esta manera de turismo motiva al visitante a aprender más de las maravillas naturales del país que visita y a respetar su ambiente natural.

Ecoturismo en la selva nublada en Costa Rica

Rubén Blades: Cuando una carrera no es suficiente...

RUBÉN BLADES

Músico, abogado, actor del cine, político y mucho más...

Cuando Rubén Blades nació en Panamá en 1948, hijo de un policía y una actriz, ¿quién habría pensado que este hombre talentoso tendría éxitos extraordinarios en campos tan diversos como la música, las leyes *(law)*, el cine y la política, y todo eso antes de cumplir cincuenta años? Se graduó en 1972 de la Escuela de Leyes de la Universidad de Panamá y tiene una Maestría de la Universidad de Harvard en Derecho Internacional. Como músico, Rubén es el rey de la salsa afro-cubana. Compositor de más de diez álbumes, el artista ha colaborado con cantantes famosos como Linda Ronstadt, Willie Colón, Ray Barreto y escritores de mucha importancia como el ganador del

Premio Nóbel de Literatura (1982), el colombiano Gabriel García Márquez. Cuando su carrera musical florecía en los años 80, Rubén nos mostró que tenía otros talentos para usarlos en el cine y la televisión. Para muchas personas, ser cantante y abogado habría sido suficiente pero no para Rubén Blades.

Entonces, comenzó en el cine en 1985 con el papel principal en *Crossover Dreams*, una película que promocionó la salsa en las discotecas norteamericanas. Desde entonces también ha aparecido en *Waiting for Salazar, The Milagro Beanfield War* (1988), *Mo' Better Blues* (1990),

Cradle Hill Rock (1999) y *All the Pretty Horses* (2000).

Cuando formó un partido político en 1992 dedicado a la justicia social, nadie dudaba la capacidad de este superhombre de gobernar Panamá. Aunque perdió su campaña presidencial en 1994, no hemos llegado al último capítulo de este hombre ejemplar.

■ **¿Cómo será?**

Imagina cómo será la oficina de una persona tan exitosa como Rubén Blades. Como el arquitecto personal de Rubén, haz una descripción detallada del espacio profesional que propones para él con el vocabulario del Capítulo 11. Debes tener en cuenta todas las necesidades de un hombre tan original como tu jefe.

■ **Un día con Rubén...**

Imagínate que eres el (la) asistente personal de Rubén. Describe un día típico, trabajando para él. Intenta usar cinco de los siguientes verbos en tu descripción: contestar, despedir, entregar, mandar mensajes electrónicos *(emails)*, firmar, llamar por teléfono, imprimir, reunirse.

13 El mundo del espectáculo:

Chapter Objectives

COMMUNICATIVE GOALS

In this chapter you will learn how to . . .

- Talk about television and other forms of popular culture
- Talk about anticipated actions
- Talk about the arts and the vocations of artists
- Talk about unplanned or accidental occurrences
- Describe completed actions and resulting conditions

STRUCTURES

- Subjunctive with purpose and time clauses
- *Se* for unplanned occurrences (No-fault *se*)
- Past participle (as adjective)

CULTURAL INFORMATION

- La cinematografía en Latinoamérica
- Oswaldo Guayasamín

Perú y Ecuador

PERÚ

Población: 27.483.864
Área: 1.285.220 kilómetros
cuadrados, casi del tamaño de Alaska
Capital: Lima, 7.451.900
Ciudades principales: Arequipa,
720.400; Trujillo, 590.200;
Chiclayo, 481.100
Moneda: el nuevo sol
Lengua: el español y el quechua
(oficiales), el aymara

ECUADOR

Población: 13.183.978
Área: 41.283.560 kilómetros
cuadrados, más o menos del
tamaño de Nevada
Capital: Quito, 1.610.800
Ciudades principales: Guayaquil,
2.148.600; Cuenca, 271.400;
Machala, 211.300
Moneda: el dólar estadounidense
Lenguas: el español y varias lenguas
indígenas, en especial, el quechua

¡Bienvenidos a Perú!

**En este video, vas a aprender de la
cultura de Perú. Después de ver el
video, contesta las siguientes
preguntas:**

1 ¿Dónde está Perú y cuál es su capital?

2 ¿Qué sabes de los incas? ¿Cuál es su historia? ¿Cuáles son
algunas de sus obras más famosas?

3 ¿Cómo viven los incas de hoy? ¿Qué producen los artesanos
indígenas?

4 ¿Por qué es importante el Río Amazonas?

5 ¿Crees que la cultura occidental ha tenido una gran influencia
en Perú de hoy día? ¿Crees que es una influencia positiva?
¿Por qué sí o por qué no?

La Plaza Independencia,
Quito, Ecuador

Cartelera de programación In this section you will learn to talk about television and movies.

Sustantivos

el anuncio commercial
el canal (TV) channel
el cine movies; movie theater
la película movie, film
  clásica classic film
la película de acción action film
  de arte art film
  de horror horror film
  de intriga (misterio) mystery film
la película extranjera foreign film
  romántica romantic film
el programa deportivo sports program
el pronóstico del tiempo weather report (forecast)

Verbos

aburrir to bore
apreciar to appreciate
dejar to leave; to let, allow
molestar to bother
poner to turn on (TV); to show (a movie)

Palabras útiles

Palabras útiles are presented to help you enrich your personal vocabulary. The words here will help you talk about television viewing.

el (la) anfitrión(-ona) (talk show) host
el (la) panelista guest on a talk show
el (la) televidente television viewer

¡A PRACTICAR!

13-1 **Películas y programas** La siguiente lista contiene títulos de películas y programas producidos en los Estados Unidos que ahora se pasan en la televisión. Indica el tipo de cada película o programa y luego, di si te gusta o no te gusta. Sigue el modelo.

MODELO: *Men in Black II*
Es una película de ciencia ficción y me gusta muchísimo. ¡Tommy Lee Jones es fabuloso!

Título de película o programa:

1. «West Wing»
2. «Beauty and the Beast»
3. «South Park»
4. «Buffy, the Vampire Slayer»
5. «Cristina»
6. *The Matrix Reloaded*
7. «Days of Our Lives»
8. «Who Wants to Marry My Dad?»
9. «Everybody Loves Raymond»
10. «Late Night with David Letterman»
11. «Monday Night Football»
12. *Evita*
13. «The Weather Update»
14. *Buena Vista Social Club*

13-2 **¡Adivina!** Éstos son los títulos de algunos programas y películas estadounidenses traducidos al español. Adivina qué programas son en inglés. Si no sabes, pregúntaselo a tu profesor(a). Después, decide qué tipo de película o programa es y compara tus respuestas con las de un(a) compañero(a) de clase. ¿Están de acuerdo?

Películas
1. *Lo que el viento se llevó*
2. *El mago de Oz*
3. *Hércules*
4. *La guerra de las galaxias*
5. *Un tranvía llamado deseo*

Programas de televisión
6. «La dama del oeste»
7. «La rueda de la fortuna»
8. «Doctor en Alaska»
9. «El expediente X»
10. «Sensación de vivir»

CULTURA
"Cristina" is a popular talk show in Spanish from the United States. The host, Cristina Saralegui, is from a family of Cuban exiles and has enjoyed many years of success with her program.

CULTURA
Evita is a musical play by Andrew Lloyd Weber and Tim Rice based on the life of Eva Perón (1919–1952), wife of Argentine dictator Juan Perón. It was made into a movie in 1996 by Alan Parker, starring Madonna as Evita and Antonio Banderas as Che Guevara.

CULTURA
Buena Vista Social Club is a documentary directed by Ry Cooder. It was released in 1999 and is based on the rediscovery of a group of aging Cuban musicians who were forgotten after the Cuban Revolution.

EN VOZ ALTA

13-3 | **Los premios** Uds. son críticos que van a seleccionar los mejores programas y películas para un premio prestigioso. Trabajando en grupos, decidan cuál es el mejor ejemplo en cada categoría. Después, anúncienle los resultados a la clase y justifiquen sus selecciones.

MODELO: programa de entrevistas
En la categoría de mejor programa de entrevistas, le damos el premio a «El Show de Cristina» porque Cristina es muy talentosa y los panelistas siempre son interesantes.

Categorías

dibujos animados
telenovela
película de horror
película romántica

documental
programa de entrevistas
película de acción

programa de concursos
programa deportivo
película de intriga

13-4 | **Entrevista** Quieres saber un poco más de tu compañero(a) de clase. Hazle las siguientes preguntas sobre la televisión y el cine. Prepárate para compartir esta información con la clase.

La televisión

1. ¿Cuántos televisores tienes en casa? ¿Con qué frecuencia miras la televisión?
2. ¿Cuál es tu programa favorito? ¿Por qué te gusta tanto?
3. Para ti, ¿qué programa de televisión es ridículo? ¿Por qué crees eso?
4. ¿Te molesta que haya tanta violencia en la televisión?
5. ¿Te quejas de la cantidad de anuncios que hay en la televisión?

El cine

1. ¿Con qué frecuencia vas al cine?
2. Si tienes un cine favorito, ¿cuál es?
3. Normalmente, ¿con quién vas al cine?
4. ¿Quién es tu actor favorito y por qué lo aprecias? ¿Quién es tu actriz favorita y por qué la aprecias?
5. ¿Viste una película buena recientemente? ¿Cuál fue?

13-5 | **Encuentra a alguien que...** Encuentra a alguien para quien sean verdaderas las siguientes oraciones. Después de encontrar a cada persona, pídele que firme tu libro (o papel). Al final, cuéntale a la clase lo que has aprendido.

MODELO: Miro la tele más de dos horas al día.
   E1: *¿Helen, miras la televisión más de dos horas al día?*
   E2: *¡Dios mío! ¡No tengo tanto tiempo libre!* (Look for someone else.)
  o E2: *Sí, miro tres telenovelas al día.* (Ask Helen to sign your book.)
 Al final E1: *Helen mira más de dos horas de televisión al día. Jason nunca va al cine. Michelle prefiere la radio a la tele...*

Nombres

1. Miro la tele más de dos horas al día.   _____
2. No tengo televisor.   _____
3. Nunca voy al cine.   _____
4. Voy al cine todas las semanas.   _____
5. Conozco a un(a) actor (actriz).   _____
6. Soy actor (actriz).   _____
7. Sigo una telenovela. Se llama _____.   _____
8. Prefiero la radio a la tele.   _____
9. Siempre miro las noticias.   _____
10. A mí me gusta mucho escuchar la radio pública (NPR). _____

¿NOS ENTENDEMOS?

Spanish speakers use **el televisor** for *television set* and **la televisión** for *television programming*. The same applies to **el radio** (the radio itself) and **la radio** (what you listen to), which is short for **la radiodifusión**.

¿NOS ENTENDEMOS?

You have already learned the difference between **la televisión** and **el televisor**. You will notice in everyday speech that it is common to use **la tele** when talking about watching TV. For example, **Voy a mirar la tele** is similar to an English speaker saying *I'm going to watch TV* or *I'm going to watch the tube,* as opposed to saying *I'm going to watch television,* which sounds a little more formal.

Lima, Perú. Son las 9:30 de una noche de febrero. Un grupo de artistas limeños *(from Lima)* están esperando el anuncio del ganador de la exposición de arte en La Galería Miraflores.

—Señoras y señores, ahora hemos llegado al momento culminante de esta magnífica exposición de arte limeño. Les pido unos segundos de silencio **para que todos podamos celebrar** este momento triunfante para uno o una de nuestros artistas. En este sobre que tengo en la mano está el nombre del ganador *(winner)* o la ganadora de esta exposición. Señoras y señores... este año la ganadora es una **pintora.** Se llama... ¡Rosario María Ramos!

—Muchas gracias. Quiero darles las gracias a todos los organizadores de la exposición, al público, a mis amigos y especialmente a mi familia. No puedo pintar **a menos que tenga** el apoyo *(support)* y la inspiración de mis padres y mis hermanos. Éste es un gran honor para mí y para mi familia. Muchas gracias a todos.

—Rosario, ¿nos puede explicar algo sobre su estilo? En su **obra** *(work)* a veces notamos una organización muy abierta, muy espontánea. En otros **cuadros** *(paintings)* las imágenes están más **cerradas,** más **controladas.**

—Bueno, en cuanto a *(in regard to)* las obras espontáneas, confieso que a veces ocurren cosas inesperadas, aun accidentales. Por ejemplo, en mi obra *Manchas de café,* yo tomaba un café antes de empezar un cuadro y de repente **se me cayó la taza.** Y ¡voilá!, tenía justo lo que buscaba para crear una escena de la vida cotidiana *(daily).*

—**Antes de que revele** todos sus secretos, Rosario, ¿nos diría cuál es su obra favorita?

—Pues sí, es otro de mis cuadros «accidentales». El cuadro se llama *Espacio en blanco.* Es una obra posmodernista que invita al espectador *(viewer)* a terminar la obra. Después de pintarla media hora, **se me acabó la pintura,** y decidí dejarla como era. Requiere la colaboración del espectador para completarla.

¿Comprendiste?

Indica si las siguientes oraciones son ciertas o falsas. Si una es falsa, corrígela.

1. La exposición solamente incluye pintores.
2. Son artistas de todo el mundo.
3. La familia es importante para la producción artística de Rosario.
4. Rosario pinta solamente obras «accidentales».
5. Generalmente, Rosario pinta dentro del estilo clásico.
6. Algunos de sus cuadros requieren la participación del espectador.

Encuentro cultural

La cinematografía en Latinoamérica

PARA PENSAR

- ¿Te gusta ir al cine? ¿Qué tipo de películas te gusta más?

- ¿Cuál fue la última película que viste? ¿Puedes describir el tema de la película?

- ¿Has visto alguna película latinoamericana últimamente? ¿Cuál?

Dirigiendo una película

En los países latinoamericanos, la gente va al cine a ver muchas películas norteamericanas. Aunque estas películas son muy populares, algunos países latinoamericanos han desarrollado una industria cinematográfica de muchísima importancia. El cine al igual que la literatura y el arte en general se han utilizado como un medio para presentar los problemas que enfrentan *(face)* las grandes ciudades en los países latinoamericanos. Con la ayuda económica de países como España, Suecia, Francia y Alemania, países como Argentina, Chile, Cuba, México, Perú y Venezuela pueden participar en los festivales de cine en todo el mundo. Por ejemplo, México ha presentado películas como *Amores Perros* (2000), donde se describe la historia de tres personas y sus relaciones personales, y se comparan estas relaciones con la vida de los perros. En la película *Y tu mamá también* (2001), se expone la vida de dos jóvenes mexicanos y una joven española en un viaje que hacen los tres juntos en busca de sus realidades. Y en la película más controversial en los últimos tiempos, *El crimen del padre Amaro* (2002), en la que un sacerdote quiere cumplir con las obligaciones de la Iglesia, pero al mismo tiempo se enamora de una muchacha; ésta tiene una madre que también tiene relaciones personales con otro sacerdote, y este sacerdote acepta limosna *(charity)* del narcotráfico.

Las películas que más se han visto de la cartelera del Festival Internacional del Nuevo Cine Latinoamericano (La Habana, Cuba)

1. *La ciudad de Dios* (Brasil, 2002). Un muchacho nace y crece en uno de los barrios más violentos de Río de Janeiro, pero puede salvarse por medio de la fotografía.

2. *El crimen del padre Amaro* (México, 2002).

3. *El coronel no tiene quien le escriba* (México, España, Francia, 1999). Está basada en el cuento del escritor colombiano Gabriel García Márquez; un viejo coronel espera la pensión *(pension)* que le prometieron, pero ésta nunca llega.

4. *El lado oscuro del corazón 2* (Argentina, España, 2001). Después de diez años, el protagonista de la película, Oliverio, sigue buscando a una mujer que pueda volar. En España, él conoce a una equilibrista *(equilibrist)* que lo ayuda a luchar contra la muerte.

5. *No se lo digas a nadie* (Perú, España, 1998). Esta película describe la vida de un muchacho de Lima; descubre que tiene tendencias homosexuales y descubre cómo logra vivir con esta vida.

PARA DISCUTIR

1. Según lo que leíste, ¿qué temas presentan las películas latinoamericanas muchas veces?

2. ¿Cuál ha sido la película mexicana más controversial en los últimos tiempos? ¿Por qué crees que haya sido *(has been)* tan controversial?

3. De las cinco películas que más se han visto, ¿cuál te gustaría ver? ¿Por qué?

4. ¿Qué tipo de película te gustaría dirigir *(to direct)* o en qué tipo de película te gustaría actuar *(to act)*? ¿Por qué?

ESTRUCTURA I Talking about anticipated actions: subjunctive with purpose and time clauses

In this section you will learn about using the present subjunctive with purpose and time clauses. Up until now, you have been focusing on the word **que** to link the main and dependent clauses. In this section you will be introduced to other conjunctions that have the same function. Although most of the verbs in the dependent clauses will be in the present subjunctive, you will learn about cases in which the present indicative must be used.

> **Conjunctions:** A conjunction is a word that links words or groups of words, such as an independent clause and a dependent clause. Conjunctions of purpose and of time are listed below along with explanations and examples of how to use them.

I. Conjunctions of purpose

| a fin de que | *so that* | a menos que | *unless* | para que | *so (that)* |
| sin que | *without* | con tal (de) que | *provided (that)* | en caso (de) que | *in case* |

Always use the subjunctive after the six conjunctions listed above.

Independent clause	**Conjunction**	**Dependent clause**
Voy al cine	con tal (de) que	vayas conmigo.
I'm going to the cinema	*provided (that)*	*you go with me.*

Note that when expressing an idea with the conjunction **aunque** *(although, even though)*, you can follow it with the indicative to state certainty or with the subjunctive to imply uncertainty.

certainty (indicative)

| **Aunque** el concierto **es** en abril, no puedo ir. | *Although the concert is in April, I can't go.* |

uncertainty (subjunctive)

| **Aunque** el concierto **sea** en abril, no puedo ir. | *Although the concert may be in April, I can't go.* |

II. Conjunctions of time

| antes (de) que | *before* | tan pronto como | *as soon as* | en cuanto | *as soon as* |
| después (de) que | *after* | cuando | *when* | hasta que | *until* |

The six conjunctions listed above may be followed by a verb in either the subjunctive or the indicative mood (see the one exception that follows). When an action, condition, or event has not yet taken place, use the subjunctive in the dependent clause. But when referring to habitual or completed actions, use the indicative in the dependent clause.

- **pending action (subjunctive)**

| Los músicos van a aplaudir **cuando llegue** el director. | *The musicians are going to applaud when the conductor arrives.* |

- **habitual action (indicative)**

| Los músicos siempre aplauden **cuando llega** el director. | *The musicians always applaud when the conductor arrives.* |

- **completed action (indicative)**

| Los músicos aplaudieron **cuando llegó** el director. | *The musicians applauded when the conductor arrived.* |

Note that there is one exception: Always use the subjunctive after **antes (de) que.**

| Los invitados van a la recepción **antes de que lleguen** los artistas. | *The guests go to the reception before the artists arrive.* |

¡A PRACTICAR!

13-6 **El documental** Completa la siguiente información presentada por el director de un documental sobre la civilización de los incas subrayando la forma correcta de cada verbo.

Vamos a hacer un documental sobre los incas, la civilización que controló gran parte de Sudamérica durante los siglos XV y XVI, hasta la conquista española. Pienso empezar muy pronto, con tal que los fotógrafos no 1. (tienen / tengan) otro proyecto. Primero vamos a Machu Picchu, a menos que 2. (hace / haga) mal tiempo. Es importante que no llueva durante la filmación para que 3. (podemos / podamos) ver bien la ciudad escondida (*hidden*) de Machu Picchu, que tiene una belleza natural especial y una arquitectura de gran valor histórico. Vamos a sacar muchas fotos allí para que las personas que miren el documental 4. (pueden / puedan) ver su esplendor. Es probable que sea difícil captar (*grasp*) este sitio en fotos. En realidad, es tan hermoso (*beautiful*) que nadie puede apreciarlo a menos que 5. (viaja / viaje) allí. Hasta que todos lo 6. (ven / vean) en persona es importante documentarlo. Siempre quiero conocer el lugar muy bien cuando 7. (hago / haga) un documental, y por eso he pasado mucho tiempo en Machu Picchu. También conozco muy bien la antigua capital de los incas, Cuzco, y pensamos ir allí después de que el equipo 8. (termina / termine) su trabajo en Machu Picchu. Tan pronto como 9. (llegamos / lleguemos) a Cuzco, vamos a sacar fotos de Sacsahuaman, una fortaleza enorme que ha durado más de quinientos años. Los espectadores van a comprender el talento de los constructores incaicos tan pronto como 10. (miran / miren) las fotos de esta estructura. Tenemos que trabajar con mucha dedicación y terminar el documental antes de que 11. (empieza / empiece) el invierno porque hace mucho frío en las montañas de Perú en el invierno.

13-7 **Otra escena de «¡No puedo más!»** ¿Qué sugerencias le dio Clara a su amigo Gregorio antes de la boda? Conjuga los verbos subrayados en el presente del subjuntivo o del indicativo.

MODELO: Compra una casa tan pronto como <u>ser</u> posible.
Compra una casa tan pronto como *sea* posible.

1. Antes de que tú y María Cristina <u>casarse</u>, piénsalo bien.
2. No compres nada muy caro sin que tu esposa lo <u>saber</u>.
3. Cuando ella <u>estar</u> enferma, haz todo lo posible para ayudarla.
4. No le des consejos a tu esposa a menos que ella te los <u>pedir</u>.
5. Habla frecuentemente con tu esposa para que Uds. <u>comprenderse</u>.
6. En caso de que tú <u>tener</u> algún problema serio, llámame, por favor.
7. Vengan a visitarme después de que Uds. <u>volver</u> de su luna de miel.
8. No tomes ninguna decisión económica hasta que tú <u>consultar</u> con ella.

13-8 Malas noticias para Mateo Completa la siguiente conversación entre dos actores de la telenovela «¡No puedo más!» Usa las conjunciones adecuadas de la lista. Cada una se usa una sola vez.

aunque   a menos que   después de que   cuando   antes de que   con tal de que

Laura: Oye, Mateo. Tengo malas noticias 1. _____ no vas a creerme.

Mateo: ¿Malas noticias? Por Dios, ¿qué pasó, Laura?

Laura: 2. _____ te lo diga, tienes que prometerme que no vas a estar enojado conmigo.

Mateo: No, mujer. Dime, ¿qué pasó?

Laura: ¿Recuerdas a María Cristina, la cantante peruana?

Mateo: Claro. La conocí en Lima 3. _____ llegamos al hotel Bolívar.

Laura: Sí, sí. Pues, ella se va a casar el próximo mes.

Mateo: ¡No me digas! Pero... ¿con quién?

Laura: Te lo digo 4. _____ te calmes, Mateo.

Mateo: Estoy calmado. Dime más.

Laura: Bueno, María Cristina va a casarse con Gregorio Vega, su novio, el que viste en Lima. Le dije a mi amiga Clara: 5. _____ le diga a Mateo que María Cristina se casa en abril, va a estar triste.

Mateo: Pues, sí, pero no puedo hacer nada 6. _____ los novios decidan no casarse.

Laura: Es verdad, no puedes hacer nada.

EN VOZ ALTA

13-9 Un secreto de Mateo Mateo está secretamente enamorado de María Cristina, la novia de Gregorio. Él no quiere que ellos se casen. ¿Qué le dice a María Cristina para que no se case con Gregorio?

1. Voy a hablar con María Cristina inmediatamente para que...
2. Ella siempre quiere saber la verdad cuando...
3. Tengo que verla antes de que...
4. Debo buscarla ahora en caso de que...
5. No puedo permitir que se case sin que...
6. Tengo que decirle la verdad aunque...
7. Es posible que no se case cuando...
8. No puedo estar tranquilo hasta que...

13-10 Planes para el fin de semana Trabajando con un(a) compañero(a) de clase, terminen las siguientes oraciones de una manera relevante para Uds.

MODELO: No voy al cine a menos que...
                    No voy al cine a menos que *tú me pagues la entrada.*
           o No voy al cine a menos que *haya alguna película interesante.*

1. Voy a ver una película este fin de semana con tal de que...
2. (No) Voy a mirar un programa deportivo a menos que...
3. Espero ver _____ con tal que...
4. Mis amigos y yo no podemos ver _____ sin que...
5. Quiero ver _____ después de que...

13-11 Entrevista Primero hazle a otro(a) compañero(a) las siguientes preguntas sobre el futuro. Luego comparte la información con la clase para ver cuáles son las respuestas más populares entre tus compañeros.

1. ¿Qué vas a hacer cuando termines tus estudios?
2. ¿Qué tienes que hacer antes de terminarlos?
3. ¿Piensas casarte algún día? (¿Sí? ¿Cuándo piensas casarte? ¿Con quién?) (¿No? ¿Prefieres vivir solo[a] o con otra persona?)
4. ¿Qué vas a hacer tan pronto como consigas un trabajo bueno?
5. ¿Vas a tener una familia grande con tal de que la puedas mantener?
6. ¿Hasta qué edad piensas trabajar? ¿Qué vas a hacer después de que te jubiles?

Escenas del Festival de Arte, Ecuador In this section you will learn how to talk about performing and visual arts and literature.

CULTURA
The cities of Manta, Quito, Guayaquil, and Cuenca represent the hubs of professional and semiprofessional theatrical and artistic activity in Ecuador. For the past eight years Manta has hosted the **Festival Internacional de Teatro.** Malayerba and La Trinchera, among the national groups that participate in this gathering, have established a significant following.

Sustantivos

la arquitectura architecture
el concierto concert
la escultura sculpture
la fotografía photography
la literatura literature

la música music
la obra (de arte) work (of art)
la ópera opera
el papel role

la pintura painting
la poesía poetry
el retrato portrait
el teatro theater

Los artistas Artists

el (la) arquitecto(a) architect
el (la) autor(a) author

el (la) escritor(a) writer
el (la) escultor(a) sculptor

el (la) fotógrafo(a) photographer
el (la) poeta poet

Verbos

dirigir to direct

esculpir / hacer escultura to sculpt

interpretar to play a role

Adjetivos

clásico(a) classical
moderno(a) modern

folklórico(a) folkloric
popular popular

Palabras útiles are presented to help you enrich your personal vocabulary. The words here will help you talk about performing and visual arts and literature.

Palabras útiles

el escenario stage
el guión script
la obra maestra masterpiece

¡A PRACTICAR!

13-12 | **Asociaciones** Da una o dos palabras de la lista del vocabulario que se relacione(n) con las siguientes vocaciones. Luego intenta formar una oración con las palabras.

> MODELO: el dramaturgo
> *el drama, el director, dirigir*
> *El dramaturgo escribió el drama que el director está dirigiendo.*

1. el poeta
2. la bailarina
3. el pintor

4. la cantante
5. el compositor
6. el músico

7. la actriz
8. el escultor

13-13 | **Mis sueños** En los siguientes cuatro párrafos, cuatro jóvenes hablan de sus esperanzas profesionales y artísticas. Completa las historias con las siguientes palabras.

ballet	escritora	poesía	papel	pintura	canción
cuadros	concierto	escultura	clásica	músico	
director	danza	drama	ópera	obra de arte	

Carlos Manuel: Yo soy Carlos y quiero ser 1. _____ en una orquesta grande algún día. Me fascina la idea de tocar en un 2. _____ muy importante. Prefiero la música moderna, pero también me gusta la música 3. _____, sobre todo la 4. _____ . Mi 5. _____ favorita es «El majo» del compositor español Enrique Granados.

Micaela: Yo soy una persona muy dramática. El 6. _____ para mí es el mejor arte para explorar la condición humana. El 7. _____ de la nueva obra teatral *Arte* va a darme el 8. _____ principal —¡estoy muy contenta! La 9. _____ de *Arte* es una mujer muy talentosa. Ella es dramaturga, pero también es poeta —escribe 10. _____ en su tiempo libre.

José Eduardo: Hola, yo soy José y me encanta pintar. Tengo una colección de 11. _____ que pinté yo mismo. Como no soy muy buen escultor, no quiero hacer 12. _____ . Mi medio preferido es la 13. _____ . Mi 14. _____ favorita es *La jungla* de Wilfredo Lam.

Tere Carmen: Yo me llamo Tere, y me encanta bailar. Yo creo que la 15. _____ es la mejor manera de expresar las emociones con el cuerpo. Aunque me gusta la danza moderna, prefiero el 16. _____ porque requiere mucha disciplina.

> **CULTURA**
> Wilfredo Lam (1902–1982) was a Cuban-born artist who spent many years of his career between Madrid, Paris, and Cuba. *La jungla* is a famous painting of his, and it caused great scandal upon being viewed for the first time.

13-14 | **Obras famosas** En grupos de cuatro personas, indiquen qué tipo de arte representan las siguientes obras y den cualquier información que tengan sobre cada una. Pregúntenle al (a la) profesor(a) o busquen en Internet si no saben algo.

1. los retratos de Frida Kahlo
2. *Carmen*
3. *Cien años de soledad* y *El coronel no tiene quien le escriba*
4. *La vida es sueño*
5. la obra de Rubén Darío
6. *Guernica*
7. *Don Quijote de la Mancha*
8. las estatuas de Botero

EN VOZ ALTA

13-15 Actividades artísticas ¿Eres artista? Escoge cuatro de las siguientes actividades artísticas que sean importantes para ti y luego explícaselas a un(a) compañero(a) de clase. Debes mencionar con qué frecuencia las haces y si tienes un papel en la producción de un proyecto específico. Luego comparte esta información con la clase. ¿Qué actividades son las más populares entre los estudiantes de tu clase?

MODELO: la poesía
Me gusta la poesía. Escribo poemas de vez en cuando. El semestre pasado escribí cinco poemas sobre mis experiencias en Bolivia. Voy a publicarlos en la revista estudiantil.

1. el teatro
2. el baile
3. la pintura
4. la música
5. la escultura

6. la fotografía
7. la televisión
8. la arquitectura
9. ¿ ?

13-16 Reacciones Forma preguntas para hacerles a dos compañeros(as) de clase sobre sus reacciones ante los siguientes medios artísticos y oportunidades. ¿Tienen mucho en común? Puedes usar los verbos de la lista para formar tus preguntas.

apreciar   aburrir   gustar   preferir   encantar   interesar   molestar   fascinar

MODELO: ir a un museo de arte moderno
E1: *¿Les interesa ir a un museo de arte moderno?*
E2: *No. A mí no me gusta el arte moderno.*
E3: *Sí. Prefiero el arte moderno. Me encantan los cuadros de Picasso.*

1. ver programas de la televisión pública
2. ir a una galería de escultura
3. asistir a funciones teatrales
4. hablar con artistas sobre su obra
5. aprender sobre las obras maestras de la pintura clásica
6. ver un espectáculo de baile folklórico
7. ir a un ballet clásico
8. visitar el taller de un(a) artista
9. escuchar música clásica
10. ver una ópera

13-17 Entrevista Primero hazle las siguientes preguntas a un(a) compañero(a) de clase. Luego comparte la información con la clase. ¿Tienen todos los estudiantes mucho en común?

1. ¿Eres una persona artística? ¿Por qué (no) es importante el arte en tu vida? ¿Has hecho algo artístico recientemente? ¿Quieres ser artista algún día? ¿Has hablado con un(a) artista profesional? ¿Es famosa esta persona?

2. ¿Te identificas con un(a) artista en particular? ¿Por qué te atrae *(attract)* el estilo o la obra de esa persona? ¿Piensas que es difícil ser artista? ¿Tiene que sufrir el artista para producir una obra buena?

3. ¿Qué piensas del arte popular? En tu opinión, ¿tiene algún mérito o importancia? ¿Es demasiado comercializado el arte de hoy? ¿Qué efecto va a tener la tecnología sobre el arte en el futuro?

Encuentro cultural

Oswaldo Guayasamín

PARA PENSAR

- ¿Te gusta la pintura? ¿Por qué sí o por qué no?
- Observa la foto y expresa tu opinión sobre el tema del cuadro.

El pintor ecuatoriano Oswaldo Guayasamín (1919–1999) dibujó y pintó desde los siete años, y a los doce años deslumbró *(dazzled)* a sus maestros y a sus compañeros por su capacidad creativa y su vocación de trabajo. Su primera exposición individual la realizó antes de graduarse. Luego se dedicó a la búsqueda de la identidad del continente americano y trataba de encontrar las raíces *(roots)* que diferenciaban a los anglosajones de los indígenas y mestizos que vivían en las tierras desde el Río Bravo hasta la Patagonia —su tierra.

Este artista ecuatoriano es uno de los más representativos del continente sudamericano. Todas sus obras constituyen un monumento dedicado a la humanidad, a los que sufren, a los desamparados *(defenseless people)* y a los inocentes. Guayasamín pintó una variedad de temas antes de crear su primera gran obra, «El camino del llanto». Los cuadros que pertenecen a esa época constituyen la selección denominada «Retrospectiva». Su técnica era impresionante. Hay retratos al óleo *(oil paintings)* hechos en solamente 20 minutos; tienen la misma calidad que las obras que Guayasamín tardaba hasta tres horas en hacer.

En las últimas décadas, Guayasamín pintó retratos de figuras públicas como Rigoberta Menchú y Danielle Mittérand. En particular, le interesaba pintar a las personas conocidas por su lucha por los derechos humanos.

PARA DISCUTIR

1. ¿Qué temas presenta Guayasamín en su obra?
2. ¿Qué buscaba el pintor con sus óleos?
3. Pensando en lo que Guayasamín ha pintado, ¿crees que se puede hablar de una ideología predominante en su obra?
4. ¿Te gusta el estilo de Guayasamín? ¿Por que sí o por qué no?

CULTURA

El término **mestizo** se ha usado desde el tiempo de la colonia española (siglo XVI) en América para referirse a los hijos de los españoles conquistadores y de las mujeres indígenas. En esa época, los mestizos no tenían ninguna clase de privilegios. No podían asistir a las universidades, no podían tener ningún cargo político ni tampoco podían ser oficiales del ejército. Además de los mestizos, durante la colonia hubo una diferencia entre los españoles nacidos en España, o «peninsulares», que tenían todos los privilegios políticos y sociales en las colonias y los nacidos en América, llamados **criollos,** quienes lucharon por obtener todos los privilegios que tenían los peninsulares. Para describir a los hijos de los blancos y los negros se usó el término **mulato** y para describir a los hijos de los indígenas y los negros se utilizó el término **zambo.**

ESTRUCTURA II Talking about unplanned or accidental occurrences: no-fault *se* construction

In addition to using **se** for reflexive constructions, impersonal expressions, and reciprocal actions, Spanish speakers also use **se** to mark events in which a person is subjected to an occurrence outside of his or her control. Rather than accepting responsibility for, say, losing one's keys, Spanish speakers have the option of portraying themselves as "unwitting victims" of the action. Consider the following:

Responsible for action
Yo perdí las llaves de mi casa.   *I lost the keys to my house.*

Victim of action
Se me perdieron las llaves de   *The keys to my house were (got)*
   mi casa.   *lost.*

I. Forming the no-fault *se* construction

In order to portray someone as a victim of circumstance, an indirect object (**me, te, le, nos, os, les**) is used to identify the person(s) to whom the event occurred. The indirect object pronoun immediately follows the **se** that begins all constructions of this type.

a + *noun* or *pronoun*	se	*indirect object pronoun*	*verb*	*subject*
A mí	se	me	olvidaron	las gafas.
A Juan	se	le	cayó	el vaso.
A nosotros	se	nos	acabó	el tiempo.

Note that the verb is always conjugated in either the third-person singular or third-person plural and normally in the preterite tense, although the verb can occur in other tenses as well. In the examples above, **el vaso, las gafas,** and **el tiempo** serve as the grammatical subjects of the sentences and require third-person conjugations of the verbs.

II. Verbs used in no-fault *se* constructions

Some commonly used verbs in the no-fault **se** constructions are:

acabar	to finish, run out	**perder (ie)**	to lose
caer	to fall	**quedar**	to remain, be left
escapar	to escape	**romper**	to break
olvidar	to forget		

With the verb **olvidar**, it is also possible to use an infinitive as the grammatical subject: **Se me olvidó entregar la tarea.** *(I forgot to hand in the homework.)* When negating these constructions, place the **no** before the **se**: **No se me olvidó entregar la tarea.** *(I didn't forget to hand in the homework.)*

It may be helpful to think of these verbs as functioning like the verbs **gustar, molestar,** and **encantar.** The only difference is that an extra **se** is added before the indirect object pronoun to stress the accidental or unintentional nature of the event. In effect, **se** makes the verb passive.

¡A PRACTICAR!

13-18 **En el taller del maestro** Imagínate que Beto es un asistente incompetente que trabaja en el taller *(workshop)* de un famoso artista de Quito. Convierte las siguientes oraciones a construcciones con el *no-fault* **se**, según el modelo.

MODELO: Beto perdió las llaves del taller. (perder)
A Beto se le perdieron las llaves del taller.

1. Beto no recordó llamar a los clientes. (olvidar)
2. Beto no compró la pintura suficiente para el proyecto. (olvidar)
3. Beto dejó caer los pinceles *(brushes)*. (caer)
4. Beto rompió las jarras *(jars)* que pintaba el maestro. (romper)
5. Beto no puede encontrar los atriles *(easels)*. (perder)
6. Beto dejó escapar al gato favorito del maestro. (escapar)

13-19 **¡Yo también quiero ser asistente!** Ahora imagínate que Carmela busca un nuevo trabajo. Ella también quiere trabajar en el taller del famoso maestro. Ella sabe que su asistente Beto tiene muchos problemas en el taller y que ella podría *(she could)* hacer su trabajo mucho mejor que Beto. Termina su historia con el *no-fault* **se**. **¡Ojo!** Es necesario usar verbos en el presente y en el pasado.

Yo soy Carmela, y quiero ser asistente del gran maestro. A mí nunca 1. _____ (caer) la pintura al suelo, y nunca 2. _____ (romper) las cosas frágiles; yo siempre tengo mucho cuidado. Cuando era niña, yo tenía un gato que 3. _____ (escapar) de la casa, pero ahora soy más responsable que antes. Tengo muy buena memoria. A mí nunca 4. _____ (olvidar) las fechas importantes. Siempre sé dónde está todo —tampoco 5. _____ (perder) las cosas importantes, como las llaves del taller. Ay, ¡caramba! Quería dejarle al maestro mi currículum, pero 6. _____ (quedar) en casa. Tengo que irme, porque tengo una cita en cinco minutos; 7. _____ (acabar) el tiempo. ¡Hasta luego!

EN VOZ ALTA

13-20 **Un día desastroso para el maestro** Un maestro bien conocido acaba de tener un día difícil. Primero, forma una oración de tipo *no-fault* **se** para explicar los eventos desafortunados que les ocurrieron a él y a su asistente. Segundo, incorpora otros detalles del día antes de narrarle toda la historia a un(a) compañero(a) de clase.

13-21 **¡A mí nunca!** Tú quieres convencer a tu compañero(a) de clase de que eres una persona muy responsable, pero claro, ¡todos somos humanos y hacemos errores de vez en cuando! Habla con él/ella sobre las siguientes preguntas, contestándolas de una manera honesta.

1. ¿Se te perdió algo alguna vez?
2. ¿Se te olvidó alguna vez una cita importante?
3. ¿A ti nunca se te rompió una cerámica o algo frágil?
4. ¿Se te perdió alguna vez algo de mucho valor?
5. ¿Nunca se te cayó un florero *(vase)* o algo parecido?
6. ¿Se te acabó alguna vez el dinero en una situación importante?

ASÍ SE DICE Describing completed actions and resulting conditions: use of the past participle as adjective

In **Capítulo 10** you learned how to form the past participle of verbs in order to generate the present perfect tense. The past participle can also be used as an adjective to modify a noun. When used as an adjective, the past participle must agree in number and in gender with the noun that it modifies.

Voy a escuchar **canciones escritas** en español.	*I'm going to listen to songs written in Spanish.*
Ramón tiene dos **cuadros pintados** en Ecuador.	*Ramón has two paintings painted in Ecuador.*

The past participle is also frequently used with the verbs **estar** and **ser.** When used with the verb **estar,** the emphasis is placed on the result of an action of the verb, as opposed to the action itself. When a past participle is used with the verb **ser,** the emphasis is placed on the action rather than the result of the action; Spanish speakers often use the preposition **por** with this agent of the action.

Compare the following examples:

Result of an action

La puerta **está cerrada.**	*The door is closed.*

Emphasis on the action itself

La puerta **fue cerrada por el dueño** de la casa.	*The door was closed by the owner of the house.*

Remember that the following verbs have irregular past participle forms:

abrir	**abierto**	morir	**muerto**
cubrir	**cubierto**	poner	**puesto**
decir	**dicho**	resolver	**resuelto**
descubrir	**descubierto**	romper	**roto**
escribir	**escrito**	ver	**visto**
hacer	**hecho**	volver	**vuelto**

¡A PRACTICAR!

13-22 **¿Cómo está la clase?** Indica si las siguientes oraciones son ciertas o falsas para tu clase en este momento.

1. Las ventanas están abiertas.
2. Todos los libros de los estudiantes están cerrados.
3. Las luces están apagadas.
4. El (La) profesor(a) está sentado(a).
5. Hay algunas palabras escritas en la pizarra.
6. Todos los estudiantes tienen los zapatos puestos.
7. Algo en la clase está roto.
8. Las persianas *(blinds)* están cerradas.
9. Los estudiantes están muertos de hambre.
10. Mi tarea para hoy ya está hecha.

13-23 **¿Quién lo hizo?** Convierte las siguientes oraciones en oraciones que contengan el verbo **ser** + participio pasado y también indica quién hizo las siguientes acciones con **por** + agente.

> MODELO: Julia puso la mochila del instructor debajo de la mesa.
> *La mochila del instructor fue puesta debajo de la mesa por Julia.*

1. Cindy resolvió los problemas con la luz.
2. Anne descubrió el secreto de un artista famoso.
3. Tim vio los cuadros en la exposición antes de clase.
4. Un ladrón *(thief)* rompió las ventanas del taller.
5. Keith puso los pinceles *(brushes)* en el escritorio del instructor.
6. Tony le hizo un anuncio a la clase.
7. Silvia dijo la verdad sobre unos cuadros misteriosos.

13-24 **Las islas Galápagos** Contesta las siguientes preguntas, usando la construcción **ser** + el participio pasado.

> MODELO: ¿Quién escribió *El origen de las especies*, basándose en los animales que existían en las islas Galápagos en Ecuador? (Charles Darwin).
> *El origen de las especies fue escrito por Charles Darwin en 1859.*

1. ¿Quién recomendó a Charles Darwin como naturalista para viajar en el barco *Beagle* y llegar hasta las islas Galápagos? (el naturalista inglés John Stevens Henslow)
2. ¿Qué animales habitaban las islas? (tortugas gigantes llamadas galápagos, iguanas y lagartijas)
3. ¿Quiénes visitaron las islas en el siglo XVIII y el siglo XIX? (en el siglo XVIII, piratas ingleses, en el siglo XIX, barcos balleneros [*whaling vessels*] estadounidenses e ingleses)
4. ¿Cuándo fueron las islas anexadas *(annexed)* a Ecuador? (en 1832)
5. ¿Cuándo fueron las islas declaradas Parque Nacional por el gobierno de Ecuador? (en 1959)

EN VOZ ALTA

13-25 **Preguntas del maestro** Imagínate que eres Beto, el asistente de un maestro bien conocido. Contesta las siguientes preguntas, indicando que todo su trabajo ya está hecho. Si hubo algún accidente, échale la culpa al gato del maestro utilizando **ser** + el participio pasado.

> MODELOS: ¿Has cerrado las ventanas del taller?
> *Sí, profesor. Todas las ventanas están cerradas.*
>
> ¿Comiste la manzana que dejé en la mesa?
> *No, la manzana fue comida por el gato.*

1. ¿Vendiste los dos cuadros?
2. ¿Has sacado la basura?
3. ¿Rompiste este pincel?
4. ¿Devolviste todos los recibos *(receipts)* del mes al banco?
5. ¿Has escrito todas las cartas?
6. ¿Descubriste aquel ratón que estaba debajo de mi escritorio?
7. ¿Abriste tú la ventana aunque hace tanto frío?
8. ¿Cubriste los cuadros que terminé ayer con las sábanas?
9. ¿Preparaste las pinturas para hoy?
10. ¿Pusiste el periódico encima de las pinturas?

13-26 **Accidentes memorables e inventados** Cuéntale a un(a) compañero(a) de clase tres accidentes memorables. Primero describe la situación antes de que ocurriera el accidente y luego indica lo que pasó.

> MODELO: *Una taza de café estaba puesta encima de algunos libros en mi escritorio.*
> *Luego se me cayó la taza sobre mi proyecto final para la clase de español.*

SÍNTESIS

¡A VER!

En este segmento del video, Sofía y Valeria hablan de la música folklórica. La conversación ocurre el día del cumpleaños de Valeria cuando ella está un poco deprimida, obstinada, y agresiva. Sin embargo, al final Valeria cambia de opinión sobre el baile folklórico.

Expresiones útiles

Las siguientes son expresiones nuevas que vas a escuchar en el video.

El folklor	Folklore
La cátedra de música	The music lecture
Me pasé	I went too far

Antes de ver

Paso 1: ¿Te gusta la música? ¿Qué tipo de música te gusta escuchar? ¿Te gusta bailar? ¿Qué tipo de música prefieres para bailar? Compara tus respuestas con las de un(a) compañero(a). ¿Tienen mucho en común?

Paso 2: ¿Conoces algunos bailes folklóricos de tu región? Y ¿de tu país? ¿Conoces bailes folklóricos de otros países? ¿Conoces a alguien que sepa un baile folklórico? Compara tus respuestas con las de un(a) compañero(a). ¿Tienen algo en común?

Después de ver

Paso 1: En **Antes de ver, Paso 1,** tu compañero(a) y tú compararon sus gustos musicales. Ahora, completa las siguientes oraciones con el infinitivo o con la forma correcta del presente del indicativo o del subjuntivo del verbo entre paréntesis. Luego indica si las oraciones son ciertas o falsas según el video y corrija las oraciones falsas.

- Aunque Sofía no _____ **(saber)** bailar, está muy emocionada con las noticias de que el grupo va a aprender un baile típico puertorriqueño. _____
- Sofía quiere aprender el baile tan pronto como _____ **(poder)** porque no sabe bailar. _____

_____

- Alejandra dice que puede ayudar a Sofía con el baile, con tal de que no _____ **(ser)** un baile muy difícil. _____

- Valeria no escucha música folklórica a menos que _____ **(venir)** de los Estados Unidos. _____
- Valeria cambia su opinión sobre el baile folklórico después de _____ **(aprender)** cómo bailarlo. _____

¿Dónde se nota el cambio en la actitud hacia la música folklórica de Valeria? Justifica tu respuesta.

_____

Paso 2: Según el video, Alejandra, Sofía y Valeria tienen opiniones distintas al principio del video. Describe la actitud de cada compañera hacia el baile folklórico.

Alejandra: _____ .

Sofía: _____ .

Valeria: _____ .

¿Qué opinas tú?

Paso 1: Con un(a) compañero(a) planeen un baile para su clase de español. Deben incluir en sus planes el tipo de música que van a tocar, el tipo de comida que van a servir, etc. Tienen que justificar sus selecciones.

Paso 2: En **Después de ver, Paso 2,** hablaste de la opinión que cada una de las compañeras tenía hacia los bailes y la música folklóricos. ¿Con quién te identificas más? ¿con Sofía, Valeria o con Alejandra? Justifica tu respuesta a un(a) compañero(a) y escucha su respuesta. ¿Eligieron la misma persona?

¡A LEER!

Strategy: Following a chronology

Diaries, travel logs, anecdotes, and short stories usually contain a series of interrelated actions and events, including the writer's opinions. These kinds of narrative descriptions require the reader to follow a chronology. The central questions implicit in most narrations are:

- What happened?
- Where, when, and how did it happen?
- To whom did it occur, why, and for how long?
- What else was going on at the same time?

Paso 1: Lee el itinerario de viaje que sigue y luego contesta las siguientes preguntas.

1. ¿Qué tipo de literatura es esta pieza?
2. ¿Qué piensa el (la) autor(a) de este viaje? ¿Vale la pena?
3. ¿En qué orden se van a visitar las obras arquitectónicas?
   <u>   2   </u> Llegar al punto más alto del camino (el paso de Warmiwañuska)
   <u>   1   </u> Tomar mate de coca para la altura
   <u>   3   </u> Caminar por las selvas tropicales de Vilcanota
   <u>   4   </u> Llegar a la Puerta del Sol (Inti Punku)
4. ¿Te gustaría caminar por el Camino Inca? ¿Por qué?

Tren de Machu Picchu a Cuzco

Templo en Machu Picchu

El Camino Inca

En este viaje vas a visitar unos de los lugares más interesantes de los Andes, como son Cuzco y Machu Picchu, adonde iremos caminando.

Duración del viaje: 6 días		
Día	**Actividades**	**Lugar**
1	**Llegada a Lima** Recepción en el aeropuerto de Lima y luego traslado al hotel	**Lima**
2	**Vuelo a Cuzco** Traslado del aeropuerto a las 7:30 de la mañana. Vuelo a Cuzco a las 10:00 de la mañana. Traslado al hotel. En el hotel van a poder descansar y tomar un poco de mate de coca para la altura. Van a visitar la Catedral de Cuzco, así como las increíbles construcciones de Sacsayhuaman, Qengo y la fortaleza de Puca Pucara. Esto es lo que queda del Imperio de los Incas.	**Cuzco**
3	**Primer día del Camino Inca** A las 6:00 de la mañana, el autobús los va a buscar y los va a llevar al punto de partida del Camino Inca (km 82). **La caminata** (*walk*) es de 2 horas hasta el almuerzo. Vamos a poder ver la ciudad de Llactapata. El camino continúa por 2 horas más hasta llegar al campamento.	**Campamento Huayllbamba**

Día	Actividades	Lugar
4	**Segundo día del Camino Inca** Hoy es el día más difícil de la caminata. Vamos a caminar 4 horas en ascenso (*going up*) hasta el punto más alto del camino, el paso de Warmiwañuska (4.200 metros). Luego, el grupo va a bajar por hora y media hasta el campamento, donde vamos a almorzar y a descansar.	Campamento Pacamayo
5	**Tercer día del Camino Inca** En este día vamos a entrar a los bosques tropicales de Vilcanota. Vamos a ascender por 1 hora el paso de Runkurakay (3.950 metros); luego el resto del camino es en descenso (*going down*). Se van a visitar 5 ruinas y el día acaba en el campamento con una ducha caliente.	Campamento Wiñay Wayna
6	**Cuarto día del Camino Inca** A las 4:30 de la mañana vamos a desayunar para comenzar a caminar. Después de hora y media de camino, llegamos a Inti Punku (Puerta del Sol), desde donde se puede ver por primera vez Machu Picchu. La visita a la ciudad dura 2 horas y luego van a tener tiempo libre para visitar esta maravilla mágica. A las 2:00 de la tarde van a tomar el autobús en el pueblo de Aguas Calientes, donde vamos a almorzar y a tomar el tren para Cuzco.	Cuzco

¡A ESCRIBIR!

Strategy: Identifying elements of a critical essay

Every day we evaluate many conditions, situations, and people. Sometimes, for personal or professional reasons, we write down our comments and opinions about them. Critical essays often appear in newspapers, magazines, and other similar publications and frequently deal with topics discussed in this chapter such as art, literature, film, and television. When beginning to write a critical essay, the following guidelines will help you get started.

1. Choose a subject or topic that interests you.
2. Write a brief introduction about the subject you choose.
3. List three or four things that you like about your subject.
4. Think of one or two things that could be done realistically to improve your subject and write these ideas down.
5. Come to a conclusion about your subject.

Paso 1: Ahora lee el siguiente ensayo que una estudiante escribió sobre el museo de historia y arte en su ciudad. Piensa en los elementos mencionados anteriormente (*above*) para ver si ella los ha incluido en su ensayo.

El Museo de Historia y Arte de mi ciudad es muy interesante. Me gustan las exposiciones de arte por artistas locales. Todos los martes a las 12:15 de la tarde, hay un evento especial en el museo. Por ejemplo, la semana pasada un señor presentó una charla interesante sobre el arte de Egipto y en dos semanas hay un taller para pintores. En verano el museo tiene conciertos de música clásica. Me gusta comer o beber algo y escuchar música. No cuesta nada entrar al museo y eso me gusta mucho. Pero también hay algo que no me gusta mucho: no cambia con suficiente frecuencia algunas de las exposiciones; duran por tres o cuatro meses. En general, creo que el Museo de Historia y Arte es muy bueno y me gusta visitarlo. Aprendo mucho allí y me divierto al mismo tiempo. Recomiendo que todos visiten este museo.

Paso 2: Trabajando con un(a) compañero(a) de clase, comenta sobre la inclusión de los elementos designados en el ensayo de la estudiante. Citando ejemplos específicos, nota la inclusión o la falta de inclusión de cada elemento.

Functions: Writing an essay;
Writing an introduction; Writing a
conclusion; Expressing an
opinion
Vocabulary: Arts; Poetry; Prose;
Musical instruments
Grammar: Verbs: subjunctive

Task: Writing a critical essay

Paso 1: Vas a escribir un ensayo crítico, teniendo en cuenta las ideas descritas en la sección anterior. Elige un tema para tu ensayo de la siguiente lista de ideas:

- una pintura famosa
- un poema
- un cuento corto
- una novela

- una obra teatral
- una película
- un programa de televisión
- un museo de arte en tu ciudad

Paso 2: Escribe el ensayo, incluyendo todos los elementos necesarios. Si necesitas ayuda con la inclusión de detalles adecuados, puedes referirte a la sección **¡A escribir!** de **Capítulo 6,** *Adding details to a paragraph.*

Paso 3: Intercambia papeles con un(a) compañero(a) de clase. Lee el ensayo de la otra persona y trata de averiguar si tiene todos los elementos necesarios. Si le falta algún elemento, infórmale a tu compañero(a).

Paso 4: Si conoces el lugar o la obra tratados *(treated)* en el ensayo de tu compañero(a), presenta tu opinión sobre ellos. Si no los conoces, hazle algunas preguntas a la otra persona para saber más sobre ellos.

¡A CONVERSAR!

Task: Discussing preferences and opinions about television viewing

Hoy día, muchas personas consideran que la televisión es el medio de comunicación más popular. Muchas personas miran la tele casi todos los días. Algunas personas tienen opiniones fuertes sobre algunos programas y hasta hay personas que hacen sus planes de acuerdo con lo que se presenta en la tele en cierto día a cierta hora.

Paso 1: Teniendo en cuenta el papel de la televisión en nuestra sociedad, pregúntale a un(a) compañero(a) de clase acerca de sus preferencias y sus hábitos con la tele. Por ejemplo:

- ¿Ve él/ella la televisión con frecuencia?
- ¿Cuántas horas a la semana pasa tu compañero(a) frente al televisor aproximadamente?
- ¿Qué tipo de programa prefiere: las comedias, las películas, los deportes, las noticias, las telenovelas, los concursos, los videos musicales, etc.? ¿Por qué tiene esa preferencia?
- ¿Qué piensa de la televisión en general? ¿Es bueno que sea tan importante en el mundo de hoy?

Paso 2: Cambien de papel para continuar la conversación. Comparen y contrasten sus opiniones.

Paso 3: Para finalizar, preséntale a la clase un resumen de las opiniones discutidas en las conversaciones.

VOCABULARIO ESENCIAL

 Track 2-13

Programas y películas Programs and movies

Sustantivos

el anuncio commercial
el canal (TV) channel
el cine movies; movie theater
la comedia comedy
los dibujos animados cartoon
el documental documentary
la función musical musical (play)
las noticias news

la película movie, film
  clásica classic film
  de acción action film
  de arte art film
  de ciencia ficción science-fiction film
  de horror horror film
  de intriga (misterio) mystery film
  del oeste Western film

  extranjera foreign film
  romántica romantic film
el programa de concursos game show
el programa de entrevistas talk show
el programa deportivo sports program
el pronóstico del tiempo weather report
  (forecast)
la telenovela soap opera

Verbos

aburrir to bore
apreciar to appreciate

dejar to leave; to let, allow
molestar to bother

poner to turn on (TV); to show (a movie)

Las artes The arts

la arquitectura architecture
el ballet ballet
la danza dance
el drama drama, play
la canción song
el concierto concert

el cuadro painting
la escultura sculpture
la fotografía photography
la literatura literature
la música music
la obra (de arte) work (of art)

la ópera opera
el papel role
la pintura painting
la poesía poetry
el retrato portrait
el teatro theater

Los artistas Artists

Sustantivos

lel actor actor
la actriz actress
el (la) arquitecto(a) architect
el (la) autor(a) author
el bailarín dancer
la bailarina dancer

el (la) cantante singer
el (la) compositor(a) composer
el (la) director(a) director
el (la) dramaturgo(a) playwright
el (la) escritor(a) writer
el (la) escultor(a) sculptor

el (la) fotógrafo(a) photographer
el (la) músico musician
el (la) pintor(a) painter
el (la) poeta poet

Verbos

dirigir to direct

esculpir / hacer escultura to sculpt

interpretar to play a role

Adjetivos

clásico(a) classical
folklórico(a) folkloric

moderno(a) modern

popular popular

Conjunciones Conjunctions

a fin de que so that
a menos que unless
antes (de) que before
aunque although, even though
con tal (de) que provided (that)

cuando when
después (de) que after
en caso (de) que in case
en cuanto as soon as
hasta que until

para que so (that)
tan pronto como as soon as
sin que without

La vida pública:

Chapter Objectives

COMMUNICATIVE GOALS

In this chapter you will learn how to . . .

- Talk about politics and elections
- Talk about future events
- Talk about political issues and the media
- Express conjecture or probability

STRUCTURES

- The future tense
- The conditional
- Present perfect subjunctive

CULTURAL INFORMATION

- El gobierno de Chile
- La libertad de prensa

Chile

CHILE

Población: 15.328.467
Área: 748.800 kilómetros
cuadrados, casi dos veces
el tamaño de Montana
Capital: Santiago, 4.939.000
Ciudades principales: Concepción,
381.000; Viña del Mar, 356.800;
Valparaíso, 326.100
Moneda: el peso
Lengua: el español

¡Bienvenidos a Chile!

En este video, vas a aprender de Chile. Después de ver el video, contesta las siguientes preguntas:

1 ¿Dónde está Chile y cuál es su capital? ¿Cómo es la geografía del país?

2 ¿Qué sabes de la economía de Chile? ¿Cuáles son dos productos de exportación importantes?

3 ¿Puedes nombrar un evento importante en la historia política de Chile? ¿Qué pasó?

4 Según el video, ¿qué problemas políticos ha sufrido el país en los últimos años?

5 ¿Qué opinas de la situación política actual de Chile comparado con los años de la dictadura de Pinochet? ¿Crees que funciona mejor un sistema de gobierno liberal o conservador?

La Plaza de la Constitución,
Santiago, Chile

El proceso político en la Plaza de Armas In this section you will learn how to talk about politics and elections.

CULTURA
The **Plaza de Armas** is the most important public commons of Santiago, Chile. The main cathedral of the city as well as the **Museo Histórico Nacional** and the central post office are located around the plaza.

¿NOS ENTENDEMOS?
Note that the verb **discutir** has two slightly different meanings in Spanish. In addition to meaning *to discuss, talk about,* it can also mean *to argue.* The verb *to support* in English translates into several different meanings in Spanish. To indicate the idea of economic, moral, or ideological support, Spanish speakers use the verb **apoyar.** The verb **soportar** in Spanish means *to tolerate, put up with.* The idea of supporting someone physically is **sostener.**

Sustantivos

el congreso congress	la dictadura dictatorship	la paz peace
el debate debate	el ejército army	el poder power
el deber duty	el gobierno government	el (la) presidente president
la democracia democracy	la guerra war	la reforma reform
el (la) dictador(a) dictator	la ley law	

Verbos

apoyar to support	discutir to argue, discuss	gobernar (ie) to govern
aprobar (ue) to approve; to pass	elegir (i, i) to elect	oponer to oppose
defender (ie) to defend	firmar to sign	votar to vote

Adjetivos

conservador(a) conservative	liberal liberal
demócrata democratic	republicano(a) republican

Palabras útiles are presented to help you enrich your personal vocabulary. The terms provided here will help you talk about politics and politicians.

Palabras útiles

el (la) alcalde(sa) mayor
la cámara de representantes (diputados) house of representatives
la constitución constitution
el (la) diputado(a) representative
el (la) gobernador(a) governor
los grupos paramilitares paramilitary groups
los guerrilleros guerrillas
la ideología ideology
el (la) ministro minister
la monarquía monarchy
el senado senate
el (la) senador(a) senator

¡A PRACTICAR!

14-1 **Definiciones** Empareja las palabras de la izquierda con la definición correcta de la derecha.

1. _____ aprobar
2. _____ el congreso
3. _____ la dictadura
4. _____ el gobierno
5. _____ los políticos
6. _____ el ejército
7. _____ las elecciones
8. _____ democrático

a. el cuerpo político que gobierna un país o un estado
b. un tipo de gobierno conservador que cuenta con el apoyo del ejército
c. un cuerpo armado que defiende el país
d. el proceso en que se determina quién va a gobernar en el futuro
e. una división del gobierno
f. una orientación política que refleja el apoyo y los intereses de los ciudadanos
g. permitir que algo se realice
h. las personas que gobiernan el país

14-2 **La vida de Salvador Allende Gossens** Pon los siguientes eventos en un orden lógico para organizar la historia de este líder chileno.

_____ Dio algunos discursos radicales mientras asistía a la escuela de medicina en la Universidad de Chile.

_____ Organizó el partido socialista de Chile y fue apoyado por el proletariado de Chile.

_____ Los ciudadanos que le apoyaban dijeron que fue asesinado.

_____ Firmó varias leyes para la reforma de tierras.

_____ Nació el 26 de julio de 1908.

_____ El gobierno de Allende defendió los derechos (*rights*) de los mineros de cobre (*copper miners*).

_____ En 1973 perdió el control del gobierno a manos de Augusto Pinochet, un general conservador que tenía el apoyo del ejército.

_____ Fue elegido presidente de Chile en 1970.

CULTURA

Salvador Allende was the first Socialist Chilean president elected by free elections in 1970. He was the president until the coup d'état in 1973 by Augusto Pinochet. Pinochet's dictatorship lasted 17 years, and many of Allende's followers were persecuted during this period. In January 2000, Ricardo Lagos was elected the first Socialist president since Salvador Allende was overthrown some 27 years earlier.

14-3 **El largo camino hacia la presidencia** Completa la historia a continuación con las palabras de la lista.

discutir   debates   republicano   reformas   deber   liberal   campaña

1. Ricardo Lagos hizo una _____ para la presidencia en Chile en el año 1999. Ganó las elecciones de enero 2000.
2. Antes de las elecciones, muchas veces hay _____ para dar a los candidatos la oportunidad de _____ sus ideas.
3. El que está opuesto a un conservador en la política es generalmente un _____.
4. En los Estados Unidos, el partido _____ es el partido más conservador.
5. Votar en las elecciones es el _____ de los ciudadanos.
6. Muchos políticos nuevos proponen _____ para mejorar una mala situación.

14-4 **Oraciones** Forma seis oraciones completas, combinando los elementos de las tres columnas.

MODELO: *El dictador aprobó el uso del poder militar para controlar el país.*

los partidos políticos	apoyar	el candidato
el presidente	elegir	el poder
el ejército	firmar	las leyes
el ciudadano	votar	las elecciones
el gobierno	gobernar	la reforma
el dictador	defender	la paz
el grupo conservador	aprobar	la dictadura

EN VOZ ALTA

14-5 **Ideas y reacciones** Después de leer las siguientes opiniones, formula una respuesta empezando con las frases de abajo. Luego compara tus reacciones con las de un(a) compañero(a) de clase. ¿Tienen mucho en común? ¡Tengan cuidado con el subjuntivo!

> MODELO: Sin un ejército, un país no puede tener poder internacional.
> *No es evidente que sin un ejército un país no pueda tener poder internacional. Costa Rica tiene mucho poder internacional sin tener ejército.*

(No) Estoy de acuerdo en que...	(No) Es evidente que...	Es (im)posible que...
(No) Dudo que...	Es una lástima que...	Es bueno (malo) que...

1. A veces hay que defender la paz con el ejército.
2. Los ciudadanos generalmente no apoyan las dictaduras.
3. Los políticos siempre mienten (*lie*).
4. Nuestro gobierno es demasiado conservador.
5. Nuestros partidos políticos representan las opiniones de todos los ciudadanos.
6. El congreso y el senado mantienen el equilibrio de poder en este país.
7. Los ciudadanos participan en las elecciones.
8. Los candidatos tienen agendas políticas llenas de promesas.
9. No hay corrupción en la política.
10. Los jóvenes son muy activos políticamente.

14-6 **¿Eres activo(a) en la política?** Completa la siguiente encuesta. Después, en grupos de cuatro personas, comparen sus respuestas. Hablen de por qué participan o no activamente en la política.

casi nunca = 0	a veces = 1	frecuentemente = 2	siempre = 3

_____ Voto.
_____ Participo en discusiones políticas.
_____ Miro los debates entre los candidatos en la tele.
_____ Escribo cartas a un(a) político(a).
_____ Me identifico con un partido político.
_____ Hago un esfuerzo para informarme sobre los candidatos antes de las elecciones.
_____ Trabajo para un(a) candidato(a) o para un(a) político(a).
_____ Las acciones del presidente de este país me afectan.
_____ Sé lo que está pasando en otros países con respecto a la política.

Interpretaciones

0–7 Debes matricularte en una clase de ciencias políticas.
8–15 Debes aprender más sobre el proceso político.
16–21 Tienes mucho conocimiento político.
22–27 ¡Vas a tener un puesto como político algún día!

14-7 **¡Ahora te toca a ti (*it's your turn*)!** Tú y un(a) compañero(a) son candidatos(as) para la presidencia. Uno de Uds. (Estudiante 1) es liberal, el (la) otro(a) (Estudiante 2), conservador(a). Sigan los puntos de vista indicados a continuación y hablen de sus diferentes puntos de vista según la información.

Estudiante 1: liberal

1. La educación en las universidades debe ser gratis.
2. Cuidar a los pobres es el deber del gobierno.
3. Debemos pagar más impuestos (*taxes*) y tener seguro médico (*health insurance*) del gobierno.
4. Es importante controlar la industria y sus efectos en el medio ambiente. Tenemos que conservar la naturaleza.

Estudiante 2: conservador(a)

1. La universidad es un privilegio. El gobierno no debe pagar estos estudios.
2. Los pobres deben buscar trabajo si quieren casa y comida.
3. El seguro médico es un negocio y el gobierno no debe pagárselo a la gente. No debemos pagar más impuestos; ya pagamos bastantes.
4. El gobierno no tiene nada que ver con la industria o el medio ambiente. Todos tenemos que ser responsables con la tierra sin leyes del gobierno.

> **¿NOS ENTENDEMOS?**
> You can also express the idea that it's a friend's turn to do something by saying **Te toca a ti.** To indicate this idea for other people, simply substitute the appropriate indirect object pronoun: **me toca a mí, les toca a ellos,** etc.

Son las 3:00 de la tarde en la Plaza de las Armas en Santiago, Chile. Allí, Marina, una estudiante ecuatoriana, reconoce a un chico que vio en la recepción de su hotel por la mañana.

Marina: Perdona. Creo que te vi esta mañana en el hotel.

Óscar: ¡Sí, es cierto! Soy Óscar.

Marina: Mucho gusto, Óscar. Soy Marina.

Óscar: Encantado. Espero que **hayas venido** (*you have come*) para **la manifestación** (*demonstration*).

Marina: ¡Ah! Por eso hay tanta gente aquí. Bueno, la verdad es que quería sacar unas fotos de la plaza, pero **aprovecharé** (*I will take advantage of*) la ocasión y **sacaré** (*I will take*) unas fotos de la manifestación.

Óscar: Mira, esto no es un espectáculo (*show*). **Protestaremos** en contra de la violación de **los derechos humanos** en nuestro país. Estamos aquí por razones bien serias.

Marina: Lo siento, Óscar. No sabía que fuera (*it was*) algo tan importante.

Óscar: Está bien. No eres de aquí, ¿verdad?

Marina: Soy de Quito, Ecuador. Vine aquí para una conferencia sobre filosofía y para hacer algo de turismo.

Óscar: ¿Filosofía? Me **interesaría** si no estuviera tan metido (*It would interest me if I weren't so involved*) en los asuntos actuales (*current*) de nuestro país.

Marina: Si la estudiaras (*If you were to study it*), **entenderías** que tiene mucho que ver con (*it has a lot to do with*) **la política.** Pero, yo tengo que confesarte que no estoy muy al día (*up to date*) con lo que pasará en las próximas **elecciones** aquí, pero sí sé lo que pasará en mi propio país.

Óscar: Si quieres yo te informo de lo que **pasará** aquí y tú me informas de lo que pasará en Ecuador. ¿Qué te parece?

Marina: ¡Trato hecho! (*It's a deal!*)

Óscar: Es bueno que nosotros **nos hayamos conocido.** ¡Así los dos **aprenderemos** algo nuevo!

> **¿NOS ENTENDEMOS?**
> To express the idea of *How about (if) . . . ?* Spanish speakers also use the expression **¿Qué tal si... ?** followed by the appropriate phrase. For example, to say *How about going to the movies on Saturday?*, one would say **¿Qué tal si vamos al cine el sábado?**

¿Comprendiste?

Contesta las siguientes preguntas en oraciones completas.

1. ¿Por qué vino Marina a la Plaza de las Armas?
2. ¿Por qué está Óscar en la plaza?
3. ¿Hay alguna relación entre la política y la filosofía?
4. ¿De dónde son los dos y qué planes tienen para el futuro?

Encuentro cultural
El gobierno de Chile

Plaza de la Moneda, enfrente del
Palacio Presidencial de la Moneda

Balcón del Palacio de la Moneda

PARA PENSAR

■ ¿Te gusta la política? ¿Por qué sí o por qué no?

■ ¿Qué opinas de los golpes de estado *(coup d'état)*? ¿Conoces algún país hispanohablante que haya tenido golpe(s) de estado?

Chile es una democracia con una constitución que estipula una rama ejecutiva y una legislatura bicameral. Aprobada *(Approved)* por un referéndum y luego enmendada *(amended)* en 1989, la constitución fue escrita y establecida con límites institucionales por mando popular *(popular rule)*.

En 1973, el comandante en jefe del ejército, el general Augusto Pinochet, violentamente derrocó *(overthrew)* al presidente Salvador Allende, que había sido elegido constitucionalmente por el pueblo. Allende murió dentro del Palacio de la Moneda ya que se negó a abandonar el gobierno durante el golpe militar *(military coup)*. Eso marcó el principio de diecisiete años de dirección militar en Chile. Este golpe de estado *(coup d'état)* y sus inesperadas repercusiones pusieron fin a un largo período de dirección constitucional en Chile y puso en marcha un régimen de facto autoritario que sería sostenido por fuerza hasta 1990.

Desde 1973 hasta 1990, y particularmente al principio del régimen militar, hubo muchas violaciones de los derechos humanos. Éstos incluyeron arrestos arbitrarios, redadas *(raids)* en hogares privados, encarcelamiento *(imprisonment)*, torturas, personas desaparecidas y exilio.

A fines del año de 1998, Augusto Pinochet fue detenido en Gran Bretaña, donde se encontraba recuperándose de una cirugía. España y muchos grupos de defensa de los derechos humanos de otros países lucharon por conseguir la extradición del ex dictador. Sin embargo, debido a su estado de salud, Inglaterra negó la extradición y Pinochet regresó a Chile. En julio de 2002, los cargos *(charges)* en contra de Pinochet fueron retirados por la corte chilena debido a su salud mental. Pinochet renunció a su cargo de senador vitalicio *(lifelong senator)*, lo cual lo protegía de ser juzgado en las cortes. En agosto de 2003, los jueces chilenos votaron a favor de dejarle a Pinochet su inmunidad *(immunity)* parlamentaria. Así que ahora es menos probable de que se pueda juzgar a Pinochet en la corte chilena.

PARA DISCUTIR

1. ¿Qué sucedió en Chile en 1973?
2. ¿Qué actividades se llevaban a cabo durante la dictadura de Pinochet?
3. ¿Cuáles son los cargos de los que se acusa a Pinochet? ¿Cuál ha sido la cronología de este caso?
4. ¿Quién es el comandante en jefe en los Estados Unidos? ¿Sabes si en la historia de los EE.UU. ha habido redadas?

ESTRUCTURA I Talking about future events: the future tense

In **Capítulo 3,** you learned to use the present indicative forms of **ir a** + *infinitive* to express actions, conditions, and events that are going to take place, for example, **Voy a viajar a Chile este verano.** *(I'm going to travel to Chile this summer.)* Spanish speakers use this construction frequently in everyday conversation. Another way to express these ideas in Spanish is to use the future tense.

I. Formation of the future tense

Regular verbs

To form the future tense of regular verbs, add these personal endings to the infinitive: **é, ás, á, emos, éis, án.**

viajar	volver	vivir	irse
viajar**é**	volver**é**	vivir**é**	me ir**é**
viajar**ás**	volver**ás**	vivir**ás**	te ir**ás**
viajar**á**	volver**á**	vivir**á**	se ir**á**
viajar**emos**	volver**emos**	vivir**emos**	nos ir**emos**
viajar**éis**	volver**éis**	vivir**éis**	os ir**éis**
viajar**án**	volver**án**	vivir**án**	se ir**án**

Verbs with different future stems from the infinitive form

Verb	Stem	Ending
decir	**dir-**	
hacer	**har-**	é
poder	**podr-**	ás
poner	**pondr-**	á
querer	**querr-**	emos
saber	**sabr-**	éis
salir	**saldr-**	án
tener	**tendr-**	
venir	**vendr-**	

Note that the future tense of **hay** is **habrá** *(there will be).*

—¿**Habrá** unas elecciones este año?	*Will there be an election this year?*
—Sí. **Tendremos** unas para nuestro club de estudiantes internacionales en marzo.	*Yes. We'll have one for our international students' club in March.*
—¿Qué **harán** los candidatos?	*What will the candidates do?*
—**Darán** un discurso de diez minutos.	*They'll give a ten-minute speech.*
—¿**Podremos** hacerles preguntas?	*Will we be able to ask questions?*
—Cómo no. ¿**Vendrás?**	*Of course. Will you come?*

II. Uses of the future tense

- Spanish speakers use the future tense to express actions, conditions, and events that will take place in the future.

Los candidatos **llegarán** a Santiago a las 11:00 de la mañana el 24 de julio. Al día siguiente, **se subirán** al autobús y **saldrán** para las otras ciudades.	*The candidates will arrive in Santiago at 11:00 in the morning July 24. The next day, they will get on the bus and they will leave for the other cities.*

- Spanish speakers also use the future tense to speculate about actions, conditions, and events that are probably taking place at the moment or will most likely occur sometime in the future. If the future of probability is expressed in a question, it carries the meaning of *I wonder* in English; if it is expressed in a statement, it means *probably*.

—¿Qué tiempo **hará** en Santiago?	*I wonder how the weather is in Santiago.*
—**Estará** a 35 grados.	*It's probably 35 degrees (centigrade).*
—Siempre hace calor allí.	*It's always hot there.*
—**Será** por la humedad.	*It's probably due to the humidity.*

¡A PRACTICAR!

14-8 | **Planes para el futuro** ¿Qué harán las siguientes personas el próximo año?

MODELO: Marina: volver a Ecuador / tomar una clase de ciencias políticas
Volverá a Ecuador. Tomará una clase de ciencias políticas.

1. Marina: terminar sus estudios universitarios / poder encontrar un buen trabajo / casarse con su novio / ir a Florida para su luna de miel / vivir en un apartamento en Quito / estar muy contenta / mirar sus fotos de Chile / recordar sus experiencias con Óscar / escribirles a sus amigos chilenos / mandarles unas tarjetas postales
2. Óscar: cumplir 21 años / comenzar a estudiar filosofía / leer sobre los grandes filósofos / trabajar para una compañía de negocios / poder salir frecuentemente con sus amigos / hacer un viaje a Ecuador para visitar a Marina y a su esposo / estar con ellos el día de su boda / darles un regalo de boda / decirles «¡Felicidades!»
3. Óscar y su novia: casarse en Santiago / vivir en Valparaíso / tener un niño / dar una fiesta grande / hacer muchos amigos / ahorrar su dinero / comprar un velero / visitar a sus amigos en Tierra del Fuego / pescar en el mar
4. nosotros: poder ir a Santiago / visitar la Chascona / viajar a Punta Arenas / ver una manifestación política en la Plaza Italia de Santiago
5. tú: terminar los estudios / salir del país / conocer al jefe del grupo ecologista *Greenpeace* / participar en una campaña mundial para mejorar el medio ambiente

CULTURA
La Chascona, a Chilean word meaning *messy-haired woman,* is also the name of a famous house in the artsy neighborhood of Bella Vista. The house La Chascona was built by 1973 Nobel Prize for Literature winner Pablo Neruda.

CULTURA
Punta Arenas is located in the far south of Chile. It is the southernmost city of importance in that country.

14-9 | **¿Qué pasará?** Completa las siguientes oraciones, usando los verbos indicados.

1. ¿Qué hará Óscar después de participar en la manifestación en Santiago?

   Él 1. _____ *(viajar) por Chile para conocer mejor su país. En la zona central* 2. _____ *(ver) el río Bío-Bío y el área donde vivían los mapuches, un grupo indígena de Chile. De norte a sur* 3. _____ *(admirar) los Andes, las montañas que definen su país. No* 4. _____ *(poder) subir al Aconcagua, el pico más alto del hemisferio, pero* 5. _____ *(tener) la oportunidad de hablar con varias personas que lo han hecho. Óscar* 6. _____ *(reunirse) con su amigo Gabriel y los dos* 7. _____ *(pescar) en uno de los muchos lagos de Chile. Ellos también* 8. _____ *(bañarse) en las aguas termales que son abundantes en la región de los lagos. Óscar* 9. _____ *(leer) poesía de Pablo Neruda y Gabriela Mistral, dos poetas chilenos que han ganado el Premio Nóbel de Literatura.*

2. ¿Qué piensa Marina mientras espera en el aeropuerto?

querer	saber	poner	venir	haber	votar	explicar

   Cuando yo llegue a Quito, 1. _____ *llamar a Marcos para que me recoja en el aeropuerto. Le* 2. _____ *todo lo que he aprendido aquí en Santiago. La próxima vez, Marcos* 3. _____ *conmigo. En Quito, nosotros* 4. _____ *todo sobre los candidatos para las próximas elecciones.* 5. _____ *elecciones en noviembre. ¡En noviembre* 6. _____ *los dos por el mejor candidato! Finalmente yo* 7. _____ *la foto de Óscar sobre mi escritorio como recuerdo de mi visita a la Plaza de la Moneda en Santiago, Chile.*

14-10 | **Cinco predicciones** Escribe cinco acciones, condiciones o eventos interesantes que pasarán en tu vida dentro de los próximos cinco años. Luego comparte tus predicciones con un(a) compañero(a). ¿Tienen mucho en común?

MODELOS: *Compraré un auto nuevo.*
Me casaré y viviré en Chile.
Viajaré a Europa con un(a) amigo(a).

14-11 | **¿Qué serán?** Mira las fotos, y luego con un(a) compañero(a) de clase inventen respuestas para contestar las preguntas. Después, hagan sus propias preguntas.

> MODELO: *Este hombre será un político. Será una persona muy importante. Estará con los ciudadanos y los periodistas. Dará un discurso político.*

¿Quién será este hombre?
¿Qué tipo de trabajo hará?
¿Será simpático o antipático, y por qué?
¿Quiénes serán las otras personas en la foto?

¿Quiénes serán estas personas?
¿De dónde serán?
¿Dónde vivirán ahora?
¿Qué harán allí?
¿Qué lenguas hablarán?
¿Cómo se divertirán?
¿Qué problemas tendrán?

14-12 | **Plan de vacaciones** Usando las frases a continuación, piensa en un plan para tus próximas vacaciones. Luego, con un(a) compañero(a) de clase, háganse preguntas sobre sus planes.

> MODELO: E1: *¿Adónde vas a ir para tus vacaciones?*
> E2: *Iré a Valparaíso. Y tú, ¿adónde irás?*
> E1: *Mi esposa y yo iremos a Viña del Mar.*

1. ¿Adónde vas a ir?
2. ¿Por qué quieres ir allá?
3. ¿Cuánto tiempo vas a estar?
4. ¿Quién va a ir contigo?
5. ¿En qué día vas a irte?
6. ¿A qué hora vas a salir?
7. ¿Dónde vas a quedarte?
8. ¿Qué vas a hacer allá?
9. ¿Cuánto va a costar el viaje?
10. ¿Qué vas a comprar en el viaje?
11. ¿Cómo vas a pagarlo?
12. ¿Cuándo vas a volver?

14-13 | **¿Qué haremos?** Forma un grupo pequeño con otros tres o cuatro compañeros. Una persona comienza, diciendo una actividad que hará en el futuro. Entonces, otro(a) compañero(a) repite lo que dijo la primera persona y luego dice lo que él/ella hará en el futuro. Continúen de la misma forma.

> MODELO: E1: *Buscaré otro trabajo.*
> E2: *Pete buscará otro trabajo y yo daré una fiesta.*
> E3: *Pete buscará otro trabajo, Camilla dará una fiesta y yo haré un viaje.*

VOCABULARIO Las preocupaciones cívicas y los medios de comunicación

Una manifestación en la Plaza Italia

LA MANIFESTACIÓN

EL CRIMEN · LA VIVIENDA · LOS IMPUESTOS · LA EDUCACIÓN · LA DROGADICCIÓN · LA GUERRA · EL DESEMPLEO · EL TERRORISMO · LA CORRUPCIÓN

CULTURA

In Chile, **La Plaza Italia** is a public place where many political protests take place. It lies just off the Alameda, a road that runs from one end of Santiago de Chile to the other.

Las preocupaciones cívicas

el aborto abortion
el (an)alfabetismo (il)literacy
la defensa defense
los derechos humanos (civiles) human (civil) rights
la (des)igualdad (in)equality
la huelga strike
la inflación inflation
la inmigración immigration
la libertad de prensa freedom of the press
la política internacional international policy

Los medios de comunicación

el Internet Internet
el noticiero newscast
el periódico newspaper
la prensa press
el reportaje report
la revista magazine

Verbos

aumentar to increase
eliminar to eliminate
informar to inform
investigar to investigate
protestar to protest
reducir to reduce

¡A PRACTICAR!

14-14 | **Definiciones** Empareja cada palabra o frase a continuación con su definición.

1. _____ el terrorismo
2. _____ la inflación
3. _____ los impuestos
4. _____ la desigualdad
5. _____ el aborto
6. _____ la libertad de prensa
7. _____ el desempleo
8. _____ la guerra
9. _____ el analfabetismo
10. _____ la huelga

a. una pelea (*fight*) entre dos fuerzas armadas
b. la terminación de un embarazo (*pregnancy*)
c. una protesta de los trabajadores
d. actos violentos de protesta
e. injusticias entre gente o grupos de gente
f. la subida (*increase*) de precios y la disminución del valor del dinero
g. la falta de conocimiento para leer o escribir
h. la falta de trabajo para todos
i. la falta de la censura (*censorship*)
j. el dinero que los ciudadanos le pagan al gobierno

14-15 | **Los medios de comunicación** Escoge la palabra adecuada de la lista a continuación para completar las siguientes oraciones.

Internet   periódico   reportaje   libertad de prensa   revista   noticiero

1. Yo soy Mario, y escribo en una _____ que sale cada mes.
2. Emilio y Maruja son reporteros para un programa de noticias de Valparaíso. Esta noche en el _____ ellos van a hacer un _____ sobre la manifestación en la Plaza Italia.
3. *La Prensa* es el nombre de un _____ que sale todas las mañanas en Santiago de Chile.
4. Yupi.com es una compañía que tiene información, tiempo y deportes sobre el mundo latino en _____.
5. Para los escritores y periodistas, la _____ es muy importante.

14-16 | **¿Qué hará esta gente para mejorar (*to improve*) el mundo?** Todas las siguientes personas harán su parte para mejorar el mundo. Completa las oraciones con la forma correcta del verbo en el futuro para especular (*to speculate*) sobre sus posibles planes.

MODELO: el congreso / reducir / el crimen en el país
El congreso reducirá el crimen en el país.

1. el nuevo candidato / eliminar / el desempleo
2. los periodistas / investigar / la corrupción en el gobierno
3. ellos / informar / al público sobre los problemas en la política internacional
4. el ministro de Defensa / aumentar / el presupuesto de la defensa nacional
5. nosotros, los estudiantes, / protestar el alto costo de la vivienda / en una manifestación en la Plaza Italia
6. el grupo Amnistía Internacional / proteger / los derechos humanos en todo el mundo
7. la guardia civil / reducir / el crimen
8. la educación sobre la salud / reducir / la drogadicción entre los jóvenes del país
9. el ministro del Interior / crear nuevas leyes / de inmigración para el país
10. los senadores / trabajar / para reducir el crimen en las ciudades

EN VOZ ALTA

14-17 **¿Cuestión nacional o internacional?** Ahora, vuelve a los temas de la actividad 14-15. Imagínate que eres consejero(a) del presidente y que tienes que decidir si las siguientes cuestiones tienen más relevancia al nivel *(level)* nacional, internacional o en los dos. Para cada tema, explica tu decisión. En grupos de tres, comparen sus respuestas.

> MODELO: los derechos humanos
>
> *Es un asunto internacional. Ahora no tenemos problemas con esta cuestión en los Estados Unidos, pero sí es un problema en otros países.*

14-18 **Entrevista con el (la) presidente** Imagínate que eres presidente de un país y que tu compañero(a) de clase es un(a) reportero(a) que quiere hacerte algunas preguntas sobre tu visión política. El (La) periodista puede usar las siguientes preguntas y luego inventar cinco más.

1. ¿Qué ha hecho Ud. recientemente para controlar el terrorismo en este país? ¿Hay mayor seguridad en los aeropuertos y en las fronteras *(borders)*? ¿Qué podemos hacer para reducir el riesgo *(risk)* en las escuelas?
2. ¿Piensa Ud. que necesitamos controlar mejor el Internet para los menores de dieciocho años? ¿Sería una cuestión de la libertad de prensa?
3. Para Ud., ¿cuál es el problema más grave que tenemos ahora en este país? ¿Qué hará para resolverlo?
4. Algunos de sus críticos dicen que Ud. debe prestar más atención a los problemas internos, en vez de los asuntos internacionales. ¿Qué ha hecho Ud. recientemente con respecto a cuestiones como la vivienda para los pobres y el seguro médico *(medical insurance)* para los ancianos?

> **¿NOS ENTENDEMOS?**
> To refer to the elderly, Spanish speakers use the term **ancianos** without conveying the literal translation of *ancient ones*. It is also common to refer to seniors as **personas de la tercera edad** o **personas mayores**.

14-19 **Un debate** Trabajando con un(a) compañero(a), preparen argumentos para un debate político. Una persona debe representar una perspectiva liberal y la otra, una posición conservadora. Cada persona tendrá dos minutos para presentar sus ideas sobre cada tema. Luego la otra persona puede reaccionar ante las ideas del (de la) otro(a) candidato(a). Intenten usar el vocabulario de esta sección.

> MODELO: la inmigración ilegal a los Estados Unidos
>
> E1: *Yo creo que el gobierno de los Estados Unidos es demasiado duro (strict) con los inmigrantes ilegales. Estos inmigrantes son trabajadores muy importantes para nuestra economía. Además, sus hijos tienen derecho a una educación en las escuelas públicas y todos deben recibir atención médica si la necesitan.*
>
> E2: *Yo no estoy de acuerdo contigo. Yo pienso que el gobierno de los Estados Unidos necesita limitar el número de inmigrantes en este país. Los inmigrantes que vienen aquí hacen que aumente el crimen y no deben tener derecho a la asistencia pública. Además, ellos toman los trabajos de la gente de este país. Es un problema grave.*

TEMAS

1. los impuestos
2. el aborto
3. la educación
4. la defensa
5. las relaciones con los países hispánicos
6. la inflación
7. las huelgas de los trabajadores descontentos *(dissatisfied)*
8. la libertad de prensa

La libertad de prensa

PARA PENSAR

- ¿Crees tú en la libertad de prensa?
- ¿Crees que hay alguna ocasión en que sea necesario que el gobierno utilice la censura?
- ¿Existen asociaciones que protejan la libertad de prensa?

Leyendo en un parque en Santiago, Chile

La libertad de prensa es uno de los elementos más importantes de la democracia. Tal como en los Estados Unidos, la primera enmienda *(amendment)* establece la libertad de expresión y de prensa en Chile. En otros países latinoamericanos su constitución garantiza derechos similares.

Bajo los regímenes autoritarios del pasado, reinaba *(ruled)* la censura gubernamental. Esos gobiernos anteriores aprobaron leyes que efectivamente quitaron la libertad de prensa. Todavía siguen vigentes *(existing)* algunas de esas leyes y siguen siendo usadas para controlar la prensa. En 1998, una periodista chilena, Paula Codou, y un presentador de televisión, Rafael Gumucio, fueron interpelados *(questioned)* por denunciar a un juez de la Corte Suprema chilena. La periodista hizo una entrevista humorística con Rafael Gumucio, en la cual se dijo que el juez era «bastante feo». El juez invocó una vieja ley sobre la seguridad del estado que protege a políticos, magistrados y militares, para demandarlos *(sue them)* por difamación.

En junio de 1998 se reunieron muchas organizaciones periodísticas en Antigua, Guatemala, para hablar del estado de la libertad de prensa. Entre los participantes estaban la Organización de Estados Americanos (OEA), la Sociedad Interamericana de Prensa (SIP) y el Centro Latinoamericano de Periodismo (CELAP). Los temas discutidos abarcaron todo lo que tuviera que ver con la libertad de prensa, incluyendo los desafíos *(challenges)* legales con los que se encuentran los periodistas en toda Latinoamérica.

En mayo de 2001, en Chile se firmó una nueva ley de prensa, que protege a los periodistas y sus opiniones. Esta ley impide que los periodistas sean juzgados en tribunales militares por sus opiniones en artículos periodísticos.

PARA DISCUTIR

1. ¿Cuál es la semejanza entre el gobierno estadounidense, el gobierno chileno y los de otros países latinoamericanos en cuanto a la libertad de prensa?
2. ¿Por qué fueron interpelados Paula Codou y Rafael Gumucio?
3. Explica qué temas se discutieron en junio 1998 en la reunión de Guatemala.
4. ¿Crees que la prensa en los Estados Unidos está controlada por algunos grupos? ¿Qué grupos?

ESTRUCTURA II Expressing conjecture or probability: the conditional

In English, we express hypothetical ideas using the word *would* with a verb (e.g., *I would travel if I had the time and money*). Spanish speakers also express these ideas by using the conditional, which you have already seen in the expression **me gustaría: Me gustaría viajar a Latinoamérica.** *(I would like to travel to Latin America.)*

I. Forming the conditional

For most verbs, add these personal endings to the infinitive: **ía, ías, ía, íamos, íais, ían.**

viajar	volver	vivir	irse
viajaría	volvería	viviría	me iría
viajarías	volverías	vivirías	te irías
viajaría	volvería	viviría	se iría
viajaríamos	volveríamos	viviríamos	nos iríamos
viajaríais	volveríais	viviríais	os iríais
viajarían	volverían	vivirían	se irían

Add the conditional endings to the irregular stems of these verbs. These are the identical stems you used to form the future tense.

Verb	Stem	Ending
decir	dir-	
hacer	har-	ía
poder	podr-	ías
poner	pondr-	ía
querer	querr-	íamos
saber	sabr-	íais
salir	saldr-	ían
tener	tendr-	
venir	vendr-	

Note that the conditional of **hay** is **habría** *(there would be).*

—¿A qué hora dijo Marina que **saldría** para Quito?

What time did Marina say she would leave for Quito?

—Dijo que lo **sabría** después de llamar al aeropuerto.

She said that she would know after calling the airport.

II. Uses of the conditional

- Spanish speakers use the conditional to express what would happen in a particular situation, given a particular set of circumstances.

—¿Qué **harías** con $1.000?	*What would you do with $1,000?*
—Yo **viajaría** a Latinoamérica.	*I would travel to Latin America.*

- Spanish speakers use the conditional with the past subjunctive *(presented in the next chapter)* to express hypothetical or contrary-to-fact statements about what would happen in a particular circumstance or under certain conditions.

In the example the *if* clause (**Si tuviéramos el dinero**) states a hypothesis, and the conditional clause (**iríamos a Santiago**) states the probable result if that hypothesis were true. You will learn more about forming *if* clauses with the past subjunctive in the next chapter.

Si tuviéramos el dinero, **iríamos** a Santiago.	*If we had the money, we would go to Santiago.*

- The conditional is also used to soften a request or to express politeness and/or respect.

¿**Podrías** ayudarme con la lectura para mañana?	*Could you help me with the reading for tomorrow?*
¿**Querría** Ud. ir con nosotros al museo?	*Would you like to go to the museum with us?*
Ud. **debería** votar en las próximas elecciones.	*You should vote in the next elections.*

- Similar to what you just learned about the future tense, Spanish speakers also use the conditional to speculate about actions, conditions, and events that probably took place *in the past*. As in the case of the future for speculation about the present, the conditional of probability also carries the meaning of *I wonder* in English; if it is expressed in a statement, it means *probably*.

—¿Qué tiempo **haría** en Santiago ayer?	*I wonder how the weather was in Santiago yesterday.*
—**Estaría** a 35 grados.	*It was probably 35 degrees (centigrade).*
—Siempre hacía calor allí.	*It was always hot there.*
—**Sería** por la humedad.	*It was probably due to the humidity.*

¡A PRACTICAR!

14-20 **¡Señora candidata, por favor!** Tú y tus amigos están asistiendo a un discurso de Ángela Montero. Uds. quieren hacerle preguntas, pero con amabilidad. Usa el condicional para formar tus preguntas.

> MODELO: decir a la gente que es necesario respetar a los jóvenes
> *¿Le diría Ud. a la gente que es necesario respetar a los jóvenes?*

1. decir a la policía que necesitamos más libertad en las manifestaciones
2. poner más énfasis en la educación pública
3. haber la posibilidad de darnos mejor empleo después de la universidad
4. (a sus asistentes) salir a los pueblos para animar a la gente a participar en las elecciones
5. querer eliminar el crimen en las ciudades

14-21 **¿Qué haría esa gente anoche?** Tú no sabes qué hacía esa gente anoche. Un amigo te pregunta, y tú tienes que contestar con el condicional del verbo entre paréntesis para especular sobre qué hacía.

> MODELO: ¿Qué haría Ángela Montero anoche? (trabajar en su campaña para la presidencia)
> *Ángela Montero trabajaría en su campaña para la presidencia anoche.*

1. ¿Qué haría el presidente anoche? (prepararse para un debate contra [against] Ángela Montero)
2. ¿Qué harían los estudiantes anoche? (hacer una manifestación en la Plaza Italia)
3. ¿Qué harían los senadores anoche? (ponerse ropa elegante para una cena del congreso)
4. ¿Qué harían los estudiantes anoche? (decir a sus amigos que es necesario votar en las próximas elecciones)

14-22 **Promesas de una candidata** Termina las oraciones de Ángela Montero, una mujer que quiere ser la próxima presidente de Chile, conjugando los infinitivos en el condicional.

> MODELO: como presidente del país / pagarles más a los profesores
> *Como presidente del país, yo les pagaría más a los profesores.*

1. con una lluvia fuerte / todos los pobres tener paraguas
2. con mucho sol / yo les dar sombreros
3. con una mujer como presidente / haber menos guerras
4. con un dictador en el poder / los ciudadanos protestar
5. con mejores escuelas / nuestros hijos poder recibir trabajos buenos
6. sin tanta violencia en las ciudades / venir más turistas
7. como presidente / yo saber reducir la inflación
8. yo como presidente / eliminar el alto nivel de desempleo en el país

14-23 **Más promesas** Termina el discurso de Ángela Montero conjugando los verbos entre paréntesis o en el futuro o el condicional.

Si yo fuera (If I were) su presidente, yo 1. _____ (reducir) los impuestos en un 10 por ciento. También yo 2. _____ (aumentar) los salarios de los empleados públicos. La semana que viene, el presidente actual y yo 3. _____ (hablar) de los abusos de los derechos humanos de los prisioneros políticos de este país. Yo personalmente 4. _____ (investigar) los casos para asegurar que ellos reciban un trato humano. Si todos nosotros protestáramos, nosotros 5. _____ (poder) cambiar esta injusticia. Si yo fuera presidente, también 6. _____ (hablar) con representantes de otras naciones sobre lo que está ocurriendo en nuestras cortes y cárceles (prisons) para atraer la atención internacional sobre este asunto. Trabajando juntos, nosotros 7. _____ (eliminar) toda la corrupción que hemos sufrido en los últimos años.

EN VOZ ALTA

14-24 **¿Qué harías tú?** ¿Qué harías durante una visita de un mes a Chile? Con un(a) compañero(a) de clase, hablen de las siguientes ideas y respondan según sus gustos. ¿Tienen mucho en común?

> MODELO: E1: ¿Irías a Santiago o a una ciudad más pequeña?
> E2: *Iría a Santiago.*
> o E2: *Iría a una ciudad pequeña en la costa.*

1. ¿Viajarías por avión o en barco?
2. ¿Comprarías muchos recuerdos?
3. ¿Participarías en una manifestación política?
4. ¿Escucharías los discursos de los candidatos?
5. ¿Qué ropa llevarías?
6. ¿Qué dirían tus padres sobre tus planes?

14-25 **Plan de reconciliación** En agosto de 2003, el presidente chileno Ricardo Lagos y su gobierno propondrían los siguientes beneficios judiciales para que todos los ciudadanos chilenos vivieran en paz y en tranquilidad. Luego, discutan lo que ustedes harían o no en esta situación.

> MODELO: el presidente / hacer varias propuestas para reconciliar al pueblo chileno
> o *El presidente haría varias propuestas para reconciliar al pueblo chileno.*

1. el presidente / dar beneficios judiciales a las personas que ayudaran a encontrar el destino de los desaparecidos
2. el presidente y el congreso / aumentar las pensiones de los familiares de los desaparecidos en un 50 por ciento.
3. el presidente / pedir prioridad a los tribunales para que estudiaran los casos de violaciones de derechos humanos primero
4. la corte chilena / reducir la pena de cárcel a aquellas personas que actuaron bajo órdenes militares

14-26 **¿Eres una persona tolerante?** Dile a un(a) compañero(a) de clase lo que tú harías en las siguientes situaciones y por qué. ¡Sean creativos!

> MODELO: Después de clase, tú vuelves a tu cuarto y tu compañero(a) ha dejado el cuarto desarreglado.
> *No haría ni diría nada porque mi cuarto siempre está desarreglado.*
> o *Yo limpiaría el cuarto porque no podría vivir en un cuarto desarreglado.*

1. Vuelves a la biblioteca y alguien se sienta en el lugar donde estudias.
2. A la 1:00 de la mañana, dos personas en otro cuarto comienzan a hablar tan fuerte que tú te despiertas.
3. Tú estás duchándote en tu baño cuando suena el teléfono.
4. Tú estás sentado junto a una piscina cuando un niño te echa agua.
5. Tú miras la cuenta en un restaurante y ves que no está correcta.

14-27 **Expresiones de cortesía** Forma una oración con el condicional para hacerle una pregunta a un(a) compañero(a) de clase en las siguientes situaciones.

> MODELO: Necesitas $10 para el fin de semana.
> *¿Podrías prestarme $10 para el fin de semana?*
> o *¿Me prestarías $10 para el fin de semana?*

1. Necesitas ayuda para un examen de matemáticas.
2. Quieres que tu amigo(a) vaya contigo al cine.
3. Quieres que tú y tu amigo(a) compartan *(share)* la cuenta en un restaurante.
4. Necesitas que tu amigo(a) te llame esta noche.
5. Quieres que tú y tu compañero(a) limpien el cuarto.
6. Quieres que un grupo de estudiantes participe en las elecciones universitarias.

ESTRUCTURA III Making references to the present: the present perfect subjunctive

The present perfect subjunctive is formed with the present subjunctive of the verb **haber** + *past participle*. The present perfect subjunctive is used in the same environments that require the use of the present subjunctive. However the present perfect subjunctive generally expresses the idea of *having done* something, and it can also mean *did* something. Consider the following examples.

Es bueno que **hayas venido.**

It's good that you have come (came).

No creo que ella **haya hecho** la tarea.

I don't believe (that) she has done (did) the homework.

Me alegro que mi mamá me **haya escrito.**

I'm happy that my mother has written (wrote) to me.

Tenemos que salir antes de que **hayas terminado.**

We'll have to leave before you have finished (finish).

¡A PRACTICAR!

14-28 **En otras palabras** Convierte los verbos subrayados al presente perfecto del subjuntivo.

MODELO: Tulia está contenta de que <u>vengas</u> con nosotros.
Tulia está contenta de que hayas venido con nosotros.

1. Óscar se alegra de que Marina <u>estudie</u> ciencias políticas.
2. No creo que todos <u>digan</u> la verdad.
3. Es bueno que <u>tengan</u> la oportunidad de informarles a los ciudadanos sobre sus ideas.
4. Es mejor que <u>votemos</u> temprano.
5. Dudo que el presidente <u>pueda</u> gobernar bien.
6. Es interesante que el senador <u>asista</u> a esta conferencia.
7. Me encanta que tú <u>vayas</u> con nosotros a la manifestación.
8. Es imposible que la candidata <u>tenga</u> suficiente dinero para la campaña.

14-29 **Apoyar a una candidata** Claudia está trabajando en la campaña de Ángela Montero. Ella habla de la campaña con su amiga Pía que ha venido para un discurso de Montero. Termina el párrafo con el presente perfecto del subjuntivo.

¡Hola, Pía! Me alegro mucho de que tú 1. _____ (venir). Es una lástima que las otras chicas no 2. _____ (poder) asistir al discurso con nosotras. Me entristece que yo no las 3. _____ (convencer) de la importancia de esta reunión. Estoy buscando a Ángela Montero ahora; espero que ella 4. _____ (llegar). Muchas veces ella viene tarde a estos eventos. Es bueno que nosotros 5. _____ (empezar) a ayudarla con la campaña porque ahora está más organizada. ¡Ven! Tenemos que buscar dónde sentarnos. ¡Ojalá el discurso no 6. _____ (comenzar) sin que llegáramos nosotras!

Ahora, Pía y Claudia están escuchando el discurso de Ángela Montero. Completa el párrafo con el presente perfecto del indicativo o del subjuntivo.

Yo 7. _____ (conocer) a todos los otros candidatos y no hay ninguno que 8. _____ (tener) tanta experiencia como yo. Mis asistentes y yo 9. _____ (contestar) francamente a todas las preguntas. Nadie duda que nosotros 10. _____ (ser) honestos con la gente. Yo espero que 11. _____ (poder) comunicar claramente mis ideas. Los discursos que nosotros 12. _____ (escuchar) en los últimos días fueron muy ambiguos. Mi padre siempre 13. _____ (decir) «vamos al grano» (let's get to the point). Creo que estas palabras me 14. _____ (servir) bastante bien durante estas elecciones. Si la gente me 15. _____ (elegir), es porque yo les 16. _____ (decir) la verdad.

EN VOZ ALTA

14-30 **¡Mentiroso!** Tu amigo Guzmán puede exagerar a veces cuando está hablando con sus amigos. Indica cuáles de las siguientes afirmaciones de él son dudosas, respondiendo con una de las expresiones de la primera columna. Si lo crees, responde con una expresión de la segunda columna.

MODELO: Yo he hablado con el presidente de los Estados Unidos.
Es dudoso que hayas hablado con el presidente de los Estados Unidos.

No creo que...	No niego *(deny)* que...
Es imposible...	Estoy seguro(a) que...
Dudo que...	Es verdad...
Es dudoso que...	No hay duda...
Es improbable...	

1. Mis padres me han comprado una bicicleta nueva.
2. He visto una película de horror.
3. Mis amigos y yo hemos conocido a un extraterrestre *(alien)*.
4. Mi hermano ha bailado con Madonna.
5. Yo he jugado en un partido profesional de baloncesto.
6. Mi padre ha corrido un maratón.
7. Mi hermano ha comprado un coche nuevo.
8. He estado en el Caribe cinco veces en el último año.
9. He comido pizza esta tarde.
10. Mis amigos me han dicho que soy mentiroso.

14-31 **Los eventos políticos en tu vida** Piensa en la política y cómo la política ha afectado tu vida últimamente. Forma oraciones para expresar tus opiniones sobre lo que ha pasado usando un elemento de cada columna a continuación. Usa el subjuntivo del presente perfecto cuando sea necesario. Después, explícale tus opiniones a un(a) compañero(a).

MODELO: *Pienso que la nueva presidente ha ayudado a los pobres porque hay menos gente viviendo en la calle hoy.*
o *Dudo que los ciudadanos de mi país hayan participado en la política. Sólo un 40 por ciento de mi ciudad votó el mes pasado.*
¡Qué lástima!

Me alegro que...	la nueva presidente	eliminar el desempleo
Estoy triste/contento(a) que...	los ciudadanos de mi país	dar muchos discursos
Pienso que...	los senadores	participar en la política
Dudo que...	la policía	ayudar a los pobres
Es probable que...	nosotros los estudiantes	disminuir el crimen
Es una lástima que...	los liberales	prohibir el aborto
Es bueno/malo que...	los conservadores	purificar el medio
Es posible que...	el (la) candidato(a) X	ambiente
		controlar la corrupción

¡A VER!

En este segmento del video, los compañeros se preparan para despedirse. Planean una última actividad juntos y también empiezan a hablar sobre sus planes para el futuro después de la vida en la Hacienda Vista Alegre.

Expresiones útiles

Las siguientes son expresiones nuevas que vas a escuchar en el video.

El folleto	The pamphlet
La portada	The cover (of a book)
La contraportada	The back cover (of a book)

Antes de ver

Paso 1: ¿Qué piensas que cada compañero(a) hará después de salir de la Hacienda Vista Alegre? Trabaja con un(a) compañero(a) para adivinar sus planes futuros.

Paso 2: ¿Qué emoción sentirá cada compañero(a) a la hora de despedirse de los demás? ¿Quién se pondrá muy triste? Y, ¿quién se pondrá feliz? Habla con un(a) compañero(a) sobre lo que opinas. ¿Están de acuerdo?

Después de ver

Paso 1: En **Antes de ver, Paso 1**, tu compañero(a) y tú adivinaron sobre lo que los compañeros harán al salir de la Hacienda Vista Alegre. ¿Adivinaron bien? Ahora empareja cada compañero con lo que piensa hacer o no hacer según lo que viste en el video. No te olvides de conjugar los verbos en el futuro.

- montar una exposición de fotos de Puerto Rico en el Museo de Arte
- quedarse en Puerto Rico para escribir un libro sobre sus tradiciones
- no volver con su ex-novio César y tal vez visitar a Antonio en Texas
- regresar a la universidad para terminar los estudios
- ir de viaje por Latinoamérica

Valeria _____.
Antonio _____.
Alejandra _____.
Sofía _____.
Javier _____.

Paso 2: En **Antes de ver, Paso 2,** tu compañero(a) y tú adivinaron las reacciones emocionales de los compañeros a la hora de despedirse. Ahora completa las siguientes oraciones según lo que viste en el video con el presente perfecto del subjuntivo para indicar por qué cada uno de los compañeros se siente feliz o triste.

- Alejandra está contenta de que _____ **(poder)** tomar tantas fotos de Puerto Rico para su exposición.
- Valeria está triste de que _____ **(conocer)** a Antonio y que ahora lo tiene que dejar.
- Javier se alegra de que _____ **(aprender)** tanto de los otros compañeros de casa.
- A Antonio le molesta que no _____ **(descubrirse)** una manera para quedarse con Valeria.
- Sofía se alegra de que _____ **(encontrar)** tanto apoyo en sus amigos.

¿Qué opinas tú?

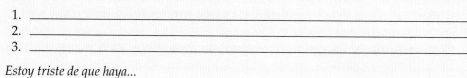

Paso 1: ¿Cuáles son tus planes para el futuro al terminar tu programa en la universidad? ¿Tienes algo en común con un(a) de los compañeros de La Hacienda Vista Alegre? ¿Quién es? Comparta tus planes con la clase. ¿Tienes planes similares a los de tus compañeros de clase?

Paso 2: ¿Cuáles son algunas experiencias en tu vida que te han puesto contento y feliz? ¿Cuáles son algunas experiencias que te han puesto triste? Sigue el modelo y escribe tres experiencias para cada emoción. Luego compara tus experiencias con las de un(a) compañero(a). ¿Tienen algo en común?

Estoy alegre de que haya...

1. _____
2. _____
3. _____

Estoy triste de que haya...

1. _____
2. _____
3. _____

¡A LEER!

Strategy: Reading complex sentences

Determining what is essential and what is nonessential in complex sentences will help you read Spanish more efficiently and effectively. As you have learned in previous reading strategies, it is not essential to understand the meaning of every single word you come across when reading in Spanish; in fact, as a learner of Spanish as a foreign language, such an expectation would be unrealistic. Instead, you should try to focus on understanding the overall meaning of sentences, which should lead you to a general understanding of the passage as a whole. When dealing with a complex sentence, the core of its meaning will come from its subject and its main verb.

Paso 1: As you turn to the following newspaper article from a popular Chilean newspaper, start by reading the title, subtitles, and first three paragraphs. Underline the subject and the main verb in each sentence. This will help you get an idea about the main point(s) of the article before you attempt to read the entire thing. As you read the rest of the article, try to identify the main subject and main verb of each sentence you come across.

En la última década del siglo XX, los salarios del llamado sexo débil crecieron *(grew)* el 70,3 por ciento frente al 46,5 por ciento de los hombres.

DISMINUYE DIFERENCIA DE SUELDOS ENTRE MUJERES Y HOMBRES

La tradicional disparidad entre los sueldos de las mujeres y de los hombres comenzó lentamente a quedar atrás durante la última década del siglo pasado. Al menos así lo confirman las cifras *(figures, numbers)* de ingreso promedio, según estadísticas oficiales de la Superintendencia de Administradoras de Fondos de Pensiones (AFP). Las cifras también indican que el sueldo de las mujeres que trabajan bajo contrato creció un 70,3 por ciento como promedio en la década, a diferencia del 46,5 por ciento real que aumentó el sueldo de los hombres en el mismo período.

La brecha *(gap)* a principios de los años noventa era de más de $63.000 entre los hombres y las mujeres, que hasta octubre de 2000 la diferencia se redujo a poco menos de $45.000 en promedio al mes. Aunque la relación sigue siendo perjudicial para las trabajadoras, la tasa de crecimiento del ingreso femenino ha sido constante. De hecho, de representar el sueldo de la mujer el 70,2 por ciento del ingreso promedio de los hombres en 1990 pasó a ser equivalente al 79,6 por ciento del mismo en 1995, hasta terminar la década representando el 85,1 por ciento del salario de los hombres. Esto equivale a decir que el sueldo de un hombre es equivalente a 1,17 sueldos de una mujer. Así, los registros previstos son un reflejo de la incorporación de la mujer al trabajo. De los casi 6 millones de personas que contribuyen al sistema de pensiones, cerca de 2.5 millones son mujeres. Según cifras de la superintendencia, la mitad de las mujeres que trabajan en forma dependiente tienen entre veinticinco y cuarenta años de edad, y se espera que su participación en el espectro laboral siga en aumento con la llegada de nuevas generaciones. El incremento de los sueldos femeninos en la última década parece respaldar *(to support)* que las mujeres están mejorando su situación dentro del mercado laboral, y que la tan rechazada discriminación pueda ser una cosa del pasado.

Paso 2: Ahora, lee el resto del artículo y contesta las siguientes preguntas.

1. ¿Cuál es el tema del artículo? ¿Qué tipo de información contiene?
2. ¿Qué cambios han tenido lugar en la última década en cuanto a la situación de los salarios de las mujeres en el mercado laboral chileno?
3. ¿Cómo ha cambiado la brecha entre los sueldos de los hombres y las mujeres en Chile en la última década?
4. Hoy día, ¿cómo se comparan los ingresos de los hombres y las mujeres en Chile? Sé específico(a).
5. Según el artículo, ¿qué edades tienen las mujeres que trabajan en el mercado laboral chileno?

Paso 3: Piensa ahora en la situación de la mujer en el mercado laboral estadounidense y contesta las siguientes preguntas.

1. ¿Crees que en el campo laboral la mujer estadounidense tiene las mismas oportunidades que el hombre? ¿Por qué sí o por qué no?
2. ¿A qué problemas se enfrenta *(faces)* la mujer estadounidense en el trabajo hoy en día?
3. ¿Crees que la situación de la mujer en el mercado laboral estadounidense ha mejorado en la última década en comparación con la de los hombres? Explica tu respuesta.

¡A ESCRIBIR!

Strategy: Writing from diagrams

In this section you will write a brief report based on information in diagrams. Diagrams present charts, tables, and graphs of specific information that can be readily understood and remembered. Written reports prepared by individuals in business, industry, government and education often include information from diagrams. It is important to learn to interpret diagrams and to express the information they contain in a succinct and clear fashion.

Paso 1: Ya sabemos que el Internet es un medio de comunicación que ha crecido mucho en los últimos años. Tiene la capacidad de facilitar la transmisión de información a una cantidad enorme de ciudadanos a través del mundo. Sin embargo, no todos disfrutan igualmente de los beneficios del Internet. Los siguientes gráficos presentan algunas estadísticas acerca del acceso al Internet que tienen diferentes sectores de la población de España. Vamos a ver que no todas las personas tienen el mismo acceso a este medio de comunicación. Estudia los tres gráficos que siguen. Nota los títulos, los colores y las categorías que aparecen en cada uno.

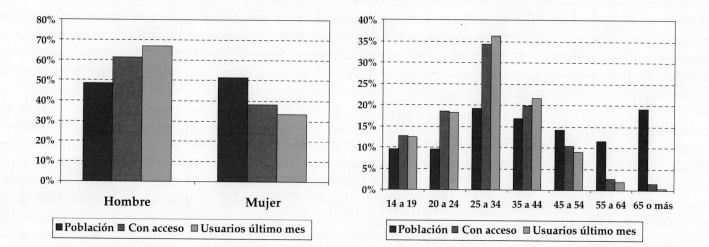

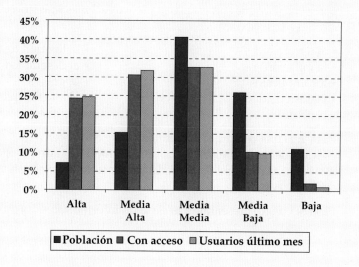

Paso 2: Basándote en la información presentada en los gráficos, contesta las preguntas que siguen.

1. ¿Cuáles son los tres factores sociales considerados en los gráficos?
2. ¿Quién tiene más acceso al Internet, los hombres o las mujeres?
3. ¿Cuáles son las edades de las personas que tienen el mayor acceso?
4. ¿Cuál de las clases sociales tiene el mayor acceso?

Task: Writing a report based on information from diagrams

Functions: Comparing and contrasting; Comparing and distinguishing
Vocabulary: Computers
Grammar: Comparisons

Paso 1: Refiriéndote a los gráficos, considera las siguientes preguntas.

- ¿Hay desigualdad en el acceso al Internet?
- ¿Por qué sí o por qué no?

Paso 2: Escribe un informe de un párrafo en el cual respondas a estas preguntas. Debes hacer lo siguiente:

- escribir una oración principal para indicar tu respuesta a la pregunta
- considerar los tres factores sociales
- mencionar algunas estadísticas específicas para apoyar tu posición
- explicar por qué hay desigualdad o no en el acceso al Internet

Paso 3: Intercambia papeles con un(a) compañero(a) de clase. Lee el informe de la otra persona para ver si Uds. han presentado la misma información y la misma conclusión. Si hay alguna diferencia, discútela con tu compañero(a).

¡A CONVERSAR!

Task: Talking about civic concerns and political issues

Algunas personas tienen más interés en la política que otras personas, pero casi todas tienen opiniones sobre varios temas políticos y preocupaciones sociales. Ahora vas a tratar con un(a) compañero(a) de los temas que Uds. consideran muy importantes en el mundo contemporáneo.

Paso 1: La siguiente lista presenta algunas preocupaciones cívicas a las que se enfrenta nuestra sociedad hoy en día. Lee la lista y escoge las tres preocupaciones que sean más graves en tu opinión. Debes pensar en algunas razones para apoyar tu posición. ¿Por qué son estas tres preocupaciones más graves que las otras? ¿Cómo afectan a la sociedad?

- el terrorismo
- la inflación
- los impuestos
- la desigualdad
- el aborto

- la libertad de prensa
- el desempleo
- la guerra
- el analfabetismo
- las huelgas

Paso 2: Habla con un(a) compañero(a) de clase acerca de las tres preocupaciones cívicas que has escogido. Si tu compañero(a) de clase no está de acuerdo en que éstas son las más graves, trata de convencerlo(la) explicándole las razones que apoyan tu opinión.

Paso 3: Luego, preséntale a la clase un informe sobre las opiniones de Uds.

La política y el voto

Sustantivos

la **campaña** campaign
el (la) **candidato(a)** candidate
el (la) **ciudadano(a)** citizen
el **Congreso** congress
el **debate** debate
el **deber** duty
la **democracia** democracy

el (la) **dictador(a)** dictator
la **dictadura** dictatorship
el **discurso** speech
el **ejército** army
las **elecciones** elections
el **gobierno** government
la **ley** law

el **partido político** political party
la **paz** peace
el **poder** power
el (la) **político** politician
el (la) **presidente** president
la **reforma** reform
el **voto** vote

Verbos

apoyar to support
aprobar (ue) to approve; to pass
defender (ie) to defend

discutir to argue, to discuss
elegir (i, i) to elect
firmar to sign

gobernar (ie) to govern
oponer to oppose
votar to vote

Adjetivos

conservador(a) conservative
demócrata democratic

liberal liberal
republicano(a) republican

Las preocupaciones cívicas

Sustantivos

el **aborto** abortion
el **(an)alfabetismo** (il)literacy
la **corrupción** corruption
el **crimen** crime
la **defensa** defense
los **derechos humanos (civiles)** human (civil)
    rights

el **(des)empleo** (un)employment
la **(des)igualdad** (in)equality
la **drogadicción** drug addiction
la **educación** education
la **guerra** war
la **huelga** strike
los **impuestos** taxes

la **inflación** inflation
la **inmigración** immigration
la **libertad de prensa** freedom of the press
la **manifestación** demonstration
la **política internacional** international policy
el **terrorismo** terrorism
la **vivienda** housing

Los medios de comunicación

el **Internet** Internet
el **noticiero** newscast
el **periódico** newspaper

la **prensa** the press
el **reportaje** journalistic report
la **revista** magazine

Verbos

aumentar to increase
eliminar to eliminate
informar to inform

investigar to investigate
protestar to protest
reducir to reduce

Los avances tecnológicos:

Chapter Objectives

COMMUNICATIVE GOALS

In this chapter you will learn how to . . .

- Talk about home electronics and computers
- Make statements in the past with the subjunctive mood
- Talk about hypothetical situations

STRUCTURES

- Past (imperfect) subjunctive
- *If* clauses

CULTURAL INFORMATION

- Las telecomunicaciones en Uruguay
- Equipos: En la palma de la mano

Uruguay

URUGUAY

Población: 3.413.329

Área: 176.220 kilómetros cuadrados, un poco más pequeño que el estado de Washington

Capital: Montevideo, 1.432.000

Ciudades principales: Salto, Rivera, Punta del Este, Minas

Moneda: el peso

Lengua: el español y el portoñol (se habla en la frontera entre Uruguay y Brasil)

¡Bienvenidos a Uruguay!

En este video, vas a aprender de Uruguay. Después de ver el video, contesta las siguientes preguntas:

1 ¿Dónde está Uruguay y cómo es su clima? ¿Cuál es el origen de sus habitantes?

2 ¿De qué es orgulloso el uruguayo?

3 ¿Es Uruguay un país urbanizado? ¿Qué sabes de Montevideo y cuál es la principal actividad económica de Uruguay?

4 Según el video, ¿cómo ha nombrado la UNESCO la ciudad de Colonia del Sacramento y por qué?

5 Según el video «Uruguay es un digno representante del mundo hispanoamericano». ¿Estás de acuerdo con ese comentario? Justifica tu respuesta.

Plaza Independencia, Montevideo, Uruguay

Una casa del siglo XXI In this section you will learn about technological innovations that we use in our homes. How many of the items pictured below are in your house?

Sustantivos

la alarma alarm
la cámara (digital) (digital) camera

el equipo equipment
el satélite satellite

Verbos

apagar to turn off
(des)conectar to (dis)connect
(des)enchufar to plug in (to unplug)

funcionar to function, work
grabar to record
prender to turn on (TV, stereo)

Adjetivos

apagado(a) off
encendido(a) on

enchufado(a) plugged in
prendido(a) on

¡A PRACTICAR!

15-1 **Una vida tecnológica** La abuela Adelaida habla de la vida de su nieta, Minia. Minia es joven y goza de *(enjoy)* muchas de la invenciones de la tecnología. Su abuela comenta sobre la vida tan fácil que tiene su nieta. Completa su historia, usando las palabras de la siguiente lista y conjugando los verbos en la forma correcta.

prender   equipo   apagado(a)   desenchufar   encendido(a)   enchufado(a)
funcionar   alarma   apagar   desconectar   control remoto   apagar

Mi nieta tiene una vida tan fácil, que a veces no me lo creo. Le encanta ver la tele. Todos los días, cuando se levanta, la 1. _____ y la deja 2. _____ todo el día. A veces yo la 3. _____, pero después de unos minutos está de nuevo 4. _____.
Minia tiene tanto 5. _____ tecnológico que tuvo que instalar una 6. _____ para nuestra seguridad. ¡Caramba! Cuando mira la tele, se sienta en el sillón con el 7. _____ en las manos. Un día, yo quiero 8. _____ todo. Voy a 9. _____ todas sus máquinas. Ojalá que deje todo 10. _____ para tener un poco de silencio. Pero nunca va a pasar. Ahora, toda su tecnología 11. _____ muy bien y yo tengo que aguantármela (to put up with it).

¿NOS ENTENDEMOS?
In Spain, the remote control may be referred to as **el mando (a distancia).** Another term for **el estéreo** is **el equipo de sonido.** A cordless phone may be referred to as **el teléfono portátil** or **el teléfono inalámbrico,** while in Spain a cell phone is called **el móvil** (short for **teléfono móvil**). In parts of Latin America it is referred to as **el celular.**

15-2 | Tipos de tecnología Indica dos o tres aparatos domésticos que corresponden a cada una de las siguientes categorías.

MODELO: la seguridad personal
la alarma, el teléfono celular

1. la diversión
2. las comunicaciones
3. la música
4. el trabajo profesional
5. los recuerdos

EN VOZ ALTA

15-3 | ¿Para qué se usa? Imagínate que tienes que describir la función de los siguientes elementos a una persona del siglo XIX (un[a] compañero[a] de clase). Explica para qué se usa cada cosa y luego cómo usarla. En algunos casos, tendrás mucho que explicarle a tu compañero(a).

1. la videocámara
2. el disco compacto
3. la antena parabólica
4. el estéreo
5. la alarma
6. el control remoto
7. el satélite
8. el teléfono celular

15-4 | Antes de que salgas de la casa Trabajando con otro(a) compañero(a) de clase, forma siete oraciones con las palabras a continuación para hacer algunas sugerencias que le darás a una persona que va a cuidar de tu casa cuando estés de vacaciones. Usa mandatos informales para tus sugerencias. La otra persona debe responder de una manera lógica.

MODELO: la alarma
E1: *Antes de entrar en la casa, asegúrate* (make sure) *de que esté apagada la alarma.*
E2: *Gracias. ¿Puedes darme el código* (code) *para apagarla?*

Verbos	**Sustantivos**	**Adjetivos**
(des)conectar	la alarma	apagado(a)
prender	el estéreo	encendido(a)
apagar	el contestador automático	enchufado(a)
grabar	el teléfono celular	abierto(a)
(des)enchufar	el control remoto	
llamar		
usar		
asegurarse		

15-5 | Opiniones Hazle las siguientes preguntas a un(a) compañero(a) de clase. ¿Tienen Uds. algo en común con respecto a la tecnología?

1. ¿Dependes mucho de la tecnología en tu casa? ¿Qué aparatos usas con frecuencia? ¿Qué aparatos usaste hoy y para qué? ¿Qué aparato te gustaría tener que no tienes ahora? ¿Por qué sería útil para ti?
2. ¿Cuáles son algunos aparatos que no usaban tus padres cuando eran jóvenes? Para ellos, ¿cuáles son los aparatos más útiles? ¿Qué aparato usas tú que no usan ellos? ¿Tienen ellos el mismo entusiasmo que tú por la tecnología? ¿Por qué sí o por qué no?
3. ¿Es la tecnología algo positivo o negativo para nuestra civilización? ¿Cuáles son algunos ejemplos de los beneficios y cuáles son los efectos negativos de la tecnología? ¿Cuáles son los avances tecnológicos más importantes del siglo XX (el avión, la computadora, los satélites, el Internet, la clonación genética, los avances en la medicina)?
4. ¿Cómo serán nuestras casas en el año 2050? ¿Habrá cambios radicales o innovaciones menores? ¿Cómo serían nuestras vidas sin los avances tecnológicos mencionados en esta sección? Si pudieras inventar una máquina nueva, ¿qué sería? ¿En qué sentido mejoraría nuestra vida?

Text audio
Track 2-16

EN CONTEXTO

Federico y Alejandra, una pareja uruguaya, están abriendo *(are opening)* una tienda de **computadoras** en Montevideo, Uruguay, donde viven los padres de Alejandra. Ahora están hablando de sus planes para el primer día de su nuevo negocio.

—¡Ay! No sé, Federico. ¿Y si no viene mucha gente?

—No te preocupes, mi amor. No habríamos abierto la tienda **si no hubiera habido** *(if there had not been)* tanta demanda. La gente vendrá.

—¿Y si no podemos pagarles a mis padres el dinero que nos prestaron?

—Tranquila. Estoy seguro de que podremos pagarles dentro de dos meses. No hay problema.

—Pero Federico, solamente tenemos la mitad *(half)* de las computadoras que pedimos. Y **las impresoras** no han llegado todavía.

—Espero que no sigas así, mi amor. Tenemos que ser optimistas. **Si tuviéramos** *(If we had)* todo en orden, no habría aventura. Tenemos que arriesgarnos *(to take a risk)* un poco.

—Para ti es fácil decir eso. No piensas en los detalles.

—Al contrario. Según mi amigo Paco, no hay mejor momento para nuestra tienda. Con tantas personas **navegando la Red** *(surfing the Internet)*, con los nuevos negocios electrónicos... , **la tecnología digital...**

—Tu amigo vive en los Estados Unidos. No creo que sea exactamente lo mismo aquí.

—Bueno, lo sabremos muy pronto, ¿eh?

¿Comprendiste?

Indica si las siguientes oraciones son ciertas o falsas. Si la oración es falsa, ¡corrígela!

1. Alejandra tiene miedo de que la tienda no vaya a tener éxito.
2. Federico ha investigado la demanda para computadoras en Montevideo.
3. La pareja tiene todos los productos que pidieron para la tienda.
4. Federico es un poco pesimista.
5. Alejandra es más realista que Federico.

Las telecomunicaciones en Uruguay

Monumento Entrevero,
Montevideo, Uruguay

Mujer hablando por el teléfono celular y usando la computadora portátil

Personas esperando para
usar el teléfono público

PARA PENSAR

■ ¿Qué aparato electrónico usas? (la computadora, los juegos electrónicos, etc.)

■ ¿Tienes un teléfono celular? ¿Cuáles son las ventajas y las desventajas *(disadvantages)* de usar un celular?

■ ¿Qué tipo de tecnología te parece la más importante? ¿Por qué?

La tecnología tiene un papel muy importante en la globalización económica mundial. Para que un país pueda integrarse económicamente al mundo, es esencial tener buenas comunicaciones. Por eso, el papel de las telecomunicaciones es cada vez más importante para este desarrollo global.

Hoy en día en Uruguay hay más de 900.000 líneas telefónicas y hay más de 400.000 personas que usan el teléfono celular y que usan la Red. Además Uruguay es uno de los países líderes en la exportación de programas de computación y de servicios de tecnología para los otros países latino-americanos, todo esto teniendo en cuenta que Uruguay es el penúltimo *(second to the last)* país en extensión de Sur América después de Suriname y que solamente tiene 3.5 millones de habitantes.

Históricamente, los países latinoamericanos han carecido de *(have lacked)* una infraestructura que pudiera apoyar las nuevas tecnologías. Durante muchos años se creía que era peligroso invertir dinero en Uruguay y otros países latinoamericanos precisamente por las malas telecomunicaciones. Este factor negativo ha desaparecido y se puede observar que en países como Uruguay, existen más de catorce proveedores de servicios de la Red y que el sistema telefónico ha sido totalmente digita-lizado, además de que existen dos estaciones de satélites.

Antel es una compañía que ofrece diferentes sistemas de telecomunicaciones y distintos tipos de servicios (instalaciones, mantenimiento y apoyo técnico) en Uruguay. Aparte existe un distribuidor de Ericsson, que le vende aparatos de telefonía al público. Uruguay ha tenido que mejorar sus tele-comunicaciones rápidamente, ya que Montevideo es la sede Administrativa del MERCOSUR. Este tratado económico firmado por Argentina, Brasil, Paraguay y Uruguay ha abierto las exportaciones e importaciones de productos. También gracias a este tratado se han eliminado *(have eliminated)* o se han reducido los aranceles *(taxes)* de productos. Este pacto económico convierte a Uruguay en un mercado de importancia estratégica.

PARA DISCUTIR

1. ¿Cuántas personas usan el teléfono celular y la Red en Uruguay?
2. ¿Por qué ha tenido Uruguay que mejorar rápidamente sus telecomunicaciones?
3. ¿Qué es MERCOSUR?
4. Algunas personas están de acuerdo con la globalización económica mientras que otro grupo de personas está en contra. ¿Qué piensas tú de la globalización económica?

Spanish speakers use the past (imperfect) subjunctive to express wishes, emotions, opinions, and uncertainty about the past.

I. Forming the past subjunctive

For all Spanish verbs, drop the **-ron** ending from the **Uds./ellos(as)** form of the preterite tense, then add the personal endings shown in boldface below.

	hablar	**venir**	**irse**
Uds., ellos(as)	hablaron	vinieron	se fueron
	hablar**a**	vinier**a**	me fuer**a**
	hablar**as**	vinier**as**	te fuer**as**
	hablar**a**	vinier**a**	se fuer**a**
	hablár**amos**	viniér**amos**	nos fué**ramos**
	hablar**ais**	vinier**ais**	os fuer**ais**
	hablar**an**	vinier**an**	se fuer**an**

The **nosotros(as)** form always has an accent mark because it is the only form in which the stress falls on the third-from-the-last syllable. Any irregularities in the third-person plural of the preterite will be maintained in the imperfect subjunctive (as demonstrated with the verbs **venir** and **irse**).

The past subjunctive has alternate forms that use **-se** instead of **-ra** endings. For example: **hablase, hablases, hablase, hablásemos, hablaseis, hablasen** and **fuese, fueses, fuese, fuésemos, fueseis, fuesen.** These forms are sometimes used in Spain and in literary works or legal documents.

II. Uses of the past subjunctive

You have learned to use the present subjunctive to express actions, conditions, and situations that take place in the present or the future. Spanish speakers use the past subjunctive to communicate the same information about the past.

In noun clauses

- To express desires, preferences, suggestions, requests, and recommendations

Federico esperaba que a Alejandra **le gustara** la idea de abrir una tienda de computadoras.

Federico hoped that Alejandra would like the idea of opening a computer store.

- To express happiness, hope, likes, complaints, worries, regret, sorrow, surprise, fear, and other emotions

Federico y Alejandra se alegraron de que su nueva tienda de computadoras **comenzara** bien.

Federico and Alejandra were glad that their new computer store was having a good start.

Federico esperaba que **hubiera** muchos clientes el primer día, pero Alejandra tenía miedo de que nadie **viniera** aquí a la tienda.

Federico hoped that there would be lots of customers the first day, but Alejandra was afraid that no one would come here to the store.

- To make impersonal expressions

Era bueno que **estuvieran** los padres de la pareja para la inauguración de la tienda.

It was good that the couple's parents were there for the opening of the store.

- To express doubt and uncertainty

Alejandra dudó que ellos **pudieran** pagarles a muchos empleados al principio.

Alejandra doubted that they could pay many employees at first.

In adjective clauses

- To express unknown and/or nonexistent conditions

Para la tienda, Federico buscaba un sitio que **tuviera** mucho espacio.

For the store, Federico looked for a site that had lots of space.

In adverbial clauses

- To express purpose and future contingency

Los padres de Federico y Alejandra les prestaron el dinero con tal de que **pudieran** devolvérselo dentro de un año.

Federico and Alejandra's parents lent them the money provided that they could pay it back to them within a year.

In making polite requests or suggestions

- In addition to the conditional tense, Spanish speakers also use the past subjunctive of verbs such as **querer, deber,** and **poder** to soften requests, to make polite suggestions, and to persuade gently.

—¿**Quisieran** Uds. acompañarnos?
Would you like to accompany us?
—Gracias, pero **debiéramos** volver.
Thank you, but we should return.
—Quizás **pudiéramos** ir otra noche.
Maybe we could go another night.

¡A PRACTICAR!

15-6 **Los recuerdos de un abuelo** Ayúdale al abuelo de Federico a contar sus recuerdos al conjugar los verbos entre paréntesis en la forma correcta del imperfecto del subjuntivo.

1. Cuando yo era niño, no teníamos computadoras. Mis padres insistían que yo _____ (estudiar) mucho.

2. Ellos querían que mi hermano y yo _____ (sacar) una beca para asistir a la universidad de Montevideo.

3. Mi padre, tu bisabuelo, trabajaba mucho para que la familia _____ (tener) las cosas básicas. ¡No teníamos tiempo para jugar, ni teníamos juegos electrónicos!

4. En aquella época no era común que la esposa _____ (trabajar) fuera de la casa.

5. Por esa razón yo empecé a trabajar cuando tenía quince años en caso de que no _____ (recibir) una beca para mis estudios universitarios.

6. Yo quería trabajar en la librería de mi tío. Más gente leía libros entonces, como no existía la televisión o el Internet. Le pedí que él me _____ (dar) un trabajo durante los fines de semana.

7. Mi madre no quería que nosotros _____ (estar) fuera de la casa los domingos, pero era el día más ocupado de la tienda.

8. En aquella época no teníamos Internet, y era importante que los estudiantes _____ (tener) y _____ (leer) todos los libros para las clases.

15-7 **Recuerdos de mi juventud** Forma oraciones sobre tu juventud, usando frases de cada grupo.

Cuando yo era joven...

1. mis padres insistían en que yo...
3. yo quería vivir en una casa que...
4. mi abuela me pedía que yo...
5. mi madre se alegraba de que la familia...

aprender a usar la computadora
estar cerca del mar / de las montañas
estudiar mucho
portarse *(to behave)* bien en la clase
no pasar demasiado tiempo al teléfono
ir de vacaciones juntos
ser amigos de por vida *(for life)*
ser honesto(a)
estar en la ciudad / en el campo
no gastar todo mi dinero en discos compactos

15-8 **Páginas de mi diario** Completa las siguientes frases y luego comparte tus experiencias con un(a) compañero(a) de clase. ¿Tienen mucho en común?

MI NIÑEZ

Cuando era niño(a), era importante que yo...
Mi(s) (papá/mamá/padres) prohibía(n) que...
No me gustaba que mi(s) (papá/mamá/padres)... , pero sí me gustaba que (él/ella/ellos)...

MI ADOLESCENCIA

De adolescente, no estaba seguro(a) de que...
Por ejemplo, dudaba que...
A veces, sentía que... ; en otras ocasiones me alegraba de que...

EN VOZ ALTA

15-9 Entrevista Hazle las siguientes preguntas a un(a) compañero(a) de clase para saber un poco sobre su niñez.

1. **La familia:** ¿Qué te gustaba que hicieran tus padres cuando eras niño(a)?
2. **La escuela:** ¿Qué te prohibían tus profesores en la escuela primaria? ¿Y en la secundaria?
3. **Los pasatiempos:** ¿Qué deportes practicabas cuando eras niño(a)? ¿En qué deportes te prohibían tus padres que participaras? ¿Por qué?
4. **La tecnología:** ¿Tenías televisor en casa cuando eras niño(a)? ¿Qué programas permitían tus padres que vieras? ¿Qué programas te prohibían que vieras? ¿Por qué? ¿Tenías computadora e Internet en casa? ¿Qué te dejaban hacer con la computadora? ¿Qué te decían que no hicieras con la computadora?

15-10 Es mejor ser cortés Imagínate que tú y un(a) compañero(a) de clase están de vacaciones en Uruguay en uno de los lugares turísticos más famosos, Punta del Este.

Yates en el puerto en Punta del Este, Uruguay

CULTURA
The largest and best known of the resorts in Uruguay is **Punta del Este,** one of South America's most glamorous and exclusive destinations. It is surrounded by yacht and fishing clubs, golf courses, casinos, and beautiful vacation homes. It has excellent beaches, perfect for swimming and sunbathing. Just offshore are **Isla Gorriti,** which has beautiful beaches and the ruins of an 18th-century fortress, and **Isla de Lobos,** a nature reserve that is home to a large sea-lion colony.

Uds. desean ser corteses con los uruguayos y por eso, usan el imperfecto del subjuntivo de los verbos **querer, deber** y **poder.** ¿Qué les dirían a las siguientes personas?

MODELO: Pides que alguien te saque una foto.
¿Pudiera sacarnos una foto?

1. Quieres que un amigo te muestre cómo usar la videocámara.
2. Un amigo uruguayo usa una palabra que no entiendes. Pídele que te la explique.
3. Estás en el Hotel Azul. Una mujer de limpieza toca a la puerta para ver si puede limpiar tu cuarto. Tú acabas de levantarte. Le pides que vuelva en una hora.
4. Llamas a un amigo por teléfono para persuadirle que vaya contigo a la Isla de Lobos para ver los lobos marinos mañana.
5. No entiendes a un muchacho que trabaja en los campos de golf de Punta del Este porque habla demasiado rápido.
6. Estás de paseo en la Isla Gorriti, visitando la fortaleza del siglo XVIII, cuando tú y tu amigo conocen a unos muchachos y los invitas a cenar en Punta del Este.
7. Después de la cena, pides permiso para volver al hotel.

VOCABULARIO La computadora

En la tienda de Federico y Alejandra In this section, you will learn how to talk about computers and their functions.

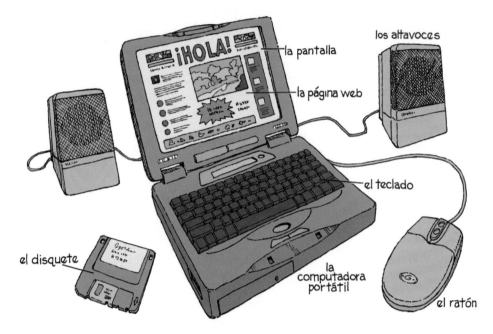

Sustantivos

el archivo file
el ciberespacio / el espacio cibernético cyberspace
la conexión connection
el correo electrónico email
el disco duro hard drive
el escáner scanner

la impresora printer
el Internet Internet
el mensaje message
el programa (de CD-ROM) (CD-ROM) program
el salón (la sala) de charla chat room

Verbos

abrir un documento (un programa) to open
   a document (program)
archivar (guardar) to save
estar conectado(a) (en línea) to be online
hacer click (sobre) to click (on)

imprimir to print
navegar la Red to surf the net
programar to program
quitar el programa to quit the program
teletrabajar to telecommute

Palabras útiles are presented to help you enrich your personal vocabulary. The words here will help you talk about computers and the Internet.

Palabras útiles

Localizador Uniforme de Recursos URL
el módem modem
la página de bienvenida (de entrada, de presentación, inicial, principal, de la Red) home page
la plataforma de operación operating platform (system)
el proveedor de servicios Internet Internet service provider
el servidor server

¡A PRACTICAR!

15-11 | **¡Socorro!** Es la segunda semana en la tienda de Federico y Alejandra. Hoy, muchos clientes llaman con problemas. Completa las oraciones con la palabra necesaria de la lista para indicar cuáles son los problemas y algunas de las recomendaciones.

computadora portátil	navegar la Red	página web	pantalla	escáner	abrir
correo electrónico	salón de charla	hacer click	Internet	conexión	
archivar mensajes	ciberespacio	imprimir	altavoces	disquete	

1. **El Sr. Ramírez:** ¡Ayúdeme, por favor, Alejandra! Voy a hacer un viaje a Punta del Este y necesito una computadora para llevar conmigo. ¿Qué me recomienda Ud.?

   Alejandra: Cómprese una 1. _____.

2. **Judith:** Alejandra, necesito algo para archivar mis documentos. No quiero archivarlos en la computadora misma. ¿Qué puedo usar?

   Alejandra: Tú necesitas un 2. _____.

3. **Juan Pablo:** Alejandra, yo quisiera escuchar música de Hugo Fattoruso con mi computadora. ¿Qué necesito?

   Alejandra: Ud. necesita unos 3. _____.

4. **La Sra. Marga:** Tengo un problema con la 4. _____ de mi computadora. No puedo ver las imágenes.

   Alejandra: Tengo que ver su computadora, Sra. Marga.

5. **José Eduardo:** Quiero navegar el 4. _____. ¿Me podría mostrar cómo hacer una 5. _____ con el Internet? Quisiera diseñar una 6. _____ con fotos de El Rosedal en los Jardines Botánicos.

   Alejandra: Mire, José Eduardo, para poner sus fotos en el 7. _____, va a necesitar un 8. _____ si no tiene una cámara digital. También necesita tener una dirección de 9. _____ para que la gente que ve su página web pueda mandarle 10. _____.

6. **Soledad:** Alejandra, yo quiero conocer al hombre de mis sueños en Internet. ¿Conoces tú algún 11. _____ para solteros?

   Alejandra: No sé, pero puedes mirar en el Internet. ¿Sabes 12. _____?

7. **Cordelia:** No quiero perder mis documentos, ¡pero no sé cómo 13. _____ en mi nueva computadora!

   Alejandra: La guía que le mandé la última semana tiene esta información en la página 29.

8. **Maruja:** Yo sé cerrar mis documentos, pero no sé cómo 14. _____ los.

   Alejandra: Para abrir tus documentos, necesitas 15. _____ con el ratón en el ícono.

9. **Eduardo Espina:** ¿Para qué es esa impresora, para 16. _____ mis documentos?

   Alejandra: Sí, señor.

15-12 | **¿Qué busca esta gente?** Ahora Federico tiene descripciones de lo que sus clientes necesitan. Ayúdale a encontrar las cosas que necesitan.

1. _____ algo para imprimir documentos
2. _____ algo con muchas teclas y letras para escribir en la computadora
3. _____ el objeto que se usa para hacer click
4. _____ lo que se usa para escribir en la computadora
5. _____ la parte de la computadora que tiene memoria

a. el disco duro
b. el programa (de Word)
c. el teclado
d. la impresora
e. el ratón

CULTURA
Punta del Este, Uruguay, is a city that lies on the coast, just 140 kilometers from Montevideo. It is a famous resort spot for the jet-set crowd from both Uruguay and Argentina. Many famous people own vacation homes there.

CULTURA
Hugo Fattoruso is one of Uruguay's most celebrated musicians. An instrumentalist, composer, and singer, he is best known to North American audiences as a member of Brazilian singer Milton Nascimento's band.

CULTURA
The Botanical Gardens in Montevideo are located near the Parque del Prado on Washington Street. These gardens boast more than 1,000 species of indigenous plants. El Rosedal, or the Rose Garden, was once the meeting place for women from high society.

¿NOS ENTENDEMOS?
With the emergence of the Internet, the Spanish language is quickly adopting and creating new vocabulary to talk about **el ciberespacio**, or *cyberspace*. Many of these words are cognates of their English counterparts. The web can be referred to as either **el Internet**, **la Telaraña mundial**, or **la Red**. One who navigates **la Red** can be called **un(a) cibernauta** or **internauta**. To surf the web can be referred to as **navegar la Red** or even **surfear**. One may visit a **salón (sala) de chat** to visit, or **chatear**, with friends around the world. Directions on a web page telling a cybernaut to "click" on an icon can be stated in at least three different ways: **hacer click**, **oprimir**, or **pulsar**.

15-13 **¿Qué necesitas?** Indica el equipo y los programas que necesitas para realizar las siguientes funciones en la computadora.

MODELO: producir una nueva versión de tu currículum
Necesito el disquete con la versión vieja, una computadora, un programa como Word y una impresora.

1. producir copias de unas fotos
2. escribir una carta
3. buscar información sobre el turismo en Uruguay
4. charlar con alguien por la computadora
5. escribir un trabajo para tu clase de inglés
6. tomar apuntes *(to take notes)* usando la computadora en la biblioteca o en la clase
7. escuchar música del Internet en tu computadora
8. imprimir copias de tu trabajo de inglés para tus amigos

EN VOZ ALTA

15-14 **¿Cuánto usas de la tecnología?** Hazle las siguientes preguntas a un(a) compañero(a) de clase para determinar cuánto él/ella usa de la tecnología.

nunca = 0   a veces = 1   frecuentemente = 2   todos los días = 3

_____ ¿Te escribes con amigos o familiares por correo electrónico?
_____ ¿Usas la computadora para escribir trabajos escritos para tus clases?
_____ ¿Haces presentaciones con la computadora?
_____ ¿Escribes páginas que aparecen en el Internet?
_____ ¿Te comunicas con gente en las salas de charla?
_____ ¿Compras cosas de un vendedor en la Telaraña (Red) mundial?
_____ ¿Navegas la Red para diversión?
_____ ¿Usas un escáner para modificar fotos?
_____ ¿Imprimes cartas o tarjetas que hiciste en la computadora?
_____ ¿Usas la computadora para programar?

INTERPRETACIONES

0–8   Debes comprarte una computadora.
9–17   Necesitas más práctica con la computadora.
18–24   ¿Quieres una entrevista con Microsoft?
25–30   Eres un(a) genio(a) con la computadora.

15-15 **Entrevista** Hazle las siguientes preguntas a un(a) compañero(a) y luego hablen sobre sus respuestas.

1. ¿Para qué actividades usas la computadora? ¿Usas la computadora más como un componente de tu trabajo o tus estudios o como una fuente de diversión? ¿Te ha simplificado la vida la computadora o es la causa de más estrés para ti?
2. ¿Es la computadora una tecnología privilegiada que se reserva solamente para los ricos? ¿Es un problema que los jóvenes sepan más que la gente mayor con respecto a la tecnología? ¿Será más fácil usar la computadora en el futuro o será tan complicado como ahora? ¿Cómo se puede asegurar que todos tengan acceso a la Red y los servicios que ofrece?
3. ¿Hay suficiente control sobre el contenido de páginas Web? ¿Qué harías si tuvieras un niño de diez años que quisiera navegar la Red? ¿Qué papel debe tener el Internet en las escuelas públicas?
4. En tu opinión, ¿son la mayoría de los programas de CD-ROM educativos o solamente para diversión? ¿Cuáles son algunos programas que te gustaría usar, pero que no has encontrado todavía en las tiendas?
5. ¿Son la computadora y el Internet novedades o representan el medio de comunicación dominante para el futuro? Explica tu respuesta.

Equipos: en la palma de la mano

PARA PENSAR

- ¿Tienes una agenda electrónica?
- ¿Crees que la agenda electrónica sea un buen producto para vender en América Latina? ¿Por qué?

Equipos
En la palma de la mano

En América Latina, el mercado de las computadoras tipo agenda electrónica (PDA o Personal Digital Asistants) deberá superar los US$ 500 millones hacia 2004, según la proyección de la consultora estadounidense IDC. Brasil y México, con dos tercios del mercado, fueron, hasta la primera mitad de 2000, los principales consumidores de estas máquinas. Los dos países continuarán al frente en los próximos años, pero México ganará espacio: aumentará su participación de un 23% a un 30%. Brasil, por su parte, caerá del 43% al 35%. El crecimiento en números absolutos será para todos. La expectativa es que los fabricantes de estos aparatos establezcan alianzas con operadoras telefónicas, lo que les dará acceso a un mayor número de usarios.

Crecimiento futuro

La participación de los países en el mercado de *PDA* en América Latina

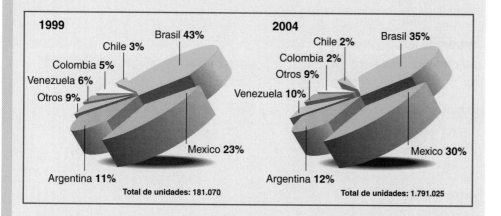

1999

Brasil **43%**
Chile **3%**
Colombia **5%**
Venezuela **6%**
Otros **9%**
Mexico **23%**
Argentina **11%**

Total de unidades: 181.070

2004

Chile **2%**
Brasil **35%**
Colombia **2%**
Otros **9%**
Venezuela **10%**
Mexico **30%**
Argentina **12%**

Total de unidades: 1.791.025

PARA DISCUTIR

1. ¿Cuántos millones de dólares se venderán en Latinoamérica en agendas electrónicas para el año 2004?
2. ¿Cuál es el porcentaje de consumidores en Brasil y en México para el año 2004?
3. ¿Entre qué compañías debe haber alianzas? ¿Por qué?
4. ¿Te parecen útiles o inútiles las agendas electrónicas? ¿Por qué?

You have seen the conditional tense used with the past subjunctive to speculate about what would happen under certain conditions **(Si tuviéramos el dinero, iríamos al Ecuador).** Now you will see how to form and use these and other hypothetical statements that are often called *if* clauses.

I. To imply that a situation is a fact or is likely to occur, however, use **si** *(if)* with a verb form in the indicative in both the *if* (dependent) clause and the conclusion (independent clause).

Factual situation

—Ya he ahorrado más de 2.000 dólares para mis vacaciones.

I've already saved more than $2,000 for my vacation.

—**Si tienes** tanto dinero, **puedes** viajar a Uruguay.

If you have so much money, you can travel to Uruguay.

Likely to occur

Si ahorro 200 dólares más, **viajaré** a ese país.

If I save 200 dollars more, I will travel to that country.

II. To imply that a situation is contrary to fact or is unlikely to occur, use **si** with a past subjunctive verb in the *if* (dependent) clause, and a conditional verb in the conclusion (independent clause).

Contrary to fact

Si tuvieras el dinero, **¿irías** a Uruguay?

If you had the money, would you go to Uruguay?

Unlikely to occur

Si yo **pagara** tu boleto, **¿irías** conmigo?

If I paid for your ticket, would you go with me?

¡A PRACTICAR!

15-16 **Si viajara a Uruguay...** ¿A ti te gustaría viajar a Uruguay algún día? Haz oraciones completas para expresar tus ideas siguiendo el modelo.

MODELO: si / viajar / Uruguay / ir / con...
Si viajara al Uruguay, iría con mi amigo Bob.

1. si / planear un viaje / Uruguay / buscar información / Internet
2. si / viajar / Uruguay / día / ir / con...
3. si / necesitar / una computadora portátil para el viaje / comprarla / en...
4. si / tener / dinero / alojarme / en Plaza Victoria
5. si / tener / problemas / hotel / hablar / con...
6. si / estar / mercado / comprar / un(a)...

CULTURA
Plaza Victoria is a hotel and conference center in the heart of the business district of Montevideo. It is near the largest shopping centers and is 25 minutes from the international airport.

15-17 **El Internet en casa** Mario es un estudiante universitario que vive en un apartamento en Montevideo con tres amigos. Completa las oraciones para saber lo que dice sobre su conexión al Internet. Escoge el presente del indicativo o el imperfecto del subjuntivo para cada verbo indicado.

1. Si yo _____ (poder) escoger el servicio de Internet para nuestro apartamento, voy a escoger Tecnet con acceso dedicado.
2. Si una persona _____ (tener) el acceso dedicado, el servicio no ocupa su línea telefónica.
3. Si la persona _____ (querer) pagar menos, puede escoger el servicio de acceso telefónico.
4. Mis compañeros y yo no podríamos sobrevivir si la computadora y el teléfono _____ (ocupar) la misma línea.
5. Con Tecnet, si pagamos 1.039,00 pesos por mes, nosotros _____ (recibir) cinco casillas de correo electrónico en @internet.com.uy.
6. Si nosotros _____ (querer) más casillas y más servicios, tendríamos que pagar más.
7. Si alguien _____ (trabajar) en casa, puede necesitar más servicios pero nosotros no los necesitamos.
8. Pues, claro que si el dinero no _____ un problema para nosotros, escogeríamos el plan con todos los servicios.
9. Si mi padre _____ (pagar) la cuenta, él querría el plan más básico, con acceso telefónico. ¡Qué horror!
10. Pienso usar el Internet todos los días, ¡si mis compañeros me _____ (dejar) usar la computadora!

> **CULTURA**
> The monetary unit of Uruguay is the peso. The U.S. dollar has been valued between 21.25 and 27.71 Uruguayan pesos in recent years.

EN VOZ ALTA

15-18 **Oportunidades y decisiones** Pregúntale a otro(a) compañero(a) de clase sobre estas posibilidades fantásticas y las decisiones que él/ella tomaría para ver si tienen mucho en común.

1. Si tuvieras el dinero y el tiempo, ¿te gustaría comprar una computadora mejor? ¿Qué tipo comprarías? ¿Para qué la usarías?
2. ¿Harías una página web en el Internet si tuvieras la oportunidad? ¿Qué información pondrías? ¿Pondrías una foto tuya en esa página?
3. Si pudieras inventar una máquina, ¿qué inventarías? ¿Por qué inventarías esta cosa?
4. Si vivieras en otro siglo, ¿en qué época querrías vivir y por qué? ¿Qué objetos de la tecnología echarías de menos *(would you miss)*?
5. Si conocieras una persona en un salón de chat, ¿qué le preguntarías?
6. Si tú y tus amigos descubrieran el secreto de la vida eterna, ¿qué harían con esta información?
7. ¿Querrías saber algo de tu vida si pudieras visitar el futuro?
8. ¿Qué haría tu mejor amigo(a) si se ganara la lotería? ¿Compartiría el dinero contigo? ¿Te compraría él/ella un nuevo estéreo u otra cosa parecida?

15-19 **¿Un mundo ideal?** Con un(a) compañero(a) de clase, hablen de las consecuencias de las siguientes situaciones y decidan si el mundo realmente sería mejor.

¿Qué pasaría si...

1. todos se cuidaran bien?
2. no hubiera guerras?
3. nadie tuviera problemas emocionales?
4. fuera posible vivir 200 años?
5. no existieran diferencias de opinión?
6. toda la gente se vistiera de la misma manera?

¡A VER!

En este segmento del video, los compañeros de casa trabajan juntos para pintar un cuadro. Mientras pintan, piensan en las experiencias que han tenido juntos en la Hacienda Vista Alegre.

Expresiones útiles

Las siguientes son expresiones nuevas que vas a escuchar en el video.

Un momento clave	A key moment
Fue como un reto	It was a drag

Antes de ver

Paso 1: ¿Cuáles son algunos de los sentimientos que experimenta la gente a la hora de despedirse de un(a) buen(a) amigo(a)? Trabaja con un(a) compañero(a) para hacer una lista de varias posibilidades.

Paso 2: ¿Cuáles son algunas de las cosas que aprendiste de tus amigos? ¿Has tenido amigos que han tenido mucha influencia en tu vida? ¿Por qué han tenido tanto valor algunas amistades? Comparte tus experiencias con un(a) compañero(a). ¿Han tenido experiencias similares?

Después de ver

Paso 1: En **Antes de ver, Paso 1**, tu compañero(a) y tú hablaron de los sentimientos de la gente a la hora de despedirse. En el video, viste cómo se sienten los compañeros. Para dar más detalles sobre los últimos momentos que los compañeros tenían juntos completa el párrafo con el infinitivo o la forma apropiada del imperfecto de subjuntivo o del pretérito de los verbos entre paréntesis.

Sofía estaba un poco triste que _____ **(terminar)** el mes de vivir juntos en la Hacienda Vista Alegre. Era obvio para ella que el mes _____ **(ser)** un momento clave para todo el grupo. Por ejemplo, era bueno que Javier _____ **(venir)** a Puerto Rico y que _____ **(escuchar)** a Sofía cuando planeaba su futuro. Alejandra dudaba que vivir con cuatro personas _____ **(poder)** convertirse en una diversión, pero así pasó. Antonio no esperaba _____ **(olvidar)** la experiencia nunca y Valeria se alegraba de que todos los compañeros _____ **(llegar)** a ser amigos.

Paso 2: En **Antes de ver, Paso 2,** tu compañero(a) y tú hablaron del valor de la amistad y la influencia que los amigos pueden tener en nuestra vida. En la Hacienda Vista Alegre, los compañeros también experimentaron esta amistad fuerte. Si no fuera por esta amistad e influencia, el futuro de cada compañero sería bien diferente. Para explicar un poco la influencia que tenían uno al otro, completa las siguientes oraciones con el imperfecto de subjuntivo o el condicional de los verbos entre paréntesis.

- Si Javier no _____ (escuchar) a Sofía, todavía seguiría su carrera de medicina.
- Si no fuera por Sofía, Valeria no _____ (apreciar) la música folklórica.
- Si Valeria no _____ (conocer) a Antonio, volvería con su ex novio César en Venezuela.
- Si no fuera por Alejandra, Sofía no _____ (tener) una fotografía para la contraportada de su libro.

¿Qué opinas tú?

Paso 1: ¿Es esto lo que esperabas que pasara a los compañeros? ¿Por qué sí o por qué no? ¿Crees que se escribirán? ¿Se hablarán por teléfono? ¿Quiénes se escribirán por correo electrónico? ¿Quiénes viajarán para visitarse? Compara tus respuestas con las de un(a) compañero(a). ¿Tienen las mismas opiniones?

Paso 2: ¿Qué harías si tú fueras uno de los compañeros? Imagínate que eres uno de los compañeros y completa la siguiente oración:

Si yo fuera _____, yo...

Comparte tu oración con la clase y justifica tu respuesta.

¡A LEER!

Strategy: Integrating your reading strategies

In previous lessons, you have learned many strategies for becoming a more proficient reader of Spanish. In this section you will practice integrating several of these reading strategies.

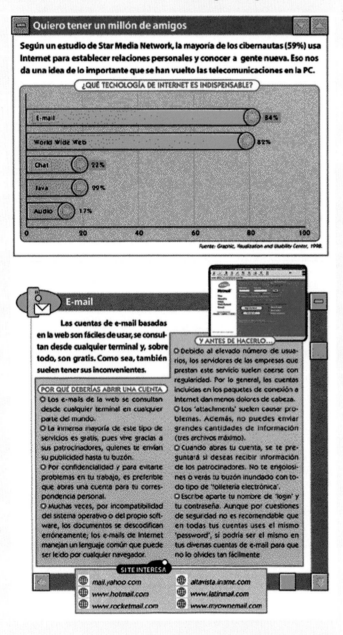

Paso 1: Antes de leer: Comprender el tema del texto

1. Mira el gráfico la izquierda. ¿Cuál de las tecnologías del Internet es la más popular?
2. En tu opinión, ¿cuál es el tema que vas a encontrar en el texto?
3. Lee el título y el primer párrafo de la sección a continuación. ¿Tienes una idea más específica del tema del texto? ¿Qué idea es?
4. Piensa en tu experiencia personal. ¿Qué sabes ya del tema?

Paso 2: Primera lectura: Comprender la idea general del texto

1. Lee rápidamente el texto para comprender la idea general de su contenido. Usa los cognados, los prefijos y los sufijos para ayudarte a comprender el significado de las palabras que no conozcas.
2. Subraya las ideas principales del texto.

Paso 3: Segunda lectura: Localizar información específica en el texto

Al leer rápidamente el texto otra vez, pon un círculo alrededor de los detalles que apoyen las ideas principales que has subrayado.

Paso 4: Tercera lectura: Verificar la comprensión total del texto

1. Contesta **sí** o **no** las preguntas que siguen.
   a. Las cuentas de email basadas en la Red son gratis. Sí No
   b. A veces hay problemas de compatibilidad con los emails del Internet. Sí No
   c. Los servidores de email suelen *(tend to)* caerse con regularidad. Sí No
   d. Es posible enviar un número ilimitado de adjuntos *(attachments)*. Sí No
   e. Es aconsejable que uses la misma contraseña *(password)* en tus diversas cuentas de email. Sí No

2. Escribe una respuesta breve a las preguntas que siguen.
   a. ¿Cuáles son algunas ventajas *(advantages)* de tener una cuenta de email basada en la Web?
   b. ¿Cuáles son algunos problemas tecnológicos que pueden ocurrir cuando envías y recibes los emails del Internet?
   c. Piensa en tu propia experiencia ahora. ¿Tienes una cuenta de email? ¿Con qué frecuencia te comunicas por email?

¡A ESCRIBIR!

Strategy: Speculating and hypothesizing

In this section, you are going to use what you have learned to write about a hypothetical situation and make a projection about what might occur under particular circumstances. After deciding on a hypothetical situation to write about, you will then outline some of the positive and/or negative consequences of this situation. This will involve speculating about the future and imagining possible outcomes that may arise from the hypothetical situation you select. Individuals in many professions prepare projections based on hypothetical situations. For example, marketing and advertising managers speculate about the success of their products, and individuals in government make projections about the effects of projects and programs.

Consider the situation of a university student:

Ojalá yo tuviera una computadora portátil. De momento, no poseo ninguna computadora, y estoy harto de hacer cola (stand in line) en los laboratorios de computadoras de la universidad. Si tuviera mi propia computadora portátil, podría navegar la Red o mirar mi correo electrónico en cualquier momento. Tendría más tiempo para estudiar o pasar con mis amigos porque no tendría que hacer cola en la universidad para usar una computadora. No importaría si estuviera en casa, en la universidad o en la casa de un amigo —siempre la tendría a mi lado. Sería mucho más fácil conectarme al Internet. También la podría llevar conmigo cuando estuviera de vacaciones en casa de mis padres o en otro sitio.

Task: Preparing a projection

Paso 1: Piensa en las siguientes situaciones hipotéticas. Luego, escoge una de ellas o inventa tu propia situación.

- tener tu propio avión
- tener tu propio yate
- ser un(a) famoso(a) músico(a) o actor (actriz)
- ser presidente de los Estados Unidos
- descubrir una cura para el cáncer
- ¿ ?

Paso 2: Ahora que has escogido una situación hipotética, piensa en lo que pasaría en el contexto que has seleccionado. Piensa en las siguientes preguntas y escribe tus ideas en una hoja de papel.

- ¿Qué harías tú?
- ¿Qué reacción tendría tu familia? ¿y tus amigos? ¿y otros estudiantes en tu universidad?
- ¿Qué ventajas tendría esta situación? ¿Qué desventajas tendría?

Paso 3: Ahora, escribe una composición acerca de lo que pasaría en la situación hipotética que has escogido. Debes incluir la información que has usado en los Pasos 1 y 2. También, podrías usar el párrafo anterior como un modelo.

Paso 4: Intercambia papeles con un(a) compañero(a) de clase. Lee la composición de la otra persona y decide si toda la información está presentada en una manera clara. También decide si todo sería igual si tú te encontraras en la situación descrita o si algunas cosas serían diferentes. Habla sobre tus reacciones con tu compañero(a).

Functions: Expressing a wish or desire; Expressing conditions; Hypothesizing
Vocabulary: Dreams & aspirations; Health: diseases & illnesses; Means of transportation; Working conditions
Grammar: Verbs: *if*-clauses

¡A CONVERSAR!

Task: Evaluating and discussing the effects of technological advances

Paso 1: Piensa en los cambios que ha provocado el creciente nivel de tecnología en los Estados Unidos (en cuanto a las computadoras, el Internet, las comunicaciones, el transporte, la medicina, el mundo financiero, los negocios y el mercado laboral, etcétera).

Paso 2: Habla con un(a) compañero(a) acerca de los efectos positivos y los negativos de la tecnología en nuestra sociedad.

Paso 3: Luego, preséntenles un resumen de sus ideas a sus compañeros de clase.

Los avances tecnológicos

Sustantivos

la alarma alarm
la antena parabólica satellite dish
la cámara (digital) (digital) camera
el contestador automático answering machine
el control remoto remote control

el disco compacto compact disc (CD)
el equipo equipment
el estéreo stereo
el satélite satellite
el teléfono celular/portátil cellular phone

la videocámara video camera
el videocasete videotape
la videocasetera VCR

Verbos

apagar to turn off
(des)conectar to (dis)connect

(des)enchufar to plug in (to unplug)
funcionar to function, work

grabar to record
prender to turn on (TV, stereo, etc.)

Adjetivos

apagado(a) off
encendido(a) on

enchufado(a) plugged in

prendido(a) on

La computadora

Sustantivos

los altavoces speakers
el archivo file
el ciberespacio / el espacio cibernético
  cyberspace
la computadora portátil laptop computer
la conexión connection
el correo electrónico email

el disco duro hard drive
el disquete diskette
el escáner scanner
la impresora printer
el Internet Internet
el mensaje message
la página Web web page

la pantalla screen
el programa (de CD-ROM) (CD-ROM) program
el ratón mouse (of a computer)
el salón (la sala) de charla chat room
el teclado keyboard

Verbos

abrir un documento (un programa) to open a
  document (program)
archivar (guardar) to save
estar conectado(a) (en línea) to be online

hacer click (sobre) to click (on)
imprimir to print
navegar la Red to surf the net
programar to program

salir del programa to quit the program
teletrabajar to telecommute

Lugar de encuentros

PLAZAS

REVISTA NO. 5

En esta edición vas a conocer a personas importantes dentro de la política y del mundo artístico, así como también aspectos culturales y económicos de países suramericanos como los de Perú, Ecuador, Chile y Uruguay. Luego vas a comparar tus ideas y opiniones con las de tus compañeros de clase y las de nuestros editores. Participa con nosotros y vas a ver que tenemos mucho en común.

- El Faro del Sur: Luces, cámara, acción
- «Tosca» por Isabel Allende
- La fantasía artística en Perú, Chile y Uruguay
- Mujeres, en cifras (Estadísticas de la Organización de las Naciones Unidas (ONU) sobre las mujeres en América Latina y el Caribe)

El Faro del Sur:
Luces, cámara, acción

Cuando los padres de Meme mueren en un accidente automovilístico, ella se ocupa de *(takes charge of)* cuidar a su hermana menor, Aneta. Esta película está cargada de emoción y cubre un período de siete u ocho años, donde las dos hermanas emprenden *(embark on)* un viaje tanto físico como espiritual para perderse y luego encontrarse en España, Uruguay y Argentina. El final dramático, la culminación de las alegrías y de las tristezas de Meme, depende del gran simbolismo del Faro del Sur para mostrar cómo estas dos chicas buscan la tranquilidad que les fue robada en el accidente donde murieron sus padres. El famoso director argentino, Eduardo Mignogna *(Sol de otoño)*, depende de la actuación de la española Ingrid Rubio como Meme y de Jimena Barón (Aneta niña) / Florencia Bertotti (Aneta adolescente) para revelar las idiosincrasias de sus relaciones con los amigos, Andy (Ricardo Darín), dueño del faro *(owner of the lighthouse)* y Dolores (Norma Aleandro), amiga de la madre de Meme y Aneta.

- ¿Cómo crees que termina la película?
- ¿Quiénes son algunos de tus directores favoritos de películas?
- ¿Qué tipos de películas te gustan?
- Escribe una reseña *(review)* de tu película favorita.

«Tosca» por Isabel Allende

Isabel Allende (1942–) nació en Lima, Perú, de padres chilenos. Empezó su carrera como periodista antes de iniciar su carrera de novelista y cuentista. Su tío, Salvador Allende, fue presidente de Chile de 1970 a 1973. Murió en el Palacio de Gobierno como resultado del golpe de estado *(coup d'état)*, después del cual subió al poder el general Augusto Pinochet. Este dictador rigió el país hasta 1990. Pasaron muchos años antes de que Isabel Allende se diera cuenta *(realized)* del impacto que su tío había tenido en su vida. Uno de los temas principales de su obra literaria es la separación de la familia debido a los conflictos políticos dentro de la sociedad latinoamericana contemporánea.

Otra característica que tienen en común sus obras es la presencia de una narradora o una protagonista femenina. En su colección *Los cuentos de Eva Luna* (1990), aparece «Tosca», cuento que narra las ironías en la vida de la protagonista, Maurizia Rugieri.

- ¿Qué opinas de los niños prodigios?
- ¿Trabajan bajo mucha presión *(pressure)* o en algo que verdaderamente les apasiona?
- ¿Cómo muestra Allende el espíritu libre e independiente de Maurizia?
- ¿Tocas algún instrumento musical? Si no, ¿te gustaría? ¿Qué instrumento?
- ¿Qué tipo de música te interesa? ¿Quién es tu cantante favorito(a)?
- ¿Con qué frecuencia asistes a espectáculos de música: conciertos, sinfonías, óperas, etc.?

«Tosca»

Su padre la sentó al piano a los cinco años y a los diez Maurizia Rugieri dio su primer recital en el club Garibaldi, vestida de organza rosada y botines de charol *(patent leather ankle boots)*, ante un público benévolo, compuesto en su mayoría por miembros de la colonia italiana. Al término de la presentación pusieron varios ramos de flores a sus pies y el presidente del club le entregó una placa conmemorativa y una muñeca de loza *(china doll)*, adornada con cintas *(ribbons)* y encajes *(lace)*.

—Te saludamos, Maurizia Rugieri, como a un genio precoz, un nuevo Mozart. Los grandes escenarios del mundo te esperan —declamó.

La niña aguardó a que *(waited until)* se callara *(quieted)* el aplauso y, por encima del llanto orgulloso *(proud crying)* de su madre, hizo oír su voz con una altanería inesperada.

—Ésta es la última vez que toco el piano. Lo que quiero ser es cantante —anunció y salió de la sala arrastrando *(dragging)* a la muñeca por un pie.

La fantasía artística en Perú, Chile y Uruguay

Los editores de *Plazas* quieren escoger un grupo de estudiantes de arte para participar en un programa de enriquecimiento cultural. El proyecto se trata de una visita a los museos principales de Lima, Santiago y Montevideo para apreciar el arte de estos países. A continuación aparece una descripción de algunos de los artistas más importantes cuyas obras te invitarán a explorar la fantasía artística, a veces abstracta, a veces basada en la realidad.

Puka Wamani

Fernando de Szyszlo (Lima, Perú)

Considerado el fundador del arte abstracto peruano, Fernando de Szyszlo (1925–) buscaba la renovación en el arte contemporáneo. Es interesante que el mismo artista no se considere un pintor abstracto porque dice que pinta lo que existe, después de un análisis profundo. Se inspiró en la poesía quechua para crear imágenes arquetípicas, evidente en su pintura *Puka Wamani* (1968), localizada en el Museo de Arte de Lima. Szyszlo es colorista y depende del contraste entre colores para distinguir entre luz *(light)* y sombra *(shadow)*.

Roberto Matta (Santiago, Chile)

Al llegar a Chile, visitarás el Museo Nacional de Bellas Artes en Santiago y verás las obras maestras de José Gil de Castro y Gonzalo Cienfuegos, entre otros. Uno de los artistas chilenos más influyentes de este siglo ha sido el surrealista Roberto Matta (1911–), quien presenta la turbulencia caótica de la vida como en *El día es un atenuado (transgression)*. Matta recibió fama internacional a través de sus viajes por varios países europeos y latinoamericanos, lo cual le dio la oportunidad de establecer amistades con algunos de los artistas predominantes de su época como Salvador Dalí.

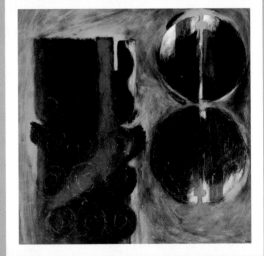

El día es un atenuado

Cambacuá

Pedro Figari (Montevideo, Uruguay)

En Montevideo, verás las obras de arte de uruguayos famosos como Pedro Figari (1861–1938). Los temas que este artista abarca incluyen los que son típicos de Latinoamérica, como los de la clase burguesa y los de escenas literarias e históricas. También utiliza como modelo en algunos cuadros las escenas de rituales con elementos africanos. Para este pintor, la función de la memoria es primordial y utiliza el paso del tiempo para evocar las impresiones del pasado. Por ejemplo, de la serie de cuadros *Cambacuá* (1923), el público puede observar los ritmos y el movimiento de la gente de descendencia africana.

- ¿Te gustaría participar en este viaje? Explica.
- ¿Cómo se refleja el contraste de luz y sombra en el cuadro de Szyszlo?
- ¿Cuál es tu interpretación de *El día es un atenuado*?

- En *Cambacuá* de Figari, ¿qué están haciendo los personajes y por qué?
- ¿Crees que el arte pictórico sea importante? ¿Por qué?

Mujeres, en cifras

Estadísticas de la Organización de las Naciones Unidas (ONU) sobre las mujeres en América Latina y el Caribe

Las siguientes cifras provienen de la CEPAL (Comisión Económica para América Latina y el Caribe), un órgano subsidiario del Consejo Económico y Social de las Naciones Unidas.

Empleo

- En las áreas urbanas el número de mujeres trabajadoras ha aumentado entre un 37% y un 50%.
- Para las mujeres sin recursos económicos una gran fuente de empleo son las microempresas y el autoempleo.
- Entre un 30% y un 60% de las microempresas en la región pertenecen a las mujeres.
- Si el nivel de educación de las mujeres mejora, así también mejora el tipo de empleo.
- Las mujeres reciben ingresos que representan el 75% de lo que ganan los hombres y en algunos países los ingresos representan el 20%, especialmente en los hogares más pobres.

Participación en empleos del Gobierno

- En la mayoría de los países de América Latina y el Caribe, la participación de las mujeres fluctúan entre un 1% y un 30% en los cargos ministeriales del gobierno.
- En países como Aruba y Ecuador, la participación de las mujeres llega hasta un 30%. En Brasil, sin embargo, la participación de las mujeres es inferior al 5% en los ministerios del gobierno federal.
- El porcentaje de mujeres electas al congreso en Latinoamérica y el Caribe fluctúa entre 3,6% y 27,6%. El país con la tasa más baja es Haití y el país con la tasa más alta es Cuba.
- En los países latinoamericanos menos de un 5% de las alcaldías están dirigidas por mujeres.
- En América Latina, en el poder judicial, el porcentaje de magistrados que forman parte de las Cortes Supremas de Justicia no es superior al 10%. En el caso de Centroamérica, el porcentaje fluctúa entre un 10% y un 22%.
- Un logro importante en el campo de la violencia es que en todos los países de América Latina y en la mayoría de países del Caribe se han aprobado leyes que condenan la violencia contra la mujer.

- ¿Qué futuro ves para las mujeres en la política en nuestro país y en los países hispanos?

- ¿Te gustaría participar en la política de tu universidad, de tu condado o de tu estado? ¿Qué te gustaría cambiar? ¿Por qué?

- ¿Qué te parece el hecho de que en Latinoamérica, el salario de las mujeres sea el 75% del de los hombres?

- ¿Sabes cuánto gana una mujer en relación con un hombre en los Estados Unidos? ¿Estás de acuerdo con esta medida? ¿Por qué sí o por qué no?

APÉNDICES

GRAMMAR GUIDE

For more detailed explanations of these grammar points, consult the Index to find the pages where they are explained fully in the body of the textbook.

ACTIVE VOICE (La voz activa) A sentence written in the active voice identifies a subject that performs the action of the verb.

Juan	cantó	la canción.
Juan	*sang*	*the song.*
subject	**verb**	**direct object**

In the sentence above Juan is the performer of the verb **cantar**.
(*See also* **Passive voice.**)

ADJECTIVES (Los adjetivos) are words that modify or describe **nouns** or **pronouns** and agree in **number** and generally in **gender** with the nouns they modify.

Las casas **azules** son **bonitas.**
*The **blue** houses are **pretty.***

Esas mujeres **mexicanas** son mis amigas **nuevas.**
*Those **Mexican** women are my **new** friends.*

Plazas es un libro **interesante** y **divertido.**
*Plazas is an **interesting** and **fun** book.*

• **Demonstrative adjectives (Los adjetivos demostrativos)** point out persons, places, or things relative to the position of the speaker. They always agree in **number** and **gender** with the **noun** they modify. The forms are: **este, esta, estos, estas / ese, esa, esos, esas / aquel, aquella, aquellos, aquellas.** There are also neuter forms that refer to generic ideas or things, and hence have no gender: **esto, eso, aquello.**

Este libro es fácil.	***This** book is easy.*
Esos libros son difíciles.	***Those** books are hard.*
Aquellos libros son pesados.	***Those** books **(over there)** are boring.*

Demonstratives may also function as **pronouns**, replacing the **noun** but still agreeing with it in **number** and **gender. Demonstrative pronouns** carry an accent mark over the syllable that would be naturally stressed anyway:

Me gustan esas blusas verdes.	*I like those green blouses.*
¿Cuáles, **éstas**?	*Which ones, **these**?*
No. Me gustan **ésas.**	*No. I like **those.***

• **Stressed possessive adjectives (Los adjetivos posesivos acentuados)** are used for emphasis and follow the noun that they modifiy. These adjectives may also function as pronouns and always agree in **number** and in **gender.** The forms are: **mío, tuyo, suyo, nuestro, vuestro, suyo.** Unless they are directly preceded by the verb **ser,** stressed possessives must be preceded by the **definite article.**

Ese perro pequeño es **mío.**	*That little dog is **mine.***
Dame el **tuyo;** el **nuestro** no funciona.	*Give me **yours; ours** doesn't work.*

• **Unstressed possessive adjectives (Los adjetivos posesivos no acentuados)** demonstrate ownership and always precede the **noun** that they modify.

La señora Elman es **mi** profesora.	*Mrs. Elman is **my** professor.*
Debemos llevar **nuestros** libros a clase.	*We should take **our** books to class.*

ADVERBS (Los adverbios) are words that modify **verbs, adjectives,** or other adverbs and, unlike **adjectives,** do not have **gender** or **number.** Here are examples of different classes of adverbs:

Practicamos **diariamente.**	*We practice **daily.** (adverb of manner)*
Ellos van a salir **pronto.**	*They will leave **soon.** (adverb of time)*
Jennifer está **afuera.**	*Jennifer is **outside.** (adverb of place)*
No quiero ir **tampoco.**	*I don't want to go **either.** (adverb of negation)*
Paco habla **demasiado.**	*Paco talks **too much.** (adverb of quantity)*

AGREEMENT (La concordancia) refers to the correspondence between parts of speech in terms of **number, gender,** and **person.** Subjects agree with their verbs; articles and adjectives agree with the nouns they modify, etc.

Todas las lenguas son interesantes.	*All languages are interesting.* (number)
Ella es bonita.	*She is pretty.* (gender)
Nosotros somos de España.	*We are from Spain.* (person)

ARTICLES (Los artículos) precede nouns and indicate whether they are definite or indefinite persons, places, or things.

- **Definite articles (Los artículos definidos)** refer to particular members of a group and are the equivalent of *the* in English. The definite articles are: **el, la, los, las.**

El hombre guapo es mi padre.	*The handsome man is my father.*
Las mujeres de esta clase son inteligentes.	*The women in this class are intelligent.*

- **Indefinite articles (Los artículos indefinidos)** refer to any unspecified member(s) of a group and are the equivalent of *a(n)* and *some.* The indefinite articles are: **un, una, unos, unas.**

Un hombre vino a nuestra casa anoche.	*A man came to our house last night.*
Unas niñas jugaban en el parque.	*Some girls were playing in the park.*

CLAUSES (Las cláusulas) are subject and verb combinations; for a sentence to be complete it must have at least one main clause.

- **Main clauses** (Independent clauses) **(Las cláusulas principales)** communicate a complete idea or thought.

Mi hermana va al hospital.	*My sister goes to the hospital.*

- **Subordinate clauses** (Dependent clauses) **(Las cláusulas subordinadas)** depend upon a main clause for their meaning to be complete.

Mi hermana va al hospital	con tal que no llueva.
My sister goes to the hospital	*provided that it's not raining.*
main clause	**subordinate clause**

In the sentence above, *provided that it's not raining* is not a complete idea without the information supplied by the main clause.

COMMANDS (Los mandatos) (*See* **Imperatives.**)

COMPARISONS (Las formas comparativas) are statements that describe one person, place, or thing relative to another in terms of quantity, quality, or manner.

- **Comparisons of equality (Las formas comparativas de igualdad)** demonstrate an equal share of a quantity or degree of a particular characteristic. These statements use a form of **tan(to)(ta)(s)** and **como.**

Ella tiene **tanto** dinero **como** Elena.	*She has **as much** money **as** Elena.*
Fernando trabaja **tanto como** Felipe.	*Fernando works **as much as** Felipe.*
Jim baila **tan** bien **como** Anne.	*Jim dances **as well as** Anne.*

- **Comparisons of inequality (Las formas comparativas de desigualdad)** indicate a difference in quantity, quality, or manner between the compared subjects. These statements use **más/menos... que** or comparative **adjectives** such as **mejor/peor, mayor/menor.**

España tiene **más** playas que México.	*Spain has **more** beaches **than** Mexico.*
Tú hablas español **mejor que** yo.	*You speak Spanish **better than** I.*

(*See also* **Superlatives.**)

CONJUGATIONS (Las conjugaciones) represent the inflected form of the verb as it is used with a particular subject or **person.**

Yo **bailo** los sábados.	*I dance on Saturdays.* (1st-person singular)
Tú **bailas** los sábados.	*You dance on Saturdays.* (2nd-person singular)
Ella **baila** los sábados.	*She dances on Saturdays.* (3rd-person singular)
Nosotros **bailamos** los sábados.	*We dance on Saturdays.* (1st-person plural)
Vosotros **bailáis** los sábados.	*You dance on Saturdays.* (2nd-person plural)
Ellos **bailan** los sábados.	*They dance on Saturdays.* (3rd-person plural)

CONJUNCTIONS (Las conjunciones) are linking words that join two independent **clauses** together.

Fuimos al centro **y** mis amigos compraron muchas cosas.
*We went downtown **and** my friends bought a lot of things.*

Yo quiero ir a la fiesta, **pero** tengo que estudiar.
*I want to go to the party, **but** I have to study.*

CONTRACTIONS (Las contracciones) in Spanish are limited to preposition/article combinations, such as **de + el = del** and **a + el = al,** or preposition/pronoun combinations such as **con + mí = conmigo** and **con + ti = contigo.**

DIRECT OBJECTS (Los objetos directos) in sentences are the direct recipients of the action of the verb. Direct objects answer the questions *What?* or *Whom?*

¿Qué hizo?	*What did she do?*
Ella hizo **la tarea.**	*She did her **homework.***
Y luego llamó a **su amiga.**	*And then called **her friend.***

(*See also* **Pronouns, Indirect object, Personal a.**)

EXCLAMATIVE WORDS (Las palabras exclamativas) communicate surprise or strong emotion. Like interrogative words, exclamatives also carry accents.

¡Qué sorpresa!	***What** a surprise!*
¡Cómo canta Miguel!	***How well** Miguel sings!*

(*See also* Interrogatives.)

GENDER (El género) is a grammatical feature of Romance languages that classifies words as either masculine or feminine. The gender of the word is sometimes used to distinguish meaning (**la papa** = *the potato,* but **el Papa** = *the Pope;* **la policía** = *the police force,* but **el policía** = *the policeman*). It is important to memorize the gender of nouns when you learn the nouns.

GERUNDS (Los gerundios) are the Spanish equivalent of the *-ing* verb form in English. Regular gerunds are created by replacing the **infinitive** endings (**-ar, -er/-ir**) with **-ando** or **-iendo.** Gerunds are often used with the verb **estar** to form the present progessive tense. The present progressive tense places emphasis on the continuing or progressive nature of an action.

Miguel está **cantando** en la ducha.　　　*Miguel is **singing** in the shower.*

(*See also* **Present participle.**)

IDIOMATIC EXPRESSIONS (Las frases idiomáticas) are phrases in Spanish that do not have a literal English equivalent.

Hace mucho frío.　　　*It is very cold. (Literally, It makes a lot of cold.)*

IMPERATIVES (Los imperativos) represent the mood used to express requests or commands. It is more direct than the **subjunctive** mood. Imperatives are commonly called commands and fall into two categories: affirmative and negative. Spanish speakers must also choose between using formal commands and informal commands based upon whether one is addressed as **usted** (formal) or **tú** (informal).

Habla conmigo.	**Talk** to me. (informal, affirmative)
No me hables.	**Don't talk to me.** (informal, negative)
Hable con la policía.	**Talk** to the police. (formal, singular, affirmative)
No hable con la policía.	**Don't talk** to the police. (formal, singular, negative)
Hablen con la policía.	**Talk** to the police. (formal, plural, affirmative)
No hablen con la policía.	**Don't talk** to the police. (formal, plural, negative)

(*See also* **Mood.**)

IMPERFECT (El imperfecto) The imperfect tense is used to make statements about the past when the speaker wants to convey the idea of 1) habitual or repeated action, 2) two actions in progress simultaneously, or 3) an event that was in progress when another action interrupted. The imperfect tense is also used to emphasize the ongoing nature of the middle of the event, as opposed to its beginning or end. Age and clock time are always expressed using the imperfect.

Cuando María **era** joven, ella **cantaba** en el coro.
*When María **was** young, she **used to sing** in the choir.*

Aquel día **llovía** mucho y el cielo **estaba** oscuro.
*That day **it was raining** a lot and the sky **was** dark.*

Juan **dormía** cuando sonó el teléfono.
Juan was sleeping when the phone rang.

(*See also* **Preterite**.)

IMPERSONAL EXPRESSIONS (Las expresiones impersonales) are statements that contain the impersonal subjects of *it* or *one*.

Es necesario estudiar.　　　　　　*It is necessary to study.*
Se necesita estudiar.　　　　　　*One needs to study.*

(*See also* **Passive voice**.)

INDEFINITE WORDS (Las palabras indefinidas) are **articles, adjectives, nouns** or **pronouns** that refer to unspecified members of a group.

Un hombre vino.　　　　　　*A man came.* (indefinite article)
Alguien vino.　　　　　　*Someone came.* (indefinite noun)
Algunas personas vinieron.　　　　*Some people came.* (indefinite adjective)
Algunas vinieron.　　　　　　*Some came.* (indefinite pronoun)

(*See also* **Articles**.)

INDICATIVE (El indicativo) The indicative is a mood, rather than a tense. The indicative is used to express ideas that are considered factual or certain and, therefore, not subject to speculation, doubt, or negation.

Josefina **es** española.　　　　　　*Josefina is Spanish.*
(present indicative)

(*See also* **Mood**.)

INDIRECT OBJECTS (Los objetos indirectos) are the indirect recipients of an action in a sentence and answer the questions *To whom?* or *For whom?* In Spanish it is common to include an indirect object **pronoun** along with the indirect object.

Yo **le** di el libro a **Sofía**.　　　　*I gave the book **to Sofia**.*
Sofía **les** guardó el libro **para sus padres**.　　*Sofia kept the book **for her parents**.*

(*See also* **Direct objects** and **Pronouns**.)

INFINITIVES (Los infinitivos) are verb forms that are uninflected or not **conjugated** according to a specific **person**. In English, infinitives are preceded by *to: to talk, to eat, to live.* Infinitives in Spanish end in **-ar (hablar)**, **-er (comer)**, and **-ir (vivir)**.

INTERROGATIVES (Las formas interrogativas) are used to pose questions and carry accent marks to distinguish them from other uses. Basic interrogative words include: **quién(es), qué, cómo, cuánto(a)(s), cuándo, por qué, dónde.**

¿Qué quieres?　　　　　　*What do you want?*
¿Cuándo llegó ella?　　　　　*When did she arrive?*
¿De **dónde** eres?　　　　　　*Where are you from?*

(*See also* **Exclamatives**.)

MOOD (El modo) is like the word *mode*, meaning *manner* or *way*. It indicates the way in which the speaker views an action, or his/her attitude toward the action. Besides the **imperative** mood, which is simply giving commands, you learn two basic moods in Spanish: the **subjunctive** and the **indicative**. Basically, the subjunctive mood communicates an attitude of uncertainty or negation toward the action, while the indicative indicates that the action is certain or factual. Within each of these moods there are many **tenses**. Hence you have the present indicative and the present subjunctive, the present perfect indicative and the present perfect subjunctive, etc.

• **Indicative mood (El indicativo)** implies that what is stated or questioned is regarded as true.

Yo **quiero** ir a la fiesta.　　　　*I **want** to go to the party.*
Quieres ir conmigo?　　　　　*Do you **want** to go with me?*

- **Subjunctive mood (El subjuntivo)** indicates a recommendation, a statement of doubt or negation, or a hypothetical situation.

Yo recomiendo que tú **vayas** a la fiesta.	*I recommend **that you go** to the party.*
Dudo que **vayas** a la fiesta.	*I doubt that **you'll go** to the party.*
No creo que **vayas** a la fiesta.	*I don't believe that **you'll go** to the party.*
Si **fueras** a la fiesta, te divertirías.	*If **you were to go** to the party, you would have a good time.*

- **Imperative mood (El imperativo)** is used to make a command or request.

¡**Ven** conmigo a la fiesta!	***Come*** *with me to the party!*

(*See also* **Indicative, Imperative,** and **Subjunctive.**)

NEGATION (La negación) takes place when a negative word, such as **no,** is placed before an affirmative sentence. In Spanish, double negatives are common.

Yolando va a cantar esta noche.	*Yolando will sing tonight.* (affirmative)
Yolando **no** va a cantar esta noche.	*Yolanda will **not** sing tonight.* (negative)
Ramón quiere algo.	*Ramón wants something.* (affirmative)
Ramón **no** quiere **nada.**	*Ramón **doesn't** want **anything.*** (negative)

NOUNS (Los sustantivos) are persons, places, things, or ideas. Names of people, countries, and cities are proper nouns and are capitalized.

Alberto	*Albert* (person)
el pueblo	*town* (place)
el diccionario	*dictionary* (thing)

ORTHOGRAPHY (La ortografía) refers to the spelling of a word or anything related to spelling such as accentuation.

PASSIVE VOICE (La voz pasiva), as compared to **active voice (la voz activa),** places emphasis on the action itself rather than the agent of the action (the person or thing that is indirectly responsible for committing the action). The passive se is used when there is no apparent agent of the action.

Luis vende los coches.	*Luis sells the cars.* (active voice)
Los coches **son vendidos por** Luis.	*The cars **are sold by** Luis.* (passive voice)
Se **venden** los coches.	*The cars **are sold.*** (passive voice)

(*See also* **Active voice.**)

PAST PARTICIPLES (Los participios pasados) are verb forms used in compound tenses such as the **present perfect.** Regular past participles are formed by dropping the **-ar** or **-er/-ir** from the **infinitive** and adding **-ado** or **-ido.** Past participles are the equivalent of verbs ending in *-ed* in English. They may also be used as **adjectives,** in which case they agree in **number** and **gender** with their nouns. Irregular past participles include: **escrito, roto, dicho, hecho, puesto, vuelto, muerto, cubierto.**

Marta ha **subido** la montaña.	*Marta has **climbed** the mountain.*
Hemos **hablado** mucho por teléfono.	*We have **talked** a lot on the phone.*
La novela **publicada** en 1995 es su mejor novela.	*The novel **published** in 1995 is her best novel.*

PERFECT TENSES (Los tiempos perfectos) communicate the idea that an action has taken place before now (present perfect) or before a moment in the past (past perfect). The perfect tenses are compound tenses consisting of the verb **haber** plus the **past participle** of a second verb.

Yo **he comido.**	*I have eaten.* (present perfect indicative)
Antes de la fiesta, yo **había comido.**	*Before the party **I had eaten.*** (past perfect indicative)
Yo espero que **hayas comido.**	*I hope that **you have eaten.*** (present perfect subjunctive)
Yo esperaba que **hubieras comido.**	*I hoped that **you had eaten.*** (past perfect subjunctive)

PERSON (La persona) refers to changes in the subject pronouns that indicate if one is speaking (first person), if one is spoken to (second person), or if one is spoken about (third person).

Yo hablo.	*I speak.* (1st-person singular)
Tú hablas.	*You speak.* (2nd-person singular)
Ud./Él/Ella habla.	*You/He/She speak.* (3rd-person singular)
Nosotros(as) hablamos.	*We speak.* (1st-person plural)
Vosotros(as) habláis.	*You speak.* (2nd-person plural)
Uds./Ellos/Ellas hablan.	*They speak.* (3rd-person plural)

PREPOSITIONS (Las preposiciones) are linking words indicating spatial or temporal relations between two words.

Ella nadaba **en** la piscina.	*She was swimming **in** the pool.*
Yo llamé **antes de** las nueve.	*I called **before** nine o'clock.*
El libro es **para** ti.	*The book is **for** you.*
Voy **a** la oficina.	*I'm going **to** the office.*
Jorge es **de** Paraguay.	*Jorge is **from** Paraguay.*

PRESENT PARTICIPLE (*See* **Gerunds.**)

PRETERITE (El pretérito) The preterite tense, as compared to the **imperfect tense,** is used to talk about past events with specific emphasis on the beginning or the end of the action, or emphasis on the completed nature of the action as a whole.

Anoche yo **empecé** a estudiar a las once y **terminé** a la una.
*Last night I **began** to study at eleven o'clock and **finished** at one o'clock.*

Esta mañana **me desperté** a las siete, **desayuné, me duché** y **vine** al campus para las ocho.
*This morning I **woke up** at seven, I **ate** breakfast, I **showered,** and I **came** to campus by eight.*

PERSONAL A (La *a* personal) The personal **a** refers to the placement of the preposition **a** before the name of a person when that person is the **direct object** of the sentence.

Voy a llamar **a** María.	*I'm going to call María.*

PRONOUNS (Los pronombres) are words that substitute for **nouns** in a sentence.

Yo quiero **éste.**	*I want **this one.** (demonstrative—points out a specific person, place or thing)*
¿**Quién** es tu amigo?	***Who** is your friend? (interrogative—used to ask questions)*
Yo voy a llamar**la.**	*I'm going to call **her.** (direct object—replaces the direct object of the sentence)*
Ella va a dar**le** el reloj.	*She is going to give **him** the watch. (indirect object—replaces the indirect object of the sentence)*
Juan **se** baña por la mañana.	*Juan bathes **himself** in the morning. (reflexive—used with reflexive verbs to show that the agent of the action is also the recipient)*
Es la mujer **que** conozco.	*She is the woman **that** I know. (relative—used to introduce a clause that describes a noun)*
Nosotros somos listos.	***We** are clever. (subject—replaces the noun that performs the action or state of a verb)*

SUBJECTS (Los sujetos) are the persons, places, or things that perform the action or state of being of a verb. The **conjugated** verb always agrees with its subject.

Carlos siempre baila solo.	***Carlos** always dances alone.*
Colorado y **California** son mis estados preferidos.	***Colorado** and **California** are my favorite states.*
La cafetera produce el café.	*The **coffee pot** makes the coffee.*

(*See also* **Active voice.**)

SUBJUNCTIVE (El subjuntivo) The subjunctive mood is used to express speculative, doubtful, or hypothetical situations. It also communicates a degree of subjectivity or influence of the main clause over the subordinate clause.

No creo que **tengas** razón.	*I don't think that **you're** right.*
Si yo **fuera** el jefe, pagaría más a mis empleados.	*If I **were** the boss, I would pay my employees more.*
Quiero que **estudies** más.	*I want **you to study** more.*

(*See also* **Mood, Indicative.**)

SUPERLATIVE STATEMENTS (Las frases superlativas) are formed by adjectives or adverbs to make comparisons among three or more members of a group. To form superlatives, add a definite article **(el, la, los, las)** before the comparative form.

Juan es **el más alto** de los tres.
Este coche es **el más rápido** de todos.

*Juan is **the tallest** of the three.*
*This car is **the fastest** of them all.*

(*See also* **Comparisons**.)

TENSES (Los tiempos) refer to the manner in which time is expressed through the **verb** of a sentence.

Yo estudio.	*I study.* (present tense)
Yo estoy estudiando.	*I am studying.* (present progressive)
Yo he estudiado.	*I have studied.* (present perfect)
Yo había estudiado.	*I had studied.* (past perfect)
Yo estudié.	*I studied.* (preterite tense)
Yo estudiaba.	*I was studying.* (imperfect tense)
Yo estudiaré	*I will study.* (future tense)

VERBS (Los verbos) are the words in a sentence that communicate an action or state of being.

Helen **es** mi amiga y ella **lee** muchas novelas.
*Helen **is** my friend and she **reads** a lot of novels.*

Auxiliary verbs (Los verbos auxiliares) or helping verbs are verbs such as **estar** and **haber** used to form the present progressive and the present perfect, respectively.

Estamos estudiando mucho para el examen mañana.
*We **are** studying a lot for the exam tomorrow.*

Helen **ha** trabajado mucho en este proyecto.
*Helen **has** worked a lot on this project.*

Reflexive verbs (Los verbos reflexivos) use reflexive **pronouns** to indicate that the person initiating the action is also the recipient of the action.

Yo **me afeito** por la mañana.

*I shave (**myself**) in the morning.*

Stem-changing verbs (Los verbos con cambios de raíz) undergo a change in the main part of the verb when conjugated. To find the stem, drop the **-ar, -er,** or **-ir** from the **infinitive: dorm-, empez-, ped-.** There are three types of stem-changing verbs: **o** to **ue, e** to **ie** and **e** to **i.**

dormir: Yo d**ue**rmo en el parque.	*I sleep in the park.* (**o** to **ue**)
empezar: Ella siempre emp**ie**za su trabajo temprano.	*She always starts her work early.* (**e** to **ie**)
pedir: ¿Por qué no p**i**des ayuda?	*Why don't you ask for help?* (**e** to **i**)

Infinitive	Present Indicative	Imperfect	Preterite	Future	Conditional	Present Subjunctive	Past Subjunctive	Commands
hablar *to speak*	hablo	hablaba	hablé	hablaré	hablaría	hable	hablara	habla (no hables)
	hablas	hablabas	hablaste	hablarás	hablarías	hables	hablaras	hable
	habla	hablaba	habló	hablará	hablaría	hable	hablara	hablad (no habléis)
	hablamos	hablábamos	hablamos	hablaremos	hablaríamos	hablemos	habláramos	hablen
	habláis	hablabais	hablásteis	hablaréis	hablaríais	habléis	hablarais	
	hablan	hablaban	hablaron	hablarán	hablarían	hablen	hablaran	
aprender *to learn*	aprendo	aprendía	aprendí	aprenderé	aprendería	aprenda	aprendiera	aprende (no aprendas)
	aprendes	aprendías	aprendiste	aprenderás	aprenderías	aprendas	aprendieras	aprenda
	aprende	aprendía	aprendió	aprenderá	aprendería	aprenda	aprendiera	aprended (no aprendáis)
	aprendemos	aprendíamos	aprendimos	aprenderemos	aprenderíamos	aprendamos	aprendiéramos	aprendan
	aprendéis	aprendíais	aprendisteis	aprenderéis	aprenderíais	aprendáis	aprendierais	
	aprenden	aprendían	aprendieron	aprenderán	aprenderían	aprendan	aprendieran	
vivir *to live*	vivo	vivía	viví	viviré	viviría	viva	viviera	vive (no vivas)
	vives	vivías	viviste	vivirás	vivirías	vivas	vivieras	viva
	vive	vivía	vivió	vivirá	viviría	viva	viviera	vivid (no viváis)
	vivimos	vivíamos	vivimos	viviremos	viviríamos	vivamos	viviéramos	vivan
	vivís	vivíais	vivisteis	viviréis	viviríais	viváis	vivierais	
	viven	vivían	vivieron	vivirán	vivirían	vivan	vivieran	

COMPOUND TENSES

Present progressive	estoy / estás / está / estamos / estáis / están	hablando	aprendiendo	viviendo
Present perfect indicative	he / has / ha / hemos / habéis / han	hablado	aprendido	vivido
Present perfect subjunctive	haya / hayas / haya / hayamos / hayáis / hayan	hablado	aprendido	vivido
Past perfect indicative	había / habías / había / habíamos / habíais / habían	hablado	aprendido	vivido

Infinitive / Present Participle / Past Participle	Present Indicative	Imperfect	Preterite	Future	Conditional	Present Subjunctive	Past Subjunctive	Commands
pensar *to think* e → ie pensando pensado	pienso piensas piensa pensamos pensáis piensan	pensaba pensabas pensaba pensábamos pensabais pensaban	pensé pensaste pensó pensamos pensasteis pensaron	pensaré pensarás pensará pensaremos pensaréis pensarán	pensaría pensarías pensaría pensaríamos pensaríais pensarían	piense pienses piense pensemos penséis piensen	pensara pensaras pensara pensáramos pensarais pensaran	piensa (no pienses) piense pensad (no penséis) piensen
acostarse *to go to bed* o → ue acostándose acostado	me acuesto te acuestas se acuesta nos acostamos os acostáis se acuestan	me acostaba te acostabas se acostaba nos acostábamos os acostabais se acostaban	me acosté te acostaste se acostó nos acostamos os acostasteis se acostaron	me acostaré te acostarás se acostará nos acostaremos os acostaréis se acostarán	me acostaría te acostarías se acostaría nos acostaríamos os acostaríais se acostarían	me acueste te acuestes se acueste nos acostemos os acostéis se acuesten	me acostara te acostaras se acostara nos acostáramos os acostarais se acostaran	acuéstate (no te acuestes) acuéstese acostaos (no os acostéis) acuéstense
sentir *to feel* e → ie, i sintiendo sentido	siento sientes siente sentimos sentís sienten	sentía sentías sentía sentíamos sentíais sentían	sentí sentiste sintió sentimos sentisteis sintieron	sentiré sentirás sentirá sentiremos sentiréis sentirán	sentiría sentirías sentiría sentiríamos sentiríais sentirían	sienta sientas sienta sintamos sintáis sientan	sintiera sintieras sintiera sintiéramos sintierais sintieran	siente (no sientas) sienta sentaos (no sintáis) sientan
pedir *to ask for* e → i, i pidiendo pedido	pido pides pide pedimos pedís piden	pedía pedías pedía pedíamos pedíais pedían	pedí pediste pidió pedimos pedisteis pidieron	pediré pedirás pedirá pediremos pediréis pedirán	pediría pedirías pediría pediríamos pediríais pedirían	pida pidas pida pidamos pidáis pidan	pidiera pidieras pidiera pidiéramos pidierais pidieran	pide (no pidas) pida pedid (no pidáis) pidan
dormir *to sleep* o → ue, u durmiendo dormido	duermo duermes duerme dormimos dormís duermen	dormía dormías dormía dormíamos dormíais dormían	dormí dormiste durmió dormimos dormisteis durmieron	dormiré dormirás dormirá dormiremos dormiréis dormirán	dormiría dormirías dormiría dormiríamos dormiríais dormirían	duerma duermas duerma durmamos durmáis duerman	durmiera durmieras durmiera durmiéramos durmierais durmieran	duerme (no duermas) duerma dormid (no durmáis) duerman

Infinitive / Present Participle / Past Participle	Present Indicative	Imperfect	Preterite	Future	Conditional	Present Subjunctive	Past Subjunctive	Commands
comenzar (e → ie) *to begin* z → c before e comenzando comenzado	comienzo comienzas comienza comenzamos comenzáis comienzan	comenzaba comenzabas comenzaba comenzábamos comenzabais comenzaban	**comencé** comenzaste comenzó comenzamos comenzasteis comenzaron	comenzaré comenzarás comenzará comenzaremos comenzaréis comenzarán	comenzaría comenzarías comenzaría comenzaríamos comenzaríais comenzarían	**comience comiences comience comencemos comencéis comiencen**	comenzara comenzaras comenzara comenzáramos comenzarais comenzaran	comienza (no **comiences**) **comience** comenzad (no **comencéis**) **comiencen**
conocer *to know* c → zc before a, o conociendo conocido	**conozco** conoces conoce conocemos conocéis conocen	conocía conocías conocía conocíamos conocíais conocían	conocí conociste conoció conocimos conocisteis conocieron	conoceré conocerás conocerá conoceremos conoceréis conocerán	conocería conocerías conocería conoceríamos conoceríais conocerían	**conozca conozcas conozca conozcamos conozcáis conozcan**	conociera conocieras conociera conociéramos conocierais conocieran	conoce (no **conozcas**) **conozca** conoced (no **conozcáis**) **conozcan**
construir *to build* i → y, y inserted before a, e, o construyendo construido	**construyo construyes construye** construimos construís **construyen**	construía construías construía construíamos construíais construían	construí construiste **construyó** construimos construisteis **construyeron**	construiré construirás construirá construiremos construiréis construirán	construiría construirías construiría construiríamos construiríais construirían	**construya construyas construya construyamos construyáis construyan**	**construyera construyeras construyera construyéramos construyerais construyeran**	**construye** (no **construyas**) **construya** construid (no **construyáis**) **construyan**
leer *to read* i → y; stressed i → í leyendo leído	leo lees lee leemos leéis leen	leía leías leía leíamos leíais leían	leí leíste **leyó** leímos leísteis **leyeron**	leeré leerás leerá leeremos leeréis **leyeron**	leería leerías leería leeríamos leeríais leerían	lea leas lea leamos leáis lean	**leyera leyeras leyera leyéramos leyerais leyeran**	lee (no leas) lea leed (no leáis) lean

Infinitive / Present Participle / Past Participle	Present Indicative	Imperfect	Preterite	Future	Conditional	Present Subjunctive	Past Subjunctive	Commands
pagar *to pay* **g → gu before e** pagando pagado	pago pagas paga pagamos pagáis pagan	pagaba pagabas pagaba pagábamos pagabais pagaban	**pagué** pagaste pagó pagamos pagasteis pagaron	pagaré pagarás pagará pagaremos pagaréis pagarán	pagaría pagarías pagaría pagaríamos pagaríais pagarían	**pague** **pagues** **pague** **paguemos** **paguéis** **paguen**	pagara pagaras pagara pagáramos pagarais pagaran	paga (no **pagues**) **pague** pagad (no **paguéis**) **paguen**
seguir (e → i, i) *to follow* **gu → g before a, o** siguiendo seguido	**sigo** sigues sigue seguimos seguís siguen	seguía seguías seguía seguíamos seguíais seguían	seguí seguiste siguió seguimos seguisteis siguieron	seguiré seguirás seguirá seguiremos seguiréis seguirán	seguiría seguirías seguiría seguiríamos seguiríais seguirían	**siga** **sigas** **siga** **sigamos** **sigáis** **sigan**	siguiera siguieras siguiera siguiéramos siguierais siguieran	sigue (no **sigas**) **siga** seguid (no **sigáis**) **sigan**
tocar *to play, to touch* **c → qu before e** tocando tocado	toco tocas toca tocamos tocáis tocan	tocaba tocabas tocaba tocábamos tocabais tocaban	**toqué** tocaste tocó tocamos tocasteis tocaron	tocaré tocará tocarás tocaremos tocaréis tocarán	tocaría tocarías tocaría tocaríamos tocaríais tocarían	**toque** **toques** **toque** **toquemos** **toquéis** **toquen**	tocara tocaras tocara tocáramos tocarais tocaran	toca (no **toques**) **toque** tocad (no **toquéis**) **toquen**

Infinitive / Present Participle / Past Participle	Present Indicative	Imperfect	Preterite	Future	Conditional	Present Subjunctive	Past Subjunctive	Commands
andar *to walk* andando andado	ando andas anda andamos andáis andan	andaba andabas andaba andábamos andabais andaban	anduve anduviste anduvo anduvimos anduvisteis anduvieron	andaré andarás andará andaremos andaréis andarán	andaría andarías andaría andaríamos andaríais andarían	ande andes ande andemos andéis anden	anduviera anduvieras anduviera anduviéramos anduvierais anduvieran	anda (no andes) ande andad (no andéis) anden
*caer *to fall* cayendo caído	caigo caes cae caemos caéis caen	caía caías caía caíamos caíais caían	caí caíste cayó caímos caísteis cayeron	caeré caerás caerá caeremos caeréis caerán	caería caerías caería caeríamos caeríais caerían	caiga caigas caiga caigamos caigáis caigan	cayera cayeras cayera cayéramos cayerais cayeran	cae (no caigas) caiga caed (no caigáis) caigan
*dar *to give* dando dado	doy das da damos dais dan	daba dabas daba dábamos dabais daban	di diste dio dimos disteis dieron	daré darás dará daremos daréis darán	daría darías daría daríamos daríais darían	dé des dé demos deis den	diera dieras diera diéramos dierais dieran	da (no des) dé dad (no deis) den
*decir *to say, tell* diciendo dicho	digo dices dice decimos decís dicen	decía decías decía decíamos decíais decían	dije dijiste dijo dijimos dijisteis dijeron	diré dirás dirá diremos diréis dirán	diría dirías diría diríamos diríais dirían	diga digas diga digamos digáis digan	dijera dijeras dijera dijéramos dijerais dijeran	di (no digas) diga decid (no digáis) digan
*estar *to be* estando estado	estoy estás está estamos estáis están	estaba estabas estaba estábamos estabais estaban	estuve estuviste estuvo estuvimos estuvisteis estuvieron	estaré estarás estará estaremos estaréis estarán	estaría estarías estaría estaríamos estaríais estarían	esté estés esté estemos estéis estén	estuviera estuvieras estuviera estuviéramos estuvierais estuvieran	está (no estés) esté estad (no estéis) estén

Infinitive / Present Participle / Past Participle	Present Indicative	Imperfect	Preterite	Future	Conditional	Present Subjunctive	Past Subjunctive	Commands
haber *to have* habiendo habido	he has ha [hay] hemos habéis han	había habías había habíamos habíais habían	hube hubiste hubo hubimos hubisteis hubieron	habré habrás habrá habremos habréis habrán	habría habrías habría habríamos habríais habrían	haya hayas haya hayamos hayáis hayan	hubiera hubieras hubiera hubiéramos hubierais hubieran	
*hacer *to make, to do* haciendo **hecho**	**hago** haces hace hacemos hacéis hacen	hacía hacías hacía hacíamos hacíais hacían	hice hiciste hizo hicimos hicisteis hicieron	haré harás hará haremos haréis harán	haría harías haría haríamos haríais harían	haga hagas haga hagamos hagáis hagan	hiciera hicieras hiciera hiciéramos hicierais hicieran	haz (no hagas) haga haced (no hagáis) hagan
ir *to go* **yendo** ido	**voy** vas va vamos vais van	**iba** ibas iba íbamos ibais iban	fui fuiste fue fuimos fuisteis fueron	iré irás irá iremos iréis irán	iría irías iría iríamos iríais irían	vaya vayas vaya vayamos vayáis vayan	fuera fueras fuera fuéramos fuerais fueran	ve (no vayas) vaya id (no vayáis) vayan
*oír *to hear* **oyendo** oído	oigo oyes oye oímos oís oyen	oía oías oía oíamos oíais oían	oí oíste oyó oímos oísteis oyeron	oiré oirás oirá oiremos oiréis oirán	oiría oirías oiría oiríamos oiríais oirían	oiga oigas oiga oigamos oigáis oigan	oyera oyeras oyera oyéramos oyerais oyeran	oye (no oigas) oiga oíd (no oigáis) oigan

Infinitive Present Participle Past Participle	Present Indicative	Imperfect	Preterite	Future	Conditional	Present Subjunctive	Past Subjunctive	Commands
poder (o → ue) can, to be able pudiendo podido	puedo puedes puede podemos podéis pueden	podía podías podía podíamos podíais podían	pude pudiste pudo pudimos pudisteis pudieron	podré podrás podrá podremos podréis podrán	podría podrías podría podríamos podríais podrían	pueda puedas pueda podamos podáis puedan	pudiera pudieras pudiera pudiéramos pudierais pudieran	
*poner to place, to put poniendo puesto	pongo pones pone ponemos ponéis ponen	ponía ponías ponía poníamos poníais ponían	puse pusiste puso pusimos pusisteis pusieron	pondré pondrás pondrá pondremos pondréis pondrán	pondría pondrías pondría pondríamos pondríais pondrían	ponga pongas ponga pongamos pongáis pongan	pusiera pusieras pusiera pusiéramos pusierais pusieran	pon (no pongas) ponga poned (no pongáis) pongan
querer (e → ie) to want, to wish queriendo querido	quiero quieres quiere queremos queréis quieren	quería querías quería queríamos queríais querían	quise quisiste quiso quisimos quisisteis quisieron	querré querrás querrá querremos querréis querrán	querría querrías querría querríamos querríais querrían	quiera quieras quiera queramos queráis quieran	quisiera quisieras quisiera quisiéramos quisierais quisieran	quiere (no quieras) quiera quered (no queráis) quieran
reír (e → i) to laugh riendo reído	río ríes ríe reímos reís ríen	reía reías reía reíamos reíais reían	reí reíste rió reímos reísteis rieron	reiré reirás reirá reiremos reiréis reirán	reiría reirías reiría reiríamos reiríais reirían	ría rías ría riamos riáis rían	riera rieras riera riéramos rierais rieran	ríe (no rías) ría reíd (no riáis) rían

Infinitive Present Participle Past Participle	Present Indicative	Imperfect	Preterite	Future	Conditional	Present Subjunctive	Past Subjunctive	Commands
*saber to know sabiendo sabido	**sé** sabes sabe sabemos sabéis saben	sabía sabías sabía sabíamos sabíais sabían	**supe** **supiste** **supo** **supimos** **supisteis** **supieron**	**sabré** **sabrás** **sabrá** **sabremos** **sabréis** **sabrán**	**sabría** **sabrías** **sabría** **sabríamos** **sabríais** **sabrían**	**sepa** **sepas** **sepa** **sepamos** **sepáis** **sepan**	supiera supieras supiera supiéramos supierais supieran	sabe (no sepas) sepa sabed (no sepáis) sepan
*salir to go out saliendo salido	**salgo** sales sale salimos salís salen	salía salías salía salíamos salíais salían	salí saliste salió salimos salisteis salieron	**saldré** **saldrás** **saldrá** **saldremos** **saldréis** **saldrán**	**saldría** **saldrías** **saldría** **saldríamos** **saldríais** **saldrían**	**salga** **salgas** **salga** **salgamos** **salgáis** **salgan**	saliera salieras saliera saliéramos salierais salieran	sal (no salgas) salga salid (no salgáis) salgan
ser to be siendo sido	**soy** **eres** **es** **somos** **sois** **son**	**era** **eras** **era** **éramos** **erais** **eran**	**fui** **fuiste** **fue** **fuimos** **fuisteis** **fueron**	seré serás será seremos seréis serán	sería serías sería seríamos seríais serían	**sea** **seas** **sea** **seamos** **seáis** **sean**	fuera fueras fuera fuéramos fuerais fueran	sé (no seas) sea sed (no seáis) sean
*tener to have teniendo tenido	**tengo** **tienes** **tiene** tenemos tenéis **tienen**	tenía tenías tenía teníamos teníais tenían	**tuve** **tuviste** **tuvo** **tuvimos** **tuvisteis** **tuvieron**	**tendré** **tendrás** **tendrá** **tendremos** **tendréis** **tendrán**	**tendría** **tendrías** **tendría** **tendríamos** **tendríais** **tendrían**	**tenga** **tengas** **tenga** **tengamos** **tengáis** **tengan**	tuviera tuvieras tuviera tuviéramos tuvierais tuvieran	ten (no tengas) tenga tened (no tengáis) tengan

Infinitive Present Participle Past Participle	Present Indicative	Imperfect	Preterite	Future	Conditional	Present Subjunctive	Past Subjunctive	Commands
*traer *to bring *trayendo *traído	**traigo** traes trae traemos traéis traen	traía traías traía traíamos traíais traían	**traje** **trajiste** **trajo** **trajimos** **trajisteis** **trajeron**	traeré traerás traerá traeremos traeréis traerán	traería traerías traería traeríamos traeríais traerían	**traiga** **traigas** **traiga** **traigamos** **traigáis** **traigan**	**trajera** **trajeras** **trajera** **trajéramos** **trajerais** **trajeran**	trae (no **traigas**) **traiga** traed (no **traigáis**) **traigan**
*venir *to come *viniendo *venido	**vengo** **vienes** **viene** venimos venís **vienen**	venía venías venía veníamos veníais venían	**vine** **viniste** **vino** **vinimos** **vinisteis** **vinieron**	**vendré** **vendrás** **vendrá** **vendremos** **vendréis** **vendrán**	**vendría** **vendrías** **vendría** **vendríamos** **vendríais** **vendrían**	**venga** **vengas** **venga** **vengamos** **vengáis** **vengan**	**viniera** **vinieras** **viniera** **viniéramos** **vinierais** **vinieran**	**ven** (no **vengas**) **venga** venid (no **vengáis**) **vengan**
*ver *to see *viendo *visto	**veo** ves ve vemos veis ven	**veía** **veías** **veía** **veíamos** **veíais** **veían**	**vi** **viste** **vio** **vimos** **visteis** **vieron**	veré verás verá veremos veréis verán	vería verías vería veríamos veríais verían	**vea** **veas** **vea** **veamos** **veáis** **vean**	**viera** **vieras** **viera** **viéramos** **vierais** **vieran**	ve (no **veas**) **vea** ved (no **veáis**) **vean**

*Verbs with irregular *yo* forms in the present indicative

GLOSARIO ESPAÑOL-INGLÉS

This Spanish-English Glossary includes all the words and expressions that appear in the text except verb forms, regular superlatives and diminutives, and most adverbs ending in **-mente.** Only meanings used in the text are given. Gender of nouns is indicated except for masculine nouns ending in **-o** and feminine nouns ending in **-a.** Feminine forms of adjectives are shown except for regular adjectives with masculine forms ending in **-o.** Verbs appear in the infinitive form. Stem changes and spelling changes are indicated in parentheses: e.g., **divertirse (ie, i); buscar (qu).** The number following each entry indicates the chapter in which the word with that particular meaning first appears. The following abbreviations are used:

adj.	adjective	*m.*	masculine	*prep.*	preposition
adv.	adverb	*f.*	feminine	*pron.*	pronoun
conj.	conjunction	*pl.*	plural	*s.*	singular
def. art.	definite article	*p.p.*	past participle		
indef. art.	indefinite article				

A

a *prep.* at, to
  a cambio de in exchange for, R4
  a fin de que *conj.* so that, 13
  a la derecha de *prep.* to the right of, 9
  a la izquierda de *prep.* to the left of, 9
  a menos que *conj.* unless, 13
  a menudo frequently, R1
  a primera vista at first sight, 10
  ¿A qué hora? At what time?, 1
  a tiempo on time, 1
  a última hora at the last minute, 8
  a veces *adv.* sometimes, 3
abajo *adv.* below, 3
abierto *p.p.* opened, 10
abogado(a) lawyer, 11
abordar to board, 9
aborto abortion, 14
abrazar(se) to hug (each other), 10
abrigo overcoat, 7
abril April, 3
abrir to open, 2
  abrir un documento (un programa) to open a document (program), 15
abrochar el cinturón de seguridad to buckle the seat belt, 9
abuela grandmother, 2
abuelo grandfather, 2
aburrido *adj.* bored, 4
aburrir to bore, 13
acabar to run out, 12
  acabar de + *infinitive* to have just (done something), 5
accesorio accessory, 7
acción *f.* action, 3
accionista *m./f.* stockbroker, 11

aceite *m.* oil, 6
acelerado *adj.* accelerated, 12
acercar (qu) to approach, move closer
acompañar to accompany, 10
acontecimiento event, R1
acostarse (ue) to go to bed, 5
acostumbrarse to get used to, 5
actividad *f.* activity, 3
actor *m.* actor, 13
actriz *f.* actress, 13
actual *adj.* current, 14
actuar to act, 13
además de in addition to, R1
Adiós. Good-bye., P
adivinanza riddle, 2
administración (*f.*) de empresas business administration, 1
¿Adónde? Where (to)?, 8
aduana customs, 9
aerolínea airline, 9
aeropuerto airport, 9
afán *m.* desire, 12
afeitarse to shave, 5
aficionado(a) fan (sports), 3
agarrar to catch, 10
agencia de viajes travel agency, 9
agente (*m./f.*) de la aerolínea airline agent, 9
agente de viajes travel agent, 9
agosto August, 3
agricultor(a) farmer, 12
agua *f.* **mineral con/sin gas** carbonated/noncarbonated mineral water, 6
aguacate *m.* avocado, 6
ahijado(a) godchild, 2
ahora *adv.* now, 1
ahorrar to save, 11
aire *m.* air, 12
  aire acondicionado air conditioning, 9
ajo garlic, 6

al aire libre outdoors, 4
  al día up to date, 14
  al lado de *prep.* next to, beside, 4
alarma alarm, 15
alcalde(sa) mayor, 14
alegrarse (de) to be glad, 12
alemán *m.* German (language), 1
alemán(ana) *adj.* German, 2
alergia allergy, 5
alfabetismo literacy, 14
alfombra carpet, 4; rug, floor covering, 8
algo something, anything, 8
algodón *m.* cotton, 7
alguien somebody, someone, anybody, anyone, 8
algún, alguno(a/os/as) some, any, 8
alianza alliance, 15
allí *adv.* there, P
alma soul, 8
almorzar (ue) to have (eat) lunch, 4
almuerzo lunch, 6
alrededor de around
altavoces *m.* speakers, 15
altiplano occidental western highlands, 8
alto *adj.* tall, 2
amable *adj.* friendly, 2
amar to love, 10
amarillo *adj.* yellow, 1
ambiente (*m.*) ameno pleasant atmosphere, R2
ambulancia ambulance, 5
amigo(a) friend, 1
amistad *f.* friendship, 10
amor *m.* love, 10
analfabetismo illiteracy, 14
analista de sistemas *m./f.* systems analyst, 11
anaranjado *adj.* orange, 1

andar en bicicleta to ride a bike, 3
anfitrión *m.* host, 8
anfitriona hostess, 8
angosto *adj.* narrow, 11
anillo ring, 7
animal *m.* animal, 12
anoche *adv.* last night, 6
anteayer *adv.* the day before yesterday, 6
antena parabólica satellite dish, 9
antes (de) que *conj.* before, 13
antiácido antacid, 5
antibiótico antibiotic, 5
antigüedad *f.* antique, 7
antipático *adj.* unpleasant, 2
anuncio commercial, 13
año year, 3
apagado *adj.* off, 15
apagar (ue) to turn off, 15
aparador *m.* shop window, 13
apartamento apartment, 1
apellido last name, 2
apenas *adv.* barely, 4
aplaudir to applaud, 10
apoyar to support, 14
apoyo support, 13
apreciar to appreciate, 13
aprender to learn, 2
apretón (*m.*) de manos handshake, 11
aprobar (ue) to approve; to pass, 14
aprovechar to take advantage, 14
apuntes *m.* notes, R1
aquél (aquélla) *adj.* that (over there), 5
aquel (aquella) *pron.* that (over there), 5
aquí *adv.* here, P
árabe *adj.* Arab, 2
aranceles *m.* taxes, 15
árbol *m.* tree, 4

archivar to file, 2; to save, 15
archivo file, 15
arena sand, 6
arete *m.* earring, 7
argentino *adj.* Argentine, 2
armario wardrobe, armoire, closet, 4
arquitecto(a) architect, 11
arquitectura architecture, 13
arreglado *adj.* neat, tidy, 9
arreglo floral floral arrangement, R4
arriesgarse (ue) to take a risk, 15
arrogante *adj.* arrogant, 2
arroyo stream, 12
arroz *m.* rice, 6
arte *m./f.* art, 1
artista *m./f.* artist, 13
artístico *adj.* artistic, 2
arzobispo archbishop, 8
ascensor *m.* elevator, 9
asesinar to assassinate, R4
Así así. So-so., P
   así como just like, 3
   Así que... So . . . , 2
asiento seat, 9
asistente de vuelo *m./f.* flight attendant, 9
asistir a to attend, 2
aspiradora vacuum cleaner, 4
aspirina aspirin, 5
asustarse to be frightened, 8
aterrizar to land, 9
atlético *adj.* athletic, 2
aumentar to increase, 14
aún *adv.* still
aunque *conj.* although, even though, 13
autobús *m.* bus *(Spain)*, P
automóvil *m.* car, P
autor(a) author, 13
avance *m.* advance, 15
ave *m.* bird, 12
avergonzado: Me pongo avergonzado. I get embarrassed., 8
avión *m.* plane, 9
avisar to warn, 8
ayer *adv.* yesterday, 6
ayudante *m./f.* assistant
ayudar(se) to help (each other), 1
azúcar *m.* sugar, 6
azul *adj.* blue, 1

B

babear to spew, R3
bailar to dance, 1
bailarín *m.* dancer, 13
bailarina dancer, 13
baile *m.* dance, 1
bajar(se) (de) to get off, 9
bajo *adj.* short (height), 2
balcón *m.* balcony, 4

ballet *m.* ballet, 13
balneario beach resort, 8
baloncesto basketball, 3
banana/banano banana, 6
banco bank, 3
banquero(a) banker, 11
banquete *m.* banquet, 10
bañarse (en la tina) to take a bath, 5
bañera bathtub, 4
barato *adj.* inexpensive, cheap, 7
bárbaro *adj.* awesome, R3
barco de carga cargo ship, 11
barrer el piso to sweep the floor, 4
barrio neighborhood, 2
Bastante bien. Rather well., P
basura trash, 12
beber to drink, 2
bebida beverage, 6
beca scholarship, 9
béisbol *m.* baseball, 3
bello *adj.* beautiful, 12
beneficios benefits, 11
besar(se) to kiss (each other), 10
biblioteca library, 1
bibliotecario(a) librarian, 1
bicicleta bicycle, 3
bien *adv.* well, fine
   Bastante bien. Rather well., P
   bien cocido well done, 6
   Bien, gracias. Fine, thanks., P
   Muy bien. Very well., P
¡Bienvenido! Welcome!, 9
bilingüe *adj.* bilingual, 2
billete *m.* ticket, 9
   billete de ida one-way ticket, 9
   billete de ida y vuelta round-trip ticket, 9
biología biology, 1
bistec *m.* steak, 6
blanco *adj.* white, 1
blusa blouse, 7
boca mouth, 5
boda wedding, 10
boleto ticket, 3
   boleto de ida one-way ticket, 9
   boleto de ida y vuelta round-trip ticket, 9
bolígrafo ballpoint pen, 1
boliviano *adj.* Bolivian, 2
bolsa purse, bag, 7
bolsillo pocket, 7
bombero(a) firefighter, 11
bonito *adj.* pretty, 2
borrador *m.* eraser, 1
bosque *m.* forest, 12
bota boot, 7
botines de charol *m.* patent leather ankle boots, R5
botón *m.* button, 7
brasileño *adj.* Brazilian, 2
brazo arm, 5

brindis *m.* toast, 8
broncearse to get a suntan, 8
bucear to scuba dive, 8
¡Buen provecho! Enjoy your meal!, 6
¡Buen viaje! Have a nice trip!, 9
Buenas noches. Good evening (night)., P
Buenas tardes. Good afternoon., P
bueno *adj.* good, 2
Buenos días. Good morning., P
bufanda scarf, 7
bufete *m.* law office, 11
búho owl, 12
buscar (qu) to look for, 1
búsqueda de trabajo job hunt, 11

C

cabello hair, 5
cabeza head, 5
cabina cabin, 9
cada *adv.* each
   cada día (semana, etc.) every day (week, etc.), 10
cadena chain, R3
cadera hip, 5
café *m.* café, 3; coffee, 6
cafetería cafeteria, 1
caimán *m.* alligator, 12
caja fuerte security box, 9
cajero automático ATM, 11
cajero(a) cashier, 11
calamares (fritos) *m.* (fried) squid, 6
calcetines *m. pl.* socks, 7
calculadora calculator, 1
calendario calendar, 1
caliente *adj.* hot (temperature), 6
callarse to quiet, R5
calle *f.* street, 3
   calle peatonal pedestrian street, R3
cama bed, 4
   cama sencilla (doble) single (double) bed, 9
cámara camera, 3
   cámara digital digital camera, 15
camarero(a) waiter (waitress), 6
camarones (fritos) *m.* (fried) shrimp, 6
cambiar to change, 7
camello camel, R3
cámara de representantes (diputados) house of representatives, 14
caminar to walk, 1
   caminar por las montañas to hike/walk in the mountains, 3
caminata walk, 7

camión *m.* bus (Mexico), P
camisa shirt, 7
camiseta T-shirt, 7
campaña campaign, 14
campesino(a) farm worker, peasant, 12
campo country, 8
   campo de fútbol (de golf) football field (golf course), 3
campus *m.* campus, 1
canadiense *adj.* Canadian, 2
canal *m.* channel (TV), 13
cancha (de tenis) (tennis) court, 3
canción *f.* song, 13
candidato(a) candidate, applicant, 11
canela cinnamon, 3
cansancio tiredness, 5
cantante *m./f.* singer, 13
cantar to sing, 1
capa de ozono ozone layer, 12
cara face, 5
caraota negra black bean, 6
carecer de to lack, 15
cargo charge, 11
cariño affection, 10
carne (de res) *f.* meat (beef), 6
carnicería butcher shop, 3
caro *adj.* expensive, 7
carpintero(a) carpenter, 11
carrera major, field of study, 1
carretera highway, 12
carro car, P
carta letter (correspondence), 2
cartera wallet, 7
cartón *m.* cardboard, 4
casa house, 4
   casa de ancianos nursing home, 2
casado *adj.* married, 2
casarse (con) to get married, to marry, 10
casi (siempre) *adv.* almost (always), 10
catarata waterfall, 12
catarro cold, 5
catorce fourteen, P
caza chase, 7
cebolla onion, 6
cebra zebra, 12
cejas eyebrows, 5
celebración *f.* celebration, 8
celebrar to celebrate, 8
cena dinner, supper, 6
cenar to have (eat) supper (dinner), 6
centro downtown, 3
   centro comercial mall, 3
   centro de negocios business center, 9
   centro estudiantil student center, 1

cepillarse los dientes to brush one's teeth, 5

cerca de *prep.* near, 4

cerebro brain, 5

cero zero, P

cerrar (ie) to close, 4

cerveza beer, 6

chaleco vest, 7

champiñón *m.* mushroom, 6

chaqueta jacket, 7

Chao. (informal) Bye., P

cheque *m.* check, 7

   cheque de viajero traveler's check, 11

¡Chévere! Cool!, 3

chico(a) boy (girl), 7

chileno *adj.* Chilean, 2

chillido screech, R3

chimenea fireplace, chimney, 4

chino Chinese (language), 1; *adj.* Chinese, 2

chipichipi *m.* thumbnail-size clam, 6

chocarse (qu) con to crash into, 8

chuleta (de cerdo) (pork) chop, 6

ciberespacio cyberspace, 15

ciclismo cycling, 3

cien/ciento one hundred, 2

cierre *m.* zipper, 7

ciervo deer, 12

cinco five, P

Cinco de Mayo Cinco de Mayo, 8

cincuenta fifty, 2

cine *m.* movie theater, 3; movies, 13

cinta ribbon, M5

cinturón *m.* belt, 7

cita date (social), 10

   cita de negocios job appointment, 1

ciudadano(a) citizen, 14

clásico *adj.* classical, 13

clavo clove, 3

cobarde *adj.* cowardly, 2

coche *m.* car, P

cocina kitchen, 4

cocinar to cook, 6

cocinero(a) cook, chef, 11

cocodrilo crocodile, 12

codo elbow, 5

cognado falso false cognate, 1

cohete *m.* rocket, 8

colina hill, 12

collar *m.* necklace, 7

colombiano *adj.* Colombian, 2

color *m.* color, 1

comedia comedy, 13

comedor *m.* dining room, 4

comenzar (ie) to start, begin, 4

comer to eat, 2

No puedo (comer) más. I can't (eat) any more.

comerciante *m./f.* merchant, 11

cómico *adj.* humorous, 2

comida food, meal, 6

¿Cómo? How? P

   ¿Cómo está usted? How are you? (formal), P

   ¿Cómo estás? How are you? (informal), P

   ¡Cómo no! Of course!, 6

   ¿Cómo se llama usted? What's your name? (formal), P

   ¿Cómo te llamas? What's your name? (informal), P

cómoda dresser, 4

comodidad *f.* comfort, R3; *pl.* ammenities, features, 9

cómodo *adj.* comfortable, 9

compañero(a) de clase classmate, 1

compañero(a) de cuarto roommate, 1

compositor(a) composer, 13

comprar to buy, 1

compras: de compras shopping, 7

comprender to understand, 2

comprometido *adj.* engaged, 10

compromiso engagement, 10

computación *f.* computer science, 1

computadora computer, 1

   computadora portátil laptop computer, 15

con *prep.* with, 4

   con destino a departing for, 9

   con permiso pardon me, excuse me, P

   con respecto a with regard to, 11

con tal (de) que *conj.* provided (that), 13

concierto concert, 13

condimento condiment, 6

condominio condominium, 4

conectar to connect, 15

conexión *f.* connection, 15

congestionado *adj.* congested, 5

congreso congress, 14

conocer(se) to know (each other); to meet, 3

conseguir (i) to get, to obtain, 4

consejero(a) advisor, 1

conservación *f.* conservation, 12

conservador(a) *adj.* conservative, 2

conservar to conserve, 12

constitución *f.* constitution, 14

construir to construct, 12

contabilidad *f.* accounting, 1

contador(a) accountant, 11

contaminación *f.* pollution, 12

contaminado *adj.* polluted, 12

contaminar to pollute, 12

contar (ue) to count; to tell, 4

   contar con to count on, 3

contento *adj.* happy, 4

   Me pongo contento. I get happy., 8

contestador automático *m.* answering machine, 15

contestar to answer, 1

contra *prep.* against, 1

contratar to hire, 11

control (*m.*) **remoto** remote control, 15

control (*m.*) **de seguridad** security, 9

copa goblet, wine glass, 6

corazón *m.* heart, 5

corbata necktie, 7

coreano *adj.* Korean, 2

correo electrónico email, 11

correr to run, 3

   correr las olas to surf, 8

corrupción *f.* corruption, 14

cortar el césped to mow the lawn, 4

corto *adj.* short (length), 2

coser to sew, R2

costa coast, 8

costar (ue) to cost, 4

costarricense *adj.* Costa Rican, 2

costo expense, 11

cotidiano *adj.* daily, 13

crear to create, R1; to found, R4

crecer to grow up, 2

crecimiento growth, 15

creer to believe, 2

crema bronceadora suntan lotion, 8

cremallera zipper, 7

criado(a) servant; maid, 11

crimen *m.* crime, 14

cruzar to cross, 9

cuaderno notebook, 1

cuadra city block, 9

cuadro painting, 4

¿Cuál(es)? Which?, P

   ¿Cuál es tu dirección? (informal) What's your address? (informal), P

   ¿Cuál es tu nombre? What's your name? (informal), P

   ¿Cuál es tu número de teléfono? What's your telephone number? (informal), P

cuando *conj.* when, 13

¿Cuándo? When?, P

¿Cuánto(a)? How much?, 8

   ¿Cuántos(as)? How many?, P

   ¿Cuánto le debo? How much do I owe you?, 7

   ¿Cuántos años tienes? How old are you?, P

cuarenta forty, 2

cuarto room, 1

   cuarto de baño bathroom, 4

cuatro four, P

cuatrocientos four hundred, 4

cubano *adj.* Cuban, 2

cuchara spoon, 6

cuchillo knife, 6

cuello neck, 5

cuenta check, bill, 6; account, 11

   cuenta corriente checking account, 11

   cuenta de ahorros savings account, 11

   La cuenta, por favor. The check, please., 6

cuento story, 4

cuero leather, 7

cuerpo humano body, 5

   Cuerpo de Paz Peace Corps, 5

cuidar(se) to take care (of oneself), 5

culebra snake, 12

cultivar to plant, 5; to cultivate; to grow (plants), 12

cumbre *f.* summit, R1

cumpleaños *m.* birthday, 8

cumplir años to have a birthday, 8

   cumplir con to honor, 10

cunita cradle, 7

cuñada sister-in-law, 2

cuñado brother-in-law, 2

currículum *m.* résumé, 11

curso course, 1

D

danza dance, 13

dar to give, 3

   dar una fiesta to give a party, 8

   dar un paseo to go for a walk, 3

   darse cuenta to realize, R5

   darse la mano to shake hands, 10

de from, of

   de cuadros plaid, 7

   ¿De dónde eres tú? Where are you from? (informal), P

   ¿De dónde es usted? Where are you from? (formal), P

   ¿De dónde? From where?, P

   de la (mañana, tarde, noche) in the (morning, afternoon/evening), 1

   de lunares polka-dotted, 7

   ¿De quién(es)? Whose?, 8

   de rayas striped, 7

   de repente suddenly, 8

   de tiempo completo full-time, 11

   de tiempo parcial part-time, 11

de vez en cuando
occasionally, 6
debajo de *prep.* under, below, 4
debate *m.* debate, 14
deber ought to, must, 2
deber *m. noun* duty, 14
debido a due to, R1
debilidad *f.* weakness, 5
decano(a) dean, 1
decir (i) to say; to tell, 4
¡No me digas más! Say no more!, 11
dedo finger, 5
dedo del pie toe, 5
defender (ie) to defend, 14
defensa defense, 14
dejar to quit, 11; to leave; to let, to allow, 13
dejar una (buena) propina to leave a (good) tip, 6
delante de *prep.* in front of, 4
delgado *adj.* thin, 2
demandar to sue, 14
demasiado *adv.* too much, 9
democracia democracy, 14
demócrata *adj.* democratic, 14
demora delay, 9
demorarse to be delayed, 13
denso *adj.* dense, 12
dentista *m./f.* dentist, 11
dependiente *m./f.* salesclerk, 7
deporte *m.* sport, 3
deportiva *adj.* sports, 3
depositar to deposit (money), 11
derecha: a la derecha de *prep.* to the right of, 9
derecho law, 1; straight, 9
derechos humanos (civiles) human (civil) rights, 14
derrocar (qu) to overthrow, 14
desafío challenge, 14
desamparado(a) defenseless person, 13
desarrollar to develop, 12
desarrollo development, 12
desayunar to have (eat) breakfast, 6
desayuno breakfast, 6
descansar to rest, 1
desconectar to disconnect, 15
desconocido *adj.* unknown
descuento discount, 7
desde *prep.* from, 1
desear to want, to wish, 1
desempleo unemployment, 14
desenchufar to unplug, 15
desenlace *m.* ending, R5
desfile *m.* parade, R1
desigualdad *f.* inequality, 14
deslumbrar to dazzle, 13
desmedro impairment, 14
desordenado *adj.* messy, 4
despedirse (i) to fire, 11
despegar to take off, 9

desperdicio waste, 12
despertador *m.* alarm clock, 4
despertarse (ie) to wake up, 5
despierto *adj.* lively, R1
desprotegido *adj.* unprotected, R4
después *adv.* afterward, 10
después (de) (que) *conj.* after, 13
destrucción *f.* destruction, 12
destrucción ambiental environmental degradation, R4
destruido *adj.* destroyed, 12
destruir to destroy, 12
desventaja disadvantage, 15
detrás de *prep.* behind, 4
día *m.* day, 1
al día up to date, 14
Día de la Independencia de España Independence Day from Spain, 1
Día de la Raza Columbus Day, 8
Día de los Muertos Day of the Dead, 1
Día de los Meyes Magos Day of the Magi (Three Kings), 8
Día de Todos los Santos All Saints' Day, 8
Día del santo saint's day, 8
día feriado *m.* holiday, 8
diagnóstico diagnosis, 5
diariamente daily, 3
dibujar to draw, 1
dibujo animado cartoon, 13
diccionario dictionary, 1
dicho *p.p.* said; told, 10
diciembre December, 3
dictador(a) dictator, 14
dictadura dictatorship, 14
diecinueve nineteen, P
dieciocho eighteen, P
dieciséis sixteen, P
diecisiete seventeen, P
diente *m.* tooth, 5
dieta diet, 5
diez ten P
dinero money, 1
diputado(a) representative, 14
director(a) director, 13
dirigir to direct, 13
disco compacto compact disc (CD), 15
disco duro hard drive, 15
disculpe pardon me, P
discurso speech, R1
discutir to argue, to discuss, 14
disfraz *m.* costume, 8
disfrazarse to wear a costume, 8
disfrutar to enjoy, 9
disquete *m.* diskette, 15
divertido *adj.* fun, R1
divorciado *adj.* divorced, 2

divorciarse (de) to get divorced (from), 10
divorcio divorce, 10
doblar to turn, 9
doce twelve, P
documental *m.* documentary, 13
dolerle (ue) (a alguien) to be painful (to someone), 5
dolor (de oídos, de cabeza) *m.* ache, pain (earache, headache), 5
domingo Sunday, 1
dominicano *adj.* Dominican (from the Dominican Republic), 2
¿Dónde? Where?, P
dormir (ue) to sleep, 4
dormirse (ue) to fall asleep, 5
dormitorio bedroom, 4
dos two, P
doscientos(as) two hundred, 4
drama *m.* drama, play, 13
dramático *adj.* dramatic, 2
dramaturgo *m./f.* playwright, 13
drogadicción *f.* drug addiction, 14
ducha shower, 4
ducharse to take a shower, 5
dueño(a) owner, R5
dulce *adj.* sweet, R1
durante *prep.* throughout
durar to last, R1

E

ecología ecology, 12
economía economics, 1
económico *adj.* economic, 5
edad *f.* age, 2
edificio building, 1
educación *f.* education, 1
efectivo cash, 7
egipcio *adj.* Egyptian, 2
ejército army, 14
el, la, los, las *def. art.* the
él *pron.* he, P
elecciones *f.* elections, 14
electricista *m./f.* electrician, 11
electrodomésticos electric appliance, 4
elefante *m.* elephant, 12
elegir (i, i) to elect, 14
eliminar to eliminate, 14
ella *pron.* she, P
ellos(as) *pron.* they, P
embajador(a) ambassador, R2
emocionado *adj.* excited, 4
empezar (ie) to begin, 4
empleado(a) employee, 11
empleo employment, 14
emprender to embark on, R5
empresa corporation; business, 11
empresa privada private company, R4
en in; on, 4

en caso (de) que *conj.* in case (of), 13
en contra against, R4
en cuanto a in regard to, 13
enamorarse (de) to fall in love (with), 10
encaje *m.* lace, R5
Encantado(a). Nice to meet you. P
encarcelamiento imprisonment, 14
encendido *adj.* on, 15
enchufado *adj.* plugged in, 15
enchufar to plug in, 15
encima de *prep.* on top of, 4
encontrar to find, 5
energía solar solar energy, 12
enero January, 3
enfermarse to get sick, 5
enfermedad *f.* illness, 5
enfermería infirmary, 9
enfermero(a) nurse, 5
enfermo *adj.* sick, 4
enfrentar to face, 13
enfrente de *prep.* across from, 9
enmendar (ie) to amend, 14
enmienda amendment, 14
enojado *adj.* angry, 4
ensalada salad, 6
enseñar to teach, 1
entender (ie) to understand, 4
entonces *adv.* then; so, 10
entrar to enter, 1
entre *prep.* between, among, 4
entremés *m.* hors d'oeuvre, 8
entrevista interview, 11
envilecido *adj.* underappreciated, R1
equilibrio balance, 12
equipaje (de mano) *m.* (carry-on) baggage, luggage, 9
equipo equipment, 15
escalera stairs, 4
escáner *m.* scanner, 15
escasez *f.* lack, shortage, 12
escenario stage, R2
escoger to choose, 9
escribir to write, 2
escrito *p.p.* written, 10
escritor(a) writer, 13
escritorio desk, 1
escuchar (música) to listen (to music), 1
escuela school, 1
escuela politécnica technical school, 1
esculpir to sculpt, 13
escultor(a) sculptor, 13
escultura sculpture, 13
hacer escultura to sculpt, 13
ese(a) *adj.* that, 5
ése(a) *pron.* that, 5
esfuerzo físico physical exertion, 5

espacio space, 4
    espacio cibernético cyberspace, 15
espalda back, 5
español *m.* Spanish (language), 1
español(a) *adj.* Spanish, 2
especialidad *(f.)* **de la casa** house specialty, 6
especialización *f.* major, 1
especies *f.* species, 12
espectáculo show, 14
espectador(a) viewer, 13
espejo mirror, 4
esperar to hope; to wait, 1
espiritualmente spiritually, 2
esposa wife, 2
esposo husband, 2
esquí *m.* **(acuático)** (water) ski, 3
esquiar (en el agua) to (water) ski, 3
está despejado/nublado it's clear/cloudy, 3
estación *f.* season, 3
estación de trenes *f.* train station, 9
estadio stadium, 3
estado libre asociado free associated state, 1
estadounidense *adj.* from the United States, 2
estante *m.* bookshelf, 4
estar to be, 3
    estar conectado(a) (en línea) to be online, 15
    estar de acuerdo to agree, 10
    estar enfermo(a) to be sick, 5
    estar resfriado(a) to have a cold, 5
    estar sano(a) to be healthy, 5
este *m.* east, 9
éste *pron.* this one, 5
este(a) *adj.* this, 5
estéreo stereo, 15
estilo style, 7
estómago stomach, 5
estornudar to sneeze, 5
Estoy a dieta. I'm on a diet., 6
    Estoy satisfecho(a). I'm satisfied. I'm full., 6
estudiante *m./f.* student, 1
estudiar to study, 1
estudio study, 1
estufa stove, 4
examen *m.* test, 1
examinar to examine, 5
éxito success, R2
explicar (qu) to explain, 9
explotar to exploit, 12
extinción: en peligro de extinción in danger of extinction, 12
extranjero *adj.* foreign, R2
extraviado *adj.* lost, R3
extrovertido *adj.* outgoing, 2

F
fábrica factory, 12
factura bill, 11
facturar el equipaje to check the luggage, 9
facultad *f.* department, 12
falda skirt, 7
falta lack, 11
familia family, R2
farmacia pharmacy, 5
faro lighthouse, R3
fax *m.* fax machine, 11
febrero February, 3
¡Felicitaciones! Congratulations!, 8
felicitar to congratulate, 10
feo *adj.* ugly, 2
ferretería hardware store, 3
fiesta (de sorpresa) (surprise) party; holiday, 8
filosofía philosophy, 1
fin *(m.)* **de semana** weekend, 1
finalmente *adv.* at last, finally, 10
finanzas personales personal finances, 11
finca farm, 12
firmar to sign, 14
física physics, 1
flan (casero) *m.* (homemade) caramel custard, 6
flor *f.* flower, 10
folklórico *adj.* folkloric, 13
fotocopiadora photocopier, 11
fotografía photography, 13
fotógrafo(a) photographer, 11
francés *m.* French (language), 1
francés(esa) *adj.* French, 2
fresco *adj.* fresh, 6
frontera border, 12
fruta fruit, 6
frutería fruit store, 3
fuego de artificio firework, 1
fuente *f.* source, 12; fountain, 4
función *f.* musical (play), 13
funcionar to function (to work), 15
furioso *adj.* furious, 4
fútbol (americano) *m.* soccer (football), 3

G
gafas de sol sunglasses, 3
ganador(a) winner, 13
ganancia earning, R2
ganar to win, 3
ganga: ¡Es una ganga! It's a bargain!, 7
garaje *m.* garage, 4
garganta throat, 5
gasolinera gas station, 3
gastar to spend (money), 7
gasto expense, R1
gato cat, 2

gemelo cufflink, 7
generoso *adj.* generous, 2
gente *f.* people, P
geografía geography, 1
geología geology, 1
gerente *m./f.* manager, 11
gimnasio gymnasium, 1
gobernador(a) governor, 14
gobernar (ie) to govern, 14
gobierno government, 14
golf *m.* golf, 3
golpe de estado *m.* coup d'etat, 14
    golpe militar military coup, 14
gordo *adj.* fat, 2
gorila *m.* gorilla, 12
gorra de béisbol baseball cap, 7
grabar to record, 15
grande *adj.* big, large, 2
gratis *adj.* free, 1
gritar to shout, 8
grupo paramilitar paramilitary group, 14
guagua bus *(Puerto Rico)*, P
guante *m.* glove, 7
guapo *adj.* good-looking, 2
guardaparques *m./f.* park ranger, 12
guardar cama to stay in bed, 5
guatemalteco *adj.* Guatemalan, 2
guerra war, 14
guerrillero *m./f.* guerrilla, 14
guión *m.* script, 13
guitarra guitar, 3
    tocar la guitarra to play the guitar, 3
gustar to be pleasing (to someone), 3
    (no) me gusta + *infinitive* I (don't) like + infinitive, 1
gusto: El gusto es mío. The pleasure is mine, P

H
haber to have (auxillary verb), 10
hablar(se) to speak, to talk (with each other), 1
hace buen tiempo it's nice, 3
    hace calor it's hot, 3
    hace fresco it's cool, 3
    hace frío it's cold, 3
    hace sol it's sunny, 3
    hace viento it's windy, 3
hacer to do; to make, 3
    hacer (un picnic, planes, ejercicio) to go on a picnic, to make plans, to exercise, 3
    hacer camping to go camping, 8
    hacer click (sobre) to click (on), 15

    hacer escala (en) to make a stop (on a flight) (in), 9
    hacer esnórquel to snorkel, 8
    hacer juego con to match, 7
    hacer la cama to make one's bed, 4
    hacer la(s) maleta(s) to pack one's suitcase(s), 9
    hacer un brindis to make a toast, 8
    hacer una fiesta to give a party, 8
    hacer una parrillada to have a cookout, 8
hacia *adv.* toward, 9
haitiano *adj.* Haitian, 2
hamburguesa hamburger, 6
hambre *f.* hunger, 5
harina de maíz corn flour, 6
hasta *adv.* up to, until, 9
    Hasta luego. See you later, P
    Hasta mañana. See you tomorrow, P
    Hasta pronto. See you soon, P
    hasta que *conj.* until, 13
hay there is, there are, P
hecho *p.p.* done; made, 10
    hechos a la medida made to order, 7
helado ice cream, 6
hermana sister, 2
hermanastra stepsister, 2
hermanastro stepbrother, 2
hermano brother, 2
hervir (ie) to boil, 3
hierba herb, 5; grass, R3
hígado liver, 5
hija daughter, 2
hijo son, 2
hipopótamo hippopotamus, 12
hipoteca mortgage, 11
hispanohablante *m./f.* native Spanish speaker
historia history, 1; story, 4
historial clínica *f.* medical history, 5
hogar *m.* home, 4
hoja leaf, 5
¡Hola! Hi! (informal), P
hombre *m.* man, 1
hombre de negocios businessman, 11
hondureño *adj.* Honduran, 2
honesto *adj.* honest, 2
hora hour, time
    ¿A qué hora? At what time?, 1
    ¿Qué hora es? What time is it?, 1
horario schedule, 9
hormiga ant, 12
horno (de microondas) (microwave) oven, 4

hotel de cuatro estrellas *m.* four-star hotel, 9
hoy *adv.* today, 1
huelga strike, 14
huérfano(a) orphan, R3
hueso bone, 5
huevo duro hard-boiled egg, 6
humanidades *f. pl.* humanities, 1
humilde *adj.* humble, 2

I
ideología ideology, 14
iglesia church, 3
igualdad *f.* equality, 14
impermeable *m.* raincoat, 7
importante *adj.* important, 12
imposible *adj.* impossible, 12
impresora printer, 11
imprimir to print, 11
impuestos taxes, 14
imunidad *f.* immunity, 14
inagotable *adj.* endless, R1
incienso incense, R3
incluir to include, 2
indeciso *adj.* indecisive, 2
indio *adj.* Indian
inflación *f.* inflation, 14
informar to inform, 14
informe *m.* report, 11
ingeniería engineering, 1
ingeniero(a) engineer, 11
inglés *m.* English (language), 1
inglés(esa) *adj.* English, 2
ingreso income, 12
inmigración *f.* passport control, immigration, 9
inodoro toilet, 4
insólito *adj.* unusual, unaccustomed, R1
intelectual *adj.* intellectual, 2
inteligente *adj.* intelligent, 2
Internet *m.* Internet, 14
interpelar to question, 14
interpretar to play a role, 13
intérprete *m./f.* interpreter, 11
intuitivo *adj.* intuitive, 2
inventar to invent, 3
inversión *f.* investment, R4
invertir (ie) to invest, R2
investigar to investigate, 14
invierno winter, 3
invitado *m./f.* guest, 8
invitar: Te invito. It's on me (my treat)., 6
inyección *f.* shot (injection), 5
ir to go, 3
   ir a pie to go on foot, 9
   ir a tomar un café to drink coffee, 3
   ir a un bar to go to a bar, 3
   ir a un club to go to a club, 3
   ir a un concierto to go to a concert, 3

ir a una discoteca to go to a disco, 3
ir a una fiesta to go to a party, 3
ir al cine to go to the movies, 3
ir de compras to go shopping, 3
ir en autobús to go by bus, 9
ir en avión to go by plane, 9
ir en barco to go by boat, 9
ir en bicicleta to go by bike, 9
ir en coche to go by car, 9
ir en metro to go by subway, 9
ir en taxi to go by taxi, 9
ir en tren to go by train, 9
irresponsable *adj.* irresponsible, 2
isla island, 9
italiano Italian (language), 1; *adj.* Italian, 2
izquierda: a la izquierda de *prep.* to the left of, 9

J
jadeo panting, 5
jaguar *m.* jaguar, 12
jamón *m.* ham, 6
japonés *m.* Japanese (language), 1
japonés(esa) *adj.* Japanese, 2
jarabe *m.* cough syrup, 5
jardín *m.* garden, 4
jeans *m. pl.* blue jeans, 7
jefe *m./f.* boss, 11
jerarquía hierarchy, 11
joven *adj.* young, 2
joya gem, R2
joyas jewelry, 7
joyería jewelry store, 3
jubilarse to retire, 11
juego game, 3
jueves *m.* Thursday, 1
juez *m./f.* judge, 10
jugador(a) player, 3
jugar (ue) to play, 4
   jugar al tenis to play tennis, 3
jugo de fruta fruit juice, 6
julio July, 3
junio June, 3

L
labios lips, 5
lado: al lado de *prep.* next to, 9
lago lake, 8
lámpara lamp, 4
lana wool, 7
langosta lobster, 6
lápiz *m.* pencil, 1
largo *adj.* long, 2
lástima: es una lástima it's a shame, 12
lavabo bathroom sink, 4
lavadora washing machine, 4

lavaplatos *m.* dishwasher, 4
lavar (los platos, la ropa, las ventanas) to wash (dishes, clothes, windows), 4
lavarse to wash up, 5
lección *f.* lesson, 1
leche *f.* milk, 6
lechuga lettuce, 6
lectura reading, R1
leer to read, 2
lejos (de) *prep.* far (away) (from), 4
lengua language, 1; tongue, 5
   lenguas extranjeras foreign languages, 1
lentillas/lentes *(m.)* **de contacto** contact lenses, 5
león *m.* lion, 12
levantar pesas to lift weights, 3
levantarse to get up, 5
levemente lightly, 11
ley *f.* law, 14
liberal *adj.* liberal, 2
libertad *f.* **de la prensa** freedom of the press, 14
librería bookstore, 1
libro (de texto) (text)book, 1
liga profesional professional league, 3
ligeramente *adv.* slightly, R2
ligero *adj.* light (meal, food), 6
limosna charity, 13
limpiar la casa to clean the house, 4
limpio *adj.* clean, 4
liquidación *f.* sale (*Lat. Am.*), reduction (in price)
listo *adj.* smart; ready, 2
literatura literature, 1
llamar to call, to phone, 1
   Me llamo... My name is . . . , P
   llamar por teléfono to make a phone call, 11
llano plain, 12
llave *f.* key, 9
llegada arrival, 9
llegar to arrive, 1
llenar to fulfill, 7; to fill out (a form), 11
llevar to wear, to carry, 7
llevar a cabo to take place, 8
llevar una vida tranquila to lead a peaceful life, 12
llevarse bien (mal) (con) to get along well (poorly) (with) each other, 10
llorar to cry, 8
llover (ue) to rain, 4
lluvia rain
lo que *pron.* what, 10
lobo wolf, 12
Localizador Uniforme de Mecursos *m.* URL, 15
lógico *adj.* logical, 12

logotipo logotype, R2
lograr to succeed
luchar por to fight for, R1
luego *adv.* then, 10
lugar *m.* place, 3
lujoso *adj.* luxurious, 7
luna de miel honeymoon, 10
lunes *m.* Monday, 1
luz *f.* light, 1

M
madrastra stepmother, 2
madre *f.* mother, 2
madrina godmother, 2
maestro(a) teacher, 1
maleta suitcase, 9
malo *adj.* bad, 2
mamá mother, 2
mamífero mammal, 12
mandar (cartas) to send (letters), 1
mando popular popular rule, 14
manifestación *f.* demonstration, 14
mano *f.* hand, 5
manta blanket, 8
mantel *m.* tablecloth, 6
mantequilla butter, 6
manzana apple, 6
mañana *adv.* tomorrow, 1
mapa *m.* map, 1
maquillarse to put on makeup, 5
mar *m.* sea, 8
marcha passing, R1
mareado *adj.* dizzy, 5
mareo dizziness, 5
mariposa butterfly, 12
mariscos shellfish, seafood, 6
marrón *adj.* brown, 1
martes *m.* Tuesday, 1
marzo March, 3
Más o menos. So-so., P
   más... que more . . . than, 6
masa dough, R2
máscara mask, 8
mascota pet, 2
masticar (qu) to chew, 5
matemáticas math, 1
matrícula tuition, 1
matrimonio marriage, 10
mayo May, 3
mayor older, 6
   el mayor oldest, 6
mayoría majority, 1
mecánico(a) mechanic, 11
mechado shredded, 6
medianoche *f.* midnight, 1
medias stockings, 7
medicina medicine, 1
médico *m./f.* physician, doctor, 5; *adj.* medical, 5
medio ambiente environment, 12
mediodía *m.* noon, 1

medio(a) hermano(a) half brother (sister), 2

medios de comunicación means of communication, 14

mejillas cheeks, 5

mejor better, 6

   el mejor best, 6

menor younger, 6

   el menor youngest, 6

menos... que less . . . than, 6

mensaje *m.* message, 15

   mensaje electrónico email, R4

menú *m.* menu, 6

mercado (al aire libre) (outdoor) market, 3

merienda snack time, 3

mes *m.* month, 3

mesa table, 4

mesita coffee (side) table, 4

metrópolis *f.* metropolis, 12

mexicano *adj.* Mexican, 2

mi *adj.* my, 2

miércoles *m.* Wednesday, 1

mil one thousand, 4

millón million, 4

ministro *m./f.* minister, 14

mío *adj.* my, mine, 7

mirar to watch, 1

   mirar la tele to watch television, 3

mirarse to look at each other, 10

mirra myrrh, R3

mismo *adj.* same, 2

mitad *f.* half, 15

mochila backpack, 1

moda: ¡Está de última moda! It's the latest style!, 7

módem *m.* modem, 15

moderno *adj.* modern, 2

molestar to bother, 13

molesto: Me pongo molesto. I get annoyed., 8

monarquía monarchy, 14

mono monkey, 12

montar a caballo to go horseback riding, 3

morado *adj.* purple, 1

moreno *adj.* dark-haired, 2

morir (ue) to die, 4

mortalidad *f.* **infantil** infant mortality, 9

mostrar (ue) to show, 7

mover (ue) to move, 3

Mucho gusto. Nice to meet you, P

muebles *m.* furniture, 4

muerte *f.* death, R2

muerto *adj.* dead, 4; *p.p.* died, 10

mujer *f.* woman, 1

   mujer de negocios businesswoman, 11

mundo world, 9

muralla de piedra stone wall, 9

murciélago bat, 12

músculo muscle, 5

museo museum, 3

música music, 1

músico *m./f.* musician, 13

muslo thigh, 5

muy *adv.* very, P

N

nacer to be born, 2

nacionalidad *f.* nationality, 2

nada nothing, not anything, at all, 8

nadar to swim, 3

nadie nobody, no one, 8

naranja orange, 6

nariz *f.* nose, 5

natación *f.* swimming, 3

naturaleza nature, 12

naturalista *m./f.* naturalist, 12

navegar la Red to surf the Net, 15

Navidad *f.* Christmas, 8

necesario *adj.* necessary, 12

necesitar to need, 1

negocios business, 1

negro *adj.* black, 1

ni... ni neither . . . nor, 8

   ni siquiera not even, 4

nicaragüense *adj.* Nicaraguan, 2

nieta granddaughter, 2

nieto grandson, 2

nieva it's snowing, 3

nieve *f.* snow, 3

ningún, ninguno(a) none, not any, 8

Noche Vieja *f.* New Year's Eve, 8

Nochebuena Christmas Eve, 8

nombre *m.* first name, 2

norte *m.* north, 9

norteamericano *adj.* North American, American, 2

nosotros(as) *pron.* we, P

noticias news, 13

noticiero newscast, 14

novecientos nine hundred, 4

noventa ninety, 2

novia girlfriend, 1; bride, 10

noviazgo courtship, 10

noviembre November, 3

novio boyfriend, 1; groom, 10

nuera daughter-in-law, 2

nuestro *adj.* our, 2

nueve nine, P

nuevo *adj.* new, 2

número number, P; shoe size, 7

nunca *adv.* never, 3

   nunca más *adv.* never again, 3

O

o *conj.* or, 3

   o... o either . . . or, 8

objeto object, 1

obra (de arte) work (of art), 13

obra maestra masterpiece, 4

obrero(a) worker; laborer, 11

océano ocean, 8

ochenta eighty, 2

ocho eight, P

ochocientos eight hundred, 4

octubre October, 3

ocupado *adj.* busy, 4

ocuparse de to take charge of, R5

oeste *m.* west, 9

oferta sale (*Lat. Am.*)

oficina office, 1

   oficina de correos post office, 3

ofrecer (zc) to offer, 9

oído inner ear, 5

ojalá que I wish that, 12

ojo eye, 5

ola wave, R1

oler to smell, 4

olvidar to forget, 8

once eleven, P

ópera opera, 13

oponer to oppose, 14

oposición *f.* competitive examination for entrance into a school or job, 1

orar to pray, 8

ordenado *adj.* neat, 4

oreja (outer) ear, 5

orgulloso *adj.* proud, R5

oro gold, R3

orquesta band, 10

orquídea orchid, 12

oso bear, 12

otoño fall, 3

otra vez *adv.* again, 10

P

paciente *adj.* patient, 2; noun *m./f.* patient, 5

padrastro stepfather, 2

padre *m.* father, 2

padrino(a) godfather (godmother), 2

pagado *adj.* paid, R1

pagar to pay, 1

   pagar a plazos to pay in installments, 11

   pagar en efectivo (con cheque) to pay in cash (by check), 7

página de bienvenida (de entrada, de presentación, inicial, principal, de la Red) home page, 15

página web web page, 15

país (*m.*) **en vías de desarrollo** developing country, 12

paisaje *m.* landscape, R2

pájaro bird, 2

palabra word, 1

palo de golf golf club, 3

pan (tostado) *m.* bread (toast), 6

panameño *adj.* Panamanian, 2

panelista *m./f.* guest on a talk show, 13

pantalla screen, 1

pantalones (cortos) *m.* pants (shorts), 7

pantera panther, 12

pantorilla calf (of leg), 5

papá *m.* father, 2

papas (fritas) (french fried) potatoes, 6

papel *m.* paper, 1; role, 13

papelería stationery store, 3

par *m.* pair, 7

para *prep.* for

   para colmo on top of that, 4

   para que *conj.* so that, 13

   ¿Para qué? For what purpose?, 8

paraguas *m.* umbrella, 7

paraguayo *adj.* Paraguayan, 2

parar(se) to stop, 9

parecer to appear, 1

parecido *adj.* similar, R1

pared *f.* wall, 4

pareja couple, 10

pariente *m./f.* relative, 2

parque *m.* park, 3

partido game, 3

   partido político political party, 14

pasado: (la semana, el mes, el año) pasado(a) last (week, month, year), 6

pasajero(a) passenger, 9

pasantía internship, R4

pasaporte *m.* passport, 9

pasar to spend (time); to pass, 1

   pasar la aspiradora to vacuum, 4

   pasar por to go through, 9

   pasarlo bien (mal) to have a good (bad) time, 8

pasatiempo pastime, 3

Pascua Easter, Passover, Christmas, 8

pasear en canoa/velero to go canoeing/sailing, 8

paseo stroll, 7

pasillo aisle, 9

paso step, 7

pastel *m.* cake, 8

pastilla pill, 5

patinar (en línea) to (in-line) skate, 3

patines (en línea) *m.* (in-line) skates, 3

patrón *m.* pattern, 7

pavo turkey, 6

paz *f.* peace, 14

peatonal *adj.* pedestrian, R3

pecho chest, 5

pedir (i, i) to ask for, 4; to order (food), 6; to request, 9

   pedir prestado to borrow, 11

pedir un aumento to ask for a raise, 11
peinarse to comb one's hair, 5
película movie, film, 13
    película clásica classic film, 13
    película de acción action film, 13
    película de arte art film, 13
    película de ciencia ficción science fiction film, 13
    película de horror horror film, 13
    película de intriga (misterio) mystery film, 13
    película del oeste western film, 13
    película extranjera foreign film, 13
    película romántica romantic film, 13
peligro: en peligro de extinción in danger of extinction, 12
peligroso *adj.* dangerous
pelo hair, 5
peluquería hair salon, 3
peluquero(a) hairstylist, 11
pensar (ie) to think, 4
pensión *f.* boardinghouse, 1
penúltimo second to the last, 15
peor worse, 6
    el peor worst, 6
pequeño *adj.* small, 2
    ¡Me quedan muy pequeños! They're too small!
perder (ie) to lose; to miss (a function), 4
perdón pardon me, excuse me, P
perezoso *adj.* lazy, 2
perezoso con tres dedos three-toed sloth, 12
perfil *m.* profile, R1
periódico newspaper, 14
periodismo journalism, 1
periodista *m./f.* journalist, 11
período de sequía dry season, 5
pero *conj.* but, 3
perro dog, 2
peruano *adj.* Peruvian, 2
pesado *adj.* heavy (meal, food), 6
pescado fish (when caught), 6
pescar (qu) to fish, 3
pestañas eyelashes, 5
petróleo petroleum, 12
pez *m.* fish (alive), 2
picar (qu) to eat appetizers; to nibble, 6; to bite, 12
pie *m.* foot, 5
piedra stone, 4
piel *f.* skin, 5
pierna leg, 5
piloto *m./f.* pilot, 9
pimentero pepper shaker, 6

pimienta pepper, 6
pincho skewer, R3
pintarse to put on makeup, 5
pintor(a) painter, 13
pintura painting, 1
piscina pool, 3
piso floor, 4
pizarra chalkboard, 1
plancha iron, 4
planchar (la ropa) to iron (clothes), 4
plataforma de operación operating platform (system), 15
plato plate, 6
    plato principal main dish, 6
playa beach, 8
plaza plaza, 3
plomero(a) plumber, 11
pluma fountain pen, 1; feather, R2
pobre *adj.* poor, 2
poder (ue) to be able, 4
    No puedo (comer) más. I can't (eat) any more., 6
poder *m.* power, 14
poesía poetry, 13
poeta *m./f.* poet, 13
policía *m.* **(mujer** *f.* **policía)** police officer, 11
política politics, 14
    política internacional international policy, 14
político *m./f.* politician, 14
pollo (asado) (roast) chicken, 6
poner to put (on), 3; to turn on (TV); to show (a movie), 13
    poner la mesa to set the table, 4
ponerse + *adjective* to become, to get + adjective, 8
    ponerse (la ropa) to put on (one's clothes), 5
popular *adj.* popular, 13
por *prep.* for
    por casualidad by the way, 11
    por ciento percent, 7
    por ejemplo for example, 11
    por eso that's why, 11
    por favor please, P
    por fin *adv.* finally, 10
    por la (mañana, tarde, noche) in the (morning, afternoon/evening), 1
    por otro lado on the other hand
    ¿Por qué? Why?, P
    porque because, 3
    por supuesto of course, 2
portarse bien (mal) to behave well (poorly), 8
portugués *m.* Portuguese (language), 1
postal *m.* postcard, 2

postre *m.* dessert, 6
practicar (qu) to practice, 1
preferir (ie) to prefer, 4
pregunta question, P
preguntar to ask (a question), 1
prenda article of clothing, 7
prender to turn on, 15
prendido *adj.* on, 15
prensa press, 14
preocupación *f.* concern, R2
preocuparse to worry, 11
preocupado *adj.* worried, 4
preparar to prepare, 6
presidente *m./f.* **de la universidad** president of the university, 1
presión *f.* pressure, R5
préstamo loan, 11
prestar to loan, 11
presupuesto budget, 11
primavera spring, 3
primero first, 10
    a primera vista at first sight, 10
    primera vez first time, 5
primo(a) cousin, 2
privado *adj.* private, 9
probarse (ue) to try on, 7
problema *m.* problem, 5
procedente de arriving from, 9
procesión *f.* parade, 8
profesión *f.* profession, 11
profesor(a) professor, 1
programa (de CD-ROM) *m.* (CD-ROM) program, 15
    programa de concursos game show, 13
    programa de entrevistas talk show, 13
    programa deportivo sports program, 13
programador(a) programmer, 11
programar to program, 15
progresista *adj.* progressive, 2
prometer to promise, 10
pronóstico del tiempo weather report (forecast), 13
propina: dejar una (buena) propina to leave a (good) tip, 6
propósito purpose, 2
proteger to protect, 12
protestar to protest, 14
proveedor *m.* **de servicios Internet** Internet service provider, 15
proyecto project, 11
pueblo town, 3
puerta door, 4; gate, 9
puerto port, 9
puertorriqueño *adj.* Puerto Rican, 2
puesto stand, 7; job, position, 11; *p.p.* put, 10

pulmones *m.* lungs, 5
pulsera bracelet, 7
punta end, R2
puro *adj.* pure, 12

Q

que *pron.* that, which, who, 3
¿Qué? What? Which?, P
    ¡Qué bueno! Wonderful!, 2
    ¡Qué casualidad! What a coincidence!, P
    ¿Qué hay? What's new? (informal), P
    ¿Qué hora es? What time is it?, 1
    ¿Qué tal? What's up? (informal), P
    ¿Qué te apetece? What would you like (to eat)?, 6
quedarle (a uno) to fit (someone), 7
    ¿Cómo me queda? How does it look?, 7
quedarse to stay, 9
quehacer doméstico *m.* chore, 4
quejarse de to complain about, 9
quemar to burn, 8
querer (ie) to want; to love, 4
    Yo quisiera... I would like . . ., 6
queso cheese, 6
quetzal *m.* bird with long beautiful feathers found in Central America, 12
quien *pron.* who, 10
    ¿Quién(es)? Who?, P
química chemistry, 1
quince fifteen, P
quinientos five hundred, 4
quinqué *m.* oil lamp, R2
quitar la mesa to clear the table, 4
quitarse to take off, 5

R

radiografía X-ray, 5
raíz *f.* root, 13
ramo bouquet, 10
rana frog, 12
ranchero(a) rancher, 11
rascacielos *m.* skyscraper, 12
rato: un buen rato a good time, 3
ratón *m.* mouse (of computer), 15
razón *f.* reason, 12
reaccionar to react, 8
real *adj.* royal, R2
rebaja sale (Spain), reduction (in price), 7
rebajar to reduce (in price), 7
rebelde *adj.* rebellious, 2
rebotar to bounce (a check), 11

recepción *f.* front desk, 9; reception, 10
recepcionista *m./f.* receptionist, 9
receta prescription, 5
recibir to receive, 2
recibo receipt, 11
reciclar to recycle, 12
recién casados *m.* newlyweds, 10
recoger (j) to pick up; to claim, 9
recomendar (ie) to recommend, 6
recordar (ue) to remember, 8
rector(a) de la universidad president of the university, 1
recursos naturales natural resources, 12
redada raid, 14
reducir to reduce, 14
reforestar to reforest, 12
reforma reform, 14
refresco soft drink, 6
refrigerador *m.* refrigerator, 4
refugio natural wildlife preserve, 12
regalar to give (as a gift), 9
regalo gift, 8
regar (ie) las plantas to water the plants, 4; to irrigate, 12
regio *adj.* great, R3
registrarse to register, 9
regresar (a casa) to return (home), 1
reinar to rule, 14
relaciones sentimentales *f.* relationships, 10
rellenar to stuff, 6
reloj *m.* clock, 1; watch, 7
rendimiento return (investment), R4
renunciar to resign, 11
reportaje *m.* report, 14
reportero(a) reporter, 11
republicano *adj.* republican, 14
reseña review, R5
reserva reservation, 9
reservado *adj.* reserved, 2
resfriarse to catch a cold, 5
resfrío cold, 5
residencia dormitory, 1
resolver (ue) to solve, resolve, 12
respeto respect, 11
responsable *adj.* responsible, 2
restaurante *m.* restaurant, 3
restaurar to refresh, 5
retrato portrayal, R3
 retrato al óleo oil painting, 13
reunión *f.* meeting, 11
reunirse con to get together with, 8; to meet, 11
revista magazine, 14

Revolución (f.) cubana Cuban Revolution, 1
rico *adj.* rich, 2; delicious, 6
ridículo *adj.* ridiculous, 12
riesgo risk, R2
rinoceronte *m.* rhinoceros, 12
río river, 8
rodeado *adj.* surrounded, 9
rodear to surround, 11
rodilla knee, 5
rojo *adj.* red, 1
romper (con) to break up (with), 10
ropa clothes, 5
rostro face, R3
rubio *adj.* blond(e), 2
rugir (j) to roar, R3
ruido noise, 12
ruso Russian (language), 1; *adj.* Russian, 2

S

sábado Saturday, 1
saber to know (how), 3
sabor *m.* flavor, 5
sabroso *adj.* tasty, 6
sacar (qu) to withdraw (money), 11
 sacar fotos to take pictures, 3
 sacar la basura to take out the garbage, 4
sagrado *adj.* sacred, 8
sal *f.* salt, 6
sala living room, 4
 sala de clase classroom, 1
 sala de conferencias / para banquetes conference/banquet room, 9
 sala de espera waiting room, 5
 sala de urgencias/emergencia emergency room, 5
salario salary, 11
salero salt shaker, 6
salida departure, 9
 salida de emergencia emergency exit, 9
salir (con) to leave, to go out (with), 3
 salir del programa to quit the program, 15
salón (la sala) de charla *m.* chat room, 15
salsa sauce, 6
salud *f.* health, 5
 ¡Salud! Cheers!, 6
saludar(se) to greet (each other), P
salvadoreño *adj.* Salvadoran, 2
sandalia sandal, 7
sándwich *m.* sandwich, 6
sano *adj.* healthy, 5
santo(a) saint, 2
sapo toad, 12
satélite *m.* satellite, 15

sciencias science, 1
secadora clothes dryer, 4
secarse (qu) to dry off, 5
sección *f.* **de (no) fumar** *f.* (non)smoking section, 9
secretario(a) secretary, 1
seda silk, 7
segundo *adj.* second, 2
seguir (i) to follow, to continue, 4
seis six, P
seiscientos six hundred, 4
selva jungle, 12
 selva nubosa tropical rain forest, 12
semana week, 1
 Semana Santa Holy Week, 8
sembrar (ie) to plant, 12
senado senate, 14
senador(a) senator, 14
sencillez *f.* simplicity, R2
sencillo *adj.* simple
sentir (ie) to be sorry, 12
 sentirse (bien/mal) to feel (good/bad), 5
señor (Sr.) Mr., sir, P
señora (Sra.) Mrs., ma'am, P
señorita (Srta.) Miss, P
separación *f.* separation, 10
separado *adj.* separated, 2
separarse (de) to separate (from), 10
septiembre September, 3
ser to be, P
servicio de habitación (cuarto) room service, 9
servidor *m.* server, 15
servilleta napkin, 6
servir (i) to serve, 4
sesenta sixty, 2
setecientos seven hundred, 4
setenta seventy, 2
si if, 15
sí yes, P
sicología psychology, 1
siempre always, 3
siete seven, P
silla chair, 1
sillón *m.* easy chair, arm chair, 4
simpático *adj.* nice, 2
sin *prep.* without, 8
 sin esfuerzo alguno effortless, 7
 sin que *conj.* without, 13
sincero *adj.* sincere, 2
sino *conj.* rather, 5
síntoma *m.* symptom, 5
sinvergüenza *m./f.* shameless person, 4
siquiatra *m./f.* psychiatrist, 11
sistema (m.) nervioso nervous system, 5
smoking *m.* tuxedo
sobre *prep.* about, R1; on; over

sobrepoblación *f.* overpopulation, 12
sobrina niece, 2
sobrino nephew, 2
sociología sociology, 1
sofá *m.* sofa, couch, 4
soldado (la mujer soldado) soldier, 11
solicitar un puesto to apply for a job, 11
solicitud *f.* application (form), 11
solo *adj.* alone, 5
sólo only, P
soltero *adj.* single, 2
sombra shade, R5
sombreado *adj.* shaded, R2
sombrero hat, 7
sopa soup, 6
sorprender to surprise, 12
sorteo raffle, 7
sótano basement, 4
su *adj.* his, her, its, their, your (formal), 2
suavidad *f.* smoothness, 3
subida climb, 5
subir to climb, to go up, 9
subsiguiente subsequent, R2
sucio *adj.* dirty, 4
suegra mother-in-law, 2
suegro father-in-law, 2
sueldo salary, 11
suéter *m.* sweater, 7
sufrir to suffer, 9
supermercado supermarket, 3
suplir to supply, 12
sur *m.* south, 9
suyo *adj.* your, yours, his, her, hers, its, 7

T

tacaño *adj.* stingy, 2
tajada slice, 6
talar to cut down (trees), 12
talla size (clothing), 7
también *adv.* also, too, 8
tampoco *adv.* neither, not either, 8
tan pronto como *conj.* as soon as, 13
tan... como as . . . as, 6
tanto(a)... como as much . . . as, 6
tantos(as)... como as many . . . as, 6
tarde *adv.* late, 1
tarea homework, 1
tarjeta card
 tarjeta de cajero automático ATM card, 11
 tarjeta de crédito credit card, 7
 tarjeta de cheque check card, 11

tarjeta de presentación business card, 2

taza cup, 3

té (helado) *m.* (iced) tea, 6

teatro theater, 13

techo roof, 4

teclado keyboard, 15

técnico *m./f.* technician, 11

tecnológico technological, 15

tela fabric, 7

teléfono celular/portátil cellular phone, 15

telenovela soap opera, 13

teletrabajar to telecommute, 15

televidente *m./f.* television viewer, 13

telón *m.* curtain, R2

temprano *adv.* early, 1

tenedor *m.* fork, 6

tener (ie) to have, P

  tener calor to be hot, 4

  tener celos to be jealous, 4

  tener dolor de cabeza to have a headache, 5

  tener escalofríos to have chills, 5

  tener éxito to be successful, 2

  tener fiebre to have a fever, 5

  tener frío to be cold, 4

  tener ganas de to feel like (doing something), 4

  tener gripe to have a cold, 5

  tener hambre to be hungry, 2

  tener lugar to take place, 6

  tener miedo (de) to be afraid (of something), 4

  tener náuseas to be nauseous, 5

  tener paciencia to be patient, 4

  tener prisa to be in a hurry, 2

  tener que to have to (do something), 3

  tener razón to be right, 2

  tener sed to be thirsty, 2

  tener sueño to be tired, sleepy, 2

  tener tos to have a cough, 5

tercero *adj.* third, 2

terminal de autobuses *f.* bus station, 9

terminar to finish, end, 1

terraza terrace, 4

terrorismo terrorism, 14

testigo *m./f.* witness, 10

tía aunt, 2

tiempo weather, 3

tienda store, 3

tienda de antigüedades (de música [de discos], de ropa) antique (music, clothing) store, 3

tierra land, earth, 12

tigre *m.* tiger, 12

tímido *adj.* shy, timid, 2

tío uncle, 2

tirar to throw, 10

tiza chalk, 1

tobillo ankle, 5

tocador *m.* dresser, 4

tocar (qu) to touch; to play an instrument, 1

todos all

  todos los años (días, meses, etc.) every year (day, month, etc.), 10

tolerante *adj.* tolerant, 2

tomar (clases/exámenes) to take (classes/tests); to drink, 1

  tomar el sol to sunbathe, 3

  tomarle la temperatura (a alguien) to take (someone's) temperature, 5

tomate *m.* tomato, 6

tonto *adj.* silly, foolish, 2

tortuga turtle, 12

tos *f.* cough, 5

toser to cough, 5

tostadora toaster, 4

trabajador(a) *adj.* hardworking, 2

trabajar to work, 1

trabajo work, 11

traductor(a) translator, 11

traer to bring, 3

tráfico traffic, 12

traje *m.* suit, 7

traje de baño bathing suit, 7

tranquilo *adj.* tranquil, peaceful, 12

transferir (ie, i) (fondos) to transfer (funds), 11

transporte *m.* público public transportation, 12

tratarse de to be about, R2

trato hecho it's a deal, 14

trece thirteen, P

treinta thirty, P

tres three, P

trescientos three hundred, 4

triste *adj.* sad, 4

tu *adj.* your (informal), 2

tú *pron.* you, P

tumba tomb, 7

turismo tourism, 1

tuyo *adj.* your, yours, 7

U

umbroso *adj.* shadowed, R2

un(a) *indef. art.* a, an

universidad *f.* university, 1

uno one, P

unos(as) *indef. art.* some

uña fingernail, 5

uruguayo *adj.* Uruguayan, 2

usar to use, 1; to wear, 7

usted(es) *pron.* you, P

V

valiente *adj.* brave, 2

valle *m.* valley, 12

vamos a ver let's see, 6

vaqueros jeans, 7

vaso glass, 6

vecino(a) neighbor, R1

vegetal *m.* vegetable, 6

veinte twenty, P

veintidós twenty-two, P

veintiséis twenty-six, P

veintitrés twenty-three, P

veintiuno twenty-one, P

vela candle, 8

vendedor(a) salesperson, 11

vender to sell, 2

venezolano *adj.* Venezuelan, 2

venir (ie) to come, 4

  ¡Venga! Come on!, 3

ventaja advantage, 7

ventana window, 4

ventanilla window, 9

ver to see, 3

  Nos vemos. See you later., P

verano summer, 3

verdad *f.* truth, 1

verde *adj.* green, 1

verdura vegetable, 6

vestido dress, 7

vestido de gala dressed elegantly, 10

vestirse (i) to get dressed, 5

veterinario *m./f.* veterinarian, 11

vez time

  a la vez at the same time, R1

  a veces sometimes, 3

  de vez en cuando occasionally, 6

  dos (tres, etc.) veces twice (three times, etc.), 10

  muchas veces often, 10

  muy pocas veces rarely, 2

  otra vez *adv.* again, 10

  una vez *adv.* once, 10

viajar to travel, 1

viaje *m.* trip, 9

vida life, 10

  vida nocturna night life, R3

videocámara video camera, 15

videocasete *m.* videotape, 15

videocasetera VCR, 15

viejo *adj.* old, 2

viernes *m.* Friday, 1

vigente *adj.* existing, 14

vinagre *m.* vinegar, 6

vino (blanco, tinto) (white, red) wine, 6

visitar to visit, 1

  visitar un museo to visit a museum, 3

visto *p.p.* seen, 10

  a primera vista at first sight, 10

viuda widow

viudo *adj.* widowed, 2; *noun* widower

vivienda housing, 4

vivir to live, 2

volcán *m.* volcano, 12

volcánico *adj.* volcanic, R3

vólibol *m.* volleyball, 3

volver (ue) to return, 4

vosotros(as) *pron.* you, P

votar to vote, 14

voto vote, 14

vuelo (sin escala) (nonstop) flight, 9

vuelto *p.p.* returned, 10

vuestro *adj.* your, yours, 2

Y

y and, 3

ya *adv.* already, 9

yerno son-in-law, 2

yo *pron.* I, P

yunta cufflink, 7

Z

zapatería shoe store, 7

zapato shoe, 7

  zapato de tacón (alto) high heels, 7

  zapato de tenis (deportivo) tennis shoe (sneaker), 3

zoología zoology, 1

zorro fox, 12

GLOSARIO INGLÉS-ESPAÑOL

A

a, an un(a) *indef. art.*
abortion aborto, 14
about sobre *prep.*, R1
accelerated acelerado *adj.*, 12
accessory accesorio, 7
accompany acompañar, 10
account cuenta, 11
accountant contador(a), 11
accounting contabilidad *f.*, 1
ache dolor *m.*, 5
across from enfrente de *prep.*, 9
act actuar, 13
action acción *f.*, 3
activity actividad *f.*, 3
actor actor *m.*, 13
actress actriz *f.*, 13
advance avance *m.*, 15
advantage ventaja, 7
advisor consejero(a), 1
affection cariño, 10
after después (de) (que) *conj.*, 13
afterward después *adv.*, 10
again otra vez *adv.*, 10
against contra *prep.*, 1; en contra, R4
age edad *f.*, 2
agree estar de acuerdo, 10
air aire *m.*, 12
air conditioning aire acondicionado, 9
airline aerolínea, 9
airline agent agente *m./f.* de la aerolínea, 9
airport aeropuerto, 9
aisle pasillo, 9
alarm alarma, 15
alarm clock despertador *m.*, 4
all todos
    All Saints' Day Día de Todos los Santos, 8
allergy alergia, 5
alliance alianza, 15
alligator caimán *m.*, 12
allow dejar, 13
almost (always) casi (siempre) *adv.*, 10
alone solo *adj.*, 5
already ya *adv.*, 9
also también *adv.*, 8
although aunque *conj.*, 13
always siempre, 3
ambassador embajador(a), R2
ambulance ambulancia, 5
amend enmendar (ie), 14
amendment enmienda, 14
ammenities comodidades *f.*, 9
among entre *prep.*, 4
and y, 3
angry enojado *adj.*, 4
animal animal *m.*, 12
ankle tobillo, 5

annoyed: I get annoyed. Me pongo molesto., 8
answer contestar, 1
answering machine contestador automático *m.*, 15
ant hormiga, 12
antacid antiácido, 5
antibiotic antibiótico, 5
antique antigüedad *f.*, 7
antique store tienda de antigüedades, 3
any algún, alguno(a/os/as), 8
anybody, anyone alguien, 8
anything algo, 8
apartment apartamento, 1
appear parecer, 1
applaud aplaudir, 10
apple manzana, 6
applicant candidato(a), 11
application (form) solicitud *f.*, 11
apply for a job solicitar un puesto, 11
appreciate apreciar, 13
approach acercar (qu)
approve; approve aprobar (ue), 14
April abril, 3
Arab árabe *adj.*, 2
archbishop arzobispo, 8
architect arquitecto(a), 11
architecture arquitectura, 13
Argentine argentino *adj.*, 2
argue discutir, 14
arm brazo, 5
arm chair sillón *m.*, 4
armoire armario, 4
army ejército, 14
around alrededor de
arrival llegada, 9
arrive llegar, 1
arriving from procedente de, 9
arrogant arrogante *adj.*, 2
art arte *m./f.*, 1
article of clothing prenda, 7
artist artista *m./f.*, 13
artistic artístico *adj.*, 2
as . . . as tan... como, 6
as many . . . as tantos(as)... como, 6
as much . . . as tanto(a)... como, 6
as soon as tan pronto como *conj.*, 13
ask (a question) preguntar, 1
ask for pedir (i, i), 4
    ask for a raise pedir un aumento, 11
aspirin aspirina, 5
assassinate asesinar, R4
assistant ayudante *m./f.*
at a *prep.*
    at first sight a primera vista, 10
    at last finalmente *adv.*, 10
    at the last minute a última hora, 8

    at the same time a la vez, R1
    At what time? ¿A qué hora?, 1
athletic atlético *adj.*, 2
ATM cajero automático, 11
    ATM card tarjeta de cajero automático, 11
atmosphere: pleasant atmosphere ambiente *m.* ameno, R2
attend asistir a, 2
August agosto, 3
aunt tía, 2
author autor(a), 13
avocado aguacate *m.*, 6
awesome bárbaro *adj.*, R3

B

back espalda, 5
backpack mochila, 1
bad malo *adj.*, 2
bag bolsa, 7
baggage (carry-on) equipaje (de mano) *m.*, 9
balance equilibrio, 12
balcony balcón *m.*, 4
ballet ballet *m.*, 13
ballpoint pen bolígrafo, 1
banana banana/banano, 6
band orquesta, 10
bank banco, 3
banker banquero(a), 11
banquet banquete *m.*, 10
    banquet room sala para banquetes, 9
barely apenas *adv.*, 4
bargain: It's a bargain! ¡Es una ganga!, 7
baseball béisbol *m.*, 3
baseball cap gorra de béisbol, 7
basement sótano, 4
basketball baloncesto, 3
bat murciélago, 12
bathing suit traje de baño, 7
bathroom cuarto de baño, 4
bathroom sink lavabo, 4
bathtub bañera, 4
be ser, P; estar, 3
    be able poder (ue), 4
    be about tratarse de, R2
    be afraid (of something) tener miedo (de), 4
    be born nacer, 2
    be cold tener frío, 4
    be delayed demorarse, 13
    be frightened asustarse, 8
    be glad alegrarse (de), 12
    be healthy estar sano(a), 5
    be hot tener calor, 4
    be hungry tener hambre, 2
    be in a hurry tener prisa, 2
    be jealous tener celos, 4
    be nauseous tener náuseas, 5

    be online estar conectado(a) (en línea), 15
    be painful (to someone) dolerle (ue) (a alguien), 5
    be patient tener paciencia, 4
    be pleasing (to someone) gustar, 3
    be right tener razón, 2
    be sick estar enfermo(a), 5
    be sleepy tener sueño, 2
    be sorry sentir (ie), 12
    be successful tener éxito, 2
    be thirsty tener sed, 2
    be tired tener sueño, 2
beach playa, 8
beach resort balneario, 8
bear oso, 12
beautiful bello *adj.*, 12
because porque, 3
become + adjective ponerse + *adjective*, 8
bed cama, 4
bedroom dormitorio, 4
beer cerveza, 6
before antes (de) que *conj.*, 13
begin comenzar (ie), empezar (ie), 4
behave well (poorly) portarse bien (mal), 8
behind detrás de *prep.*, 4
believe creer, 2
below abajo *adv.*, 3; debajo de *prep.*, 4
belt cinturón *m.*, 7
benefits beneficios, 11
beside al lado de *prep.*, 4
best el mejor, 6
better mejor, 6
between entre *prep.*, 4
beverage bebida, 6
bicycle bicicleta, 3
big grande *adj.*, 2
bilingual bilingüe *adj.*, 2
bill cuenta, 6; factura, 11
biology biología, 1
bird pájaro, 2; ave *m.*, 12
    bird with long beautiful feathers found in Central America quetzal *m.*, 12
birthday cumpleaños *m.*, 8
bite picar (qu), 12
black bean caraota negra, 6
black negro *adj.*, 1
blanket manta, 8
blond(e) rubio *adj.*, 2
blouse blusa, 7
blue azul *adj.*, 1
blue jeans jeans *m. pl.*, 7
board abordar, 9
boardinghouse pensión *f.*, 1
body cuerpo humano, 5
boil hervir (ie), 3
Bolivian boliviano *adj.*, 2

bone hueso, 5
book (text) libro (de texto), 1
bookshelf estante *m.*, 4
bookstore librería, 1
boot bota, 7
    patent leather ankle boots
        botines de charol *m.*, R5
border frontera, 12
bore aburrir, 13
bored aburrido *adj.*, 4
borrow pedir prestado, 11
boss jefe *m./f.*, 11
bother molestar, 13
bounce (a check) rebotar, 11
bouquet ramo, 10
boy chico, 7
boyfriend novio, 1
bracelet pulsera, 7
brain cerebro, 5
brave valiente *adj.*, 2
Brazilian brasileño *adj.*, 2
bread (toast) pan (tostado) *m.*, 6
break up (with) romper (con), 10
breakfast desayuno, 6
bride novia, 10
bring traer, 3
brother hermano, 2
brother-in-law cuñado, 2
brown marrón *adj.*, 1
brush one's teeth cepillarse los
    dientes, 5
buckle the seat belt abrochar el
    cinturón de seguridad, 9
budget presupuesto, 11
building edificio, 1
burn quemar, 8
bus autobús *m. (Spain)*, P;
    camión *m. (Mexico)*, P;
    guagua *(Puerto Rico)*, P
bus station terminal de
    autobuses *f.*, 9
business negocios, 1; empresa, 11
    business administration
        administración *f.*
        de empresas, 1
    business card tarjeta
        de presentación, 2
    business center centro
        de negocios, 9
    businessman hombre
        de negocios, 11
    businesswoman mujer
        de negocios, 11
busy ocupado *adj.*, 4
but pero *conj.*, 3
butcher shop carnicería, 3
butter mantequilla, 6
butterfly mariposa, 12
button botón *m.*, 7
buy comprar, 1
by the way por casualidad,
    11
Bye. Chao. *(informal)*, P

C

cabin cabina, 9
café café *m.*, 3

cafeteria cafetería, 1
cake pastel *m.*, 8
calculator calculadora, 1
calendar calendario, 1
calf (of leg) pantorilla, 5
call llamar, 1
camel camello, R3
camera cámara, 3
campaign campaña, 14
campus campus *m.*, 1
Canadian canadiense *adj.*, 2
candidate candidato(a), 11
candle vela, 8
car automóvil *m.*; carro; coche
    m., P
caramel custard (homemade)
    flan (casero) *m.*, 6
card tarjeta
cardboard cartón *m.*, 4
cargo ship barco de carga, 11
carpet alfombra, 4
carpenter carpintero(a), 11
carry llevar, 7
cartoon dibujo animado, 13
cash efectivo, 7
cashier cajero(a), 11
cat gato, 2
catch a cold resfriarse, 5
catch agarrar, 10
celebrate celebrar, 8
celebration celebración *f.*, 8
cellular phone teléfono celular/
    portátil, 15
chain cadena, R3
chair silla, 1
chalk tiza, 1
chalkboard pizarra, 1
challenge desafío, 14
change cambiar, 7
channel (TV) canal *m.*, 13
charge cargo, 11
charity limosna, 13
chase caza, 7
chat room salón (la sala) de
    charla *m.*, 15
cheap barato *adj.*, 7
check cuenta, 6; cheque *m.*, 7
    check card tarjeta de cheque, 11
    The check, please. La cuenta,
        por favor., 6
check the luggage facturar el
    equipaje, 9
checking account cuenta
    corriente, 11
cheeks mejillas, 5
Cheers! ¡Salud! , 6
cheese queso, 6
chemistry química, 1
chest pecho, 5
chew masticar (qu), 5
chicken (roast) pollo (asado), 6
Chilean chileno *adj.*, 2
chimney chimenea, 4
Chinese chino *adj.*, 2; (language)
    chino, 1
choose escoger, 9
chore quehacer doméstico *m.*, 4

Christmas Eve Nochebuena, 8
Christmas Pascua, Navidad *f.*, 8
church iglesia, 3
cinnamon canela, 3
citizen ciudadano(a), 14
city block cuadra, 9
claim recoger (j), 9
clam: thumbnail-size clam
    chipichipi *m.*, 6
classical clásico *adj.*, 13
classmate compañero(a)
    de clase, 1
classroom sala de clase, 1
clean limpio *adj.*, 4
clean the house limpiar la casa, 4
clear the table quitar la mesa, 4
clear: it's clear está despejado, 3
click (on) hacer click (sobre), 15
climb subida, 5
    climb subir, 9
clock reloj *m.*, 1
close cerrar (ie), 4
closet armario, 4
clothes dryer secadora, 4
clothes ropa, 5
clothing store tienda de ropa, 3
cloudy: it's cloudy está
    nublado, 3
clove clavo, 3
coast costa, 8
coffee café *m.*, 6
coincidence: What a coincidence!
    ¡Qué casualidad!, P
cold resfrío, catarro, 5
    it's cold hace frío, 3
Colombian colombiano *adj.*, 2
color color *m.*, 1
Columbus Day Día de la Raza, 8
comb one's hair peinarse, 5
come venir (ie), 4
    Come on! ¡Venga! , 3
comedy comedia, 13
comfort comodidad *f.*, R3
comfortable cómodo *adj.*, 9
commercial anuncio, 13
compact disc (CD) disco
    compacto, 15
company: private company
    empresa privada, R4
competitive examination for
    entrance into a school
    or job oposición *f.*, 1
complain about quejarse de, 9
composer compositor(a), 13
computer computadora, 1
computer science computación
    f., 1
concern preocupación *f.*, R2
concert concierto, 13
condiment condimento, 6
condominium condominio, 4
conference room sala de
    conferencias, 9
congested congestionado *adj.*, 5
congratulate felicitar, 10
    Congratulations!
        ¡Felicitaciones!, 8

congress congreso, 14
connect conectar, 15
connection conexión *f.*, 15
conservation conservación *f.*, 12
conservative conservador(a)
    adj., 2
conserve conservar, 12
constitution constitución *f.*, 14
construct construir, 12
contact lenses lentillas/lentes *m.*
    de contacto, 5
continue seguir (i), 4
cook cocinar, 6
cook, chef cocinero(a), 11
Cool! ¡Chévere!, 3
cool: it's cool hace fresco, 3
corn flour harina de maíz, 6
corporation empresa, 11
corruption corrupción *f.*, 14
cost costar (ue), 4
Costa Rican costarricense *adj.*, 2
costume disfraz *m.*, 8
cotton algodón *m.*, 7
couch sofá *m.*, 4
cough syrup jarabe *m.*, 5
cough tos *f.*, 5
    cough toser, 5
count contar (ue), 4
    count on contar con, 3
country campo, 8
coup d'etat golpe de estado *m.*, 14
couple pareja, 10
course curso, 1
court (tennis) cancha (de tenis), 3
courtship noviazgo, 10
cousin primo(a), 2
cowardly cobarde *adj.*, 2
cradle cunita, 7
crash into chocarse (qu) con, 8
create crear, R1
credit card tarjeta de crédito, 7
crime crimen *m.*, 14
crocodile cocodrilo, 12
cross cruzar, 9
cry llorar, 8
Cuban cubano *adj.*, 2
    Cuban Revolution
        Revolución *f.* cubana, 1
cufflink gemelo, yunta, 7
cultivate cultivar, 12
cup taza, 3
current actual *adj.*, 14
curtain telón *m.*, R2
customs aduana, 9
cut down (trees) talar, 12
cyberspace espacio cibernético,
    ciberespacio, 15
cycling ciclismo, 3

D

daily cotidiano *adj.*, 13; *adv.*
    diariamente, 3
dance bailar, 1
    dance baile *m.*, 1; danza, 13
dancer bailarín *m.*, bailarina, 13
dangerous peligroso *adj.*
dark-haired moreno *adj.*, 2

date (social) cita, 10
daughter hija, 2
daughter-in-law nuera, 2
day before yesterday anteayer *adv.*, 6
day día *m.*, 1
    Day of the Dead Día de los Muertos, 1
    Day of the Magi (Three Kings) Día de los Reyes Magos, 8
dazzle deslumbrar, 13
dead muerto *adj.*, 4
deal: it's a deal trato hecho, 14
dean decano(a), 1
death muerte *f.*, R2
debate debate *m.*, 14
December diciembre, 3
deer ciervo, 12
defend defender (ie), 14
defense defensa, 14
defenseless person desamparado(a), 13
delay demora, 9
delicious rico *adj.*, 6
democracy democracia, 14
democratic demócrata *adj.*, 14
demonstration manifestación *f.*, 14
dense denso *adj.*, 12
dentist dentista *m./f.*, 11
departing for con destino a, 9
department facultad *f.*, 12
departure salida, 9
deposit (money) depositar, 11
desire afán *m.*, 12
desk escritorio, 1
dessert postre *m.*, 6
destroy destruir, 12
destroyed destruido *adj.*, 12
destruction destrucción *f.*, 12
develop desarrollar, 12
development desarrollo, 12
    developing country país *m.* en vías de desarrollo, 12
diagnosis diagnóstico, 5
dictator dictador(a), 14
dictatorship dictadura, 14
dictionary diccionario, 1
die morir (ue), 4
died *p.p.* muerto, 10
diet dieta, 5
digital camera cámara digital, 15
dining room comedor *m.*, 4
dinner cena, 6
direct dirigir, 13
director director(a), 13
dirty sucio *adj.*, 4
disadvantage desventaja, 15
disconnect desconectar, 15
discount descuento, 7
discuss discutir, 14
dishwasher lavaplatos *m.*, 4
diskette disquete *m.*, 15
divorce divorcio, 10
divorced divorciado *adj.*, 2
dizziness mareo, 5

dizzy mareado *adj.*, 5
do hacer, 3
doctor médico *m./f.*, 5
documentary documental *m.*, 13
dog perro, 2
Dominican (from the Dominican Republic) dominicano *adj.*, 2
done hecho *p.p.*, 10
door puerta, 4
dormitory residencia, 1
double bed cama doble, 9
dough masa, R2
downtown centro, 3
drama drama *m.*, 13
dramatic dramático *adj.*, 2
draw dibujar, 1
dress vestido, 7
    dressed elegantly vestido de gala, 10
dresser cómoda, tocador *m.*, 4
drink tomar, 1; beber, 2
    drink coffee ir a tomar un café, 3
drug addiction drogadicción *f.*, 14
dry off secarse (qu), 5
dry season período de sequía, 5
due to debido a, R1
duty deber *m.* noun, 14

E
each cada *adv.*
ear (outer) oreja, 5; (inner) oído, 5
earache dolor de oídos *m.*, 5
early temprano *adv.*, 1
earning ganancia, R2
earring arete *m.*, 7
earth tierra, 12
east este *m.*, 9
Easter Pascua, 8
easy chair sillón *m.*, 4
eat comer, 2
    eat appetizers picar (qu), 6
    eat breakfast desayunar, 6
    eat lunch almorzar (ue), 4
    eat supper (dinner) cenar, 6
    I can't (eat) any more. No puedo (comer) más., 6
ecology ecología, 12
economic económico *adj.*, 5
economics economía, 1
education educación *f.*, 1
effortless sin esfuerzo alguno, 7
egg: hard-boiled egg huevo duro, 6
Egyptian egipcio *adj.*, 2
eight hundred ochocientos, 4
eight ocho, P
eighteen dieciocho, P
eighty ochenta, 2
either . . . or o... o, 8
elbow codo, 5
elect elegir (i, i), 14
elections elecciones *f.*, 14
electric appliance electrodomésticos, 4
electrician electricista *m./f.*, 11

elephant elefante *m.*, 12
elevator ascensor *m.*, 9
eleven once, P
eliminate eliminar, 14
email mensaje electrónico, R4; correo electrónico, 11
embark on emprender, M5
embarrassed: I get embarrassed. Me pongo avergonzado., 8
emergency exit salida de emergencia, 9
emergency room sala de urgencias/emergencia, 5
employee empleado(a), 11
employment empleo, 14
end punta, R2
    end terminar, 1
ending desenlace *m.*, R5
endless inagotable *adj.*, R1
engaged comprometido *adj.*, 10
engagement compromiso, 10
engineer ingeniero(a), 11
engineering ingeniería, 1
English (language) inglés *m.*, 1; inglés(esa) *adj.*, 2
enjoy disfrutar, 9
    Enjoy your meal! ¡Buen provecho!, 6
enter entrar, 1
environment medio ambiente, 12
environmental degradation destrucción ambiental, R4
equality igualdad *f.*, 14
equipment equipo, 15
eraser borrador *m.*, 1
even though aunque *conj.*, 13
event acontecimiento, R1
every day (week, etc.) cada día (semana, etc.), 10
    every year (day, month, etc.) todos los años (días, meses, etc.), 10
examine examinar, 5
excited emocionado *adj.*, 4
excuse me perdón, con permiso, P
exercise hacer ejercicio, 3
existing vigente *adj.*, 14
expense gasto, R1; costo, 11
expensive caro *adj.*, 7
explain explicar (qu), 9
exploit explotar, 12
extinction: in danger of extinction en peligro de extinción, 12
eye ojo, 5
eyebrows cejas, 5
eyelashes pestañas, 5

F
fabric tela, 7
face enfrentar, 13
    rostro, R3; cara, 5
factory fábrica, 12
fall asleep dormirse (ue), 5
fall in love (with) enamorarse (de), 10
fall otoño, 3

false cognate cognado falso, 1
family familia, R2
fan (sports) aficionado(a), 3
far (away) (from) lejos (de) *prep.*, 4
farm finca, 12
farm worker campesino(a), 12
farmer agricultor(a), 12
fat gordo *adj.*, 2
father papá, padre, *m.*, 2
father-in-law suegro, 2
fax machine fax *m.*, 11
feather pluma, R2
features comodidades *f.*, 9
February febrero, 3
feel (good/bad) sentirse (bien/mal), 5
feel like (doing something) tener ganas de, 4
fifteen quince, P
fifty cincuenta, 2
fight for luchar por, R1
file archivar, 2
    archivo, 15
fill out (a form) llenar, 11
film película, 13
    action film película de acción, 13
    art film película de arte, 13
    classic film película clásica, 13
    foreign film película extranjera , 13
    horror film película de horror, 13
    mystery film película de intriga (misterio), 13
    romantic film película romántica, 13
    science fiction film película de ciencia ficción, 13
    western film película del oeste, 13
finally por fin, finalmente *adv.*, 10
find encontrar, 5
fine bien *adv.*
    Fine, thanks. Bien, gracias., P
finger dedo, 5
fingernail uña, 5
finish terminar, 1
fire despedirse (i), 11
firefighter bombero(a), 11
fireplace chimenea, 4
firework fuego de artificio, 1
first name nombre *m.*, 2
first primero, 10
    first time primera vez, 5
fish pescar (qu), 3
    (alive) pez *m.*, 2
    (when caught) pescado, 6
fit (someone) quedarle (a uno), 7
five cinco, P
five hundred quinientos, 4
flavor sabor *m.*, 5
flight (nonstop) vuelo (sin escala), 9
flight attendant asistente de vuelo *m./f.*, 9

floor covering alfombra, 8
floor piso, 4
floral arrangement arreglo
    floral, R4
flower flor f., 10
folkloric folklórico adj., 13
follow seguir (i), 4
food comida, 6
foolish tonto adj., 2
foot pie m., 5
football field campo de
    fútbol, 3
for para, por, prep.
    for example por ejemplo, 11
    For what purpose? ¿Para
        qué?, 8
foreign extranjero adj., R2
    foreign languages lenguas
        extranjeras, 1
forest bosque m., 12
forget olvidar, 8
fork tenedor m., 6
forty cuarenta, 2
found crear, R4
fountain fuente f., 4
fountain pen pluma, 1
four cuatro, P
four hundred cuatrocientos, 4
fourteen catorce, P
fox zorro, 12
free gratis adj., 1
    free associated state estado
        libre asociado, 1
    freedom of the press libertad f.
        de la prensa, 14
French (language) francés m., 1;
    francés(esa) adj., 2
frequently a menudo, R1
fresh fresco adj., 6
Friday viernes m., 1
friend amigo(a), 1
friendly amable adj., 2
friendship amistad f., 10
frog rana, 12
from de, desde prep., 1
    From where? ¿De dónde?, P
front desk recepción f., 9
fruit fruta, 6
fruit juice jugo de fruta, 6
fruit store frutería, 3
fulfill llenar, 7
full-time de tiempo completo, 11
fun divertido adj., R1
function (to work) funcionar, 15
furious furioso adj., 4
furniture muebles m., 4

G

game juego, partido, 3
game show programa de
    concursos, 13
garage garaje m., 4
garden jardín m., 4
garlic ajo, 6
gas station gasolinera, 3
gate puerta, 9
gem joya, R2

generous generoso adj., 2
geography geografía, 1
geology geología, 1
German (language) alemán m.,
    1; alemán(ana) adj., 2
get conseguir (i), 4; + adjective
    ponerse + adjective, 8
    get a suntan broncearse, 8
    get along well (poorly)
        (with) each other llevarse
        bien (mal) (con), 10
    get divorced (from) divorciarse
        (de), 10
    get dressed vestirse (i), 5
    get married casarse (con), 10
    get off bajar(se) (de), 9
    get sick enfermarse, 5
    get together with reunirse
        con, 8
    get up levantarse, 5
    get used to acostumbrarse, 5
gift regalo, 8
girl chica, 7
girlfriend novia, 1
give dar, 3
    give (as a gift) regalar, 9
    give a party dar/hacer una
        fiesta, 8
glass vaso, 6
glove guante m., 7
go ir, 3
    go by bike (boat, bus, car,
        plane, subway, taxi, train)
        ir en bicicleta (barco,
        autobús, coche, avión,
        metro, taxi, tren), 9
    go camping hacer camping, 8
    go canoeing/sailing pasear
        en canoa/velero, 8
    go for a walk dar un paseo, 3
    go horseback riding montar
        a caballo, 3
    go on a picnic hacer un
        picnic, 3
    go on foot ir a pie, 9
    go out (with) salir (con), 3
    go shopping ir de compras, 3
    go through pasar por, 9
    go to a bar (club, concert,
        disco, party) ir a un bar
        (club, concierto, discoteca,
        party), 3
    go to bed acostarse (ue), 5
    go to the movies ir al cine, 3
    go up subir, 9
goblet copa, 6
godchild ahijado(a), 2
godfather padrino, 2
godmother madrina, padrina
    2
gold oro, R3
golf golf m., 3
    golf club palo de golf, 3
    golf course campo de golf, 3
good bueno adj., 2
    Good afternoon. Buenas
        tardes., P

Good evening (night).
    Buenas noches., P
    Good morning. Buenos días., P
Good-bye. Adiós., P
good-looking guapo adj., 2
gorilla gorila m., 12
govern gobernar (ie), 14
government gobierno, 14
governor gobernador(a), 14
granddaughter nieta, 2
grandfather abuelo, 2
grandmother abuela, 2
grandson nieto, 2
grass hierba, R3
great regio adj., R3
green verde adj., 1
greet (each other) saludar(se), P
groom novio, 10
grow (plants) cultivar, 12
grow up crecer, 2
growth crecimiento, 15
Guatemalan guatemalteco adj., 2
guerrilla guerrillero m./f., 14
guest invitado m./f., 8
    guest on a talk show
        panelista m./f., 13
guitar guitarra, 3
gymnasium gimnasio, 1

H

hair cabello, pelo, 5
hair salon peluquería, 3
hairstylist peluquero(a), 11
Haitian haitiano adj., 2
half brother (sister) medio(a)
    hermano(a), 2
half mitad f., 15
ham jamón m., 6
hamburger hamburguesa, 6
hand mano f., 5
handshake apretón m. de
    manos, 11
happy contento adj., 4
    I get happy. Me pongo
        contento., 8
hard drive disco duro, 15
hardware store ferretería, 3
hardworking trabajador(a) adj.,
    2
hat sombrero, 7
have tener (ie), P; (auxillary verb)
    haber, 10
    have a birthday cumplir
        años, 8
    have a cold estar resfriado(a),
        tener gripe, 5
    have a cookout hacer una
        parrillada, 8
    have a cough tener tos, 5
    have a fever tener fiebre, 5
    have a good (bad) time
        pasarlo bien (mal), 8
    have a headache tener dolor
        de cabeza, 5
    Have a nice trip! ¡Buen viaje!,
        9
    have chills tener escalofríos, 5

have just (done something)
    acabar de + infinitive, 5
have to (do something) tener
    que, 3
he él pron., P
head cabeza, 5
headache dolor de cabeza m., 5
health salud f., 5
healthy sano adj., 5
heart corazón m., 5
heavy (meal, food) pesado adj., 6
help (each other) ayudar(se), 1
her su adj., 2
herb hierba, 5
here aquí adv., P
hers suyo adj., 7
Hi! ¡Hola!, P
hierarchy jerarquía, 11
high heels zapato de tacón
    (alto), 7
highway carretera, 12
hike in the mountains caminar
    por las montañas, 3
hill colina, 12
hip cadera, 5
hippopotamus hipopótamo, 12
hire contratar, 11
his su adj., 2; suyo adj., 7
history historia, 1
holiday fiesta, día feriado m., 8
Holy Week Semana Santa, 8
home hogar m., 4
home page página de bienvenida
    (de entrada, de presentación,
    inicial, principal, de la Red),
    15
homework tarea, 1
Honduran hondureño adj., 2
honest honesto adj., 2
honeymoon luna de miel, 10
honor cumplir con, 10
hope esperar, 1
hors d'oeuvre entremés m., 8
host anfitrión m., 8
hostess anfitriona, 8
hot (temperature) caliente adj., 6
    it's hot hace calor, 3
hotel: four-star hotel hotel de
    cuatro estrellas m., 9
hour hora, 1
house casa, 4
    house of representatives
        cámara de representantes
        (diputados), 14
    house specialty especialidad f.
        de la casa, 6
housing vivienda, 4
How ¿Cómo?, P
    How are you? ¿Cómo está
        usted?, ¿Cómo estás?, P
    How does it look? ¿Cómo me
        queda?, 7
    How many? ¿Cuántos(as)?,
        P
    How much do I owe you?
        ¿Cuánto le debo?, 7
    How much? ¿Cuánto(a)?, 8

How old are you? ¿Cuántos años tienes?, P
hug (each other) abrazar(se), 10
human (civil) rights derechos humanos (civiles), 14
humanities humanidades *f. pl.*, 1
humble humilde *adj.*, 2
humorous cómico *adj.*, 2
hunger hambre *f.*, 5
husband esposo, 2

I

I yo *pron.*, P
ice cream helado, 6
ideology ideología, 14
if si, 15
illiteracy analfabetismo, 14
illness enfermedad *f.*, 5
immigration inmigración *f.*, 9
immunity imunidad *f.*, 14
impairment desmedro, 14
important importante *adj.*, 12
impossible imposible *adj.*, 12
imprisonment encarcelamiento, 14
in en, 4
   in addition to además de, R1
   in case (of) en caso (de) que *conj.*, 13
   in exchange for a cambio de, R4
   in front of delante de *prep.*, 4
   in regard to en cuanto a, 13
   in the (morning, afternoon/ evening) de/por la (mañana, tarde, noche), 1
incense incienso, R3
include incluir, 2
income ingreso, 12
increase aumentar, 14
indecisive indeciso *adj.*, 2
Independence Day
   from Spain Día de la Independencia de España, 1
Indian indio *adj.*
inequality desigualdad *f.*, 14
inexpensive barato *adj.*, 7
infirmary enfermería, 9
inflation inflación *f.*, 14
inform informar, 14
intellectual intelectual *adj.*, 2
intelligent inteligente *adj.*, 2
international policy política internacional, 14
Internet Internet *m.*, 14
   Internet service provider proveedor *m.* de servicios Internet, 15
internship pasantía, R4
interpreter intérprete *m./f.*, 11
interview entrevista, 11
intuitive intuitivo *adj.*, 2
invent inventar, 3
invest invertir (ie), R2
investigate investigar, 14
investment inversión *f.*, R4
iron plancha, 4

iron (clothes) planchar (la ropa), 4
irresponsible irresponsable *adj.*, 2
irrigate regar (ie) las plantas, 12
island isla, 9
Italian (language), italiano, 1; italiano, *adj.*, 2
its su *adj.*, 2; suyo *adj.*, 7

J

jacket chaqueta, 7
jaguar jaguar *m.*, 12
January enero, 3
Japanese (language) japonés *m.*, 1; japonés(esa) *adj.*, 2
jeans vaqueros, 7
jewelry joyas, 7
jewelry store joyería, 3
job puesto, 11
   job appointment cita de negocios, 1
   job hunt búsqueda de trabajo, 11
journalism periodismo, 1
journalist periodista *m./f.*, 11
judge juez *m./f.*, 10
July julio, 3
June junio, 3
jungle selva, 12
just like así como, 3

K

key llave *f.*, 9
keyboard teclado, 15
kiss (each other) besar(se), 10
kitchen cocina , 4
knee rodilla, 5
knife cuchillo, 6
know (each other) conocer(se), 3
   know (how) saber, 3
Korean coreano *adj.*, 2

L

laborer obrero(a), 11
lace encaje *m.*, R5
lack carecer de, 15
   falta, 11; escasez *f.*, 12
lake lago, 8
lamp lámpara, 4
land aterrizar, 9
   tierra, 12
landscape paisaje *m.*, R2
language lengua, 1
laptop computer computadora portátil, 15
large grande *adj.*, 2
last durar, R1
   last (week, month, year) (la semana, el mes, el año) pasado(a), 6
   last name apellido, 2
   last night anoche *adv.*, 6
late tarde *adv.*, 1
law derecho, 1; ley *f.*, 14
law office bufete *m.*, 11
lawyer abogado(a), 11
lazy perezoso *adj.*, 2

lead a peaceful life llevar una vida tranquila, 12
leaf hoja, 5
league: professional league liga profesional, 3
learn aprender, 2
leather cuero, 7
leave salir, 3; dejar, 13
   leave a (good) tip dejar una (buena) propina, 6
left: to the left of a la izquierda de *prep.*, 9
leg pierna, 5
less . . . than menos... que, 6
lesson lección *f.*, 1
let dejar, 13
let's see vamos a ver, 6
letter (correspondence) carta, 2
lettuce lechuga, 6
liberal liberal *adj.*, 2
librarian bibliotecario(a), 1
library biblioteca, 1
life vida, 10
lift weights levantar pesas, 3
light (meal, food) ligero *adj.*, 6
light luz *f.*, 1
lighthouse faro, R3
lightly levemente, 11
like: I (don't) like + infinitive (no) me gusta + *infinitive*, 1
lion león *m.*, 12
lips labios, 5
listen (to music) escuchar (música), 1
literacy alfabetismo, 14
literature literatura, 1
live vivir, 2
lively despierto *adj.*, R1
liver hígado, 5
living room sala, 4
loan préstamo, 11
   prestar, 11
lobster langosta, 6
logical lógico *adj.*, 12
logotype logotipo, R2
long largo *adj.*, 2
look for buscar (qu), 1
   look at each other mirarse, 10
lose perder (ie), 4
lost extraviado *adj.*, R3
love querer (ie), 4; amar, 10
   amor *m.*, 10
lunch almuerzo, 6
lungs pulmones *m.*, 5
luxurious lujoso *adj.*, 7

M

made hecho *p.p.*, 10
   made to order hechos a la medida, 7
magazine revista, 14
main dish plato principal, 6
major especialización *f.*, 1
   major, field of study carrera, 1
majority mayoría, 1
make hacer, 3

make a phone call llamar por teléfono, 11
make a stop (on a flight) (in) hacer escala (en), 9
make a toast hacer un brindis, 8
make one's bed hacer la cama, 4
make plans hacer planes, 3
mall centro comercial, 3
mammal mamífero, 12
man hombre *m.*, 1
manager gerente *m./f.*, 11
map mapa *m.*, 1
March marzo, 3
market (outdoor) mercado (al aire libre), 3
marriage matrimonio, 10
married casado *adj.*, 2
marry casanse (con), 10
mask máscara, 8
masterpiece obra maestra, 4
match hacer juego con, 7
math matemáticas, 1
May mayo, 3
mayor alcalde(sa), 14
meal comida, 6
means of communication medios de comunicación, 14
meat (beef) carne (de res) *f.*, 6
mechanic mecánico(a), 11
medical médico *adj.*, 2
   medical history historial clínica *f.*, 5
medicine medicina, 1
meet conocer(se), 3; reunirse con, 11
meeting reunión *f.*, 11
menu menú *m.*, 6
merchant comerciante *m./f.*, 11
message mensaje *m.*, 15
messy desordenado *adj.*, 4
metropolis metrópolis *f.*, 12
Mexican mexicano *adj.*, 2
midnight medianoche *f.*, 1
military coup golpe militar, 14
milk leche *f.*, 6
million millón, 4
mine mío *adj.*, 7
minister ministro *m./f.*, 14
mirror espejo, 4
miss (a function) perder (ie), 4
Miss señorita (Srta.), P
modem módem *m.*, 15
modern moderno *adj.*, 2
monarchy monarquía, 14
Monday lunes *m.*, 1
money dinero, 1
monkey mono, 12
month mes *m.*, 3
more . . . than más... que, 6
mortality: infant mortality mortalidad *f.* infantil, 9
mortgage hipoteca, 11
mother madre *f.*, 2
mother mamá, 2
mother-in-law suegra, 2

mouse (of computer) ratón *m.*, 15
mouth boca, 5
move mover (ue), 3
movie película, 13
    movie theater cine *m.*, 3
    movies cine *m.*, 13
mow the lawn cortar el césped, 4
Mr., sir señor (Sr.), P
Mrs., ma'am señora (Sra.), P
muscle músculo, 5
museum museo, 3
mushroom champiñón *m.*, 6
music música, 1
    music store tienda de música (de discos), 3
musical (play) función *f.*, 13
musician músico *m./f.*, 13
must deber, 2
my mi *adj.*, 2; mío, 7
myrrh mirra, R3

N

name: My name is . . . Me llamo..., P
napkin servilleta, 6
narrow angosto *adj.*, 11
nationality nacionalidad *f.*, 2
native Spanish speaker hispanohablante *m./f.*
natural resources recursos naturales, 12
naturalist naturalista *m./f.*, 12
nature naturaleza, 12
near cerca de *prep.*, 4
neat ordenado *adj.*, 4; arreglado *adj.*, 9
necessary necesario *adj.*, 12
neck cuello, 5
necklace collar *m.*, 7
necktie corbata, 7
need necesitar, 1
neighbor vecino(a), R1
neighborhood barrio, 2
neither . . . nor ni... ni, 8
    neither, not either, 8 tampoco *adv.*, 8
nephew sobrino, 2
nervous system sistema *m.* nervioso, 5
never nunca *adv.*, 3
    never again nunca más *adv.*, 3
new nuevo *adj.*, 2
    New Year's Eve Noche Vieja *f.*, 8
newlyweds recién casados *m.*, 10
news noticias, 13
newscast noticiero, 14
newspaper periódico, 14
next to al lado de *prep.*, 9
nibble picar (qu), 6
Nicaraguan nicaragüense *adj.*, 2
nice simpático *adj.*, 2
    it's nice hace buen tiempo, 3
    Nice to meet you. Encantado(a)., Mucho gusto., P

niece sobrina, 2
night life vida nocturna, R3
nine hundred novecientos, 4
nine nueve, P
nineteen diecinueve, P
ninety noventa, 2
nobody, no one nadie, 8
noise ruido, 12
none, not any ningún, ninguno(a), 8
nonsmoking section sección *f.* de no fumar *f.*, 9
noon mediodía *m.*, 1
North American norteamericano *adj.*, 2
north norte *m.*, 9
nose nariz *f.*, 5
not even ni siquiera, 4
notebook cuaderno, 1
notes apuntes *m.*, R1
nothing, not anything, at all nada, 8
November noviembre, 3
now ahora *adv.*, 1
number número, P
nurse enfermero(a), 5
nursing home casa de ancianos, 2

O

object objeto, 1
obtain conseguir (i), 4
occasionally de vez en cuando, 6
ocean océano, 8
October octubre, 3
of de
    of course por supuesto, 2; ¡Cómo no!, 6
off apagado *adj.*, 15
offer ofrecer (zc), 9
office oficina, 1
often muchas veces, 10
oil aceite *m.*, 6
oil lamp quinqué *m.*, R2
oil painting retrato al óleo, 13
old viejo *adj.*, 2
older mayor, 6
oldest el mayor, 6
on en, 4; encendido *adj.*, prendido *adj.*, 15; sobre *prep.*
    on the other hand por otro lado
    on time a tiempo, 1
    on top of encima de *prep.*, 4
    on top of that para colmo, 4
once una vez *adv.*, 10
one hundred cien/ciento, 2
one thousand mil, 4
one uno, P
one-way ticket billete/boleto de ida, 9
onion cebolla, 6
only sólo, P
open abrir, 2
    open a document (program) abrir un documento (un programa), 15

opened abierto *p.p.*, 10
opera ópera, 13
operating platform (system) plataforma de operación, 15
oppose oponer, 14
or o *conj.*, 3
orange anaranjado *adj.*, 1
orange naranja, 6
orchid orquídea, 12
order (food) pedir (i, i), 6
orphan huérfano(a), R3
ought to deber, 2
our nuestro *adj.*, 2
outdoors al aire libre, 4
outgoing extrovertido *adj.*, 2
oven (microwave) horno (de microondas), 4
over sobre *prep.*
overcoat abrigo, 7
overpopulation sobrepoblación *f.*, 12
overthrow derrocar (qu), 14
owl búho, 12
owner dueño(a), R5
ozone layer capa de ozono, 12

P

pack one's suitcase(s) hacer la(s) maleta(s), 9
paid pagado *adj.*, R1
pain dolor *m.*, 5
painter pintor(a), 13
painting pintura, 1; cuadro, 4
pair par *m.*, 7
Panamanian panameño *adj.*, 2
panther pantera, 12
panting jadeo, 5
pants (shorts) pantalones (cortos) *m.*, 7
paper papel *m.*, 1
parade desfile *m.*, R1; procesión *f.*, 8
Paraguayan paraguayo *adj.*, 2
paramilitary group grupo paramilitar, 14
pardon me disculpe, con permiso, perdón, P
park parque *m.*, 3
park ranger guardaparques *m./f.*, 12
part-time de tiempo parcial, 11
party (surprise) fiesta (de sorpresa), 8
pass pasar, 1; aprobar (ue), 14
passenger pasajero(a), 9
passing marcha, R1
Passover Pascua, 8
passport pasaporte *m.*, 9
    passport control inmigración *f.*, 9
pastime pasatiempo, 3
patient paciente *adj.*, 2; paciente *m./f.*, 5
pattern patrón *m.*, 7
pay pagar, 1

pay in cash (by check) pagar en efectivo (con cheque), 7
pay in installments pagar a plazos, 11
peace paz *f.*, 14
    Peace Corps Cuerpo de Paz, 5
peaceful tranquilo *adj.*, 12
peasant campesino(a), 12
pedestrian peatonal *adj.*, R3
    pedestrian street calle peatonal, R3
pencil lápiz *m.*, 1
people gente *f.*, P
pepper pimienta, 6
pepper shaker pimentero, 6
percent por ciento, 7
personal finances finanzas personales, 11
Peruvian peruano *adj.*, 2
pet mascota, 2
petroleum petróleo, 12
pharmacy farmacia, 5
philosophy filosofía, 1
phone llamar, 1
photocopier fotocopiadora, 11
photographer fotógrafo(a), 11
photography fotografía, 13
physical exertion esfuerzo físico, 5
physician médico *m./f.*, 5
physics física, 1
pick up recoger (j), 9
pill pastilla, 5
pilot piloto *m./f.*, 9
place lugar *m.*, 3
plaid de cuadros, 7
plain llano, 12
plane avión *m.*, 9
plant cultivar, 5; sembrar (ie), 12
plate plato, 6
play drama *m.*, 13
play jugar (ue), 4
    play a role interpretar, 13
    play an instrument tocar (qu), 1
    play tennis jugar al tenis, 3
    play the guitar tocar la guitarra, 3
player jugador(a), 3
playwright dramaturgo *m./f.*, 13
plaza plaza, 3
please por favor, P
pleasure: The pleasure is mine. El gusto es mío., P
plug in enchufar, 15
    plugged in enchufado *adj.*, 15
plumber plomero(a), 11
pocket bolsillo, 7
poet poeta *m./f.*, 13
poetry poesía, 13
police officer policía *m.* (mujer *f.* policía), 11
political party partido político, 14
politician político *m./f.*, 14
politics política, 14

polka-dotted de lunares, 7
pollute contaminar, 12
polluted contaminado *adj.*, 12
pollution contaminación *f.*, 12
pool piscina, 3
poor pobre *adj.*, 2
popular popular *adj.*, 13
    popular rule mando popular, 14
pork chop chuleta de cerdo, 6
port puerto, 9
portrayal retrato, R3
Portuguese (language) portugués *m.*, 1
position puesto, 11
post office oficina de correos, 3
postcard postal *m.*, 2
potatoes (french fried) papas (fritas), 6
power poder *m.*, 14
practice practicar (qu), 1
pray orar, 8
prefer preferir (ie), 4
prepare preparar, 6
prescription receta, 5
president of the university rector(a)/presidente *m./f.* de la universidad, 1
press prensa, 14
pressure presión *f.*, R5
pretty bonito *adj.*, 2
print imprimir, 11
printer impresora, 11
private privado *adj.*, 9
problem problema *m.*, 5
profession profesión *f.*, 11
professor profesor(a), 1
profile perfil *m.*, R1
program programar, 15
    (CD-ROM) programa (de CD-ROM) *m.*, 15
programmer programador(a), 11
progressive progresista *adj.*, 2
project proyecto, 11
promise prometer, 10
protect proteger, 12
protest protestar, 14
proud orgulloso *adj.*, R5
provided (that) con tal (de) que *conj.*, 13
psychiatrist siquiatra *m./f.*, 11
psychology sicología, 1
public transportation transporte público *m.*, 12
Puerto Rican puertorriqueño *adj.*, 2
pure puro *adj.*, 12
purple morado *adj.*, 1
purpose propósito, 2
purse bolsa, 7
put puesto *p.p.*, 10
put (on) poner, 3
    put on (one's clothes) ponerse (la ropa), 5
    put on makeup pintarse, maquillarse, 5

Q

question interpelar, 14
    pregunta, P
quiet callarse, R5
quit dejar, 11
    quit the program salir del programa, 15

R

raffle sorteo, 7
raid redada, 14
rain llover (ue), 4
rain lluvia
    rain forest selva nubosa tropical, 12
raincoat impermeable *m.*, 7
rancher ranchero(a), 11
rarely muy pocas veces, 2
rather sino *conj.*, 5
    Rather well. Bastante bien., P
react reaccionar, 8
read leer, 2
reading lectura, R1
ready listo *adj.*, 2
realize darse cuenta, R5
reason razón *f.*, 12
rebellious rebelde *adj.*, 2
receipt recibo, 11
receive recibir, 2
reception recepción *f.*, 10
receptionist recepcionista *m./f.*, 9
recommend recomendar (ie), 6
record grabar, 15
recycle reciclar, 12
red rojo *adj.*, 1
reduce reducir, 14
    reduce (in price) rebajar, 7
reforest reforestar, 12
reform reforma, 14
refresh restaurar, 5
refrigerator refrigerador *m.*, 4
register registrarse, 9
relationships relaciones sentimentales *f.*, 10
relative pariente *m./f.*, 2
remember recordar (ue), 8
remote control control *m.* remoto, 15
report informe *m.*, 11; reportaje *m.*, 14
reporter reportero(a), 11
representative diputado(a), 14
republican republicano *adj.*, 14
request pedir (i, i), 9
reservation reserva, 9
reserved reservado *adj.*, 2
resign renunciar, 11
respect respeto, 11
responsible responsable *adj.*, 2
rest descansar, 1
restaurant restaurante *m.*, 3
résumé currículum *m.*, 11
retire jubilarse, 11
return volver (ue), 4
    return (home) regresar (a casa), 1

return (investment) rendimiento, R4
returned vuelto *p.p.*, 10
review reseña, R5
rhinoceros rinoceronte *m.*, 12
ribbon cinta, R5
rice arroz *m.*, 6
rich rico *adj.*, 2
riddle adivinanza, 2
ride a bike andar en bicicleta, 3
ridiculous ridículo *adj.*, 12
right: to the right of a la derecha de *prep.*, 9
ring anillo, 7
risk riesgo, R2
river río, 8
roar rugir (j), R3
rocket cohete *m.*, 8
role papel *m.*, 13
roof techo, 4
room cuarto, 1
    room service servicio de habitación (cuarto), 9
    roommate compañero(a) de cuarto, 1
root raíz *f.*, 13
round-trip ticket billete/ boleto de ida y vuelta, 9
royal real *adj.*, R2
rug alfombra, 8
rule reinar, 14
run correr, 3
    run out acabar, 12
Russian (language), ruso, 1; ruso *adj.*, 2

S

sacred sagrado *adj.*, 8
sad triste *adj.*, 4
said dicho *p.p.*, 10
saint santo(a), 2
    saint's day Día del santo, 8
salad ensalada, 6
salary salario, sueldo, 11
sale oferta, liquidación *f. (Lat. Am.)*; rebaja *(Spain)*, 7
salesclerk/person dependiente *m./f.*, 7; vendedor(a), 11
salt sal *f.*, 6
salt shaker salero, 6
Salvadoran salvadoreño *adj.*, 2
same mismo *adj.*, 2
sand arena, 6
sandal sandalia, 7
sandwich sándwich *m.*, 6
satellite dish antena parabólica, 9
satellite satélite *m.*, 15
satisfied: I'm satisfied. I'm full. Estoy satisfecho(a)., 6
Saturday sábado, 1
sauce salsa, 6
save ahorrar, 11; archivar, 15
savings account cuenta de ahorros, 11
say decir (i), 4

Say no more! ¡No me digas más!, 11
scanner escáner *m.*, 15
scarf bufanda, 7
schedule horario, 9
scholarship beca, 9
school escuela, 1
science sciencias, 1
screech chillido, R3
screen pantalla, 1
script guión *m.*, 13
scuba dive bucear, 8
sculpt esculpir, hacer escultura, 13
sculptor escultor(a), 13
sculpture escultura, 13
sea mar *m.*, 8
seafood mariscos, 6
season estación *f.*, 3
seat asiento, 9
second segundo *adj.*, 2
second to the last penúltimo, 15
secretary secretario(a), 1
security control *m.* de seguridad, 9
    security box caja fuerte, 9
see ver, 3
    See you later. Hasta luego., Nos vemos., P
    See you soon. Hasta pronto., P
    See you tomorrow. Hasta mañana., P
seen visto *p.p.*, 10
sell vender, 2
senate senado, 14
senator senador(a), 14
send (letters) mandar (cartas), 1
separate (from) separarse (de), 10
separated separado *adj.*, 2
separation separación *f.*, 10
September septiembre, 3
servant criado(a), 11
serve servir (i), 4
server servidor *m.*, 15
set the table poner la mesa, 4
seven hundred setecientos, 4
seven siete, P
seventeen diecisiete, P
seventy setenta, 2
sew coser, R2
shade sombra, R5
shaded sombreado *adj.*, R2
shadowed umbroso *adj.*, R2
shake hands darse la mano, 10
shame: it's a shame es una lástima, 12
shameless person sinvergüenza *m./f.*, 4
shave afeitarse, 5
she ella *pron.*, P
shellfish mariscos, 6
shirt camisa, 7
shoe zapato, 7
    shoe size número, 7
    shoe store zapatería, 7
shop window aparador *m.*, 13
shopping de compras, 7

short (height) bajo *adj.*, 2; **(length)** corto *adj.*, 2

shortage escasez *f.*, 12

shot (injection) inyección *f.*, 5

shout gritar, 8

show espectáculo, 14

show mostrar (ue), 7

show (a movie) poner, 13

shower ducha, 4

shredded mechado, 6

shrimp (fried) camarones (fritos) *m.*, 6

shy tímido *adj.*, 2

sick enfermo *adj.*, 4

sign firmar, 14

silk seda, 7

silly tonto *adj.*, 2

similar parecido *adj.*, R1

simple sencillo *adj.*

simplicity sencillez *f.*, R2

sincere sincero *adj.*, 2

sing cantar, 1

singer cantante *m./f.*, 13

single soltero *adj.*, 2

single bed cama sencilla, 9

sister hermana, 2

sister-in-law cuñada, 2

six hundred seiscientos, 4

six seis, P

sixteen dieciséis, P

sixty sesenta, 2

size (clothing) talla, 7

skate (in-line) patinar (en línea), 3 patines (en línea) *m.*, 3

skewer pincho, R3

ski (water) esquí *m.* (acuático), 3 esquiar (en el agua), 3

skin piel *f.*, 5

skirt falda, 7

skyscraper rascacielos *m.*, 12

sleep dormir (ue), 4

slice tajada, 6

slightly ligeramente *adv.*, R2

small pequeño *adj.*, 2

smart listo *adj.*, 2

smell oler, 4

smoking section sección *f.* de fumar *f.*, 9

smoothness suavidad *f.*, 3

snack time merienda, 3

snake culebra, 12

sneeze estornudar, 5

snorkel hacer esnórquel, 8

snow nieve *f.*, 3

it's snowing nieva, 3

so entonces *adv.*, 10

So . . . Así que..., 2

So-so. Así así., Más o menos., P

so that a fin de que, para que *conj.*, 13

soap opera telenovela, 13

soccer (football) fútbol (americano) *m.*, 3

sociology sociología, 1

socks calcetines *m. pl.*, 7

sofa sofá *m.*, 4

soft drink refresco, 6

solar energy energía solar, 12

soldier soldado (la mujer soldado), 11

solve, resolve resolver (ue), 12

some unos(as) *indef. art.*; algún, alguno(a/os/as), 8

somebody, someone alguien, 8

something algo, 8

sometimes a veces *adv.*, 3

son hijo, 2

song canción *f.*, 13

son-in-law yerno, 2

soul alma, 8

soup sopa, 6

source fuente *f.*, 12

south sur *m.*, 9

space espacio, 4

Spanish (language) español *m.*, 1; español(a) *adj.*, 2

speak (with each other) hablar(se), 1

speakers altavoces *m.*, 15

species especies *f.*, 12

speech discurso, R1

spend (money) gastar, 7

spend (time) pasar, 1

spew babear, R3

spiritually espiritualmente, 2

spoon cuchara, 6

sport deporte *m.*, 3

sports deportiva *adj.*, 3

sports program programa deportivo, 13

spring primavera, 3

squid (fried) calamares (fritos) *m.*, 6

stadium estadio, 3

stage escenario, R2

stairs escalera, 4

stand puesto, 7

start comenzar (ie), 4

stationery store papelería, 3

stay quedarse, 9

stay in bed guardar cama, 5

steak bistec *m.*, 6

step paso, 7

stepbrother hermanastro, 2

stepfather padrastro, 2

stepmother madrastra, 2

stepsister hermanastra, 2

stereo estéreo, 15

still aún *adv.*

stingy tacaño *adj.*, 2

stockbroker accionista *m./f.*, 11

stockings medias, 7

stomach estómago, 5

stone piedra, 4

stone wall muralla de piedra, 9

stop parar(se), 9

store tienda, 3

story cuento; historia, 4

stove estufa, 4

straight derecho, 9

stream arroyo, 12

street calle *f.*, 3

strike huelga, 14

striped de rayas, 7

stroll paseo, 7

student estudiante *m./f.*, 1

student center centro estudiantil, 1

study estudiar, 1

study estudio, 1

stuff rellenar, 6

style estilo, 7

It's the latest style! ¡Está de última moda!, 7

subsequent subsiguiente, R2

succeed lograr

success éxito, R2

suddenly de repente, 8

sue demandar, 14

suffer sufrir, 9

sugar azúcar *m.*, 6

suit traje *m.*, 7

suitcase maleta, 9

summer verano, 3

summit cumbre *f.*, R1

sunbathe tomar el sol, 3

Sunday domingo, 1

sunglasses gafas de sol, 3

sunny: it's sunny hace sol, 3

suntan lotion crema bronceadora, 8

supermarket supermercado, 3

supper cena, 6

supply suplir, 12

support apoyar, 14

support apoyo, 13

surf correr las olas, 8

surf the Net navegar la Red, 15

surprise sorprender, 12

surround rodear, 11

surrounded rodeado *adj.*, 9

sweater suéter *m.*, 7

sweep the floor barrer el piso, 4

sweet dulce *adj.*, R1

swim nadar, 3

swimming natación *f.*, 3

symptom síntoma *m.*, 5

systems analyst analista de sistemas *m./f.*, 11

T

table mesa, 4

table (side) mesita coffee, 4

tablecloth mantel *m.*, 6

take (classes/tests) tomar (clases/exámenes), 1

take (someone's) temperature tomarle la temperatura (a alguien), 5

take a bath bañarse (en la tina), 5

take a risk arriesgarse (ue), 15

take a shower ducharse, 5

take advantage aprovechar, 14

take care (of oneself) cuidar(se), 5

take charge of ocuparse de, R5

take off quitarse, 5; despegar, 9

take out the garbage sacar la basura, 4

take pictures sacar fotos, 3

take place tener lugar, 6; llevar a cabo, 8

talk (with each other) hablar(se), 1

talk show programa de entrevistas, 13

tall alto *adj.*, 2

tasty sabroso *adj.*, 6

taxes impuestos, 14; aranceles *m.*, 15

tea (iced) té (helado) *m.*, 6

teach enseñar, 1

teacher maestro(a), 1

technical school escuela politécnica, 1

technician técnico *m./f.*, 11

technological tecnológico, 15

telecommute teletrabajar, 15

television viewer televidente *m./f.*, 13

tell contar (ue), 4; decir (i), 4

ten diez, P

tennis shoe (sneaker) zapato de tenis (deportivo), 3

terrace terraza, 4

terrorism terrorismo, 14

test examen *m.*, 1

that ese(a) *adj.*, 5; **(over there)** aquel (aquella) *adj.*, 5

that que *pron.*, 3; ése(a) *pron.*, 5; **(over there)** aquél (aquélla) *pron.*, 5

that's why por eso, 11

the el, la, los, las *def. art.*

theater teatro, 13

their su *adj.*, 2

then luego, entonces *adv.*, 10

there allí *adv.*, P

there is, there are hay, P

they ellos(as) *pron.*, P

thigh muslo, 5

thin delgado *adj.*, 2

think pensar (ie), 4

third tercero *adj.*, 2

thirteen trece, P

thirty treinta, P

this este(a) *adj.*, 5

this one éste *pron.*, 5

three hundred trescientos, 4

three tres, P

three-toed sloth perezoso con tres dedos, 12

throat garganta, 5

throughout durante *prep.*

throw tirar, 10

Thursday jueves *m.*, 1

ticket boleto, 3; billete *m.*, 9

tidy arreglado *adj.*, 9

tiger tigre *m.*, 12

time hora; vez

a good time un buen rato, 3

timid tímido *adj.*, 2

tiredness cansancio, 5
to a *prep.*
toad sapo, 12
toast brindis *m.*, 8
toaster tostadora, 4
today hoy *adv.*, 1
toe dedo del pie, 5
toilet inodoro, 4
tolerant tolerante *adj.*, 2
tomato tomate *m.*, 6
tomb tumba, 7
tomorrow mañana *adv.*, 1
tongue lengua, 5
too también *adv.*, 8
   too much demasiado *adv.*, 9
tooth diente *m.*, 5
touch tocar (qu), 1
tourism turismo, 1
toward hacia *adv.*, 9
town pueblo, 3
traffic tráfico, 12
train station estación de trenes *f.*, 9
tranquil tranquilo *adj.*, 12
transfer (funds) transferir (ie, i) (fondos), 11
translator traductor(a), 11
trash basura, 12
travel viajar, 1
   travel agency agencia de viajes, 9
   travel agent agente de viajes, 9
   traveler's check cheque de viajero, 11
tree árbol *m.*, 4
trip viaje *m.*, 9
truth verdad *f.*, 1
try on probarse (ue), 7
T-shirt camiseta, 7
Tuesday martes *m.*, 1
tuition matrícula, 1
turkey pavo, 6
turn doblar, 9
   turn off apagar (ue), 15
   turn on prender, 15; **(TV)** poner, 13
turtle tortuga, 12
tuxedo smoking *m.*
twelve doce, P
twenty veinte, P
twenty-one veintiuno, P
twenty-six veintiséis, P
twenty-three veintitrés, P
twenty-two veintidós, P
twice (three times, etc.) dos (tres, etc.) veces, 10
two dos, P
two hundred doscientos(as), 4

U

ugly feo *adj.*, 2
umbrella paraguas *m.*, 7
uncle tío, 2
under debajo de *prep.*, 4
underappreciated envilecido *adj.*, R1

understand comprender, 2; entender (ie), 4
unemployment desempleo, 14
United States: from the United States estadounidense *adj.*, 2
university universidad *f.*, 1
unknown desconocido *adj.*
unless a menos que *conj.*, 13
unpleasant antipático *adj.*, 2
unplug desenchufar, 15
unprotected desprotegido *adj.*, R4
until hasta *adv.*, 9; hasta que *conj.*, 13
unusual, unaccustomed insólito *adj.*, R1
up to hasta *adv.*, 9
   up to date al día, 14
URL Localizador Uniforme de Mecursos *m.*, 15
Uruguayan uruguayo *adj.*, 2
use usar, 1

V

vacuum pasar la aspiradora, 4
   vacuum cleaner aspiradora, 4
valley valle *m.*, 12
VCR videocasetera, 15
vegetable verdura, vegetal *m.*, 6
Venezuelan venezolano *adj.*, 2
very muy *adv.*, P
   Very well. Muy bien., P
vest chaleco, 7
veterinarian veterinario *m./f.*, 11
video camera videocámara, 15
videotape videocasete *m.*, 15
viewer espectador(a), 13
vinegar vinagre *m.*, 6
visit visitar, 1
   visit a museum visitar un museo, 3
volcanic volcánico *adj.*, R3
volcano volcán *m.*, 12
volleyball vólibol *m.*, 3
vote votar, 14
   vote voto, 14
wait esperar, 1
waiter (waitress) camarero(a), 6
waiting room sala de espera, 5
wake up despertarse (ie), 5
walk caminar, 1
   walk caminata, 7
   walk in the mountains caminar por las montañas, 3
wall pared *f.*, 4
wallet cartera, 7
want desear, 1; querer (ie), 4
war guerra, 14
wardrobe armario, 4
warn avisar, 8
wash (dishes, clothes, windows) lavar (los platos, la ropa, las ventanas), 4
   wash up lavarse, 5
washing machine lavadora, 4
waste desperdicio, 12
watch mirar, 1

watch reloj *m.*, 7
   watch television mirar la tele, 3
water the plants regar (ie) las plantas, 4
water: carbonated/noncarbonated mineral water agua *f.* mineral con/sin gas, 6
waterfall catarata, 12
wave ola, R1
we nosotros(as) *pron.*, P
weakness debilidad *f.*, 5
wear llevar, usar, 7
   wear a costume disfrazarse, 8
weather tiempo, 3
   weather report (forecast) pronóstico del tiempo, 13
web page página web, 15
wedding boda, 10
Wednesday miércoles *m.*, 1
week semana, 1
weekend fin *m.* de semana, 1
Welcome! ¡Bienvenido!, 9
well bien *adv.*
   well done bien cocido, 6
west oeste *m.*, 9
western highlands altiplano occidental, 8
what lo que *pron.*, 10
   What time is it? ¿Qué hora es?, 1
   What would you like (to eat)? ¿Qué te apetece?, 6
What? Which? ¿Qué?, P
   What's new? (informal) ¿Qué hay?, P
   What's up? (informal) ¿Qué tal?, P
   What's your address? (informal) ¿Cuál es tu dirección? (informal), P
   What's your name? ¿Cómo se llama usted?, ¿Cuál es tu nombre?, ¿Cómo te llamas?, P
   What's your telephone number? (informal) ¿Cuál es tu número de teléfono?, P
when cuando *conj.*, 13
   When? ¿Cuándo?, P
Where? ¿Dónde?, P
   Where (to)? ¿Adónde?, 8
   Where are you from? ¿De dónde es usted?, ¿De dónde eres tú?, P
which que *pron.*, 3
   Which? ¿Cuál(es)?, P
white blanco *adj.*, 1
who que *pron.*, 3; quien *pron.*, 10
   Who? ¿Quién(es)?, P
Whose? ¿De quién(es)?, 8
Why? ¿Por qué?, P
widow viuda
widowed viudo *adj.*, 2

watch reloj *m.*, 7

widower viudo
wife esposa, 2
wildlife preserve refugio natural, 12
win ganar, 3
window ventana, 4; ventanilla, 9
windy: it's windy hace viento, 3
wine (white, red) vino (blanco, tinto), 6
wine glass copa, 6
winner ganador(a), 13
winter invierno, 3
wish desear, 1
   I wish that ojalá que, 12
with con *prep.*, 4
   with regard to con respecto a, 11
withdraw (money) sacar (qu), 11
without sin *prep.*, 8; sin que *conj.*, 13
witness testigo *m./f.*, 10
wolf lobo, 12
woman mujer *f.*, 1
Wonderful! ¡Qué bueno! , 2
wool lana, 7
word palabra, 1
work trabajar, 1
   work trabajo, 11
   work (of art) obra (de arte), 13
worker obrero(a), 11
world mundo, 9
worried preocupado *adj.*, 4
worry preocuparse, 11
worse peor, 6
worst el peor, 6
write escribir, 2
writer escritor(a), 13
written escrito *p.p.*, 10

X

X-ray radiografía, 5

Y

year año, 3
yellow amarillo *adj.*, 1
yes sí, P
yesterday ayer *adv.*, 6
you tú, usted(es), vosotros(as) *pron.*, P
young joven *adj.*, 2
younger menor, 6
youngest el menor, 6
your (formal) su *adj.*, 2; vuestro *adj.*, 2; tuyo, suyo *adj.*, 7
yours vuestro *adj.*, 2; tuyo, suyo *adj.*, 7

Z

zebra cebra, 12
zero cero, P
zipper cremallera, cierre *m.*, 7
zoology zoología, 1

A

+ **el**, 86
personal, 82, 92, 360
with time, 39
abrir, past participle, 296, 313, 394
acabar de + *infinitive*, 148
academic courses, 32
accent marks, use of, 14, 121, 144, 156, 212, 262, 275, 295, 305, 436
actions
completed, 394
in progress, 124
reciprocal, 298
activities
daily, 145, 165
outdoor, 237, 253
work-related, 325, 345
addresses and telephone numbers, exchanging, 14
adjectival clauses, 360
adjectives
agreement of, 24, 53, 59–60
demonstrative, 156
descriptive, 59–60, 123, 136, 177, 191, 207, 223, 283, 373, 388
past participles as, 394
placement of, 60, 73
possessive, 53, 202
with **estar**, 123, 152
with **ser**, 57, 152
adverbs, 302
of frequency, 239, 302, 313
of place, 271
of sequence, 302, 313
of time, 39, 181, 191, 302, 313
with **estar**, 123
affirmative
commands, 121, 121, 274–275
expressions, 240–241, 253
affixes, 160
age, expressing, 16, 67
air travel, 256, 283
Alegría, Claribel, 286
alguno(a,os,as), 240
Alhambra, La, 192
Allende, Salvador, 405
Almodóvar, Pedro, 114
almorzar, present tense, 113
alphabet, Spanish, 20
anatomy. *See* human body
animals, 364, 373
answering questions, 5, 21
appliances, electrical and electronic, 108, 136, 432, 440, 451
-**ar** verbs, 35
conditional tense, 417

formal commands, 274–275
future tense, 409
imperfect tense, 214
informal commands, 275
past participle, 295
present participles, 124
present subjunctive, 334
present tense, 35
preterite tense, 180
Argentina, Mar del Plata, 287
articles, definite and indefinite, 29, 82, 144, 149, 202
arts
fine, 388, 401
movies and television, 380, 381, 382, 384, 401
ask questions, 5, 14, 231

B

background knowledge, use in anticipating content, 219–220
balboa, 323
banking, 331, 345
Barrios de Chamorro, Violeta, 374
beach activities, 237, 253
beverages, 170, 191
bilingual dictionary, using a, 162
Blades, Rubén, 377
body, parts of, 140, 144, 165
Bogotá, Colombia, 87
Bolivia, La Paz, 8, 143
Botero, Fernando, 93, 105
buen(o), 60
"Buena Vista Social Club," 381
buildings
town, 84, 101, 271, 283
university, 32, 47
business practices, 316, 325, 327, 329, 345

C

-**car** verbs
formal commands, 274–275
present subjunctive, 334
preterite tense, 180
careers. *See* professions
celebrations, 226, 253
Central America, map, 19
Chichicastenango, 230
Chile, government in, 405, 408
chores, household, 118, 136
chronology, following a, 398
Churro Manía, 193
cinematography in Latin America, 384
classroom items, 2447
clothes, 198, 223
size chart, 209

clustering words, 132
coffee, 89, 168, 297
cognates, 60, 191, 207
college buildings, 32, 47
Colombia
Bogotá, 87
coffee, 89
Colón Free Trade Zone, 324
colors, 24, 47
combining sentences, 99
comenzar (ie)
formal commands, 274
present subjunctive, 334
present tense, 113
preterite, 180
comer
commands, 121, 275
past participle, 295
present participle, 124
present tense, 65
preterite tense, 180
commands
affirmative informal (**tú**), 121, 212
formal, 274–275
negative informal, 275
communications, public, 413
comparatives, 172–173
complex sentences, reading, 426
computers, 440, 443, 451
conditional tense, 417–418
conjunctions, 99, 385, 401
conocer
present tense, 90
versus **saber**, 92
conservation, 356, 373
context, use in predicting content, 98
contractions, 53, 86
Costa Rica
ecology of, 352, 359, 376
Golfito, 364
countries, 18, 31
countryside, 237, 253, 348, 352
courses, academic, 31–32, 47
courtship, 290, 313
creer, past participle, 295
"Cristina," 381
¿cuál(es)?, 14, 231
cuando, 234
¿cuántos(as)?, 14, 231
Cuba, 265, 268, 285
cubrir, past participle, 394
cultural information
Arzobispo Óscar Arnulfo Romero, 239
las bodas en el mundo hispano, 301
Bolivia y la salud, 143

el café en Colombia y en el mundo, 89
el Canal de Panamá, 320
Chichicastenango, 230
la cinematografía en Latinoamérica, 384
la comida típica venezolana, 171
de compras en Buenos Aires, 201
Costa Rica: estación biológica La Selva, 359
Costa Rica: puros ingredientes naturales, 352
Cuba: Escuela Latinoamericana de Ciencias Médicas, 265
los deportes en el mundo hispano, 81
la educación en Latinoamérica y España, 34
equipos: en la palma de la mano, 443
el español en los Estados Unidos, 28
estancia, 216
la familia hispana, 62
Gaudí y su obra, 112
el gobierno de Chile, 408
guayabera, 263
la libertad de prensa, 416
el lugar de encuentro: las plazas, 7
marimba, 232
mojito cubano, 263
el mundo hispánico, 17
los nombres y apellidos en español, 56
los novios en los países hispanoamericanos, 294
Oswaldo Guayasamín, 391
pizza a la piedra, 205
los postres venezolanos, 179
protocolo en los negocios del mundo hispanohablante, 329
Puerto Rico: Estado Libre Asociado, 273
quinceañera, 227
la República Dominicana, 260
¿Ser informal o formal? ¿Tú o usted?, 9
el sistema de 24 horas, 41
el tango argentino, 210
las telecomunicaciones en Uruguay, 435
tradición de hierbas: yerba mate en Paraguay

y las hojas de coca **en los Andes,** 155
viviendas en Latinoamérica y España, 120
Curaméricas, 194
curandero(a), 149

D

daily activities, expressing, 145, 165
Dalí, Salvador, 128
dar
   formal commands, 274
   present subjunctive, 336
   present tense, 90
   preterite tense, 204
Darío, Rubén, 299
dates, 127
days, 39, 47
de
   + **el,** 53
   indicating possession, 53, 73, 201
   with dates, 127
   with numbers, 172
   with superlatives, 174
deber, 65, 116
decir
   conditional tense, 417
   future tense, 409
   past participle, 296, 313, 394
   present tense, 113
   preterite tense, 204
   tú command, 121
definite articles, 29, 82, 144, 149, 202
demonstrative adjectives and pronouns, 156
denial, expressing, 330
descubrir, past participle, 394
diagrams, writing from, 427
direct object, 92
   pronouns, 211–212
directions, requesting and giving, 270–271, 281, 283
dislikes and likes, expressing, 38, 82
divertirse
   imperfect tense, 214
   present subjunctive, 335
   preterite tense, 184
doler, 149
Dominican Republic, 256, 259, 260
dormir
   commands, 275
   past participle, 295
   present participle, 124
   present subjunctive, 335
   present tense, 113
   preterite tense, 184
double object pronouns, 266
doubt, expressing, 330, 360, 436

E

e → i stem-changing verbs, 113, 124, 335
e → ie stem-changing verbs, 113
Ecuador, artistic centers in, 388
editing your writing, 221

education in Latin America and Spain, 34
elapsed time, 244
elections, 404, 429
El Salvador, 234, 239, 286
emotion
   changes in, 226
   expressing, 330, 353, 436
en, 28
endearment, terms of, 293
entertainment
   fine arts, 388, 401
   movies and television, 380, 381, 382, 384, 401
environmental issues, 348, 356, 373
equal comparisons, 173
-er verbs
   conditional tense, 417
   formal commands, 274–275
   future tense, 409
   imperfect tense, 214
   informal commands, 274–275
   past participle, 295
   present participles, 124
   present subjunctive, 334
   present tense, 65
   preterite tense, 180, 181
escribir
   past participle, 296, 313, 394
   present participle, 124
   present subjunctive, 334
   vosotros command, 121
essay writing, 370
estar
   formal commands, 274
   present subjunctive, 336
   present tense, 90
   preterite tense, 204
   uses of, 123
   vs. **ser,** 152
   weather expressions with, 94
estudiar
   present participles, 124
"Evita," 381

F

family relationships, 50, 62
farewells, 5, 21
films, 380
fine arts, 388, 401
food, 168, 170, 171, 177, 178, 191, 205
formal commands, 274–275
format clues, using, 280
Franco, Francisco, 128
freedom of the press, 416
frequency, adverbs of, 239, 302, 313
furniture, 108, 136
future tense, 409–410

G

-gar verbs
   formal commands, 274, 275
   present subjunctive, 334
   preterite tense, 180
García Lorca, Federico, 195
García Márquez, Gabriel, 93
Gaudí, Antonio, 112

gender of nouns, 29, 59
geography, rural and urban, 348, 352, 373
Golfito, Costa Rica, 364
good-bye, 5
Goya, Francisco, 128
grammar
   affirmative and negative expressions, 240–241
   affirmative **tú** commands, 121
   el alfabeto en español, 20
   common uses of the verb **ser,** 57
   comparatives and superlatives, 172–174
   conditional tense, 417–418
   contraction **a + el = al,** 86
   definite and indefinite articles, 29
   demonstrative adjectives and pronouns, 156
   direct object pronouns, 211–212
   double object pronouns, 266
   el español en los Estados Unidos, 28
   formal and negative **tú** commands, 274–275
   formation of present subjunctive and statements of volition, 334–337
   future tense, 409–410
   gustar + infinitive, 38, 82
   gustar + noun, 82
   how to make nouns plural, 29
   if clauses, 444
   imperfect tense, 214–215
   indirect object pronouns, 261–262
   ir a + destination or infinitive, 86
   negative **tú** commands, 275
   no-fault **se,** 392
   por versus **para,** 321–322
   present perfect in subjunctive mood, 421
   present perfect tense, 295–296
   present subjunctive with statements of volition, 334–337
   present tense of **-er** and **-ir** verbs, 65
   present tense of regular **-ar** verbs, 35
   present tense of stem-changing verbs, 113
   preterite of regular verbs, 180
   preterite vs. the imperfect, 233–234
   question words and inflection, 5, 14
   relative pronouns, 305
   reflexive pronouns and present tense of reflexive verbs, 144–145
   ser, present tense, 10, 57
   ser vs. **estar,** 152

statements in the past with subjunctive mood, 436
subject pronouns, 10
subjunctive following verbs of emotion, impersonal expressions, and **ojalá,** 353
subjunctive mood, 330
subjunctive with purpose and time clauses, 385
subjunctive with verbs, expressions of uncertainty, and adjective clauses, 360
   tener, present tense, 16, 67
   verb **estar,** 123
   verb form **hay,** 12
   verbs irregular in the preterite, 204
   verbs with irregular **yo** forms, 90
   verbs with stem changes in the preterite, 184
gran(de), 60
greeting and meeting people, 4, 21
guayabera, 263
Guayasamín, Oswaldo, 391
gustar, 38, 82

H

haber, present tense, 295
hablar
   commands, 274–275
   imperfect subjunctive, 436
   past participle, 295
   present tense, 35
   preterite tense, 180
   vosotros command, 121
hace... que, 244
hacer
   conditional tense, 417
   future tense, 409
   imperfect tense, 214
   past participle, 296, 313, 394
   present subjunctive, 334
   present tense, 90
   preterite tense, 204
   tú command, 121
   weather expressions with, 94
have just, to, 148
hay, 12
   conditional tense, 417
   future tense, 409
   imperfect tense, 214
   present subjunctive, 336
   preterite tense, 204
health issues, 149, 165
herbs, 155
holidays, 226,
hotels, 268, 283
household
   appliances and electronics, 108, 136, 432, 440, 451
   chores, 118, 136
   rooms and furnishings, 108, 136
human body, 140, 144, 165
hypothetical situations, expressing, 360, 417–418, 444, 449

I

Iberian peninsula, 19
idea map, writing from, 343
idioms, 75, 101, 207, 223, 256,
    283, 313, 345, 373
    with **tener,** 67, 75, 116, 116,
    136
if clauses, 418, 444
illnesses and treatments, 149,
    165
imperfect subjunctive, 436–437
imperfect tense, 214–215
    uses of, 215
    versus preterite tense,
    233–234
impersonal expressions, 353, 436
indefinite articles, 29
indicative mood, 330, 334
    versus subjunctive, 385, 443
indirect object pronouns, 82,
    149, 261–262, 392
infinitives, 35, 145, 337
informal commands
    affirmative, 121
    negative, 275
integrating reading strategies,
    448
interrogative words, 14, 21,
    231, 253, 407
introductions, 4, 21
ir
    + **a,** 86, 233
    commands, 274–275
    imperfect tense, 214
    present participles, 124
    present subjunctive, 336
    present tense, 82
    preterite tense, 204
    tú command, 121
-**ir** verbs
    conditional tense, 417
    formal commands, 274–275
    future tense, 409
    imperfect tense, 214
    informal commands, 274–275
    past participle, 295
    present subjunctive, 334
    present tense, 65
    preterite tense, 180, 181, 184
irregular
    comparatives, 172
    superlatives, 174
irregular verbs
    conditional tense, 417
    formal commands, 274
    future tense, 409
    past participles, 295–296,
    313, 394
    present subjunctive, 336
    in preterite tense, 204
    stem-changing, 113, 124,
    184, 334–335
    tú commands, 121
    yo forms, 90, 124, 262
irse
    conditional tense, 417
    future tense, 409
    imperfect subjunctive, 436
las Islas Bahías, 296

J

job hunting, 325, 345
jugar
    imperfect tense, 214
    present tense, 113

L

Lam, Wilfredo, 389
landscape, rural and urban,
    348, 352, 373
languages, 31, 47
La Paz, Bolivia, 8
La Selva, Costa Rica, 359
lavarse, present subjunctive, 334
leer, past participle, 295
levantarse, present tense, 144
likes and dislikes, expressing,
    38, 82
llegar
    formal commands, 274
    past participle, 295
    present subjunctive, 334
    preterite, 180
llevar, uses of, 142
lodging, 268
lo que, 305

M

mal(o), 60
Managua, Nicaragua, 299
maps
    Central America, 19
    Europe, 31
    Iberian peninsula, 19
    San Juan, Puerto Rico, 270
    South America, 18
    Spain, 19
    United States, 18
Mar del Plata, Argentina, 199,
    287
marital status, 50, 290
marriage, 290, 299, 301, 304,
    313
más (...) que, 172
Mayan, 297
meals, 168, 171, 191
medicine, 149, 165
meeting and greeting people,
    4
menos (...) que, 172
mientras, 233
mojito cubano, 263
money, 331, 345
Monteverde, Costa Rica, 362
months, 94, 101
Morazán, Francisco, 290
morir, past participle, 296,
    313, 394
movies, 380, 384, 401

N

names, Spanish, 56
Naranjo, Carmen, 368
nationality, 57, 63, 75
negation, 173, 212, 240–241,
    262, 275, 360, 392
negative
    expressions, 240–241, 253
    informal commands, 275

neuter demonstrative pronouns,
    156
news media, 413, 429
Nicaragua, 297, 299
ninguno(a,os,as), 241
no-fault **se,** 392
nouns, gender of, 29, 59
numbers
    0–30, 12, 21
    30–100, 64, 75
    100 and higher, 127, 136

O

o → u, 27
o → ue stem-changing verbs,
    113, 124
office work, 325, 327, 329, 345
ojalá (que), 353
organizational features of a pas-
    sage and skimming, 188
organizing ideas, 45
outdoor activities, 237, 253
ownership, 53

P

pain, discussing, 149
Panama, 316
    Canal, 320, 324
    currency, 323
Panamerican Highway, 324
para versus **por,** 321–322
participles
    past, 295–296, 394
    present, 124
past subjunctive, 436–437
past, talking about, 181, 214–215
pastimes, 78, 101, 237, 253
Paz, Octavio, 104
pedir
    present participle, 124
    present subjunctive, 336
    present tense, 113
pensar (ie)
    past participle, 295
    present subjunctive, 335
    present tense, 113
    preterite tense, 180
people, describing, 24, 47, 59–60
performing arts, 388, 401
personal
    finances, 331, 345
    hygiene, 145, 165
personality traits, 60, 75
pets, 50, 75
physical characteristics, 59–60, 75
Picasso, Pablo, 128
Piedras Blancas National Park,
    362
plazas, 7
places
    in a town, 84, 101, 271, 283
    on a campus, 32
pluralization, 29
poder
    conditional tense, 417
    future tense, 409
    present subjunctive, 335
    present tense, 113
    preterite tense, 204, 234

polite requests, 436
politics, 404, 429
pollution, 356
poner
    conditional tense, 417
    future tense, 409
    past participle, 296, 313, 394
    present tense, 90
    preterite tense, 204
    tú command, 121
ponerse + adjective, 226
por vs. **para,** 321–322, 394
possession, indicating, 53, 67,
    73, 202
possessive adjectives, 14, 53,
    202
preferir (ie), present tense,
    113
prefixes, 160
prepositions
    of location, 270
prereading, 188
present participles, 124
present perfect
    indicative, 295–296
    subjunctive, 421
present progressive tense, 124
present subjunctive, 334–337
present tense
    -**ar** verbs, 35
    -**er** and -**ir** verbs, 65
    irregular **yo** forms, 90, 124,
    262
    stem-changing verbs, 113
    uses of, 35
press
    freedom of, 416
    media, 413, 429
preterite tense
    -**ar** verbs, 180
    -**er** and -**ir** verbs, 180
    irregular
        verbs, 204, 184
        yo forms, 181
    uses of, 181, 204, 215
    versus imperfect tense,
    233–234
professions, 57, 316, 345
pronouns
    demonstrative, 156
    direct object, 211–212
    double object, 266
    indirect object, 82, 149,
    261–262, 392
    placement of, 275, 275, 337,
    392
    reflexive, 144–145
    relative, 305
    subject, 10, 21
    with **tú** commands, 121
public policy issues, 413, 429
Puerto Rico, 270, 273, 284
Punta del Este, Uruguay, 439
purpose, clauses of, 385, 436

Q

quantity, adjectives of, 60
que, 305
¿qué tal si... ?, 407

querer (ie)
  conditional tense, 417
  future tense, 409
  present tense, 113
  preterite tense, 204, 234
questions, asking, 5, 14, 21, 39, 231
quien, 305
¿quién(es)?, 14, 231

R

reading strategies
  clustering words, 132
  complex sentences. 426
  following a chronology, 398
  guessing meaning from word roots, 248
  guessing unfamiliar words and phrases, 342
  integrating strategies, 448
  organizational features of a passage and skimming, 188
  recognizing Spanish affixes, 160
  recognizing cognates, 44
  skimming and scanning, 72
  summarizing a passage, 310
  understanding the writer's perspective, 368
  using background knowledge to anticipate content, 219
  using context to predict content, 98
  using format clues, 280
recent past, 148
reciprocal actions, 298
reflexive pronouns, 144–145, 298
reflexive verbs
  object pronouns with, 212
  present tense, 144–145
reír
  past participle, 295
  -se, 184
relationships
  family, 50, 62
  indicating, 53
  interpersonal, 290, 292, 293, 313
relative pronouns, 305
República Dominicana, 285
resolver, past participle, 394
restaurants, 168, 170, 177
romper, past participle, 394
rooms, 108

S

saber
  conditional tense, 417
  formal commands, 274
  future tense, 409
  present subjunctive, 336
  present tense, 90
  preterite tense, 204, 234
  versus **conocer,** 92
sacar, formal commands, 274
salir
  conditional tense, 417
  future tense, 409

present tense, 90
  tú command, 121
San Carlos de Bariloche, 199
Santa Fe de Bogotá, 87
se, no-fault, 392
seasons, 94, 101
sequence, adverbs of, 302, 313
ser
  formal commands, 274
  imperfect tense, 214
  present subjunctive, 336
  present tense, 10, 57
  preterite tense, 204
  tú command, 121
  uses of, 57, 123
  vs. **estar,** 152
servir
  present participle, 124
  present subjunctive, 336
  present tense, 113
  preterite tense, 184
shopping, 201, 207, 223
sizes, 209
skimming and scanning, 72
social issues, 413, 429
South America, map, 18
Spain
  education in, 34
  government, 110
  map, 19
Spanish in the United States, 28
Spanish-speaking world, 17–19, 34
Spanish word order, 73
speculation, expressing, 410, 418, 449
sports, 78, 81, 101, 237, 253
stem-changing verbs
  present tense, 113, 124
  preterite tense, 180, 184
stressed possessives, 202
subject pronouns, 10, 21
subjunctive mood
  statements in the past with, 436
  uses of, 334–337, 330, 353, 385, 421
  versus indicative, 330, 334, 385
  versus infinitives, 337
summarizing, 250–251
superlatives, 174
suffixes, 160

T

tango, 210
tan(to)... como, 173
technology, 432, 440, 443
telephone numbers, 15
television, 380, 381, 382, 401
tener
  conditional tense, 417
  future tense, 409
  idioms with, 67, 75, 116, 136
  present tense, 10, 67
  preterite tense, 204, 234
  + **que** + *infinitive,* 116
  tú command, 121
  uses of, 67
terms of endearment, 293

time
  clauses, 385
  expressions, 39, 57, 233, 302, 313
  of day, 39
  duration, 244, 321
  official, 41
  past, 181, 191
  telling, 39, 41
titles, personal, 5, 9
toast, making a, 226
tocar, 180, 406
topic sentences, 134
traer
  past participle, 295
  present participle, 124
  present tense, 90
  preterite tense, 204
transportation, means of, 256, 271, 283
travel, by air, 256, 283
tú
  commands, 121, 275
  versus **usted,** 8, 9
24-hour clock, 41

U

uncertainty, expressing, 330, 360, 385, 436
unequal comparisons, 172
unfamiliar words and phrases, 342
United States, map, 18
university buildings, 32
uno, 12, 60
urban landscape, 348
Uruguay
  Punta del Este, 439
  telecommunications in, 435
usted, 5
  versus **tú,** 8, 9

V

vallenato, 93
Velásquez, Diego, 128
venir (ie)
  conditional tense, 417
  formal commands, 274
  future tense, 409
  imperfect subjunctive, 436
  preterite tense, 204
  tú command, 121
ver
  imperfect tense, 214
  past participle, 296, 313, 394
  present tense, 90
verbs
  -ar, 35
  -er and **-ir,** 65
  irregular
    commands, 121, 274
    conditional tense, 417
    future tense, 409
    past participles, 295–296, 394
    present subjunctive, 336
    preterite tense, 204, 184

    stem-changing, 113, 124, 184, 334–335
    yo forms, 90, 124, 262
  no-fault **se** constructions, 392
  of emotion, 353
  of uncertainty, 360
  of volition, 337
  reflexive, 144–145
  stem-changing, 113, 124, 184
viajar
  conditional tense, 417
  future tense, 409
vivir
  commands, 275
  conditional tense, 417
  future tense, 409
  past participle, 295
  present tense, 65
  preterite tense, 180
vocabulary
  los animales y el refugio natural, 364
  las artes, 388
  los avances tecnológicos, 432
  las características físicas y la personalidad, 60
  la casa, 108
  en la clase, 24
  colores, 24
  la comida, 168
  de compras, 207
  la computadora, 440
  la conservación y la explotación, 356
  el cuerpo humano, 140
  los deportes y los pasatiempos, 78
  los doce meses y las estaciones, 94
  la familia, 50
  fiestas y celebraciones, 226
  las finanzas personales, 331
  la geografía rural y urbana, 348
  el hotel, 268
  indicaciones, 270
  lenguas extranjeras, otras materias y lugares universitarios, 31–32
  los lugares, 84
  las nacionalidades, 63
  los números del 0 al 30, 12
  los números 31 a 100, 69
  los números 100 y más, 127
  la oficina, el trabajo y la búsqueda de un puesto, 325
  palabras interrogativas, 14
  la playa y el campo, 237
  la política y el voto, 404
  las preocupaciones cívicas y los medios de comunicación, 413
  las profesiones y los oficios, 316
  programas y películas, 380
  los quehaceres domésticos, 118
  la recepción, 299

las relaciones sentimentales, 290
el restaurante, 177
la ropa, 198
la salud, 149
saludos y despedidas, 4
viajar en avión, 256
volition/influence, expressing, 330, 334–337, 436
volver
  conditional tense, 417
  formal commands, 274
  future tense, 409
  past participle, 296, 313, 394
  present tense, 113
  preterite tense, 180

vosotros(as), 10, 200
  command, 121

W

weather expressions, 94, 101
wedding
  customs, 301, 304
  reception, 299, 313
weekdays, 39
wildlife reserve, 364, 373
word clusters, 132
word order, 73, 145, 212, 240–241, 261, 275, 302, 337
word roots, 248
writing
  adding details, 189

combining sentences, 99
critical essay, 399
editing, 221
from an idea map, 343
from diagrams, 427
organizing ideas, 45
persuasive essay, 370
Spanish word order, 73
speculating and hypothesizing, 449
summary, 250–251
topic sentences, 134
using a bilingual dictionary, 162

using commands to give directions, 281
using expressions of frequency in descriptions of activities, 311

Y

y → e, 27
years, 127

Z

-zar verbs
  formal commands, 274, 275
  present subjunctive, 334
  preterite tense, 180

Text/Realia Credits

102: Reprinted by permission of Center for Latino Studies in the Americas, http://www.usfca.edu/celasa; **132:** "70m²" by Lourdes Vijande. Reprinted from *El País Semanal*, Madrid, Spain, October 10, 1999; **133:** "Concepto urbano" by Isabel Núñez. Reprinted from *El País Semanal*, Madrid, Spain, April 11, 1999; **161:** "Los cinco mandamientos de la automedicación" by Juan Manuel Barberá. Reprinted from *Quo*, Madrid, Spain, no. 14, November 1996; **188:** "Oda al tomate" by Pablo Neruda. Reprinted from *Odas elementales* by permission of Editorial Losada; **193:** Art and photos reprinted by permission of Ariel Acosta-Rubio. © Churro mania; **194:** Art, logo, and web elements reprinted by permission of Jennifer Babula, Curaméricas; **195:** *La casa de Bernarda Alba* by Federico García Lorca © Herederos de Federico García Lorca. From *Obras Completas* (Galaxia Gutenberg, 1996 edition). All rights reserved. Rights and permissions, on behalf of William Peter Kosmas, Esq. **220:** "La primavera la moda altera" by Marisol Abejón. Reprinted from *CNR*, Madrid, Spain, no. 25, March 1999; **249:** "Guía del viajero: Guatemala" by Cristina Morató. Reprinted from *Rutas del mundo*, Barcelona, Spain, no. 33, November 1992; **280:** "Los mejores destinos: Noches calientes en La Habana" by Guillem Gayà. Reprinted from *CNR*, Madrid, Spain, no. 16, July 1998; **286:** Reprinted from FLOWERS FROM THE VOLCANO, by Claribel Alegría, translated by Carolyn Forché, by permission of the University of Pittsburgh Press. © 1982 by Claribel Alegría and Carolyn Forché; **310:** "Casino Sampedrano exalta a 'Novios del año.'" Reprinted from *La Prensa Honduras*, February 17, 1998; **369:** *Responso para el niño Juan Manuel* (fragment) by Carmen Naranjo. Published by Editorial Universitaria Centroamericana, San José, Costa Rica, 1991. Reprinted by permission of Consejo Superior Universitario Centroamericano; **374:** Content and web elements provided by Cristina Chamorro Barrios, Fundación Violeta Barrios de Chamorro; **426:** "Disminuye diferencia de sueldos entre mujeres y hombres" by Sandra Rojas W. Reprinted from *La tercera*, Santiago, Chile, January 9, 2000; **443:** "En la palma de la mano." Reprinted from *Revista América Economía*, Miami, April 19, 2001; **453:** "Tosca" (fragment) by Isabel Allende. Reprinted from *Los cuentos de Eva Luna*, Barcelona, Spain, 1991.

Photo Credits

PRELIMINARY CHAPTER
2: © Jeremy Horner/CORBIS; **3:** © Martin Roger/CORBIS; right: Andre Jenny/Alamy

CHAPTER 1
22–23: © Gail Mooney/CORBIS; **26:** © Randy Taylor/Index Stock Imagery; **34:** © Heinle; **37:** © Royalty-Free/CORBIS; **38:** © Andrea Boohe/Index Stock Imagery; **41:** © Owen Franken/CORBIS.

CHAPTER 2
48–49: © Heinle; **62:** © Frank Herholdt/GETTY (Taxi); **64:** © Reuters New Media Inc/CORBIS.

CHAPTER 3
76–77: © Dave Simchock/Vagabond Vistas; **81:** Jean-Yves Ruzzniewski/CORBIS; **89:** © Royalty-Free/CORBIS; **98:** © Reuters NewMedia/CORBIS.

MAGAZINE 1
102 top right: © Randy Taylor/Index Stock Imagery; **102** bottom right: © Walter Bibikow/Index Stock Imagery; **104:** © William Coupon/CORBIS; **105:** © Marianne Hass/CORBIS.

CHAPTER 4
106–107: © Lorenzo Armendariz/LatinFocus.com; **109:** Miquel Riopa/Lightroom Photos; **110:** © Archivo Iconografico, S.A./CORBIS; **112:** © Color Point Studio/Index Stock Imagery; **120** top left: © Kindra Clineff/Index Stock Imagery; **120** top right: © Peter Adams /Index Stock Imagery; **120** bottom: © Chad Ehlers/Index Stock Imagery; **128** top left: *The Triangular Hour* Salvador Dali. Private Collection/Art Resource, NY. © 2003 Salvador Dali, Gala-Salvador Dali Foundation/Artists Rights Society (ARS), New York.; **128** top right: *Les Meininas* Diego Rodriquez Velasquez, 1656. Museo de Prado, Madrid. Scala/Art Resource, NY; **128** bottom left: *Duelo a garrotatos* Francesco de Goya Y Lucientes. Private Collection. Eric Lessing/Art Resource, NY; **128** bottom right: *Guernica* Picasso, 1937. Museo Nacional Centro de Arte Reina Sofia, Madrid, Spain. Photo: John Bigelow Taylor/Art Resource, NY. © 2003 Estate of

Pablo Picasso/Artists Rights Society (ARS), New York.; **132** top: © IPS/Index Stock Imagery; **132** bottom: ThinkStock LLC/Index Stock Imagery.

CHAPTER 5
138–139: © Jeremy Horner/CORBIS; **143:** © Penny Tweedy/CORBIS; **155:** © Gustavo Gilabert/CORBIS.

CHAPTER 6
166–167: Andre Jenny/Alamy; **171:** © Pablo Corral/CORBIS; **179** left: © Heinle; **179** right: © David Burch/Index Stock Imagery; **188:** © James A. Sugar/CORBIS.

MAGAZINE 2
192 top and bottom: © Heinle; **194:** © Garry Adams/Index Stock Imagery; **195:** a.g.e. footstock.

CHAPTER 7
196–197: R. Kord/Robertstock.com; **201:** © Hubert Stadler/CORBIS; **208:** © Heinle; **210:** © Abilio Lope/CORBIS.

CHAPTER 8
224–225: © Jan Butchofsky-Houser/CORBIS; **230:** © Galen Rowell/CORBIS; **233:** © Suzanne Murphy-Larronde; **239:** © Leif Skoogfors/CORBIS.

CHAPTER 9
254–255: © Wolfgang Kaehler/CORBIS; **260:** © Timothy O'Keefe/Index Stock Imagery; **265:** Jose Azel/AURORA; **273:** © Dave G. Houser/CORBIS.

MAGAZINE 3
284: © Alan Blessta/Index Stock Imagery; **285** top: © Steve Dunwell/Index Stock Imagery; **285** center: © Leslie Harris/Index Stock Imagery; **285** bottom: © Scott Christopher/Index Stock Imagery; **286:** Courtesy of Curbstone Press, Willimantic, CT; **287** top: © Jimmy Dorantes/LatinFocus.com; **287** bottom: © Garry Adams/Index Stock Imagery.

CHAPTER 10
288–289: © Carl & Ann Purcell/CORBIS; **294:** © C/B Productions/CORBIS; **301:** © Greg Williams/ LatinFocus.com.

CHAPTER 11
314–315: © Danny Lehman/CORBIS; **320** left: © Barry Winker/Index Stock Imagery; **320** right: © Jeff Greenberg/Index Stock Imagery; **329:** © Heinle.

CHAPTER 12
346–347: © Martin Rogers/CORBIS; **352** left: © Phil Savoie/Index Stock Imagery; **352** center: © Robert Houser/Index Stock Imagery; **352** right: © Eric Sanford/Index Stock Imagery; **359** left: © RO-MA Stock/Index Stock Imagery; **359** right: © William Ervin/Index Stock Imagery.

MAGAZINE 4
375 top, center, and bottom; **376** top and bottom: © Heinle; **377:** © AFP/CORBIS.

CHAPTER 13
378–379: © Pablo Corral V/CORBIS; **384:** © Heinle; **391:** © Victor Engelbert; **398** left and right: © Heinle.

CHAPTER 14
402–403: Gonzalez/Laif/AURORA; **408** left and right: © Heinle; **412** left: © Carrion Carlos/CORBIS SYGMA; **412** right: © Victor Engelbert; **416:** © Heinle.

CHAPTER 15
430–431: © Pablo Corral V/CORBIS; **435** left: © Timothy O'Keefe/Index Stock Imagery; **435** center: © Arni Katz/Index Stock Imagery; **435** right: © Heinle; **439:** © Timothy O'Keefe/Index Stock Imagery.

MAGAZINE 5
453: Fotex/Shooting Star; **454** top, center and bottom: Christie's Images; **455** left, center and right: © Heinle.

Word stress and written accents

In Spanish the natural stress of words most commonly occurs on the second-to-the-last syllable, and the last syllable—and more commonly on the former. Words that deviate from the norm must carry a written accent mark, known as the **acento ortográfico,** to indicate where the stress of the word falls. The following three principles describe where word stress occurs and when a written accent is necessary:

1. The pronunciation of words that end in a vowel or in the consonants **n** or **s** are stressed on the second-to-the-last syllable:

   problem   pro-**ble**-ma   trabajo   tra-**ba**-jo

   resumen   re-**su**-men   bailas   **bai**-las

2. Words that end in a consonant other than **n** or **s** are stressed on the last syllable:

   bailar   bai-**lar**   similar   si-mi-**lar**

   normal   nor-**mal**   reloj   re-**loj**

3. If a word does not follow one of the first principles described above, the word is an exception to the norm and must carry a written accent to indicate where the stress falls:

   sofá   árbol   comerás   menú   función

Dividing syllables in a word

Dividing syllables in Spanish can be summarized in four principles for both consonants and vowels:

Consonants

1. Spanish is a language that favors the pronunciation of vowels over consonants. The simplest syllable is formed by the combination of a consonant and a vowel (rather than a vowel and a consonant):

   mi   tu   la   su

2. If a consonant is found between two vowels, it is united with the second vowel:

   baila   bai-la   oro   o-**ro**